What's New in This Edition

Except for Appendix A, "How IBM Developed the Personal Computer," this edition has been *entirely* rewritten from scratch. Although the core computer technologies remain much the same, we've highlighted coverage of the following new content:

- **Microprocessors**: Evolution of x86 architecture to the latest beasts, including Pentium Pro, MMX, Pentium II, clone processors on the horizon (AMD, Cyrix, IBM, Texas Instruments, IDT), local bus and cache technology, RISC/CISC difference and confluence, multiprocessor systems and the future. See Chapter 6, "Enhancing Your Understanding by Messing Around (Exploring and Tinkering)."

- **Disks**: Removable hard disks, super-floppies, flopticals, magneto-opticals, CD-RW, from DVD-ROM to DVD-RAM. See Chapters 9, "You Can Never Have Too Much Closet (or Data Storage) Space," and 11, "Bigger Is Better in Ballrooms and in a PC's Memory."

- **Memory**: ROM (mask programmed, EPROM, EEPROM, and so on), RAM (flash, EDO, FPM, SDRAM, SGRAM, VRAM, WRAM). Cache, video, expanded, disk controller, NIC, and printer memory. See Chapter 12, "Getting Your PC's Attention: Input Devices."

- **Display**: Thin CRT, LCD (double scan and active matrix); latest standards; video image RAM. See Chapter 14, "Getting It All Down on Paper: Printers."

- **Input/Output**: Universal Serial Bus (USB), FireWire, Advanced Graphics Port (AGP), CardBus (zoomed video, CIS, card and socket services), enhanced SCSI coverage, detailed PCI architecture, and system chips. See Chapter 18, "Understanding How Humans Instruct PCs."

- **Operating Systems and Programming**: Windows family including Windows 98 and Windows CE, Windows memory models compared, OS/2 Warp, Linux, UNIX, Java virtual machine; assembly language, code reuse (linking, modularity, libraries, object-oriented programming). See Chapters 19, "Some PCs Can Understand Speech and Talk to Us," and 20, "How to 'Wow' a Human."

Peter Norton®

- **Multimedia**: Audio and video compression/decompression techniques, audio-video hard disks, audio synthesis, speech recognition and synthesis, wave guide technology, 3D modeling, virtual reality (force transducers, data mining, and so on). See Chapters 21, "Special Storage Hardware Needs for Multimedia," 22, "Immersive PC Experiences," and 23, "Why Mobile PCs Must Be Different."

- **Portables**: Space constraints on components, proprietary parts, upgrading issues, battery technologies. See Chapter 26, "PCs that Think They're Mainframes: Multiprocessor PCs and Other Servers."

- **Networking and Communications**: Network topologies (bus, star, modified star, ring, linking LANs), video conferencing, whiteboard, group calendaring and scheduling; modem standards and specifications, data compression and error correction, ISDN, T1, xSDL, cable and fiber-optic connection to the Super Highway, satellite communications. See Chapters 27, "You Can Touch the World, and It May Touch You, Too!" and 28, "Looking Back and Looking Ahead."

Peter Nortons'®
Inside the PC,
Seventh Edition

Peter Norton
John Goodman

SAMS 201 West 103rd Street
PUBLISHING Indianapolis, Indiana 46290

Copyright © 1997 by Peter Norton®

SEVENTH EDITION

International Standard Book Number: 0-672-31041-4

Library of Congress Catalog Card Number: 96-72009

2000 99 98   4 3 2

Interpretation of the printing code: the rightmost double-digit number is the year of the book's printing; the rightmost single-digit, the number of the book's printing. For example, a printing code of 97-1 shows that the first printing of the book occurred in 1997.

Composed in Goudy and MCPdigital by Macmillan Computer Publishing

Printed in the United States of America

President:	Richard K. Swadley
Publisher:	John Pierce
Executive Editor:	Angela Wethington
Managing Editor:	Thomas Hayes
Indexing Manager:	Ginny Bess
Director of Software and User Services:	Cheryl Willoughby

Acquisitions Editor
Sunthar Visuvalingam

Development Editor
Sunthar Visuvalingam

Project Editor
Tonya Simpson

Copy Editors
Tom Dinse
Julie McNamee
Colleen Williams

Indexers
Cheryl Jackson
Chris Wilcox

Technical Reviewers
Matt Butler
Brian Zucker

Editorial Coordinators
Mandie Rowell
Katie Wise

Technical Edit Coordinator
Lynette Quinn

Editorial Assistants
Carol Ackerman
Andi Richter
Rhonda Tinch-Mize
Karen Williams

Cover Designer
Karen Ruggles

Book Designer
Gary Adair

Copy Writer
David Reichwein

Production Team Supervisor
Andy Stone

Production
Bryan Flores
Julie Geeting
Kay Hoskin
Christy Lemasters
Darlena Murray
Julie Searls
Sossity Smith

Overview

Contents

Part III   The Stand-Alone PC   129

7   Understanding PC Processors   131

8   How Your PC "Thinks"   155

Acknowledgments

Creating a wholly new version of an old standard can be a daunting task. I was fortunate to have the assistance of many people in this effort.

Foremost among them is Dr. John M. Goodman. My editor, Sunthar Visuvalingam, and I invited him to completely rethink this book from a new perspective and then to execute his plan for it.

We both want to thank wholeheartedly the many people who assisted us, often surprisingly generously. Dell Computer provided our sample desktop and laptop systems shown and described at various points in the book. You can learn more about their fine products by going to their Web site (http://www.dell.com). In addition to this physical support, they also made available their in-house expertise. Brian Zucker, who is Manager of Performance and Architecture for the Dell Dimension Group, served as our primary technical resource on the project. Also of invaluable help was Jim Kelsey, Senior Software Engineer at SystemSoft Corp. Matt Butler served as the first of several technical reviewers who examined all of the text to assure its accuracy and completeness.

John Lunsford, John Omahen, Ray Lischner, and Scott H. A. Clark read portions of the manuscript and shared some of their specialized knowledge with us. We also want to thank Judy Fernandes for her contributions to the book. Finally, we want to thank Mike Spilo, Robert Mankin, Mark Elpers, Paul Gaske, and Chris David for many extended telephone and e-mail conversations that were most illuminating.

Once the manuscript arrived at the publisher, many additional talented and dedicated people contributed their special skills to making this the best possible book. The Executive Editor Angela Wethington, Project Editor Tonya Simpson, Graphics Supervisor Mary Beth Wakefield, and Development Editor Sunthar Visuvalingam were chief among them. However, we also want to thank the copy editors Julie McNamee and Colleen Williams for their keen eyes and careful defense of the needs of a less-than-fully knowledgeable reader. Without that help, many places in the book would have been harder to understand.

We also want to acknowledge with great thanks for their patient efforts to shepherd this book through what was an unexpectedly protracted and, at times, trying process our agents Bill Gladstone, Matt Wagner, and the rest of the good folks at Waterside Productions.

Introduction

You're about to embark on an amazing voyage of discovery, understanding, and productivity. Welcome!

From the day it first appeared, the IBM PC stirred excitement and fascination: The PC marked the coming of age of "personal" computing, a drastic change from the days when all computers were managed by other people who doled out computer power to users on an as-needed, as-available basis. Today, the PC is the tool without equal for helping business and professional people improve their personal performance and the quality of their work. Students of almost all ages and other home-based users have successfully expanded personal computing into near ubiquity. The exploding home-PC market has accelerated the development of an ever-growing range of applications from word processors for homework, to technologies that allow people to actually work at home. Users also have utilized the technology to find recipes, play with games, work on their education, and research topics.

The original IBM PC also spawned a great many other computers—some from IBM, but most from the makers of IBM-compatible computers—that make up the PC family. In fact, when I first wrote this book, it was actually called *Inside the IBM PC*, but the strong influence that companies other than IBM now exert on the PC industry inspired me to change the title a few years ago. The term *PC* is now universally used in the computer industry to refer to any IBM-compatible computer, and that's exactly how I use the term in this book.

I am excited and enthusiastic about the PC family; I want you to be, too. I want to lead you into understanding the workings of this marvelous machine and to share with you the excitement of knowing what it is, how it works, and what it can do. Armed with that knowledge, you'll be positioned to make intelligent decisions about computers for yourself, your family, or your company.

Many new personal computer users try to ignore DOS. They concentrate on learning just the one or two applications they work with every day. A word processor or database manager, however, can't locate and correct errors in the disk directory structure; these programs can't rescue a file that you deleted by mistake, and they can't detect and remove a virus that has infected your disk. The more you know about DOS, the safer your data will be. You also can significantly improve the overall performance of your system with DOS.

Tell Us What You Think!

As a reader, you are the most important critic and commentator of our books. We value your opinion and want to know what we're doing right, what we could do better, what areas you'd like to see us publish in, and any other words of wisdom you're willing to pass our way. You can help us make strong books that meet your needs and give you the computer guidance you require.

Do you have access to the World Wide Web? Then check out our site at http://www.mcp.com.

> **Note:** If you have a technical question about this book, call the technical support line at 317-581-3833 or send e-mail to support@mcp.com.

As the team leader of the group that created this book, I welcome your comments. You can fax, e-mail, or write me directly to let me know what you did or didn't like about this book—as well as what we can do to make our books stronger. Here's the information:

Fax: 317-581-4669

E-mail: awethington@iquest.net

Mail: Angela Wethington
            Comments Department
            Sams Publishing
            201 W. 103rd Street
            Indianapolis, IN 46290

My Approach

If you know anything about me or the first edition of this book, you know that I made my reputation by explaining the technical wizardry of the PC. In the early days of the PC, that was what PC users needed most—an inside technical explanation of how the PC worked. The world of the PC has matured and changed since then—a lot—and so have the needs of mainstream PC users. I haven't changed my approach, however, and it occurs to me that you might want to know how I look at what I do.

From my perspective, the most useful approach to a subject such as this one has always been to assume that you, my reader, are an intelligent, curious, and productive person. That means that you'll never find me endlessly repeating elementary stuff, as though my books were "for dummies," and you're spared from all the dysfunctional oversimplification and condescension that such writing makes inevitable.

I like to write in the same way that I talk, and you may already know that my conversational approach was something of a novelty back when this book was first published. I don't mind saying that I'm proud to see my basic belief—that people can talk about technology like people, not like machines—has been adopted by hundreds of other writers, including my competitors. I think you'll intuitively agree that you'll learn more about your computer from "talking" with me about it than you would if just I handed you pages of technical lists and hieroglyphic diagrams and told you that the test will be on Wednesday. But, when this book premiered, that's exactly what most computer documentation was like.

I would never, of course, suggest that computer professionals have maintained their personal job security by keeping computers as mystical and unfathomable as possible. But I will observe that many companies have experienced notable jumps in productivity at all levels when certain types of technology management people are made obsolete. These companies have taken steps to empower everyday computer users to make many of their own decisions, to solve their own problems. You may not be employed by a large multilevel company, or you may be a student and not employed at all, but this book will lead you to the same power and enable you to make the same sorts of productivity jumps by giving you a personal, direct, and complete understanding of your PC.

About This Book

This isn't a book for people who are having trouble finding the on/off switch on their computers. Instead, it's for people who have enough experience and curiosity to begin examining in greater depth these wonderful machines. My goal is to make understanding the PC easy as well as fun.

This is, more than anything else, a book written to help you learn what you really need to know about the PC. You can successfully use a PC without really understanding it. However, the better you understand your PC, the better equipped you are to realize the potential in the machine and—don't forget this—to deal with emergencies that can arise when working with a PC. After all, when something goes wrong, the better you understand the machine, the more likely you are to make the right moves to fix the problem and reduce its adverse impact on you and your business.

There are many reasons you might want to understand the inner workings of your PC. One reason, a really good one, is simply for the intellectual satisfaction and sense of mastery that comes with understanding the tools with which you work. Another is to open up new realms for yourself. After all, there is plenty of demand these days for people who have PC savvy. But perhaps the most practical reason is the one that I suggested before. By analogy, think back to the early days of the automobile when you had to be an amateur mechanic to safely set out on a journey by car. It doesn't take the skills of a mechanic to drive a car today because cars have been tamed for everyday use. I'd like it to be that way with computers, but, frankly, computing hasn't yet progressed quite that far. Today, to safely and successfully use a personal computer, you need at least some degree of expertise; the more expertise you have, the better you can deal with the crises that sometimes arise.

Vitally important, too, in today's economy, is the realization that by understanding what goes on inside your PC, you'll be much better equipped to make intelligent decisions when it comes time to pull out your or your company's wallet. You won't end up paying for what you won't use, and you'll really minimize your risk of "driving home with an Edsel," when you can look at technological trends and understand where things are and where they're likely headed. With high technology, more than anything else, advances tend to antiquate much of what came before. Last year's innovation will probably be this year's low-end model, and in the grand scheme of things, we wouldn't want it any other way. For you and me personally, however, this type of evolution-by-replacement can make buying equipment extremely stressful. By the time we're finished here, you'll be in a strong position when it comes time to analyze all of your purchase options and make a purchase choice that will give you the most for your buck—the greatest longevity.

Finally, PCs are now an integral part of our lives. Children learn to use them in schools, at home, or at a public library. Even some homeless people now have "home pages" on the World Wide Web.

You may not see yourself becoming all that heavily invested in computing as a part of your life, but it certainly is an ever-increasing part of most of our lives, and it appears that computers will be even more at the core of our children's lives. Thus, to understand your PC is in a way to understand more fully the social and technical environment in which we live. That puts the contents of this book right up there in importance: on a par with that to be found in books on politics, economics, and the history of our civilization.

For Readers of the Previous Edition(s)

If you already own a copy of a previous edition of *Peter Norton's Inside the PC*, some natural questions you'll be asking yourself are these: "Do I need yet another version of this book? What's new here that I want? And if I do buy this version, is there any reason to save the previous version(s) I have?" Here are my answers.

What's new in this edition? Literally everything. This is a completely new look at the topic. We started at ground zero and rebuilt this exposition from the bottom up, using a wholly new notion of what was appropriate to include and what was not. Every word you read here, and every figure you see were prepared especially for this edition.

We did this for a couple of reasons. One is that the world of PCs has changed dramatically. It was time to update this book in more than just minor ways. A second reason was that the writing team now includes a new player, with a new set of perspectives and perceptions about the relative importance of different issues. The changes in our industry motivated the new look for this book; Dr. John Goodman executed it.

New Topics and New Organization

PCs are no longer just hackers' toys, nor even mere programmers' tools. They have become nearly "ubiquitous information appliances." (That phrase, literally, is one commonly cited vision of where PCs are going, even if they aren't yet quite there.)

Today, as never before, you can use a PC quite successfully without much or any appreciation of what is inside it. That this has happened is no accident. Many companies have expended enormous efforts trying to make PCs so easy to use that you won't have to think about how they do their jobs.

Still, you can be even more effective if you do understand them—more effective as a PC user, and especially more effective when it comes to choosing additions or upgrades to your PC's hardware or software.

That understanding now can be harder than ever to acquire. In part, this is because there is so much more to know; and in part, it is because some of the new ideas are so complex and arcane. However, I firmly believe that any intelligent person who wants to understand these topics can, if only they give them some focused attention, and if only someone—in this case me—is there to guide their learning.

Look at the Table of Contents. This book gives you first a fast overview, then a much more in-depth treatment. It is broken into Parts to help you know how the different topics relate to one another.

New to this edition is all the material on what goes on when one PC connects to another, or to the Internet. Also new is the Part devoted to mobile PCs and the chapters on natural language processing. The Part on multimedia PCs has been greatly expanded over that in the previous edition—reflecting the emergence of the multimedia PC as the most common configuration being sold today, and because the multimedia technologies are at the core of the much-vaunted coming "convergence" of PCs, telecommunications, entertainment, and the conversion of homes and offices into "smart" homes and "smart" offices.

New Angles on Old Topics

When PCs were simply stand-alone machines, a look inside could be just that. It could be confined to an exploration of what each part of your PC is and does, and how it is able to do those things. But now, with PCs connected to the world, mainly through the Internet, and with local area networking becoming common not only in offices, but also in homes, any in-depth look inside a PC must be extended. In a sense, we will dive into the PC and then find ourselves coming out "the other side" where I will show you in addition to what we found inside the PC itself, also the world of technical marvels to which your PC gives you access.

Thus, this edition clearly separates the inside-inside story on PCs from the inside-and-out-the-other-side story, and then gives you considerable details about both. Mobile PCs have gained a newfound prominence—in many cases replacing desktop PCs, rather than merely supplementing them. These portable machines have, in many ways, a story all their own. In this edition, they get their own Part to make this clear.

Also, as our industry matures and as the focus of my exploration with you in this book changes, some topics that were central in previous editions become merely background material or warm-up events before the main show in this edition. Thus, for example, you will find that I explain what DOS is and how it still underlies the Windows operating system most of you are using. But you won't find nearly the focus on DOS that has been in the book's previous editions.

What's Not Still Here

Something had to go. Not only could we not put in everything we said before, plus all the new material without making this book so large and heavy that you wouldn't even want to pick it up, it was time for some things to go. I don't mean to suggest that those things are no longer true, or even that they no longer matter. It simply is the case that they no longer deserve the prominence they had in earlier editions.

So, if you own previous editions of this book, I hope you will keep them and keep them handy. You may well find that something I said in one of them was said in just the right way for you to understand it most easily. Or there may be a table or figure there that made some details apparent that you cannot so easily find in the current edition.

Sometimes when you approach a new topic, you will find it easier to understand if you read what I say about it here, in this version, and then go back and compare that to what I said in a previous version. Two different statements of the same thing sometimes makes a point clear that you might otherwise miss.

Navigation Aids for Our Journey

Some people think they'll get lost in a book as big as this one. Well now, I wouldn't want that to happen. So I've made sure you'll have plenty of ways to keep the big picture in view, and to find each nook or cranny that especially interests you.

The table of contents is a good place to start. Or, if you want to find some specific bit of information, check the index. That is an especially good way to find something when you remember reading it, but can't recall where in the book you found it. Also look at the jump table on the inside front cover. That points you directly to certain hot topics, and points out some that may be treated partially in each of several chapters.

Technical Note: Some of you want really detailed, technical information—the "real goodies," as you might put it. And there is quite a lot of that in here. Just look for paragraphs that look like this one, with this icon beside them.

Maybe really "hard" stuff frightens you. Should you avoid these paragraphs? Perhaps, but I suggest you try reading a few and see. You might find that you are able to understand more than you thought you could. And you might even enjoy them. On the other hand, I've been careful to be sure that your overall grasp of the book's story line will not suffer if you skip these paragraphs entirely.

Historical Aside: Some of you are more interested in the broad picture, and would enjoy some historical anecdotes. You'll want to keep a lookout for paragraphs that look like this one. Not only will you find some interesting background to today's technology, you may also discover the reasons that we still must do certain things the way we do, because of past decisions whose influence still lingers.

Tip: Looking for some hot tips? I have them in here, too. This is how they will appear in the body of the book.

Note: Sometimes I have a note flagged in the manner of this paragraph. These are not necessarily technical points, nor are they asides. They are just something I found—well—noteworthy.

Standards: The PC field is full of jargon and other things that may confuse you. Fortunately, there are some standards that help us keep things straight. Whenever you see this type of paragraph, please read it carefully. It will help you keep out of many of the potholes you might otherwise fall into on our journey.

Warning: Speaking of tripping up, there are some important cautionary notes. These are warnings I give you so you won't hurt yourself, your PC, or your data. Please read them carefully, also, and follow them every time they apply. You'll be glad you did, and so will I.

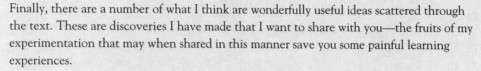

Peter's Principles: Point the Way

Finally, there are a number of what I think are wonderfully useful ideas scattered through the text. These are discoveries I have made that I want to share with you—the fruits of my experimentation that may when shared in this manner save you some painful learning experiences.

To help you find them, I have given each one a title, like the one above this paragraph.

A Point of View

Where you stand often defines what you can see. That's true when you are out hiking in the mountains, and it is no less true when you come with me on a "hike" through PC land.

If you're looking for interesting and useful technical information about the PC from the inside out, you won't be disappointed. I am dedicated to making this book a guide to what makes the PC tick. But, just as the hardware has changed dramatically over the past couple of years—and seems poised for more, even more dramatic changes in the next few years—so has the focus of the user. The Internet is all the rage and for some pretty good reasons. PCs today can be understood only in the context of these larger changes. To that end, I shall address both the technology as it is and as it seems likely to be in the near future, and also how all this is changing what PC users are doing, thinking, and wanting.

A lot of this book focuses on hardware. That is the stuff you can see, feel, heft, and for which you feel pretty sure you got something for your money. But software is also important. In fact, without good software, your PC's hardware is good only as a doorstop or decoration.

So some chapters will take you into hardware depths and practically ignore the software, while others will assume the hardware and explain the technologies behind today's operating systems and application programs. You can discover which chapters serve which purposes pretty well just from the table of contents, and I will point out the relationships among different parts and chapters in this book from time to time in the text, as well.

At the end of several chapters, you'll find some suggestions for things you may want to think about or try. These exercises are examples of what I think it is the most powerful way to get to know your PC. Get in and get your hands dirty—figuratively, at least. This is so important, in fact, that I have devoted an entire chapter to teaching you how to do this safely and effectively. See Chapter 6, "Enhancing Your Understanding by Messing Around (Exploring and Tinkering)." If you have never played around much inside your PC, you might want to wait until after you read that chapter before you start tinkering.

I

The Big
Picture

1

The View
From Afar

Peter Norton®

Welcome to a grand adventure! This book is going to take you on a tour inside the modern PC. You'll learn how it is built (and why), how it works (at least in a general sense), and gain insight into where this amazing technology is headed.

The knowledge you will gain will empower you in several ways. You'll become a more educated consumer, better able to make wise choices when selecting or upgrading your PC. When the inevitable problems arise, you'll be better equipped to understand what is happening and thus to take appropriate corrective actions. And your new insights will help you position yourself on this incredible, ever-breaking wave of new technology so that you won't, as surfers say, "wipe out."

I thought it might be best to start with a simple question: What is a PC? This turns out to be an important question, and the answer is more complicated than you might have imagined. Exploring some of the richness in this idea is the purpose of this chapter. The insights and knowledge you will gain from reading this chapter will help you put the information in the rest of the book into context, and thereby will help you understand it and make the best use of it.

When I reflected on what a PC is, I realized that there are at least three important ways to view the subject. First, PCs are, as the words say, "personal," and they are "computers." But examining that apparently simple description can lead you to some surprising places. Second, PCs might be about to become something new and unexpected. We might be, to use accurately an overly popular phrase, in a time of *shifting paradigms*. And third, PCs have a history that defines them and, it turns out, limits them in some ways. After you understand that history, you will find that it will make everything else about PCs easier to understand as well.

So let's begin our adventure.

Who's In Charge Here?

What does it mean for a computer to be a "personal computer"? "Well," you might say, "isn't that obvious?" Just look at the words. It is some sort of computer, whatever that is, and it is mine. (Or maybe it is ours, if you share your PC with a few other people.)

Yes. That's it. The first key fact is: *You* are in charge of your PC. What's important to realize is that this key fact has aspects that are both wonderful and terrible.

You Are In Charge

You are in charge means that your computer is at your beck and call. You get to decide what your PC does and when. You can even decide that for awhile it is going to do nothing at all. That is a radical change in how computer use is decided. Before there were personal computers, virtually all the computers that existed were owned by companies and were such valuable resources that they had to be kept busy all the time. This is still true of so-called "mainframe computers" and even of many of the somewhat smaller "minicomputers."

But then again, *you are in charge* means that you don't have a flock of people wearing white lab coats hovering over your PC, making sure that it is working optimally at all times. You must notice when something about it goes amiss. And then, you must fix whatever is wrong, or at least know enough to find someone else to fix it.

Not Every Computer You Personally Use Is a PC

But wait a minute. Not every computer you personally use is a PC. Did you know that your microwave oven has a computer inside it? Your wrist watch might also. Even a toaster can have a computer watching the bread and deciding when it is time to pop it up. Are they all PCs? Not the way I see it.

Your car and your home audio system are even more complicated. If they are of a recent vintage, they almost certainly contain one (or more than one) computer. Yet even they are not, in my view, PCs. In fact, even though nearly every modern consumer electronic device, kitchen appliance, and piece of office equipment is built around a computer, I assert that they aren't PCs, at least as that term is used in this industry—and as I am going to use it in this book—for one simple reason.

As useful as these devices might be, and the many others like them with which we fill our homes and offices, they each are able to do just one thing. You can't play music on your microwave oven. You wouldn't try to compose a letter using your wrist watch, and your toaster is useless for creating and using a database. But a PC can do all those things and much, much more.

So, for now, I'll exclude from the collection of objects called PCs any such single-purpose tool, no matter how much computing power might lie inside it. That "embedded computer" might be quite sophisticated, and its programming might be quite impressive, but if you, the user of the device, cannot alter its programming in some significant ways (which you might do by loading a new program written by someone else), then it isn't a personal computer.

I can't leave this topic, however, without noting that soon many of these devices might start to look a lot like PCs, even though they still won't work quite like one. If Bill Gates has his way, your washing machine, coffee maker, and many others of the accouterments of your life will someday soon sport a Windows interface, and they will be able to hook up to your PC and even to the Internet. You learn a bit more about this trend in Chapter 17, "Understanding PC Operating Systems."

Some PCs Aren't, It Turns Out, Very Personal After All

On the other hand, some PCs aren't simply used by one or a very few people. They have grown to be so powerful that many companies are now using PCs as network servers, for example. Those PCs can be used by thousands of people, and they might indeed have a staff of possibly white-lab-coat–wearing folks hovering over them day and night, ensuring that they keep doing their jobs correctly.

These machines are, however, simply very capable PCs that have been put to work as replacements for minicomputers or, occasionally, even for mainframe computers. They're still PCs because you *could* use them personally and they are otherwise just like "normal" PCs. Therefore, the descriptions and explanations in this book do apply to them.

So maybe just looking at the words "personal" and "computer" isn't enough to let you figure out which devices are PCs and which aren't. Instead, you might have to look a little more broadly at the question. Which leads me to a term that is getting bandied about quite a lot these days: the "information appliance."

A Grand Vision for the Future

I mentioned that there is a possible paradigm shift going on. That term refers to a change in one's assumptions about the world. And this is a pretty accurate description of what has rocked the PC industry in the past two years, and that now seems increasingly likely to rock our entire society. The emergence of the Internet (and the related development of intranets) is changing everything. It is driving the development of new PC hardware and software, and it threatens to alter in some fundamental ways how people go about living their lives.

I said there is a possible paradigm shift going on. Don't I know? Actually, no, I don't and neither does anyone else. Not yet. When paradigms shift, what was obvious before becomes not only not obvious afterward; it often comes to be seen as obviously false. But during the process of the shift, where the truth lies is not clear to anyone.

What's the Old Paradigm?

If there is a shift going on, what might it be? Well, up until fairly recently, if you asked someone who was supposed to know such things what a PC was you'd probably get an answer something like this: "A PC, at least an IBM-compatible PC (which is what most of them are), is an arrangement of particular kinds of computing hardware pieces plus a collection of software programs designed to run on that hardware. It is a tool that you use to do word processing, create and manipulate spreadsheets, store and retrieve data using a database application, or several similar tasks." Yet more recently the answer might have included a reference to the PC's growing capacity for helping artists create interesting visual effects or for a musician to compose and perform electronic music.

In each case the PC is viewed as a tool, consisting of a particular type and configuration of hardware pieces, activated by one or more programs that were specially written for use on that type of computing hardware and that one stores on the PC. What that PC can do is dictated entirely by what hardware pieces it has and what programs it contains.

What's the New Paradigm?

Now, however, a growing number of people are beginning to claim that the important fact about a PC is that it is just one of a wide variety of tools that can be used to access the Internet, that it is interchangeable with many similar objects, and that what particular 'net tool you happen to have is not nearly as important as what you can get access to by using it. Granted, if you want to make good music, your PC must have some suitable music-generating hardware parts, but you might not even have to own *any* software applications to do that job; you might be able to get whatever you need from the Internet.

Even more radically, people are talking about using PCs as "transparent information appliances," by which they mean something like this: If you want to know some fact, say what the weather is in Newark, New Jersey, today or how many members of the Screen Actors Guild have red hair, you will seek that answer from the (by then) universal network of interconnected computers. You won't pay much more attention to the device you use to achieve this access than you now do to your telephone when you call Directory Assistance to learn someone's phone number or a theater to learn when its next show begins.

Taking things a big step further, the Media Lab at MIT, among others, is exploring the notion of "smart clothes." You might, they say, have a computer in your shoe, a keyboard on your belt, and a small video camera in your glasses frame. When you walked into a room and someone walked up to you, your computer would compute from the video image who that person is. To do this it would have to access one of your personal databases (which might be in the computer inside your shoe, or it might be one which it would access across the universal network). Then, before that person even said hello to you, your computer-in-a-shoe would be able to whisper that person's name in your ear. Furthermore, if you wished and had so directed it, the computer would also remind you when you last met that person and what you had talked about.

Your car might use the Global Positioning Satellite System to keep track of where it is at all times, and any time your child (or anyone else) drove it outside of whatever region you had prescribed, your car would take the initiative to call you—using the Internet, of course—and let you know where it had been taken.

Any time you went to the doctor's office, while you were waiting, you could just pick up the nearest computing tablet (of which there would be several for patients to use) and log in. Voilà! Your own, familiar computer desktop would be displayed on this stranger's tablet, ready for you to use just as you would on your home or office PC.

Ubiquitous Computing

Another phrase that has been used to describe this brave new world is "ubiquitous computing." That means you will never be out of touch with the grand universal network and, through it with all the computers you have rights to use anywhere in the world. And not only that, but unless you have instructed that net (using some computer, somewhere of course) that you don't want to be disturbed, it will notify you of any of a wide variety of events that you had told it you would find interesting. These could range from a holding in your stock portfolio whose price was going up or going down more than a preset amount, to someone ringing your home or office telephone (and who then could be connected to your personal phone or to any nearby phone extension, if you wanted), to your child getting a fever. In that last case your child would, presumably, be wearing smart clothes that monitored her vital signs. And, whenever they went out of a safe range, it would contact you via the 'net and, if necessary, call the paramedics as well.

In this new vision of things, the question "What is a PC?" is just not very important anymore. No longer does the answer to that question have very much to do with what you can accomplish by using just the PC you possess. Now, the interesting questions are all about what information you can access (or have brought to your attention) via the 'net, and what tasks you can perform on or over the 'net. The PC—why, it's just how you connect to the 'net. As such, the question of just what that PC is, itself, simply isn't very interesting anymore.

Clearly, this is a vision of a possible future. Equally clearly, it is an overstatement—one that is meant to make a point. Still, it seems quite clear that something like this can happen. Most of the technological pieces are either in place or being worked on in some laboratory. But whether this actually is what people will want and will pay to have is yet to be determined. (You are, of course, one of those people who will decide this issue. So it behooves you to learn about it and then make an educated choice. When you have, you'll want to assert your point of view on these issues every chance you get, in particular by making a careful choice of what software and hardware you will buy.) Your future possibilities will be determined, in part, by *your* buying and other decisions today.

The Importance of Interoperability

If this grand vision of a world of fully interconnected computers and of software that can be anywhere and yet be used by anyone is to come to pass, then in order to let you use any computer, anywhere in the world to do any of the things you might have done at your home or office, it will be necessary that all those computers be fully "interoperable." That means that no longer will PCs run only PC software, Macintosh computers run Mac software, and UNIX computers run UNIX software. Every computing device will run any program.

If that sounds like a pipe dream, guess again. We are almost to that point right now. Or at least some people claim that we are. You will learn more about that hot topic in Chapter 27, "You Can Touch the World, and It May Touch You, Too!," and Chapter 28, "Looking Back and Looking Ahead."

The Simply Interactive PC (SIPC) and Some Other Acronyms

One of the things that often bothers newcomers to PCs the most is the heavy load of acronyms that they encounter. Jargon (and acronyms are just one form that jargon can take) is common in almost every area of human endeavor. It serves at least two purposes. The first (and laudable) one is that it is a form of shorthand. After one knows what the acronym (or other jargon item) means, then mentioning it recalls the entire definition and its context. This makes for more efficient communication. The second purpose of most jargon (and I find it a much more regrettable one) is that the insiders in a field will use it as a weapon to intimidate, and a barrier to exclude, the outsiders. This latter use of jargon is just human nature. So you must expect to have a job learning the insider language that applies to PCs, just as you would in any other field with comparable complexity.

> **Tip:** Still, the level of jargon and, even worse, the number of acronyms used in the personal computer field is unusually high. Any time you encounter an acronym, or even just a word or phrase that you suspect means something other than what it appears to mean at first glance, look in the Index for a reference to the place in this book where I discuss the concept in more detail.

The SIPC term mentioned in the heading for this section refers to a "vision" that Microsoft is sponsoring. It is not actually a design standard (as is the case for many of the things referred to by acronyms), but is instead merely a statement of a concept detailing how Microsoft hopes to see PCs develop from their present status as useful, but sometimes awkward, devices to information appliances that are so simple to use that most folks will forget they ever had to learn how to use them.

A few other recently introduced acronyms you might encounter are *ACPI* and *HID*. The first stands for Advanced Configuration and Power Interface. This is a serious, formal standard that describes in a very detailed fashion how the hardware of a truly modern PC must function so that the latest PC software (in particular, the about-to-be-released versions of Windows) will be able to control the hardware appropriately. In particular, it refers to the ways in which the software can cause portions of the hardware to turn on or off when the user presses appropriate keys or when a suitable time interval has passed. This is the formal specification that defines how PC makers and PC programmers are going to be required to support the newest Microsoft-defined PC behavior, called "OnNow." (Makers of PCs don't really have to design their products to meet this specification, but if they don't, Microsoft won't let them use its logo in advertising the products. Microsoft feels [apparently correctly] that this is enough of a club to force most PC makers into line.)

The second of these new acronyms, HID, is a different sort of beast. It stands for Human Interface Device. That is, HID is simply a fancy (or insider-speak) way to refer to any device with which humans interact and that also can interact with a PC. Obvious examples include the PC's keyboard and mouse. Less obvious ones are a telephone, a VCR, and a postage meter. Each of these can be used as a stand-alone appliance, but each of them (at least in future versions) can also be hooked to a PC. If you do hook them up to a PC, then it will have to know how to interact with that device. And to define all such interactions, Microsoft has defined several HID classes. After your PC knows what HID class a device is, it knows how to operate the device and thus how to respond to the human-initiated interactions that device is capable of supporting.

But enough of this for now. You will learn about much of the other jargon used in the PC world soon enough, and by putting it in its proper context, later in the book, the meanings will be much clearer than they possibly could be if I tried to define them all right here.

So let us return to our original purpose in this chapter, clarifying the definition of a PC. Because PCs aren't yet fully transparent universal information appliances, we have to look at yet another definition of what they are.

The Historical Perspective

Personal computers of any sort are a recent phenomenon. Many say that the first one was the MITS Altair computer, created in 1974. It was a big box with a tiny capability. The user interface was just a lot of little switches and lights on the front panel. You could demonstrate the principles behind the operation of any computer, but you really couldn't do much computing.

An amazingly short time later, the Apple Computer company was born and its Apple II became the definition of what a computer was for an entire generation of school children and quite a few people outside of schools. At about the same time several other companies made small computers that were quite distinct from one another in their designs, but which all ran an operating system called CP/M. (You learn a little bit about what an operating system is in Chapter 5, "How to Get Your PC to Understand You," and revisit that subject in more depth in Chapter 17.

These computers could do quite a few useful tasks, but learning how to use them required a level of dedication that relatively few people wanted to bring to bear. Still, they were successful products and people did a lot of work using them.

1981 saw a quantum jump in the capability of small computers. IBM's original PC (that was their name for it, which we presume stood for personal computer), cost about the same as many of the other small computers on the market, but it was in some important ways technologically a big step forward. That fact was not at all obvious to many people at the time, but it became quite clear within about one or two years after the PC's introduction.

What Hath IBM Wrought?

When it introduced its PC, IBM did two things that were totally out of character. First, it told everyone almost all the details about how its PC was built. It did this to invite others to make computing hardware pieces that would work with its PC. A lot of companies took IBM up on its offer. Second, it bought the PC's operating system from Microsoft, and its license agreement with Microsoft let Microsoft license that operating system to other companies that made small computers as well as to IBM.

At first, IBM offered only a very limited number of optional hardware pieces and software programs that one could buy for its PC. This meant that although the basic design was a marvel of technological progress (for its time), the kinds of things one could actually *do* with a PC were quite limited.

However, very soon the marketplace was overflowing with PC add-ons that could enable a PC to do almost anything. In short order the IBM PC became hugely popular. It soon far outsold all the competition put together. And just as the Volkswagen "beetle" is history's most customized car, the IBM PC soon became history's most customized computer.

That no doubt made the folks at IBM very happy. What happened next did not. Some people said to themselves, "Because IBM has told us all about how they build their PC, we could build ones just like them. And we could do it cheaper. And we can buy our microprocessor chips from Intel and our operating system from Microsoft (and the other parts from yet other manufacturers), so IBM can't stop us." All of which was absolutely true. Of course, one major reason why those "clone makers" could create and sell their products more inexpensively was that they didn't have to pay for all the engineering effort IBM had expended to create the PC design and the pieces that went into making one.

In a very few years we had a whole industry making computers that were so nearly alike that they all could run the same programs and one could freely exchange data between them (carrying the data on diskettes, usually). And equally significantly, soon no one manufacturer, including IBM, could claim total control of that "industry standard PC" design.

The result is now history. The dominant small computer became some sort of PC compatible or PC clone. And the number of them grew way beyond anything that anyone at IBM had ever thought possible. This fact has both some wonderful and some terrible consequences.

How History Binds Us

This market development defined the PC quite precisely and unchangeably as any small computer that conformed to IBM's general design and that would run the same programs that could run on any other PC. This did not include the Apple II or most of the CP/M machines. Some of those companies became makers of clone PCs. Others, including Apple, persisted in making small computers using only their own proprietary designs. Many of them went out of business. Apple has hung in there—so far, and in the process introduced some technically marvelous machines of its own, but it never again achieved the importance in the overall small computer market that it once had.

The downside of these events is that this industry standard became pretty much the definition of what was acceptable as a small computer, especially for use in business. And as the years went on and ever more people got those PC-compatible computers, this standard became ever more solidly entrenched. Now almost no company dares to introduce a new computer design or a new operating system design for the PC that isn't fully "backward compatible." By this we mean that those new computers or PCs running those new operating systems will be able to run virtually any program that could run on any earlier PC or PC-compatible computer. This has been very important in terms of letting PC owners feel free to upgrade to the newer machine or newer operating system, but it also has served as a heavy anchor limiting companies' freedom to innovate.

Intel, the company that made the microprocessor IBM chose to put at the heart of its original PC, and the company that still makes most of the CPU (central processing unit) chips for PCs today, has ridden this huge wave of computer industry growth precisely because it promised vociferously that every x86 family member is totally backward compatible with the original 8088. (You can find out all about what the x86 family is in Chapter 7, "Understanding PC Processors.")

Similarly, Microsoft, by being the vendor with the operating system that IBM used, rode the same wave to dominate the computer operating system market. And its family of first DOS, then DOS plus Windows, and now (in name at least) Windows-only operating systems are, de facto, the industry standards for PC operating systems.

By contrast, IBM, which started this whole show, is now only a peripheral player. It no longer can single-handedly set any meaningful standards for the industry. And, not only is it not the only maker of PCs, it isn't even the one that makes the largest number of units each year. That crown belongs to Compaq, as it has for several years.

These developments led someone to coin the term, "the Wintel monopoly." And for now, that pretty accurately sums up where we are.

Another Answer to Our Question

This leads us to the final form of the Historical Perspective on the question, "What is a PC?" And the answer has now evolved to something like this: It is a general-purpose computer that contains a central processing unit that is compatible with Intel's x86 family and which will run some version of Microsoft's Windows. (Some of the older models of PC can run only very early versions of Windows, but they were able to run at least Windows 1.x so they still qualify under this definition as a PC. On the other hand, some of the newest appliances and "personal digital assistants" can run Windows CE, but because they are not general-purpose computers, I'd say they aren't really PCs.)

So finally, you have three answers to the question "What is a PC?" and they could hardly be more different. The first says a PC is any computer you personally control and can significantly reprogram. The second says it is any of a broad class of Internet-access tools. The third says it must be Intel and Microsoft Windows compatible. Are they all true? Yes, at least for now.

If the grand vision described earlier (and at the core of the second definition of a PC) really comes about, the Wintel monopoly will have been broken. And there are signs that this might be about to happen, although it certainly will take many years to accomplish that fully. This trend is another thing discussed in more detail in Chapter 27.

The Bottom Line: What You Must Know and Why

Who needs to know all these things? Perhaps you do. Understanding how we got where we are, as an industry, and having some insight into where we probably are going in the near future will explain a lot of what is happening now. And it will help you see which of the hot, new products (hardware or software) are likely to be important, and which are likely to serve only niche markets or which might bloom briefly and then pass from the scene.

And clearly, if you can see ahead of time which "hot new" technologies are likely to have a lasting impact and which are not, then you can choose to invest more heavily in the former and steer clear of the latter. That will get you the best return on your investment in both PC hardware and software, especially over the long haul.

But to have those good effects, your knowledge must be fairly deep about certain aspects of the PC's design, as well as about how its software is built and operates. And, it should come as no surprise that giving you that information is exactly what the rest of this book is all about.

Can You Learn It All?

When I first began working with PCs shortly after IBM first introduced them in 1981, they weren't very complicated. It was perfectly practical for one individual to aspire to understanding in full detail every aspect of the design of the PC hardware, as well as learning how nearly all PC software was programmed.

Back then, PCs were rare, and very few companies made anything to do with PCs. That's why it was all so simple. Now, however, PCs are a *very* big business. Furthermore, PCs are now frequently connected to one another or to other, different computers. This makes understanding the big picture and all the details in it a much harder task.

Arguably, modern PCs—including their natural extensions via the Internet and other similar computer-to-computer connections—have become as a whole the most complex creation of mankind in all of our history. Certainly, they form the most complex and sophisticated consumer appliance and business tool ever devised.

This complex creation was not made by a single company, or even by a few companies. A huge number of companies and their brilliant, talented, and hard-working employees were needed to build it all. This means that there are far too many diverse products that enhance or work with PCs for any one individual to understand them all fully.

Indeed, to write this book, I needed the help of several people with expertise that went beyond mine in various ways. You'll find them mentioned in my acknowledgments in the front of this book.

But please don't despair. You *can* learn enough. You can learn at least the basics of how a PC is built and how it works, and you can learn the principles behind the programs it can use. You can learn how networks of PCs are created and, at least generally, how they operate. And those kinds of knowledge are exactly what you must learn to be empowered in the ways I mentioned at the beginning of this chapter.

The OBE (Out-of-Box Experience) and You

With the push to make PCs into a sort of "information appliance," hardware vendors have begun to give serious attention to various ways of helping the new owners of their products have an easy time setting them up and getting them to work. The jargon term for this is the OBE, which is defined as the "Out-of-Box Experience." It refers to the overall experience you are likely to have when you take home a new box containing some PC accessory—or even an entire new PC—open it up, and try to get it to work.

The goal, of course, is to make one's OBE an easy and satisfying one. Achieving that goal has turned out to be quite a challenge for the manufacturers. And, as often happens with laudable but difficult developments, even before a vendor's engineering department has worked out how to give the customer a good OBE, their marketing department will very likely start trumpeting to one and all that their products now offer a great OBE. So, my advice to you is this: *Caveat emptor*. Or, in common speech: Don't believe everything you read or hear—especially from a manufacturer or salesman.

No matter how nice they say your OBE will be, you must plan on spending some time getting to know your new PC (or PC part) and its capabilities rather intimately. And then you will find that it takes even more time if you want to be able to upgrade those capabilities.

One error too many people make is to choose a PC based on how easy it is said to be to upgrade it later on. And in the process they can let themselves be talked into buying a PC with lesser capabilities than they really know they need (in order to avoid having to spend so much money up front). This rarely works out as smoothly as you will have been told.

That said, I must ask: When was the last time you "upgraded" your washing machine or television set without simply replacing it? Probably you never have done that. The ease of setup and use of most appliances goes hand in hand with an inflexibility in their capabilities. PCs are different. And you may be happy that they are. (The so-called Network PCs and NCs have software flexibility, but little or no hardware flexibility. You will learn more about them in Chapter 27.

In practical terms this might mean that, unless you are very confident of your abilities to work inside the PC system unit, you should never buy a PC with less RAM than you will need to run the programs you want to use in the next six months. (After that the whole PC might be obsolete, or you might save so much on the new RAM you need by waiting until you need it—because prices on almost all PC parts have historically fallen quite rapidly—that you can afford to pay someone to install it.) At the end of Chapter 11, "Bigger is Better in Ballrooms and in a PC's Memory," I give you some specific suggestions on how much RAM is enough. Also, be sure you buy as much storage space (as big a hard disk) as you can afford. That is another item that sounds easier to upgrade than it can turn out to be in practice.

A Method and Plan for Our Journey

Okay. You should now have a fairly good idea of what a PC is (and what it is not). And you know something of how this industry came to be and where it is headed, at least in very general terms.

Now you must know a bit more about how this book is organized, and how you might choose to organize your safari into the deepest, darkest parts of your PC, and on into the strange new world that opens up beyond it.

Like many other books about computers, this one is both a general learning tool and a reference tool. That is, it can be read from cover to cover, in a totally linear manner, or you can browse in it, or dip in first here, then there, until you get the specific facts you want or need to find.

Here I shall explain the book's organization and point out some of the navigation tools it contains. After that, choosing the particular path that you want to follow is up to you. (If, for example, you have some burning questions you need answered, first check the index for those topics. Then dive right into the parts of the book that seem most likely to answer your questions. But if you find yourself feeling lost while reading in those places, just come back here and pick another path.)

As you can see from the Table of Contents, the book is divided into eight parts and two appendixes. Furthermore, throughout each part you will find that the material has been "layered" and peppered with "signposts" for your convenience.

PCs and the World in Eight Parts

Part I, "The Big Picture," looks at PCs from the outside. That is, it tells you about them without actually referring to the nitty-gritty details.

Part II, "A First Look Inside Your PC," is just a fast trip into the interior. Think of it as a chance to get your feet wet, or in another metaphor, as a high-altitude pass over the territory, to let you get a general sense of the "lay of the land."

The story continues in Part III, "The Stand-Alone PC." If yours is a fairly basic PC, and if it never is connected to another computer, then these parts will have most of what you need to understand its construction and function.

Part IV, "PC Programs: From Machine Language Bytes to Natural Human Speech," is a bit different. It returns to something closer to the flavor of Part I, but this time goes a lot deeper into how computers in general, and PCs in particular, are programmed.

Next come three parts that describe the main ways in which some PCs are different from their simpler brethren. Part V, "Splendiferous Multimedia PCs," describes fancy PCs. Part VI, "PCs Are Frequent Fliers, Too," focuses on mobile PCs. Finally, Part VII, "The Connected PC," explains the special features of PCs that connect to other computers.

Part VIII, "PCs, the Internet, the Future, and You," takes you beyond merely going *inside* your PC. It takes you, in effect, out of the other side of your PC into the wide world beyond.

Use the Layers to Fine-Tune Your Trek

Watch the icons as you read this book. There are three main levels on which the text is written. There is the basic story, which is suitable for any reader. There are historical asides that might interest only readers who are not in a tearing hurry to find some instantly useful facts, but instead are more leisurely readers seeking enjoyable anecdotes and background information. And there are the particularly technical portions, clearly marked so you can either avoid them (if you fear they might spook you), or hone in on them (if you know you are a "geek" or "techno-nerd" and want to find the absolute last word on a topic). Some other icons I also use are described in the introduction.

And, of course, don't forget the Index. That's often the best way to find the information you want in the fastest possible way.

Have a great trip!

2

How (Almost) Any Computer Works

Peter Norton®

Computers are tools used to process information. (In the next chapter, I explain exactly what I mean by *information*. For now, I shall assume that you have at least a pretty good notion of what it is.) Having said that fairly obvious yet basic fact about computers, I have actually implied quite a bit about how they must be built. Let me explain.

The Logical Parts of Any Computer

First, if you are going to process some information, you must be able to get into the computer the information to be processed. So all computers must have a functional part (or more than one) that serves as an input path for information.

Second, processing information is pretty pointless if you never get to find out the results of the processing. So all computers must have another functional part (or more than one) that serves as an output path for the processed information.

Third, and this might be said to be the (logically) most central part, there must be some part that can do the information processing. We call this part the information processing part.

Fourth, it wouldn't be possible to do any information processing if every bit of it that came in went back out immediately. The information must linger for at least a while so the computer can work on it. This implies that all computers must have some sort of information holding part (or parts).

There is another reason why some information-holding mechanism is necessary: The computer must know what it is to do. That means that somewhere inside it must be a place where the instructions about the processing it is to do can be kept. That takes more information holding.

Finally, there must be some part that controls what all the other parts do. Leave this out, and you have something that is almost a computer, but not quite. It has all the parts it needs to do everything, but no "head" to tell it when to do them.

To repeat myself a little more concisely: Every computer has a means for information input, a means for information output, a place for information to linger while it is waiting to be processed, a portion that does the processing, and finally, a portion that directs the work of all the other parts.

When you get into the details of how a particular computer is built, you will find some significant differences. And this book concerns itself with the details of how only PCs are built, which is why the chapter title doesn't promise that you will learn the details of every computer ever built. Funny thing, though: If you count only how many mainframe computers have been built, how many minicomputers, and how many of each kind of smaller computer, then add together all the varieties of PC, you will find that their total numbers far exceed all the other computers ever built. So to understand PCs is to understand almost all computers.

Actually, I have left out one very important logical part, because it isn't also a functional part as such. I mentioned that there must be some place in which to store programs. Those programs themselves can be thought of as yet another logical part. They differ from the other parts, though, in that for all the other parts, you must have some actual hardware of some sort. Programs, in their purest form, are merely abstract collections of numbers. True, they will end up residing in some physical medium somewhere, but you never need to possess physically that program-containing medium; all you really need is an ability to retrieve those numbers from it and transport them into your PC. (This is, for example, what you often end up doing when your PC is connected to the Internet.)

Functional Hardware Parts of a PC

That was a pretty fast overview of how a computer is built. Now I am going to go back over each of these five functional physical parts of any computer in a bit more detail, this time showing you what pieces of a PC typify each one.

Information Input Devices

The input device you probably use most often on your PC is the keyboard. You also input information any time you load a program from a disk or CD-ROM. Most PCs have a floppy disk drive. Some also have tape drives or removable cartridge drives (such as a ZIP drive). When you bring information on a floppy disk, tape, or ZIP cartridge, or CD-ROM disc from some other computer to your PC, the drive that lets your PC get to that information is another form of input device.

You might be confused a bit here. You might be thinking that a floppy disk, CD-ROM, or a ZIP drive is a place where information is held. That is true, but it is not the point I am trying to make here. I am talking about the *functional input parts* of a computer; not about the physical pieces of which it is composed. Sometimes a physical piece can serve in two or more different functional roles. That is the case, for example, for a disk drive. When you bring information to your PC from some other computer on a floppy disk, then that disk drive serves, at that time, as an input device. I'll explain a bit later in this chapter how that same physical piece can also serve as an information-holding device or an output device, depending on what you are doing with it. (Your hard drive could conceivably also serve as an input device, but only if you remove it from one PC and then install it in your PC. Because hard drives don't normally migrate between PCs, we normally consider them to be only information-holding devices, not input or output devices.)

Another very common way to put information into your computer, although you might not have thought of it in those terms before, is by moving and clicking your mouse (or, of course, doing the equivalent things by using a trackpad, trackball, graphics tablet, or joystick).

Technical Note: Of all these, the joystick is in some ways the most deceptive. You might have thought of it only as a way to play a computer game. But in some very significant commercial applications, that same hardware has been used to give feedback on the actions of a numerically controlled machine tool. In that context, the "game port adapter" (to which normally a joystick is connected) is quite properly described as a "four-channel analog-to-digital input device with an additional four purely digital inputs." Quite a mouthful, isn't it?

Other types of input some people use these days include scanners, video cameras, microphones, and video cassette recorders. These are the essential inputs for creating multimedia presentations on a PC.

Connect your PC to another computer, and you are likely to use that connection as a means of getting even more information into your PC. Such connections include a local area network, a mainframe host session connection, or using a modem to connect your PC to an electronic bulletin board, information service (such as America Online), or an Internet service provider. In effect, when you are connected to any such information service or Internet access point, you are connecting your PC to any and all of the other computers "out there" whose information content you are now able to access. So, in effect, they all become "input devices" that are "attached" (albeit temporarily) to your PC.

Of course, these same remote computers can also be used as recipients of information from your PC. But that is the subject of the next section, "Information Output Devices."

These are merely examples of some of the more common PC input devices. After you understand the concept, I am sure you can think of at least a few more you've heard about, and possibly even some you personally have used.

Information Output Devices

The most common output device for a PC is the monitor, on which words and pictures can be displayed for the PC user to see. It is a very efficient output device because it can display a lot of information at once, and it can alter that displayed information quite rapidly.

Another form of output is a printer. In the early days of computers, almost all output that was in human-readable form was printed on paper. If that were still the case, and if all the information that is now shown on screens had to be printed, I think the planet would have no trees left. But when you do need to keep some output for later reading, printing to paper is a convenient way to accomplish that.

Remember that not all printers print only words. In fact, a very large portion of PC output to printers today is in the form of highly formatted pages of text (which is to say, information about how the individual letters are to look and where they are to be placed is sent to the printer) and those pages can also include photographic or other images.

But not all computer output must be put into a form that humans can read. Indeed, it is essential that we be able to put much of it out in a computer-readable form. Every time you save your work to disk—at least if the disk in question can be removed from your PC and attached to some other computer—you have created some output that some computer (yours or another) could later use for input. So your PC's floppy disk drives can serve as output devices. (And, as you learned in the preceding section, they also can serve as input devices. It just depends on what you are doing with them.)

We don't normally count saving files on the PC's hard disk as output, because you can't easily take your hard disk out and put it in another PC. (This is not to say that can't be done; just that it is not normally done.) But when you save a file to a floppy disk, to tape, or to a disk cartridge, and if you plan to take the information you put on those media to some other computer so that the content can be loaded into that other computer, then those acts on your PC are clearly information output.

Multimedia creations often show up as output to audio loudspeakers (in addition to showing their images on the monitor), or they can be saved to a recordable CD (called a CDR disk) or on a video cassette recorder. Or perhaps you have given a presentation in which your PC was attached to a liquid crystal display panel on an overhead projector or to a video projector, as well as to a sound system so an entire room full of people could see and hear what you had created. That is just another form of computer output. And, of course, any time you connect your PC to another computer (over a local area network or a modem connection), you can use that link for output (or for input).

Finally, let me describe a really far-out kind of PC output. Attach your PC to an appropriate machine tool (and supply it with suitable raw material) and you can use it to craft real, three-dimensional objects of almost any shape. One example might be using a computer-controlled milling machine with a block of brass as the raw material. From this setup, it would be possible to make a model car, a fancy wrench, or whatever you might imagine made of brass by the operation of milling it. (Milling is a special class of cutting operations.)

The immediate output of your PC in this case is the flow of numbers to the tool that cause it to do its job. But in another sense, the ultimate output is the object created. So in that sense, the entire machine tool subsystem (with its supply of raw material) is an information output device for your PC. This is analogous to the way one often uses a PC with a printer and its supply of paper to make what amounts to a small book.

Eventually, most manufactured items might be made under the control of a PC in just such a fashion. This just-in-time approach has the very great advantage that only the parts that are going to be used are made, and each one can be custom crafted to meet the most exacting details of the customer's every whim.

Information Processing Devices

Most of the work of information processing is done by a device called the arithmetic-logic unit (ALU), which is only a part of what is on the particular integrated circuit chip we call the central processing unit (CPU).

In the original IBM PC, that CPU chip was a part made by the Intel Corporation and they called it an 8088. Chapter 7, "Understanding PC Processors," tells you about all the other CPUs that have been used in later models of IBM PCs or in various PC-compatible and clone PC computers. And you'll learn there about some of the processors that have been used in some computers that aren't what we are calling a PC.

The name *central processing unit* suggests that there might be other processors in your PC, elsewhere than at the center of the action. And, indeed, there are. A typical PC contains about half a dozen (and often many more) separate microprocessors, each doing its own, separate job.

The central processor is so important that often people refer to their entire PC by just the name of its CPU. For example, if you say you have a Pentium machine, or a 486, you are doing that. This shorthand way of speaking is understandable and quite acceptable because the nature of the CPU prescribes most of the details for how all the other parts must be built.

Chapter 5, "How to Get Your PC to Understand You," explains what types of processing the CPU chip is capable of doing. For now, just know that it is the physical part that does most of whatever information processing is done in your PC.

Information-Holding Devices

Earlier in this chapter, I mentioned several reasons why any computer must be able to hold information, at least briefly. One is to have it hang around long enough to be acted upon (processed). The other is that the instructions specifying what processing is to be done must be held inside the computer in order for them to be acted upon.

Once again, I am focusing here on the essential *function* in any computer of the parts that hold information. The same devices that can serve this function might also be able to serve the function of carrying information to (or from) another computer, as was described in the preceding two sections. In doing so they will, of course, have to retain that information during its transit to (or from) the remote computer, but they are not by that fact serving as what I am here calling the essential information-holding function of the computer, but rather as a suitably persistent medium of data transfer.

Because both types of information (data to be processed and instructions on what processing is to be done) are just numbers, they can both be held in the same information-holding devices. And in PCs, that is precisely what is done. (Some computers have been built that kept programs *exclusively* in one set of devices and data *exclusively* in another. That sort of "computer architecture" has not proven to be as useful as the one used in PCs, in which the two kinds of information are held in the same set of devices.)

> **Technical Note:** The computers I'm referring to in the previous paragraph that keep programs and data apart *always* are ones in which even when the data or programs are in RAM, they are kept apart in separate blocks of RAM. Nothing says you cannot keep all your programs on one particular hard disk and your data on another, for example, if you want to do this. And some folks think that doing so is a very good idea because it makes their strategy for backups work more easily. But that type of separation is an optional one implemented by the computer's user; not one that is enforced by its very design and construction.

Chapter 18, "Understanding How Humans Instruct PCs," explains how sometimes the identity of these two types of information becomes even more confused—when data can act as instructions, or instruction can be treated as just so much more data.

Right now, I want to point out a different way to divide the places in a PC where information is held: in a three-way division.

The first is a set of places that keep information that never changes. The second is a set of places that forgets any information it contains whenever you turn your PC off or reboot it. The third is a set of places that can keep information for a long time, and yet can enable that information to be changed.

Non-Volatile Electronic Memory

The first set of places for information holding are some very high-speed ones whose content cannot be changed. In a PC, this is any number of non-volatile electronic memory chips. There must be at least one of these because there must be at least a little bit of permanently and instantly available information to let the PC know how to start working when you first turn it on. Other programs that are held in non-volatile electronic memory include ones that are needed to activate the various hardware parts (such as the input and output devices) and that are used too often to make it worthwhile to get fresh copies of them from a disk whenever they are needed.

Some non-volatile electronic memory chips have their information content manufactured into them when they first are built. It can never be changed. We call these chips Read-Only Memory (ROM) chips. Other non-volatile electronic memory chips hold their information content for long periods of time without needing an outside power source, yet are able to have that information changed when necessary. As a generic group, these can be referred to as NVRAM (Non-Volatile, Random-Access Memory) chips. Other names are also often used for these chips, each one describing how a particular kind of NVRAM chip is built. These names include EEPROM, Flash RAM (or Flash ROM), and FERAM (or FEROM). You'll learn more about each of these technologies in Chapter 11, "Bigger Is Better in Ballrooms and in a PC's Memory."

Volatile Electronic Memory

The second set of places is where your PC keeps information only temporarily. These places forget whatever information they contain any time you reset or turn off your computer. In a PC, these are found in some larger number of electronic read-write memory chips. Because it is possible to go directly to any of the stored bits of information in these chips, they are called *random-access memory* (RAM) chips. Often in modern PCs, small groups of these chips are mounted on little plug-in circuit cards, and those assemblies are called *memory modules*. (Several different types of these memory modules exist, some called SIMMs and some called DIMMs. They are not all interchangeable; when adding more of them, you must get just the right kind for your PC.)

Both volatile and non-volatile electronic information-holding devices (ROM and RAM) are covered in much more detail in Chapter 11. For now, the most important other thing you must know about these devices is that they work very quickly—almost as fast as the CPU chip, and a whole lot faster than the third type of information storage device.

I've pointed out that this second group of memory chips (the volatile electronic ones) forget easily. That can be disastrous if your PC becomes "hung" and must be reset when you are in the middle of some long task and have forgotten to save your work. But it also can be a blessing if your PC is so confused that it cannot do anything (which is what being "hung" really means). In that case, you can clear out all that confusing mess simply by rebooting it and let it start afresh.

Because in modern PCs the CPU often runs too fast even for the RAM and ROM chips, some smaller amount of extra-fast RAM is needed to keep the CPU from having to twiddle its thumbs, chew its fingernails, or otherwise waste time waiting for the information it needs to reach it.

This faster RAM is organized into something called *cache memory*. In 486 and later processors, some of that cache memory is actually located on the CPU chip. And often, more of it is placed on the motherboard. You learn more about those details in Chapters 4, "Understanding Your PC's Parts," and 7, "Understanding PC Processors."

Disk Storage

The third set of places to store information is in the various types of disk (or tape) drives on your PC or remotely on some other computer. The good news about these places is that they can accept new information, and they can preserve it even when your PC is shut off. The bad news is that they cannot take or deliver back that information nearly fast enough to satisfy the CPU. So before any of the information is used as a program of instructions or as data to be processed, it must be loaded from that remote location into someplace in the PC's RAM.

A useful shorthand to keep clearly in mind the differing nature of the fast information-holding places and the slow ones is to call the former ones "memory" and the latter ones "storage." From now on in this book I will do just that, and in fact, that is a standard distinction used almost all the time throughout the PC industry. Chapters 9, "You Can Never Have Too Much Closet (or Data Storage) Space," and 10, "Digging Deeper into Disks" are all about PC storage. Chapter 11 talks exclusively about PC memory.

Warning: Let me repeat myself: Memory and storage are two entirely different things. Many folks who are new to the PC business get them confused. If you do, you will have no end of trouble trying to understand how your PC is built and how it works. So repeat this until you get it clearly in your mind: Memory is the fast information-holding place (made up of RAM and ROM). Storage is the long-term information-holding place (often made up of magnetic or optical disks or tapes).

Typically in a PC, you will have tens or hundreds of times as much capacity in storage as you have in memory. For example, a pretty good system these days might have between 16 and 64 megabytes (MB) of RAM (and a small fraction of that much ROM), and it might have several gigabytes (GB) of disk storage. One GB is the same as 1024MB.

Control Devices

Computers process information. They don't just do it automatically; something must direct their various parts to do their jobs. The input section must be told to bring in the information to be processed. It also must be told to bring in the instructions describing the processing to be done. Both of these are placed in an information-holding place.

The part of your PC that causes all this to happen is referred to as the *control portion*. Most of it is located on the CPU chip, along with the processor part (and, perhaps, an extra-fast memory part, called "cache memory"). Some other portions of the control part are on some other integrated circuit chips elsewhere in the PC (including ones commonly referred to by the names "chip set" and "embedded controller" chips).

Without a control portion, your PC would be no more than a fancy calculator. After all, any calculator has a means for information input—pressing the number keys (0–9) and the operations keys (+, –, ×, and ÷). It has a means of information output (the numerical display). It has an information-holding device, at least large enough to hold the numbers it is using in the current calculation. And it obviously has processing power enough to do those calculations. What it lacks is any part that can push the various buttons automatically.

Technical Note: Before the days of personal computers, we used desktop calculators. Some did only the things today's simple "four-function" calculators can do. Others were called "programmable calculators." These machines were, in essence, small computers but of a very limited sort. They had only a tiny amount of RAM, and they were useful only for very small programs. Changing their programs was also a lot more of a hassle than is the case for modern PCs.

Today you can buy modern equivalents to those machines, such as the popular Hewlett-Packard Model 48G programmable calculator with graphical display. These are not PCs, yet like all computers, they have the same five essential hardware aspects to their construction.

A key difference between most such programmable calculators and the more flexible PCs is that in the programmable calculators the programs are kept totally separate from the data. This means, among other things, that the program's instructions cannot be changed as a result of some calculation that it performs. Although this is not often done in a PC, it is possible, and that flexibility is, at times, very important.

What Makes a Computer More than a Calculator?

Here is where programs fit into the story. Even with all the different hardware parts I described earlier, if it has no programs to run, a computer will do nothing. (Well, if you want, it can serve as a pretty good doorstop or boat anchor. To be precise, I should have said that it will do no computing.)

A program is nothing more than a precise prescription for what is to be done. In mathematical language, we say that it implements an algorithm (which is just a fancy word for a set of rules for doing something).

Ah, if only making really good, error-free computer programs were as simple as that sounds.

Two Problems Programmers Face

Two things make writing computer programs harder than writing instructions to another human being. The first is that, unlike human beings, computer chips are able to "understand" and act on only a very few, rather simple instructions. So any task must be broken down into minute detail before it is ready to hand to a computer for execution. The second problem arises from the difficulty people have in anticipating absolutely every possible thing that might happen.

A perfect computer program must have specific instructions built in saying precisely what is to be done in each and every possible situation that could arise, no matter how unlikely some of them might be. Figuring out all those possibilities is, to say the least, a challenge to the best minds. And deciding what actions are to be taken, and incorporating the correct instructions to make those actions happen for every single contingency, without even once making a mistake, is asking for a perfection mere humans cannot seem to master.

In fact, many computer programs are now so complex that despite literally hundreds of millions of tests run on each one, some "bugs" are never found, simply because the conditions that would expose them never occur in those tests. And because computers run so rapidly, and there are so many PCs in existence with such a wide diversity of add-on parts and running such an eclectic mix of software, even those rare bugs can surface, sometimes years after the product's introduction, in many thousands of computers.

An Example of the Problems

To get some sense of just how hard this might be, let's play a little game. Pretend that you are asked to tell a willing, but very literal-minded and not too smart child to do some task. Let's say, taking out the trash.

First you might write the task like this:

1. Go to kitchen.
2. Get kitchen waste basket.
3. Take waste basket to trash container outside house.
4. Return kitchen waste basket to the kitchen.
5. Come back here.

That would suffice for you and me; in fact, it might be insultingly over-specific. But for the prospective executor of this task, it might be appallingly vague.

Look at the first instruction. We can assume that the child knows how to walk. But where is the kitchen? How will the child recognize it when he gets there? Then how is he to know what the kitchen waste basket looks like?

We might assume that once he has the waste basket he will know how to pick it up and carry it. But does he know the way to the outside trash container? You probably must spell it all out for him.

And then consider this: Suppose that when he gets to the back door it is closed. Did you remember to tell him to check for that, and if it is, to open the door before trying to go out? (And to close it after himself?) If you don't put in that sort of contingency checking and contingent instructions, the child might end up trying to open a door that is already open (and getting stuck at that point, unable to comply with what you have said he should do), or trying to walk through a closed door. Neither will work. Either will stop the execution of the program right there.

And so on. I don't think I need to carry this much further for you to get the general idea that writing computer programs takes a much more precise and attentive approach than directing human beings.

Two Ways Computer Designers Make Computer Programmers' Jobs Easier

To help programmers get their jobs done with fewer errors, either of omission (leaving out needed code to deal with unlikely conditions) or commission (including erroneous code), computer designers have come up with two general strategies. The first is to make the computer chips understand more and more complex instructions. That saves the programmer from having to break down each task quite so far into its elemental substeps. The second method is to create programs that write programs. The human programmer writes only a general schema for what the program is to do. The "compiler" then crafts the actual "machine language" program from those more general instructions.

The first of these strategies goes by several names, each describing a different way of approaching the same problem. The data handling and processing portions of a microprocessor chip are built with functional parts (such as the ALU) that can respond only to some very primitive commands. The instruction decoder (which is a key part of the control section of the processor chip) can be built to read instructions that assume more complex actions, and by reference to some "micro-code" stored on the chip, translate those instructions into the more primitive ones on which the functional processing parts can act.

This general strategy can be applied in several ways. One way, in which the complexity of the apparent processor instruction set is only minimally more complex than what the actual functional parts use, is called Reduced Instruction Set Computer (RISC) design. Another way, and the one used in the CPUs that are at the heart of almost all PCs built today, is to use that microcode instruction decomposition and elaboration strategy more heavily. The result is that the set of things the programmer can ask of the CPU is greatly expanded. This approach is called Complex Instruction Set Computer (CISC) design. Finally, we are beginning to see some processor chips that are designed to pack many elemental instructions into one, very long instruction. This very long instruction word (VLIW) strategy hasn't yet made it into mainstream PCs, but it very likely will within another generation or two.

Chapter 7 briefly describes the different CPU chips that have been or are now being used in PCs. That chapter also identifies which are more nearly pure CISC and which have more RISC in their designs.

The second strategy, crafting computer programs to write computer programs, also carries several names such as assemblers, interpreters, and compilers. You learn more about each of these in Chapter 18. In that and Chapter 19, "Some PCs Can Understand Speech and Talk to Us," you will learn about another, related strategy which, in effect, bridges the other two. In this strategy, the crafting of computer programs is broken down into layers of code. Each layer "clothes" the processor and all the layers beneath it with a new appearance, and that new appearance includes the apparent capability to understand and perform even more complex tasks.

Summary

In this chapter, you have gotten a pretty good sense of what the five functional parts of any computer are (input, output, information holding places, processing, and control) and how they can be exemplified in the pieces that make up your PC. (These five functional parts are supported by some additional, and quite necessary, parts such as the power supply and box and other hardware that holds all the pieces together.) Also, you now should have at least a glimmering of both how complex the job of instructing a computer is and of some of the general strategies computer hardware and software engineers have devised to deal with that complexity.

These are topics you will return to in more depth later in this book. Chapter 4 goes over all of these hardware parts in a little more detail and in the actual context in which they appear in a PC. There you learn why a power supply is vital, even though it doesn't do any of the essential tasks of the functional parts; why PCs have a motherboard and, usually, several daughter boards; the purpose of having a system unit with some parts inside and some outside it; and a lot more. Then, in Chapters 7–16, 21, and 23–26, you will find each of the individual parts discussed in much greater detail. Chapters 5, 18, and 27 explain the ins and outs of the PC programs that activate all this hardware and cause it to do all the things you or I want it to do.

For now, though, you have gotten enough of an understanding of both the problems and their solutions that you can move on to examine in more depth just what information is and just what it means to process data.

3

Understanding Bits, Nybbles, and Bytes

Peter Norton®

You cannot really understand how a PC, or any other computer, is built and how it works unless you first learn what information is. That, after all, is the raw material a computer works with. In this chapter I'll explain what information is. Also, we'll explore the many ways in which it is represented inside a PC. At the very end of this chapter, I'll explain how data and data processing (which is, after all, what PCs are used for) are related to information.

What Is Information?

You probably think you know what information is, at least in a general sense. And, no doubt, you do. But can you define it precisely? Probably not. In the day-to-day workings of the world, most people never need to know this, and so they've never thought about it.

Mathematicians do study such things, and they have come up with a really clear way to understand information. They say that information can best be understood as what it takes to answer a question.

The advantage of putting it this way is that it then becomes possible to compute exactly how much information you must have in order to answer particular questions. This then enables the computer designer to know how to build information holding places that are adequate for holding the needed information.

Measuring Information

The simplest type of question is one that can be answered either yes or no, and the amount of information needed to specify the correct answer is the minimum possible amount of information. We call it one *bit*. (If you like to think in terms of the ideas of quantum physics, the bit could be said to be the quantum of information.)

In mathematical terms, the value of the bit can be either a one or a zero. That could stand for true or false, or for yes or no. And in electrical engineering terms that bit's value could be represented by a voltage somewhere that is either high or low. Similarly, in a magnetic information storage medium (such as a disk or tape, for example), the same bit's value could be stored by magnetizing a region of the medium in some specified direction or in the opposite direction. Many other means for storing information are also possible, and we'll discover at least a few later in this story.

The marvelous next fact (which isn't initially obvious) about information is that we can measure precisely, in bits, the amount of information needed to answer any question. The way to decide how many bits you need is to break down the complex question into a series of yes-no questions. If you do this in the optimal way (that is, in the way that requires the fewest possible yes-no questions), then the number of bits of information you require is indicated by the number of elemental (yes-no) questions you used to represent the complex question.

How Big Is a Fact?

How many bits do you need to store a fact? That depends on how many possible facts you want to discriminate.

Consider one famous example: Paul Revere needed to receive a short but important message. He chose to have his associate hang some lighted lamps in a church tower. Longfellow immortalized the message as, "One if by land and two if by sea." This was a simple, special-purpose code. Computers work in much the same way, only they use a somewhat more complex and general-purpose code.

Actually, Paul's code was a little more complex than the phrase suggests. There were three possibilities, and the lamp code had to be able to communicate at each moment one of these three statements:

- "The British are not yet coming." (Zero lamps)
- "The British are coming by land." (One lamp)
- "The British are coming by sea." (Two lamps)

Paul chose to use one more lamp for each possibility after the first. This is like counting on your fingers. This works well if the number of possibilities is small. It would have been impossible for Paul to use that strategy if he had needed to distinguish among 100 facts, let alone the thousands or millions that computers handle.

The way to get around that problem is to use what mathematicians call *place-value numbering*. The common decimal numbering system is one example. The binary numbering system is another (binary numbering is used in the construction of computers). The next example will help make this concept clear.

The Size of a Numeric Fact

Suppose someone calls you on the telephone and asks you how old you are (to the nearest year). You could tell them, or you could make them guess. If you do the latter, and if you say you answer only *yes* or *no* in response to various questions, then here is the questioner's best strategy. (This assumes that over the phone the questioner is unable to get any idea of how old you are, but because you are a human, it is reasonable to guess that you are less than 128 years old.)

The first question is, "Are you at least 64 years old?" If the answer is *yes*, then the second question is, "Are you at least 96 years old?" However, if the answer to the first question is *no*, the second question would be, "Are you at least 32 years old?" The successive questions will further narrow the range until by the seventh question you will have revealed your age, accurate to the year. (See Figure 3.1 for the numbers to choose for each question.)

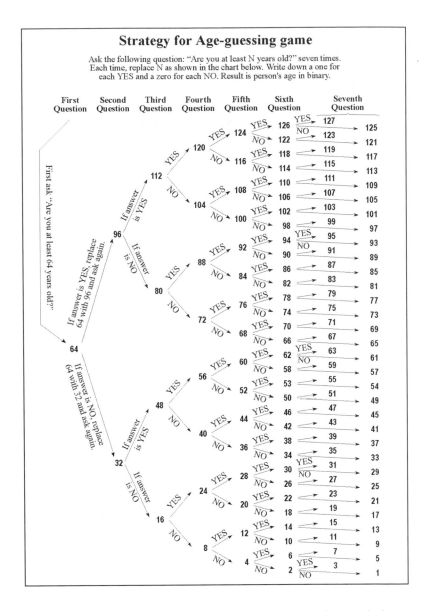

Figure 3.1.
Optimal strategy for the age-guessing game.

As the questioner gets the answers to each of the seven questions, he or she simply records them, writing a one for every *yes* and zero for every *no*. The resulting 7-bit binary number is the person's age. This procedure works because the first question is the most significant one. That is, it determines the most about the person's age. And if, like most of us, the questioner writes down the answer bits from left to right, the result will be a binary number stated in the usual way, with the most significant bit (MSB) on the left end of the number.

Here is what that process might look like. Assume you are 35 years old. Here are the answers you would give: "Are you at least 64 years old?" (no), 32 (yes), 48 (no), 40 (no), 36 (no), 34 (yes), 35 (yes). Your age (in binary) would be written 0100011.

This is an example of a place-value number. The first place is worth 64. The next is worth 32, then 16, and so on all the way to the last place, which is worth 1. By the *worth* of a place, I mean simply that you must multiply the value in that place (in binary this is always a zero or a one) by the worth of that place and add all the products to get the value of the number. In the example, add no 64s, one 32, no 16s, no 8s, no 4s, one 2, and one 1. The result of this addition (32 + 2 + 1) is 35.

When you answer seven yes-no questions, you are giving the questioner seven bits of information. Therefore, it takes seven bits to specify the age of a human being (assuming that age is less than 128). And that means that seven bits is the size of this numeric fact.

The general rule is this: The number of bits of information in a number is given by the number of places you need to represent that number in binary notation (which is to say, by using a place-value numbering system that uses only ones and zeros).

But wait a minute, you might say, this is all well and good for numbers, but how much information is there in a non-numeric fact? That is an important question, because most things for which we use computers these days involves at least some information that is not naturally stated in a numeric form.

The Size of a Non-Numeric Fact

To decide how much information a non-numeric fact contains, you first must decide how you will represent non-numeric information. To see one way in which it might be done, consider this very common use for a computer—word processing.

In word processing you create and manipulate documents. A word processing document normally isn't filled just with numbers. It is filled with words, and they are made up of letters separated by spaces and punctuation symbols. One way to represent such a document is as a string of symbols (letters, numbers, punctuation symbols, special symbols to represent the end of a line, tabs, and other similar ideas). How much information is there in such a document?

If you write down all the possible symbols that could occur in the document, you'll see how many different ones there are (disregarding how often each one occurs). Then you could give each of those unique symbols a numeric label. Now, I claim it is easy to see how many simple questions, like those used to fix your age, it would take to pick each symbol out of that character set. Here is how.

Suppose you had a document with 43 different symbols occurring in it. This means you have a *character set* with 43 members. You could label those symbols with the numbers from 0 to 42. After you have specified this collection of symbols and their order, you can designate any particular one of them by a number that gives its location in the collection. We call such a number a pointer. The size of the non-numeric fact that you are indicating—for example, the size of the letter *j*—is now considered to be simply the size of the binary number needed as a pointer to pick out the specified character from this collection of symbols. And the size of the entire document is the number of symbols it contains times the size of each pointer.

It is important to realize that these pointer values make sense only in the context of a given collection of symbols. Therefore, you must have that collection in hand before you can use this strategy. You will return to this point in more depth in the section "Symbols and Codes" later in this chapter.

Table 3.1 shows how many bits you need for a pointer that can pick out one member of a collection of symbols. In our sample case, the answer is six bits, because 43 is less than 64. (With six bits, you could pick out each member of a collection of up to 64 symbols. You can pick out the members of a collection with only 43 members by thinking of them as the first 43 members of those 64. You could not get away with using a five-bit number as a pointer, because that would let you discriminate only among members of a set of 32 items.)

Table 3.1. How big is a fact?

Number of possibilities this fact can distinguish	Number of bits needed to hold this fact
2	1
4	2
8	3
16	4
32	5
64	6
128	7
256	8
.	
.	
.	
65,536	16
.	
.	
.	
1,048,576	20

This strategy provides a way to represent symbols as numbers (pointers into collections of symbols). In the process, it also provides a measure of just how big a fact you need to specify those symbols. That is, it measures their information content. Each symbol holds as many bits of information as the size of the pointer needed to pick it out of the collection of symbols to which it belongs.

This also provides a way to transform the original document (a string of symbols) into a string of pointers (numbers). In the example, each pointer would be six bits long. In that case, the entire document would be six bits times the number of pointers (which is the same as the number of symbols, and this time I mean the total number of symbols in the document, not just the number of unique symbols). This is a form you could hold in a computer. This is a form much like the one actually used by typical word processors.

How Much Space Does Information Need?

Now you know the size of information in a mathematical sense—that is, how many bits you need to specify a certain fact. But how much room does it take to hold this information inside a computer? That depends, of course, on exactly how those information-holding spaces are built.

All PCs are built on the assumption that every information-holding place will contain a binary number. That is, each location can hold either a one or a zero. In this case, you need at least as many locations to hold a number as there are bits in that number.

Technical Note: Because the information-holding spaces in PCs are organized into groups of eight bits (called bytes), sometimes a number will fit into some number of bytes with some space left over. In that case, any remaining highest-order bit locations are simply filled in with zeros. (That is true for positive numbers. For negative numbers, which typically are represented in a "ones-complement" style, the filled-in bit locations would all receive ones.)

The alternative to binary information-holding places is to put information in locations that could each represent more than two values. That lets one hold more information in fewer locations.

If each location could have three discernible states (say a low voltage, a medium voltage, and a high voltage), then the numbers would be held in those locations using a ternary (base three) numbering system. This system is distinctly more space efficient than binary in that fewer locations are needed to hold the same amount of information. However, building reliable and inexpensive information-holding cells that operate on any higher number base than two has proven to be very difficult. Therefore, all modern computers use only binary number holding places.

Technical Note: We can put a precise value on the higher efficiency of ternary information holding places, as compared to binary ones. It takes N binary number (bit) locations to hold numbers up to 2^N. And it is possible to hold numbers up to 3^M in M ternary locations. If $2^N = 3^M$, then the two collections of locations can hold the same range of numbers, but that implies that the ratio N/M is equal to (log 3)/(log 2), or about 1.58. This means that each ternary location can hold approximately 1.58 bits of information. A similar calculation shows that in a base-5 (quinary) system each location holds about 2.32 bits.

Technical Note: You might have noticed that the relationship between the number of bits held in one cell and the number base implies that you could hold an enormous amount of information in a single cell just by using some very high number base. But doing that means that you would have to be able to distinguish as many different possibilities for the value held in each cell as the base of that numbering system.

What if you chose a number base such as one million? Could you hold a value that could take on any of a million possibilities in one cell? If the value were held as a voltage, that would mean the cell might hold voltages between zero and one volt, and you would have to be able to set and read that voltage accurate to one microvolt. And indeed, you could do this—in principle. But in practice, you'd find that the inevitable noise in the circuit would probably swamp the tiny variations you intended to hold in that cell. Therefore, you couldn't reliably place there and then later retrieve numbers with that fine-grained a resolution after all. Or, if you could, the circuit would work far too slowly to be useful in a computer.

This chain of reasoning hints at what is perhaps the biggest advantage of any digital circuits: They eliminate the effect of noise altogether. This is very important. At every stage of a digital circuit, the values are represented by voltages that inevitably will vary somewhat from their ideal values. That variation is called *noise*. But when those values are sensed by the next digital portion of the circuit, that portion makes decisions that are simple, black-and-white, go/no go decisions about what the values are. And it then re-creates those voltage values more nearly at their ideal levels.

This means that you can copy digital data any number of times and be reasonably sure that it still has exactly the same information content that it had when you started out. This is in sharp contrast to what happens in analog circuitry. If you try to copy an analog tape recording of music, for example, and then copy the copy and keep on repeating this process hundreds of times, you will most likely end up with a tape recording that contains nothing but noise. All the original information will have been lost beneath the huge overlay of noise.

To accomplish this noise-defying act, the digital elements of the circuit must each have a generous difference between significant input values. This is how it is possible for each stage to throw away the minor variations from the nominal values and be sure it isn't throwing away anything significant. And the faster you want that circuitry to make these noise-discarding decisions, the larger the differences must be between significantly different input levels. In the end, this is why computer circuit designers have settled on binary circuits as the basic elements. They have the simplest decisions to make ("Is this level high or is it low?") and, therefore, they can make them most rapidly.

Historical Aside: In the early days of computers, designers experimented with many different schemes. Some were tried out only in laboratories; others actually made it into commercial production.

In some computers the numbers were held in a hybrid of decimal and binary called "binary coded decimal," or BCD. In this scheme numbers are regarded as decimal (base 10) numbers. They are composed of digits, each having a value of 0 to 9. Then the actual information holding cells are built using four binary bits to represent each decimal digit. (Looking back at Table 3.1 you can see that four is the minimum number of bits that must be used to hold a pointer capable of discriminating among ten possible values for a particular digit.)

This probably seems like a pretty natural way to design a computer. After all, most people think in decimal numbers, and so they probably will provide numbers to the computer mostly in decimal form and want to see the results of its calculations also in decimal form. Thus, it seemed perfectly normal to build a computer to work with numbers solely as decimal quantities.

Unfortunately, this is not a very efficient way to hold numbers. To hold numbers up to a billion (a thousand-million), you must be able to hold nine-digit decimal values. That means you need four-times-nine (which is 36) places to put a bit. If, on the other hand, you used only pure binary numbers, you could get away with only 30 places. The disadvantage to using binary numbers comes in the conversions that must be performed to figure out what binary number corresponds to each decimal number and the reverse.

When computers were used mostly to do a lot of very simple calculations (mainly payroll and other accounting applications), the conversion effort was a significant part of the total information-processing work they performed. Therefore, designing those computers to work directly with decimal numbers actually did make sense.

continues

Now that computers do so many other things, such as word processing (manipulating abstract symbols), manipulating graphics, and creating music—and even when they are used to do mathematics on numbers, they typically do a lot of calculations with them—the conversion of decimal input numbers to binary and converting them back for output is a very minor part of their information-processing work. Therefore, for these computers, space efficiency in the information holding places is much more important than avoiding number base conversions. This is the main reason why all modern computers are built to hold numbers exclusively as pure binary numbers.

Putting more information into fewer memory cells by using a number base other than binary is only one way to reduce the number of memory cells you need. It is not, in fact, normally used. One way that often is used is to remove redundancy. This very different approach is explained in the following section.

Document Size, Redundancy, and Information Content

I told you earlier that information is what is contained in the answers to some questions. Another way of viewing it is as news. That is, if you get some information, and then you get the same message over again, the second time it carries no (new) information. The relationship between the two points of view is clear when you consider that the repetition of a message doesn't help you answer any more questions than you could by using only the first copy. This shows that an exact repeat of some message does not really deliver twice the original information content. Furthermore, many messages deliver less information than they might appear to hold at first glance.

Real documents often contain *redundancy*. That is, knowing some of the document enables you to predict the missing parts with an accuracy that is better than chance. (Try reading a paragraph in which all the vowels have been left out. You can do surprisingly well.) This means that you must encode only some fraction of the symbols in the document to know all of what it contains. And that means the true information content of the document might be significantly less than the raw size (number of symbols times bits per symbol).

Note: Here is a paragraph of simple English with all the vowels removed. Can you read it? After you try, check your understanding by going to the end of the chapter where you will find the same paragraph with its vowels restored.

Ths s tst. f y cn rd ths prgrph, nd gt th mnng t lst mstly rght, y hv shwn tht nglsh s rdndnt t sch dgr tht lvng t ll th vwls dsn't stp y frm rdng t prtty wll.

For convenience, most word processors put every symbol you enter directly into your documents. They make no attempt to reduce the document size to the bare minimum. This saves time, but it bloats the documents which, among other things, wastes disk storage space.

Most of the time that is just fine, but sometimes you want to minimize the size of your files. You might plan to send some of them over a phone line and want to minimize the time and cost that this will require. Or you might find yourself running out of space on your hard disk.

Technical Note: Various strategies are available to take advantage of redundancy. One is an *archiving* program. Such a program can take several files, squeeze out nearly all the redundancy in each one, and then combine them all into a single file with many fewer bytes than the original collection of files. ARC, PKZIP, and LHA are some very popular programs for this purpose.

Another approach is a software or hardware data-compression disk interface product (also called an "on-the-fly file data compressor"). These products squeeze out the redundancy in files as they are stored on your disk or tape drives, and then they expand them back to their original, redundant form as the files are read from the tape or disk.

One of the early leaders in this field is Stac. Its compression products are used by many tape drive manufacturers. Its retail product, Stacker, is a device driver that creates the illusion that you have a much larger disk drive than the actual physical size of your disk. (Typical compression ratios run about 2:1, with some files compressing to as little as a tenth their full size, and others compressing hardly at all.)

Stacker does its magic entirely transparently. After it is installed, you won't know it is doing anything; you'll simply experience having an apparently larger, and often somewhat faster, hard drive at the relatively slight cost of using up some of what turns out to be a very precious first megabyte of memory in your PC's RAM.

Things can become even more subtle. The information content of a file might depend on who is looking at it. If you have never seen a document before, it will contain much that is news to you. This means it will contain a lot of information. You could not guess all of its content without using a lot of yes-no questions. Essentially, you must see every symbol in the document, or nearly every one. And that means that the information content of the document is close to being the number of symbols it contains times the information content of each symbol. And because you can't predict all those symbols, the information content of each one is simply the size of the pointer you need to pick out that particular symbol from the character set being used.

Someone who knew ahead of time that this document was one of a certain small group of documents might find that it contained very little information. All that person needs in order to know all of what it contains is to figure out which one of the given sets of documents this one is. This will take a rather small number of questions (at least the number indicated in Table 3.1 for the size of the group of known documents). For that person, the document could be adequately replaced with just one pointer number. The size of that number is all the information that document contains *for that person*.

> **Note:** To see how powerful this approach can be, imagine that you work in an office that creates custom documents out of a limited number of standard parts (pieces of boilerplate text) along with a customer-specific header. You could replace each custom document with just that header followed by a short list of small numbers, one number per standard part you were including. The numbers could be small because each one only needs to contain enough information to indicate which of the limited number of standard parts it represents.
>
> This shortened representation of the document is adequate for you to re-create the full document. This means you need store only this small file on your hard disk to enable you to print out the full document any time you want.
>
> To put numbers to this, suppose your office used only 256 standard document parts. Each one could be any length. Suppose they averaged 10,000 bytes. Because an 8-bit pointer (one byte) would suffice to indicate any one of the 256 documents (2^8=256), your custom documents could each simply consist of the customer-specific header followed by a string of bytes, one per standard part to be included. This would enable you to compress your documents for storage on average by a ratio of 10,000:1.
>
> Of course, because your customers don't have your collection of standard parts, you must assemble the full document for them before you can ship it.
>
> Is such an approach actually practical? Yes. Something much like this is often used in law offices, by architectural specifiers, and in the writing of computer programs, for example.

Bits, Bytes, Nybbles, and Words

Early teletypewriters used five or six bits per symbol. They were severely restricted, therefore, in the number of distinct symbols a message could contain (they were limited to 32 or 64 possibilities). To see just how restrictive this is, consider the following facts: There are 26 letters in the alphabet used by English language writers, and every one of them comes in an uppercase (capital letter) form and a lowercase (uncapitalized) form. In addition, we use 10 numerals and quite a few punctuation symbols (for example, the period, comma, semicolon, colon, plus and minus signs, apostrophe, quotation mark, and so on). Count them. Just the ones I have mentioned here come to 70 distinct characters, and this is too many for a six-bit code. Even leaving out the lowercase letters, you'll have 44 characters, which is too many for a five-bit code.

In order to accommodate all these symbols in messages, for most of the past century the standard has been to use seven bits. That allows 128 symbols, which is enough for all the lowercase and uppercase letters in the English alphabet, all 10 digits, and a generous assortment of punctuation symbols. This standard (which now has the formal name of the American Standard Code for Information Interchange, or ASCII) uses only 96 of the 128 possibilities for these printable symbols. The remaining 32 characters are reserved for various *control characters*. These latter values encode the carriage return (start typing at the left margin once again), the line feed (move the paper up a line), tab, backspace, vertical tab, and so on. The ASCII standard also includes symbols to indicate the end of a message and the famous code number 7, to ring the bell on the teletypewriter. Presumably, this last one was needed to get the attention of the person to whom the message was being sent. (I go into more detail about the control characters and printable characters included in ASCII in the section "Symbols and Codes," later in this chapter.)

Starting with the IBM 360 series of mainframe computers in the early 1960s, the most commonly handled chunk of information was a group of eight bits, which has been named the *byte*. Many other mainframe and minicomputer makers used other size chunks, but all modern PCs have used the byte exclusively as the smallest chunk of information commonly passed around inside the machine, or between one PC and another.

Although they never explained it this way, I am sure the engineers at IBM were concerned with two things when they decided to switch from 7-bit symbols to 8-bit ones. First, this change let them use symbol sets with twice as many symbols, and that was a welcome enriching of the possibilities. Second, this was a more efficient use of the possibilities for addressing bits within a minimal chunk of information.

Occasionally, dealing with half a byte as a unit of information is useful. This is enough, for example, to encode a single decimal digit. Some droll person, noting the resemblance of byte and bite, decided that this four-bit chunk should be called the *nybble*. This name became popular and is now considered official.

More powerful PCs can also handle groups of two, four, or even eight bytes at a time. There is a name for these larger groupings of bits. That name is *word*. Unfortunately, unlike a byte, a word is an ill-defined amount of information.

Technical Note: This is not unlike English. Each letter, number, or punctuation symbol takes up roughly the same amount of room, but a word can be as small as a single letter or an almost unlimited number of letters. (Consider the words *I* and *a* and then remember the famous 34-letter word *Supercalifragilisticexpialidocious*; there are also a good many less artificial words that are nearly that long.) Things are not quite that bad in the world of computers; but still, a computer word is far from being a clearly defined constant.

One notion of a computer word is that it contains as many bits as the computer can process internally all at once. This rule makes the size of a word dependent on which computer you are talking about.

Another popular idea has been that one computer word has as many bits as can be carried at once across that computer's data bus. (The next chapter introduces you to the notion of a computer bus in detail.) This definition also gives us a size that depends on the particular model of PC.

If you use the first of these definitions, you can say the earliest PCs had 16-bit words, more modern ones have 32-bit words, and the Pentium and Pentium Pro have 64-bit words. By the second definition, the earliest PCs had 8-bit words, and again the most modern ones have 32-bit or 64-bit words.

Either of these definitions can lead to confusion. The good news is that all the different models of PCs are more alike than different, so choosing one definition for word size and sticking to it can help you keep your sanity.

Fortunately, most people have settled on 16 bits as the size of a PC's "word," independent of which model of PC they are discussing. Thus, in programming one often speaks of handling words, double words (32 bits, referred to as DWORDs) and quadruple words (64 bits, referred to as QWORDs). However, these definitions are not universally used. So be careful when reading technical descriptions of PC hardware. A *word* might be something different than you expect.

Historical Aside: Historically, some mainframe computers have had rather peculiar word sizes. Sizes such as 12, 36, and 72 bits have been used. Notice that none of these is an integral power of two. This is unfortunate, because somewhere the computer must be able to hold addresses that are pointers to locations of bits within each of its information-holding places. Those pointers are binary numbers, so if the word size is, for example, 72 bits, then each pointer must have seven bits. This would allow pointing to individual bits within words that held up to 128 bits. This excess capacity is, in a sense, wasted. Fortunately, engineering common sense has come to the fore in the design of PCs. All of them use only 16-bit words or some other integral power-of-two number of bits per word.

Don't confuse the use of 36 bits or 72 bits here with the fact that modern PCs use SIMMs or DIMMs, which hold 36 or 72 bits. In these older computers all those bits were part of the real data being held in those word locations. In PCs that use 36-bit or 72-bit SIMMs or DIMMs one out of every nine bits is used for error control (parity) or for error correction (ECC). Only the remaining 32 or 64 bits are used to hold actual data.

Representing Numbers and Strings

Information-holding places in a PC hold only binary numbers, but those numbers stand for something. Whether that something being represented is a number or something non-numeric, some group of bytes must be used. The strategy most commonly used to hold non-numeric information is simpler than that for numbers because having several definitions of how to hold a number has proven more efficient, with each of the different ways being used in particular contexts. I'll explain the details of how numbers are held first, and then explain how non-numeric entities are held.

How Numbers Are Held in a PC

Mathematicians distinguish among several types of numbers. The ones you probably use every day are *counting numbers*, *integers* and *real numbers*. Counting numbers are, of course, the ones you use to count things. That is, they are the whole numbers beginning with zero (1, 2, 3…). Integers are simply the counting numbers and the negatives of the counting numbers. Real numbers include integers and every other number you commonly use (for example, 45, –17.3, 862.1457). Either type of number can be arbitrarily large.

Computer engineers categorize numbers a little differently. They speak of short and long integers and short and long real numbers, for example. They also often distinguish integers that are always positive from those that are allowed to take on either positive or negative values.

Counting Numbers and Integers

The exact definition of what's a short integer and what's a long integer varies a little between different computer designs, and sometimes between different computer languages for the same computer. The key point of difference with the mathematical definition is that although mathematical integers can be of any size, computer integers are limited to some maximum size, based on the number of information-holding places to be allocated to each one.

Short integers typically are held in a pair of bytes (16 bits). If a short integer is construed as a counting number, that means its value can be anything from 0 to 65,535. Or, if it can be either positive or negative, then one bit must be used for the sign. That cuts down the largest size positive or negative number to about half the foregoing value. Now the range is from –32,768 to +32,767.

Long integers typically are held in four-byte locations (32 bits). For counting numbers (which cannot be negative) this gives a range of 0 to 4,294,967,296. For integers, therefore, the range is from –2,147,483,648 to +2,147,483,647.

When giving the values of these long and short integers, the common notation uses hexadecimal numbers. (I explain exactly what these are in the next section. For now you just need to know that hexadecimal, or base-16, numbers use two symbols chosen from the numerals 0–9 and the letters A–F to represent the value of one byte.) Thus, a short integer might be written as 4F12h or AE3Dh, and a long integer as 12784A3Fh or 83D21F09h. (The trailing lowercase letter *h* is merely one of the conventional ways to distinguish a hexadecimal number from a decimal number.)

Negative integers can be represented in two different ways. In one plan, the first, or high-order bit is called the *sign bit*. Its value is zero for positive numbers and one for negative numbers. The remaining bits are used to hold the absolute value of the number. Thus, +45 would be represented as the binary number 0000000000101101 and the number –45 as 1000000000101101. I'll call this the "ordinary" way to represent a signed binary number.

But the more commonly used way to represent negative numbers is what we call the *ones-complement* of the representation I have just described. To generate this representation for any negative number you first figure out what the "ordinary" representation would be, then flip all the bits ("complement" them) from zero to one or from one to zero, and finally you add one to the result.

Why would one want to do something so weird as using a ones-complement notation? For simplicity, actually. Let me explain why this is so.

Table 3.2 shows you a dozen numbers starting with +5 at the top and decreasing by one on each succeeding line down to –6 at the bottom. Each of these numbers is shown as a decimal value in the first column, as an ordinary binary number in the second column, and in ones-complement notation in the third column.

Table 3.2. Three ways to represent integer numbers.

Decimal value	"Obvious" binary notation	Ones-complement binary notation
5	0000000000000101	0000000000000101
4	0000000000000100	0000000000000100
3	0000000000000011	0000000000000011
2	0000000000000010	0000000000000010
1	0000000000000001	0000000000000001
0	0000000000000000	0000000000000000
–1	1000000000000001	1111111111111111
–2	1000000000000010	1111111111111110
–3	1000000000000011	1111111111111101
–4	1000000000000100	1111111111111100
–5	1000000000000101	1111111111111011
–6	1000000000000110	1111111111111010

In both the second and third columns the first bit is the sign bit, with a one indicating a negative value. What is nice about the ones-complement notation is that the sign bit is, in a sense, automatic. Notice that if you start anywhere in the table and add one to the value in the third column (treating all the bits, including the sign bit, as if this was simply a 16-bit positive integer) you'll get the number on the line just above. Similarly, if you subtract one you'll get the number just below. This works whether the starting point is a positive or a negative value.

However, if you try this in the middle column you'll find that you must use different rules for negative and positive numbers. That makes those ordinary binary numbers much more complicated to use in doing arithmetic. So, computers typically are built to spend the effort to figure out the ones-complement form of negative values, knowing they will more than save it back in the ease with which arithmetic operations can be done on them later on.

Real Numbers

Storing real numbers is much trickier than storing integers or counting numbers. Because in everyday use we let these numbers be as large as we like or as small as we like, they potentially have an unlimitedly large number of possibilities. Setting aside unlimitedly large blocks of information-holding places for each one is not practical. Therefore, some decisions have to be made about how to represent these numbers adequately.

One thing you'll realize if you think about how real numbers are used is that normally for very large numbers we don't care much about the fine details, whereas for very small numbers, the size of "negligible portion" becomes correspondingly smaller. For example, in dealing with the federal budget, pennies just don't count. Even dollars are commonly considered too tiny to matter. As the late Senator Everett Dirkson once put it, "You add a million dollars here, a million dollars there, and pretty soon you are talking about some real money."

At an opposite extreme, atomic physicists and chemists often must ponder very tiny structures in atoms and molecules. The difference to them between two different sizes can matter when it is only 0.000 000 001 meter, or even less. And nuclear physicists commonly talk about distances thousands of times shorter than this.

How can one possibly devise a representation of numbers that will encompass such a wide range? The only reasonable way is by holding the number in three parts. The first part indicates whether the number is positive or negative. The second part indicates how large the number is. The third part describes what the actual number is, to some defined relative accuracy.

Technical Note: In mathematical terms, this looks like a product of these three terms:

- Sign (plus or minus)
- An integer power of 16
- A number between 1/16 and one

The use of powers of 16 (rather than, say, powers of 10) has to do with engineering efficiency. Because 16 is two to the fourth power, multiplying a number by an integral power of 16 in binary notation merely means moving the decimal point to the right or left by some multiple of four places.

Each of these portions is given a definite number of holding places in the computer. Because the first part, called the *sign*, indicates only one bit of information (plus or minus), it needs only a single bit as its holding place. The next part, called the *exponent*, and the final part, called the *mantissa*, each could potentially use an arbitrarily large number of holding places. However, for practical reasons they are each limited to definite, and sometimes uncomfortably small, values. What are called *single-precision real numbers* commonly are represented using seven bit locations for the exponent and 24 for the mantissa. Together these take up a single four-byte group of information-holding locations.

These limited spaces imply limits on the numbers that can be represented. Those limits are often not important, but occasionally they can matter, sometimes a lot.

Technical Note: With seven bits for the exponent, one of which is used for the sign of the exponent, and 24 bits for the mantissa, the largest positive number that can be represented is $+16^{63}$. The smallest positive number is $+16^{-64}$. The range of size of negative numbers is about the same. The accuracy with which any number can be represented will vary from one part in 2^{24} down to one part in 2^{20}.

These facts translate into decimal terms as follows: The maximum positive number is about 7.24×10^{75}. The minimum positive number is about 1.16×10^{-77}. The relative accuracy with which any number can be represented ranges from about one part in four million to about one part in a million, or from about six to seven significant figures.

When it is necessary to hold numbers with greater relative precision than the single-precision real number format allows, many computer programs allow the use of double-precision real numbers. In this format, the sign still gets one bit and the exponent (including its sign bit) still gets seven bits, thus filling up the first byte. The difference comes in the mantissa, which is now given 56 bits. This enables you to hold numbers in the same general range of sizes, but now with precision equivalent to 16 or 17 significant decimal digits rather than the merely six or seven significant decimal digits that are possible with single-precision numbers.

Strings of Non-Numeric Information

Another way to organize bytes into larger groups is used in creating what are called *strings*. A string is a collection of bytes, strung out one after another, which go together logically. A string can be of any length. (Abstractly speaking, a string can have any length at all. But a string that gets held inside a computer must not have a length greater than some maximum size that depends on the particular computer program that was used to define the string. Typically, maximum string lengths are at least 32,768.)

There are two ways that are often used to indicate the length of a string of bytes encoding a string. One is to put the length as an integer into the first few bytes. The other is to end the string with a special symbol that is reserved for only that use. The advantage of the first strategy is that you can see the length of the string immediately. The advantage of the latter strategy is that you can have, in principle, strings of any length you want. However, in order to discern what length a particular string has, you must examine every one of the symbols in it until you come across that special string-terminating symbol.

Symbols and Codes

Codes are a way to convey information. If you know the code, you can read the information. I've already discussed Paul Revere's code. His was created for just one occasion. The codes I am going to discuss in this section were created for more general purposes.

Any code, in the sense I am using the term here, can be represented by a table or list of symbols or characters that are to be encoded. The particular symbols used, their order, the encoding defined for each symbol, and the total number of symbols defines that particular coding scheme.

Tip: In order not to be confused by all this talk of bits, bytes, symbols, characters sets, and codes, you must keep clearly in mind that the symbols you want to represent are *not* what are held in your PC. Only a coded version of them can be put there. If you actually look at the contents of your PC's memory, you'll find only a lot of numbers. (Depending on the tool you use to do this looking, the numbers might be translated into other symbols, but that is only because the tool assumes that the numbers represent characters in some coded character set.)

Morse code is one well-known encoding scheme. Its original purpose was to send messages consisting of letters, numbers, and some punctuation symbols from one place to another using a single wire (and its electrical return path) and some rather crude signaling devices.

What actually is sent from one place to another is a succession of short and long pulses (called *dits* and *dahs*, respectively), each separated from its neighbors by either a long or a short interval. An interval equal in length to a dit is used to separate the dits and dahs of one letter (or other symbol). A dah-length interval is used to separate the symbols from one another. Morse code indicates what symbol a given pattern of dits and dahs means. If you know the code, reconstructing the message is easy—but you must know the code.

Morse code is not very useful in PCs because Morse code uses a variable-length string of dits and dahs to represent the symbols. PCs have fixed-size places to hold information (bytes); therefore, they work best if they use a code that also has a fixed size per symbol.

You'll encounter three common codes in the technical documentation on PCs:

- Hexadecimal
- ASCII
- EBCDIC

The hexadecimal code is used to make writing binary numbers easier. ASCII is the most common coding used when documents are held in a PC. EBCDIC is an alternative coding scheme sometimes used for computer-held documents. (This last one will not be used anywhere in this book outside this chapter, although it is referred to in some PC documentation.)

If you are using a PC with non-English language software, you might be using yet another coding scheme. In fact, there are several ways in which foreign languages are accommodated in PCs. Some simply use variants of ASCII. Others use a special double-byte encoding. A new standard way is starting to encompass and ultimately replace all those possibilities. Its name is Unicode. I'll describe it in more detail in just a moment.

Hexadecimal Numbers

The first of the three most common coding schemes is *hexadecimal numbering*, which is a base-16 method of counting. As you have now learned, it takes 16 distinct symbols to represent the "digits" of a number in base-16. Because there are only 10 distinct Arabic numerals, those have been augmented with the first six capital letters of the English alphabet to get the 16 symbols needed to represent hexadecimal numbers (see Table 3.3).

Table 3.3. The first 16 numbers in three number bases.

Decimal	Binary				Hexadecimal
0	0	0	0	0	0
1	0	0	0	1	1
2	0	0	1	0	2
3	0	0	1	1	3
4	0	1	0	0	4
5	0	1	0	1	5
6	0	1	1	0	6
7	0	1	1	1	7

Decimal	Binary				Hexadecimal
8	1	0	0	0	8
9	1	0	0	1	9
10	1	0	1	0	A
11	1	0	1	1	B
12	1	1	0	0	C
13	1	1	0	1	D
14	1	1	1	0	E
15	1	1	1	1	F

The advantages of using hexadecimal are twofold: First, it is an economical way to write large binary numbers. Second, the translation between hexadecimal and binary is so trivial, anyone can learn to do it flawlessly.

Any binary number can be written as a string of bits. A four-byte number is a string of 32 bits. This takes a lot of space and time to write, and it is very hard to read accurately. Group those bits into fours. Now replace each of the groups of four bits with the equivalent hexadecimal numeral according to Table 3.3. What you get is an eight-numeral hexadecimal number. This is much easier to write and read accurately!

Converting numbers from hexadecimal to binary is equally simple. Just replace each hexadecimal numeral by its equivalent string of four bits.

For example, the binary number

01101011001101011000110010100001

can be grouped into fours of bits as

0110 1011 0011 0101 1000 1100 1010 0001

This can, in turn, be written as a hexadecimal number. Look up each group of four bits in Table 3.3 and replace it with its hex equivalent. Putting a lowercase *h* at the end (to indicate a hexadecimal number), you'll get this:

6B358CA1h

Now test your work. Using Table 3.3, convert the final hexadecimal number back into the original binary one.

You'll encounter many hexadecimal numbers in documents on various aspects of PCs and PC programs. That's because the important addresses are simpler to write and say when they are expressed in hexadecimal form.

You can recognize a hexadecimal number in two ways. If it contains some normal decimal digits (0, 1, … 9) and some capital letters (A through F), it is almost certainly a hexadecimal number. Sometimes authors will add the letter *h* or *H* after the number. The usual convention is to use a lowercase *h*, as in this book. Another convention is to make the hexadecimal number begin with one of the familiar decimal digits by tacking a zero onto the beginning of the number if necessary (or to put 0x in front of every hexadecimal number). Thus, the hexadecimal number A would be written 0Ah (or 0xA). Notice that the hexadecimal number 5 and the decimal number 5 are the same. Putting the h after a hexadecimal number less than 10 (decimal) isn't necessary.

Unfortunately, not all authors play by these rules. In some cases, you simply have to go by the context and guess.

Technical Note: Engineers love hexadecimal as a way to represent addresses in a PC. For them, the important point is not that the special numbers are written so simply. It is that the binary number into which you can easily convert the hexadecimal number actually represents the arrangement of low and high voltages on the wires in the PC.

The ASCII and Extended ASCII Codes

The next common code you'll encounter in PCs is called the American Standard Code for Information Interchange, abbreviated ASCII. This is the code that was developed first for teletypewriters, and it now is the almost universally accepted code for storing information in a PC. If you look at the actual contents of one of your documents in memory (or on a PC disk), you usually must translate the numbers you find there according to this code to see what the document says (see Figure 3.2). (Some programs use a different coding scheme, called EBCDIC when creating documents. I'll explain this code in just a few moments.)

Of course, because ASCII is so commonly used, many utility programs exist to help you translate ASCII-encoded information back into a more readable form for humans. One of the earliest of these utility programs for DOS is one of the external commands that has shipped with DOS from the very beginning. Its name is DEBUG. You'll meet this program and learn how to use it safely for this purpose in Chapter 6, "Enhancing Your Understanding by Messing Around (Exploring and Tinkering)."

Vern Buerg has written a shareware program called LIST, which displays information from ASCII-encoded PC disk files superbly well. It often is licensed by software companies and included with their products to help customers read the online documentation or READ.ME files.

Figure 3.2.
The ASCII character set, including the standard mnemonics and the IBM Graphics symbols for the 33 ASCII control characters.

		Control Codes		ASCII Printable Characters						
		00	10	20	30	40	50	60	70	Hex
Hex	Dec	0	16	32	48	64	80	96	112	Dec
0	0	NUL	DLE ►		0	@	P	`	p	
1	1	SOH ☺	DC1 ◄	!	1	A	Q	a	q	
2	2	STX ☻	DC2 ↕	"	2	B	R	b	r	
3	3	ETX ♥	DC3 ‼	#	3	C	S	c	s	
4	4	EOT ♦	DC4 ¶	$	4	D	T	d	t	
5	5	ENQ ♣	NAK §	%	5	E	U	e	u	
6	6	ACK ♠	SYN ▬	&	6	F	V	f	v	
7	7	BEL •	ETB ↨	'	7	G	W	g	w	
8	8	BS ◘	CAN ↑	(	8	H	X	h	x	
9	9	HT ○	EM ↓	)	9	I	Y	i	y	
A	10	LF ◙	SUB →	*	:	J	Z	j	z	
B	11	VT ♂	ESC ←	+	;	K	[	k	{	
C	12	FF ♀	FS ∟	,	<	L	\	l	|	
D	13	CR ♪	GS ↔	-	=	M	]	m	}	
E	14	SO ♫	RS ▲	.	>	N	^	n	~	
F	15	SI ☼	US ▼	/	?	O	_	o	⌂	

ASCII uses only seven bits per symbol. When you create a pure-ASCII document on a PC, typically the most significant bit of each byte is simply set to zero and ignored. This means there can be only 128 different characters (symbols) in the ASCII character set. About one-quarter of these (those with values 0 through 31, and 127) are reserved, according to the ASCII definition, for control characters. The rest are printable. (Some of the control code characters have onscreen representations. Whether you see those symbols or have an action performed depends on the context in which your PC encounters those "control code" byte values.) Those symbols and the ASCII control code mnemonics are shown in Figure 3.2. Add the decimal or hexadecimal number at the left of a row to the corresponding number at the top of a column in order to get the ASCII code value for the symbol shown where that row and column intersect. Table 3.4, later in this chapter, shows the standard definitions for the ASCII control codes.

IBM's Extensions to ASCII

When IBM designed its PC, it decided to extend the standard ASCII code in two ways. First, because the PC moves information around most of the time in byte-sized blocks, IBM decided to create a standard set of meanings for what are sometimes called the upper-ASCII characters—that is, those with code values between 128 and 255 (80h to FFh). It built these definitions into both its PC video display adapters and its PC printers. Furthermore, IBM created a set of symbols to be used to represent onscreen the first 32 ASCII characters and the one at position 127. Normally, these values are used only to control computer processes, but in the IBM PC it is possible, in some situations, to send them to the video display subsystem and see them interpreted onscreen as the symbols shown beside those positions in Figure 3.2. Figure 3.3 shows the "upper-ASCII" character set IBM chose. Some, but not all, of those symbols can also be printed on many printers.

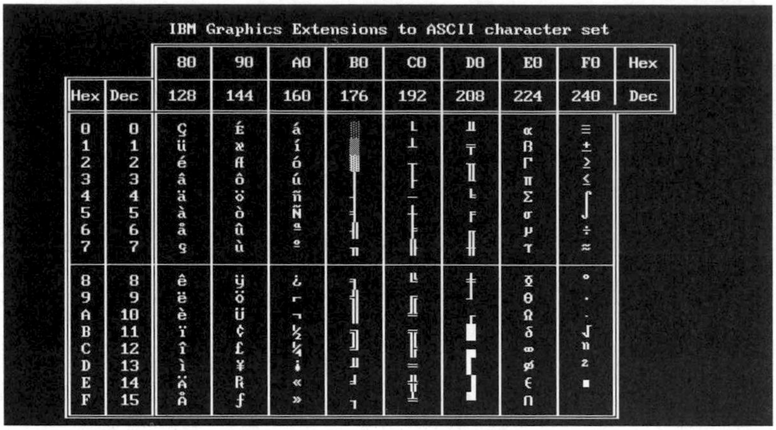

IBM Graphics Extensions to ASCII character set

		80	90	A0	B0	C0	D0	E0	F0	Hex
Hex	Dec	128	144	160	176	192	208	224	240	Dec
0	0	Ç	É	á	░	└	╨	α	≡	
1	1	ü	æ	í	▒	┴	╤	ß	±	
2	2	é	Æ	ó	▓	┬	╥	Γ	≥	
3	3	â	ô	ú	│	├	╙	π	≤	
4	4	ä	ö	ñ	┤	─	╘	Σ	⌠	
5	5	à	ò	Ñ	╡	┼	╒	σ	⌡	
6	6	å	û	ª	╢	╞	╓	µ	÷	
7	7	ç	ù	º	╖	╟	╫	τ	≈	
8	8	ê	ÿ	¿	╕	╚	╪	Φ	°	
9	9	ë	Ö	⌐	╣	╔	┘	Θ	∙	
A	10	è	Ü	¬	║	╩	┌	Ω	·	
B	11	ï	¢	½	╗	╦	█	δ	√	
C	12	î	£	¼	╝	╠	▄	∞	ⁿ	
D	13	ì	¥	¡	╜	═	▌	φ	²	
E	14	Ä	₧	«	╛	╬	▐	ε	■	
F	15	Å	ƒ	»	┐	╧	▀	∩		

Figure 3.3.
IBM's definitions for the "upper-ASCII" character set.

IBM's Line-Drawing Characters

One small group of characters in IBM's extensions to the ASCII code are particularly noteworthy. These are the line-drawing characters.

Any time you look at a computer display and see a menu or data entry screen composed solely of letters and numbers plus some boxes around some of them, it is quite likely that you are looking at these special characters. (This used to be quite certain, before the popularity of Windows and other graphical user interfaces. Many computers used in businesses are still running DOS programs with pure-text displays for data entry and other applications, in part because these programs need only the least expensive video display adapters and monochrome monitors.)

IBM included the line-drawing characters precisely so that it would be possible to do more interesting and useful displays for business applications than would have been the case if the only printable characters were the letters, numbers, and normal punctuation characters.

The IBM line-drawing characters are shown in Figure 3.3 at locations 179 through 218. Why 40 characters just for drawing lines? Because they wanted enough flexibility to draw single- or double-line boxes. Not only do they need four corner pieces plus a top (or bottom) and side character for each line style, they also need characters that represent where one line style meets another in all possible ways. Finally, the characters at positions 176–178 and 219–223 are there to permit drawing very bold lines.

Other Extensions to ASCII

Even before IBM's PC (and the many clones to it), there were small computers. Apple II was one popular brand. Many different brands of small computers running the CP/M operating software were also popular. These computers all held information internally in bytes.

Because they held bytes of information, they were able to use a code (or character set) with twice as many elements as ASCII. Each manufacturer of these small computers was free to decide independently how to use those extra possibilities.

Epson, Hewlett-Packard, and IBM all make printers for PCs, but each of them chose a different way to translate extended-ASCII character values into printable symbols. If you print something from DOS on one of these printers (unless you have told it to use the IBM set of extended-ASCII symbols in place of its own native set), you might be quite surprised by what you see on the printed page. It might not at all reflect what you saw onscreen.

Some word processors, most notably WordStar, use that eighth bit to indicate the end of every word. Viewing programs such as LIST have an option to mask off that bit, thus treating it as a zero no matter what its actual value might be. This makes viewing WordStar files much easier.

Not everything in your PC uses ASCII coding. In particular, programs in files use what might be regarded as the CPU's native language, which is all numbers. Therefore, LIST will not help you make much sense of them, although DEBUG can help some.

A Totally Other Coding Scheme: EBCDIC

Some manufacturers developed their own codes totally independent of the ASCII definition. One notable example is IBM. When IBM introduced the use of bytes in its 360 series of mainframe computers, it also introduced a new character encoding. Instead of adding the ASCII code as it did later with the PC, IBM created a whole new code called the Extended Binary Coded Decimal Interchange Code, or EBCDIC for short.

This would be only a historical curiosity except that IBM still uses this code on some of its larger computers—it used the code on its stand-alone DisplayWriter word processors, and it used it in the DisplayWrite word processing program for the PC. EBCDIC has become an alternative standard for document interchange, represented in the standard called Document Content Architecture, Revisable Format Text (or DCA/RFT). Figure 3.4 shows the EBCDIC character set. Notice that it lacks some of the symbols in IBM's extended ASCII for PCs. More importantly, the symbols it shares with ASCII are assigned to very different numbers.

Viewing an EBCDIC-encoded document requires a special viewer. Otherwise, you must either use the program that created the document or convert it to a format suitable for some other program to read and use.

Figure 3.4.
*The EBCDIC
character set.*

Hex	Dec	Control Codes				EBCDIC		Printable Characters		
		00	10	20	30	40	50	60	70	Hex
		0	16	32	48	64	80	96	112	Dec
0	0	NUL	DLE	DS		SP	&	-		Alternate Code Assignments
1	1	SOH	DC1	SOS		RSP		/		
2	2	STX	DC2	FS	SYN					
3	3	ETX	DC3	WUS	IR					
4	4	SEL	ENP	INP	PP					ENP or RES
5	5	HT	NL	LF	TRN					INP or BYP
6	6		BS	ETB	NBS					
7	7	DEL	POC	ESC	EOT					
8	8	GE	CAN		SBS					
9	9	SPS	EM		IT					
A	10	RPT	UBS	SM	RFF	¢	!	|	:	SM or SW
B	11	VT	CU1	FMT	CU3	.	$	,	#	
C	12	FF	IFS		DC4	<	*	%	@	
D	13	CR	IGS	ENQ	NAK	(	)	_	'	
E	14	SO	IRS	ACK		+	;	>	=	
F	15	SI	ITB	BEL	SUB	|	¬	?	"	ITB or IUS

Hex	Dec	Upper half of EBCDIC character set								Hex
		00	10	20	30	40	50	60	70	Hex
		0	16	32	48	64	80	96	112	Dec
0	0					{	}	\	0	
1	1		a	j	~	A	J	NSP	1	
2	2		b	k	s	B	K	S	2	
3	3		c	l	t	C	L	T	3	
4	4		d	m	u	D	M	U	4	
5	5		e	n	v	E	N	V	5	
6	6		f	o	w	F	O	W	6	
7	7		g	p	x	G	P	X	7	
8	8		h	q	y	H	Q	Y	8	
9	9		i	r	z	I	R	Z	9	
A	10					SHY				
B	11									
C	12									
D	13									
E	14									
F	15								EO	

Control Codes

I've mentioned several times that a portion of the ASCII code is reserved for control characters. Any useful computer coding scheme must use some of its definitions for symbols or characters that stand for actions rather than for printable entities. These include actions such as ending a line, returning the printing position to the left margin, moving to the next tab (in any of four directions—horizontally or vertically, forward or backward).

Other special codes stand for various forms for indicating the beginning or the end of a message (SOH, STX, ETX, EOT, GS, RS, US, EM, and ETB). Another special code (ENQ) lets the message-sending computer ask the message-receiving computer to give a standardized response. Four quite important control codes for PCs are the acknowledge or negative-acknowledge (ACK or NAK) codes, the escape code (ESC), and the null code (NUL). The first pair is used by the receiving computer to let the sending computer know whether a message has been received correctly, among other uses. The escape code often signals that the following symbols are to be interpreted according to some other special scheme. The null code is often used to signal the end of a string of characters.

Table 3.4 shows all of the officially defined control codes and their two- or three-letter mnemonics. These definitions are codified in an American National Standards Institute document, ANSI X3.4-1986.

Table 3.4. The standard meanings for the ASCII control codes.

ASCII Value Decimal (Hex)	Keyboard Equivalent	Mnemonic Name	Description
0(0h)	Ctrl+@	NULL	Null
1(1h)	Ctrl+A	SOH	Start of heading
2(2h)	Ctrl+B	STX	Start of text
3(3h)	Ctrl+C	ETX	End of text
4(4h)	Ctrl+D	EOT	End of transmission
5(5h)	Ctrl+E	ENQ	Enquire
6(6h)	Ctrl+F	ACK	Acknowledge
7(7h)	Ctrl+G	BEL	Bell
8(8h)	Ctrl+H	BS	Backspace
9(9h)	Ctrl+I	HT	Horizontal tab
10(Ah)	Ctrl+J	LF	Line feed
11(Bh)	Ctrl+K	VT	Vertical tab
12(Ch)	Ctrl+L	FF	Form feed (new page)
13(Dh)	Ctrl+M	CR	Carriage return
14(Eh)	Ctrl+N	SO	Shift out
15(Fh)	Ctrl+O	SI	Shift in
16(10h)	Ctrl+P	DLE	Data link escape
17(11h)	Ctrl+Q	DC1	Device control 1
18(12h)	Ctrl+R	DC2	Device control 2
19(13h)	Ctrl+S	DC3	Device control 3
20(14h)	Ctrl+T	DC4	Device control 4

continues

Table 3.4. continued

ASCII Value Decimal (Hex)	Keyboard Equivalent	Mnemonic Name	Description
21(15h)	Ctrl+U	NAK	Negative acknowledge
22(16h)	Ctrl+V	SYN	Synchronous idle
23(17h)	Ctrl+W	ETB	End of transmission block
24(18h)	Ctrl+X	CAN	Cancel
25(19h)	Ctrl+Y	EM	End of medium
26(1Ah)	Ctrl+Z	SUB	Substitute
27(1Bh)	Ctrl+[	ESC	Escape
28(1Ch)	Ctrl+\	FS	Form separator
29(1Dh)	Ctrl+]	GS	Group separator
30(1Eh)	Ctrl+^	RS	Record separator
31(1Fh)	Ctrl+_	US	Unit separator
127(3Fh)	Alt+127	DEL	Delete

In Table 3.4, note that Ctrl+x means to press and hold the Ctrl key while pressing the x key, and Alt+127 means to press and hold the Alt key while pressing the 1, 2, and 3 keys successively.

Unicode

By now you understand why the early five- and six-bit teletype codes weren't adequate to do the job of encoding all the messages and data that needed to be sent or that are now being handled on our PCs. What might be less obvious to you is why even an eight-bit code such as IBM's extended ASCII or EBCDIC aren't really what we need. In this section, I hope to clarify for you the ways in which eight-bit codes are proving to be hopelessly limited, as well as show you what is soon going to replace them, at least in some contexts.

If everyone on the planet spoke and wrote only in English, none of what I just said would be true. But that clearly is not reality. By one count, there are almost 6,800 different human languages. Eventually, we need to be able to communicate in every one of them using a PC. And to do that, some serious improvements must be made in the information-encoding strategy we use.

The importance of this point is becoming clearer and clearer. At first, people tried some simple tricks to extend extended-ASCII. That was enough for awhile, but soon the difficulties of using those tricks outweighed their advantages. And in any case, it was becoming apparent that these types of tricks just wouldn't do at all for the broader task ahead.

In the beginning, the heavy users of computers of all kinds were all people who used a language based on an alphabet, usually one that was quite similar to the one used for English. Simple variations on the ASCII code table were worked out, one for each language, so that the set of symbols would include all the special letters and accents used in that country. These "code pages" could then be loaded into a PC, and it would be ready to work with text in that language.

However, this strategy can work only if two conditions are met. First, the computer in question must be used for only one of these languages at a time. Second, the languages must be based on alphabets not too dissimilar to that of English.

However, there are some very important languages that use too many different characters to fit into even a 256-element character set. This is clearly true for the Asian languages that are based on ideographs. What you might not realize is that this also holds true for many other languages, such as Farsi (used in Iran), where the forms of characters are altered in important ways depending on their grammatical context.

At first, people thought they could solve this problem by devising ever more complex character sets, one per language to be encoded. And the really difficult languages were handled by making up short character strings that would encode each of the more exotic characters.

One difficulty with this approach is that not all symbols are contained in a single-size information chunk. We are back to the problem I mentioned with using Morse code. Another difficulty is that there are still many different encoding schemes, each one tuned to the needs of some particular language, and none will work for arbitrary mixed-language documents.

Obviously (in retrospect, at least) the solution ultimately must be to devise an entirely new encoding scheme—one that will have enough capacity to hold all of the symbols used in any of the 6,800 languages of the people on this planet. This is exactly what has been done. The result of this effort is *Unicode*.

Unicode is a complex subject. It has been developed in a lengthy process, including input from linguists and computer scientists around the world. It is being codified in several documents issued by several international standards groups, each document describing some aspect of Unicode. The designers of Unicode have taken great pains to be sure that this strategy has enough room to grow in order to make it last a very long time.

The basic approach is to represent each symbol in Unicode with a 16-bit number. This means that it is possible to represent every symbol in a pair of bytes (which is one computer "word" in the most common definition of that term for PCs). Normally, this would allow representing at most 65,536 distinct characters or symbols. This set of symbol possibilities is called, in Unicode jargon, the *Basic Multilingual Plane*, or BMP. This space is very large but, the designers thought, it might someday prove to be inadequate. Therefore, they built in a way to extend this representation even further.

When you use only two-byte (16-bit) numbers to represent Unicode characters, what is called *UCS-2 encoding* is being used. However, the standard enables inserting within the body of some UCS-2-encoded text some UCS-4 characters. To do this, two 1,024 location blocks are reserved in the BMP. Each of those locations cannot be used to represent any symbol. Instead, pairs of those numbers, one chosen from each group, will be used to encode up to about a million UCS-4 characters.

Why, you might wonder, not simply use four bytes per character from the outset? The answer is quite simple. That is too wasteful of space. Almost all the time you can get away with double-byte characters, and only when you need to use something more exotic will you have to dedicate four bytes per symbol.

The details of Unicode are well beyond anything I want to go into here. If you are interested, you can find most of them on the World Wide Web. Point your browser to the Unicode home page at the following Uniform Resource Locator (URL), and follow the links you find there:

```
http://www.stonehand.com/unicode.html
```

Is Unicode being used today? Most certainly. If you are running Windows 95 or Window 98, you are using it (probably without knowing that you are). Every directory entry pointing to a file on your disk drive is stored using Unicode. And Office95 and Office97 use Unicode extensively in the document files they create. This makes it much easier for these programs to support users with different language needs. You set your language preference once (and it is recorded in the Windows registry). Thereafter every program you use, including Windows Explorer, will show you displays in your language, interpreted from the Unicode representation.

What Is Data and How Is It Processed?

This has been a long chapter. You have learned not only what bits, bytes, and nybbles are, you also learned what information is and how it can be measured and stored. What's left to discuss about information in the most general sense is its relationship to data and data processing. This is the other piece of the puzzle you must understand in order to appreciate how a PC is built and how it operates.

Data is, in many ways, the same thing as information. The difference is mostly just one of perspective. Data is information that we consider a raw resource to be mined for the precious gems of information it contains. The point of much information processing is to take some mass of data and reorganize it in such a way that the valuable information in it is clearly revealed. Sometimes this reorganization is done automatically by a computer, under the control of some program. Other times the reorganization is done in a more interactive manner.

This description clearly applies to the types of statistical analysis that were the bread and butter of computing in the early days. However, today we do so many different things with PCs—does this description apply to graphic artists creating stunning visuals, or to musicians composing and performing music on a PC? How about what I am doing now—writing this book?

Yes, I think the description is still apt. For example, when I write this paragraph, I am taking some data I hold in my head and delivering it to the PC in a particular fashion. Therefore, I do some of the data mining in my brain. But I then expect the PC to capture that output and hold it for my editor's, and eventually my reader's benefit. After I have put the thoughts down, I often find I must use the PC as a tool to help me rearrange or modify those thoughts in an effort to make their meanings even clearer.

Note: Remember the test earlier in the chapter? Here is the same paragraph with the vowels put back in. See how closely you got the meaning of this paragraph from the earlier version with no vowels.

This is a test. If you can read this paragraph, and get the meaning at least mostly right, you have shown that English is redundant to such a degree that leaving out all the vowels doesn't stop you from reading it pretty well.

II

A First
Look Inside
Your PC

4

Understanding Your PC's Parts

Peter Norton®

At this point you have learned an overview of the PC industry and its role in our larger society. You also have at least a general notion of how any computer is designed and works. You also know something about what information is and how data is processed. It finally is time to get down and dirty, to go inside the PC and see how the parts look and what they are. The previous chapters focused on functionality and logical organization. This one focuses on the physical parts and how they are interconnected.

A PC as a "Chamber Orchestra"

Some people, and perhaps you, find computers intimidating. They feel reluctant to open the box and muck around inside. Others relish doing this. Whichever group you belong to (or even if you don't identify with either), you must know one very important fact up front and keep it clearly in mind as you continue on your safari into PC land.

Peter's Principle: Look at the Parts Separately and Then at Their Interconnections

The simple, but overwhelmingly important fact is that PCs are made up of many parts, and each part is much simpler than the whole. To understand a PC, therefore, you are well advised to look first at the simpler parts that make it up. But to make sense of those explorations, you must also keep in the back of your mind some image of the interconnection and interaction of all these parts.

In this chapter you will meet the parts that make up a typical PC, and you will see the scheme by which they are interconnected. These introductions are fairly cursory, but they will give you that necessary background image of the whole as the sum of its parts. The following chapters (especially those in Parts III, V, and VII) take you through a much more intimate look at each of the different parts of the PC one at a time.

If you see a PC as some wonderfully capable multifunctional machine, you might believe that understanding how it works is almost impossible. Breaking up that image into many parts will be very helpful. Each of those parts might also be quite wonderful, but none is nearly as complex as the overall combination. Now look at each part in turn. Understand the parts, one by one, in as much detail as you want, then see how they fit together and work as a whole. This is the most direct way to an overall understanding of the total PC.

I also want to give you some important cautionary tips. You really don't want to hurt either yourself or your PC, so whenever you open up the case, remember the following precautions.

Warning: First, don't open up your monitor. It is a special-purpose television set, and as such it contains dangerous voltages. Let a specialist do any needed repairs there. Also, don't open up your PC's power supply. It doesn't contain anything you can fix.

However, do feel free to open your PC's system unit and probe around inside. Just remember, when you do so, follow these critically important steps:

1. Turn off the PC.

2. Touch an unpainted metal part of the case (to discharge any static electrical charge you might have picked up) before *each* time you touch anything else inside the PC.

3. Keep a record of anything you change so you can put that back as it was in case you have only made things worse.

The Three Main Pieces

Most PCs have a lot in common. The essential core of the typical desktop PC comes in three pieces: a keyboard, a monitor, and one other box called the system unit. Of course, you might also have a printer and a mouse and other things, but nearly every PC has these three parts, and it must have them in order to do anything useful.

This is not to say that other PC designs are not possible. For example, a laptop computer has all three of these parts bundled into a single unit, mainly for convenience in carrying it around. In Part VI, "PCs Are Frequent Fliers, Too," I will go into detail on the many design differences between portable, laptop, and palmtop computers. This chapter focuses on the more typical desktop systems, such as that shown in Figure 4.1, which happens to be a fine mainstream system (in terms of its features and price) made by Dell Computer Corporation.

The system shown in this figure is fairly typical of today's high-end desktop systems. The larger-than-typical monitor is one that would serve well the needs of anyone doing a lot of graphics-intensive work, including desktop publishing. I'll be using this Dell XPS M200s system for most of the examples throughout the rest of this book.

Some PCs have system units that are thinner than the one shown in the picture. Those are called low-profile PCs, and the idea is that you can slip the system unit under your monitor without having the monitor stick up uncomfortably high above your desktop. Other PCs have system units that are particularly short; they sometimes are referred to as baby PCs. And some older units have system units that are larger than the one shown in the picture. IBM's original AT is one example.

Figure 4.1.

A typical desktop PC has three main pieces: the keyboard, monitor, and system unit. This PC system is a Dell model XPX M200s with an optional Dell UltraScan 20 TX monitor.

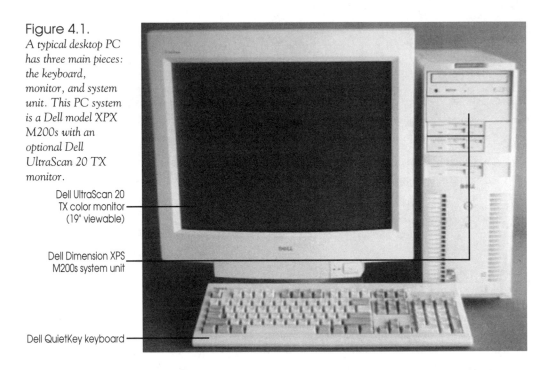

Dell UltraScan 20 TX color monitor (19" viewable)

Dell Dimension XPS M200s system unit

Dell QuietKey keyboard

Some PC manufacturers turn the system unit on its end. These are called *tower systems* (or mini-tower systems for particularly short system units). Although it is possible to turn almost any desktop system on its end, the ones designed for use in that position usually have some design details that make them preferable for that usage. For example, they often have a broad foot that keeps them from tipping over, and they have one or all of the disk drive bays rotated 90 degrees from the orientation used in desktop units.

Peter's Principle: Cleanliness Is Good

Any PC will work better and last longer if it stays reasonably clean inside. I don't mean that you must open it up and clean its insides frequently. (Although cleaning the inside whenever you have some other reason to open it up might be a good idea; normally that will be sufficient.) I suggest that you try to keep dust and dirt from getting into your PC in the first place.

For example, don't put any PC directly on the floor—even if it is a tower unit. If you want to put it beside your desk, put it on top of a low box or other support. This keeps the vents where air goes into the PC away from the bottom few inches of air in the room, because that is where most of the dust and dirt will be found. However, if you support your PC above the floor, be sure whatever you use will not make the PC more likely to tip over.

PCs come in many shapes and sizes. Just glance at the catalogs of some vendors that make and sell PCs. Which form you choose limits in some ways which options you can put into that PC, but in general how they are built internally and how they work is pretty much the same as in the traditional desktop unit shown in Figure 4.1.

What Goes Inside the Box

There might be only three main pieces to a typical PC, but one of those pieces, the *system unit*, is a pretty complex object. It contains many other, smaller objects. It also contains the essential interconnection infrastructure that lets those pieces work together amicably.

> **Architecture:** A theme that I shall return to over and over again in this book is that PCs are made by many manufacturers out of pieces made by other, even more numerous manufacturers. This diversity is the source of much of the flexibility and power of PCs. It has allowed each customer to buy a PC that includes almost any conceivable collection of features that the customer wants (is willing to pay for).

This diversity is also the principal source of most people's problems with their PCs. I will go into more detail on this point in the section "Controlling Chaos," later in this chapter.

This diversity came about, and it could only have come about, after there were some industry-wide agreements about how the pieces should interconnect. I discuss that point in the section "Information Rides the Bus," later in this chapter. But first I must explain just what all those pieces are that live inside the typical (or not-so-typical) PC's system unit.

A Platform to Build Upon: The Motherboard

Every PC has one printed circuit card in it that serves as its foundation. This circuit card is the *motherboard*. (Well, if it doesn't have any places in which to plug other printed circuit cards, it technically is called a *mainboard*. That term can be used to refer to the main printed circuit board in any PC, but because almost all of them have places in which to plug other boards, the term motherboard has become the more common term for this item, even in those relatively few cases in which it really is only a mainboard.)

The motherboard very likely will contain some of the integrated circuits (chips) that provide certain functional aspects of the PC, though how much of your PC's functionality is there depends very much on what make and model you have. But whatever its other design features, the main purpose of the motherboard is to interconnect the several functional parts of the PC. To this end it has several special connectors into which other pieces can be plugged. Some of these (the ones into which other printed circuit cards are plugged) are called *input/output (I/O) slots*, because plugging in boards like these is the most common way to connect to the PC's input-output bus (over which path these cards communicate with the rest of the motherboard). Others are simply called connectors.

Figure 4.2 shows the motherboard from our example desktop system. The callouts indicate where you can find various key features. In this figure, you see the motherboard removed from its case and viewed from a position above and in front of it.

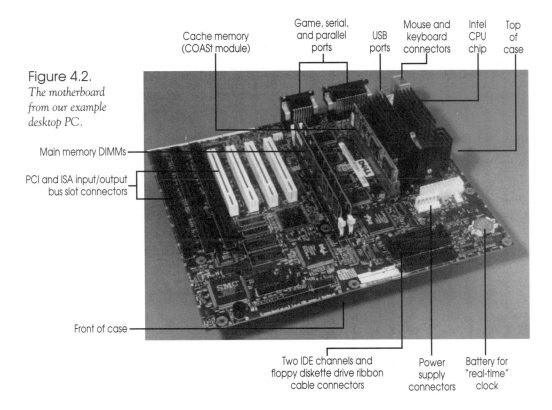

Figure 4.2.
The motherboard from our example desktop PC.

This motherboard, like most, has the CPU (the central processing unit) mounted on it. The CPU is a large integrated circuit chip that does much of the work of the PC, and which directs most of the rest of its activity. In this PC, as is increasingly common these days, that chip is hidden under a large *heat sink*, which is the finned object near the upper-right corner of the picture. (The heat sink serves to remove heat from the CPU efficiently, thus keeping it from "cooking" itself. I'll tell you more about this topic later in this chapter.)

The long rectangular objects at the top-left are the *I/O (input/output) slot connectors*. On this motherboard are three PCI slots (the smaller connectors) and three more ISA (Industry Standard Architecture) slots. Plug-in cards carrying any of a wide variety of functional parts can be plugged into one of these slots. You'll get to meet the variety of I/O slot designs that have been used in PCs in Chapter 14, "Understanding Standard PC Input and Output."

In the opposite corner of the motherboard are connectors for cables to the floppy diskette drives and to any IDE (Integrated Device Electronics) or EIDE (Enhanced IDE) peripheral devices you might have mounted inside the system unit. Also in this corner of the motherboard is both the battery-backed up "real-time" clock that keeps track of the date and time when your PC is turned off, and the system clock that dictates when each step of each instruction (or almost any other action that happens inside the PC when it is turned on) takes place.

Near the CPU are some connectors with small circuit cards in them. Each of those cards carries several integrated circuit chips. One of these cards holds the Level 2 (L2) cache and the other two hold the main memory subsystem (the RAM) for this PC. The cache memory is on what is called a Cache On A Stick (COASt) module. Each of the other two little cards is called a SIMM (Single Inline Memory Module) or a DIMM (Dual Inline Memory Module). The motherboard in Figure 4.2 happens to have DIMMs, as is typical of most modern PCs.

A few other medium-size integrated circuit chips supply the main ROM memory for the PC. These *motherboard BIOS ROM* chips contain the programs that are used whenever the PC boots and whenever other programs must activate any of the standard hardware pieces that make up this PC.

Near the top center of the motherboard are a few integrated circuit chips and some connectors that stick through the back panel of the PC. The printer, mouse, and keyboard attach to these connectors. The circuits on the motherboard implement what is known as the serial and parallel I/O ports for this machine, as well as the keyboard interface and a special "bus-mouse interface." Not every PC has all of these features built into the motherboard, though the keyboard interface is nearly always there.

The other large chips on the motherboard contain what is known variously as the *chipset* or the *glue logic*. These are electronic circuits that are needed to transfer information from one part of the motherboard to another. They also include the function of figuring out which location is being addressed in either the RAM or ROM and then commanding the corresponding chips, SIMMs, or DIMMs to supply the information at that location (or, in the case of RAM, it can mean commanding the chips, SIMMs, or DIMMs to accept information to be held in that location).

Finally, many small connectors are scattered around the motherboard and a few "jumper blocks." The connectors receive small plugs attached to cables that go to the front panel's lights and switches, the disk drives that are mounted in the system unit's drive bays, and the power supply.

Most motherboards are flexible in what they can be set up to do. There are two ways you can tell a motherboard which of its options you want to invoke. For some, you must place shorting jumper plugs across certain pairs of pins on the jumper blocks. (Or, in some PC motherboard designs, you will find some small switches that must be set.) You invoke the rest of the options by running a setup program, which often is located in the motherboard BIOS ROM chips when you boot the PC. The only way to be sure which jumpers or switch positions do what is to check the manual that came with your motherboard or system unit. Don't guess. And don't just try things without knowing what you are doing. You could disable your PC totally if you made arbitrary (and incorrect) changes to these settings.

Figure 4.3 shows a close-up view of the configuration jumpers on this motherboard. Here the jumpers are used on groups of three pins. In one position each jumper shorts the pin the center of its group to the left-hand pin; in the other position it shorts the center pin to the right-hand pin. In this way it acts like a switch that can be flipped from one position (shorting to the left) to another (shorting to the right). We call a switch that does this a *single-pole, double-throw switch*.

The jumpers you see in this figure are a little unusual in that they have extensions that serve as handles. Similar jumpers are included on many plug-in option cards and disk drives. In most cases, the jumpers that come with those devices are much shorter, and barely enclose the full length of the pins that they connect.

Figure 4.3.
Motherboard configuration jumpers.

Figure 4.4 shows a close-up view of the CPU chip out of its socket, looking at it from below. Notice the many pins that go into the socket and the labeling put on the chip by Intel.

The heat sink is a relatively massive piece of aluminum with fins molded into it that is attached to the back of the chip. (The chip extends just barely outside the pattern of pins and is quite thin from top to bottom, while the heat sink extends to the right in this figure well beyond the edge of the CPU chip, and with its fins is very much thicker from top to bottom.)

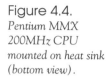

Figure 4.4.
*Pentium MMX
200MHz CPU
mounted on heat sink
(bottom view).*

I discuss why some motherboards have more and some have less functionality built into their circuitry later in this chapter, in the section, "The Motherboard: Active or Passive." Now, I want to describe some of the key pieces that usually are plugged into the motherboard.

You Must Feed Your PC: The Power Supply

In some ways, the most fundamental piece attached to the motherboard is the power supply. After all, without electricity, the computer can do nothing. The power supply has three jobs to do:

1. Convert wall outlet AC electrical power into suitable DC voltages.
2. Monitor those DC voltages.
3. Remove the heat that results from the consumption of that electrical power.

This is easy enough to say, but for you really to understand what these things mean, I must tell you a bit more.

From AC to DC, and Holding Some Energy in Reserve

The power supply's first job is to accept energy from the electric utility company via the power cord. It converts this raw energy to direct current (DC) at several different voltages, and it stores some of that energy so it can bridge over small intervals in which the electric power input stops.

Figure 4.5 shows the power supply for our example desktop PC. Notice that it has several output connectors. The largest go to one or more connectors on the motherboard. These connectors carry at least four voltages (+12 volts, +5 volts, –5 volts, and –12 volts), and in modern PCs they also can carry one or more other, lower voltages (3.3 and 2.8 volts are common). This is because several chips on the motherboard need those different voltages to do their jobs correctly. Manufacturers have started using lower voltages because as CPU speeds have increased, one way to prevent them from simply cooking themselves to death is to make them capable of running on a lower voltage. We'll return to this point in Chapter 7, "Understanding PC Processors."

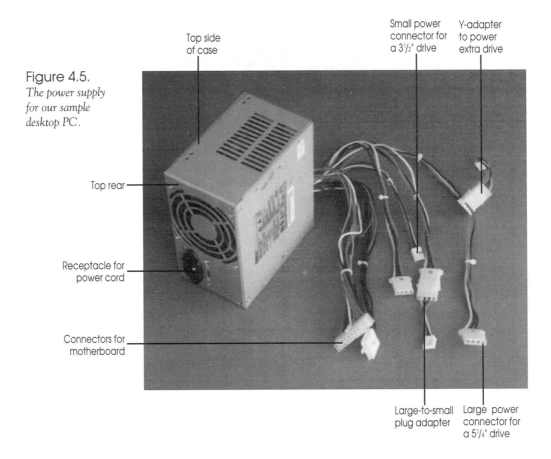

Figure 4.5.
The power supply for our sample desktop PC.

Top side of case

Small power connector for a 3½" drive

Y-adapter to power extra drive

Top rear

Receptacle for power cord

Connectors for motherboard

Large-to-small plug adapter

Large power connector for a 5¼" drive

The other connectors on the power supply are used to power disk drives. Most modern PCs can accept at least one or two floppy diskette drives and up to four IDE or EIDE hard, CD-ROM, LS-120, tape, ZIP, or other kinds of drive. Each of these devices needs electrical power to do its job, and none of them gets that power from the motherboard. Instead, they use power connectors that hook directly to the power supply. (The drives also connect to the motherboard through one or more cables that carry data to and from the drives.)

In most PCs the power supply comes with as many drive connectors as there are spaces to put drives, but if yours did not, you can buy adapters that let you connect more drives than the power supply maker intended. Just be careful that you don't overload the power supply, or it might not function correctly, and then your whole PC becomes useless until you replace that power supply with a more capable one.

The electrical power coming from the wall socket is alternating current (AC). This means that the voltage across the wires in the power cord varies smoothly from zero, up to some maximum positive value, down to zero, further down to about the same maximum negative value, and then back up to zero. And it continues this pattern, repeating in the U.S. 60 times per second. Some other countries use AC with a different frequency; 50 cycles per second is another common value. Because the voltage is repeatedly going to zero, for times that are short in human terms but which are nearly eternal for the very rapid circuits in a PC, the power supply must store up enough energy to at least bridge across those mini-brownouts that come 120 times each second.

A typical PC power supply can keep the PC going for considerably longer than that, though often not for as much as one second. You can buy special power supplies that incorporate a battery and battery charger, and these uninterruptible power supplies (UPS) can keep the PC working much longer during a power outage—sometimes for more than an hour.

Tip: If you don't have a UPS built into your PC, I suggest you consider very seriously getting an external UPS into which you can plug your PC. Nothing is worse than losing your data, and everyone eventually experiences a power outage. Murphy's Law suggests that when it happens to you it will happen just when you are working on something really important and just before you remember to save your work. Having a UPS that keeps your PC going when all the lights go out around you can be a truly wonderful thing. Of course, the main reason this is wonderful is because it gives you a chance to save your work and shut your PC down before the UPS runs out of stored energy. Some modern UPSs can shut down the PC automatically if you don't happen to be around when the wall power fails.

If you don't have a UPS either built in or external to your PC, I hope you plug your PC into a power strip that contains a really good surge arrestor. This is a set of devices that can limit the maximum voltage that will come in from the power line to your PC's power supply. Without it, your PC might die some day simply because lightning struck a power line many miles from your home or office, or because some big electric motor was turned off at just the wrong moment in a building near yours.

Monitoring the PC's Power and Rebooting

The second job of the PC's power supply is to monitor the quality of the DC voltages it is supplying to the other parts of the PC. Whenever any of these voltages deviates from its nominal value by more than a preset amount (typically 5 percent), the power supply will indicate this to the motherboard.

The power supply tells the motherboard that its output voltages are within range by raising a voltage on one of the wires going into the motherboard power supply connector. This wire is called the *power-good line*. When you first turn on your PC, the power supply starts to work. When it has all its output DC voltages stabilized at their nominal values and after some short time delay, it raises the power-good line's voltage. That signals the CPU to start computing.

Whenever the power supply sees that line's voltage fall below some critical value, it will lower the voltage on the power-good line. In response to that, the computer simply resets itself, and when that line's voltage returns to the high state, the CPU will again start computing as if the PC had just been turned on. This action is called *rebooting*.

Tip: If your PC reboots itself from time to time for no obvious reason, one possible cause is an inadequate power supply. You might have plugged into your PC more power-hungry components than it was meant to support, or you might have a particularly poor supply of AC electricity to the PC from the wall socket. Or, of course, your PC's power supply could be in the process of dying!

One way to implement a reset button on a PC is simply to hook up a momentary contact switch so that when you press it, it shorts this power-good line to ground. That simulates the power supply saying that the DC voltages are not right and reboots the PC.

Buying Tip: One way discount PC vendors sometimes shave their costs is by including very low wattage power supplies. When you are comparison shopping, be sure to ask about the number of watts and the number of disk drive connectors on the power supply in each PC you are considering buying.

Getting the Heat Out

Finally, the PC's power supply has one or more fans in it to remove waste heat from the PC. It not only must remove the heat it generates in converting the AC input power to DC, it usually must remove almost all the energy used by all the other parts of the PC. Except for a tiny amount of electric energy that makes its way outside the PC through the attached cables to the monitor, keyboard, printer, and other peripheral devices, all the electric energy that the power supply dumps into the motherboard and the disk drives is used by those parts, which, in using it, convert that energy ultimately to heat.

The power supply makers incorporate a fan they think is large enough to remove all the waste heat that will result from both its operation and the consumption inside the system unit of the power it supplies. However, often that fan is not really enough to ensure the optimum health of your PC. This is especially true if you have a "loaded" PC with many plug-in cards, any plug-in cards that have a lot of power-hungry components on them, or a CPU that runs at a high clock frequency.

Power-hungry plug-in cards might include some of the video graphics accelerator cards with lots of RAM on them. Power-hungry CPU chips include almost any chips that run at more than about 33MHz. For any such CPU chip a heat sink is essential, and often a fan is added as well.

If your CPU becomes too hot, it might self-destruct. (Or, if you are very lucky, it might only turn down its clock speed to some very low frequency and make your PC crawl through its tasks—or it might actually shut down altogether and refuse to do anything until it cools off. This last behavior is what you'll get with the latest CPU chips from Intel.)

If the CPU chip, or any other electronic component, becomes almost hot enough to die or stop working, it will have a much shorter life before it ultimately does die. Although this is true of all electronic components, the CPU chip is the single chip that dissipates the most power in most PCs, and thus is the one that will get the hottest unless it is kept cool by a heat sink with or without a fan.

A good heat sink can keep the CPU chip quite cool. Instead of nearly burning yourself if you touch it after it has been on for a while, you might barely be able to detect any warmth from it at all.

A heat sink with an attached fan might do an even better job of cooling the CPU, although sometimes the amount of heat sink metal that is removed to make room for the fan makes the combination less effective than the heat sink would have been by itself. And if you decide to buy a PC that has a CPU heat sink with a fan, be careful: The shafts of some of these CPU cooler fans merely turn in a bushing. Other, more expensive fans use ball bearings to support the shaft. The bushing design often leads to a premature fan failure—and a fan that won't turn isn't doing you any good at all. This problem, combined with the capability of a really large heat sink to do as much cooling as a smaller fan-cooled one, has led Dell, for one, to avoid CPU fans completely in its current machines. In this way, not only does it get adequate cooling, but by avoiding fan failures it increases the mean time between overall system failures (MTBF) for its PCs.

Some of the latest PCs from other manufacturers have CPU fans with speed monitors on them. Each time you boot your PC you will see a report on the screen (if you look at just the right time) telling you how fast that fan is turning.

After you have made sure your CPU chip won't overheat, you also might want to look into adding one or more fans to keep the rest of the parts of your PC cool. This isn't really necessary for a run-of-the-mill PC without much in the way of special, power-hungry "goodies" added inside it. It is a very good idea if you have a top-of-the-line screamer of a PC with all the bells and whistles you could stuff into it. Our sample desktop PC has an extra fan besides the one in the power supply, just to be sure it keeps cool enough inside.

One other issue concerning PC fans is noise—most of them put out more than you want them to. It is possible to buy special power supplies with extra-large and super-quiet fans. And you can, if you look around enough, find similar quiet and very capable fans to install in your PC where they will cool the plug-in cards. The only fan that usually makes too little noise to hear is the one on your CPU chip. (Which is a pity, because it is the fan that is most likely to fail, and if you could hear it, you might be able to notice when it stopped working and then fix or replace it.)

Room to Grow: Slots and Bays

Any functional part of your PC that lives inside the PC system unit and that isn't on the motherboard must be attached to the motherboard somehow in order to let information flow between those pieces and the circuits on the motherboard. Normally that means the parts in question will either be mounted in a drive bay or they will be mounted on printed circuit cards that are plugged into one of the motherboard's I/O slot connectors. The parts mounted in the drive bays connect via some special cables to corresponding connectors on the motherboard.

The pieces of the PC that go outside the box also must connect to the motherboard. They do so either via some connectors on the motherboard that stick through the back panel (used mostly for the keyboard, mouse, or other pointing device, and serial and parallel port devices such as modems and printers), or else by plugging into connectors on the backs of printed circuit cards that are themselves plugged into one of the motherboard I/O slot connectors. (This latter practice led to the term *input/output slot connectors*.) Modern PCs usually have some special connectors on the motherboard for the internal floppy and IDE drives.

Figure 4.6 shows the floppy diskette drive, as well as the hard disk and CD-ROM drives that normally ship with the Dell system shown in Figure 4.1, along with the cables that connect those drives to the special motherboard drive connectors. Those connectors are shown in Figure 4.2, near the lower-right corner and again, closer up, in Figure 4.3.

Figure 4.6.
The several drives normally included in our sample desktop PC.

3 1/2" floppy diskette drive

3 1/2" hard disk drive

5 1/4" CD-ROM drive

What are plugged into the I/O slot connectors? In general, cards that perform some sort of input or output function are plugged in here (which is, after all, why these are called I/O slots). The most common plug-in card is a video display adapter. Some PCs have this functionality built into the motherboard, but most do not. And, as I will discuss in more detail shortly, this is often a good thing. The video display subsystem consists of this card, the monitor that attaches to it, and the cable that goes between them.

Figure 4.7 shows one of the video adapters that is shipped with our sample desktop computer system. In this case it is a PCI bus accelerated video card with 4MB of video RAM, suitable for both computer-game and relatively high-end business graphics use. There are other, more or less expensive video display adapters available for customers who want either more or less capability than this adapter offers. See Chapter 13, "Seeing the Results: PC Displays," for details on the very wide variety of PC display subsystems that have been marketed over the years.

Figure 4.7.
The PCI video display adapter for our sample desktop PC.

Some other common plug-in cards include an internal modem, a network interface card (NIC), and a SCSI host adapter. Figure 4.8 shows one of each of these. Notice that the internal modem plugs into an ISA slot, whereas the other two cards plug into PCI slots. The reason for this difference is that the modem must carry data at only a relatively modest speed, compared to what is optimum for the network adapter and the SCSI host adapter. Details on each of these technologies are covered in Chapters 15, "Understanding Standard PC Input and Output," 16, "Faster Ways to Get Information Into and Out of Your PC," 24, "The PC Reaches Out, Part One: Modems and More," and 25, "The PC Reaches Out, Part Two: Through the NIC Node."

Figure 4.8.
*Some more plug-in
option cards for our
example desktop PC.*

 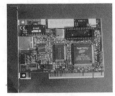 

ISA internal modem   PCI network interface   PCI SCSI host adapter

It wouldn't be possible to give a comprehensive list here of all the other types of plug-in cards that you can add to a PC. Suffice it to say that if you can imagine something a PC might do, somebody has probably made a plug-in card to facilitate that function.

A few of the more common plug-in cards include cards to connect a scanner, cards to play and record sounds, cards to increase the quality of the sounds made by those other sound cards, MIDI interface cards for serious musicians, process control cards for chemical engineers, and the list goes on and on. (Sometimes you can get more than one kind of functionality on a single plug-in card. Those are, naturally, referred to as "multifunction" I/O cards.) You will learn about many of these cards in later chapters in this book, and the rest you will be able to understand from their manufacturer's literature after you have learned about the ones I describe.

Many people are concerned about whether they can upgrade their PCs at a later time. As I suggested in Chapter 1, this is not always a wise thing to do, but it does sometimes make sense. The ultimate limit on what upgrading you can do in a given PC system unit and with a given motherboard will be set by three things:

- The power supply wattage
- The number and type of I/O slot connectors on the motherboard
- The number and size of the drive bays (and which of them are accessible from the front panel)

A few years ago, one PC manufacturer captured this concern by saying, "All my customers seem to care about is the number of watts, slots, and bays we give them."

If your present case, power supply, and motherboard are not ones that will gracefully accept the upgrades you want, you might be able to change one, two, or all three of these things. Mostly standard "AT style" replacement PC cases come with a power supply that is sufficient for almost anything you'd care to put into them. Extra high power (or extra low-noise, or extra efficient) power supplies are also available. And if you need more slots, you might want to upgrade your motherboard and probably get a better CPU and many other important improvements at the same time.

What Goes Outside the Box

Not every part of a PC can go inside the system unit. The keyboard, monitor, and printer of most PCs are located outside the system. And some people connect an external modem, a scanner, external disk drives, and many other types of peripheral devices outside the system unit.

Figure 4.1 shows the standard keyboard and one of the optional monitors that come with our sample Dell desktop computer. I'll describe some of the other popular choices for external input and output devices in Chapters 12–14, "Getting Your PC's Attention: Input Devices," "Seeing the Results: PC Displays," and "Getting It All Down on Paper: Printers."

Information Rides the Bus

At the beginning of this chapter I told you in part why it is important that you realize a PC is composed of many quasi-independent subpieces. Now I am going to discuss another reason.

The many pieces that make up your PC often come from many different manufacturers. This is true even when you buy the PC completely assembled from a vendor, such as Dell, that ships all the pieces of your PC system in a single box. They simply have assembled that PC out of the separate parts for you.

Alternatively, you can buy separate parts and assemble your own PC. You might save a few dollars doing this, but you would sacrifice the convenience of having a ready-to-run PC immediately, and more importantly, you would lose the substantial benefits of getting a pre-tested system and of having a warranty on the operation of that system by the company that sold it to you. If you become your own "system integrator" (which is what it means to assemble a PC from pieces), then you are the responsible party when the pieces seem not to be working together properly.

However, although I don't necessarily recommend that you build your own PC, I want to point out that it is possible. And what makes it possible is the notion of having standard interfaces between the various parts. That is what it takes to let pieces made, at least potentially, by different manufacturers connect and work. The common name for any such standard information transfer interface is a *bus*.

A Bus Implies a Standard

Any time you connect one piece of computer hardware to another, if you expect them to work together, the interface between the two (where they plug together—which is the essence of an information bus) must meet four conditions: The two halves of the interface must be physically, logically, and electrically compatible, and the signals must be timed suitably.

Let me explain each of these points in turn. The first one is pretty obvious. If you try to push a plug with 15 pins into a socket with only 9 holes, it just won't go. Likewise, two plugs with 15 pins won't connect; one of them must be a 15-hole socket.

The second one is less obvious, until you think about it. Even when the connectors mate properly, there must be agreement between the manufacturers that, for example, data is going to go out of device A on pin number three and come into device B on socket hole number three.

The third condition is yet more subtle. If I intend to send data from device A to device B, the makers of both must agree on what levels of voltage and current shall be available on each power-supplying pin (and, of course, on which side is supplying power and which is using it). Furthermore, with respect to all the pins that carry data, the manufacturers must agree on the voltage levels that mean a zero bit or a one bit.

The final condition is merely a refinement of the third one. It says that the two device makers also must agree that when they put a signal on any of the pins it will stay there for some prescribed amount of time, and perhaps that it will not rise or fall in voltage either faster or slower than some prescribed speeds.

Any time we have such an agreement among computer hardware makers we call it a *bus definition*. This applies especially if the agreement is not just between a few companies but is shared by the entire industry.

Historical Aside: Some bus standards are created after a lengthy negotiation between companies, possibly under the aegis of some national or international standards organization. Others just happen when one company makes a lot of one kind of device [call it A] (and, at first, all the other devices [B] that can connect to it), and then many other companies jump into the marketplace, offering their alternative devices to connect to the first maker's device A.

The first way, via a standards committee, is necessary when many companies want to enter a new marketplace more or less at once. That is how the VESA I/O bus and the SCSI interface were defined and refined through several versions (see Chapter 16 for more details).

Traditionally the other way standards arise, by a *de facto* standard-creating process, is exemplified by how IBM came to define most aspects of what we today call a PC. IBM published its design for the original PC in 1981 (and again in 1983 for the PC/XT, and in 1985 for the PC/AT) with the hope of inducing others to make plug-in cards that would work in a PC. Not only did that happen, but the PC clone makers also used that information to help them make products that would directly compete with IBM's PCs. And thus was born what we now call the *industry standard architecture* (ISA) I/O slot definition, and more generally, the standard notion of what constitutes a PC.

Recently, a third way to create a standard has emerged as the most common method. In this variation, one company solicits input from several or many other companies. Then the first company publishes its notion of a new standard. If the company doing so is very prominent (for example, Microsoft or Intel), then very likely this new standard will be adopted by a lot of companies (including at least those that were consulted during its creation) and a new industry standard will have been born.

I am using the term *bus standard* a bit more broadly than some authors have. I include any standardized interface between two kinds of PC hardware that must be able to connect and work together. Other authors have limited the term to only a few of the more famous buses, such as the I/O bus, which in its several forms is called by the jargon acronyms ISA, EISA, VESA, MCA, and PCI.

By my broader usage, there are a lot of buses in your PC. Although some have received a lot of attention, and their names are, if not household words, at least relatively familiar jargon, others you might never have heard of before. The ISA bus and PCI bus variant forms of the I/O slot connector are two examples of famous PC buses. The IDE standard for connecting to disk drives is another. Likewise, you probably have heard of the standards called the serial and parallel ports. Other, less familiar PC buses include the MFM and RLL disk interfaces (now pretty much obsolete), the video interface (between the monitor and the display adapter or, more accurately, between each of them and the intervening cable), the SCSI device interface (between host adapter and cable and from cable to SCSI slave device), the infrared device standard, and so on. (That last one is interestingly different in that its physical definition relates to how two devices "attach" via light waves instead of by direct contact.)

You will learn a whole lot more about these and many other PC buses in the chapters to come. In particular, you will find this topic treated in Chapters 15 and 16.

The Motherboard: Active or Passive

When reading literature on PCs you might run across the phrases "Passive Backplane" and "Active Motherboard." What do these mean, and why should you care?

Any printed circuit card that carries electronic chips that actually do something to the data passing through them is considered an *active* piece of computing hardware. Any board that only passes signals along, possibly amplifying them so they can provide strong enough signals for several receiving boards, is considered *passive*.

Any printed circuit card that has sockets into which other printed circuit cards can be plugged may be called a *motherboard*. The cards that plug into it are called *daughter boards*.

Architecture: Curiously, if those cards can have other cards plugged into them, these last cards are not referred to as granddaughter boards. Instead, they are still just daughter boards. I suppose the logic is that any card can be a mother and have daughters, and that we needn't look at the possibilities of more generations when referring to these cards.

What kind of mainboard does a PC use? That depends on which PC you are talking about. Almost any possibility has been tried at some time. Each strategy has some very significant advantages and disadvantages. Hitting the right balance for a particular group of customers is the difficult goal pursued by every PC manufacturer.

If you have a PC with only one printed circuit card it would be said to have an active *mainboard*. That board wouldn't be a motherboard, technically, because it has no daughters. In saying this I remind you that all useful printed circuit cards must have connectors of some kind on them to let signals and power get onto and off of the card. But if only cables plug in, and not other printed circuit cards, then it isn't truly a motherboard. Also, even though memory modules—SIMMs and DIMMs—are small printed circuit cards carrying memory chips, we don't normally consider them to be daughter boards. Therefore, a mainboard that has connectors only for cables and memory modules would still not be considered a motherboard.

The usual type of PC that might use this design is a portable one. The advantages to using a mainboard in a portable PC include being able to make such a mainboard a very special, custom shape and size, designed to fit perfectly the particular laptop's case and having no board-to-board connectors to work loose over time and cause reliability problems. Perhaps the main disadvantage is that this is a custom board and can be used only in this one PC design, and thus is necessarily going to be made in relatively small volume. That means it will be more expensive than a standard design that is made in the millions and is used in many different PCs. The second and related disadvantage is that this PC will not be flexible to upgrade. It is what it is, and it always will be exactly that until it dies or is thrown away. Finally, if any portion of the circuitry on this mainboard dies, you might end up having to replace the entire board because repairs often cost more than a whole new board.

The opposite extreme is a passive backplane motherboard. In this design the motherboard simply carries other cards, and all the computing work is done in the circuits on those cards. This provides the absolute maximum flexibility, but it also costs the most to build, is the least reliable, and might not perform as well as nearly any other design one might choose. The performance penalty, if there is one, will happen because signals must travel from one card to another via a third card (the motherboard), instead of traveling directly. All such transfers take time. (The time penalty might be even greater than you'd imagine if the transfer must proceed at a bus speed dictated by the backplane when it could have gone faster over a direct link from, for example, the CPU chip to main memory.) A few PCs were built with more or less pure passive backplane designs, but they did not succeed very well in the mass PC marketplace.

This brings us to the middle ground on which almost all PCs fall. In these designs the mainboard is an active motherboard; that is, it carries daughter cards and it carries its own set of active circuitry.

A variant form of this design might be referred to as a "bent" motherboard. This is actually a motherboard with one slot, and in that slot a card with more slots. In effect, this second card is merely a bent-up portion of the motherboard. All the plug-in daughter boards go into the slots on that second card, and thus end up parallel to the motherboard. This design is mainly used for "low-profile" system units. The most important issue in the design of this type of mainboard is to strike the right balance between what goes on the motherboard and what is left for the daughter boards to supply. Putting more functionality on the motherboard lowers the manufacturing cost and increases its reliability. However, doing so also makes the board less flexible in terms of the PC configurations it supports and makes upgrading it harder.

Historical Aside: When IBM first designed the original PC, which had just such an active motherboard, its choice of that design was to a certain extent forced by circumstance. At the time most of the integrated circuits available, other than the central processor, were what are now termed either small-scale integrated circuit (SSI) or medium-scale integrated circuit (MSI) chips. Each one could do only a very few logical operations on the signals presented to it. (The standard measure of complexity in an integrated circuit chip is the number of elemental logic circuits, called "logic gates," that it carries. SSI chips have at most a handful; MSI chips might have a few dozen. In contrast, today's very large-scale integrated circuit chips [VLSI chips] have many millions of gates on each one.)

Thus, the IBM engineers had to nearly fill the entire motherboard with a host of these SSI and MSI chips just to create the necessary glue logic to interconnect the central processor (CPU chip) and the rest of the parts of the PC. Almost everything else functional had to be relegated to an "option card," as IBM termed the plug-in daughter boards for the PC.

After the PC became a grand success, the companies that made integrated circuit chips found that it was economical for them to create new large-scale integrated circuit (LSI) chips and even very large-scale integrated circuit (VLSI) chips that incorporated all the functionality of the dozens of glue logic chips in the original PC's design. Thus was born what we now refer to as "the chip set." And with that innovation making much more complex mainboards became a possibility.

The early clone PC manufacturers tried to distinguish their machines from IBM's by a combination of distinguishing features and lower prices. The marketplace soon demanded, very loudly, that all PCs be essentially identical functionally. This pressure helped establish the lowest-common denominator clone PC as the industry standard. And its relatively simple motherboard was, for a long time, the only kind to be found in most PCs.

Architecture: For several decades many complex appliances and other machines have had computers embedded in them. At first these were, for the most part, special-purpose computers, designed just for a specific use, such as a traffic signal controller running all the lights at an intersection, or a point-of-sale terminal (which is the modern equivalent of a cash register).

Recently, using what is a more-or-less standard PC for these applications has become quite popular. The only ways in which these PCs differ from a desktop machine are that they are usually packaged on a single printed circuit board, and their programs are commonly loaded into some read-only memory (ROM) chips, instead of being on a disk.

The advantages to the manufacturer of using a standard PC design is simple: These machines are so similar to desktop PCs that the programs for them can be created and tested on desktop PCs and then put into ROM chips to be loaded into the embedded PCs only when they are finished and fully tested.

The printed circuit boards that comprise these PCs can be about the size of a common page of office letterhead (8.5×11 inches) or they can be not much bigger than a common business card. The size is dictated mostly by the functionality that must be included and by the overall size of the machine into which the PC is to be embedded.

These PC printed circuit boards are mainboard designs that will no doubt undergo further changes. But they aren't really a part of our main story, because these PCs aren't available for general-purpose use. Instead, they are fully dedicated to performing the computations needed to run the appliance or other machine in which they are embedded.

As CPU chips and memory chips began to be run at faster and faster clock speeds, the design of the good-old-fashioned clone PC motherboard became unbearably limiting. But having several different clone PC makers "improve" that design, each in its own way, wasn't a very appealing prospect.

Intel, as the maker of the vast majority of CPU chips for PCs, had perhaps the greatest stake in helping solve this problem. With input from Microsoft and several other industry leaders, Intel came up with some new prototype motherboard designs. These designs included new layout standards and new Intel chip sets (VLSI implementations of the glue logic) for each.

At first, Intel seemed only to want to help clone PC makers save engineering costs, get new PC designs to market faster, and of course sell more CPU chips and motherboard chip sets. Soon, though, Intel became one of the main suppliers of complete motherboards for the clone market. It is not yet the dominant supplier, but its chip sets have become almost *de facto* standards, used in most of the newer motherboard designs from all the major clone PC makers, and the motherboards themselves are most often designed to conform to Intel's published standards. The most recent Intel standard for full-size desktop PC motherboards is called the ATX, version 2.01. The most recent Intel standard for low-profile PCs is its NLX design. You can learn more about these design standards by pointing your Web browser at one of these URLs:

```
http://www.intel.com/design/motherbd/atx.htm

http://www.teleport.com/~atx/index.htm

http://www.intel.com/design/motherbd/nlx.htm

http://www.teleport.com/~nlx/
```

Controlling Chaos

The most wonderful fact about PCs is that their open design has led to a truly vast marketplace with a huge number of vendors making a rapidly expanding variety of both hardware and software. The resulting mix-and-match environment has given PCs enormous flexibility and power. But it also has, inevitably, produced chaos.

This chaos must be managed or PCs will be so complex and difficult to set up and keep running that only a tiny fraction of the potential users will be willing to endure the needed effort. To prevent that curtailing of a booming market, the industry leaders have tried several things. Some of those companies proposed new standards for how a PC should be built. Other times, these companies—normally fierce competitors—have cooperated in the development of new industry standards for PC design.

The Critical, Limited Resources in a PC

In Chapter 8, "How Your PC 'Thinks,'" you will learn about the details of the PC's design. You will learn about the several kinds of "resources" that a PC offers to its constituent parts and the programs that run within it. (I'll explain just what a "resource" means in this context in just a moment.) Each piece of hardware and software must use some of one or more of these resources. Managing their demands and resolving conflicting requests for resources is a major task in today's PCs.

With some exceptions, only one bit of hardware can use any given resource at a time. When that resource is allocated to that device, only that device can use it until its allocation is canceled. And often those allocations cannot be canceled until the next time you reboot your PC. The exceptions include the possibility that some devices that normally would use an IRQ line, for example, can be operated in a polling manner, so as to free up that IRQ for some other device to use. This strategy, which is often used for printers to free up an otherwise occupied IRQ, is explained fully in Chapter 8. Another exception is that in systems with an advanced bus, such as PCI, it is possible for the system to see which cards are in which slots, and as a consequence, for cards plugged into different slots on that bus to use the same interrupts.

The following are the PC's critical, and limited, resources:

- The memory addresses that the CPU can see
- The input/output (I/O) port addresses it can use

- The interrupt request lines (IRQs) through which external hardware can get the CPU's attention
- The direct memory access (DMA) channels by which data can flow without the CPUs direct intervention

PC disk drives are divided further into logical drives, each of which gets its own letter designation. That lettering constitutes another critical, limited PC resource.

Tip: If your PC is part of a network, and if there are many shared directories on remote PCs, you can easily run out of drive letters on your PC to which to map those remote drives. This can be a serious problem if you are running Windows 3.x on top of DOS, but if you are running Windows 95 there is a simple solution. Just don't map all those remote drives. You can still access the unmapped drives through the Network Neighborhood, either on the desktop or in the Windows Explorer.

When only engineers and other "techy" types used PCs, manufacturers could get away with requiring every user to understand all this, and those companies could reasonably expect the PC users to open the box and move jumpers or flip switches to set up the motherboard and each option card so they wouldn't conflict with one another. Now that PCs are mass-market items, that just won't do.

The industry's response has been to develop several *plug-and-play* (PnP) standards. These form a framework for making PCs more or less auto-configuring. This attempt has been only partially successful, mainly because of the need to keep including older hardware and software that was designed before there were any PnP standards.

The first fully PnP-compatible operating system for the PC, Windows 95, does an admirable job of recognizing the hardware you put in your PC, supplying the resources required for each piece, and resolving conflicting resource requests. But it is far from perfect. When it works, it is wonderful. When it doesn't, the user must get involved in solving the resulting problems, and often Windows 95 makes that process less easy than one would wish. (Thus, you will often hear this variation on plug-and-play: "plug-and-pray.")

Windows NT doesn't yet have plug-and-play support. But when Windows NT version 5 appears, it is supposed to have fully as much PnP capability as Windows 98 will at around the same time. Furthermore, both Windows 98 and Windows NT 5 are expected to share a common device driver model (referred to by the jargon term "Win32 Driver Model" or WDM). This will mean that manufacturers of PC add-in devices will no longer have to write two version of the device driver software for each of the products. More importantly to PC users, this development, if or when it comes to pass, will mean that they can move up to the greater stability of Windows NT without having to sacrifice good support for a wide range of PC add-in products, and also get the ease of (at least fairly good) plug-and-play auto-configuration.

Peter's Principle: How to Record Your PC's Resource Usage in a File

From the Windows 95 Start button on the taskbar, select Settings | Control Panel | System. The System Properties dialog box will appear. Select the Device Manager tab, and click the Print button. Select All Devices and System Summary, and click OK. This will let you print out a listing of pretty much all that Windows knows about the resource usage in your machine.

To keep this information in electronic form for ready comparison with other snapshots, print it to a file. If you haven't already done so, set up a printer definition for the purpose. To do that, from the Start button select Settings | Printers. In the resulting Explorer frame you will see Add Printer; select it. The wizard that pops up will walk you through the necessary steps. Choose Local Printer of type Generic/Text Only. Choose to Keep Existing Driver and for the printer's connection, choose FILE: (which means print to a file).

Now return to the Device Manager, and this time, before you print the summary, use the Print Setup button to select your Generic/Text Only printer. You will be prompted for a filename and location. Choose some folder that you reserve for configuration information and a filename that shows you what date you took this snapshot of your PC.

If you do this both before and after each time you install new hardware, you can see from a file comparison of these snapshots just what Windows changed to accommodate the new hardware. If it isn't what you think should have changed, this will probably give you the information you'll need to help resolve any problems that might have resulted from installing the new hardware.

Why ISA Means Chaos

The biggest headache for the designer of any new PC is the success of all the earlier designs. That success means that many millions of prospective customers for the new PC design will already have a PC and that most of those PC owners will want to move some or all of the peripheral devices and plug-in cards from their older machine to the newer one. The headaches come from trying to make the new design accommodate those older parts.

This is a particular problem for plug-in cards designed for the original ISA bus. That bus design, unlike many newer I/O bus standards, didn't allow for the sharing of IRQ lines or DMA channels. And the cards designed for the ISA bus in the past typically didn't have any provision built in to let the motherboard turn them off or reassign their resource usage if that usage conflicted with another card in the system. A recent trend, even with so-called "legacy" ISA cards, is for them to include some plug-and-play controllability.

The ISA bus design didn't contemplate having the system configure the cards, nor having it disable them. But if the cards themselves include the proper provisions, a more modern PC can use those cards as fully compatible plug-and-play cards, even when they are plugged into an ISA slot.

Modern PCs are expected to spot any new hardware and adapt themselves to it, and sometimes they can. But ISA cards, in particular the older, non-PnP compatible ones, are resource consumers that the newer PCs can't control. Even worse, the PC motherboard can't even know, without some help, what resources this type of card is using. That means the use of these cards can totally defeat the automatically self-configuring PC.

One solution to this quandary is for the operating system to know a lot of technical detail about most of the popular legacy ISA cards. If you simply tell such an OS (and Windows 95 is one) that your PC has such-and-such ISA card installed, it can summon up the necessary information from its legacy database, and then it might be able to configure the device drivers for that card, as well as avoid using any of the resources taken by that card for any other purposes. Finally, if you intend to install a legacy ISA card in your PC, and it is such an oddball one that the OS doesn't know about it, you can inform the OS about the needs of that card manually. In Windows 95 you do this by going into the Device Manager (in the System section of Control Panel) and clicking Properties and then Reserve Resources—you can do this, that is, if you know the technical details about that card yourself. I hope you have the documentation for it or can contact the card's manufacturer. If not, you may simply be unable to make that card work in your PC (or if it does, it might mess up some other aspect of the PC's functioning).

The Limitations Imposed by the ISA Bus Standard

The continuing use of the ISA bus in modern PCs presents several difficulties. The lack of plug-and-play support is only one. A plug-in option card designed merely to the original ISA specification will have these, now unnecessarily limiting, features:

- Only 16 data lines, thus limiting data transfers to two bytes at a time
- Only 8.33MHz maximum clock speed
- No sharing of interrupts or DMA channels between cards in different slots
- No provision for configuring the card's use of regions of main memory, I/O port addresses, IRQ lines, or DMA channels by the system
- No provision for being disabled by the system in case of resource conflicts

This specification needed to be improved before a truly modern PC could emerge. These improvements have come in an evolutionary process, with several intermediate standards being introduced (and having variable market success) before we finally have gotten to the present situation. And, of course, even that is just a way-station on the way to some future, even-better PC design.

IBM's Micro Channel Architecture (MCA)

IBM was the first to begin the process of forging what we now see as the solution to this problem. It was trying to solve not only this problem, but also an even more troublesome difficulty it was experiencing. When it found itself losing market share to the PC clone makers, IBM loudly declared that it was going to stop making PCs altogether, and instead it would make some new machines called PS/2s.

When one examined the details of the announcement, and even more, when one looked at the new machines themselves, it became clear that these new PS/2 machines were, for the most part, just PCs in disguise. But the PS/2 models 40 and above did introduce one really new, and very significant, piece of PC architecture. They had a novel I/O slot design. IBM called this the Micro Channel Architecture (MCA), and it announced that MCA would be its new standard for the I/O interface on all its new machines from the (high-end) PS/2 models up through its mainframes.

This new design went well beyond simply changing the I/O slot connectors. It added many more pins to each, so many more functions could be supported. And the MCA design had a major impact on the way the motherboard and the software running on the PC interacted with cards plugged into these new slots.

The following are the key advantages of the MCA design:

- The capability to ask each card plugged into the bus to identify itself
- The capability of the motherboard to disable any MCA card inserted into a slot, if its resource requirements could not be met without conflict
- The capability to share interrupt requests on the same IRQ line

IBM registered every maker of MCA cards, giving each one a unique code number by which those cards would identify their function. (This is not like Ethernet cards, for example, which each carry an identification code that is unique to each card. The MCA identity code merely defines the type of card.) Manufacturers inform an MCA machine about the capabilities and resource requirements of each of their MCA plug-in cards through a small Adapter Description File (ADF) that they ship with each card.

Although this clearly was a superior design technically, this new PC design was not a smashing success commercially for a variety of reasons.

Historical Aside: In retrospect it's pretty clear why MCA was a bust. For one thing, the MCA slots wouldn't accept any of the ISA cards. So there was no backward compatibility to this design. For another, IBM took a much more aggressive stance toward its patents on

continues

this design. IBM said that any company wanting to license them would have to also pay a license fee for any past use of IBM patents in clone PCs—a price that was far too high for the major clone makers to accept. (Previously IBM had simply not pursued license fees from clone PC makers for the IBM-owned patents that obviously were being infringed. That might have been mostly out of fear of antitrust suits by the federal government—a fear now much reduced by IBM's greatly decreased market share for PCs.)

Whatever the reasons, MCA-based PC designs didn't make much of an impact. And even IBM has quietly dropped most of its support of that design.

The EISA Experiment

The major clone PC makers responded to IBM's MCA initiative with one of their own. They came up with an enhancement to the original ISA I/O bus design called the Enhanced Industry Standard Architecture (EISA) bus. This standard used a new connector design that accepted both older, legacy ISA cards and newly designed EISA cards. The former would go into the slot only a short way and make contact with only half of the leads. The newer cards went in all the way and contacted every lead. In this fashion the bus slots were able to offer all the new functionality of the MCA design, and yet provide full backward compatibility with legacy ISA plug-in cards.

However, this also meant that EISA machines could achieve the fully automatic self-configuration like that possible with MCA machines only if they didn't have any ISA cards plugged in. Or if one did plug in ISA cards, those cards had to be described to the PC's operating system by the creation of a small file of information on the resources it used. Some ISA card makers provided these EISA configuration (CFG) files on request. More did not. Some generic ones were created to describe the most popular legacy ISA cards, and these got widely distributed on bulletin boards and, more recently, on the Internet.

If every option card's CFG file is available, one can run an EISA Configuration Utility (ECU) program and by using those files, plus information it learns by directly interrogating the EISA cards, it will be able to see which cards need which resources. After reserving whatever resources the ISA cards needed, the ECU program will choose and set the resource usage of the EISA cards. If there is some possible configuration without conflict, the ECU will find it and make it happen. If not, some of the cards will simply be disabled.

EISA machines are more expensive to build than ISA ones, and although their advantages were many, so were their drawbacks. Most limiting was the fact that the EISA bus, like the ISA bus, was limited to 8.33MHz. And yet, in early EISA machines, it was expected to carry all the data traffic from the CPU to main memory. As processor speeds rose dramatically, this limitation made it necessary to at least supplement the EISA bus.

You will learn more about most of the important supplements that have been tried (and in some cases are still in use) in Chapter 16. With suitable supplementation, the EISA bus is still a very good input/output bus, and many of these modern, supplement-EISA bus-based PCs are in use today, mainly as file servers.

PCMCIA and the PC Card

Another development that occurred at about the same time, and which at first seemed quite independent of these new bus designs, later converged with them in the modern plug-and-play PC. That is a technology that started out as a means for adding more RAM or ROM to microprocessor-based game machines. Only later did it become one of the popular features on a portable PC, and it is just now becoming an option that is available for a significant number of desktop PCs.

This development originally went by the cumbersome name PCMCIA cards. The PC Memory Card International Association began as a trade association of several manufacturers of RAM and ROM chips. They designed a credit-card size carrier for memory chips with a connector on one end, and they published a specification for these cards, as well as the slot into which they would fit. When it became clear that this was a convenient form factor for adding something to a portable PC, other manufacturers joined the PCMCIA, and they began the push to broaden the applicability of this standard. For example, Hewlett-Packard and Western Digital, among others, produced miniaturized hard disks that fit on these cards and figured out how to support them through appropriate device driver software. Manufacturers of other PC peripherals, including modems and network interface cards, also saw an opportunity here.

Historical Aside: Initially, when IBM saw the opportunities, it decided that a good name for these PC add-ons would be PC Cards, and it trademarked that name. When the other members of the PCMCIA decided that they would like to use a less cumbersome designation for these cards, they asked IBM's permission to use the name PC Card. IBM at first hesitated, wanting to keep that neat name for its own, exclusive use. Later IBM relented, seeing that its fortunes and that of the industry would both be furthered by sharing that name. So now the official name for what used to be called PCMCIA cards is PC Card, and now the slots into which they plug are called either PC Card or Card Bus slots. (This last name implies an improved version of the PC Card standard that supports 32-bit data transfers in parallel.)

The PC Card design has undergone many developments, leading to two fully standardized and one proprietary form factor, called Type I, Type II, and Type III cards. They are all the same size, but differ in thickness. A PC Card slot can be made to accept a single Type I card, a single Type II card, or a pair of Type I cards. Certain manufacturers have also built oversize slots that can accept a Type III card, or two Type I cards, or one each of Type I and Type II.

I'll tell you more about PC Cards in Chapter 23, "Why Mobile PCs Must Be Different," because so far they are far more common in this context than in desktop or server PCs.

Plug and Play

There is a constant theme to all of these enhancements to the original PC architecture. It is to make the machine do more of what it is good at (detail work) and let the human operator concentrate on what humans are good for (seeing the big picture and the general application of the PC to some task humans value).

This means that, starting with the MCA and EISA designs, PCs have been more and more capable of doing just work rather than requiring extensive configuration tweaking by the user first. That makes for a better OOBE (which, as you will remember from the discussion in Chapter 1, stands for Out of Box Experience), and for easier upgrades as well.

All of these developments have been guided by a vision of a PC that is fully automatic in its configuration. The name given to this vision by the industry is plug-and-play. The difficulty in implementing this vision has been two-fold. One is to incorporate backward compatibility—which means the capability to use older, legacy devices with even the newest PC—and the other is preserving the open marketplace with all its wild and woolly freedom for innovation.

One way in which these issues are being dealt with is by the publication of a large number of standards by several different organizations. The Video Electronics Standards Association (VESA) is one, as is the Institute for Electric and Electronic Engineering (IEEE). Microsoft is another. Intel is yet another.

Often, standards that are first proposed by one company, such as IBM, Hewlett-Packard, Microsoft, or Intel, are later adopted by an official, independent standards organization. Sometimes this happens because the corporate developer of the standard requests it. At other times, the user community essentially has had to wrest control of the standard from the corporate developer and give it to the standards body. Either way it happens, the advantage to giving an independent standards body control of a standard is that this pretty well guarantees that no company can control the standard and improvements to it to their competitive advantage over the other companies in the industry.

The Essentials of Plug-and-Play

Plug-and-play is first and foremost a philosophy describing how a PC "should" operate without needing much in the way of user setup effort. More formally described, plug-and-play is a whole series of formal standards describing a number of ways to achieving this goal. And only PCs that conform to these standards are entitled to be described by the trademarked term, plug-and-play. Plug-and-play builds upon the pioneering work of mainframe computer designers and developers of the MCA, EISA, and PC Card bus standards, and it also goes well beyond all of them.

Essential to this effort is the notion that every part of a PC (whether it is built onto the motherboard or is added to the PC on a plug-in option card or by plugging it into some other connector) shall have a device identifier. This *device ID* implies all the technical details that the PnP controlling software must know about the device. For some devices it identifies them as being able to be turned on or off and perhaps to have some or all of their resource usage controlled by the PnP management software. For other devices it indicates that they are old (legacy) ISA cards or otherwise are inherently unable to be disabled or controlled.

The PC must learn about all of the PnP devices it contains. So one of the jobs that must be done during the bootup process is *enumeration* of all those devices. Responsibility for this task is divided among several different players. The PCI controller chip has this job for devices plugged into PCI slots. Likewise, the EISA bus controller chip will report on EISA cards installed into those slots (if your PC has any of them). And PC Cards identify themselves to the PC Card controlling software as soon as they are plugged in. The PnP BIOS coordinates all this information and adds to it information for devices that are built into the motherboard, attached across the IDE bus plus the keyboard and a few other devices.

If you are running Windows 95, go into the Control Panel, System dialog box. Click the Device Manager tab, and select the View Devices By Connection radio button. Now click the plus sign in front of Plug and Play BIOS to see all the sources of this information and how the BIOS brings them all together.

After the devices in the system have been enumerated, two more tasks remain. One is to decide which ones get which resources. This is the job of the *arbitrators*. Once again, the overall task has been divided up so those subsystems, such as the PCI or EISA buses or the PC Card bus, can take care of the work for the devices they handle. The system arbitrator will do the rest. Finally, a *configurator* program must go out and set up each configurable PnP device so it uses the resources that have been assigned to it. The configurator will also configure the device drivers for any non-configurable legacy ISA devices (at least for those for which the necessary information has been supplied) so they will access those devices via the resources they are known to use.

If, when you look at the Device Manager tab in the System Properties dialog box, you see any device listed with an exclamation point in a yellow circle on top of it, that device is in conflict with some other device. (So you will likely see either none of these symbols or more than one.) That is a sign that you must help the system resolve things because it has tried and failed to do so on its own.

Alternatively, you might see some devices listed with a black X in a red circle over them. These are disabled devices. If you didn't choose to disable them yourself, then Windows did so in order to resolve some resource conflict.

By highlighting one of the devices with the exclamation point or red X over it and then clicking the Properties button, you'll call up a dialog box that might tell you just what the problem is. Go to the Resources tab and see if it lists the conflict.

Sometimes you will be able to alter the resource usage manually right in that dialog box in order to remove the conflict. Other times, after you have discovered what the conflict is, a general knowledge of what resources different devices use and of how those uses can be altered (by jumpers, switches, or running some software program) will let you quickly resolve the problem.

The more worrisome cases are when Windows hasn't even noticed there is a conflict. This can happen when you have legacy devices, if those devices haven't been described properly to Windows. Only by knowing what resources those devices use and then making sure that Windows is reserving the required resources for those devices, can you eliminate that source of problems.

Of course, if you are running the older Windows 3.x and DOS or just DOS as your operating system, instead of Windows 95, then you most likely won't have the advantages of plug-and-play. (A software add-on package for Windows 3.x is available that gives partial plug-and-play capability, but it isn't a standard part of that operating environment.) Without plug-and-play support, you're totally on your own identifying and resolving resource allocation conflicts. And after you do that a few times, you really will appreciate a machine that can do that chore for you, even if it works correctly most of the time.

Summary: IBM's Grand Innovation

This chapter has pointed out that PCs are collections of parts, each one doing its job independently of the others but all coordinated by the "lead player"   the CPU. What is both most wonderful and most terrible about PCs is that IBM (in its wisdom or folly) did something totally uncharacteristic when it introduced the PC. Namely, it told the world how it built them, and thus told the world how they either could build parts to work with the PC, or actually clone PCs.

The former possibility led to the vast array of optional hardware for PCs. This opened up the market as nothing else could have. That was very good for IBM. The latter possibility, however, soon became a reality and IBM not only lost its leadership position as a maker of PCs, it almost left that marketplace altogether. It is still there, but only as one of many manufacturers of "IBM-compatible" PCs.

What Parts Are Where in *Your* PC; Some Things to Think About and Try

I've told you about a lot of things that might be inside your PC or attached to it. What pieces do you actually have? The only way to know for sure is to look.

First, look at the externally attached pieces. They are pretty much obvious. You surely have a keyboard and, most likely, a mouse. You might have one or two monitors. Do you have any external drives? Make a list of all these pieces, and leave room beside each one to record all the resources it must have to do its job.

Now, if you are running Windows 95, look at the Device Manager listing you printed out if you followed my tip earlier in this chapter. That will show you all the resource allocations that Windows has managed or is otherwise aware of.

Finally, nothing replaces actually opening up the system unit and peering inside. You might have to remove some of the pieces in order to see just what they are. Just be sure you follow the cautions I set out near the beginning of this chapter when you do so.

Making this sort of exploratory trip inside your PC will help you visualize the parts as I describe them in more detail later in this book. If you also list the pieces and their resource uses, you will have taken the first necessary step to troubleshoot any difficulties you might have later when you install new hardware or when some portion of your PC starts misbehaving. And, when you have finished that exploration, you will be ready to learn how PCs and people communicate. In particular, in the next chapter, you will learn how programmers tell PCs what they are to do.

5

How to Get Your PC to Understand You

Peter Norton®

You must be able to communicate with your PC. But whenever you try to communicate with any other entity, whether it is another person or a machine, you must have some language you share with that other entity. It could be your native language, the native language of the other entity, or some common third language. Or, of course, you could employ the services of a translator.

The next question is, what language is your PC's native tongue? (I'll get to the other obvious questions—such as "If I don't understand its language, and it doesn't understand mine, what common-ground language might we use?" and "Where do I find a translator?"—in Chapter 18, "Understanding How Humans Instruct PCs.")

What Language Does Your PC Understand?

There is only one language your PC can directly utilize: its "machine language," which is just a bunch of numbers. Every PC program is made up of a lot of these numbers. In other words, if you use a diagnostic program to look at a fragment of a program (which is what you might consider "text" in this special language), all you will see, usually, is just a lot of numbers. The PC reads these numbers as binary values, but for human convenience, most programs that display these numbers show them as pairs of hexadecimal symbols, each pair representing the binary value held in a one-byte location.

You will usually look at such a program fragment either in the PC's main memory or on one of its disk drives. (You'll learn more about how to use several different programs that can display and manipulate these numbers in the next chapter.) Figure 5.1 shows one such display of a program fragment in its hexadecimal form. This figure was generated by capturing the output from the DOS "external command" DEBUG. This is a program that has been included with every version of DOS, and is also available in Windows 95 and Windows 98.

The first column, consisting of two groups of four hexadecimal symbols separated by a colon, indicates (in this case) a particular location in the PC's main memory. The 16 pairs of hexadecimal symbols just to the right of the location numbers are the values at that and the following 15 locations. The characters that appear at the right are the ASCII characters corresponding to some of those values (with a period standing in for any ASCII character that isn't a number, a letter, or a common punctuation mark); however, often these characters have no real meaning when you're looking at a program.

Figure 5.1.
DEBUG's display of the contents of some locations in a PC's main memory.

```
>debug
-d 0715:0180
0715:0180  2E FF 2E 18 01 E8 25 00-1E 0E 2E FF 2E 1C 01 E8   ......%.........
0715:0190  1B 00 1E 0E 2E FF 2E 20-01 E8 11 00 1E 0E 2E FF   ....... ........
0715:01A0  2E 24 01 E8 07 00 1E 0E-2E FF 2E 28 01 9C 2E 80   .$.........(....
0715:01B0  3E 34 01 00 74 1A 50 53-B4 07 2E FF 1E 30 01 0B   >4..t.PS.....0..
0715:01C0  C0 75 0B B4 05 2E FF 1E-30 01 0B C0 74 04 5B 58   .u......0...t.[X
0715:01D0  9D C3 EB FE EA 35 01 16-07 50 A0 86 05 0A C0 75   .....5...P.....u
0715:01E0  03 58 F9 C3 E8 A8 00 E8-23 00 26 C6 06 86 05 00   .X......#.&.....
0715:01F0  E8 03 00 58 F8 C3 32 FF-8A 1E 8B 05 B8 03 58 CD   ...X..2.......X.
-q
```

DEBUG, like most similar low-level PC diagnostic programs, can also be made to display a version of the meaning of these numbers. In Figure 5.2, you see the contents of the beginning of that same region of this PC's main memory, but this time displayed in a form known as *assembly language*. This is a more-or-less readable language for humans, but one that has been especially designed to be easy to translate into real machine language. (You'll learn more about assembly languages and other computer languages in Chapter 18.)

Each line in Figure 5.2 represents one machine language instruction. The first column in this figure, as in Figure 5.1, shows a location in memory. The second column shows the actual numbers stored in that and enough of the subsequent locations to make up one entire instruction. (Those numbers are shown here in hexadecimal format). The rest of that line is that instruction as it is written in assembly language. (Because this display takes up more space, one screenful in this format covers fewer memory locations than the display shown in Figure 5.1.)

Figure 5.2.

A DEBUG's "disassembly" display of the same memory region.

```
>debug
-u 0715:0180
0715:0180 2E           CS:
0715:0181 FF2E1801      JMP      FAR [0118]
0715:0185 E82500        CALL     01AD
0715:0188 1E            PUSH     DS
0715:0189 0E            PUSH     CS
0715:018A 2E            CS:
0715:018B FF2E1C01      JMP      FAR [011C]
0715:018F E81B00        CALL     01AD
0715:0192 1E            PUSH     DS
0715:0193 0E            PUSH     CS
0715:0194 2E            CS:
0715:0195 FF2E2001      JMP      FAR [0120]
0715:0199 E81100        CALL     01AD
0715:019C 1E            PUSH     DS
0715:019D 0E            PUSH     CS
0715:019E 2E            CS:
0715:019F FF2E2401      JMP      FAR [0124]
```

From the number of hexadecimal symbols in the second column, you can see that these instructions vary in length from one byte (two symbols) up to four bytes.

How Big Are the Words in PC Machine Language?

The numbers that represent a computer's machine language come in natural groupings, called instructions. Some are only one byte long. Others can stretch for up to about a dozen bytes. The maximum length of an instruction for your PC depends on which kind of central processor chip it has.

When the PC's central processing unit (CPU) reads one of these strings of numbers, it analyzes the first byte to decide how many bytes are in this particular instruction and then reads the rest of those bytes. Next, it looks at a table of super-detailed instructions, called the *microcode*, that is built into the CPU to find out what that particular instruction is asking it to do. Finally, it does that task.

In most modern PC CPUs, many of the more common instructions are "understood" and executed directly by the CPU, without having to look up any microcode. Only the most complex or least frequently used instructions force the CPU to refer to its microcode library. In Chapter 7, "Understanding PC Processors," I will explain more fully the difference between CISC and RISC processors. That discussion will cover the notion of microcode in more detail.

Technical Note: A very important point to realize is that because every instruction is just a group of numbers, you can't tell by looking at them whether they are part of some instructions or merely just data, and—more importantly—neither can your PC's CPU.

This becomes much more than just an interesting bit of trivia when you realize that it means your PC can do computations and logical operations on data that, in another context, can be considered a program. Therefore, your PC can create or modify programs as well as simply execute them. This capability is vital to the process of translating programs from a human-friendly language into real machine language.

What Can Your PC Do, at the Lowest Level?

What can one instruction command a PC to do? Not much. Basically, in a single instruction, all the CPU can do usually is some little bit of arithmetic or one logical operation. For example, it can add a few numbers. It can move a number, or even move a whole string of bytes, from one place to another. It also can compare two numbers and decide which one is larger. That's just about it. Well, some of the more recent and powerful CPU chips can do some fairly fancy bits of logic or arithmetic in a single, rather complex instruction, but I hope you are getting the idea that it can't do something really complex, like check your spelling or compute your tax liability. To do such things requires an entire program with many, many instructions.

Still, even though a CPU can do only a relatively few and fairly simple operations, inherent in them is the power to accomplish all the manifold and wonderful things PCs can be made to accomplish. Provided, of course, that enough of the correct instructions are strung together properly (and presuming that the correct combination of peripheral hardware is in place and working).

Where Are Instructions and Data Kept?

In order for the CPU to execute instructions, they must be kept somewhere the CPU can get at them—quickly. The CPU is always in a hurry, and if you value your PC's speed, as most folks do, you never want its CPU to have to "twiddle its fingers" waiting for its next instruction to arrive. Likewise, for the CPU to process some data, it must be kept where the CPU can get at it—again, quickly.

In practice, this means that every bit of data and all the instructions that the CPU executes to process the data must be in some part of the machine's RAM (Random Access Memory) or ROM (Read-Only Memory) at the time the processing takes place. RAM and ROM are very fast electronic holding places for numbers, and they are composed of small integrated circuit chips.

Historical Aside: When PCs were first introduced, the RAM chips that were available and (relatively) inexpensive were about as fast as the CPU chips. Over the years since then, the CPU chips have gotten faster much more rapidly than affordable RAM chips. So now it is common to have some small amount of super-fast RAM in between the CPU and the main RAM or ROM chips. This small area is called the *cache*, and it helps keep the CPU supplied with data and instructions (and to take from the CPU processed data) at the full speed of the CPU. I'll explain cache memory in more detail in Chapter 11, "Bigger Is Better in Ballrooms and in a PC's Memory."

There are two reasons why you don't want to keep all your data and programs in RAM all the time. The first has to do with the inherent nature of RAM and ROM. The second has to do with their cost.

Programs or data that are kept in ROM cannot be changed. Therefore, ROM is only a suitable place to keep things that don't need to change. This is OK for any program you expect to run often and for data that is fixed (for example, the value of pi, or the conversion factor from centimeters to inches), but not for most of the data with which you work.

Programs or data that are kept in RAM can be altered at will. But, unfortunately, they also can be altered in other ways. In particular, when you shut off your computer, or even merely reboot it, all the contents of RAM are lost.

For this reason, there are magnetic and optical disk drives (and tape drives and other media) for the semi-permanent storage of both programs and data. These types of media, except for read-only optical disks (called CD-ROMs), enable you to alter their contents. In between such alterations they faithfully hold the contents more or less indefinitely—at least for several years—even when you turn off power to them.

The matters of relative cost and relative speed also enter in. When PCs were new, RAM and ROM chips and magnetic disks cost a whole lot more than they do today. In fact, the ratio of cost for the two kinds of information holding places, per unit of information held, has stayed more or less constant, with magnetic media having an advantage of close to 100:1 over electronic media. Optical media have, in the past, been more expensive than magnetic, but they are coming down in cost to where they are competitive with magnetic media today. However, with all the improvements in each of these areas, only the electronic information-holding devices have any hope of keeping up with today's speedy CPU chips.

Today, because RAM costs just a few dollars per megabyte and the typical CPU chips cost about a hundred times as much, it is reasonable to have several dozen, or perhaps a hundred megabytes, of RAM. However, for about the same expenditure you can buy several gigabytes (thousands of megabytes) or tens of gigabytes of magnetic or optical disk capacity. Therefore, it has become quite common to have many dozen megabytes of RAM and several gigabytes of disk storage space on a good PC.

What Is a BIOS ROM and Why Do I Need One?

Some programs must be kept where the CPU can find them without having to load them off of a disk drive (in particular, those programs that are used to start the PC). Until it has gone through quite an extensive Power On Self-Test (POST) process, your PC doesn't even know that it has any disk drives to work with at all.

For this reason, that startup (POST) program is kept in a Read-Only Memory chip (ROM) called the motherboard Basic Input-Output System (BIOS) ROM. The contents of this ROM are located in a special region of the CPU's memory address space—one where the CPU automatically goes when it first wakes up in order to find out what it is to do.

Certain other programs are also kept in the motherboard BIOS ROM. In fact, it gets its name from these other programs. Their job is to activate the standard PC hardware, such as reading keystrokes from the keyboard, putting information on the video display, sending information to the printer, and so on.

Looking Ahead: As you'll learn in more detail in Chapter 18, computer designers have learned that it makes everyone's task easier if the actual details of operating the hardware are handled by one programmer or one group of programmers, and the details of what you want that hardware to do are handled by a different individual or group. The first programmer(s) write something called a *device driver*. The second write what is most often called an *application program*.

The device driver programs that actually command the hardware to work are so often called upon by application programs (and by the operating system, which is another kind of program that sits in between the other two) that it is more efficient to always keep them in memory than to go fetch a copy of them each time you want to operate the hardware. The collection of programs that performs the most basic information input (such as reading keystrokes) and output (such as writing to the screen) is called the Basic Input-Output System, and it is the main resident in the motherboard BIOS ROM.

Some PCs also have their hardware setup programs located in a portion of the motherboard BIOS ROM. They can also have other programs in other ROMs. I'll mention a few of these in the section "Other Tasks, Other BIOSs," later in this chapter, and you'll see several other examples in later chapters.

Technical Note: Occasionally, you might need to change one or more of the programs that are kept in one of these ROMs, but by the nature of a true Read-Only Memory chip, that just isn't possible. Therefore, you might have to replace one such chip with another one that has been manufactured with the updated program in it.

Until recently, that was the only way to upgrade your PC's BIOS ROM or any other ROMs it might have. Now, though, you have available another strategy—the use of what is sometimes called an *EEPROM*, which stands for Electrically Erasable Programmable Read-Only Memory; or *NVRAM*, which stands for Nonvolatile Random Access Memory. Yet another term for this kind of memory is *Flash ROM* (or *Flash RAM*). This term comes from the notion that you can update an entire collection of locations in one fell swoop—an operation that is sometimes called "flashing" the chip.

These changeable, yet semi-permanent memory devices often are integrated circuit chips that have been specially built to enable them to hold information indefinitely, even if no electrical power is supplied to them. Yet, by special means (involving higher voltages applied briefly to special programming pins), they are able to have that information changed.

Alternatively, this facility may be provided simply as a small amount of normal RAM that has a tiny battery built right into the chip itself in order to enable it to remember its contents even when external power is removed. The choice of which kind of nonvolatile memory technology to use is dictated by the relative costs of each kind, as well as the anticipated frequency of updates plus the anticipated time periods during which external power will be unavailable. Each manufacturer must go through a design evaluation to conclude which kind to use in its PCs.

No matter how the long-term information-holding arrangement is constructed, and no matter which programs are kept there, these programs are called *firmware*. This name suggests their basic nature (in that they are a kind of software), yet they are intrinsically linked to some particular piece of hardware as well.

Programs That Get Loaded Off a Disk; Firmware That Can "Disappear"

If you always want your PC to do exactly the same task over and over, then it would be best if you simply put the program needed for that task into firmware. However, most of us use our PCs some-times to do one task, and other times to do different things. For us, the most sensible course is to store the programs for each of these purposes on a disk drive and load each of them into memory (RAM) only when we need it.

Conversely, sometimes you might want a program that really must be in ROM to be able to disap-pear. One example is the Setup program. If you can call that program up at any time with some hot-key sequence, you could summon it accidentally. And, if at that moment you were in the middle of some important work and you hadn't saved that work, you could end up losing it all. This is because most setup programs don't let you exit from them without rebooting.

Note: Dell uses two different strategies in this regard. In its Optiplex computers it saves the system state, including even the video display, before entering the Setup program. Then, after you finish making whatever changes you want to make there, you are permitted to return to exactly the point in your work that you were when you left it to go into the Setup program.

Dell's Dimension line of computers follows the more usual industry practice of forcing the user to reboot the PC upon each exit from the Setup program. However, Dell protects the user from the sort of accidental data loss described earlier by only allowing one to enter the Setup program during the boot process.

Another case in point is when you perform memory management. In Chapter 11, I explain just why this is so, and how you can make ROMs, or even just portions of a ROM, disappear from the CPU's view.

Data Available on Demand Versus Data That's Always Available

Just as some programs must be kept in memory all the time, either because the CPU can't access a disk to get them without already having them to use or because the CPU will be using them often, some data values must be kept always at hand. And, just as most programs are kept on disks most of the time, so is most data.

The only data your PC must have instant access to, or access to before it can access the disk drives, are details about how the PC is configured, including the parameters that describe the disk drives attached to it. This type of data typically is stored in what is commonly known as the CMOS, which stands for Complementary Metal Oxide Semiconductor, which is a particular kind of integrated circuit manufacturing technology.

You might wonder why this data isn't simply stored in the BIOS ROM along with the POST program that uses it. The reason is simple. The POST program never changes. So it can be (and usually is) stored in an utterly unchangeable ROM chip. The configuration data I'm referring to here is subject to change, so it must be stored in some changeable, yet non-volatile memory. And that is exactly what the "CMOS" is.

Historical Aside: The key advantage to the CMOS chip manufacturing technology is the very low power needed to operate chips that are made using it. When PCs were young, this technology was relatively expensive, so it was used only when it really was needed. IBM decided when it introduced its PC/AT to use this technology to provide a small amount of ordinary "static" RAM that was made nonvolatile by having associated with it a small battery. This combination of a battery plus a CMOS chip was soon nicknamed "the PC's CMOS." That name has stuck, even though now most of the integrated circuits in every part of your PC are manufactured by a variation of the same CMOS technology.

All the other data your PC uses is stored on some disk, somewhere. This might be the hard disk inside your PC's system unit or a floppy disk you put into the A: drive, or it might be on a disk on some remote computer you access across the Internet. From the point of view of your CPU, there is no difference. These are all examples of data that can be made available upon demand but that aren't where the CPU can use them instantly.

Other Tasks, Other BIOSs

I have told you how these special hardware device drivers that control the standard PC hardware are normally placed into the BIOS ROM on the PC's motherboard. There are some other tasks that are done by similar device driver programs that can be located in other ROMs or can be programs that are loaded off a disk drive, just like any application program.

One example of a program that lives in a special ROM is the video display adapter's BIOS. The original IBM PC came with device drivers to operate either the original monochrome character display or the earliest color graphics adapter as a part of the motherboard BIOS ROM.

Now, though, almost no one uses either of these video display adapters. A few PC manufacturers have built in better video display circuits to their motherboards, and in those cases they have incorporated alternative device drivers to operate that alternative video circuitry right into the motherboard BIOS ROM.

More commonly, PCs are built with plug-in video display adapters. These option cards almost always carry a video BIOS ROM as well as the video display circuitry. By a special technique that I will explain in Chapter 8, "How Your PC 'Thinks'," each time you reboot your PC, the POST program looks for these "option ROMs" and, in effect, logically bonds them seamlessly with the programs in the motherboard BIOS ROM.

Still other BIOS programs don't need to be in a ROM. An example of this is the mouse driver. Normally, when your PC boots, it loads from the disk (at some fairly advanced point in the boot process) a small program that knows how to take information from the mouse and convey it to application programs as well as how to put a mouse cursor on the video display. That bit of BIOS code ends up somewhere in your PC's RAM where it stays until the next time you reboot.

How Mere Humans Can Manage All This

If you are getting the idea that a PC is stunningly complex, you are quite right. Arguably, individual computers (mainframes, minicomputers, and PCs), and even more the whole interconnected set of computers that make up the Internet (many of which are PCs), are mankind's most complex creation yet. And it all has been done by ordinary mortals. Complexity can be understood by nearly everyone who tries, if only they consider it one piece at a time.

In the chapters before this one I've given you an overview of computers, and specifically of the various pieces of hardware that make up a typical PC. In this chapter I gave you an overview of the native language of any computer. These overviews provide a context for understanding the details you will learn in the later chapters, where I go back over each of these areas in much greater detail.

Part III, "The Stand-Alone PC," covers all the hardware issues plus the operating system software that activates it. Part IV, "PC Programs: From Machine Language Bytes to Natural Human Speech," covers the rest of the software story. Part V, "Splendiferous Multimedia PCs," extends the discussion to the PCs that have been optimized for multimedia uses—which it turns out is fast becoming almost every PC sold today. Part VI, "PCs Are Frequent Fliers, Too," explains what is different about portable and laptop computers. Part VII, "The Connected PC," explains the details of how PCs get connected to one another and to other computers. And finally, Part VIII, "PCs, the Internet, the Future, and You," tells what is different now that our PCs are connected to so many other computers, and then attempts to tie everything I've told you together.

However, before I go into any of those detailed areas, I want to show you just how you can safely explore the information spaces within your PC. Which, of course, leads us to the next chapter.

6

Enhancing
Your
Understanding
by Messing
Around
(Exploring and
Tinkering)

Peter Norton®

Most people learn better when they actually experience something, instead of simply reading about it. The text and figures in a book like this can take you only so far. To get a deeper understanding of how your (and for that matter, any one else's) PC works, you must "get your hands dirty."

In part, this means opening up the box and looking around inside. When you do that, I hope you always remember to follow the cautions I gave you near the beginning of Chapter 4, "Understanding Your PC's Parts." They are important. Following them will save you much grief and might save your PC and its data from damage. I'll repeat those cautions and explain them in more depth in just a moment.

This chapter shows you how to explore inside your PC in another sense. We'll go on a journey into its information spaces. Here you will get to look at things you cannot see directly with your unaided eyes. And this turns out to be crucial to your gaining a full understanding of your PC.

Why Is This Valuable? And, Is It Dangerous?

You might be reluctant to try some of the experiments I suggest. You might think you don't need to do them, or you might fear hurting something if you do them wrong. I'll admit it up front: Some of the techniques I am about to explain can damage data. None of them will, however, harm your PC's hardware in any permanent way. So, although it might appear that I am encouraging "the giving of chain saws to babies," I actually am going to show you how to protect yourself and your computer quite fully before you start doing anything that is even possibly dangerous.

How to Protect Your Hardware (and Yourself)

The first line of defense against hardware damage is common sense and an awareness of the possibilities for static electricity damage. Oh yes, and a heightened awareness of exactly what changes, if any, you are making in the way the inner pieces are connected, both electrically and physically.

Please remember that there are two principal boxes that make up your PC. One is the monitor and the other is the system unit.

Warning: As I told you previously, you *really* don't want to open up your monitor. There is actual, physical danger there, and furthermore, there is nothing going on inside it that you must see or fiddle with in order to further your understanding of how a PC works.

The system box, on the other hand, was designed to be opened by anyone. If you own the PC, then you have a perfect right to open it up. And that is going to be necessary in order to understand its construction and workings fully. If you are merely the user of a PC that belongs to someone else (such as your company), see if you can get permission to go exploring inside or to participate in a class in which such an exploration is done for and with everyone in the class.

The system unit is the only really important part of your PC for you to open up. The other pieces, such as your printer, mouse, or scanner might or might not be safe to open. And usually you won't learn much of importance if you do open them.

Now what about that static electricity hazard? It turns out that you are a lot more dangerous to your PC than it is to you; at least in terms of what could go wrong when you open up the system unit. The voltages used by the integrated circuit chips in your PC's system unit are anywhere from a little less than 3 volts up to 12 volts. These are so low that you won't hurt yourself touching any of them. On the other hand, people normally walk around with static electric charges of several hundred volts, or up to several thousand on a dry, cold day. That is more than enough to totally fry the delicate innards of your computer's chips.

An electric current won't flow unless there is a voltage difference to drive it. Therefore, the actual voltage of your body isn't very important by itself. What matters is how much difference there is between the voltage at your fingertip and the voltage at the places you are about to touch. If you first touch the power supply or an unpainted portion of the metal chassis of your PC system unit, and then touch whatever you want inside, you will by this first step have brought your entire body (including your fingers) to essentially the same voltage as the chips you'll be touching. In this case, no damage will be done.

If you get a nasty, or even a painful shock when you touch the case, be glad. That shock might have pained you, but it could have killed your PC's inner workings if they had received it instead of you.

If the pain of those shocks is just too great to bear, then there are several steps you can take. First, you must think about reducing the static electric charge you carry around. You can get static-reducing carpet or a chair pad and put it where you sit or stand when you work on your PC. An even easier solution is to get some fabric softener, dilute it with three to four times as much water as softener, and then spray the diluted mixture on the carpet. Repeat this as necessary, probably no more often than once a month, and then only in especially dry weather.

You can reduce your personal pain from these shocks another way. Get a one million ohm radio resistor. (Radio Shack is one convenient source.) The exact value of the resistor is not important; anything from a few hundred thousand ohms to a few million will do, and the wattage rating of the resistor is also unimportant.

Hold one end of the resistor and touch the other end to the chassis before you reach over and touch the chassis directly. This will let your excess electric charge bleed off more slowly, and you won't even feel the resulting current. It might take a second or two, but you'll very quickly be discharged and thus safe to explore inside your PC. (Please still touch the chassis directly before reaching inside, just to be sure you are discharged fully.)

Every time you move around your room, you are potentially picking up more static charge. This is why you must re-discharge yourself *each and every time* you are about to reach inside the PC. Likewise, if you are carrying an option card and are about to install it, by touching the case while you hold the card you are ensuring that the card and the case are at the same voltage. It is then safe to insert the card.

Well, it is safe to plug the card in if the PC is turned off. By turning off your PC and perhaps unplugging the power cord from the back of the PC's system unit, you'll guarantee not only that the PC won't make any voltages to harm you, both it and you also won't be able to deliver any harmful electric shocks to any option cards or other add-ons you plug into it.

Now, about those changes to the connections of the inner pieces: If you do choose to unplug something, or to unscrew something, please record carefully just what the connection looked like before you made that change. (Some people find taking Polaroid photos a handy way to capture some of this information.) Then, if something you attempted doesn't work out, you can at least put it back the way it was.

Often a particularly troublesome kind of connection in this regard are the places where flat, multi-conductor "ribbon" cables attach to printed circuit boards. Typically there will be a field of gold-plated pins sticking up from the board. On the end of the cable is a rectangular block of plastic with some holes in one side. You plug in the cable by pressing the block down over the pins.

Two types of problem can arise. One is when the plug is turned around 180 degrees. The other is when it gets offset from the correct position by exactly the spacing of one pair of pins (typically just one-tenth of an inch). Doing either of these things will mean that the wires in the cable connect with the wrong pins, or they fail to connect with any pins.

Two things can help: First, the usual practice is to identify one of the pins as the "number one" pin. This is often shown by a small numeral 1 printed next to that pin on the printed circuit card. (It also is usually indicated by having a square bit of copper on the board into which the pin is soldered, instead of the round ones used for all the other pins.) Ordinarily the number one wire in the ribbon cable has a different color insulation than the rest of the cable. (Sometimes this stripe of color on one edge of the cable is blue, sometimes black, and sometimes red. Or you might find that all the wires are different colors, in a rainbow pattern. In that case, the brown wire will be number one.)

If you are really lucky, the manufacturer of both the cable and the board with the field of pins will have taken one more precaution to keep you from plugging in the cable incorrectly. If they did, there will be one or more missing pins and one or more of the holes in the block will be plugged up (at locations that match up with the missing pins). This arrangement of missing pins and matching plugged up holes ensures that the block can only be plugged onto the pins in the correct position and orientation. Figure 6.1 shows just such a ribbon cable and its connectors. In this case one pin is missing and one hole is plugged up. We say that this cable is "keyed" to ensure that it is installed correctly.

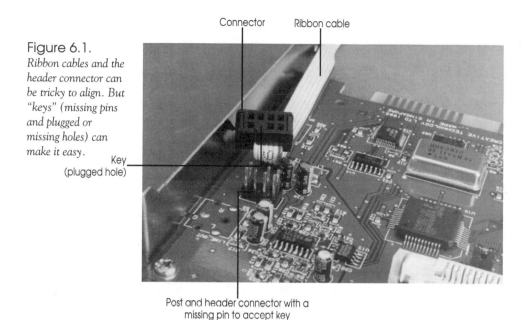

Connector   Ribbon cable

Figure 6.1.
Ribbon cables and the header connector can be tricky to align. But "keys" (missing pins and plugged or missing holes) can make it easy.

Key
(plugged hole)

Post and header connector with a
missing pin to accept key

Another trouble some people have, and that is closely related to the difficulty I just described with ribbon cables, has to do with placing or moving shorting jumpers. These are little blocks that contain a metal strap. You shove them down over a pair of pins and they short those two pins together. (They are sort of like a two-wire ribbon cable connector without the ribbon cable.) But, of course, if you miss the correct pair of pins, you won't short what needs to be shorted, and you may short something else that shouldn't be shorted. The only solution to this problem is to get a bright light and, if you need it, a strong pair of glasses or a magnifying glass. Then look very closely at what you are doing.

How to Protect Your Data

Because you are about to go inside your PC, either physically or logically (through the use of some diagnostic program), and because in that process you possibly could damage some of your data, your common sense should tell you to protect your data against that possible harm. There is really only one good way to do that. You must make—*and test*—backups of your data.

Just as a dentist might say, "You only have to floss the teeth you wish to keep," I'll point out that you must back up only the data you don't want to lose. That might sound trivial, but it is not.

By now, most PC users know they should do backups. And, in fact, many people—perhaps most people who use PCs—do create backups. But most of them use a poorly thought-out process for that purpose. They typically just toss a tape in the backup drive on Friday afternoon, click on some backup program, and expect it to do all the work. On Monday morning they put the tape away, confident that all their work is now safe.

I have several concerns about this strategy. First, these people are vulnerable all week long. What if disaster strikes midweek? This type of PC user stands to lose all the work he or she has done so far that week. (And, of course, if a fire burns down the building over the weekend, both the PC and the backup tape in its drive will be lost.)

Second, this strategy does too much. It commonly will back up *all* the files on your PC. The problem with doing too much is that you will soon fill up the tape. Then, one is strongly tempted to reuse the tape later on; otherwise, the cost of all the tapes you must buy can become onerous, not to mention the space to store them all. But if you find out later that the only valid backup copies of some file are not the most recent ones, you might well be out of luck. If the tape that held that valid and potentially useful backup has already been reused... Oops!

An improvement is to use a backup program that can be configured to back up only data files, or better still, only data files that have changed since the last backup. If you choose this last approach, you are making "incremental" backups only. That is, in fact, my favorite strategy. It does mean that you must save all your backups to be sure you will have access to the latest copy of any file you may lose or damage.

There is one more problem with the most common backup strategy (and it is one that affects almost every backup strategy anyone uses): The backup strategy doesn't take into account the fact—and it is a fact   that backups don't always work correctly. Sometimes, even though the backup was "verified" by the tape backup program, when you go to restore the files the tape presumably contains, you find that some or all of them are simply unreadable.

To be safe, you *must* test your backup strategy. Test it fully the first time you do it, and then test random samples of the backups you make after that.

To me, the only valid test of a backup's integrity is to restore the files to some different place than their origin, and then compare each restored file with its original. *Only if every single one of the restored files matches its original exactly is your backup strategy working satisfactorily.*

Tip: One simple way to do this is to restore all or a portion of your backup file set to another disk drive than the one on which the originals reside. If you only have a C: drive, create a fake D: drive by using these DOS commands:

```
MD C:\ROOT-D
SUBST D: C:\ROOT-D
```

You must do the first step only once; after that, the directory will exist. But you must do the second step each time you reboot if you want to use that directory as a stand-in for the root of a fictitious D: drive. If you already have a D: drive (perhaps a CD-ROM), then you can use any letter you like that isn't already in use. If you are running just DOS or DOS and Windows 3.*x*, you might have to add a `LASTDRIVE` line to your `CONFIG.SYS` file to have enough drive letters available for this strategy to work.

Now you can back up files from C: and restore them to D: without overwriting the originals on C:. Next, use a file comparison program to check that each file on D: is identical to its source on C:. If you don't have room for all the files in your backups to fit on D: (which will be the case if your C drive is over half full), then just restore some of them, test their integrity, erase them, and then restore some more, and so on, until you have tested all the backed up files. (Remember to delete the last group of restored files after you compare them. Otherwise you may end up backing them up inadvertently in your next backup session.)

After you verify one time that your basic backup strategy works for all the files, you can relax a little. But don't neglect to check at least a random sampling of the files you back up at later sessions, to be sure that they also have full integrity. This simple precaution takes some time and effort, but it will catch many problems before they become full-fledged disasters.

Don't forget to keep one full set of backups off site. That means in some other building, far enough away from your PC that if the building burns down or is robbed, flooded, or whatever, your spare set of backups will still be safe. Insurance can replace all the hardware; it can even replace the programs you own, but nothing other than a valid set of backups will replace your data. There just is no other way to go.

So what do I do, and what do I recommend that you do? My choice is to use my backups also as archival storage. I back up only those files that change; but I back them up often. I choose to use disks for the purpose. Originally I used 5^1/$_4$-inch 360KB floppies; now I am up to using 3^1/$_2$-inch 120MB ultra-high-density floppies. I also have used ZIP drives, Bernoulli cartridges, and SyQuest cartridges at various times in the past. You'll learn more about these high-capacity removable disk drives in Chapter 10, "Digging Deeper Into Disks." I usually do these mini-backups many times a day. Each one takes just a few seconds after I get my routine down. This has often saved me many hours of grief, or worse.

An Introduction to DEBUG

Back when the PC was young and most of the people using one were programmers, engineers, or other "techy" types, a tool program was bundled with DOS to help programmers find and eliminate flaws, or "bugs," from their programs. That tool's name was DEBUG.

How to Run (and How to Quit) DEBUG

DEBUG still is a part of DOS, and it even comes with Windows 95 and Windows 98. It is hardly a user-friendly program. If you simply type DEBUG at the DOS prompt and press Enter (or double-click DEBUG.EXE in the Windows 95 Explorer), you will be confronted with just a hyphen as a prompt. That is DEBUG's way of letting you know it is ready to do something for you. What you must do next is supposed to be something you already know.

There are two ways you can get a little bit of help from DEBUG itself. First, if you type DEBUG /? and press Enter at the DOS prompt, you'll get a very brief statement about the legal syntax for invoking the program. Second, if you are at the hyphen prompt and type ? and press Enter you will get a list of legal commands you can type there.

Peter's Principle: Nothing Beats Knowing How to Stop

The most important thing to know about any program is how to get it to quit. To get DEBUG to quit, type q and press Enter when you are at the hyphen prompt.

DEBUG is a very useful snooping tool. You can use it to look at the contents of any place you want in the first megabyte of your PC's memory, or at any file or sector on any disk attached to the PC. A *sector* is a physical location on the disk; a *file* is a logical construct stored there. You'll find more details on these notions in Chapter 9, "You Can Never Have Too Much Closet (or Data Storage) Space."

The reason DEBUG is limited to looking at the first megabyte has to do with its history. It is what we now call a "real-mode," or "16-bit" program. As such, it cannot see any more than the first megabyte of RAM—a restriction shared by all real-mode programs unless they have been enhanced with a "DOS extender."

Using DEBUG to Look at Memory Locations

You saw in Chapter 5, "How to Get Your PC to Understand You," (Figures 5.1 and 5.2) two examples of using DEBUG to look at a location in memory. One shows what is called the dump display; the other shows a program disassembly (or, to help you associate the word with the letter u that is the DEBUG command to generate it, you can call this an unassembly). In the first display, you see the actual numeric values held at each physical memory location. In the second display, those values are interpreted as instructions, much as the CPU might interpret them.

To snoop in the memory in your PC, you must know how to state a memory address in a form DE-BUG can use. It uses is a special way of specifying a location called *segment:offset notation*. An address in this form consists of four hexadecimal symbols (numerals 0 through 9 and letters A through F) followed by a colon and four more hexadecimal symbols.

The actual memory address indicated in this way is computed as follows: Multiply the number before the colon by 16, and then add the number after the colon. This is simpler than it might at first appear, because 16 is the number base for hexadecimal numbers. So just as multiplying by ten in decimal arithmetic means simply moving the decimal point over one place or the addition of a trailing zero, in hexadecimal multiplying by 16 can also be done by a simple shifting over of the decimal point or the addition of a trailing zero.

Here is an example showing just how to do the math: Suppose the address you want to convert from segment:offset form is 3754:2698. Using the rule I just gave about how to multiply by 16 in hexadecimal, you will easily see that the actual memory address pointed to by our example segment:offset value is equal to the hexadecimal number (37540+2698)h. When you remember how to add hexadecimal numbers, this works out to 39BD8h. (The trailing lowercase h shows that this is a hexadecimal number.) You can use the calculator that comes with Windows to convert this to a decimal value if you want, in which case you'll see that that number is the same as the decimal number 236,504.

If you are finding all this confusing, you might want to review the section on hexadecimal numbers in Chapter 3, "Understanding Bits, Nybbles, and Bytes." And, you might find it helpful to study the addition table for hexadecimal numbers in Figure 6.2. This figure also shows the example used in this section in a form that might look more like addition problems you have seen before.

How do you know at which memory addresses you should snoop to see something interesting? Well, the first step is to go to a DOS prompt (either by booting your computer to DOS without Windows or by opening a DOS prompt window inside Windows). Then enter the command MEM /D /P. This will display all the programs currently running in the first megabyte of your machine's main memory. The first column in the MEM display shows the segment portion of the address. Suppose that one of the lines begins with the number 1234. Then, if you snoop at 1234:0000, you'll see the beginning of that program. Actually, the first 16 bytes at this address are the memory control block for the program. I'll explain just what this means in Chapter 11, "Bigger Is Better in Ballrooms and in a PC's Memory."

You can practice your hexadecimal arithmetic abilities by looking at several successive memory control blocks. (These are the 16-byte regions that start at each of the segment addresses shown in the left column of the MEM /D display.) The fourth and fifth bytes in each block (at address segment:0003 and segment:0004) can be combined to give the size of the memory region "controlled" by this memory control block.

Figure 6.2.
Addition table for hexadecimal numbers.

	0	1	2	3	4	5	6	7	8	9	A	B	C	D	E	F
0	0	1	2	3	4	5	6	7	8	9	A	B	C	D	E	F
1	1	2	3	4	5	6	7	8	9	A	B	C	D	E	F	10
2	2	3	4	5	6	7	8	9	A	B	C	D	E	F	10	11
3	3	4	5	6	7	8	9	A	B	C	D	E	F	10	11	12
4	4	5	6	7	8	9	A	B	C	D	E	F	10	11	12	13
5	5	6	7	8	9	A	B	C	D	E	F	10	11	12	13	14
6	6	7	8	9	A	B	C	D	E	F	10	11	12	13	14	15
7	7	8	9	A	B	C	D	E	F	10	11	12	13	14	15	16
8	8	9	A	B	C	D	E	F	10	11	12	13	14	15	16	17
9	9	A	B	C	D	E	F	10	11	12	13	14	15	16	17	18
A	A	B	C	D	E	F	10	11	12	13	14	15	16	17	18	19
B	B	C	D	E	F	10	11	12	13	14	15	16	17	18	19	1A
C	C	D	E	F	10	11	12	13	14	15	16	17	18	19	1A	1B
D	D	E	F	10	11	12	13	14	15	16	17	18	19	1A	1B	1C
E	E	F	10	11	12	13	14	15	16	17	18	19	1A	1B	1C	1D
F	F	10	11	12	13	14	15	16	17	18	19	1A	1B	1C	1D	1E

```
Example:   3754:2698 = 37540h + 2698h

               37540h
             + 2698h
             _____
               39BD8h = 236,504  (decimal)
```

A simple way to combine them is to put the two hexadecimal symbols at segment:0004 in front of those at segment:0003 and read the result as a four-symbol hexadecimal number. This is the length of the controlled memory region, expressed in "paragraphs," where a paragraph means the same thing as 16 bytes.

The length of the controlled region does not include the memory control block itself. Therefore, to get the segment address of the next memory control block, you must add just the segment portion of the address of this block to the length of the region it controls (in paragraphs), plus one paragraph for the length of the memory control block itself.

In Figure 6.3, you see some real-life examples (taken from the machine on which I am writing this). I produced this figure by first running the MEM command to see where the memory control blocks were. Then, for each one, I ran the d segment:0000 command within DEBUG (at the hyphen prompt). I redirected the output to a file and edited out all but the first line of output after each DEBUG output, plus I edited off the end of each line of DEBUG output, so only the hexadecimal values show. Then I imported this data into CorelDRAW! and finished the rest of the figure. The boldface numbers in each long line are the fourth and fifth entries in that memory control block. And, as you can see, they can be used to compute the address of the next block.

Figure 6.3.
Using DEBUG to see the contents of some memory control blocks and the hexadecimal addition needed to find the next one.

```
-d  020D:0000
020D:0000   4D 08 00 05 07 04 F7 44-53 44 00 74 03 80 CB 02

              020Dh + 0705h + 1 = 0913h

-d  0913:0000
0913:0000   4D 08 00 04 00 2B C2 00-53 43 06 2E 01 46 06 2E

              0913h + 0004h + 1 = 0918h

-d  0918:0000
0918:0000   4D 26 0C 01 00 33 C0 26-43 4F 4D 4D 41 4E 44 00

              0918h + 0001h + 1 = 091Ah

-d  091A:0000
091A:0000   4D CF 0B 16 00 45 4D 50-3D 63 3A 5C 77 69 6E 64

              091Ah + 0016h + 1 = 0931h

-d  0931:0000
0931:0000   4D 32 09 34 01 00 00 00-4E 41 56 42 4F 4F 54 00

              0931h + 0134h + 1 = 0A66h

-d  0A66:0000
0A66:0000   4D 67 0A 67 01 00 00 00-44 4F 53 4B 45 59 00 00

              0A66h + 0167h + 1 = 0BCEh

-d  0BCE:0000
0BCE:0000   4D CF 0B 42 00 43 48 4F-48 4B 54 52 41 50 00 20
```

What I just did is essentially what the MEM program did to generate its /D display. (And it was from the MEM program's display that I found the memory control block addresses in the first place.) MEM had to look in those same exact places in memory, extract those length numbers, and do the same arithmetic in order to know where to look for the next line of its output. It got the rest of the information on each line by reading and interpreting the rest of the information in each memory control block.

In Chapter 11, you'll find out more about some of the interesting memory locations you can examine in this way. Right now I want to point out some of the other things you can do with this program to further your education.

Other Things You Can Do with DEBUG

Looking at memory is not all you can do with DEBUG, not by a long shot. It has 23 different commands it can execute. The d command merely displays the information it finds in memory. The u (unassemble) command, as you saw in Figure 5.2, interprets that information and then displays the result. Other commands, in particular e (edit) and f (fill), let you alter the information that is held in memory.

Warning: You might put some information into a place in memory that the PC must have to hold some other information. In this way you could make your PC very confused, and perhaps hang. If that happens, you can recover simply by rebooting the PC. Of course, this means that you shouldn't do this type of experimenting while you have any unsaved data in another program.

Perhaps the worst thing that could happen would be if you were to alter the image in main memory of the FAT table for one of your disk drives. If you did this without realizing it, and if afterward you wrote anything to that disk, you could lose some of the files stored on that disk. So, in general, I'd recommend that you feel free to *look* at the contents of any memory location, but only alter ones whose purpose you are pretty sure you understand.

Still other DEBUG commands let you see information from a disk drive (or alter that drive's contents). The l (standing for load) command will bring in one or more sectors of information from an absolute sector address on a disk and place that information in memory. After it is there, you can use the d command to display that information.

This works, but a far easier way to look at disks, if you have a copy of the Norton Utilities, is to use the Norton Disk Editor. I will explain how that is done in the section "Using the Norton Disk Editor," later in this chapter.

You can also read input from a port or send output to a port, and you can read or set the CPU's registers using DEBUG. (You'll learn in Chapter 8, "How Your PC 'Thinks'," just what registers and ports are.)

Furthermore, you can make the PC run a program by using the proper DEBUG commands. Doing these things will give you a better sense of how your PC does them itself. But please be careful. I strongly suggest that you begin your playing around with disks by using a "scratch" floppy disk—that is, any disk whose contents you don't care about. (If you have a disk whose contents you want to look at but want to be sure you don't alter, then first make a DISKCOPY of it and then do your snooping on the copy.)

Because this isn't a book focused on DOS and DOS utilities, I won't take the time to explain in detail all the things you can do with DEBUG. Instead, I am going to move on to some other tools you might want to use for snooping around your PC.

Note: If you want to find out more about DOS, I suggest you look at *Peter Norton's Complete Guide to DOS 6.22, 6th Edition*, published by Sams Publishing, ISBN 0-672-30614-X.

QBASIC Snooping Basics

If you have any version of MS-DOS up through 6.22, or PC-DOS up through 5.1, then you have a copy of BASIC or QBASIC. These are computer programming languages that were designed to be particularly easy to learn and use.

Historical Aside

In fact, up until quite recently, the one common feature of all personal computers was that they came bundled with some version of the BASIC language. This is what got the company started by Bill Gates and Paul Allen, Microsoft, going. Their successes with DOS and Windows came later on.

Using BASIC, you can read or write the contents of memory, send or receive information via an I/O port, or access a disk drive. You can even, with the addition of a suitable linkable library, read or set the registers in the CPU. In short, you can do all the same things I told you that DEBUG would let you do. But where is the advantage?

Although there is no kind of snooping you can do with BASIC that you couldn't do with DEBUG, BASIC offers some other important capabilities. They come into play when you decide that you would like to manipulate the information you have just retrieved. BASIC is a programming language. Recent versions are quite full featured; in fact, there have been nearly as many business programs written in BASIC as have been written in the more currently fashionable languages such as C and C++.

This is not a book on DOS and its utility programs. It also is not a book on programming. Therefore, I am not going to teach you how to write BASIC programs. In Appendix B, "Some Sample Programs," however, you'll find a couple of small BASIC programs you might want to study and then type into your BASIC interpreter or compiler

Using the Norton Disk Editor

Finally, I cannot end this chapter without telling you about one of my all-time favorite PC exploration tools—the disk editor, DiskEdit, that comes with the Norton Utilities.

Historical Aside

Peter Norton started his career in the personal computer field with an observation about human nature. People make mistakes.

continues

He noticed that the designers of the first PCs and of the early versions of DOS didn't really allow for that. The designers assumed that every PC user would, like them, know all the ins and outs of the machine and its software, and that the user never would do something unless he or she knew what effect it would have and that the user really intended for that effect to occur.

But, as Peter noticed, this wasn't always the case. In fact, a lot of early PC users came to great grief by erasing files they wished they hadn't erased. And from an understanding of just how the PC stored files, and how it "erased" them, Peter realized that it was quite possible to "unerase" files—at least much of the time.

So Peter built a tool to do just that. And then he went on to build several other tools that might be useful to ordinary PC users. This was the beginnings of the Norton Utilities.

That Peter's perception was correct has long since been proven by the enormous success of the Norton Utilities. Eventually, the company Peter started to develop and market this product, Peter Norton Computing, Inc., became so valuable that the Symantec Corporation made Peter an offer he couldn't refuse. (Or at least he didn't.) They bought his company, and that is the source of the biggest part of Peter's fortune today.

Before Peter Norton could write the Norton Utilities and its famous unerase tool, he had to understand how PC disks are organized at a very deep and intimate level. The tool he created to help himself do that is what finally became the Norton Disk Editor.

As I explained earlier, you can look at almost anything you want on a disk simply by using DEBUG—at least you can if you know what you are doing with it. But it isn't easy.

Peter Norton's genius, in large part, lay in visualizing a very good way to display the information hidden on PC disk drives. And a refined version of that method is embodied in the screens you will see when you run the Norton DiskEdit program. (I recall that when I saw each new version of the Norton Utilities I would marvel at how the developers had managed to improve on something already so marvelous, and yet do so in a way that didn't lose any of what made the product marvelous in its previous versions.)

When you start the program, it might tell you that it is configured in read-only mode. That is wonderful. It means you can play around all you like, and you will never hurt any of the data on your disk drives.

This is all the more important because if you were to change just one crucial byte on a disk, you could render it totally inaccessible to DOS. The only way to recover from that sort of error is to use either DiskEdit or the Norton Disk Doctor (or some similar program) to set that critical byte back to the right value.

There are several different places you could mess up the disk's data in ways that would keep DOS from using it. One advantage to using the Norton Disk Doctor to recover from such an error is that it knows pretty much all those places and can quite likely set them all back to their proper contents with little or no input on your part.

If your copy of DiskEdit isn't set to read-only mode, then setting it to that mode is your first order of business. Go into the main screen (shown in Figure 6.4) and from the drop-down Tools menu, select Configuration.

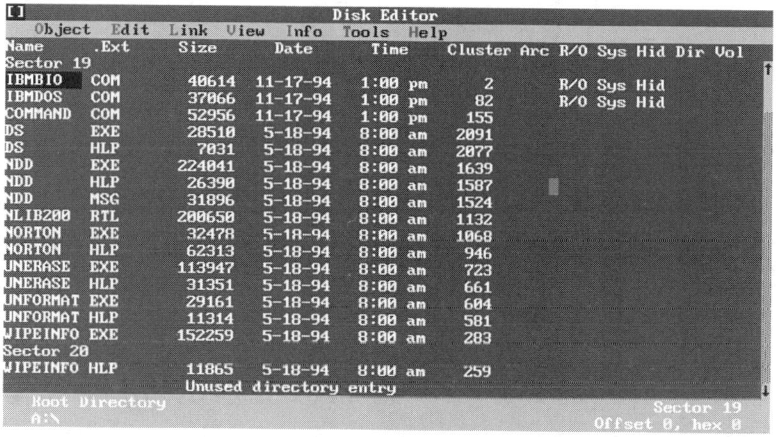

Figure 6.4.
The Norton DiskEdit program's main screen.

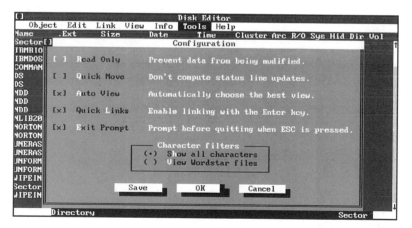

Figure 6.5 shows the screen that pops up next and indicates the checkbox you will want to select to protect yourself. If there is an × in it, you are safe. Now press the OK button and you are ready to start exploring.

Figure 6.5.
Save yourself grief; prevent DiskEdit from doing any harm.

Rather than walk you through a lengthy exploration of a diskette at this point, I would rather encourage you to, as the title of this chapter puts it, mess around a bit. Try out the various menu items in the DiskEdit program. Now that you have verified that it is in the safe read-only mode, you know you won't do any damage. So just play with it. Try anything that comes to mind.

If you become comfortable with it, and assuming that the diskette in the A: drive doesn't contain anything you highly value, then you might want to set the program to its read-write mode. You'll be asked to confirm any changes you make before they are written to the disk; by using the program this way, you'll be able to develop a feel for it before you actually must use it to recover some lost data.

I'll give you some hints on what to try in the next section. After you have read Chapter 9, you'll no doubt be able to think of many more.

Some More Things to Think About and Try

Here are a few suggestions to get your PC snooping going. After you have done them, perhaps you can come up with more on your own.

Looking at the "DOS Clock" Values in the BIOS Data Area

Using either DEBUG or a BASIC program you have written, retrieve the values held at memory locations 0040:006C through 0040:006F. Now do it again. You'll notice that the numbers you get change each time you do it. These four locations hold a long integer number that tells how many times the PC's motherboard "timer" circuit has "ticked" since the PC was last rebooted. The timer ticks are events that happen once every 55 milliseconds. Knowing that, can you write a BASIC program to retrieve them and then display the time of day? (You'll have to give that program the current time when you start it. After that, it should be able to update the display on its own, using the information from these memory locations. This is what most onscreen PC clock programs do.)

Looking at the CMOS "Real-Time Clock" Values

Again using either DEBUG or a BASIC program, send a number to I/O port address 70h. The value you send will be an address in the CMOS nonvolatile RAM. Now read a byte in from I/O port address 71h. That is, the byte held at that address in the CMOS. The first 10 bytes (at addresses 00h through 09h) in the CMOS hold the current time according to the "real-time clock" on the motherboard. This is where the PC keeps track of time when it is turned off. One of the tasks your PC performs during the boot process is reading these locations to set the main operating system clock.

Thereafter, that clock keeps time by reference to the timer tick BIOS data area locations you examined in the previous paragraph.

Warning: There are two points I particularly want to have you notice here. If you don't attend to both these points, you could render your PC unable to boot because you inappropriately altered the contents of the nonvolatile RAM.

The first point is that the addresses I have given you are stated in hexadecimal notation. Address 70h is the same as 112 in decimal, for example. Be careful when you enter them to use the number base expected by the program you are using. DEBUG normally expects all numbers to be entered in hexadecimal. BASIC normally expects all numbers to be decimal ones, unless you precede them with &H.

The second point is that you are going to send data only to port 70h (which is port 112 in decimal). You'll be reading data only from port 71h (113 decimal). If you accidentally write data to port 71h, you will alter the contents of the CMOS instead of inspecting them.

If you do mess up the contents of your CMOS, this won't keep your PC from booting. A checksum in the CMOS allows the POST to discover whether this data has been messed up. If so, the POST will restore the factory default values and go on to boot up the PC. But this means, of course, that all of the configuration information you provided through the Setup program will have been lost.

You'll have to reenter manually such things as the types of drives you have and any nondefault choices you might have made in other areas of the CMOS. For this reason, it is only prudent for you first to go into the CMOS setup program, inspect all the values displayed there (on each of the many pages, if your PC's setup program has many pages), and write down on paper all the values you see displayed. That way you have a record from which you can help your PC rebuild its CMOS to the state it was in before you messed it up.

If you retrieve this data (and it will take you 10 separate accesses to the CMOS to do so), then you'll find you can interpret it to get the time your PC thinks it is, without having to enter the current time manually. The format for this information is as follows: The first byte (at address 0) holds the current second. The third byte (address 2) holds the current minute. The fifth byte (address 4) holds the current hour. (Addresses 1, 3, and 5 hold the same information for the alarm time, if you have set one.) The seventh byte (address 6) holds the day of the week in numeric form (Sunday = 1). The next two bytes hold the date and current month. The last byte (address 9) holds the current year.

Two decimal digits are held in each of these bytes in what is called a *packed BCD format.* That is, each nybble (four bits) holds one decimal digit. Therefore, when the value is written in hexadecimal, you can simply pretend it is in decimal and read it directly.

> **Technical Note:** Alternatively, you can say that the tens place of the two-digit decimal value is the binary value divided by 16, with the fractional part discarded. The units place of the two-digit decimal value is the binary value modulo 16. This formulation suggests what calculations you'll have to do in a BASIC program to unpack the packed BCD values into a normal decimal value.

Here is one place, incidentally, where the now-infamous "Year 2000" problem pops up. Location 9 in the CMOS is only big enough to hold the last two digits of the year. Therefore, if you only look there, you (and your PC) won't be able to tell the difference between the year 2000 and the year 1900 (or 2100). There are other storage locations in the nonvolatile RAM that weren't at first designated for any particular use. One of these is now used to hold the century in modern PCs.

Just which CMOS location holds the century value can depend on what brand of computer you have. If yours is an IBM PS/2, for example, the century (two-decimal digit) value is held (as a packed BCD number) in CMOS location 37h. Most other PCs hold that value at CMOS location 32h. See if you can find out where this information is held in your PC.

Snooping Around on Your Disk Drives

If you have a copy of the Norton Utilities, use the DiskEdit program to look at a floppy disk. From the Tools menu, select Configuration. Be sure the checkbox for Read Only is checked. This will keep you from accidentally altering something important on one of your disk drives.

Next, from the Object menu, choose Drive, and then your logical A: drive. (That is, the Logical Disks radio button should be selected—have a dot in it—and then from the list of logical disks, choose A:.)

Notice that there is no Partition Table on a floppy disk. (That option on the Objects menu is grayed out.) The first sector of a floppy disk is the Boot Sector.

Look at the contents of that Boot Sector (by selecting it from the Object menu). The Norton Disk Editor, by default, will display a table of information about that disk that it has read from the boot sector. You can see the actual hexadecimal values stored in that sector by pressing the F2 function key, or by selecting View as Hex from the View menu. Notice that near the beginning of the boot sector you will see ASCII characters spelling out the name of the operating system, and its version, that was used to format this disk.

Now try looking at your C: drive. Here you'll find a partition table. If you have a physical disk (that is, one actual piece of spinning hardware) divided into two or more logical disks, then the partition table shows you the beginnings of that logical division. (If three or more drive letters are allocated to this physical disk, most likely you'll find additional partition tables, called *extended partition tables*, further out on the disk.)

Now try looking at a directory. Again, you can have it displayed in a very readable format (the default directory display) or in hexadecimal if you want to see what really is stored in each location within each entry. This is particularly interesting to do if you are running Windows 95 and have some files with long names.

You can jump from one interesting place to another on the disk. Keep watching the location indications at the bottom of the screen as you do so. Often, the easiest way to jump is to highlight some piece of information and then press Enter. You will be transported to another location on the disk involving that particular piece of information. Using the Link menu is another way to jump around.

Yet Other Things to Try

When you tire of these experiments—and they might not be all that fascinating to you until you have read Chapter 9—you can return to this narrative and continue your journey there. Any time along the way that some idea for an experiment pops into your mind, I encourage you to put the book down, go to your PC, and try it. This is, without a doubt, the very best way to learn about these intricate and fascinating machines.

Summary

Hands-on learning is the very best kind. What you hear you remember for awhile. What you hear and see, you remember longer. What you hear, see, and experience in every other possible way, you remember for the longest and it leads most directly to a real sense of understanding.

Fortunately, getting this very valuable hands-on experience with various aspects of your PC is not all that hard. In this chapter I have shown you, first, how to protect yourself, your PC, and your data from harm while you are experimenting. Next, I pointed out how to use DEBUG, BASIC, and the Norton Disk Editor to explore the ways information is held both in your PC's main memory and on its disk drives. And finally, I gave you a few "exercises for the reader." (You will find my answers to those exercises in Appendix B, "Some Sample Programs.")

III

The
Stand-Alone
PC

Peter Norton ®

7

Understanding PC Processors

Peter Norton®

The original IBM PC was built around an Intel 8088 chip as its central processing unit (CPU). This was not the first microprocessor that Intel made, and it was not the only kind Intel sold, even back then. It certainly wasn't the only one on the market. However, after the IBM PC (and its clones) swept the marketplace, Intel's 8088 became pretty much the only processor chip most people needed to know about.

Historical Aside: This is, of course, not completely true. Apple, Atari, Commodore, and some other companies made non-IBM-compatible personal computers that were still selling fairly well. In a short time, though, all of these small computer makers (except Apple) fell by the wayside, and Apple's market share never rose very far past 10 percent of the personal computers sold each year. So the fact that Apple's computers were built using non-Intel-designed CPU chips was and continues to be only a minor side note in the history of this industry.

That was then. This is now. And, oh boy, now sure is different.

Today there are at least four major makers of independent, competing, and yet compatible designs of CPU chips for PCs: Intel, Advanced Micro Devices (AMD), Integrated Device Technology (IDT), and Cyrix. All but IDT offer more than one design. So now, instead of a relatively simple story about a single vendor's products, there is a plethora of processors from multiple manufacturers to consider.

This chapter gives you an overview of this crowd of PC processor possibilities, and perhaps some insight into how you can navigate your way through the resulting confusion to find the perfect processor for your PC.

Intel, IBM, and You

At the beginning of the PC revolution, IBM was the leader and Intel and Microsoft were the most important of several major suppliers to IBM. That picture has now been turned upside down.

Historical Aside: Before the PC, IBM made virtually all the parts for its own computers. It was then the highest volume producer of integrated circuits (ICs) on the planet. However, because it used almost all the chips it produced, IBM usually wasn't even listed in industry statistics about the largest IC producers.

Therefore, buying CPU chips from Intel was just one more of the radical things IBM did to create its PC. But IBM hedged its bets. IBM bought a significant fraction of Intel's stock so that it would be at least one of the most important owners of that company. And IBM negotiated a contract that let it produce CPU chips in its own fabrication plants based on the Intel designs.

This arrangement was just one of several licensing agreements Intel struck with other IC makers. At that point in Intel's and the industry's development, the existence of such "second-source" agreements was crucial in helping a manufacturer convince its customers to buy its product. This meant that if Intel, for example, were unable to make enough of its chips at some point in time, then some other manufacturer could be relied upon to step in and fill the need. That was the only way system makers could feel comfortable in deciding to base their products on a particular company's IC design.

Now, Intel is its own second-source producer; that is, it has fabrication plants scattered around the world. Therefore, if one plant ever is unable to make high-quality chips (as happened in 1981 after Mount St. Helens blew her volcanic top just a few miles from the Intel IC fabrication plant in Oregon), the other plants can continue to churn out lots and lots of ICs. Intel is now fiercely possessive of its intellectual property and market share. It has terminated most of its second-source licensing agreements and has gone to court more than once to defend its right to be the exclusive manufacturer of its designs.

In response, several other makers of ICs have gone to great pains to create what are referred to as "clean room" designs. That is, designs for ICs whose functionality is sufficiently close enough to that of an Intel design that it can be substituted for the Intel version. Yet the details of how it is built are derived without direct reference to any aspect of how Intel builds its ICs. In this way, those manufacturers are able to skirt the intellectual property laws and make and market their Intel-compatible chips legally.

Intel still holds a commanding lead in the race to supply all the CPUs needed for the tens of millions of PCs produced each year. However, AMD is becoming about as significant in this marketplace as Apple is in the overall PC marketplace. And Cyrix, with help from its fabrication partners, IBM and Texas Instruments, is beginning to make significant inroads also. A newcomer to the race is Integrated Device Technology and its Centaur Technology subsidiary.

Furthermore, the not-really compatible CPU family referred to by the name "Power PC" is adding to the pressure on Intel. Power PC–based personal computers from Apple and other manufacturers are often able to run PC programs, and in any case have become important, if minor, offerings in the PC marketplace.

As always happens when markets are open and competitive, the consumer comes out the ultimate winner. Intel has been forced by its perception of threat from AMD, Cyrix, and others to lower its prices, add features, and accelerate the development of new designs, and the competitors still are nipping at Intel's heels. So the race goes on, while we sit back and reap the benefits.

The *x86* Family Tree

You cannot understand present PC processors without knowing something of their family history. The reason for this necessity is precisely the qualities of similarity and compatibility that have made these many, quite different, processors a "family." Intel named its line of CPU chips for PCs the x86 family. This includes (so far) at least a dozen major models introduced over the past 20 years.

The point of calling this a family of CPU chips is that they share many things in common. Their basic architecture has evolved over time, but it still reflects a particular approach to making a CPU. The way memory is addressed is fundamentally the same, though later models have more ways of doing so. Similarly, the instructions that the CPU understands (its native language, in other words) is the same, although again the later models have added substantially to the original vocabulary.

There is an important reason for this constancy. Intel didn't want to upset a very valuable apple cart. When the original IBM PC became a smash hit, Intel had a wonderful and rapidly expanding market for its products. But if it had introduced new, better, but incompatible designs for its subsequent microprocessors, there would have been a substantial risk that those new designs would not be acceptable to the marketplace. Indeed, all the clone PC experience to date has strongly suggested that the backward compatibility of every new PC is one of the most essential qualities it must have in order to succeed.

And all that means that we are still saddled with some (unfortunate) architectural decisions the Intel designers made nearly a quarter-century ago. The most prominent of these was the way Intel's designers decided to expand the address space from what had been commonplace in even earlier models of microprocessor.

PC Prehistory

Before there were PCs, there were some other small computers. The Apple II was the king in schools. Various brands of CP/M machines ran many small businesses. All of these microprocessor-based small computers had two things in common. They all handled information internally in 8-bit (one byte) chunks, and they all used no more than 64KB of RAM. (Well, with some clever page-switching mechanisms, some of them managed to use up to 128KB, but this was quite rare.)

When it came time to create a new generation of microprocessors, one thing that was obviously needed was to enable them to address more memory. The reason for the 64KB limit previously was simply that the memory addresses always had to fit into a two-byte *register* (information holding space) inside the processor. To get a larger amount of addressable memory meant using larger memory address pointers.

It might, in retrospect, seem obvious that the next step should be to double the length of the memory address pointers. That would jump the upper limit of RAM up from 64KB to 4GB (which, until very recently, was the maximum amount you could put on a PC, Macintosh, or any other microcomputer). The CPU chip designers at Motorola opted for exactly that choice at about the same time Intel's designers were making their choice in a very different way.

You must understand that there was a very powerful conflicting pressure on the Intel designers. They wanted to make it as easy as possible to transfer business programs from the earlier CP/M machines (many of which used Intel CPU chips) to their new machines. And one way they felt they could facilitate that process was to make their new CPU chips address memory in a rather odd way. (This strategy was understandable, but it seemed odd even then, and it seems odder still today.)

In Chapter 8, "How Your PC 'Thinks,'" and in Chapter 11, "Bigger Is Better in Ballrooms and In a PC's Memory," I'll tell you all about the Intel segment:offset method of combining two 16-bit numbers to get a single 20-bit number for addressing memory. For now, I'll just note that this strategy served Intel's goal. It did make it easy to "port" programs from CP/M to the PC, but it also imposed an upper limit of 1MB to the amount of RAM any computer using these new Intel chips could have. (At the time, this didn't seem so harsh a limit. After all, it was a factor of 16 larger than anything anyone had been able to use previously.)

Where the PC Began: Intel's 8086 and 8088

PC history starts with Intel's introduction of the 8086 CPU chip in 1979 and the 8088 the following year. These chips handled information internally in 16-bit (two-byte) chunks—twice as much as had been the case for the previous generation of microprocessor chips. The 8086 had 16-bit registers (information holding places) internally, and it had 16 data pins to carry information onto and off of the chip. The 8088 differed from this only in that it had just eight data pins and an internal mechanism to let it move data in and out in single bytes, while still computing with that information internally in two-byte chunks.

IBM chose the 8088 as the CPU for its new PC (which it introduced in August of 1981) over the slightly more powerful 8086, in part because having only eight data lines meant that all the ancillary circuits could be only half as complex as would be needed to support 16 data lines. In today's terms the difference is trivial. At the time that difference really *was* a big deal in both engineering and financial terms.

Many Stops Along the Way

As you know, the PC was a great success. And with it, Intel's fortune was greatly boosted. So, of course, Intel wanted very much to continue to be the preferred supplier of CPU chips for all of IBM's later PC models. To do that, Intel needed to keep coming out with improved versions of its 8086 CPU chip. Intel gave the subsequent members of the family names like 80186, 80286, and 80386. Each new member had substantial improvements in some of its features. (The 80186 was never used as the CPU in any model of IBM PC, for some arcane reasons. All the rest were.) Building on this naming pattern, Intel dubbed the whole family of chips its x86 family.

And to make selling the idea of these chips to the mass market easier, Intel's marketing folks dropped the 80 off the front end. Now they talked only of their 386 and said to look for "Intel Inside."

The 386 was eventually made in two flavors, the 386SX and the 386DX. The next chip in the family also came in two flavors, the 486SX and 486DX. (The suffixes in the two cases meant very different things, but to Intel's marketers they were just memorable labels and didn't have to carry any additional meaning, per se.)

Historical Aside: Each new generation of integrated circuits is noticeably more powerful than its predecessors because each one is more complex. This has been possible only because the industry is constantly learning new and better ways to make the features on those chips smaller and at the same time make the size of the overall wafers on which the chips are created ever larger.

Gordon Moore, who was one of Intel's founders and its chief executive at the time, made an interesting observation about this back in the late 1960s. He said he had noticed that if one plotted the industry's progress on semi-logarithmic paper (that is, with a scale that allots equal horizontal space to equal *intervals* of time, and equal vertical space to equal *ratios* of performance or size), then the points representing the complexity or fineness of scale of ICs and their date of development would lie very nearly on a straight line. Another way to say this is that the economically feasible chips get about 100 times more complex every decade. (And a related statement is that the price of a given level of complexity falls to about half every 18 months or so.)

What I find most remarkable about this so-called "Moore's Law" is that it has *no* basis in any known physical facts. Instead, it seems to be an observation about the rate of human invention as much as anything. This rate of progress has continued for many decades now, and still it shows no signs of stopping. Every time we seem to be about to run into an absolute brick wall, in terms of some physical limit on what a particular integrated circuit manufacturing process can achieve, someone invents a new process that skirts that limitation. Truly this "law" is a remarkable observation—and so far it is completely inexplicable.

The feature-set improvements in this progression of chips came in several areas. First, each new type of chip worked faster than all its predecessors. Second, most new generations introduced at least a few new instructions (new words or phrases in the CPU's native language). Third, the size of the chunks of data being handled internally or being shipped in and out of the chip increased in several steps. Fourth, some new ways to address memory were added.

Of all of these changes, perhaps the most historically significant is the innovation in memory access that was introduced with the 386. The 80286 already had introduced a version of what Intel called "protected mode." This was a way to access more than just 1MB of RAM. The 286 version of protected mode allowed access of up to 16MB. The 386 supported this mode of access, plus another one that pushed the upper limit all the way up to 4GB (4,096MB). But of much greater importance, the 386 also introduced a new mechanism called *paging* by which the relationship between actual, physical memory addresses and the logical addresses seen by the CPU could be manipulated almost arbitrarily.

I'll tell you all about both protected mode (in both its 286 and 386 flavors) and memory paging in Chapter 11.

The effect of these two improvements was to foster a whole new generation of software, all of which requires at least a 386-level CPU to run. This is why the 386 marks a watershed point in the development of the Intel x86 CPU family. At no time since then (and it has been a dozen years since the 386 was introduced in 1985) has there been an improvement in the x86 CPUs so great as to obsolete all previous generations of software as thoroughly as was the case with the 386. You can run nearly any PC program on the market today on an archaic, 386-based PC—if you have sufficient patience. (Today's PCs are a whole lot faster than the old, 386-based models, but they aren't capable of doing much that the earlier PCs couldn't do if given enough time.)

The next most significant feature upgrade was the increase in the size of information chunks that could be handled at once. From the initial 16-bit chunk for internal handling and 8-bit chunks for input and output, the x86 processors were extended by the time of the 386 to handle information internally and for input-output in 32-bit chunks. They still could put out or bring in just one byte, but they also could transfer up to four bytes in parallel. And almost all the processing internally proceeded four bytes at a time.

By the time the 486 was introduced in 1989, the increased complexity that was made possible by new developments in integrated circuit manufacturing techniques allowed the chip designers to bring on-board the chip all the math processing power that up to that time had been relegated to a secondary "floating-point coprocessor" chip. Furthermore, they added a small amount of what we now refer to as Level One (L1) cache memory. This is some very fast RAM that acts as a sort of loading dock where information can be parked briefly while it is on its way into or out of the CPU chip.

At around this time Intel decided to let 0no one else make chips that used its designs. AMD, in particular, fought back, claiming that it had a legal right under an earlier licensing agreement to make copies of any future Intel CPU chips. The resolution of that case finally allowed AMD to sell 386-like chips, but not 486-like ones. So AMD simply created its own, differently designed, but functionally equivalent "clones" to the Intel 486SX chips. And, for perfectly good marketing reasons, AMD called them 486SX chips—just as Intel had done for its chips.

Intel didn't like that (naturally). It wanted people to think only of Intel when they thought about a 386-based or a 486-based PC. About this time, Intel started the now famous "Intel Inside" advertising campaign. Intel tried to claim that AMD was infringing its copyright on the names 386 and 486. But the courts disagreed, saying one couldn't copyright a number. This is why the next member of the x86 family carries the moniker *Pentium*. Because that name is not a word, it can be (and has been) copyrighted by Intel, and it cannot be used by other chip makers to name their products.

Pentium

Intel's Pentium CPU chip was introduced in 1993. It upped the ante for motherboard makers because it sported 64 input/output pins. This meant it could move information on and off the chip eight bytes at a time. Also, it doubled the amount of cache memory on the CPU chip. But now, instead of one 16KB cache, it has two 8KB caches—one for data and the other for instructions. This change helps the cache serve its main purpose of keeping significant information readily at hand, thus reducing the number of main memory accesses that are needed. (And that helps performance, because each main memory access makes the CPU wait, instead of being able to sail along processing at its full speed. Internally, however, the Pentium moves data around and processes it in 32-bit chunks. The principal exception to this is that the floating-point unit handles 64-bit chunks.

As with each other member of this family, the Pentium supports all the instructions of every previous x86 processor, and it sports a few new ones all its own. But the most significant fact about the Pentium is simply that it can run faster than any 486.

A major reason for the increased speed is that, in addition to using a somewhat faster clock frequency so that it executes more instructions per second in each internal part, it also has the capability to process two instructions at a time. Actually, it can process two integer instructions simultaneously, but only one floating-point instruction at a time. This is accomplished by having two integer processing units (each very much like the corresponding parts of a 486), and one floating-point execution unit (which is an improved version of the one in the 486).

Technical Note: This capability to overlap the execution of separate instructions is an extension of an earlier idea called *pipelining*. In pipelining, the various stages of performing an instruction are broken up, with dedicated circuitry on the chip doing each instruction. The chip is designed so that while one section is executing an instruction, another section is gathering the data to be processed by the next instruction, a third is figuring out (decoding) what is to be done to perform the instruction after that.

In a way, pipelining is similar to an assembly line or an automated car wash. When some local group assembles a group of volunteers to raise money by washing cars, the cars usually are washed one at a time. However, automated car wash machines do several cars at once. While one is being rinsed, another is being washed, yet another is dried or waxed, and so forth. It is a production line. The time to wash any one car remains about the same, but more cars can pass through the automated car wash each hour than can be washed by a single team of people working on one car at a time.

Intel's CPU designs have incorporated pipelining in varying degrees almost from the very beginning. The extent and sophistication of the pipelining has, however, been greatly increased with each succeeding generation. And now with what amounts to multiple assembly lines in parallel, each is fed from a set of preprocessors that decode instructions and gather data. Then, through feeding a set of postprocessors that put the processed data back into memory, the Pentium raised the performance that is possible much more than you would expect if you only looked at the clock speed.

The Pentium shows what is called a "super-scalar" increase in performance over the 486. With the early members of the x86 family, Intel increased speed mostly by making each new CPU chip run faster than its predecessors. But with the Pentium, the major speed improvements could be attributed to something else—in this case, the doubling up of the integer execution units.

Pentium Pro

The Pentium Pro was the next member of this chip family. There are several ways in which this chip is an improvement over the Pentium, and at least one in which it is not.

The Pentium Pro is a module that incorporates two integrated circuit chips. Therefore, although it looks superficially like a larger version of the Pentium, it actually has the functionality of the Pentium plus a so-called "L2" or level-two cache inside it. Also, there are two data buses connected to the CPU chip: one going to the L2 cache chip and the other to the outside world (that is, to the system motherboard). If you wanted to have even more cache memory than this design affords, you could add a third level of cache memory on the motherboard, in exact analogy to the second level of cache common on 486 or Pentium motherboards. (So far, though, no one is doing this on a commercial motherboard.)

A second level (L2) of cache adds more speedy RAM to the cache that comes built into the Pentium chip, as a way of still increasing the speed of the system. But until the Pentium Pro, one bottleneck was the speed with which the CPU chip could communicate with the L2 cache. That bottleneck has been eliminated in this new design. (However, it would still persist in the communication with the third-level cache, if you were to have a system with that feature.)

Another improvement is the incorporation of a variation on pipelining, called *speculative execution* or, as Intel prefers to call it, *Dynamic Execution*. This feature lets the logic pieces inside the CPU keep busy more of the time. If there is nothing to be done on the instructions that would normally come next (for example, because they involve some data that must be fetched from main memory), then the logic unit will pick out a future instruction whose data is already on hand and figure out what the result of that instruction would be. That result is held in reserve, and if that instruction actually gets to be executed with the anticipated data, then the result is instantly made available. Otherwise, that result is discarded, and the logic unit's efforts are wasted. But then again, that unit couldn't have been doing anything more useful, so nothing really is lost.

Although instructions are often executed out of order, their results are always made available to subsequent instructions only in the originally specified order. That makes this process work transparently; the programmer and the user don't need to be concerned with how the CPU is able to act as though it is working more quickly—they simply will notice that it does.

Technical Note: The utility of speculative execution depends on several things. First, most computer programs, most of the time, execute the instructions that are held in successive memory addresses one after the other, in the same order in which they are held in memory. But every once in awhile, the program will "jump" (also called "branch") to another location in memory to get the next instruction to be executed.

Speculative execution works well for sequential instructions. It also can work well for a branch instruction if only the execution unit is clever enough to guess correctly which way the branch will go. The decision ultimately depends on the results of some calculation or comparison. Because the execution unit cannot know in advance how the branch calculation is going to come out, it must guess. CPU designers spend a lot of time trying to figure out clever ways of doing this guessing in order to maximize the percentage of the time that their chosen process will guess correctly. Specialized hardware branch prediction is now a part of all of Intel's x86 CPUs (and their clones, as well).

This works well enough that speculative execution almost always gives some performance benefit. That benefit can be much enhanced if the programs being processed are of a special type. The most recent versions of PC operating systems support a concept known as *threads*. This is the idea that you can sometimes divide the work in a program into several related, yet at least partially independent, tasks. Each of those tasks is called a thread or a process.

Now the programmer writes code to cause the processor to perform the work of each thread. And the compiler does what it can to interleave these threads, so that they will proceed in parallel. Now, if the CPU picks up a number of instructions out of main memory it may be able to schedule the instructions for one thread to go through one execution unit and those for the other thread to go through the second execution unit. Because of the relative independence of the two processes, there are likely to be almost no times when any of the instructions that have been executed in this fashion will turn out to have been "wasted."

Achieving this clever routing of instructions through the two parallel execution units in the Pentium requires careful coordination between the programmer and the compiler (which must be specially designed to do this type of optimization), and it also takes a good deal of luck. It won't work all the time. But if it works even a good fraction of the time, that will translate to a significant jump in performance.

Finally, the sub-unit in the CPU that handles information going in and out on the bus that connects the CPU to the system board has been modified to give priority to information being fetched from the external memory over information being sent out. Intel explains that its simulations show that this prioritizing of memory accesses speeds up the overall working of the system more than any other method it has tried.

> **Buying Tip:** The overall effect of these changes is to greatly increase the Pentium Pro's performance over that of the Pentium, but only for certain types of programs. Specifically, multithreaded, protected-mode (so-called "32-bit") programs run faster. But, unfortunately, many older, so-called "16-bit" programs actually run more slowly. Therefore, users of Windows NT (or OS/2 or any flavor of UNIX) mainly find benefits to using the Pentium Pro. Users of Windows 95 (or of DOS, either alone or in combination with Windows 3.*x*) may find it disadvantageous to switch to a Pentium Pro, depending upon the particular mix of 16-bit and 32-bit applications they are using.

Pentium with MMX

Intel next enhanced the Pentium instruction set with a new class of instructions call *multimedia extensions* (MMX). These are 57 new integer instructions and several new data types. The common theme is to let a programmer pack multiple data items into one 64-bit package and then perform at one time whatever operation is specified by one of the new MMX instructions on all those data items. The new data types range from one in which eight bytes of data are packed together to a single 64-bit piece of data.

The name "multimedia extensions" for these new instructions suggests that they mostly are of importance for people writing or using game programs or video presentations. And at least initially, that is mostly where they are being used. However, the MMX instructions can also be quite helpful in other contexts. Microsoft's Office 97 is said to use them to very good advantage.

The Pentium MMX differs from the original Pentium in one other way, and as it turns out, this much-less-heralded difference is probably responsible for more of its performance gains than the inclusion of MMX support. That change is a doubling in the size of the L1 cache to 32KB. This most likely is more important because most programs don't use MMX instructions. That will, no doubt, change over time as programmers become more comfortable with what MMX can do for their programs. But at least for awhile, the MMX support is going to benefit a very limited class of users, while the added L1 cache will significantly benefit virtually every user.

Intel holds no proprietary rights to the MMX technology. In order to encourage programmers to write programs to this new standard, Intel has decided to share the technology with the industry. This means that competing chip makers can incorporate MMX technology in their chips as well (and some already have).

> **Technical Note:** Intel implemented the MMX instructions in a novel way. It has those instructions temporarily take over the 64-bit floating-point register whenever a program wants to perform some MMX operation. Then, that register is returned to the floating-

continues

point unit to use when it next must process a floating-point instruction. Therefore, although the actual logic units that do the information processing for MMX and floating-point operations are separate, they share the register in which the data on which they work is held. For more details, point your browser to

```
http://mmx.com/sites/mmx/index.htm
```

The effect of this new technology is to speed up certain classes of programs. In particular, it may be useful for multimedia applications that include visually complex graphics tasks as well as full-motion video and high-quality sound. You will learn more about these types of programs in Part V, "Splendiferous Multimedia PCs" (Chapters 20 through 22).

In terms of its impact on the marketplace, the Pentium with MMX only widened the gap between the perceptions of Windows 95 users and Windows NT users about which Intel processor was best for them. This made the choice of a new PC harder for anyone not firmly committed to one or the other operating system. But that situation soon changed.

Pentium II

In the middle of 1996, Intel brought out its next x86 family member, the Pentium II. Effectively, the Pentium II simply is a Pentium Pro with some slight tweaks to its design to enable it to handle 16-bit programs more speedily, plus the MMX technology. All this is packaged along with a totally separate chip for the L2 cache in an entirely new form factor called the Single Edge Contact (SEC) cartridge, which plugs into an entirely different type of CPU socket called Slot One. The L2 chip, now that it is on a separate chip, instead of sharing space with the CPU as was the case for the Pentium Pro, has been expanded in size to 32KB—twice the size that was on the Pentium Pro.

Unfortunately the CPU's private bus to the L2 cache in the Pentium II runs at only half the CPU clock frequency, unlike the Pentium Pro where it runs at the full speed of the CPU clock. We can speculate that perhaps Intel felt that it would be able to raise clock speeds on the CPU faster than it could on the RAM that makes up the L2 cache. However, that is just speculation. Whatever the reason, this reduced speed of communication between the CPU and L2 cache makes for a bottleneck that can limit the overall Pentium II's performance. Even with this throttling of the CPU to L2 cache bus, having that bus separate from the CPU to main memory bus is a great advantage. The CPU to L2 cache bus runs faster than the main memory bus, and because the two are independent of one another, they can operate on different data simultaneously.

Technical Note: There is one other improvement in both the Pentium Pro and the Pentium II, but just how significant it will be is yet to be seen. The memory address space has been enlarged. Every chip from the 386 to the Pentium could potentially address up to

4GB (4,096MB) of physical RAM, and they could address, in a logical sense, up to 4TB (terabytes—a terabyte is a thousand gigabytes, or a million megabytes) of virtual memory. These limits were expanded by a factor of 16 in the Pentium Pro and Pentium II.

So far, though, no one has built any PCs with anywhere near 4GB of RAM; therefore, just how important this will turn out to be remains to be seen. Furthermore, today's popular PC operating systems cannot take advantage of the larger memory space. The Pentium II might become an obsolete chip long before anyone wants to put that much memory in their PC.

Essentially, the new Single-Edge Cartridge (SEC) processor housing design bears the same relationship to its predecessors as the SIMM or DIMM does to the individual memory chip. In early PCs, you had to plug in great fields of memory chips; a total of 36 chips was common. Then, manufacturers started putting groups of chips on little printed circuit boards called SIMMs or DIMMs, standing for Single (or Double) Inline Memory Modules. Similarly, the SEC cartridge is a printed circuit board with the CPU and L2 cache chips mounted on it and with contacts along one edge. The whole thing is encapsulated, so it looks like a single oversized chip (but with contacts poking out only on one edge).

There are several reasons to applaud the new Pentium II design. For one, this is a reconvergence of the two processor design paths represented by the Pentium Pro and the Pentium with MMX. No longer will there be different "best" Intel processors for different groups of customers. If you can afford a Pentium II, that will be as good as it gets (for now).

One drawback to the new design is the flip side of another of its benefits. In order to make good electrical contact, each pin on a chip must be firmly gripped by its contacts in the socket. As the CPU chips have become more and more complex, the number of those contacts has escalated. Several years ago it became unfeasible to simply push them into their sockets. It became necessary to have special Zero Insertion Force (ZIF) sockets instead. These sport a lever that you flip from one extreme position to another to release the chip, and then back again to lock the chip into the socket (see Figure 7.1). This design works, but it is expensive to manufacture.

Figure 7.1 shows two views of a Pentium MMX processor with a heat sink attached, and also a view of the Zero Insertion Force (ZIF) Socket 7 into which it is plugged. This socket is particularly important. It was introduced for the first Pentium processors (the first of the "fifth-generation" CPUs), and still serves the Pentium MMX, which is a late fifth-generation CPU. The Intel sixth-generation CPUs use two other sockets. Their early sixth-generation design, the Pentium Pro, uses a Socket 8, and their later sixth-generation design, the Pentium II, introduced the new Slot One socket. But all the clone sixth-generation CPUs from AMD, Cyrix, and IDT/Centaur still use Socket 7. Because Intel has declined to license its Slot One design to these companies, Socket 7 (or perhaps Socket 8) will have to serve the clone makers for some time to come.

Figure 7.1.
An Intel Pentium
MMX processor with
attached heat sink and
the Socket 7 into
which it gets plugged.

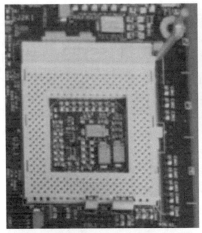

The new Pentium II's SCE design enables the chip to be inserted into a socket that resembles the one for a memory module. The required insertion and extraction forces are reasonable, and still the socket can be nearly as cheap to make as a SIMM socket.

The downside to all this is that the Pentium II requires a completely redesigned motherboard—and it's *not* much of an upgrade from the existing Pentium or Pentium Pro motherboard. On the other hand, this new socket design will permit the creation of new motherboards in the future that will run with much faster system bus clock speeds. The Socket 7-based motherboards are not likely to be able to raise that speed much above 100MHz.

Competitive CPUs that promise to give much or all of the performance gains of the Pentium II in a package that can be put into an older Pentium-style motherboard are coming on the market. (You'll learn more about them in the section "What If It Isn't Intel Inside?," later in this chapter.)

A Further Complication (CPU Steppings and Other Submodel Variations)

In all the preceding narrative, I have glossed over one very important point. Since the beginning of the time covered so far in this chapter, whenever Intel introduced a new and improved processor—at least if the improvements were major—it would give that new processor a new model number. And many months or even several years would go by between each of these introductions. This is no longer the case.

All along Intel has, from time to time, improved its CPU designs in minor ways. These might be likened to reprintings of a book, with the major revisions corresponding to new editions. And, just as publishers often use the opportunity of a new printing to correct typographic and other minor errors in a book, so does Intel use these revisions of the masks used to "print" the integrated circuits to make corrections (and other integrated circuit manufacturers do this as well). These corrections to its manufacturing process remove some of the "bugs" in its chip designs. These iterations are called *chip steppings*. In order to really know the capabilities and limitations of your CPU, you must know not only its model number, but also from which step it was made.

Now the situation gets even muddier. Intel lately has been flooding the market with new processor submodels. For the most part, these involve different clock speeds at which they operate. However, some also involve different packages (such as the tape-bond chips that are sold to notebook computer makers) or other variations in the way the chip operates.

I have described the major generations in the x86 family. A complete list of all the members would, however, have many times this many entries. Fortunately, a typical user normally can ignore the subtle details of the submodel differences. You'll learn some of the unique qualities of the chips used in portable computers in Part VI, "PCs are Frequent Fliers, Too."

Others Yet to Come

We can be sure of one thing in this industry: The pace of change is relentless. More and better is always on the way. We'll surely see several more generations of CPU from Intel before the end of the century.

What might we expect those later CPUs to offer that today's don't? For one thing, more speed. That is almost a given. Also, they will include a lot more processing power, and in more varieties. Expect digital signal processors to be included alongside the general-purpose processors we now have. This will facilitate voice recognition and speech synthesis so that we'll be able to converse with our PCs in a quite natural manner.

Finally, look for future chips to include much more self-test circuitry. This is essential, because already they are too complex to be tested fully by any external test machine.

What If It Isn't Intel Inside?

So far in this chapter I have barely mentioned all the other makers of CPU chips for PCs other than Intel. That is mostly because Intel has such a lion's share of the market. But I can't stop there; you wouldn't get the full picture. There are alternatives to having an Intel processor inside your PC, and some of them make very good sense.

Another reason I have emphasized the Intel designs is because they exemplify most of the industry's trends. When you understand all that Intel has to offer, you'll find yourself well prepared to evaluate where the competition's offerings fit in.

When you are number two (or three or four) in a market dominated by the number-one supplier, one of your main tools for convincing people to buy your product is to offer a lower price for the same quality and quantity of goods. This is nicely exemplified by the "clone" processor market.

Up until very recently, the most successful clone CPU chip makers limited themselves to making cheaper or faster versions of what were essentially Intel design-equivalent chips. The details of the designs for these chips differed enough from Intel's to avoid patent or copyright infringement, but the basic philosophy behind their designs was the same. Now, however, in their latest designs, and with the entrance of IDT/Centaur to this marketplace, we have the option of choosing from some truly new, alternative CPU designs that are still fully compatible functionally with Intel's x86 CPUs.

Advanced Micro Devices (AMD)

Advanced Micro Devices (AMD), Intel's primary second-source supplier for its earlier x86 chips, has offered faster, yet cheaper and fully compatible CPU chips for many years. Its 386 designs were essentially identical to Intel's. The AMD 486SX was different but arguably a better design than Intel's, and it certainly ran faster and cost a lot less.

AMD's next offering was something more than a 486, but not quite the same as Intel's Pentium. AMD named it the Am5x86, which sounds like another generation up from the 486. In fact, however, this chip is merely an enhanced 486. It plugs into the same socket as a 486 and is therefore restricted to a 32-bit I/O bus. Still, in other ways it resembles a Pentium. In particular, it supports an enhanced instruction set comparable to that in the Pentium. Still, it was a significant upgrade for 486 users, and it achieved a degree of market acceptance, even though its performance is noticeably less than a Pentium at the same clock speed. Mainly, though, the Am5x86 was a stop-gap for AMD until it could introduce its real response to the Pentium, which Intel called the AMD-K5.

The AMD-K5 is functionally a twin of the Pentium. It plugs into the identical socket and can be used in the same motherboards. (You might have to upgrade your motherboard BIOS to fully support the K5.) When you do this, you'll see a performance that is also fully comparable to what the same motherboard would yield when a Pentium of the same speed rating is installed.

Where things become confusing, and in a way more interesting, is the next generation. AMD was planning an ambitious new chip design that differed significantly from Intel's sixth-generation design, yet would deliver equal or greater performance and total compatibility. Creating that chip proved to be a tough job.

AMD helped itself by buying NextGen. Then it put the entire NextGen design team to work helping create the AMD-K6, which was introduced in 1996.

The design of these chips differs from Intel's in many ways, and AMD claims that it potentially can offer significant performance improvements over Intel's Pentium Pro and Pentium II designs. Third-party benchmarks support the contention that the K6 is at least the equal of the Intel designs.

An important distinction for a potential end-user of the AMD-K6 to note is that, unlike the Pentium II, the K6 uses a so-called Socket 7 motherboard, which is what the Pentium design uses, whereas Intel's Pentium II comes in its new SEC package and must be used with a totally new motherboard design. This distinction has enabled AMD to sell its product to manufacturers who would rather not have to offer and support both a Socket 7 (Pentium-style) motherboard and an SEC (Pentium II-style) motherboard. This distinction also means that Pentium owners may be able to upgrade to something close to Pentium II performance simply by swapping CPU chips, and perhaps upgrading their motherboard BIOS chips.

> **Warning:** There is a caveat I must add to the suggestion that you can upgrade a motherboard from a Pentium to an AMD-K6 processor. The CPU socket is the same, but there may be some other ways in which the motherboard must be modified to work properly with the AMD chip. Non-Intel motherboards often have some jumpers to allow just such modifications to certain voltage levels and in some cases to some processor ID pin numbers. Intel motherboards (unsurprisingly) do not.
>
> If you want to try such an upgrade, check your motherboard manual to be sure it will accommodate the change gracefully. Also check with either the motherboard maker or the manufacturer of your motherboard BIOS to see if the BIOS must be upgraded at the same time.

AMD recently scored quite a coup in getting Compaq, the number-one PC maker, to offer systems with AMD CPU chips. Still, AMD is only a minor player; the vast majority of PCs still contain Intel CPUs, and that will remain true for many years to come.

Cyrix, IBM, and Texas Instruments

Another, smaller, Intel competitor is Cyrix. This company has developed a strong design team, and it has contracted with Texas Instruments and IBM Microelectronics for fabrication services. The IBM contract also lets IBM use Cyrix designs in the other CPU chips IBM makes under its own label. Recently National Semiconductor purchased Cyrix, but until the complete integration of that acquisition, the Cyrix name will still appear on the chips they designed and marketed.

Cyrix has two sixth-generation products currently on the market. One, the Cyrix 6x86, is comparable to the Pentium Pro. The other, the Cyrix 6x86MX, is comparable to the Pentium II. Both fit in a Socket 7 motherboard. The pinout of the 6x86 is identical to Intel's original Pentium (sometimes referred to as the P54C). Cyrix's 6x86MX has the same pinout as Intel's Pentium MMX (which is also known as the P55C).

The term *pinout*, in case you were wondering, is simply the jargon term for which pins serve what function on an integrated circuit chip. Saying that two CPU chips have the same pinout implies that either of them can be placed into a particular motherboard and, with perhaps some tweaks to the motherboard jumpers, each will function properly.

The designs of these Cyrix chips differ significantly from both Intel's and AMD's designs. However, the performance is comparable. In practice, this means that each of the three companies' designs will be better for some tasks than its competitors, and worse for others—but in all cases they are quite comparable. For a typical end user, there shouldn't be much reason to prefer one over another, except of course for the price (and the less easily quantified matter of vendor support, because some vendors use only one manufacturer's CPUs in their systems).

Another issue to consider is the fact that only Intel CPUs work in Intel motherboards, and according to some observers, the Intel motherboards have shown themselves to have significantly higher quality than those from their competitors. Not all observers support this particular point of view, but it is one to consider when evaluating your alternatives.

Cyrix also offers something it calls the MediaGX processor, which is, according to Cyrix, the next wave in CPU chips. It incorporates on the chip with the CPU complete video and sound systems and PCI bus control circuitry. This combination chip is not intended for the type of high-end workstation that commonly uses a Pentium II or Pentium Pro today. Instead, the MediaGX is targeted toward the very low-cost end of the market, yet with significant multimedia support built in to enable manufacturers to make new, proprietary designs for under $1,000 multimedia PCs. Compaq is the only supplier at this time offering a MediaGX-based PC (its Presario 2100), and Cyrix isn't yet selling these chips directly to end users, retail dealers, or value-added resellers (VARs).

Integrated Device Technology and Centaur Technology

Integrated Device Technology (IDT) has established itself as a major vendor of memory parts and other integrated circuits. Recently they set up a wholly-owned subsidiary called Centaur Technology. This company has, so far, just one product: The WinChip C6 microprocessor.

The WinChip C6 is functionally a clone of Intel's Pentium MMX. However, it is a pure RISC design. (I explain that jargon term in some detail later in the section, "It's an Increasingly RISC-y Business.") By some clever innovations, they have made this chip very much smaller than the Pentium, yet—they say—as fast and as powerful. This is the new kid on the block, and as such must still prove itself. If it delivers as much as Centaur promises, this will soon become a serious competitor for Intel's Pentium MMX. And Centaur's next offering might be even more interesting.

Other Intel Competitors

This doesn't exhaust the list of competitors to Intel in the CPU market. Most notable is the Apple-IBM-Motorola consortium that produces the PowerPC chips. These are not x86-compatible CPUs, although they can be made to emulate x86 chips through software.

It's an Increasingly RISC-y Business

The x86 processors "understand" (can execute) any of a very large set of instructions. Over 100 different instruction types exist, and most of them can accept modifiers, which essentially turn one instruction type into a family of instruction types. In all, a program can tell the processor to do literally several hundred different things. Some of these things are extremely simple; others are pretty complicated. (However, none of them is nearly as complicated as what is implicit in nearly any, even moderately complicated, human language sentence.)

You learned in Chapter 5, "How to Get Your PC to Understand You," that the individual instructions for the x86 processors vary in length from one to over a dozen bytes. The simplest actions are encoded in single-byte instructions. The most complex one, with all its modifiers, can stretch way out—to 20 bytes in an extreme case.

These characteristics are typical of what is referred to as a Complex Instruction Set Computer (CISC). And with each new generation of x86 processor, CISC computers are becoming more and more complex. But curiously, at the same time they also are becoming more and more like a Reduced Instruction Set Computer (RISC) machine. RISC machines are characterized by a relatively meager set of individual instructions, all of which are exactly the same length.

For many years there has been a debate in the computer science world about the relative merits of these two ways to design a processor. The resolution of that debate is turning out to be more of a merger than the declaration of a winner.

The RISC advocates point out that although this type of machine cannot do as many different things in one instruction, instructions can be decoded into logical unit operations more quickly because they are of a uniform size. On average, a RISC instruction takes fewer clock cycles to be executed than an average CISC instruction. In fact, RISC machines commonly can perform several of their instructions each clock cycle, whereas a CISC machine might take more than 100 clock cycles to perform a single particularly complex instruction.

CISC advocates have maintained that their favored processor design has two big advantages. First, they claim that programming a CISC processor is easier because it "understands" more of the things a programmer regards as elemental operations. Second, if it is built correctly, a CISC processor can do the overall tasks just as fast, or maybe even faster, than a comparable RISC machine because its more complex instructions can encode the task in so many fewer instructions.

There is some truth on both sides, of course. 10 or 20 years ago, all the very high-performance "workstations" used by engineers, programmers, and graphic artists were built around a RISC processor (or more than one). Now it is possible to buy a CISC-based PC that performs at the workstation level.

To get to this point, the makers of CISC processors have been incorporating in their designs many of the aspects of RISC design. In some cases (the AMD-K6 is an example of this), the processor can break down the complex x86 instructions that the programmer thinks it uses into many, smaller RISC instructions that are what its logical units actually execute. In effect, the RISC-based machine is built to emulate a CISC machine.

This is, indeed, a pretty good way to describe the Intel Pentium Pro and Pentium II processor designs. So even Intel, up to now the foremost proponent of the CISC approach, has chosen to use the RISC approach at the microcode level to create what appears to programs to be a very fast CISC machine, but which works internally as a RISC one.

Even in less extreme cases, the modern CISC processor uses concepts such as pipelining and speculative execution, which were first developed for RISC machines.

The picture gets more muddled when you learn that the newest development goes in a third direction, referred to as Very Long Instruction Word (VLIW) computing. Here the idea is to put many relatively simple instructions together into one long instruction, and then build the processor so that it can process all of them at once. If it is done right, this can provide the best of both the RISC and the CISC approaches. Hewlett-Packard and Intel have been collaborating on a new processor design that uses this approach. We can expect to see it on the market within the next two or three years.

However, the bottom line question for many of us is "Do I care?" My simple answer is "No." If the computer does what you want it to do, then unless you are a heavy-duty programmer or a chip designer, you really don't care how it is capable of accomplishing its feats at this level—other than, perhaps, to satisfy your intellectual curiosity. It certainly isn't a reasonable basis for making a purchasing decision for most of us.

If you want to learn more about the details of how your PC's CPU chip actually works at this level, you can find a good deal of information at the Web site of its manufacturer. Here are some URLs you might want to look at:

```
http://www.intel.com/intel/product/index.htm
```

```
http://www.amd.com/
```

```
http://www.cyrix.com/
```

Are More Brains Better Than One?

Much of the thrust of processor development has focused on getting them to run faster. This has worked stupendously well. However, if you want a computer that goes faster than the fastest available processor can run, there is a way—and only really one way—to accomplish this: Use more processors at once.

Multiprocessing, as this approach is termed, is nothing new. Mainframe computers did this decades ago. As PCs are becoming more capable and are getting assigned to ever more complex tasks, it is becoming common to give some of them additional power in the same way.

This works, sometimes. But it isn't appropriate for all PC applications. Furthermore, in order for this approach to work, several things must be true. First, the individual processors must be designed in a way that permits them to cooperate with one another. The system design must support multiprocessing. And, finally, the programs must be rewritten to utilize this power.

This is a complex subject. I'll return to it in Chapter 26, "PCs That Think They're Mainframes: Multiprocessor PCs and Other Servers." For now I just want to point out that this is one way in which speeding up a PC without having to speed up the processor itself is sometimes possible.

Before leaving this discussion, I want to anticipate and clear up one possible confusion: This multiprocessing idea involves using several comparable CPU chips, each doing comparable work. It is completely independent of another idea that is used every day in all our PCs, namely having subprocessors dedicated to doing subtasks. That strategy is the subject of the next section.

Other Processors in Your PC

This entire chapter up to this point has focused on the CPU; which is, after all, the processor at the center of what your PC does. However, it is certainly not the only processor inside a typical PC.

In the distant past (about 20 or 30 years ago), if one wanted to design a subassembly for a complicated apparatus, and if that subassembly had to do some logical operations to perform its task, then the designer would create a custom array of logic chips that would do just the one thing needed for that subassembly's operation. This no longer is the best way to proceed. Now, it is much more common, and much cheaper, for a manufacturer to use an embedded processor. This is a processor that, in some other contexts, could do any of a wide variety of tasks, but in this particular context does just one because it has a single program built right into it.

One of these little embedded processors controls the keyboard for your PC. Another controls the floppy disk drives. Yet another creates the video signals needed to put images on the monitor. Others control the PCI bus and the SCSI bus, as well as generate sounds or do other specialized tasks.

For the most part, the processors used in these applications are not the same ones used as CPUs. But as some of those subtasks become more complicated, and as the earlier generations of CPU chips become less expensive, some of the CPU designs are finding a second life after they have become hopelessly too slow for CPU usage—as embedded controllers of peripheral PC subsystems.

I'm not going to go into a lot of detail about how any of these many, dedicated embedded processors does its job. You will, however, see many of them mentioned in later chapters as I describe the subsystems they control.

Major and Minor Improvements

PC processors have improved in two ways: They have become faster, and they have become more complex.

The x86 chips made today run a lot faster than their predecessors. The first PC used a 5MHz clock frequency. Today's best machines run more than 300MHz, with still faster ones promised soon. The Pentium II, for example, is hugely more complex than the 8086. The Pentium II has nearly 7,500,000 transistors on the chip; the 8086 had only 29,000. But not every improvement is a major one. Some are valuable, yet only minor in nature.

The two biggest landmark events in the x86 family's history are certainly the introduction of protected mode in the 80286 and the introduction of virtual 86 mode and memory paging in the 386. Everything else pales by comparison.

For the PC user, this means that when software which exploited all the 386 could do became popular, any older CPU-based PC really was obsolete. But even today, you can run any of today's software you want on even the oldest 386-based PC, if only you have enough RAM installed (and not all 386 motherboards would let you do this), and provided you have enough patience. (Not many of us have enough patience, so the issue of being able to install enough RAM is mostly moot.)

When to Upgrade Your PC

That last discussion brings us to an important issue that every PC user must face sooner or later. Should I upgrade my PC now?

You can always find an article in a trade magazine that praises some newly improved PC as having the best performance or the greatest new features. That doesn't mean you must rush out and buy each new machine as soon as it comes on the market.

Most folks are well served by their PC, even though it might be several years old. Remember, the trade press exists to sell magazines, and it does that by making each improvement sound like a revolution.

Two Rules of Thumb for When to Upgrade a PC

For my money, the only important upgrades are ones that either give you some new functionality you really want or at least double the speed with which your PC can do what it did before. For example, if you don't have a CD-ROM drive now, you probably must upgrade to a machine that does have one—or else add one to your present PC. And if your present PC doesn't have a VESA or PCI bus, then moving up to a new motherboard that does have PCI and new video and hard disk controller cards to take advantage of that new bus will certainly be beneficial.

Although reviewers love to measure performance and declare one PC "a clear winner" over the others because of its 10 percent greater speed, the truth is that most users won't notice anything less than about a doubling of speed, which is why I set this as my rough measure of when upgrading just to increase speed is worth it.

Upgrading Versus Buying a New System

When you notice that you can get a truly significant increase either in functionality or speed, you must then decide whether to upgrade your existing PC or simply replace it with a newer, bigger, better model. That decision is often not an easy one.

One thing to look at is which pieces you must replace to get the functionality or performance you want. If you only must add an option card or plug in a new drive, then you should upgrade. But if you must replace the processor, you usually also will want to replace the motherboard. And at that point you are getting pretty close to justifying the purchase of a whole new PC.

You often can move some of the pieces from your old PC into the new one and use them there. This is especially true for disk drives (including ZIP drives, optical drives, and so on), and it might be true for a sound card, PCI-bus video card, or network interface card. It is often not true for an obsolete ISA-bus based video card. Today's systems often bundle in the video or sound circuitry, if not on the motherboard, then on an included option card. The old card you have might not function correctly with the new, faster PC.

For some practical advice on what to do with your old PC, I'd refer you to the Appendix of *Peter Norton's Upgrading and Repairing Your PC*, also by Sams Publishing (ISBN: 0-672-31140-2).

8

How
Your PC
"Thinks"

Peter Norton®

In the past, the folks at IBM have been extremely careful to make the point that computers don't think; only people do. Recently, even as their Deep Blue computer beat Gary Kasparov at chess, they still insisted that it didn't think; instead, it just computed the right moves to make. The members of Gary's team often felt otherwise.

And very possibly you, too, believe that your PC "thinks." Well, it doesn't, at least according to the experts on the subject, but what it does do often looks like thinking to most of us. This chapter introduces just what the PC does that so much resembles thinking.

What Is a Computer Architecture?

People who design computers often speak of the *architecture* of a given computer. What are they talking about? Isn't architecture something that applies to buildings and not to computers?

My dictionary says, as its third definition, that an architect is "the designer of anything." And it says, in its sixth definition, that architecture is "the structure of anything." So the architecture of a computer is just a fancy way of referring to how its parts are arranged.

In Chapter 2, "How (Almost) Any Computer Works," I showed you the basic components of a PC and explained how they work together to create a computing machine. Here I want to go a bit deeper and tell you a little bit about how those parts are built and also how they are connected.

Also I am going to take the opportunity to teach you some of the more important jargon that so litters this field. Knowing what the terms mean can make lots of things you read turn from apparent gibberish into something that is merely curiously obtuse, or—if you are very lucky (or work at it a bit)—into something that you actually understand.

It All Begins with the CPU

The core of any computer's design is its CPU. The designer of this chip ends up defining in many important ways what is possible for this computer. For example, the CPU has only so many pins on it. Their number, and their specific uses, define how much memory it can be connected to, what particular sorts of information manipulation it can perform, whether or not it responds to events outside itself when they occur, and so on.

The x86 family of CPU chips have many common features. That common set of features defines the x86 architecture, and the PC architecture is a subset of the x86 architecture.

Details of the x86 CPU's Architecture

I could easily fill the rest of this book with arcane details about how the various x86 processors work. But if I did, your eyes would glaze over, and in any case you don't need to know all those things in order to get an accurate, if general, notion of how the processors do their jobs. So I am going to limit myself here to just an overview of the most important architectural features of these chips. I will, in this process, blur some of the lines between different parts of the CPU or lump several related parts together. This will let you see a unified picture that applies to all the members of the family more clearly than would be the case if I pointed out all the detailed ways in which the family members differ from one another.

Architecture: For the rest of this chapter I will be referring many times to the x86 chip family members. By this designation I mean the Intel family of microprocessor, but I also include any of the clone CPU chips that have been built by Intel's competitors, such as the AMD and Cyrix chips I described in the last chapter. For simplicity, I shall omit saying this each time it might apply. If your PC uses one of the clone chips, realize that probably what I am saying about the x86 chips also applies to the CPU chip in your PC.

The Bus Interface Unit

Pretend you are "visiting" the CPU. Your first impressions will be a view from the outside, followed by what you see as you enter the "lobby." The actual CPU is connected to the outside world, in logical terms, by a portion of its internal circuitry we call the bus interface unit. This section listens to some of the pins, looking for input signals; speaks to the outside world on some other pins; and for some pins can do either listening or speaking, depending on the state of signal on yet another pin.

This section of the CPU is also responsible for *buffering* the input and output signals. This means that it contains amplifiers to make the output signals strong enough to be heard by any number of receiving circuits, up to some specified maximum. It also contains receivers capable of detecting the input signals while extracting very little power from their sources.

In some members of the x86 family, the bus interface unit also must translate voltage levels. In those chips, the external circuitry might operate from a 5 volt power supply, while the internal circuitry might be running on a 3.3 volt or 2.8 volt power supply. This means that the valid level of a binary "one" on any of the external pins is around 2 volts but the corresponding level on an internal connection is closer to one volt. (In both cases, the level for a "zero" is a voltage very near zero.) The bus interface unit's receivers and output amplifiers are designed to accept and generate the correct voltage signals for each of its input and output connections, depending on whether they connect to the internal CPU circuits or to the outside world.

Finally, some members of the x86 family have internal clocks that run at some multiple of the external clock. The bus interface unit is also responsible for generating the internal clock from the external one, and for keeping information flowing into and out of the CPU in synchrony with both those clock frequencies.

Separating Instructions from Data

When the signals get inside the CPU, they must be routed to the correct internal parts. If you think of a CPU as analogous to a factory, this is the job done in a factory by the receiving clerk. If you'd rather think of the CPU as analogous to an office, this job is that of the receptionist.

The incoming signals consist of a mixture of two kinds of information: instructions and data. (Think of orders for finished goods and raw material, if you prefer the factory analogy. Think of employees who do the office work and clients on whom they perform their services if you prefer the office analogy.)

Instructions are placed in a queue for the instruction decoder. ("Go over to Window 3 and wait in line, please.") Data, on the other hand, is parked in some waiting rooms, called *registers*. ("Follow me. Now, please wait in here. Someone will be with you shortly.")

Figuring Out What to Do and Making It Happen

The instructions are taken out of the queue, interpreted, and put to work by a group of parts called the code prefetch unit, the instruction decoder, and the control unit. I will refer to this collection of parts from here on simply as the *instruction handler*. This section of the CPU has several jobs to perform.

First, because the x86 processors are Complex Instruction Set Computer (CISC) machines, their instructions come in a variety of lengths. The shortest is a single byte; the longest can consist of well over a dozen bytes.

The instruction handler examines the first byte and from what value it contains deduces how many bytes there are to this particular instruction. It must then make sure that the rest of the bytes of this instruction are ready for its further use, and if they are not, invoke the help of other sections of the CPU to go out to main memory and fetch them.

Next, the instruction handler must decide what data this instruction needs. Some instructions carry some or all of their data inside themselves. These are called *immediate* data items. Other instructions operate on data that is already present in one or more of the CPU registers. Yet others operate on, or return results to, locations outside the CPU in main memory. The instruction handler must ensure that the data items needed by this instruction are in place and ready to be operated on. If they are not, the instruction handler must arrange for them to be fetched into the CPU.

Finally, the instruction handler has the job of figuring out just what the instruction is telling the CPU to do and then activating the relevant parts of the CPU to get that job done. The simplest instructions correspond directly to some elementary task that some element of the CPU's circuitry can do. Certain of the more recent members of the x86 family have specialized circuitry dedicated to performing even some of the more complex instructions—if they are used often enough. This is done to make the CPU execute those instructions as fast as possible.

On the other hand, most of the instructions an x86 processor understands require multiple actions by different parts of the computing machinery in the CPU. The instruction decoder looks up these steps in an internal library called the *microcode store*. It then delivers those microinstructions to the relevant parts of the CPU for execution.

Registers Are Temporary Information Holding Places

Registers are important in any processor. As I explained to you in Chapter 2, every computer—and a microprocessor such as an x86 processor, which is actually a full computer in its own right—must have some place to hold information while it is being processed.

The x86 family members have different numbers of registers, of different sizes. The original 8086 and 8088 designs include 14 registers, each capable of holding a single 16-bit number. The latest Pentium II has many more registers. Most of the Pentium II's registers hold 64-bit numbers; a few hold many more bits. (In the case of these largest registers, called translation lookaside buffers, only a portion of the bits it holds are visible to a program running on the CPU. The rest are hidden from the program's view, but are accessible to the CPU to help it do its job more quickly.)

One reason for the much larger number of registers in the most recent x86 family members is that they have gotten so complex that some special, extra registers were needed to facilitate automatic testing of the processor at the end of its production cycle—as they attempt to make certain that it works before it leaves Intel's hands. Another reason is that these models include, in addition to the hardware needed to do the basic computing job they were designed to do, other hardware referred to as the *system management* hardware, which supports various special operations such as powering down to save power during times of inactivity.

To keep my story as simple as possible, I am going to focus at first just on the set of registers that were defined for the 8086. All the registers that were added in later members of the x86 family are similar to these, at least in concept. I will introduce some of those other registers when I discuss the functions that they serve. In the 8086 (and 8088), the 14 registers can be grouped into five categories. Here is a brief description of each category and the names of the corresponding registers.

General-Purpose Registers

Of the 8086's 14 registers, four are designated as general-purpose registers. These are mainly used for data values being processed. That is, they can be added to, subtracted from, or multiplied by one another. They can be compared with one another, or a number in a general-purpose register can be combined with a number somewhere out in main memory. There are still other ways in which this data can be processed.

If the instruction being executed needs only one byte of data, that byte can reside in either half of a general-purpose register, and it can be accessed by that instruction without altering whatever byte value is in the other half of that register.

These registers have simple names. When they are used as full, 16-bit wide registers, they are called AX, BX, CX, and DX. (You may think of X in this context as standing for *extended*.) When you want to refer to just one half of a register, the lower half is called AL, BL, CL, or DL. The upper half is referred to as AH, BH, CH, or DH.

Technical Note: You might think that these names were chosen just because they are the first four letters of our alphabet. That might be so, but they also have mnemonic value. (That is, they have longer names that are suggested by these short ones.) These four registers, despite being called general-purpose, have some restrictions on their use and some customary uses. Here are the details.

The AX (or AH plus AL) register is most often used as the *accumulator*—the place where the result of some calculation ends up. For example, you can add the value in some other register or in a memory location to the value in the A register and the result will wind up replacing the value originally in the A register.

The BX register is often used to hold the segment portion of an address. When it is used for this you may think of it as the *base* register, because the segment address value indicates the beginning (or base) of a region of memory. The BX register (or BL or BH) may also be used to hold data of other sorts.

The CX register is normally used to hold a number that indicates how many times some operation has been done. When that number reaches a specified target value, the program must jump to a different place in the program. And only if the count of operations that have been performed so far is held in this particular register is it possible to do the necessary comparison and jump in a single instruction.

The DX register (or DH and DL) commonly is called the *data* register. It sometimes is used to hold a port address. Other times it is used in combination with AX to hold a 32-bit number (for example, the result of multiplying together two 16-bit numbers).

If the preceding paragraphs seem like gibberish to you, don't worry. I will explain all about segment addresses, flag bits, and jump instructions in just a moment.

The Flags Register

One very special register is called the *flags register*. It is simply a place that holds a collection of 16 individual bits, each of which indicates some fact. One of the simplest examples of a flag bit's meaning is the one that indicates whether the last comparison of two bytes found that they were or were not equal. Other flags indicate whether the result of the last arithmetic operation was positive or negative, whether it was zero, or whether it overflowed the capacity of the register. Still other flags indicate something about the state of the processor. Examples of this include these: Is the processor supposed to respond to or ignore external interrupts; is it supposed to run in single-step mode; or when processing a string of bytes, is it working its way "up" the string or "down" the string?

Because the more recent members of the x86 family have wider registers for both data and flags, they have even more conditions that are represented by flags.

The Instruction Pointer

Another special register holds the address in main memory of the instruction currently being executed. Its name, of course, is the *instruction pointer* register (and it is given the designation IP). The value in this register *implies* the location in main memory where the instruction being executed is held; to get the actual location you must combine this value in a suitable fashion with a value in another register, called a *code segment register*.

The value that is held in the instruction register gets changed in either of two ways. One we refer to as the normal flow of control and the other as a branch.

The Normal Flow of Control

Unless the instruction being executed causes something different to happen, the value in this register, sometimes called the Program Counter, is automatically increased by the length of the current instruction each time an instruction is completed. This is done because in most cases the next instruction to be executed is held in main memory right after the current instruction. The complexity to pushing the pointer up a variable amount comes from the fact that the x86 processors are CISC (Complex Instruction Set Computing) devices, with variable-length instructions.

Branch Instructions

About 10 percent of the time this is not true. In those cases, the current instruction might tell the CPU to fetch its next instruction from some other location. These instructions are called branch instructions, or jump instructions, and they come in two types. One kind is unconditional branch instructions in which the next location is always different from the normal flow of control. The others, called conditional branch instructions, decide whether to jump to a new location or simply fall through to the next instruction after this one. These instructions usually base their decision upon the value of one of the flag bits. Figure 8.1 shows both the normal flow of control for a program and also both kinds of branch in a graphical manner.

Figure 8.1.
The normal flow of control and how branch instructions sometimes alter that flow.

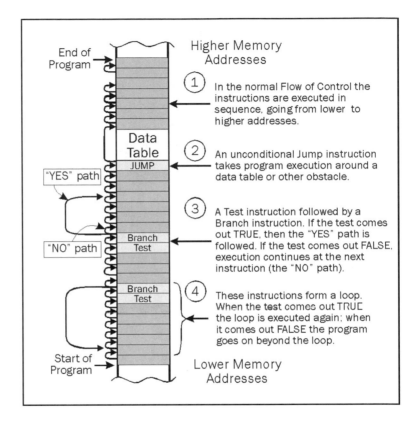

1. In the normal Flow of Control the instructions are executed in sequence, going from lower to higher addresses.

2. An unconditional Jump instruction takes program execution around a data table or other obstacle.

3. A Test instruction followed by a Branch instruction. If the test comes out TRUE, then the "YES" path is followed. If the test comes out FALSE, execution continues at the next instruction (the "NO" path).

4. These instructions form a loop. When the test comes out TRUE the loop is executed again; when it comes out FALSE the program goes on beyond the loop.

Other Pointer Registers

Two more of the original 8086's 14 registers are also pointer registers. One is called the base pointer register (BP); the other is called the stack pointer register (SP). Each of them holds a number that is used as the segment portion of an address if the processor is running in real mode. In protected mode that number is called a selector, but it serves a similar function. Either way it is used to point to the beginning of a region of memory that is used for a stack. I'll explain just what that means later in this chapter.

Index Registers

Two of the registers were designed for use in moving strings of data (many-byte sequences of arbitrary length). One called the source index register (SI) might hold the address of the beginning of a string you want to move, for example. The other register in this class called the destination index register (DI) holds the address to which that string will be moved. The number of bytes to be moved is usually held in the CX (Count) register. In addition to their use in moving entire strings of data, these registers can also be used to indicate a location within an array of numerical data or in a number of other ways.

Segment Registers

Finally, the last class is the segment registers. There are four of these in the 8086. These are very special-purpose registers used only in performing address calculations. Later, in the section called "Calculating Addresses," I explain all about the different ways in which the values in any of these registers get used in address calculations. Right now I simply want to tell you the names of the different registers and describe what types of addresses might be pointed to by use of its value.

The first is the code segment register (CS). CS holds a value that is combined with the value in the instruction register to point to the next instruction to be executed. The next register is the data segment register (DS). Normally DS is used to point to a region of memory in which data values are being held. It can be combined with a number in the BX, SI, or DI registers, for example, to specify a particular byte or word of data. The third register is called the extra segment register (ES). It is, as its name suggests, simply an extra segment register provided for whatever purpose the programmer wants, although it most naturally gets used in connection with string operations. The last register is called the stack segment register (SS). The value in this register is combined with the value in the stack pointer (SP) register to point to the current "stack." The SS register can also be used in combination with the BP register for certain instructions.

The Arithmetic-Logic Unit (ALU) and Its Kin

It is convenient, at the level of understanding I'm trying to give you, to lump together another collection of logical subparts of the CPU. These include the Arithmetic-Logic Unit (ALU) and some other portions that do similar things. The ALU is the part that actually adds, subtracts, or multiplies integer values. It also can compare two numbers to determine whether they are identical and if not, to decide which one is larger.

Simple Integer Operations

One other thing the ALU can do is shift the bits around in a number. Think of the contents of a 16-bit register as 16 individual bits (think of tiny people) sitting on 16 chairs in a row. The first kind of shift, called an *arithmetic shift*, just makes each bit get up and move one place to the right or left; the end bit that finds itself without a place to "sit down" simply is lost (and a zero bit is moved in at the opposite end of the register). Another kind of shift, called a *circular shift*, takes the bit that falls out of one end and stuffs it back in the opposite end. This type of bit shifting comes in very handy when multiplying numbers, and also for certain logic operations. Trust me: Programmers often find this capability vital for their programs.

Dedicated Hardware for More Complex Tasks

More recent members of the x86 family have greatly expanded the range of arithmetic and logical operations that can be accomplished by dedicated hardware. The reason for doing this is simply to make the CPU do its job more rapidly. A 486DX is faster than a 386DX even when their clock speeds are the same, just because the more complex CPU has the capacity to do more complex operations in the same number of clock cycles. (The same can be said of a Pentium II versus a Pentium. Every Pentium of any flavor runs faster than any 386, but they compute more rapidly than the simple clock speed comparison would suggest.)

Floating-Point Operations

For example, starting with the 486DX, a separate set of circuits has been devoted to processing floating-point numbers. This additional hardware consists of two parts. One is a set of eight very wide (80-bit) registers that are specifically designed to hold floating-point numbers. The other is the set of logic gates (and the special microcode instructions that activate them) that are arranged so as to do the actual floating-point arithmetic.

MMX Enhancements

The newest wrinkle in the x86 processors is the inclusion of the so-called MMX instructions. These "multimedia extensions" to the rest of the x86 instruction set are *simple instruction multiple data* (SIMD) instructions. In a Pentium MMX or Pentium II processor, these instructions cause special additional circuits in the CPU to do different things with the numbers held in one of the 80-bit floating-point registers than the normal floating-point calculation circuits do. Specifically, the MMX instructions can treat the value held in a floating-point register as eight 8-bit numbers, four 16-bit numbers, two 32-bit numbers, or a single 64-bit number. (In every MMX instruction 32 bits of the floating-point register just aren't used.)

In all but the last case (where the data is a single 64-bit number), you have multiple, potentially independent values sitting side-by-side in a register. Now, by using an MMX (SIMD) instruction, you cause whatever you do to one of these groups of numbers to be done also to the others, and these actions all occur at the same time.

This strategy of using SIMD instructions isn't really any great help for normal computing. Ordinarily you want to apply a given instruction on a particular set of numbers, then go on to do something else with the next set of numbers. But some problems involve a very large number of instances in which you want to do the exact same process on different sets of numbers. For example, if you are engaged in video conferencing, speedy compression and decompression of the video signal is essential. The mathematical operations involved in both compression and decompression are naturals for being speeded up by SIMD (that is, MMX) technology. Other applications include advanced graphics image processing where you might, for example, be applying a texture map to a surface.

The MMX instructions are treated as integer instructions, although they manipulate values held in the floating-point registers. The significance of this is that those advanced members of the x86 family that sport MMX also have multiple integer instruction execution units and only one floating-point instruction execution unit. So these processors can do a single floating-point instruction and two integer instructions simultaneously. Well, if the integer instructions are MMX ones, the CPU cannot also do a floating-point instruction at that time, but it can still do a normal integer instruction and an MMX one, in parallel.

These advantages only accrue to programs that are written to take advantage of them. The same thing applies to the floating-point hardware enhancements. Only programs that are aware of these processor enhancements, and have been redesigned to use them, will run faster. Only certain kinds of programs benefit from that type of redesign.

But in time, many, many programs have come to use the floating-point hardware. Running these programs on a 486SX- or a 386-based PC, which doesn't have the floating-point hardware built in, is painful. The programs must invoke emulation programs to accomplish the effect of the missing special-purpose hardware, and those emulation programs are always tremendously slow compared to the dedicated hardware.

At this time, MMX is new. Not very many programs use it. But in time it might come to be a very popular way to speed up common multimedia applications, some games, and certain business and scientific applications, as well.

Calculating Addresses

I mentioned in discussing the instruction register that the value it contains, taken alone, doesn't indicate where in memory the instruction it points to is located. Every time an x86 processor wants to refer to memory, whether to retrieve an instruction or to get or put some data item there, it must go through a more or less complex process involving at least two register values to decide where it must go. And often (in protected mode), the CPU must not only use those values from two (or more) registers, it must also access up to three different data tables in memory before it knows what actual, physical memory address is implied.

Going from Abstraction to Reality

There are several reasons for the complexity of address calculations in an x86 processor. Perhaps the most fundamental reason is that these processors deal in several different kinds of memory address space.

At the physical level (what actually happens to real, physical objects in your PC), memory locations are addressed by voltages on wires that connect to each memory module or chip. These signals are derived from the voltages on corresponding pins of the CPU. If you look at the voltages on those CPU pins, labeling the ones that are high as "ones" and the others as "zeros," the binary number you get is what we refer to as the *physical address*.

Technical Note: Some of those CPU address pins have their signals directly routed to the memory modules. (They pass through some other integrated circuits that amplify them, but they go straight through those amplifiers and are not mixed with other signals in the process.)

Others of the CPU address pin signals get combined in circuits called *memory address decoders* whose job it is to decide which, if any, of the different memory chips or modules your PC has is supposed to be activated just now. All of those modules (or chips) get all the other signals, and the active module (or chip) uses them to decide which location within itself to access.

Figure 8.2 shows this relationship schematically. In this diagram the PC is assumed to have just two 32MB modules, each with 64 data lines. This is, in fact, exactly what I have in the Dell Pentium MMX computer that I am using to write this book.

The CPU, with its 65 data wires, connects to eight bytes of memory at a time. This means that the three least-significant bits of any address may be ignored in pointing to locations in main memory. They are only used internally by the CPU to decide which of the eight bytes it just read is the one it wants to begin working with. That fact reduces the number of address wires we need to connect to each 32MB memory module from 25 to 22. Furthermore, it is possible (and usual) to make the address pins on the memory modules serve double duty. At one instant they read a "row" address and at a different instant a "column" address. That lets the module makers get away with, in this case, just 11 address pins, plus one pin to indicate whether these address lines were reading the first 11 bits of the address (lines A3 through A13) or the remaining 6 bits (A14 through A24).

The signal lines on the memory modules labeled *Chip Enable* are used to turn the integrated circuits in this module on or off. The voltage on this line will either make the module responsive to signals on the rest of its input lines, or it will make the module go into a sort of stasis in which it ignores all its other inputs and creates no output signals.

The memory address decoder gets all the rest of the address lines—in this case seven lines (A25 through 31). That is enough bits to point to any of 128 different "banks" of memory. This computer, however, has only two banks. With 32MB in each bank, that is enough for today's programs (though certainly not too much!). The memory address decoder must examine the signals on all seven lines in order not to activate those memory modules unless all of those lines except the first one have zero-level signals on them. The level on the first one is then used to decide which of the two memory banks to activate.

Figure 8.2.
How the CPU's physical address lines are connected to the banks of memory modules.

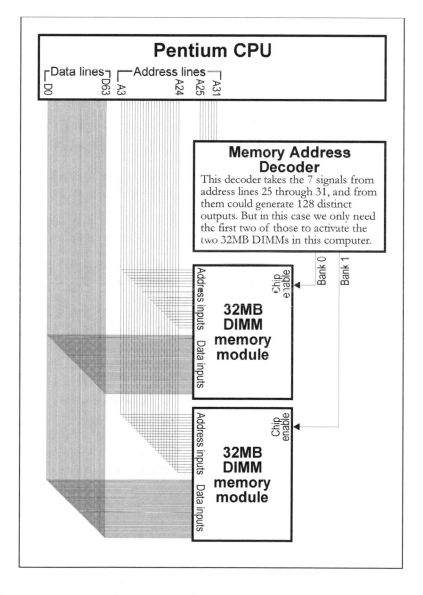

Pentium CPU

Data lines — Address lines

D0 D63 A3 A24 A25 A31

Memory Address Decoder

This decoder takes the 7 signals from address lines 25 through 31, and from them could generate 128 distinct outputs. But in this case we only need the first two of those to activate the two 32MB DIMMs in this computer.

Bank 0   Bank 1

Address inputs   Data inputs   Chip enable

32MB DIMM memory module

Address inputs   Data inputs   Chip enable

32MB DIMM memory module

What Addresses Do Programs Use?

PC programs don't use physical addresses. The x86 family of processors doesn't enable them to. Instead, they must use at least one level of indirection. The actual physical address is generated by combining two or more numbers according to one of several strategies. Because of this complexity you will run across the terms *logical address* (also known as the *virtual address*), *linear address*, and *physical address*. I'll explain each one of these concepts in the following sections.

Calculating Physical Addresses in Real Mode

You have already met the simplest of the x86 strategies for computing a memory address. In Chapter 6, "Enhancing Your Understanding by Messing Around (Exploring and Tinkering)," I told you that memory addresses in real mode are expressed in programs as logical addresses, each of which is composed of a segment value and an offset. Figure 6.2 shows how those two 16-bit numbers are combined to generate one 20-bit number (or in some cases the result might be a 21-bit number) that points to the actual address in physical memory.

To repeat what I said there, the segment value is multiplied by 16 (in hexadecimal that means simply shoved left one space) and then added to the offset value to get the physical address value. There are 65,536 possible values for the segment number and an equal number of possibilities for the offset. This means that a particular value for the segment portion of the address indicates a particular 64k-byte region of memory. The offset value indicates a particular one of those locations. The upper portion of Figure 8.3, later in this chapter, shows this algorithm. (The number written above as 64k—which is a very common practice in works about PCs—is equal to 65,536. This is so because any time you see k or M in reference to an amount of memory or storage in a PC, the k means not the usual 1000, but rather the tenth power of two, which is 1024, and likewise the M doesn't mean one million, but rather the twentieth power of two, which is 1,048,576.)

Technical Note: An important point to realize is that there are many different logical addresses (by which I mean a pair of 16-bit numbers, one for segment and one for offset) that point to each physical memory address. If I simply increase the segment value by 1 and decrease the offset value by 16, the physical address remains unchanged. Thus, the logical address 01A0:4C67h is exactly the same as the logical address 01A1:4C57h. I have put the lowercase letter *h* behind each address to remind you that these are hexadecimal numbers. Normally, just having two four-digit numbers connected by a colon implies this, but I want to make this point very clear. That should also make it clear to you that the offset value 4C57h is exactly 16 less than the offset value 4C67h, because the two numbers differ by only one in the "sixteens" place.

Calculating Physical Addresses in 286-Protected Mode

All but the earliest members of the x86 family of processors have more than one mode in which they can operate. They all "wake up" in real mode, and in that mode they use exactly the strategy just described to calculate physical addresses.

After several special and necessary data tables have been built in memory, it is possible for any member of the x86 family more advanced than the 80186 to go into some version of protected-mode operation. In these modes (and there are three of them), the numbers held in the segment registers are not simply multiplied and added to the offset value to point to a memory location. The use of the numbers in the segment registers in any of the protected modes is so different from their use in real mode that we use a different name to refer to those values. They now are called *selectors* instead of segment values.

Unlike a segment value, which points to a particular 64k-byte region of memory, a selector just points to one line in a data structure called a descriptor table. That line contains several numbers. One of them points to the beginning of the region of memory in question. Another says how long that region is. Others indicate certain special properties (called access rights) that region of memory has when it is accessed via that selector value.

The name *segment* still refers to the region of memory pointed to by a particular value in the segment register. But because the process for getting from the selector value to the segment position in memory address space is more convoluted, it is no longer appropriate to use the same name for both.

There are three advantages to this strategy. First, we can have any selector value we want point to any region of memory we want. (No longer is there any necessary connection between the regions of memory specified by two selector values that differ by some fixed amount.) The second advantage is that the size of the segment referred to by a selector value is not fixed. It can be as short, in some cases, as 1 byte or, in certain other cases, as long as 4GB. Finally, the presence of the access rights in the descriptor table allows the CPU to control the kinds of access to this region of memory that will be permitted when it is accessed via this selector.

The name *logical address* is still attached to the combination of two 4-character hexadecimal numbers separated by a colon. The first one is now called the selector instead of the segment; the second one is still called the offset, and indeed it still means the number of bytes into the segment from its beginning, wherever that may be. Figure 8.3 shows the contrast between how one gets from a real-mode logical address to the corresponding physical address in real mode and in 286-protected mode.

Calculating Physical Addresses in 386-Protected Mode

In 386-protected mode the approach is the same, but the details of what the bits in the descriptor table entries represent differs a little. The 386 and all later members of the x86 family can run in either 286- or 386-protected mode, or in a third protected mode called virtual 86 mode (V86 mode).

The differences between 286-protected mode descriptors and those used in 386-protected mode are shown in Figure 8.4.

Figure 8.3.
From a logical (a selector:offset pair of numbers) address to a linear address in real mode versus in protected mode.

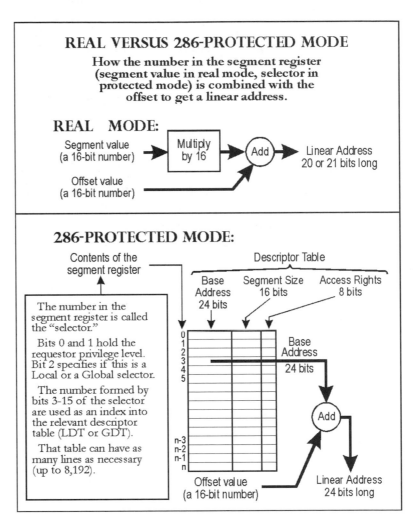

Calculating Physical Addresses in Virtual 86 Mode

Virtual 86 mode is a sort of strange beast. In this mode, which is always used in conjunction with 386 protected mode, the running program thinks it is running on an 8086 processor in real mode, while in fact the processor is in protected mode, and the operating system is running in 386 protected mode and serving a role described as a virtual 86 monitor.

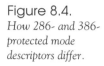

Figure 8.4.
*How 286- and 386-
protected mode
descriptors differ.*

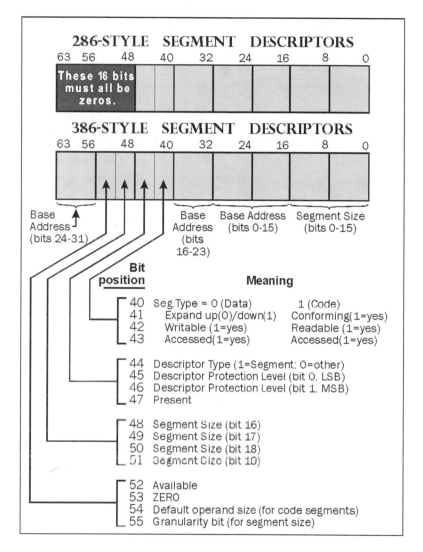

The advantage of this mode of CPU operation is that it lets you run old DOS programs that were written to run in real mode, while having the advantages of protected mode. (I'll describe a bit of what those advantages are in the next section.) Furthermore, it lets you run several such programs, each in its own DOS box, without any of them knowing that the others exist. This is what is done when you run an old DOS application under Windows 3.x or Windows 9x, for example.

How Paging Complicates Address Calculations

Also, in the 386 and all later members of the x86 family there is one more complication to memory address calculations. It is called *paging,* and it introduces the third kind of memory address. The selector value combined with the offset is still called the logical address. That is what programs actually use. What you get by adding the offset to the base address in the line of the descriptor table pointed to by the selector is now called the linear address. In the 80286, that was the same as the physical address. In the later x86 processors it need not be the same.

The notion here is the following: A physical address is what gets specified by the voltages on the address pins of the CPU chip. It is one of some large number of locations in what we call the processor's physical memory address space.

When paging is in use, the linear address is simply an abstract location in some hypothetical memory address space. Getting from a linear address to a physical one is done by a process analogous to, but a bit more complicated than, the way we got from a selector value to a segment address.

The 32-bit linear address gets broken up into three parts. The most significant 10 bits are used as a directory index. The next most significant 10 bits are the table index. The least significant 12 bits are used as the offset. The relationship between these three numbers and the actual physical address is indicated in Figure 8.5.

Enforcing Protections

The name *protected mode* is suggestive. Something is being protected somehow. But what and how? The whole reason for protected mode is to facilitate good multitasking. In any multitasking system (think of a Windows machine running several programs at once), several programs might each think it is the only program in existence, and yet they all are able to run together in the same PC without interfering with one another. Or at least, that is the idea.

For this to work, it is necessary for something to keep the various programs from conflicting. Some master program must be in charge. That master program is the operating system (for example, Windows).

That is not enough, however. When an operating system launches an application on a PC, in real mode, the application program can do anything it likes. It can read or write to any portion of memory, can send information out any port, or write all over the screen. There is no way for the operating system to prevent this, for sure. This is why Intel devised the various protected modes for its x86 processors. The idea was not new; it was a direct borrowing from mainframe computer experience (as was the notion of paging), but this was the first time it was applied at the microcomputer level.

The basic notion is that each program is assigned some protection level, and it can only do whatever that level of program is allowed to do. There are four levels of protection, from zero to three, and programs are assigned to one of these four rings. The core of the operating system gets to run at ring zero, and normally in protected mode, only that set of programs is allowed to run there. All application programs normally run in ring three. So far, no operating system has made much use of rings one or two, but they are there in every x86 processor, just waiting for some clever programmer to find a use for them.

Figure 8.5.
From a linear address to a physical address when paging is active.

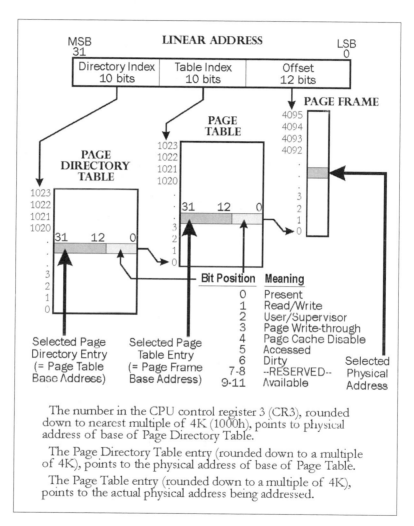

The number in the CPU control register 3 (CR3), rounded down to nearest multiple of 4K (1000h), points to physical address of base of Page Directory Table.

The Page Directory Table entry (rounded down to a multiple of 4K), points to the physical address of base of Page Table.

The Page Table entry (rounded down to a multiple of 4K), points to the actual physical address being addressed.

Furthermore, each segment of memory (recall that now those are the regions specified by lines in descriptor tables) is given certain access rights. Only programs that have the correct level of privilege can change those access rights, and only operations that the access rights permit are allowed to happen.

Who enforces all these rules? The CPU does. That is why this discussion is here, under the CPU's internal architecture, and why in particular under the discussion of address calculations, for the same circuitry in the CPU that computes addresses also checks to be sure that the instruction about to be executed doesn't violate any of the rules.

When a rule violation occurs it is referred to as an *exception*. These are further classified as faults, traps, and aborts. When any of these exceptions occurs, the CPU stops doing what the program says to do, and instead it goes off and does something else. (Just how it does this is very similar to how it responds to external or software interrupts, and I will describe the mechanism in some detail later in this chapter.)

The most infamous of the exceptions is the one called a *General Protection Fault (of type 13)*. This generally results in an error message on the screen and leads to shutting down the offending application program. You might think that Windows bombs a lot. It does, but not nearly as much as it would without the hardware support that is built into every x86 processor for protection enforcement.

Technical Note: This discussion is not complete. I haven't told you about the differences between the global descriptor table (GDT) and the local descriptor table (LDT), nor about the Task State Segment (TSS) and Input-Output Permission Level (IOPL) data structures. Those details are not vital to your general understanding of how the CPU functions and to describe them really would make your eyes glaze over.

The Level 1 Cache

The last of the key functional groups in the CPU to discuss is the Level 1 (L1) memory cache. This has been a feature of the x86 CPUs starting with the 486.

Technical Note: Actually, a form of caching (for addresses) was used even earlier in the translation look-aside buffers (TLBs) in the 386—and that form is also present in all later members of the x86 family. However, this caching is mostly hidden from view in a way that the data and instruction caching I am speaking about here is not.

The Level 1 cache is a small amount of very fast RAM located inside the CPU chip. It is used to provide a temporary holding place for all the data and instructions that have recently been brought in from, or sent out to, main memory. There are two ways such a fast, temporary holding place can speed things up. One applies when writes from the CPU to main memory are cached. The other applies when reads are cached.

The first way a cache can help is when information is to be written to main memory. The cache can accept that information and then let the CPU get on with its work immediately. The cache controller circuitry is then responsible for seeing that this information is later transferred out to its proper place in main memory.

The second way a cache can speed things up is when the information in a given memory location is read by the CPU more than once. The first time there is no speedup, but the second time (and any later times) the CPU asks for that same location's value. If that value is still in the cache memory, the cache controller can serve it up almost instantaneously.

The principal limitation on the effectiveness of cache memory comes from the fact that it is only a tiny fraction of the size of main memory. So only a tiny fraction of the most recently accessed locations in main memory will have their values still in the cache memory.

Memory Caching Didn't Always Make Sense

When PCs were new, building any cache memory into the CPU wouldn't have been worth it. That was true for two reasons. First, it adds complexity, and the manufacturing processes of the time could barely make chips complex enough to serve as CPUs. And second, those chips ran so slowly that main memory could easily keep up with them. Now, however, the CPU chips can run as much as four times faster than the memory chips on even the fastest motherboards, and the needed complexity for a memory cache can be afforded relatively easily.

Careful study of actual everyday computer programs has shown that they very often reuse the same instructions, and even the same data items, over and over again. This comes about because it often is very helpful to the programmer to use "loops" in the program in which some task is done over and over until some desired result is achieved. If the loop is small enough that all of its instructions and all the data referred to within the loop fit inside the cache memory, then during the execution of that loop the CPU can run at its very top speed without ever having to wait for a relatively slow access to main memory.

In any case, if the running program wants to write some information out to memory, it can simply hand it off to the cache unit and then continue its work. The cache unit will take care of getting that information out to main memory eventually, as soon as the much slower external circuitry allows it to do so.

Making Cache Memory More Effective

A small pool of cache memory can be organized and utilized in several different ways. Each of these different techniques has different implications, both on how expensive the cache memory is to build and on how effective it is in operation.

Naturally, a lot of jargon is used to describe all the variations. Some of the names you will run across include read caching, read-ahead caching, write-through caching, deferred write and read caching, fully associative caches, direct mapped caches, and set associative caches. The set associative caches also come in two-way, four-way, and other subdesignations. Finally, the latest wrinkle is to separate the cache into two pieces: one dedicated to caching instructions and the other dedicated to caching data.

Explaining all these variations on this theme in detail would take far too much space, and you don't really need to understand them if all you seek is a general understanding of how PCs work and the ability to be a savvy consumer. You can be pretty sure that the CPU makers are building in what their research says is the most effective kind and amount of cache they can include, and they still will be able to make the chips using today's technology.

The Architecture That Goes Around the CPU

At this point you should have a pretty good idea of what the functional parts of the CPU are and how they work together. What we still need to examine to complete this discussion of the PC architecture is how the external parts of the PC are arranged. The most important of these is main memory. The next most important are the input/output ports. Everything else communicates with the CPU via one of these two structures.

Memory

Main memory and the CPU are the places in a PC where all the computing action takes place. This is true because data and programs must be in some portion of the main memory before the CPU can do anything with them. Some of the programs and a little bit of data may live there perpetually. Most of them are just brought into that space when they are needed and then either discarded (in the case of programs) or saved to a permanent storage location (in the case of data), after which the memory space they had occupied is once more available to be used by new programs and data.

Main memory in a PC is a mixture of RAM, ROM, and vacant potentiality. That is, your PC's CPU chip can address a physical memory address space of fixed size. At some of the locations in that space are random-access, read-or-write memory chips (RAM). At some other locations are read-only (or read-mostly) memory chips (ROM or non-volatile RAM, called NVRAM). And for most of the memory address space, nothing is there at all.

This hasn't always been so. When PCs were new, memory was a lot more expensive, per byte, than it now is, but the early PCs couldn't address more than a total of one megabyte. So, many owners of these early PCs had their machine's memory address space at least mostly filled with RAM or ROM.

The Maximum Size of Physical Memory

Modern PCs can address *many* more memory locations. Starting with the 386, they could potentially use up to 4GB of memory, and the Pentium Pro and Pentium II chips can, in theory, use up to 64GB of memory. Even at today's relatively low cost for memory, I don't know of anyone who is pushing those limits very closely—yet.

Modern members of the x86 processor family have two other address spaces, referred to as virtual (or logical) memory and linear memory. Linear memory address space is usually the same size as physical memory address space. The virtual memory address space, on the other hand, is enormously larger still. I will explain just why this is so in Chapter 11, "Bigger Is Better in Ballrooms and in a PC's Memory."

The potential size of the CPU's physical memory address space is not the same as the maximum memory you can add to your PC. The reason is because PC makers don't connect all the address lines (either directly or via memory address decoders) to sockets. They don't need to, because none of their customers want to put in as much memory as the CPU can address. (Even if they did, no current operating systems could use all that memory. Windows, for example, in all its flavors is, so far, limited to using a maximum of 2GB of memory.)

Level 2 (or Level 3) Cache

At the end of the discussion of the CPU architecture, I described the Level 1 memory cache that is included in all recent x86 family members. The idea of using a memory cache in a PC actually goes back even farther than the 486DX, which was the earliest of those cache-enabled x86 processors. When the CPU chips became significantly faster than the fastest reasonably affordable DRAM chips, people started to be interested in having some cache memory, but at that point it still wasn't feasible for the CPU makers to put it on their CPU chips.

The first PC implementations of this idea were on 386-based machines. The motherboard in these PCs included some additional, extra-high speed (and extra costly) RAM chips, plus a specialized integrated circuit called a cache controller. For those PCs this was the one and only memory cache it could have.

The size of this memory cache is mainly limited by how much money the motherboard maker thinks its customers want to spend for the performance gain which that much added memory will provide, rather than being limited as the L1 cache is even today by the amount of room and "spare" complexity available on the CPU chip. (The more cache the better, but after some point, the improvement in performance grows only slightly for even rather large additions to the size of the memory cache.)

This meant that even when Intel and the other CPU makers started putting a small amount of cache RAM inside the CPU, motherboard makers found it helped their sales to include a second level of memory cache on the motherboard—provided that this Level 2 (L2) cache was considerably larger than the L1 cache inside the CPU.

A given amount of memory in an L2 cache is not nearly as effective as the same amount of L1 cache for the simple reason that the external clock frequency on modern CPUs is only a fraction of the internal clock frequency. Still, it can be a useful addition to a motherboard, because it normally can deliver data or accept data in a single clock cycle, and often the DRAM that makes up the bulk of main memory requires two or more clock cycles to do those same things.

Partly to address this limitation on the effectiveness of L2 cache on the motherboard, and to get a larger high-speed cache than they could manage to put on the CPU chip itself, Intel's Pentium Pro introduced the concept of a module that contains two chips, closely integrated together inside the module. The bus from the CPU chip is now divided into two buses: One to the outside world and the other to the L2 cache chip that is inside the CPU module with the CPU chip.

Not only is the CPU to L2 cache bus capable of running at the full internal clock speed of the CPU, it also is completely independent of the CPU to motherboard bus, meaning that two different data transactions can be happening on the two buses at the same time. Intel's term for this is dual-independent bus (DIB).

The Pentium II also has an L2 cache memory chip next to the CPU chip inside the processor module, but in this case the CPU to L2 cache bus runs at half the internal CPU clock speed, so this L2 bus is less effective than that in the Pentium Pro. But both are more effective than the L2 cache on the motherboard of a Pentium PC.

For those who want the ultimate in memory caching, a Pentium II machine could have a third level of caching (an L3 cache) on the motherboard, in addition to the second-level cache on the separate chip inside the CPU module and the L1 cache on the CPU chip itself, although so far no commercial motherboards offer this feature. Each lower level of cache would be larger, in part to make up for its being slightly slower to access than the next higher level. The combination of all three levels of memory cache is the ultimate today in this technology.

Cache Coherency Problems

The idea of cache memory is a very good one. But a few potential snags must be avoided. A serious one can arise whenever two or more devices might be reading and writing to the same bank of main memory. This could be a problem in either of two ways. Suppose the CPU reads the values held at several memory locations. It then does some computations that lead it to place new values in some of those locations. If another microprocessor comes along and reads those same values after the CPU read them, but before the CPU writes back the altered values, that other microprocessor could potentially end up overwriting those changes with its own changes, and thus lose the effect of the CPU's changes.

Another way that a problem can arise is if the CPU calls for the contents of a certain memory location and the cache controller sees that its cache contains a previous reading of that value. It then will supply the CPU with that value without taking the time to go out and re-read it. That is, after all, just what the cache controller is supposed to do—that is what makes having a cache valuable. If, however, in the interim some other device has altered the value that is being held in that memory location, the cache controller will be giving the CPU a wrong value to work with.

Every PC ever built, other than IBM's PC Jr., has had a feature called direct memory access, or DMA. (I'll explain more about why this can be wonderful—or not, depending on the particular kind of PC you have—in the section "Why DMA Fell from Favor," later in this chapter.) DMA means having a secondary microprocessor that is capable of accepting a command from the CPU to move some data from one place in memory to another—or to or from an input/output port. The DMA processor does this task while the CPU goes on about its business. And some of the most recent and most powerful PCs now have more than one CPU chip, with all the CPUs sharing the same pool of main memory.

Either way, whether because you have multiple CPU chips or because your PC is using the DMA strategy (or perhaps some other "bus mastering" device such as a high-speed SCSI host adapter), it is entirely possible that at times the contents of main memory will be changed by something other than the CPU's cache controller (or the motherboard L2 or L3 cache controller if your PC has one of those devices). Whenever this happens, a cache controller that is connected to this memory must know about this fact and at the minimum, it must "invalidate" the image of those memory values that it is holding in its cache memory until it can replace them with a freshly read copy of the new values.

The only way that this *cache coherency* can be maintained is for the cache controller that is connected directly to the main memory pool to watch every access to that pool by whatever device may be doing it. This allows the cache controller to see if any address that is being accessed is one that is currently being imaged in the cache memory this cache controller is managing. So, every cache controller is, in fact, built to do this sort of *bus snooping* to see who else might be writing to memory besides itself.

The other type of cache coherency problem that can arise is in a way more subtle. If the CPU tries to write to a memory address where there is some ROM or one where there is nothing at all, it clearly cannot make that location hold the value it sends out. If, however, the cache controller doesn't know that, it may hold the information written out by the CPU as though it were a valid image of what is actually in main memory at that address. As long as that image stays in the cache memory, the CPU will get that value any time it tries to read it back. If it waits long enough that the cache contents are completely replaced, however, the CPU will discover the real value (if any) that is being held in that location.

The only way to avoid this problem is to tell the cache controller up front which areas of physical memory address space are *cacheable* (meaning they have actual RAM there) and which are not cacheable (meaning either they have nothing there or they have ROM there). It can be—indeed it almost always is—very useful to do read caching for ROMs, but it is *never* good to allow write caching of memory locations that are occupied by ROMs.

Modern PC BIOS setup programs often include a section in which you can inform the cache controller which regions of memory you want it to cache. If that section is initialized properly, nothing will go amiss for this reason. But if you mess with those settings and get them wrong, you could be in for some nasty surprises somewhere down the road.

Stacks

I pointed out earlier that the CPU must have some temporary holding places for information it is processing. That is why it has registers. Sometimes, however, it doesn't have nearly enough registers to hold all the information it must have temporarily stashed somewhere.

This is especially true for a PC that is doing multitasking. This simulation of doing more than one thing at a time is accomplished by doing a little bit on one task, then switching to another task and doing a little on it, then switching to a third task, and so on.

Each time the CPU switches from working on one task to working on another one, it must save the values that are contained in every register for the first task and load those registers with the values they last had for the next task it is going to work on. The CPU accomplishes this by using *stacks*. This is not the only time stacks are used, by any means, but it is one of the most dramatic uses for them.

A stack is a simple concept. Think of a stack of dishes. When you want to put away freshly washed dishes, you stack them in a cupboard. When you want to take out some dishes, you take them off the top of the stack. The last dish you put on the stack becomes the first one you will take off.

In a computer a stack is implemented simply as a region of memory plus a register that holds an address pointer. When an item is to be "pushed" onto the stack, the item gets written to the location indicated by the address pointer, then the value of the address pointer is reduced by one. That makes the next item to be pushed onto the stack go into the next lower memory address. Alternatively, when an item is "popped" off the stack, it is read from the location pointed to by the register's contents, after which that register's contents are increased by one. Figure 8.6 shows how this concept is implemented in PCs.

The maximum size of a stack is set first by the size of numbers the relevant register can hold, and second by the initial value of the stack pointer (which normally is the same as the size of the memory area that has been set aside for that stack). Almost always the latter limit is far more severe than the former, although it is possible to make a very large stack that would use almost the entire possible range of the stack pointer.

Figure 8.6.
How a PC's stack works.

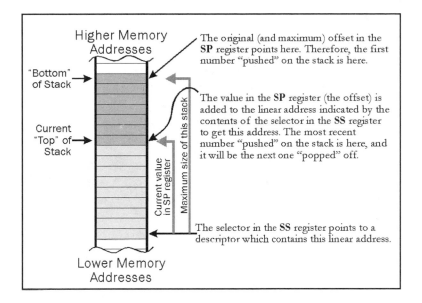

If a program ever attempts to push more information onto the stack than it can hold, that stack pointer value will have to go negative, the CPU will notice this, and, before it can happen, the CPU will cause an exception.

A PC must always have some stack ready for use. The CPU holds the pointer to the current location in the stack in its stack pointer (SP) register. That value is an offset into the segment pointed to or indicated by the value held in the stack segment (SS) register.

Any well-written program will create and use a private stack as one of its first actions. The reason for this is that the programmer cannot know how much space is left on the pre-existing stack. This is done simply by allocating some memory for the private stack, then "pushing" the value presently in the stack pointer and stack segment registers onto the pre-existing stack and then loading the SP and SS registers with new values pointing to this newly allocated memory region. At the end of its work, the program will pop the old value off the stack and the CPU will be restored to its prior state. (It also is necessary to push onto the stack the contents of any register that the program will be altering, and then pop them back off at the end.)

Any number of stacks can be defined in a PC at any moment, but only one of them will be the *current* stack. That is the one pointed to by the logical address [SP]:[SS] (by this notation I mean the two numbers held in those two registers joined by a colon).

> **Technical Note:** As an aside, note that there is another stack in all recent x86 processors. That is a special stack of eight 80-bit registers inside the CPU that are used in connection with floating-point number manipulation and—in the Pentium MMX and Pentium II—when executing MMX instructions. This stack is normally used only by MMX and floating-point math instructions, and it is entirely different from the "regular" stack created out of a portion of main memory and used by POP and PUSH instructions.

This notion of stacks is a very important one for PC programming. It allows programs to be written that are far more complex than would be possible if only the registers in the CPU could be used as temporary information holding places. The whole idea of multitasking would be utterly infeasible without stacks.

Ports

When the CPU forms a physical address on its address pins, that address normally refers to some location in memory address space. But by simply changing the voltage on another pin (the Memory or I/O pin) from high to low the CPU can signal that it intends the address pin value to be interpreted as a location in a totally different logical space.

Because the primary use for these other locations is to move information between the CPU and other parts of the PC, including some totally outside the PC, we call this logical space the space of the PC's input/output ports. And although the addresses in this new space are indicated by voltages on the same address pins that are used to indicate memory addresses, the I/O port space is quite different from the physical memory address space.

For one thing, I/O port address space is very much smaller. Every member of the x86 family from the earliest 8086 or 8088 to the latest Pentium II has the same size I/O port address space, namely 64k (65,536) byte-wide locations. This is because when it is doing an I/O operation the CPU uses only the bottom 16 address lines.

Furthermore, there are none of the complexities of selectors or paging associated with I/O port addresses. Because there are only 64k port addresses (each one byte wide), only a single 16-bit number is needed to point to a desired port. That number can be loaded into any of the general-purpose registers in the CPU, although some instructions assume that the port address will be loaded into the DX register.

Because all the x86 processors but the 8088 can read and write two or more (up to eight) bytes of information from memory at a time, they can also read or write the same number of successive port locations in one operation. And, as with memory locations, the processor can only address locations in the port address space with a resolution equal to the width of its data bus. (That is, the Pentium can only address ports in blocks of eight, although it can send information in or out any single byte-wide port if that is desired.)

What Makes I/O Ports Different from Memory Locations

The main distinction between an I/O port and a location in memory is what happens to data that is sent there. When you send a succession of bytes to a port, usually each of them will go on to some receiving hardware. When you read from a port, you might get a different value each time you read it (and none of them need be any of the values you sent out to that port), for what you see is whatever was last sent in to that location from the outside. This behavior is in stark contrast to that of a true memory location, where what is there is whatever you last wrote to that place, and that is what you will get if you read from that place. That is not to say that it is impossible to put memory chips at I/O port locations. That is simply not done often.

Memory Mapped I/O as an Alternative to Using Ports

What about the opposite "misuse" of an address, in which some I/O gadget is placed at a location in the memory address space instead of in I/O port address space? This not only can be done, it often has proven to be quite useful. No difficult trick is involved in making the port-like hardware respond as if it were memory. You just invert the signal on the MEM/IO# line and the port hardware will think all memory accesses are port accesses and vice versa.

The reason this can be useful has to do with the very different speeds with which the ISA I/O bus and the memory bus operate. To get maximum speed out of an I/O device, it used to be necessary to make it "memory-mapped," which is to say, make it appear in the CPU's memory address space.

Unfortunately, this also leads to some considerable complexity that you don't have to deal with when the hardware is connected to a real port address. Because of the many ways in which linear memory addresses can be shifted around in physical memory address space both by the selector/descriptor table strategy and by paging, it can all too easily happen that the port hardware will seem to bounce around all over the linear memory map—or it might even disappear altogether. This is not at all what you want an I/O device to do, for the programs that intend to talk to it must know where to find it before they can function successfully. Fortunately, now that we have fast I/O possible via the PCI bus, there is no longer enough gain in using this memory-mapped I/O strategy to make up for the complexity. Now all the I/O hardware that needs real speed is put on the PCI bus.

Speed Issues for Ports

Originally the ports were connected to the CPU data and address pins in exactly the same manner as memory chips. But later, as CPU and memory speeds increased, the paths for data flow to memory and to I/O were made quite separate. They join right at the CPU, but away from that point they operate independently and at quite different speeds.

For example, a modern high-end PC uses a memory bus that runs at 66MHz (and an internal CPU clock of, currently, up to 300MHz), but every PC is designed to run the Industry Standard Architecture (ISA) input/output bus at the same sedate 8.33MHz or less. This is done to ensure that even the oldest PC plug-in cards will be capable of operating properly in even the newest PCs.

Modern PCs do have other, faster I/O buses—most notably the PCI bus. I will tell you all about these alternative I/O channels in Chapter 16, "Faster Ways to Get Information Into and Out of Your PC."

Interrupts: The Driving Force

At this point you have seen all the essential parts that make up a PC. Thus, you have seen its basic architecture, at least in a static sense. What you haven't heard about yet are some of the key dynamic aspects to its architecture. In the rest of this chapter I will explain what these dynamic aspects are and how they work. The first of these, and in some ways the most important, is the concept of interrupts.

Polling Versus Interrupts

Imagine a small flower shop in a mall. The proprietor of this shop must serve the customers when they visit, but in between customers she must go back into the back room and take care of paperwork. How does she know when to stop doing paperwork and come out to serve a customer?

The owner can use two fundamental strategies. One is to interrupt herself at regular intervals, get up from her desk and go out front to see if there may be some customers out there desiring service. This is called *polling*. This strategy works, but it is terribly inefficient for two reasons. First, when a customer walks in, he or she must wait until the next time the owner happens to stop working on the paperwork and comes out to discover the customer. Second, when there are no customers, the owner cannot work steadily on the paperwork, but instead must waste time every few minutes coming out to look and notice that there aren't any customers waiting for help.

The obvious solution, in the case of a flower shop, is to put in a sensor that will be triggered each time a customer walks through the door. One common way this is done is by a light and photocell pair on opposite sides of the door. The light beam is broken by an entering (or exiting) customer, and that causes a bell to ring, alerting the owner in the back room that it is time to come out and help the customer. This costs more than the polling method. The shop owner must buy and install the sensor and bell, but it saves money in the long run by enabling the shop owner to work more efficiently.

Intel included something very much like this in the first 8086 processor and in every x86 processor since then. The details of how it implemented this idea are particularly clever.

Interrupt Vector Table

Intel built the x86 processors so that when they are operating in real mode and any one of 256 different kinds of events occurs, the CPU will finish the present instruction it is executing, it will stop what it is doing, save a marker so it can pick up where it left off, and then it will start doing some specified task that is appropriate to the kind of interrupting event that just occurred.

Intel did this is by making the CPU, when it is interrupted, first discern what type of interrupt has happened, and then go to a specific address very low in the memory address space. From that location it picks up a pointer to another location, and at that second location it finds a program that directs it in the proper handling of this kind of interrupting event.

Notice the indirection: Intel could have said, if an interruption of type 75 occurs, go to this specific address and do whatever the program there dictates. Instead, it said, pick up the pointer value in slot 75 of a special interrupt vector table (IVT) and execute the program to which that pointer points.

This indirection has several advantages, not the least of which is that it lets you change how the CPU will respond to a given type of interrupt on-the-fly. All you must do is change the pointer value for that kind of interrupt from one that points to program A to one that points to program B, and the CPU will alter its behavior accordingly.

Figure 8.7 shows schematically how an interrupt is processed by reference to the IVT. By Intel's mandate, the IVT occupies the first 1,024 bytes of main memory address space. That size means that each of the 256 interrupt types gets a 4-byte number, which is just what we need to specify a logical address (in segment:offset form).

This location for the IVT is, in real mode, the first 1KB of the CPU's actual, physical memory address space. In protected mode, or in virtual 86 mode, it is the first 1KB of the CPU's linear memory address space, which may be some very different region of the actual, physical memory.

In Figure 8.7 you see on the left the first 10 slots (4 bytes each) of the interrupt vector table with the actual logical addresses they held on a particular PC when I was creating this figure. On the right you see a memory map for that PC. On the memory map I have indicated not only the location of the interrupt vector table, but also where the DOS and BIOS data area is, just above the IVT. And above that you see the region occupied by DOS. Then there is a region I have shaded a bit more darkly in which the programs that are called for by the CONFIG.SYS and AUTOEXEC.BAT files are loaded. After all that has been assembled in memory, the PC is ready to run a real, useful application program.

Figure 8.7.

The interrupt vector table and how it is used.

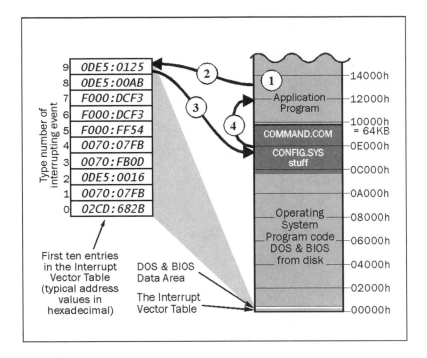

First ten entries in the Interrupt Vector Table (typical address values in hexadecimal)

DOS & BIOS Data Area

The Interrupt Vector Table

Figure 8.7 shows the four steps that always happen when there is an interrupt:

1. The application program is executing along when it is interrupted by a keystroke.

2. Because this is an interrupt of type 9, the CPU first saves its place, then goes to the IVT (slot 9) and retrieves the address of an interrupt service routine that will be able to handle this interrupt.

3. As it happens, in this example, that ISR is one of the programs that was loaded in response to some line in the PC's startup files.

4. When that ISR finishes its work, it tells the CPU (by executing a special instruction called return from interrupt [IRET]) to go back to what it was doing before, and the CPU resumes executing the application program.

How Do Interrupts Happen?

In my analogy of the small shop in the mall I indicated that an interrupt might be used to signal some external event (in that case, the arrival of a customer). In PCs, some interrupts happen because of an external event. Others happen because a program says they happen. Yet others happen because the CPU says they should happen.

Hardware Interrupts

The first kind of interrupts, called hardware interrupts, is the principal means by which anything outside the CPU can get its attention. For example, each time you type a key on the keyboard, it sends a signal to the PC system unit. Special circuitry inside the system unit (called the keyboard controller) notices that signal, and in turn it alerts the CPU to the arrival of a keystroke.

There are only two pins on the CPU by which a hardware interrupt may be signaled: the normal interrupt input (whose pin name is INTR) and the nonmaskable interrupt (with a pin name of NMI). However, many more than that number of different kinds of hardware events might need CPU attention. This seems like a problem. Fortunately, the standard PC design (PC architecture) includes a solution to this problem.

A standard part of the motherboard circuitry that surrounds every PC's CPU is a subsystem we call the interrupt controller. In the original PCs and PC/XTs, it could accept signals from any of eight input lines and send an interrupt signal to the CPU. Then, when the CPU acknowledged receipt of that signal, the interrupt controller would tell it from which of the eight possible sources that particular interrupt signal had come. In the IBM PC/AT and all later PC designs the number of inputs to the interrupt controller has been increased from 8 to 15 or 16. I say 15 *or* 16 because one of the interrupt inputs is used to collect together eight of the others, but in some situations it can also be used in its own right.

The input/output bus carries within it 9 of these 16 interrupt request (IRQ) lines. Any device plugged into a slot on the I/O bus can inform the CPU of its need for attention via one of these lines. The rest of these IRQ lines are reserved for use on the motherboard by, for example, the keyboard controller.

Cards plugged in to the ISA bus slots cannot normally share an IRQ line. Each IRQ line must be used for only one card. Cards plugged in to the PCI slots, or in to a CardBus slot, on the other hand, usually can share interrupts with other cards also plugged in to these more modern buses. Any of the interrupts caused by a signal on an IRQ line ultimately arrives at the CPU on its INTR pin. The nonmaskable interrupt (NMI) pin is normally used only for the PC's reset circuitry.

The difference between nonmaskable and normal interrupts is this: When a maskable interrupt is asserted, the processor can ignore it if it has been told to ignore interrupts. The fact that an interrupt is pending is remembered until the processor is ready to act on the request. This is much like an adult who says to the child tugging on her sleeve, "Not now, dear. I will talk to you as soon as I finish talking on the phone."

The nonmaskable interrupt is used when no delay can be tolerated. This is more like a fire alarm. The reset circuitry uses this means of interrupting the processor because it is sure to work, even if the processor gets totally confused and would otherwise stay in an "I don't wish to respond to interrupts right now" state indefinitely.

Software Interrupts

Intel decided it would also be a very good thing if a program could, in the course of its operation, cause an interrupt to happen. This would interrupt the running program and invoke another, special program to handle the type of event corresponding to the type of interrupt the running program had asserted.

The advantage of this approach is easy to demonstrate. The writer of an application program can know that at a certain point his program must send some information to the screen. But the program (and the programmer) need not know in detail just how to do that. All the program must do is assert the proper type of interrupt, with the correct values in the certain registers to indicate what is to be sent to the screen, and the program invoked by that interrupt will then do the job. This is just one simple example of a much larger principle we will meet again in Chapter 18, "Understanding How Humans Instruct PCs," namely a sort of divide-and-conquer strategy.

The programmer who writes the program that must write something to the screen need not understand anything about how that will be done. The programmer who writes the program that does that job needn't know anything about why this particular bit of information must be written to the screen at this time.

CPU Exceptions

After it had this mechanism in place, Intel found it convenient to use that mechanism to handle problems the CPU might detect on its own. For example, if a program attempts to access some memory it isn't entitled to access (often referred to as a general protection fault or a page fault), it will trigger a suitable interrupt. The corresponding program that is invoked can then put up a dialog box telling the PC user what has gone wrong, and it can terminate the program that ran amok.

Interrupt Service Routines

The programs that respond when an interrupt happens are called, quite naturally, interrupt service routines (ISRs). One ISR must be designated for each of the 256 possible interrupts, or at least there must be one for any of them that might happen. However, nothing says these 256 programs all must be different programs. Usually, a great many of them are in fact all the same, single, simple ISR.

As I indicated in Figure 8.7, when an ISR is invoked, it runs until it is finished, at which point it executes a special RET (which stands for return from interrupt) instruction. The CPU understands that instruction to mean, "Please resume doing whatever you were doing before."

The very simplest ISR consists of nothing more than just one RET instruction. That is a "do nothing" ISR. After you have one such instruction in memory somewhere, you can simply make the IVT entries for any interrupts you want to ignore point to that RET instruction.

When Interrupts Interrupt an ISR

Nothing in what I have written so far indicates that ISRs are immune to being interrupted themselves. Sometimes they must not be interrupted for a very short time after they start executing, and in that case they can simply turn on the mask that inhibits interrupts. However, it is considered very bad PC programming practice to let that PC run in this state any longer than absolutely necessary.

As a result, it is quite common for an ISR to be interrupted. When that happens, it is suspended in just the same fashion as the original application program was suspended when that original ISR was invoked, and now a new ISR gets invoked. When it finishes its work and executes an RET instruction, the CPU will pick up what it was doing when it last got interrupted, which in this case means resuming what the first ISR was doing. Only when that one finishes its work will the CPU be able to go back to the application program.

Layers Upon Layers of ISR

Not only can interrupts interrupt an interrupt service routine, it is also quite common for one ISR to call another one, which calls yet another one, and so forth. The way this comes about is that when each ISR is loaded into memory, it replaces the address in certain slots in the IVT with its own address. If it was written properly, it first copies the address that was once there into some holding place within itself. Then, if later another ISR is loaded into memory that wants to handle that same type of interrupt, it will do all the same things.

Why would more than one ISR want to handle the same interrupt? A good example is the case of the keyboard interrupt. Many programs might be watching to see whether you have just typed their hot key. If you have, they will spring into action and do something useful for you. If not, they must not let that keystroke disappear. Instead, they simply hand off the news of this interrupt to whatever ISR had previously been installed to handle this kind of interruption. Figure 8.8 shows an example of this.

The process begins with the same situation as that shown in Figure 8.7. But now a TSR (terminate and stay resident) program has been loaded on top of all the programs loaded by the startup files, before the application program was started. So, when the interruption comes along the following occurs:

1. The CPU looks in slot 9 in the IVT.
2. Where it finds itself directed by the new address there to execute the TSR program.
3. When the TSR finishes checking the keystroke (in particular, if it isn't going to do something with that keystroke).
4. The TSR will call the original ISR.

Figure 8.8.
How layers of ISRs cooperate in handling an interrupt.

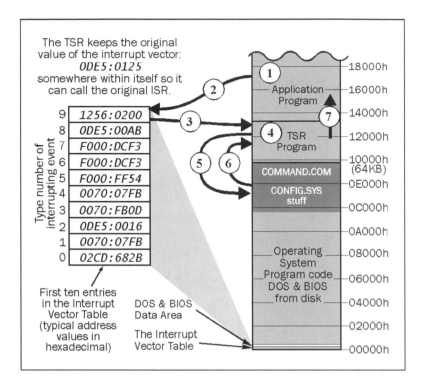

5. Which will do whatever it would have done anyway. When the ISR finishes, it executes an IRET instruction.

6. But this time, instead of making the CPU resume the application, this only makes the CPU resume the TSR program. But that program executes another IRET instruction.

7. And this time the CPU does return to executing the original application.

BIOS Services in ROM

Where does your PC get its ISRs? Every PC ships from the factory with a motherboard BIOS ROM. This chip (or pair of chips, usually) contains many different things. Most of what it contains, however, is a collection of ISRs to do the most basic things every PC must be able to do, such as responding to keyboard input and writing to a monochrome (or the now obsolete CGA color) screen. As I will explain in more detail near the end of this chapter, the entries in the Interrupt Vector Table (IVT) are initially set up to point to these ISRs.

Many PCs have some additional BIOS ROMs located on plug-in cards. One common example is a video card, which today almost always includes a fairly hefty BIOS ROM. This ROM contains alternative ISRs to handle screen output using the hardware on that card. A part of what must happen early in the boot process is for this card to place the addresses of its ISRs into the IVT in place of the addresses of the default screen handler ISRs in the motherboard BIOS ROM.

DOS and BIOS Services in RAM

Many additional ISRs are loaded into memory when you load the operating system. From one point of view, almost all of what any operating system is can be described as just one of a huge collection of ISRs. Most of the services that the operating system performs for programs are provided either by an ISR within the operating system, or by one that is located in some BIOS ROM.

When you load a terminate-and-stay resident device driver (for example, a mouse driver), that is yet another ISR. In almost every such case, not only is the program loaded into memory in a fashion that ensures it will hang around until it is needed, but also it must stuff its own starting address into the proper slot in the IVT, so that it will be activated at the appropriate moments.

Technical Note: The one common exception to this rule is the class of device drivers known as *block devices*. These are the device drivers that create phantom disks (for example, a RAM disk) or that activate special types of disks for use with your PC. They usually link themselves into the operating system both by stuffing some entries in the IVT, but more importantly by also inserting themselves into a *linked list* that is called the device driver chain.

Interrupts are one of the most important ways that things are caused to happen in a PC other than by direct action of the CPU. Another special feature in the standard PC architecture that functions in a somewhat similar manner is the DMA channel.

What Is a DMA Channel?

For the most part, each time a byte of information is moved from one place to another within the PC's main memory or between a memory location and an I/O port, it gets there in two steps. The first step is for the CPU to read that byte into some register within itself. The second step is to write that byte back out to its final destination.

This works, but it has two drawbacks. The first is that the CPU cannot be doing anything else while it is moving that byte around. The second is the fact that it takes two distinct steps to make the move. For moving a single byte this is not so bad, but when you have a whole flock of bytes to move, it certainly isn't wonderful.

Several kinds of devices in a PC do want to do just that sort of many-byte information transfers. The floppy disk was the first. Sound cards do this a lot—so much so that they often use more than one

DMA channel. Likewise, scanners generally use a DMA channel, and who knows what new devices might want to do this as well.

Realizing this, the designers of the original PC decided to incorporate an additional microprocessor dedicated to solving exactly this kind of problem. The processor in question is called the Direct Memory Access (DMA) controller. With a DMA controller present, the CPU can hasten its work by telling the DMA controller that it is to move a certain number of bytes from successive memory locations starting at one address to successive memory locations starting at some other address. It also has the option to tell the DMA controller to send out a certain number of bytes from successive memory locations to a particular port address, again starting at some specified memory address.

The final option is that it can tell the DMA controller to receive a designated number of bytes in from a particular port address and deposit those values in successive memory addresses, starting at some specified address. Each time the DMA controller sets up one of these transfers, it must do so over what is referred to as a DMA channel. That simply means that a particular portion of the DMA controller is assigned to this transfer task.

The DMA controller, however, doesn't get to pick which part does which transfer. Instead, the requesting device (the CPU or some I/O hardware) must specify the channel that will be used. This means that these channels are a precious resource, and conflicts in requests for them can keep them from being used to their full capacity.

So far, not many devices need DMA channels in a PC, so the issue of running out of DMA channels is not nearly as urgent as that of running out of IRQs. However, that happy situation might not last. As more and more devices that often must move large numbers of bytes are attached to our PCs, we might soon find ourselves wondering where on the DMA controller we can possibly find a channel to hook them up.

Why DMA Fell From Favor

At first DMA was wonderful. The floppy disk controller in the original PC used it, and it helped even that relatively slow device work more quickly and reliably. When they came along some years later, some hard disk controllers and SCSI host adapters used DMA as well.

Then things began to change. The CPUs got faster, but the ISA I/O bus couldn't speed up. Well, it did speed up a little bit, from the original roughly 4.77MHz to the PC/AT's higher 8.33MHz, but that was it. Any of the clone PC manufacturers who ran their I/O bus at a faster speed (and some did crank up the speed as high as 12MHz) were tempting fate, for surely some of the plug-in cards their customers would try in those slots would fail simply because they couldn't keep up with that higher-than-standard clock rate.

As CPU speeds increased, so did the speed of main memory, although the latter speed didn't increase quite as fast or as far. The speed of the bus from CPU to memory crept up from 8MHz to

16MHz and then to 33MHz and finally to 66MHz (with some other steps along the way). The ISA bus, however, still ran at a measly 8MHz. This meant that the DMA controller (in particular when it was sending information out from memory to a port or receiving information into memory from a port) was quite thoroughly frustrated by the slow I/O bus speed. Although it could do the job without needing constant attention from the CPU, it couldn't do the job nearly as quickly as the CPU could by tossing the bytes out to a memory-mapped I/O device. So programmed I/O to memory-mapped I/O devices became all the rage. (DMA was still useful for memory-to-memory transfers. These simply weren't needed as often as the memory-to-or-from-port transfers.)

How DMA Made Its Comeback

DMA has bounded back, and it is an even better solution now than it was in the first PCs. The reason is simply that we now have I/O bus technologies (the PCI bus and the CardBus) that can transfer data to and from I/O devices at speeds that are more nearly comparable to those on the main memory bus. Now, once more, the DMA strategy is a sound time-saver for the CPU and overall.

DMA also has been improved, so it uses the available bus bandwidth even more efficiently. The newest version, called Ultra DMA, can transfer data to IDE devices at speeds up to a full 33 megabytes per second (MBps)—twice the old maximum speed.

What all this means for the PC user is that DMA channels matter once more. They are once again the preferred way to carry large blocks of data into or out of I/O devices, and more and more we will see those devices using this strategy.

Keeping Up with the Clock

PC clock speeds are mentioned a lot. In fact, for many years one of the most prominent numbers in any PC advertisement was clock speed. ("Buy our nifty new 266MHz Pentium Pro computer.") Just what is that speed? And what parts of the PC actually run at that speed? Are there other clocks in a PC? If so, what do they do? These are the questions I will answer for you in this section.

Asynchronous Versus Synchronous Computers

Although they are amazingly fast, electronic circuits do need some time to operate. Just how much time each one needs varies from sample to sample. It is possible to make a computer that has no clocks in it. Such a computer would run just as fast as each individual piece within it would let it. Data requested from memory would get used just as soon as it showed up wherever it had been asked to show up. The results of calculations would be stashed back into main memory just as soon as they were available. Never would any part wait unnecessarily long, just because it wasn't yet time to move on according to some central clock.

Such an asynchronous computer is possible to design and build, but it sure isn't easy. A far simpler way to design a computer is to synchronize each of the parts to some central clock or "heartbeat." As long as this clock ticks slowly enough, you can be quite sure that every part will have completed its assigned tasks before the next tick comes along and tells the parts to move on to their next steps. Synchronous computers are so much easier to design and build that nearly every computer built today is an example of such a design. Certainly every PC is.

Different Clocks for Different Purposes

This doesn't mean that all the parts must march to the beat of the same drum, however. It is perfectly possible, and has now become quite standard, to have a multiplicity of clocks in a PC, each one used for a different purpose. Here is a quick rundown on the most important clocks in PCs. Your PC surely has all of the ones I will mention, and it might also have a few more.

The CPU Clock

The most famous clock is one that "ticks" inside the CPU chip. This is the 266MHz (or 300MHz, or 100MHz or whatever your PC may have) that you hear so much about. It measures how fast the fastest part of your PC runs. Mostly these days the CPU inner core runs at this speed and nothing else in the PC comes close. Well, if you have a Pentium Pro, its L2 cache, which is located inside the CPU module, also runs at this speed. In the Pentium II, the L2 cache runs at half the CPU clock speed. For all other x86 processors, the external cache runs at the same speed as the main memory bus.

The bus from the CPU to main memory commonly runs at some fraction of the CPU clock speed. Or, to put this more properly, the CPU runs at a multiple of the external bus speed. That is, the actual clock circuit that controls this speed is located outside the CPU and the CPU simply synchronizes its not-very-constant frequency clock to a fixed multiple of that external clock signal.

For example, a 200MHz Pentium MMX machine, which is one of the fastest machines widely available as I write this, has a main memory clock speed of 66MHz. This means the internal clock is running at precisely three times the external clock. The even faster 266MHz machines use the same external clock speed, but are designed to run with their internal clock synchronized at precisely four times the external clock speed.

The Main Memory Clock

The same clock that drives the CPU also drives the main memory modules and all the associated circuitry. Frequently only the external (L2 or L3) memory cache actually is capable of keeping up with this fast a clock. The slower DRAM chips that make up the bulk of main memory are enabled to run more slowly by the insertion of one or more "wait states." These are delays between the clock cycle in which the CPU or external cache controller asks something of a memory chip and the clock cycle in which it expects to find the result of the requested operation.

The Input/Output (I/O) Bus Clocks

As I have mentioned many times now, the Industry Standard Architecture (ISA) input/output bus is required to run no more rapidly than 8.33MHz. This signal is derived from the same clock as the main memory clock by dividing by, in the case of our sample systems with a 66MHz memory clock frequency, a factor of eight. The ISA clock speed is this slow in order to make sure that even very old ISA plug-in cards will function correctly when they are plugged in to an ISA slot in even the latest and greatest PC.

But today's PCs also have one or more additional I/O buses, and these buses typically operate at a faster speed than the ISA bus, although usually not quite as fast as main memory. The PCI bus can operate at up to 33MHz in the fastest of today's PCs, just half the speed of the main memory clock.

Other Clocks in Your PC

Many of the subsystems in your PC must work in synchrony with a clock that runs at some different frequency. For one example, the video monitor scans the electron beam across and down the face of the display at a frequency set by the desired resolution of the image and the acceptable refresh rate. (If these terms mean nothing to you, see Chapter 13, "Seeing the Results: PC Displays," for a complete explanation of them.)

The disk drives need clocks at special frequencies that are a fixed multiple of the rate at which their disk platters turn. A modem needs a clock that will make it put out or take in bits at the correct speed for the transmission rate it is trying to achieve.

There can be as many different clocks as there are different pieces of hardware with differing speed capabilities and requirements. (You can't make the part go faster than it is capable of running, and in some cases you mustn't let it go either slower or faster than the standard speed for that sort of gadget.)

What Does *Super-Scalar* Mean?

When bragging about how much faster a new PC is than the older ones it has replaced, the manufacturers often point to its *super-scalar* performance. What does that mean? Quite simply, it means that if the clock speed on the new PC is the same as on the old PC, the new one will run programs faster anyway. If the new PC's clock is twice the speed of the old one, the new PC will run programs more than twice as fast as the old one. That is, the performance goes up faster than the clock speed.

(If it went up in direct proportion to the clock speed, the performance would be said to scale with the clock speed. Going up faster is, thus, super-scalar.)

There can be many different reasons for super-scalar performance. Usually, it comes from some combination of improvements such as having more execution units, having a bigger instruction pipeline, or having a better L1 memory cache. It may also come from having some part of the CPU "speculatively execute" instructions whose turn hasn't yet come, in the hopes that they will be needed later. At that future time, if those results are needed, they can be stuffed into the flow without waiting for them to execute. Or, perhaps the new PC actually uses more CPU chips than the older one.

Whatever the reason, super-scalar in simple terms just means the new PC works faster than you might have imagined. This is a good thing, but is not nearly as mysterious as the name might make it seem.

How Your PC Wakes Up and Prepares Itself for Work

The last topic I want to cover in this chapter is a brief description of what your PC must go through between the time you flip on the power switch and the time it is ready for you to run your first application program. This process is called *booting* the PC, from the whimsical notion of the impossible task of lifting oneself by one's own bootstraps.

Fortunately, all PCs (as well as modern, larger computers) come with the capability to get themselves started without all that fuss and effort by a human being. The reason they are able to do that lies in two features of their architecture. One is a portion of how the x86 processors are designed. The other is in the contents of a particular program that the motherboard BIOS chips contain.

Just as Intel hard-wired the x86 processors to look in the first 1KB of main memory for the interrupt vector table, they also hard-wired the address at which it will look for instructions when it first wakes up. The designated address is exactly 16 bytes below the top of the first megabyte, which is the only region of memory that an x86 processor can access when it first wakes up in real mode.

So, if only the PC maker will arrange to have the motherboard BIOS ROM show up in the CPU's memory address space in the region just below 1MB, and if it contains an appropriate program starting at that special address, that boot program will automatically run each time the PC is turned on or reset.

Because a PC program normally progresses through memory from lower addresses to higher, and because the starting address is only 16 bytes below the absolute upper end of the first megabyte of memory (which is all that any PC can see when it first wakes up), it would seem at first glance that the boot program would have to be impossibly short. In fact, one of the very first things the boot program does is an unconditional jump to some address a good deal further below this "ceiling" but still somewhere inside the motherboard BIOS ROM.

Next, the boot program begins checking to see whether all the standard parts of the PC are present and seem to be working normally. Before it gets very far into this process, it fills in the first 16 slots in the IVT with pointers to ISRs elsewhere in the motherboard BIOS. After that has been done, the boot program enables the maskable interrupts, so the machine can respond to, for example, keystrokes from the keyboard.

Also along the way, the motherboard BIOS program checks to see whether a special video BIOS chip is located on a plug-in video card. If it is, the boot program transfers control of the PC to that program, which uses this opportunity to place its ISR addresses into the correct slots in the IVT. When that has been accomplished, the video card can be used to display information on the screen. That video BIOS program commonly displays a copyright message as the first message on the screen. Then it returns control to the motherboard BIOS boot program.

The boot program now checks main memory to see how much of it there is, and to be sure it all works correctly. Some PCs do a more thorough job of checking memory at this stage than others, which explains why some PCs can have flaky memory and yet pass this step in the boot process. They may reveal the deficiencies of the memory at a later stage, either when a memory management program loads and does a more careful check of main memory, or perhaps only by failing in the middle of some important task you are doing.

Around this time, the boot program usually also offers the user a chance to suspend the boot program and enter the BIOS setup program. This lets you go into a special set of screens that display and enable you to alter configuration settings that are stored in the motherboard CMOS.

The boot program continues by building some data tables in the DOS and BIOS data area, a region of main memory just above the IVT. This area holds, among other things, a concise record of the number of serial and parallel ports, floppy disks, and other standard pieces of hardware in this PC.

Now the boot program has finished its power-on self test (POST) section and it is ready to look for an operating system and load it into memory. If it succeeds in doing this, it will then turn over control of the PC to that operating system, and the boot program's job will be done. If the boot program cannot find an operating system, it typically will simply stop with a message saying that you should insert a bootable diskette in the A: drive and press any key to restart the boot process.

In all PCs built more than a few years ago, the boot program would always look for the operating system in a standard set of places and always in the same order. That sequence was: First look on the first floppy diskette drive (A:) and then on the first hard drive (C:). If you don't find an operating system in either of those places give up (or in IBM-brand PCs only, run the BASIC interpreter located in a special motherboard ROM).

Many modern PCs are more flexible, and in their BIOS setup program, you can tell it which devices you want it to check and in what order. The possible boot devices now commonly include the A: and B: floppy diskette drives (which could also be the new high-capacity "super"-floppy drives referred to either as a:drives or LS120 drives), the C: hard drive, or a CD-ROM drive attached to either the primary or secondary IDE chain.

Peter's Principle: A Simple Antivirus Safety Net

One way to minimize the likelihood of getting your PC infected by a so-called boot sector virus is to specify that it not try booting from A: or B:. That way it won't accidentally load a boot virus simply because you forgot to take an infected diskette out of the floppy drive before rebooting. When you must boot from a floppy, you can simply first enter the BIOS setup program and reset this choice to allow booting from the floppy diskette drive, and then be sure that the diskette you use is virus-free.

In the next chapter I'll explain the various data structures that are to be found on PC diskettes and hard disks. After you understand that you will see fairly easily why and how the boot program can load the operating system. The process starts when the boot program loads the very first sector (512 bytes long) from the disk or diskette and then executes the program it contains. However, before doing that, the boot program checks to see that there is a special "signature" byte sequence 55h AAh at the end of the boot sector. If there is, the boot program assumes that the rest of the sector contains a valid startup program and the other information necessary to continue the search for an operating system on that disk(ette).

Some Things to Think About and Try

Look at the screen during the boot process. Also watch the lights indicating disk access. See which parts of the boot process that I just described you can identify. A flashing of the access light for the floppy diskette drives or the hard drive might indicate simply that the boot program was checking to see that those drives are responding to commands. Or, if the access light comes on and stays on for several seconds, the boot program might be trying to read information from a disk in that drive. A "ka-thunk" sound from a printer probably means it was reset by a signal sent to it from the CPU at the boot programs behest. And, of course, you should see the amount of main memory being counted onscreen as it is being checked.

9

You Can
Never Have
Too Much
Closet (or
Data Storage)
Space

Peter Norton®

Now that you understand how your PC "thinks," it's time to talk storage—that's where all the programs your computer uses to "think" and all the data it "thinks about" are kept. *Storage* is the collection of places where information is kept, long-term. It is in sharp contrast to *memory*, which is the place where you must put that same information (programs and data) before the CPU can do anything with it.

I pointed out this distinction in Chapter 2, "How (Almost) Any Computer Works," and I can't overstress its importance. This distinction is absolutely the standard industry usage for these two terms, and keeping the concepts clearly separate is vital. (If you find yourself having trouble with this one, you might be reassured to know that nearly all new PC users have that problem, but almost all of them manage to overcome it in a short time.)

This chapter is about the long-term information holding places, *storage*. Not about memory. (That is the subject of Chapter 11, "Bigger Is Better in Ballrooms and in a PC's Memory.") The concept of storage is a broad one. It covers many different kinds of long-term information holding devices. Because the first storage technology that was commonly used on PCs was the diskette drive, the PC has been designed mostly to view all the rest of these holding devices (including CD-ROMs, Flash memory cards, and tape drives) as though they, too, were disk drives.

In fact, this generalization has been taken so far that distant computers you access over a network or over the Internet often appear to you as just additional disk drives attached to your local PC. This makes using those diverse resources so much simpler.

Traditional PC Disk Drives

Before going into non-disks that look like disks to a PC, you should first understand actual PC disk drives. The first drives were floppy diskette drives. Later came hard drives, and then removable drives of various types. In the next section, I'll explain a little bit about the floppy diskette technologies used in PCs, followed by a section discussing hard disks.

 Standards: You might have noticed that I use the term *diskette* whenever I refer to a floppy, and *disk* only when I refer to a hard disk. This usage is not totally standard, but it should help you keep clear the differences between these different technologies.

Diskette Drives for PCs

The essence of any magnetic disk storage device is that it contains one or more circular disks. These disks are coated with a material that responds to magnetic fields to enable information to be stored there. The disks are mounted on a spindle and they turn under a head (or heads) that can move radially in toward the axis of rotation or out toward the edge of the disk. Normally in PC disk drives, the head is moved to a suitable position, it sits still while the disk spins past it and the information is written to or read from the surface in bursts. Figure 9.1 shows this arrangement, albeit with a much exaggerated scale. Normally the head is tiny, and the bursts of magnetic data recorded in the surface, even if they were visible (which they are not) would be so tiny and close together that they wouldn't be clearly distinguishable in this figure.

Figure 9.1.
As the disk turns under the stationary read-write head, that head passes along a track past sectors of recorded information on the surface of the disk.

A read/write head writes and reads magnetic tracks in the surface coating on the disk platter.

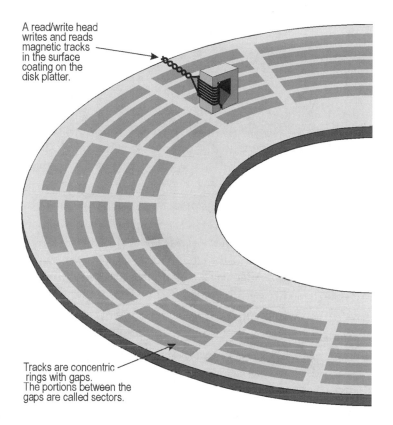

Tracks are concentric rings with gaps. The portions between the gaps are called sectors.

Getting a diskette drive was an extra-cost option for buyers of the first PCs (and hard disks simply weren't available at all). Having a floppy diskette drive (or even two of them) became standard quickly. Not only did these devices provide a means for storing programs and data for the long haul, they also proved to be a very convenient way to exchange information with other people.

The original PC floppy diskette drives were physically larger than the ones that most of us use today ($5 \frac{1}{4}$-inch instead of $3 \frac{1}{2}$-inch) and yet they could hold only a small fraction of what modern diskettes can. What you see when you pick one up and remove it from its protective paper jacket is a stiff, square paper folder with a large hole in the middle and several small notches on some of the edges.

Inside the square paper folder is a thin disc of clear plastic (usually mylar) that has been coated on both sides with a very thin layer of magnetic iron oxide. This magnetic coating is very similar to the coating on an audio tape. The disc actually is "floppy," that is, it is very flexible. But when it is in its sleeve the whole assembly is moderately rigid. The diskette drive spindle grabs the disc through the large, round center hole. The read-write head actually slides on the surface of the disc as it moves toward the center or away from it, along the length of the oblong hole you see at the bottom of the sleeve. (The details of how data gets stored on a diskette, in terms of tracks and sectors, is quite similar to how it gets stored on a hard disk. I will explain both in the section "DOS Disk Overview," later in this chapter.)

The original PC diskette drives could only read and write data to one side of a diskette, and they didn't use the available surface area as efficiently as later models. This meant those drives could store at most 160KB on a diskette.

We've come a long way since then. The most common diskettes today use 3 $\frac{1}{2}$-inch diameter discs that are much better protected in hard plastic housings, with a metal shutter to cover the hole where the read-write head contacts the vulnerable surface of the disc, and with a metal hub bonded to the disc to let the drive hold and turn it more precisely.

One result of these improvements is that these 3 $\frac{1}{2}$-inch diskettes can hold either 720KB or 1.44MB of information per diskette. Indeed, with simply an alteration in how the data is recorded, Microsoft and IBM each came up with (different) ways to push that capacity to something closer to 2MB per diskette, while still using standard diskettes and standard diskette drives. (Microsoft calls their format MDF, for Microsoft Distribution Format, and they intend that it be used only for their distribution of programs to save themselves the cost of more diskettes. IBM calls their new format XDF, for Extended Diskette Format, and they also use it only for software distribution.)

A few manufacturers introduced a higher-density standard diskette that held 2.88MB per diskette. Unfortunately, a special drive was needed to use them, because their magnetic coating requires stronger magnetic fields for writing, and special circuitry was required to understand their different read-head signals to read them.

This specialness was fatal. Very few people wanted to replace their floppy drives just to double the capacity. Furthermore, if they did start using those special extra-high density diskettes, then their diskettes wouldn't be useful for giving files to other folks who didn't have those special drives in their PCs. This theme of "we don't want it if it isn't compatible with everything that has gone before" has been a resounding chorus from the PC user community to the manufacturers. It took them awhile, but now most of the manufacturers know the folly of trying to give people something that isn't fully backward compatible. I'll explain about the latest attempt, the LS120 drive, later.

Hard Disks for PCs

Hard disks are like floppies, except that the media are, well, hard. Called a *platter*, these rigid disks are made of aluminum or glass. They are much thicker than a floppy's disc, but the coating of magnetic material is comparably thin. Some hard disks have just one platter. Some have several, all mounted on the same spindle and spun together.

The huge significance of the rigidity of a hard disk's platters is that after you have recorded some information on it, it is relatively easy to find your way back to the same spot to read the information. Floppies stretch and swell with changes in temperature and humidity. Hard disk platters don't—or at least they don't as much. This fact has allowed the makers of hard disks to use read-write heads that are much smaller than those in a floppy diskette drive, and that allows them to pack the information on the disk surface much more densely than is feasible on a floppy.

When PCs were new, adding a hard disk wasn't an option. Hard disks existed and were sometimes installed on small business computers, but only the priciest of those pre-PC machines sported one. Adding a 5MB hard disk to a PC could easily double its cost. By the time the PC/XT came along, IBM realized that the larger capacity and speed of hard disks was becoming a necessity.

The earliest PC hard disks were two-part contraptions. The drive itself, with an attached printed circuit card, sat in the disk drive bay. It connected via two data cables to a controller card that was plugged into one of the I/O slots on the motherboard. In its earliest form, these drives and the drive-controller interface were often described by the nickname for the data-encoding technology, MFM (Modified Frequency Modulation), which is the same data-encoding strategy that was used then, and is still used for floppy disks.

Technical Note: You might have a picture of magnetic data recording that is overly simple. You might think that the bits of data are recorded directly in the surface of the medium with 1s represented by little regions of "north" magnetization and 0s represented by little regions of "south" magnetization.

Unfortunately, disk heads excel at seeing changes in state of the medium, but are not so hot at noticing the state itself. Thus, any time you pass the head of a disk drive over a spot where the magnetization changes in direction or strength, the circuitry gets a signal that is easy to spot and to which it can then respond. But if you try recording a long field of magnetic 0s (or of magnetic 1s), the data detection apparatus has no change-signals to notice, and would likely get lost at least in terms of how many 0s in a row (or 1s in a row) it had seen. It might even get confused as to whether it was currently looking at a 0 or a 1.

The right way to record digital data is first to *encode* it. This means replacing long, unchanging patterns of 0s and 1s with patterns that do change regularly, thus better compensating for the disk head's inherent limitations.

Many encoding schemes have been used over the years. They sported monikers such as MFM and RLL (run-length-limited). Each scheme was "better" than the ones before it, in terms of how much data it could cram into a given space on the disk.

All floppy diskette drives use MFM encoding exclusively. Hard disk makers have now pretty well settled on some form of RLL, with "2,7 RLL" being the most popular.

The next generation of PC drives used an improved data-encoding method called *RLL* (*Run-Length-Limited encoding*), and those drives required new controller cards as well. Although some further improvements in data encoding were made after that generation, essentially all modern hard disks use a version of RLL data encoding.

Drives were improved in other ways. The MFM and RLL drives were followed by ESDI (Enhanced Small Device Interface) and SCSI (Small Computer System Interface) hard drives. ESDI is much like the MFM or RLL interface, but with some improvements that make it possible for these drives to have larger capacity and greater speed.

ESDI was popular for a short time, but it died away quickly when IDE (Integrated Device Electronics) drives appeared on the market. This trend was greatly accelerated when the improved EIDE (Enhanced Integrated Device Electronics) drives came along. These drives have the matching controller electronics moved from the plug-in I/O card to the circuit card on the side of the drive itself.

SCSI is not so much a way of interfacing to a hard drive as it is a tiny, one-computer local area network. Attaching a SCSI device of any type (and hard disks are only one of the many kinds of devices that can have a SCSI interface) to a PC requires the use of a *SCSI Host Adapter*. This is a plug-in card that mediates between the activity on the SCSI bus and that on the PC's I/O bus. Both ESDI and IDE (or EIDE) drives offer great ease of use—you just plug them in and they work. SCSI drives, on the other hand, offer the possibility of greater capacity and speed, but at the cost of greater difficulty in initially getting them to work in a PC.

EIDE and SCSI each has its advantages, and so both will probably be around for a long while. (One possible replacement for either may be drives that we see in the next couple of years that will work with the new IEEE 1492 "Firewire" bus standard.)

In Chapter 15, "Understanding Standard PC Input and Output," you'll learn more about all these different interface and bus standards. You'll find out why you might want to choose one type of hard drive over another. Later in this chapter, you'll learn how to handle a PC with multiple hard drives, including a mix of IDE and SCSI drives.

Understanding the DOS Perspective (and Why This Still Matters)

The first PCs came with a choice of operating systems, but the hands-down winner of consumer preference turned out to be PC DOS. IBM and Microsoft jointly created DOS and worked together on improvements for all the versions up to 5.0. Only since then have MS-DOS and IBM's PC DOS become somewhat different.

Why am I wasting your time talking about DOS? Isn't Windows all the new thing, now? As you will learn in more detail in Chapter 17, "Understanding PC Operating Systems," in many ways plain old

DOS, Windows on top of DOS, or Windows 95 (with DOS hidden inside) are essentially the same type of beast. At their core, and in particular, in their view of disks, they are just different flavors of DOS. Beginning with the version of Windows 95 known as OSR2 (Operating System Release 2), Microsoft has introduced a significant variation in how DOS works with hard disks—even though DOS is still the underlying operating system.

Other operating systems like Windows NT, OS/2, and Linux look at disks differently. All of them are capable of reading and writing DOS disks as well as ones that are formatted in their own special ways. Therefore, understanding how DOS views a disk is very important. And, it is going to continue to be important for a very long time.

When I refer to DOS, I am referring not only to what a purist might consider the "actual" DOS portion of the operating system, but also to those files that come on a DOS system disk and act as a portion of an operating system for your PC plus the portions of the motherboard BIOS that deal with disks. That includes the BIOS, the DOS kernel, the DOS file system, the DOS command interpreter, and—in DOS versions starting with 6 in which data compression was a built-in feature—the DOS data compression engine. (It does not include the external DOS commands, which are the many separate applet programs also shipped on a DOS disk, like FORMAT.COM.) In a Windows 95 or 98 machine, this refers to all the layers of system software from the motherboard BIOS on the bottom all the way up to the GUI (graphical user interface) on the top, or at least to those portions of these layers that have anything to do with handling disk drives.

DOS Disk Overview

The *Disk Operating System* (DOS) is an operating system whose special focus is managing disk drives. To DOS, the most fundamental unit of information storage is a *sector*. A sector is a clump of 512 bytes of information. Other sizes of sector are certainly conceivable. Indeed, some people have used other sector sizes (usually some power of 2 times 512 bytes), but without help from an add-on device driver, DOS cannot utilize any disk that uses a non-standard sector size.

Physical Structure of a Disk Drive

Look back at Figure 9.1, and then also look at Figure 9.2. In each of these figures, the short arcs of darker gray on the disk represent individual sectors. All the sectors around a disk at a given distance from the center form a *track*. The number of sectors in a track varies from one disk capacity to another, but every DOS disk has its information stored as some number of concentric tracks, each made up of a different number of sectors. (This is almost, but not quite, like the grooves on a record. The difference is that record grooves spiral inward, while tracks on a floppy or hard disk are concentric rings.)

Figure 9.2.

The location and numbering of disk heads (surfaces) and cylinders on a hard disk.

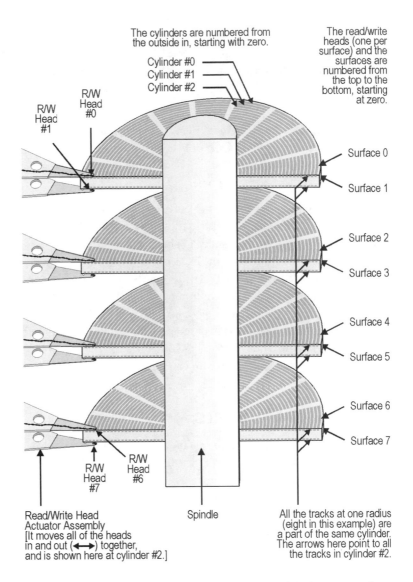

The cylinders are numbered from the outside in, starting with zero.

Cylinder #0
Cylinder #1
Cylinder #2

The read/write heads (one per surface) and the surfaces are numbered from the top to the bottom, starting at zero.

R/W Head #1
R/W Head #0

Surface 0
Surface 1
Surface 2
Surface 3
Surface 4
Surface 5
Surface 6
Surface 7

R/W Head #7
R/W Head #6

Read/Write Head Actuator Assembly [It moves all of the heads in and out (◄─►) together, and is shown here at cylinder #2.]

Spindle

All the tracks at one radius (eight in this example) are a part of the same cylinder. The arrows here point to all the tracks in cylinder #2.

Most floppy diskettes have information recorded on both sides. Most hard disks have more than two recordable surfaces because they usually have multiple platters mounted on the same spindle with two recordable surfaces on at least most of those platters. (Sometimes the outermost surfaces, the top side of the top platter and the bottom side of the bottom platter, are reserved for special purposes and cannot be used to store the user's information.) The collection of all the tracks at the same distance from the spindle on all the recordable surfaces is called a *cylinder*.

Technical Note: DOS and the PC BIOS were designed from the outset with the notion that the various disks they would manage might have differing numbers of heads, differing numbers of sectors per track, and differing numbers of cylinders. What DOS and the BIOS can't comprehend is a disk that has a different number of sectors on different tracks. And yet that is, in fact, just how most modern hard disks are built.

In these disks, because the outer tracks are longer than the inner ones, it is possible to put more sectors on those longer, outer tracks than on the shorter, inner tracks without quite crowding the individual bits together too closely in either place. Manufacturers commonly divide the tracks into two or more "zones" and put the same number of sectors on all the tracks within a zone, but a different number on the tracks in neighboring zones.

There are two ways in which such a disk can be made to work with DOS, and hence with PCs. One is by making the disk somehow pretend to be constructed differently than it really is. The other, more modern method is to use *Logical Block Addressing* (LBA) to connect it to the PC.

In the first strategy, the disk controller electronics first organize into one long chain all the locations on the disk at which information can be stored. It assigns a logical block number (starting with 0) to each of those locations. Next, the drive electronics creates a fictitious drive geometry. This fictitious drive has an almost arbitrary set of numbers representing its supposed number of heads, sectors per track, and cylinders. Every logical block number is converted into an equivalent location on the fictitious drive, and that is the pseudo-physical address used for that information when dealing with DOS.

In the second strategy, an extra layer is added to DOS to let it deal directly with a disk that is organized as a one-dimensional chain of logical blocks. That avoids all the messiness of fictitious drive geometries and, more importantly, it allows one to use much larger disks than DOS and the BIOS can natively understand.

Now let's focus on how this lowest-level information structure of tracks, sectors, and cylinders gets imposed on a disk, and how it is further organized into logical subsections by DOS.

Physical Versus Logical Formatting of Disks

This section deals with a sometimes confusing distinction between what is called the "physical formatting" and the "logical formatting" of a disk. Both processes consist simply of storing some special information on the disk, but the two processes store information that is used for very different purposes.

A freshly made diskette or hard disk has nothing stored on it. In that state, DOS can't use the disk at all. Two (or in the case of hard disks, three) steps must be taken first. The first step is the physical formatting of the medium. The second step for floppies, and the third step for hard disks, is the logical formatting. Hard disks add a step in between these two called *partitioning*. (I'll explain partitioning later in the chapter.)

None of the information that gets put on a disk during the physical or DOS logical formatting is anything you can read or use as a program or data in your PC. Instead, the disk drive needs this information to be able to store your data in an orderly manner, and thus to be able to retrieve your data again when it is needed. I like to think of a disk as being like a parking lot for information. If you attempt to store data there, you will get, if anything, a complete mess. Just as if you let people park their cars in a large, freshly paved lot, they will likely jam them in and later be unable either to find their cars, or get them out.

How the Physical Format Information Is Used

So the first step you must take with a new parking lot or disk drive is to define where, precisely, the parking places (for cars or information) are going to be. In a parking lot, this is accomplished by painting stripes to mark all the individual parking places, and to organize them into rows. On a disk, it is accomplished by recording "empty" sectors of information in each of the places where information is to go. This level of organization is called the *physical formatting* of the drive.

After the physical formatting is complete, every single sector in which information might ultimately get stored will be written to the disk surface. Each sector will have a header region that includes numbers indicating where on the disk this sector is located. Each sector will have a data section that is 512 placeholder bytes. And, each sector will have a section at the tail end for either a CRC value or for a few bytes of ECC. (Just what those jargon terms mean and why we must place those numbers there is something I'll explain in the later sections dealing with defects on a disk. Bear with me for now.)

How the DOS Logical Format Information Is Used

The second step in preparing a floppy (and third for a hard disk) is imposing the logical format. That means simply putting some special information that DOS needs to manage that disk into some of those sectors that were created in the first step—sectors that are now empty but available for information storage. In terms of our parking lot analogy, this is like building a valet parking system. A valet parking enterprise needs some way to find where in the lot each car has been parked so it can be quickly returned to its owner upon demand. Similarly, DOS must keep track of every file it stores on the disk so it can get that file's contents back whenever you, or a program you run, wants it.

DOS does this job by building three data tables on the disk. These are the *file allocation table* (FAT), a backup FAT to be used if the first FAT gets damaged, and the *root directory*. DOS also adds some information into the very first sector of each disk drive to inform it about the size of this disk and some of its other properties, and also to facilitate loading the DOS operating system from this disk, should that later be desired.

How Each Kind of Format Gets Installed

Floppy diskettes are supplied from the factory either with no formatting or with both low- and high-level formatting already in place. In either case, you can redo both levels of formatting quite simply by running the DOS FORMAT command. Hard disks are different. They once came from the factory completely unformatted.

Now, with all the disk controller electronics integrated onto each hard disk drive, hard disks have the low-level formatting already in place. After a hard disk is installed in a PC, and before it can have the DOS formatting installed, it must be *partitioned*. This is true even if the whole disk will be used as a single partition. (You'll learn why this is true and more about partitioning in the next chapter.)

Because the hard disk makers aren't sure how you will be using their disks with DOS, and in particular don't know how you want them partitioned, they rarely do the DOS level of formatting for you. (Of course, if you buy your PC with both the disks and a bunch of software installed, then that system maker has had to do the partitioning, DOS-level formatting, and software loading.)

When the partitioning information is in place, the DOS logical format can be put on the disk, one partition at a time (if it has more than one) using the DOS FORMAT command. Because the low-level formatting has already been done, the FORMAT command need only insert the DOS-specific data into the defined sectors.

Dealing with Defects on a Disk

No physical systems people build, and certainly none as complex as a disk drive, turn out exactly as planned. There are always some defects inherent in the device. But PC users demand total perfection in the performance of their disk drives. When you store information there, you want it to come back 100 percent accurate, right down to the very last bit. Anything less, and some perhaps vital part of your PC's operating system may fail, or you might lose some critical document. How can this gap be bridged? A part of the answer is what makes digital computers so special.

Why "Digital" Equals "Apparently Perfect"

As I said in Chapter 3, "Understanding Bits, Nybbles, and Bytes," at every stage of digital circuits, the numerical values they handle are represented by voltages that inevitably will vary somewhat from their ideal values. That variation is what we call *noise*. But when those values are sensed by each digital portion of the circuit simple, black-and-white, go-nogo decisions are made about what the values are. Each portion also re-creates those voltage values as close to their ideal levels as possible.

This means that you can copy digital data any number of times and be reasonably sure that it still has exactly the same information content that it had when you started out—the noise is eliminated, leaving a perfect copy of the original.

The Two Tricks Used in Disk Data Storage to Ensure Integrity

In terms of disk storage, the same notions apply, with some special considerations. Not only do the digital circuits essentially guarantee that the data you send through them gets to its destination unchanged, disk drives also have special provisions to ensure that when information is stored and then later read back, it can be checked to ensure its integrity.

Disk drives do this in two ways. First, they check all the information holding places on the disk during the low-level format, and again during the high-level format, to be sure that each sector will hold and return information faithfully. Any sectors incapable of doing this are marked as bad and are never used. Second, some extra, redundant information is stored along with your "real" information. When your data is read back from the disk, the drive checks it against the extra information to be sure that what it thinks it saw stored there is valid.

How Bad Sectors Are Tracked

There are several important differences in the ways that these things are done on floppy diskettes and on hard disks. On a floppy diskette, any bad sectors are simply marked as bad and the diskette's actual capacity is reduced by the number of bad sectors.

Modern hard disks, however, almost always appear to be perfect. They accomplish this by having more sectors for information storage than they tell you about. Some spare sectors are held in reserve, and whenever the disk controller detects a bad sector, it can replace that sector, in a functional sense, with one of the spare sectors. Different disks and different disk controllers use slightly different strategies. Some, for example, have a few spare sectors at the end of each track. Others just have a pool of spare sectors at the end of the entire chain of logical block addresses. Either way, the disk controllers usually manage to hide the defective sectors completely.

In fact, the only way you are likely to see any bad sectors on a hard drive is if it a very old one, or if a sector goes bad while it is holding some of your data. A very old hard disk might not have been built with all the modern hardware for hiding defects, and if a sector goes bad while it is holding some data, the drive might not be capable of substituting another sector for it without losing the data that had been stored in the sector that just failed.

Integrity Maintenance

The beginning of each sector on a floppy diskette contains a few bytes of data for the sole use of the disk drive. These are the address of the sector, plus an indication of whether the sector is bad. Then comes 512 bytes of space for your information. Finally, two bytes make up a special, extra number, called the *cyclical redundancy check* (CRC) number. Each time your information is written, this extra number is added.

Each time your information is read, the disk controller first checks the lead-in bytes to be sure it is reading the correct sector. Then, it reads the data and re-computes what the CRC value should be. Finally, it looks at the actual CRC value on the disk. If the two numbers are equal, the controller concludes that it read that sector correctly.

If the CRC the drive reads doesn't equal the CRC it computes from the data it read, it may try re-reading that sector. But after doing that a few times and still getting the same mismatch, the only thing the disk controller and operating system can do is announce their failure and prevent you from using the damaged data. That is what has happened when you see the dread message, `Error reading drive A: Abort, Retry, or Fail`.

Hard disks handle much more data than floppies, both because they can store so much more, and also because they can move information onto and off of their disks much more rapidly. They also encounter many more errors than floppies, but if a hard drive just gave up whenever it misread data, it wouldn't be a useful device at all. Fortunately, our PC hard drives hide at least 99 percent of all mistakes they make.

Instead of merely calculating a CRC value for each sector, hard disks compute a short string of *error correction codes* (ECC). When a read error occurs, the most likely cause is a pinpoint defect on the disk's surface. That defect will mess up just a few bits in the 4,096 bits that make up a sector's 512 bytes. More importantly, the "bad bits" will all be close together. Some very clever mathematicians and engineers worked out a scheme for ECC that would allow them to not only detect when a mistake is made, but to know exactly what and where the error is. Each bit must be either a 1 or a 0; if you know exactly which bits are wrong, you can compensate for them just by reversing those individual values.

This is why it seems like our hard disks work perfectly almost all the time. Actually, errors occur several times a day, typically, but they are fixed automatically and transparently. On a typical PC, no more than a few times per year does a real error get through and actually cause some problem.

Figure 9.3 shows the anatomy of a hard disk sector. This picture is also a good representation of the anatomy of a sector on a floppy diskette, except that the region that is labeled in this figure as containing ECC numbers is a little shorter on a floppy and holds only a CRC number.

The Logical Structure of a DOS Disk

Now you know how sectors get on disks in the first place. You know something about the internal structure of each sector. What you haven't learned yet, though, is how DOS manages to keep track of all the files you have loaded into all those sectors. I told you the names of the structures it builds a few pages ago (the boot record, FAT, and root directory). Now I will explain just what each one is and how DOS uses it.

Figure 9.3.
*The anatomy of a
hard disk sector.*

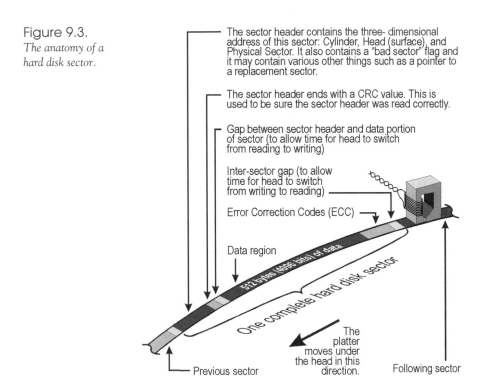

The sector header contains the three- dimensional
address of this sector: Cylinder, Head (surface), and
Physical Sector. It also contains a "bad sector" flag and
it may contain various other things such as a pointer to
a replacement sector.

The sector header ends with a CRC value. This is
used to be sure the sector header was read correctly.

Gap between sector header and data portion
of sector (to allow time for head to switch
from reading to writing)

Inter-sector gap (to allow
time for head to switch
from writing to reading)

Error Correction Codes (ECC)

Data region

512 bytes (4096 bits) of data

One complete hard disk sector

The
platter
moves under
the head in this
direction.

Previous sector

Following sector

Figure 9.4 shows the logical structure that every formatted DOS diskette or hard disk has. This structure is the complete description of what is on a DOS-formatted floppy. A hard disk drive can be
logically divided—partitioned—in such a way that it appears to actually contain several hard disks.
Thus, your C: drive and your D: drive could, actually, both exist inside the same physical hard disk
case. I'll talk more about partitioning in the next chapter.

Figure 9.4.
*The four essential
regions within any
DOS-formatted
logical disk drive.*

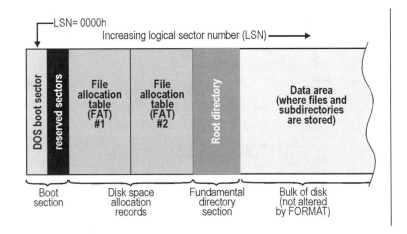

LSN= 0000h

Increasing logical sector number (LSN) ⟶

| DOS boot sector | reserved sectors | File allocation table (FAT) #1 | File allocation table (FAT) #2 | Root directory | Data area (where files and subdirectories are stored) |

Boot
section

Disk space
allocation
records

Fundamental
directory
section

Bulk of disk
(not altered
by FORMAT)

The Boot Record

The very first sector on any DOS floppy, and the very first sector in each logical drive on a hard disk is where DOS (or any other PC operating system) puts the *boot record*. Every boot record written by a given version of DOS is precisely the same, except for the contents of a small data table. (Because that table holds information on the size of that drive, and some other things, that part of the boot record must be different on different drives.) With that one exception, a floppy's boot record is the same as that on a hard drive.

Because this boot record ordinarily is exactly 512 bytes long, it also is sometimes called the *boot sector* or, to distinguish it from the *master boot record* (MBR), it might be called the *DOS boot sector*. You'll meet the MBR in detail in "Digging Deeper into Disks," an early section of the next chapter.

Most of the boot record is a program used to help start up your computer, assuming we're talking about the disk you are booting it from. That's why it carries the name *boot record*. If the disk doesn't have the operating system on it, and if you try to start up from it anyway, the program will put up the message, Non-System disk or disk error. Replace and strike any key when ready.

Figure 9.5 shows how this boot record's information is displayed by Norton Disk Editor. Here you see just the contents of the data table for the DOS boot record on the C drive of the hard disk, in a particular Dell Latitude XPi CD M166ST portable's 2GB hard disk.

Figure 9.5.
The DOS Boot Record from a typical Windows 95 hard disk's C drive is displayed by Norton Disk Editor.

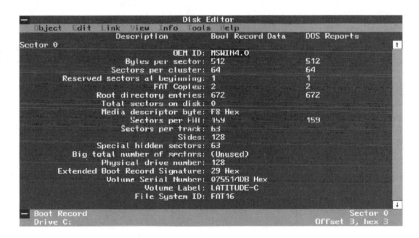

The data table in the DOS boot record, called the *BIOS parameter block* (BPB), records some essential numbers that DOS must know about this disk. This is the data that Norton Disk Editor showed in Figure 9.5. It includes the number of bytes per sector, the total number of sectors on the disk, the number of copies of the FAT, the type of FAT (12-, 16-, or 32-bit), the number of sectors per FAT, the number of sectors in the root directory, plus a few miscellaneous other facts about this disk. As you can see, mostly this data table is telling DOS where on the disk to find its special data structures, and how much other space there is in which to store your data.

Technical Note: One of the numbers in the BPB that often confuses people is the number of "reserved" sectors. This is the number of sectors at the beginning of this logical volume that are reserved for the boot program. So far in all DOS versions, the boot program is only one sector long. That goes for Windows 95 also—if you use the 16-bit FAT (FAT16) on your hard disk. Any Windows 95 or 98 logical disk drive that uses the new 32-bit FAT (FAT32) will have a boot record that is more than a single sector. In fact, in addition to the boot program itself taking up two sectors, these volumes store additional system information in a couple of other sectors. For all these reasons, the number of reserved sectors on a FAT32 volume is likely to be substantially more than on a FAT16 volume.

The "hidden sectors" number may also seem strange. This is the number of sectors on the disk before the first logical volume, and is something I will discuss more in the section "Master Boot Record and Partitions," in the next chapter.

The Data Area

The next area of the disk I must explain is actually the last area in sequence, and by far the largest one. But until you understand this area's function and structure, my description of the other two areas won't make much sense. The Data Area is where DOS stores your data. In fact, it includes all the space in the logical disk drive that isn't taken up in one of the system structures (the boot record, FAT, and root directory).

Block Devices Versus Character Devices

DOS handles data in two different ways, depending on the type of place that data is coming from or going to. When you type on the keyboard or send characters to the screen, you really want DOS to notice and act upon each and every keystroke and send each character to the screen as soon as it can. On the other hand, when you are sending data to or from a disk drive, it is perfectly acceptable to have DOS handle the data in fairly substantial chunks. And, because it is much more efficient for DOS to do that, it lumps together 512 bytes of data into a package (called a *block*) and sends all of them at once.

Sectors Versus Clusters on a Disk Drive

DOS sends data to, or retrieves it from a disk one sector at a time. (Well, sometimes it may handle multiple, consecutive sectors in a single operation, but at a very low hardware level, the disk drive itself is capable of handling only individual sectors, neither more nor less.) DOS uses logical sector numbers to address everything on the disk (including the system information in the boot record, FAT, and root directory). DOS starts this numbering at one (1) for the first logical sector in a disk drive.

Technical Note: A block and a sector are each 512 byte units of information. However, the DOS logical sector number is not to be confused with the logical block number. The difference is this: The disk drive tracks the logical block numbers for the entire drive. So this is ultimately the unit in which the BIOS must talk to the disk drive if it is using the LBA access strategy. (If it uses the fictitious geometry strategy, the BIOS uses a combination of three numbers, representing the head, sector, and cylinder on that fictitious drive while the disk drive itself always uses the logical block number.)

DOS, on the other hand, tracks the logical sector number within a DOS logical disk drive. That is some portion of a disk, but not necessarily all of a disk. The only time the two are the same is on a floppy diskette, or some other medium that is mimicking a floppy diskette.

But at another level, when it comes to keeping track of the files stored on a disk, DOS uses a different strategy. This entails using another, often larger unit of data called a *cluster* or an *allocation unit*. A cluster is a collection of sectors of data (and they are, in fact, ones that contain successive blocks of data in a particular file). That collection occupies a space on the drive that is the minimum size portion of the logical disk drive that can be allocated to a given file's use by DOS.

So, in the DOS view, a logical disk drive consists of the system areas (boot record, FAT, and root directory) followed by some number of identical-size clusters into which it can store data. The purpose of the FAT and root directory is simply to hold the records that let DOS keep track of the information stored in the disk's data area clusters.

The File Allocation Table (FAT)

The *File Allocation Table* (FAT) is the principal structure by which DOS keeps track of what is using which portions of a logical disk. Every DOS logical disk drive (that is, each "thing" to which DOS assigns a drive letter designation) has a FAT. In fact, each such drive usually has two copies of that FAT.

Technical Note: Having two copies of the FAT protects you against certain types of possible problems that might lead to data loss. Every time DOS must access a file, it checks the entries in the first FAT to see where to go. If it is writing data onto the disk, it updates both the first FAT and the second FAT. (There can be an exception to this for FAT32 partitions, but this is the usual case.)

However, if DOS gets an error reading the first FAT, it will automatically try to get the information it needs from the second FAT. Because it never reads the second FAT until it really needs it, DOS might not notice if the second FAT itself gets damaged until it is too late to do anything about it.

continues

The only ways you can learn about a problem with reading or writing the first FAT is if there is also an error in reading the second FAT—in which case the problems are very serious and you may never recover your data—or if you run a utility like Microsoft ScanDisk or Norton Disk Doctor to diagnose possible problems with your disk.

If there are any problems with reading either FAT, or if they aren't identical, the program will tell you. Depending on which tool you use, you might be able to properly repair the FATs and make the two copies identical once more.

It is prudent to check for problems on your disk drives on a regular basis, and the Norton Utilities and Windows 98 both allow you to have your PC do this automatically at intervals you establish. If problems are fixed shortly after they occur, your data might never be endangered. If you never check for trouble, you still might not be totally out of luck— but it will require a lot of time and some skill using a tool like Norton Disk Editor to try to recover your data.

The FAT is simply a huge table of numbers, each the address of a single cluster. These address numbers are assigned consecutively, starting at 2 for the first cluster after the root directory. The FAT has an entry for each cluster, which tells DOS that cluster's current status.

This can be one of several special values. If the value is 0, the cluster is currently unused and available. An End of File (EOF) value means that this cluster is in use, and the file using it has the end of its information stored here as well. A third special number signals to DOS that this cluster is "bad"— meaning it cannot safely be used to store information. Any other number in the FAT is a signal that the cluster is in use, storing information from a file, and that the information for that file continues in another cluster—specifically the one whose address number is stored at this location in the FAT.

Figure 9.6 shows a portion of a FAT table with some typical values in it. (This display is another screen capture from Norton Disk Editor.)

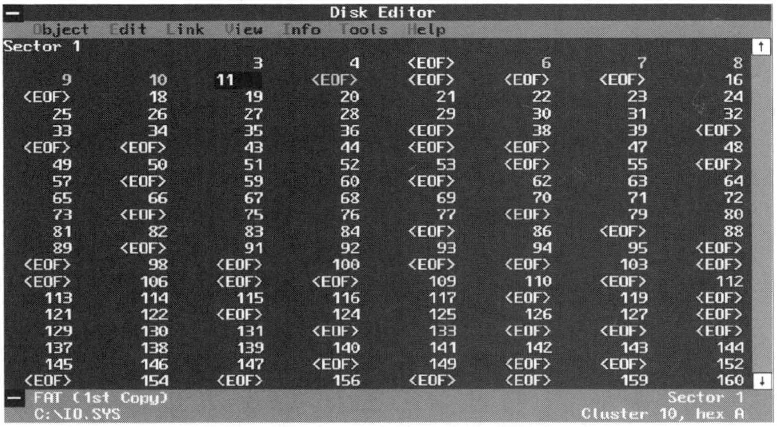

Figure 9.6.

A portion of a typical FAT is displayed by the Norton Disk Editor program.

Here you see one number for each entry in the FAT. The information at the bottom of the screen shows that we are looking at the first copy of the FAT table, and in particular, at the very beginning of that table. The legend at the bottom tells us that the file whose data is stored partly in cluster 10 is c:\IO.SYS, one of the key boot files on this PC. Look at the upper part of the figure. The first two locations are blank, corresponding to the two reserved cluster numbers 0 and 1. Cluster number 2 holds the number 3, meaning that the first file on the disk has data stored beginning in cluster 2 and continuing into cluster 3. The number there shows us that the file also continues on into cluster 4. But, in cluster 4 instead of a number we see the designation <EOF>, which stands for end of file. So, we know the first file's data ends somewhere inside cluster number 4. Similarly, the file that starts in cluster 15 ends in cluster 16. But the file that starts in cluster 17 goes on all the way to cluster 36.

I am sure you can figure out the rest of what this figure has to tell you about the assignment of clusters near the beginning of this disk. All the files shown in Figure 9.6 are *unfragmented* files. That is, their data is stored in consecutive clusters. A *fragmented* file has its contents stored in clusters that are not consecutive on the disk. For example, such a file might occupy clusters 3, 4, 17, 18, 28, 356, and 357. That would be a *cluster chain* comprised of seven sectors in four contiguous groups, and all of them together would be the total cluster chain for this file. Figure 9.7 shows a hypothetical FAT with several unfragmented files and one fragmented one.

Figure 9.7.
This hypothetical FAT shows some unfragmented files and one that is fragmented.

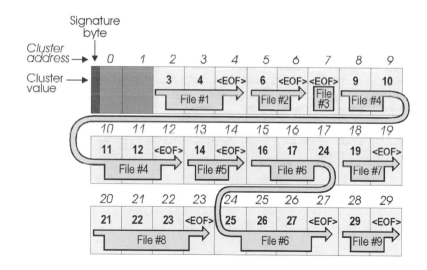

A FAT like this might be created in many ways. One way to get this result could be the following scenario: First, create a file that has too much data to fit into two clusters, but not enough to fill up three. That is File #1 in the figure, and its contents occupy clusters 2 through 4. Then, create another file with between 1 and 2 clusters worth of data in it (File #2). This file's contents go into clusters 5 and 6.

Now, create a short file (File #3) and put its contents into cluster 7. Short, in this context, just means its length is less than one cluster can hold.

The next file, File #4, is a larger file, using four clusters and spilling over into a fifth (clusters 8–12). File #6 originally filled up two clusters completely and a portion of a third one (clusters 15–17). Then, before any more data was added to File #6, File #7 was created and it used the next two clusters (18 and 19). File #8 was also created, using four more clusters (20–23). Now, after Files #7 and #8 have been created, File #6 is again opened and additional data is written into it. But there is no room for it to grow where it is, so DOS fragments it, putting the additional data in the next available cluster (in this case, cluster number 24). When that operation is finished, all the clusters have been used up through number 27, so when a new file (File #9) is created, it goes into clusters 28 and 29. If your head just spun reading this paragraph, be assured that the disk drive's heads do too—a severely fragmented hard disk will force the drive head to zip back and forth repeatedly to read or write a file. Head movements use a comparatively huge amount of time, and a badly fragmented disk will definitely reduce your system's performance.

How Big Is Your PC's FAT?

FAT tables come in three "flavors," each with a different size for its entries. So to figure out how big your FAT is, you must find out which of three strategies is used in each one of the FATs on the disks in your PC, and discover what the overall size of each one is.

The original DOS FATs used 12-bit numbers for each cluster entry, and DOS still uses 12-bit FATs for all floppy diskettes. (This is crucial, for it lets you read even very old floppies that might have data stored on them from the early days of DOS.) Furthermore, DOS also uses 12-bit FATs for any hard disk volume of less than 16MB.

A number with 12 bits suffices for storing values from zero to 4093. Several of these values are reserved, so all cluster addresses must be in the range from 2 to 4086. If DOS tried to keep track of every sector of data individually, this limit would mean that it could manage data only on a disk whose data capacity was quite small. You can get the actual value by multiplying 512 bytes (the amount in one sector) times 4085 (the maximum number of clusters)—just a little more than 2MB. That's larger than most floppy diskettes, but a lot smaller than any hard disk.

So, DOS can keep track of every single sector of data on a floppy diskette. But on a hard disk it must clump the data together into larger blocks (clusters). For simplicity, on hard disks of any size up to about 8MB capacity, DOS uses a cluster size of 2KB (four sectors per cluster). Notice that 8MB is about the largest disk that DOS can track with 12-bit FAT entries and this size of cluster. So, when it sees a hard disk volume between 8MB and 16MB, it simply clumps the data together into larger clusters—with eight sectors in each cluster, instead of only four. This makes the cluster size 4KB. This strategy similarly requires any disk between 16MB and 32MB to use 8KB clusters.

That was fine when hard disks were commonly no larger than 10MB, or perhaps 20MB. Now, with hard disk capacity measured in GB, this strategy would mean ridiculously large clusters.

So, starting around DOS version 3, a second style of FAT was introduced. (The exact point in the development of DOS varied with the many different clone-specific versions introduced around that time, which is why I used this wording here.) These newer-style FATs use 16-bit numbers for cluster entries. DOS versions from then until now still use 12-bit FATs on floppies, but they use 16-bit FATs on any hard disk volume that can hold more than 16MB—but less than 2GB—of data.

Technical Note: Why do cluster numbers start at two? The more usual choice for counting is to start at one or—if you are a mathematician or computer engineer—perhaps at zero. We can't start at zero, because the entry value must point to a cluster address, and zero is disallowed, because a zero entry value for a cluster means that cluster is available for data storage. But we could start with one. Why not do so?

The answer is that DOS wants to see a very special "signature" byte at the beginning of a FAT to let it know that this is a FAT, and what kind of FAT it is. The designers of DOS decided to use up the first two cluster-entry-sized places in the FAT for this purpose. (If the cluster entry size is $1\,{}^{1}/_{2}$ bytes, they add a hexadecimal value FFFFh to the end of the signature byte. If the cluster entries each occupy 2 full bytes, the signature byte is augmented by FFFFFFh.) Now, when you take the cluster address value times the cluster size you get the position within the FAT where that cluster's entry starts.

The DOS designers decided to use clusters with at least four sectors in them (thus, a cluster size of at least 2KB) for all FAT16 hard disks. That size suffices for any hard disk with less than a 128MB total capacity. After that, every time the total capacity doubles, DOS doubles the cluster size. The largest logical disk drives that DOS can handle comfortably have capacities of up to 2GB. For such a large volume, the cluster size is 32KB. That means that even if a file contains only a single byte of data, writing it to the disk uses one entire 32KB region of the disk, making that area unavailable for any other file's data storage.

The ever-increasing size of hard disks has caused the DOS and Windows designers to face the limits imposed by the 16-bit FAT structure. The first solution to these problems was introduced by IBM in OS/2's High Performance File System (HPFS). Another solution was introduced by Microsoft with the Windows NT File System (NTFS). Both of these perform FAT-like tasks in completely new ways. As such, they make disks formatted with those file systems largely inaccessible to DOS or Windows 95 programs.

The most recent solution to these large-disk problems was introduced by Microsoft in its OSR2 release of Windows 95—FAT32. As the name suggests, FAT32 is pretty much like the earlier 12-bit and 16-bit FAT structures, just expanded to accommodate larger cluster entry values (each using 32 bits, or 4 bytes, of space in the FAT) and as a consequence allows pointing to many more clusters. There are several consequences of this change, and some other added new features that make this quite a new and different disk drive format.

Windows 95 doesn't format logical drives with this new 32-bit FAT format unless you choose to have it do so. When you first run FDISK, if your hard disk has any volume that is larger than 512MB, you will have a chance to turn on this feature. From then on (unless you turn it off), FDISK will format all larger than 512MB logical volumes with a 32-bit FAT structure. The default format is still the 16-bit format, because after you format a disk volume with FAT32, it will no longer be accessible by DOS or any older version of Windows. But Windows 95, OSR2, and Windows 98 can and do work fine with all three FAT-structured logical disk drives.

The Root Directory

The final part of the system area on a DOS logical disk drive is the *root directory*. The root directory is a part of the system area for all but the new FAT32. That new format moves the root directory out of the system area and treats it just like a subdirectory. The root directory serves much the same purpose as the directory board that you can find in the lobby of most large office buildings. The directory board tells you the office number to use to enter a specific set of offices. It doesn't mean that this room is the only one that a company uses, but that this is the company's lobby or entry point. Similarly, the root directory entries in a DOS file system point to the beginnings of several files. In addition to those pointers, the root directory entries also hold the names of those files, their sizes, and some additional information about them.

What the root directory doesn't do is tell you the details about all the places on this disk drive where a given file's information may be stored. That is the purpose of the FAT. There can be several kinds of entries in a directory. I'll describe all of them in a moment, but I want first to focus on one special kind: the subdirectory.

Subdirectories

Large hard disks hold lots of files—far too many to keep track of sensibly if all their names were listed in a single place. The designers of DOS allowed for this by including (starting with DOS version 3) the notion of subdirectories. These are files that are pointed to by entries in the root directory (or in some other subdirectory), but their contents are treated as an additional file directory listing.

In almost all respects, the contents of these subdirectory files have a form that is identical to that of the contents of the root directory. But there are a few key differences. One difference is that only the root directory can have an entry for the logical volume's name (the volume label entry). Another is that every subdirectory contains two special pseudo-directory entries.

The names of these pseudo-directory entries are very odd. One has the name ".."—by which I mean its full name is simply a single period. The other has the name ".."—two periods. These are not like the periods you see between the name and extension of a file. If you look at a directory's contents with the DOS DIR command, you won't see those periods, but you will see the periods that make up these special pseudo-directory names.

The single-period entry is a synonym for the subdirectory in which it is found. The double-period entry is a pointer to the directory (root or sub-) that is the "parent" of this directory. That is, the directory that contains an entry pointing to the file whose contents are this subdirectory. Figure 9.8 graphically shows this relationship.

Figure 9.8.
How subdirectories point to their parents and to their children.

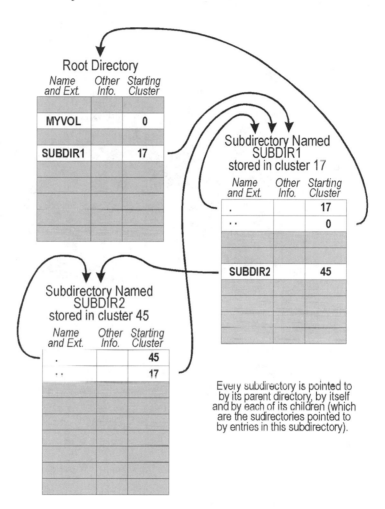

Every subdirectory is pointed to by its parent directory, by itself and by each of its children (which are the subdirectories pointed to by entries in this subdirectory).

The Different Types of DOS Directory Entries and What They Contain

You probably are quite familiar with at least one view of a directory. If you use Windows 95, you might have seen only the view shown by Windows Explorer. If you use DOS, with or without Windows 3.x, you will have seen a directory's contents in the form shown by the DOS DIR command.

But whether you use Windows Explorer or the DOS DIR command, you aren't seeing all of what is contained in those directory entries. And, you certainly aren't seeing how that information is arranged.

The information in a subdirectory is stored in exactly the same format as is used in the root directory. Figure 9.9 shows a subdirectory's contents using the DOS DIR command, but using a command prompt in a DOS window within windows 95 (what is sometimes called a *DOS box*).

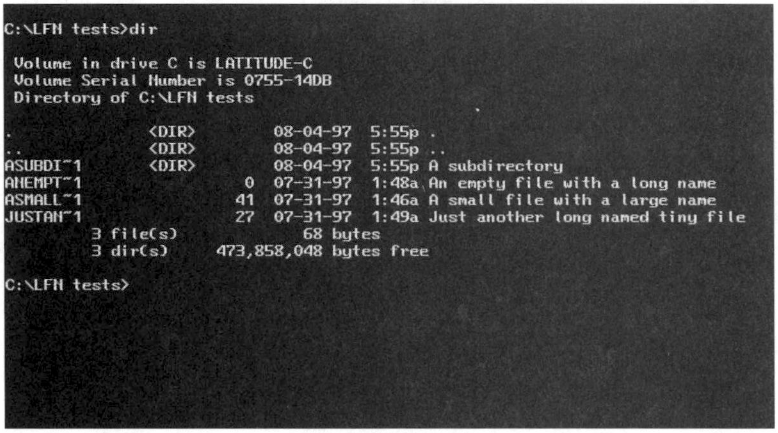

Figure 9.9.
The DOS DIR command issued inside a DOS window also shows the long filenames, but still much information is invisible.

```
C:\LFN tests>dir

 Volume in drive C is LATITUDE-C
 Volume Serial Number is 0755-14DB
 Directory of C:\LFN tests

.              <DIR>         08-04-97   5:55p .
..             <DIR>         08-04-97   5:55p ..
ASUBDI~1       <DIR>         08-04-97   5:55p A subdirectory
ANEMPT~1             0       07-31-97   1:48a An empty file with a long name
ASMALL~1            41       07-31-97   1:46a A small file with a large name
JUSTAN~1            27       07-31-97   1:49a Just another long named tiny file
          3 file(s)             68 bytes
          3 dir(s)     473,858,048 bytes free

C:\LFN tests>
```

The listing in Figure 9.9 shows the names of the files and subdirectories in this directory (including the two, special pseudo-directory entries with the names "." and "..") and a size for each item, plus a time and date on which it was last modified.

Notice that the sizes shown for the directory entries are all 0. That is not actually true, but it is what the designers of DOS and Windows decided to show you when presenting this information. Subdirectories are files and they have length, but that length just isn't shown here. You can figure out their length by looking in the FAT to see how many clusters they occupy.

To see the full contents of a directory entry, you must use some type of disk snooping tool. As I explained in Chapter 6, "Enhancing Your Understanding by Messing Around (Exploring and Tinkering)," you can use the DOS DEBUG program to do this. But it's far easier, and a good deal safer, to use a special-purpose utility program like Norton Disk Editor.

This program initially starts up in a read-only mode that makes it ultimately safe to use for disk snooping. If ever you must change something on a disk and want to have absolute control over what you are doing, simply switch into write-enabled mode, and you can do whatever you must do with precision and confidence. Even then, you will be prompted before you are allowed to change anything on the disk permanently.

Figure 9.10 shows the same subdirectory shown in 9.9, but this time you see all its contents in as human-readable a form as possible. This is the default way that Norton Disk Editor shows directory listings.

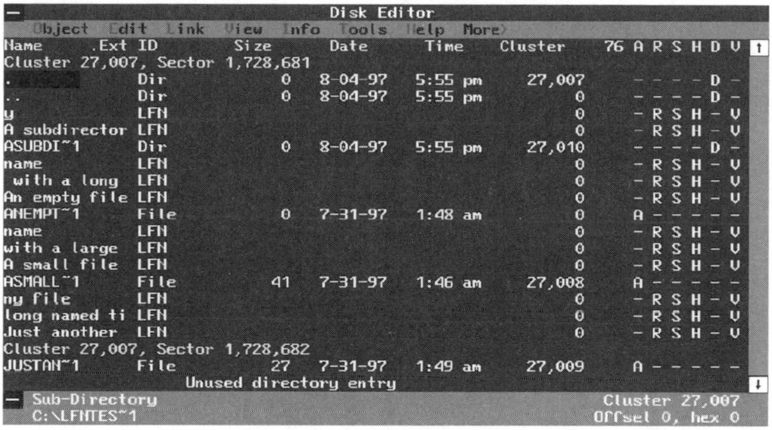

Figure 9.10.
Norton Disk Editor can display all the information in this subdirectory in a readable form.

Here you can see that the directory entry contains more than just the name and extension, the file size, and the date and time of last modification. In particular, it contains some file attributes and a cluster address where this file's contents begin on the disk.

Notice that the entry with a single period as its name points to cluster 27,007, and this directory entry is in cluster 27,007. Also notice that the entry with the double period as its name points to cluster number 0. There is no such cluster, but this means simply that the parent directory for this directory is not in a data cluster; it is the root directory located in the system area of the disk.

Directory Entry Structure and File Attributes

Now you've seen a subdirectory in different ways, and it's time to look at the contents of a single entry in detail. Each entry in the root directory, and each entry in any subdirectory, is exactly 32 bytes long. Some of those entries hold filenames and information DOS needs to find that file's content, plus other information about the file. Some entries hold similar information about subdirectories. And, some entries serve other purposes (including, in Windows 95 and 98, storing pieces of the long filename that belongs to a file pointed to by some other entry in this directory). I will explain first the entries that are used to point to files.

The first 11 bytes of this type of DOS directory entry are used to store the name of the file to which this entry points. That name is broken up by DOS into two parts. The first eight bytes hold eight characters (letters, numerals, or certain symbols) that form the name itself. The next three bytes hold a three-character extension to that name. The DOS file-naming rules require the name to have at least one non-space character, and they permit a maximum of eight characters. If the name is less than eight characters long, it gets padded with space characters to fill out the eight locations in the directory entry. Similarly, the extension can have anywhere from zero to three characters. The remaining locations, if any, in the directory entry are simply filled with space characters.

The 12th byte in the directory entry stores the file attributes. Of these eight bits, six are used by DOS. (Some network operating systems like Novell use one or both of the extra two attribute bits.) The DOS attributes include

- Archive attribute (A): This indicates a file that has been opened by a program in a fashion that enabled the program to change the file's contents. DOS sets this archive bit to ON when the file is opened. Backup programs frequently turn it OFF when they back up the file. If you use this strategy, then only the files with this bit ON must be a part of your next incremental backup.

- Directory attribute (D): This indicates that this directory entry points to a subdirectory rather than to a file.

- Volume attribute (V): This is used on just one directory entry in the root directory. That one holds the name of this disk volume. (This attribute also gets used for Windows 95 long filenames, as you will learn in the next section.)

- System attribute (S): This indicates a file that is a part of the operating system (DOS) or it can be a file that has been flagged in this manner by an application program (for example, this is often done as a part of a copy-protection scheme).

- Hidden attribute (H): These files (and those with the S bit set ON) are not to be displayed in a normal DIR listing.

- Read-only attribute (R): This indicates to DOS that this file is not to be modified. Of course, because this is only a bit in a byte stored on the disk, any program could change this bit, and then DOS will freely let it modify this file. This is mostly used to protect against human error—that is, to help keep you from inadvertently erasing or altering key files.

Notice that having a file labeled with one or more of these attributes can make perfect sense. For example, most files that are tagged as "system" files are also tagged with the "hidden" and "read-only" flags. But it makes less sense (or so it would seem) to make the volume label have any other attributes, except perhaps the read-only attribute. In fact, just such an "implausible" combination of attributes (RSHV) is used by Windows 95 to flag directory entries that are part of a long filename.

The next 10 locations in the directory entry used to be called simply reserved. On a FAT32 volume some of them are used for a portion of the file's first cluster address and for the dates and times at which the file was last accessed or modified.

All versions of DOS and Windows use the remaining 10 bytes in the same ways. First comes a pair of bytes for the time when this file was created. That information is stored as three binary numbers simply packed in side-by-side. The first five bits give the hour, the next four the minute, and the last five the number of seconds divided by two. The next pair of bytes store the date on which this file was created in a similar "packed bit" format. This time there are seven bits for the year, four for the month, and five for the day.

This 32-bit "FileTime" field is followed by a couple of bytes that hold the cluster address of the start of this file's data. For a 32-bit FAT disk this is only the low-order (least significant) 16 bits of the address. The high-order 16 bits are stored elsewhere, in two of what used to be called the reserved bytes. (In some earlier versions of DOS, those two bytes were used to hold what was then called a file's "extended attributes.")

The last four bytes of each directory entry hold a 32-bit binary number saying how long this file is in bytes. That would seem to suggest that DOS can handle files that are up to 4GB long. Unfortunately, that isn't quite the case. FAT32-enabled DOS can, but earlier versions were limited to only half that much (before Windows 95 [OSR2]) or even less.

In addition to the directory entries that point to files and those that point to subdirectories, there can be just one directory entry, and only in the root directory, of the third type: a volume label. In this directory entry, the name is used as the volume name (without a period inserted between the eighth and ninth characters, as is done for filenames and subdirectory names). The rest of the fields in this entry are not used.

Starting with Windows 95, there is a fourth kind of directory entry. This is one that holds a portion of a long filename.

How Windows 95's Long Filenames Have Altered Things

Before Windows 95, DOS and Windows 3.x limited all filenames to the old "8.3" standard. That is, they could have up to eight characters in the filename itself, plus up to three characters for the extension. Windows 95, in contrast, finally allowed filenames to be anything you like, up to 254 characters long.

The old DOS standard let one use only uppercase letters, A–Z, numerals, 0–9, and any of the following symbols:

$ % ' - _ @ ~ ` ! ( ) { } ^ # &

Any time you entered a lowercase letter in a filename, DOS would simply convert it to uppercase. It was possible to use a space within a DOS filename or extension (as well as at the end of the name or at the end of the extension), but many DOS programs are unable to deal with the resulting filename appropriately. (Certain other ASCII and extended ASCII characters can also be used without causing DOS any problems, but many programs will fail to recognize those names and might do unpredictable things to the corresponding files. Understandably, Microsoft recommends against trying these tricks with filenames.)

The new standard for long filenames adds to the list of allowable characters the following symbols:

+ , ; = [ ]

Furthermore, in a long filename you are allowed to mix upper- and lowercase letters freely, embed spaces wherever you like, and use as many periods as you like. (It is important that you realize, however, that when Windows looks at those long filenames it ignores case in deciding whether this filename matches some other filename.) Microsoft continues to recommend against using extended ASCII characters in long filenames.

Windows 95 was made capable of working with long filenames by a rather clever strategy. For every file with a long name (LFN), it automatically creates an alias, which is also called the generated short filename (SFN). That short filename conforms to the old DOS file naming rules, with the additional constraint that it may not contain any embedded space characters.

Then when DOS is creating that file, it makes a principal directory entry for that file whose name field is filled with this generated short name. That directory entry is preceded by one or more special directory entries that hold pieces of the long filename.

Each 32-byte LFN directory entry can hold at most 13 characters of the long filename. This is because those entries store the filename in a 2-byte Unicode format. (See Chapter 3 for more on Unicode), and because some of the 32 bytes are used for other purposes.

The first byte of the directory entry has a number that is the counting number of the pieces of this particular long filename. (That is, the LFN directory entry that comes just before the SFN entry carries a value of 1 in this location.) The last entry for each LFN has the ordinal number you would expect (one more than the one just below it), but with 128 added to its value. (This just means the most significant bit is set to 1 instead of 0.) Windows 95 can use this to help it find the end of an LFN.

The attribute byte in an LFN entry (the 12th byte in the directory entry) now holds the special combination of attributes RSHV, and the 13th byte (called the *type* byte) always contains a 0. The 14th byte carries a checksum based upon the SFN. This is another tool Windows 95 uses to help keep LFNs associated with the right SFN.

The 27th and 28th bytes of the directory entry in an SFN entry hold the starting cluster in the data area where this file's content is stored. In the LFN entries this field is set to 0. All the remaining 26 bytes in the directory entry are used to store the LFN in Unicode, 2 bytes per character. This is the only place in the directory that you will see Unicode characters (refer to Figure 9.10).

How Windows 95 Generates Short Filenames

You learned that Windows 95 creates a short filename (SFN) alias for each file with a long filename (LFN). But how Windows 95 does this isn't so obvious, and certainly can cause you some grief if you don't understand it.

If the file's "long" name is short enough that it fits in the old-style 8.3 naming scheme, then Windows 95 just uses that name as its SFN, changing any lowercase letters to uppercase in the process. If the name is longer, or if it includes spaces or multiple periods, then the SFN gets more complex.

There absolutely must not be two files in the same directory with the same short filename or the same long filename. If there were, Windows wouldn't know which one you meant (nor would you) when you wanted to access one of them. This rule forces Windows to do some pretty odd things with the SFNs.

For long names, Windows first strips out the spaces, uppercases what remains, and then uses the first eight characters of the name and three characters of the extension to form the SFN. For these purposes, if a name has only one period and that one is the very first character—which is a legal LFN—then Windows treats it as having a name with no extension. The SFN is, therefore, built from the first eight characters of the long filename after that initial period. If the filename has one or more periods after the first character position, then Windows 95 treats all the long name after the last period as the extension, and forms the SFN extension from the first three characters of whatever follows that last period.

If the SFN it generates is not unique in this directory, then Windows forces it to be by lopping off two or more of the final characters of the name and substituting a tilde character (~) followed by a one, two, or more digit number, with that number being chosen to be as small as possible and yet force the SFN to be unique. So, for example, the long filename Program File List.DOC might have a corresponding SFN of PROGRA~1.DOC. Letter to Mother on 9-11-95.DOC might SFN as LETTER~1.DOC. (In this second example, you can see that if you have several letters to mother, and you name them all the same, except for the date, you will have difficulty telling the files apart from within an earlier version of DOS. All of the long filenames in this directory will be SFN'd as LETTER~x.DOC, where x is the number of LETTER files in the directory. If you have more than nine such files, subsequent SFNs will appear as LETTE~xx.DOC, where xx is a two-digit number, and so on.)

The most subtle, and in some ways most confusing, aspect of the way Windows generates short filenames is that it will not necessarily generate the same name for a given file in two different locations. So when you copy a file from one directory to another, its long filename will go across unchanged, but its short filename might change, depending on what other files are already in the target directory.

Following all these new rules requires Windows to do a lot more writing and rewriting of the directories. In the past when a program altered one file, the operating system only needed to rewrite the one disk sector in which the directory entry for that file resided. Now it might have to rewrite the entire directory, depending on just what changes have been made to the file in question. Similarly, many programs, such as word processors, will open a temporary file, work in it, and then close it and after deleting the original file, rename the temporary file to the original file's name. That was pretty simple when each file involved only one directory entry. Now, if the file in question has a long filename, lots of entries might have to be rewritten.

Perhaps now you understand why many old, LFN-unaware DOS and Windows programs can get messed up trying to work with Windows 95 and long filenames. They haven't a clue. And if you aren't careful, they can destroy the long filenames of other files in the same directory with ones they are working on.

The DOS DIR Command as a Rosetta Stone

Previously, Figure 9.9 showed that the DIR command, when it is issued inside a DOS window in Windows 95, will display both the short and long filenames. If you are using Windows 95, are a committed "hacker" and like your old, DOS-based programming tools, you can use this fact to your advantage.

Shell out of your old-style program and have the DIR command redirect its output to a file. Then, back inside your program, read that file and you can match up all the long filenames with the short filename they happen to have in this particular directory. In a way, this is very much like how linguists used the famous Rosetta stone to learn the translations from Egyptian hieroglyphics to Greek.

Sorting and Searching with Long Filenames

The somewhat arbitrary and variable SFNs associated with long filenames also lead to some oddities in sorting files or searching for them. The DOS command DIR /O:N, for example, is supposed to list the files in a directory in alphabetical order. It does so, but it uses the short filenames in deciding what that order should be. This can, and often is, different from what you would get if you looked at the long filename.

And, a search for a "wildcard name" such as *1.* will match all files with a numeral one as the last non-space character in their short filename as well as any that have a numeral one followed by a period in their long filename. So you must be attentive to these and similar details if you want to understand why programs that search for short filenames under Windows 95 produce the results they do.

What DOS Does When You Delete a File

When you delete a file, DOS doesn't erase it from your hard disk. Instead, it does two simple things. First, it sets to 0 the value in all the cluster locations in the FAT that "belong" to that file. Second, it changes the very first entry in the (SFN) directory entry for this file from the ASCII value representing the letter, number, or symbol in the filename to the special value E5h. In decimal, this value is 229, and it is the extended ASCII value for the Greek lowercase sigma (σ).

These two steps tell DOS or Windows that this directory entry and those clusters in the data area are now available for reuse. But until they are reused, almost all the directory information and all the file's contents are still in place on your disk.

So, if only you could replace the first character of the filename, and then guess correctly which clusters used to belong to this file, you could make it appear once more. Starting with version 6, DOS lets you set up *deletion tracking* or *deletion sentry*. These are two different strategies for protecting you from losing an important file by an accidental deletion.

Delete tracking simply records for each file you delete what clusters it was using and what the first character of its filename was. Then, if you want to undelete it, you can—provided no other file's content has been written into any of those clusters and nothing has overwritten this directory entry in the meantime.

Delete sentry actually moves files you think you are deleting to a special, hidden directory. Then, if you want to undelete them, it simply moves them back. (Moving a file doesn't actually involve any moving of the file's contents. It just means creating a new directory entry in the target directory that points to the original file's chain of clusters, and then deleting the original directory entry.)

At first it looks like everyone should always use the delete sentry strategy. In fact, Windows 95 by default does essentially this. It moves all the files you delete into the Recycle Bin. That is just a new, fancy name for the hidden directory that delete sentry used in DOS 6.*x*. But there is a downside to this strategy. It means that when you delete a file you aren't actually freeing up any space on your disk. To do that you must also empty the Recycle Bin (or empty the delete sentry's hidden directory).

And actually, you don't need either strategy to let you undelete a file—most of the time. After all, if you recently deleted it, you probably know what the first character of its name was. The directory entry still contains the cluster number where the file's contents start and its size (which implies how many clusters it occupies). The only tricky part for a multi-cluster file is deciding which other clusters contain the rest of its content. If you only deleted this one file before you tried to undelete it, the chances are very good they are the next however many clusters you need that are currently marked as available in the FAT. That will be true even if the file was fragmented, and it certainly is true for unfragmented files.

Peter's Principle: Undelete Difficulties

The only time you are likely to have trouble undeleting a file is when you try to do it just after deleting a whole bunch of files, and then only if the file you want was fragmented. Or, of course, if you have written something else to the disk in the places formerly occupied by the file you want to undelete. You can make your computer run faster and also make it easier to undelete files whenever you want no matter what deletion protection strategy you are using (if any), simply by periodically defragmenting all the files on your hard disk.

DOS and Windows 95 include a tool to do this called DEFRAG. The Norton Utilities includes an even more capable version of the same program called Speed Disk. Whatever tool you use, if you are running Windows 95 or 98 you must use a defragmenter that was designed to retain your long filenames, or they may be deleted during the defragment process. Far, far more deadly, a defragmenter that was created before FAT32 existed *will destroy* the data on a FAT32 drive—you must only use FAT32-aware utilities on FAT32 volumes.

Learning About File Formats

Files store your data, but not every file stores just what you think it does. In this section I am going to explain some of the variety of file formats and suggest some ways you might explore them on your own.

ASCII Text Files

The simplest files contain almost exactly what you might expect them to. These are what we call *pure ASCII text files*. Examples include your PC's startup files, CONFIG.SYS, AUTOEXEC.BAT (both found in the root directory of your boot disk), and if you have Windows 3.*x*, WIN.INI and SYSTEM.INI (both in your Windows directory). If you have Windows 95 or 98, you might have these files, or you might not. But you certainly have one called MSDOS.SYS (in the root directory of the boot disk) that is also a pure ASCII text file. (DOS and Windows 3.*x* users will also have a file called MSDOS.SYS, but it is a hidden, system file and it is most certainly *not* a pure ASCII text file.)

Other ASCII text files are the various INI files used by many Windows (and some other) programs to store their initialization data. The distinguishing mark of these files is that, in addition to being pure ASCII files, they have a structure very much like that of WIN.INI and SYSTEM.INI. They are composed of blocks of text with each block beginning with a title enclosed in square brackets.

You can see what is in a pure ASCII text file by using the DOS command TYPE. For example, this command will display the contents of your CONFIG.SYS file (if you have one):

```
TYPE C:\CONFIG.SYS
```

If your CONFIG.SYS file is large, the first lines may scroll off the screen. To prevent that, you can add a pipe command and the DOS command MORE. Now the command line will read like this, which will show you the contents of that file one screenful at a time:

```
TYPE C:\CONFIG.SYS ¦ MORE
```

You can apply this technique to any pure ASCII text file and you will find the screen image easy to read. (It may be a bit harder to understand, but that is another story altogether.)

Although this strategy for viewing an ASCII text file works, it's not as easy as using a program built specially for the purpose. In the next section I will discuss the LIST program, which is my personal favorite tool for this use.

Displaying ASCII text files works so well because they contain almost nothing but simple, displayable text characters taken from the ASCII character set. (If you don't recall just what an ASCII character is, refer to Chapter 3.)

Although these files contain almost only ASCII displayable text characters, there are some exceptions to that rule. They almost always include some special control characters to indicate the end of a line of text. In text files prepared for PCs, that usually means the lines are terminated by a pair of control characters, one to say "move back to the left margin" and one to say "move down a line." These are termed the *carriage return* (CR) and *line feed* (LF) control characters and they have the ASCII values of 13 and 10, respectively (which are Dh and Ah, in case you are looking inside the file with a snooping tool that displays the contents in hexadecimal).

Many text files also contain tab characters that have an ASCII value of 9. They stand for a variable number of space characters—whatever is needed to move the next character in the file to a column just past the next "tab stop." Not all programs that use ASCII text files will interpret these tab characters in the same way. The DOS TYPE command and many programming languages, for example, assume that the tab stops should be at multiples of eight columns. Many word processors assume a default spacing of five characters, and most of them also let you set the tabs wherever you want.

One other control character that is often used in text files is the *end-of-page character*. Another name for this is *form feed* (meaning that it signals a printer when to eject a page and start a new one), from which it carries the abbreviation FF. Its ASCII value is 12 (Ch). The TYPE command ignores this character.

It used to be universal that all text files would end with a special end of file character. That is the Ctrl+Z (Control+Z) character, which has the ASCII value of 26 (1Ah). Before DOS, in CP/M machines there was no other way to know where the end of a file was. Now that the DOS directory entry keeps track of the file length to the byte, it isn't necessary to include a Ctrl+Z character. But if that character is present, the DOS TYPE command will assume that it is an end-of-file mark and stop processing a file there.

ASCII text files also vary in how they represent paragraphs. Some will put all of a paragraph on a single line, and then put a single pair of CR and LF control characters after it to indicate the beginning of the next paragraph. Others will use a CR-LF pair to signal the end of a line within a paragraph and a pair of CR-LF pairs to signal a new paragraph. Still others may use tabs to indent paragraphs or lines. All of these still qualify for the name pure ASCII text files, but they also may go by names such as MS-DOS text, DOS text with layout, or some other variation.

Non-ASCII (Binary) Files

In the universe of files on PCs, ASCII text files are a very small minority. All the rest are called *binary files*. They contain at least some non-ASCII characters (which is to say, they have bytes of data whose most significant bit is set to one, and thus they represent an extended ASCII character) or they contain some control characters other than the simple CR, LF, TAB, and FF. You could use the DOS TYPE command on them, but if you do the results may startle you. Quite literally.

Your computer may display some of what you expect, plus a lot of other strange characters. Also, it might beep at you many times. And, it might stop displaying information before it reaches the end of the file.

If a binary file contains only ASCII characters and extended ASCII characters (and the usual control characters CR, LF, TAB and perhaps FF), it is possible to display their contents with the TYPE command. But what you will see might not be what you would expect. The reason is that there are many different definitions for the extended ASCII characters. If the file was prepared using one definition and if the TYPE command uses another, then you might be surprised by what shows up on the screen.

The cause of the beeps, huge blank areas, and perhaps a sudden termination of the output is likely to be the presence of some other control characters. The Bell code (ASCII value 7) will cause your PC to beep. The Vertical Tab character (VT) with ASCII value 11 (Bh) may jump the cursor vertically on the screen. And, if the TYPE command encounters a Ctrl+Z (EOF) character (ASCII value 26, or 1Ah) it will stop right there.

All those things are perfectly normal. They just mean that the TYPE command is not the optimal way to look at the contents of those files.

Sometimes you will know something about how the file got created. For example, if it is a Word for Windows document file it most likely will have an extension of .DOC. The best tool to use to look at this or any other word processing document file is the word processor that created it. Spreadsheet files are best looked at in the spreadsheet program that created them, and so on.

Peter's Principle: File Snooping

What if you don't know what program created the file, or don't have that program? Is there a universal file snooping tool you might use? My favorite such program is Vern Buerg's fine LIST program. It began as a simple shareware file viewing program. It now has grown up into a full-fledged file viewing and management program with two versions called LIST Plus and LIST Enhanced. You can learn more about it (and about Vern Buerg) at his Web site:

http://www.buerg.com/software.html

You also can download a copy of LIST from his Web site. Like all shareware, you are supposed to pay a registration fee for it if you find it useful. Please do.

Why Binary Files Are Different

Binary files are not like ASCII files for the simple reason that they hold something other than just text. Even the word processing files, for which text is the main point, also hold other things.

Word Processing Files

Why aren't word processing document files just what I typed into the document? A word processing document file must contain not only the textual content, but also the formatting information. And, many modern word processors go further by including pictures, drawings, outline headings, and summary information.

Database and Spreadsheet Files

Database files must keep information in records. That can be done in any of several ways. Some special ASCII control characters seem to have been designed for just this purpose. They bear names such as record separator and group separator. But the fact is, most PC database programs don't use them. Some database programs format the records into fixed-length blocks. Others separate the records with special characters—just not the ones the ASCII code says they should.

Spreadsheet files are simply special-purpose database files. Their records are displayed differently, but the essential file storage ideas are very similar. Of course, the format particulars vary with the particular spreadsheet program you use. (One reason so many programs use their own file formats is to try to inhibit competitors from decoding their file formats and thus be able to use those data files with a competing product.)

If you have a database file you want to snoop inside, use LIST (or DEBUG, or whatever tool you choose) and look for things you recognize. If you find blocks of recognizable text items separated by regions of garbage, and if the distance from one recognizable block to the next is constant, then most likely you are looking at a fixed-length record database (or spreadsheet) file. The apparent garbage is actually numbers stored as binary values rather than as the ASCII representation of the numerals.

Program Files

Another important type of binary file you will encounter are program files. These contain instructions to the PC in the language it understands: machine language instructions. So, of course it is not readily readable by humans. One easy thing to look for is the first couple of characters. If they are MZ, then this is likely to be an MS-DOS EXE file, which is to say either a DOS program or a Windows program. (If you see a message a short distance into the file that reads either This program requires Microsoft Windows or This program cannot be run in DOS mode then you are looking at a Windows executable program.)

Some of these program files have the extension .EXE. Others are .DLL files or .OVR files or some other extension. But all of them are programs. (Files with extension .COM are a simpler kind of program file. They don't have the MZ signature at the start, and they are supposed to be no larger than 64KB. They are, in fact, simply images of the bytes that are deposited into the RAM when you run them. EXE files, on the other hand, have a "relocation header" at the beginning that specifies what parts of their content go where in memory when they are loaded.)

Other Binary Files

There are still other kinds of files that are essentially binary. These include image files, sound files, and more.

Warning: The essential thing to know about all these binary files is that their precise content matters. You must not alter even one byte or they may become unusable. (This is in sharp contrast to a pure ASCII text file, for which in most cases a minor alteration is no big deal.)

So feel free to snoop around your PC's disk drives, looking inside all manner of files, but to save yourself much grief, please use a tool that won't alter their contents.

Summary

In this chapter, we've begun an extensive exploration of how your PC meets the task of reliably storing and retrieving the millions of bytes of data that you require of it. I hope you've begun to understand the various structures that make this possible, along with their strengths and limitations, and how those impact your own productivity. In the next chapter, we'll step back to move forward—applying the knowledge of the disk's data area that you've learned here to the disk's vital system areas. Then we'll go on to examine some of the newest technologies that are making hard disks both more efficient and more reliable. Finally, we'll take a good look at the other hardware—CD-ROMs, tape drives, and so on—that have been devised to meet your storage needs.

10

Digging Deeper Into Disks

Peter Norton®

Up to this point almost everything that I have told you about disks applies to every kind of disk that your PC can use, from the oldest floppies to new EIDE and SCSI drives, and even to most CD-ROM drives. Now I will discuss what makes hard disks different. I also will cover the ways in which the other kinds of disk-like objects we use with our PCs are different from floppy and hard disks.

How Hard Disks Are Different

In the preceding chapter, I told you about the physical differences between floppy disks and hard disks. I pointed out that hard disks have rigid platters and use feedback servomechanisms to position the read-write heads, which enables you to store data much more densely on them. I also pointed out that although floppy disks protect data with a cyclical redundancy check (CRC) value, hard disks go an extra step and use error correction codes (ECC), allowing them to not only detect errors but also usually to correct those errors on-the-fly.

Now I'll cover the logical differences between floppy diskettes and hard disks as they are seen by the motherboard BIOS and DOS. All other disk-like devices are made to look either like floppies or like hard disks in these respects, so understanding these differences is quite important.

Master Boot Record and Partitions

The most important difference between a floppy diskette and a hard disk, from the perspective of the motherboard BIOS, is that the BIOS assumes all floppy diskettes contain a single logical disk volume or partition, but that all hard disks are partitioned into four parts, some of which are primary logical volumes, hidden, or extended partitions with multiple logical volumes.

It is quite possible for a partition to have zero size, but the BIOS assumes they are all defined, and it looks first for those definitions before it can begin to use any of the volumes. The way this is implemented is quite simple. The first sector on any hard disk contains a simple program and data file in a standard format. This program and data file together are called the master boot record (MBR).

Figure 10.1 shows Norton Disk Editor's default view of an MBR. In this case, you see that only two of the four partitions have any size, but all four lines in the data table are present nonetheless.

On this particular disk the primary partition (C:) holds 1.3GB and the extended partition holds about three quarters of a gigabyte in a single logical disk drive (D:)—this information is in the last column. The first column of this data table shows what kind of partition each one is. The name BIGDOS means a primary DOS partition that is larger than 32MB, which was the maximum size DOS could handle. The name EXTEND means a DOS-extended partition.

The second column shows that only one of the four partitions is flagged as bootable. (A synonym for bootable in this context is *active*.) This is the partition in which the PC BIOS will look for a boot sector and operating system files to boot your PC. If you could mark more than one of the four partitions as active, the BIOS wouldn't know which one to use. If you don't mark any of them as active, it won't attempt to boot the PC from this hard disk. Most PC BIOSes can only boot from the first hard disk—the one that gets the drive letter C:—or from a floppy or, in some cases, from a CD-ROM. A major exception to this is PCs that use only SCSI hard disks. In that case, a special BIOS on the SCSI host adapter can be enabled which allows the PC to boot from one of the SCSI devices. However, a PC that contains both IDE and SCSI drives can only boot from an IDE device or floppy—the PC's internal BIOS won't give up control to the SCSI BIOS if it sees that any IDE hard drive is available. If none of the IDE drives is bootable and no system floppy diskette is present, the PC will not boot at all.

Figure 10.1.
A typical partition table for a moderately large hard drive, as shown by Norton Disk Editor.

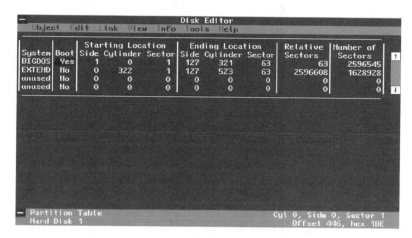

Only primary partitions can be bootable under DOS or Windows, and DOS can understand only one primary partition. You can create other primary partitions to use with other operating systems. A DOS primary partition also can contain only a single logical disk volume. DOS can understand exactly one additional partition, of the type DOS-Extended. That partition can contain any number of logical disk volumes—limited only by the number of letters in the alphabet. Figure 10.2 illustrates this and shows how a hypothetical hard disk might be divided into three partitions. The third partition shown is a UNIX partition which cannot be seen by DOS at all. If it is marked as bootable, the DOS partitions will disappear, and the PC will boot into UNIX.) Some operating systems can see—and use—DOS partitions. OS/2, Windows NT, and Linux each has its own native file system, but each has also been designed to work with DOS, too.

Figure 10.2 also shows two special cylinders after the end of the data area. Not every hard drive will have these. They are created by certain types of disk controllers. The diagnostic cylinder is used, as its name suggests, for disk diagnostics. The other cylinder, if it exists, is used by the disk controller to store information for its own internal use.

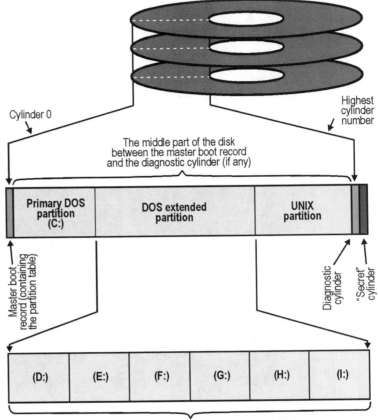

Figure 10.2.
A hypothetical hard drive partitioning for multiple DOS drives, plus a UNIX partition.

DOS-Extended Partitions Tables

I said that you could divide a DOS-extended partition into multiple logical disk drives. How is this done? Simply extend the notion of partitioning. The first sector in a DOS-extended partition is a special sector called an extended partition table. This is similar to the MBR with some significant differences. For example, there is no boot program in an extended partition table.

Managing Multiple PC Disk Drives

Modern PCs can support multiple disk drives or disk-like devices. How that is done is the subject of this section. I won't explain here the intricacies of all the different kinds of disk attachments, but I will tell you how DOS will handle each one.

How Disk Drives Attach to PCs

Modern PC motherboards have several special connectors for attaching disk drives. They also can have one or more option cards plugged into the I/O bus with additional connectors for some other kinds of disk drives.

Floppy Diskette Drives

Floppy diskette drives attach to the motherboard via a 34-wire ribbon cable. You can attach zero, one, or two floppy diskette drives and how you physically connect each determines whether a drive becomes A: or B:. The ribbon cable has two connectors, and a floppy diskette drive hooked up to the middle connector becomes B:, while the one at the end of the cable is always A:.

IDE Devices

Integrated device electronics (IDE) devices are connected to the PC motherboard via another special connector, or they can be connected to an option card plugged into the PC's I/O bus. The latest version of the IDE specification allows for four IDE channels, each one capable of supporting two IDE devices.

Most modern PCs have one or more IDE or EIDE internal hard drives, and a jumper on each drive's circuit board determines whether the drive functions as a master or as a slave. The first hard drive on each of the IDE channels is always that channel's master. The newest plug-and-play BIOSes enable the jumper to specify a "cable select" mode, which enables the BIOS to command the drive to be either a master or a slave, whichever is needed to avoid conflicts with other devices in the system. It is important that only one device acts as master and one as slave on each IDE channel, so you must pay careful attention to the settings of these jumpers.

The cable that connects hard drives to the motherboard is similar to, but wider than, the floppy drive cable. It has three connectors (two for drives, one for the motherboard), and most are keyed to prevent plugging it in backward. If no key-tab is present, one of the wires of the cable will be marked with a color—usually red. On the motherboard and the drives, one end of the connection socket will be marked 1 (or 2); the red side of the cable always connects closest to the 1- or 2-marked side of the socket. Unlike floppies, however, each hard drive's jumper settings identify it and it doesn't matter whether a drive is plugged into the end or middle of the cable.

An IDE CD-ROM drive also has IDE select jumpers. It may also have a 4-pin audio cable connector to carry the analog signal from an audio CD to the sound card in the PC.

In some PCs the primary and secondary IDE channels are nearly equivalent. You may put any device you want on either cable, paying attention to have only one master and one slave on each one. The exception to this, generally, is that the drive from which you want to boot must almost always be on the primary IDE channel.

In other PCs, the two IDE channels have very different properties. The primary one is set up as a fast EIDE channel; the secondary one is merely an older-style IDE channel. If yours is like this, you must put the hard drives on the primary chain and the CD-ROM drive or other slow devices on the secondary channel.

Even if your PC treats each IDE channel nearly the same, it might do so in a manner that still will force you to put the fast devices on one IDE cable and the slower ones on the other cable. This is because some PCs, while able to run either IDE cable at high speed, can do so only for messages meant for one of the two devices on that cable. If your PC can't make that distinction, it will have to slow down all messages to the speed that is acceptable to the slower of the two devices attached to the cable. This could make your hard drive crawl instead of fly if it shares an IDE channel of this type with a (much slower) CD-ROM drive.

SCSI Devices

The other popular way to attach a disk drive to a PC is via a SCSI interface. You can find all the details on this interface in Chapter 15, "Understanding Standard PC Input and Output," but here I want to show you a few essentials about how this interface connects disk drives and PCs.

SCSI devices have all their controller electronics on board the device itself. In addition, they have special hardware that can operate over a SCSI bus with a SCSI host adapter. Macintosh computers have a SCSI host adapter built into them. A few PCs have SCSI host adapters built into their motherboards, but a much more common strategy is to put that optional circuitry on a plug-in card. Because the SCSI host adapter may potentially be transferring data rapidly to or from a hard drive, you should plug it in to a fast input/output bus. Currently, the most popular choice is the PCI bus.

The PCI SCSI host adapter card has a connector on the rear panel for external SCSI devices and two connectors on the upper edge of the card for internal SCSI devices. Only one of the two internal connectors may be used at a time, however. They are both provided to allow connecting to either Wide or Ultra-Wide SCSI devices. (The rear-panel connector follows the Ultra-Wide standard, but a suitable cable can adapt that connection down to the narrower SCSI standards.)

A SCSI host adapter can communicate simultaneously with up to seven SCSI 1 devices, or up to 15 Wide- or Ultra-Wide devices. Each device must be assigned a unique SCSI identification number between 0 and 7 or 15. Traditionally the highest ID number is reserved for the host adapter. All the rest are up for grabs by the attached devices.

Making Sense Out of Chaos

Now you know how to physically connect lots of disk drives to a PC, but how are these all managed? What happens to the drive letters? Can you boot from any of those disk drives? These are serious questions with nonobvious answers. Fortunately, they are not difficult to answer.

How DOS Assigns Drive Letters

Floppy disk drives normally show up as drives A: and B:. This is unalterable in most PCs. Hard disks and other disk drives get drive letters beginning with C:. DOS will assign C: to the first hard disk it finds. As I mentioned above, because it looks first at the primary IDE channel for a master device, that is where you should put your main internal IDE or EIDE hard disk.

DOS will assign D: to the primary DOS partition of the next physical hard disk, if it finds more than one. This includes both other hard drives on the IDE chains and SCSI hard disks. DOS keeps this up for as many physical hard disks as it can find. DOS then assigns the next drive letter to the first logical drive inside any DOS-extended partition on the first hard drive. The next letters go to any other logical disk drives in that same partition. Then DOS goes through the logical disk drives inside the DOS-extended partition on the second hard disk, then on to the third hard disk, and so on.

Only after it has assigned drive letters to all the hard disk volumes it can find will DOS assign a drive letter to any other disk-like devices. These include super-floppy drives that attach via the IDE chains, CD-ROM drives, and so on. Drives with compressed data (using DriveSpace or some equivalent product) get drive letters assigned in a special fashion. I'll cover those rules later in this chapter in the section called "Data Compression."

Overriding certain rules is sometimes possible, but most of the time you will find that this is the necessary order for the drive letters in your system. One consequence is that you must be careful about introducing removable media drives that would appear alphabetically earlier than any nonremovable drives.

Windows 95 users can move some drives around rather easily, although some of the DOS rules I mentioned above cannot be. To make a CD-ROM drive be O: (for optical disc), for example, rather than, say, E:, you simply must go into Control Panel | System | Device Manager, and select the drive in question. Then go to the Properties display | Settings tab. You will find that it displays the current drive letter assigned to this drive and offers you two windows in which you can set the lowest and highest letters you want it to have. Set them both to O:, click OK, and you are finished after you reboot your PC. (Remember, DOS and Windows assign all drive letters at startup. The only exception is with special hot-dockable drives.)

How Big Should My C: Drive Be?

Many people wonder how large to make their C: drive and whether to create additional logical disk drives on the first physical hard drive. Many PC vendors ship their products with just a single partition (that is C:) on the installed hard drive.

Keep several important considerations in mind when you are looking at this issue. None of them are simple decisions. You will have to make some judgment calls. This is okay because there are no really right or wrong answers.

First, having too many files and directories on one disk can make finding things much harder than necessary. If you partition your disk drives and put like files together in each partition or logical disk drive, they will have a level of organization one higher than the subdirectories off the root directory. You might think of this as putting file cabinets that contain material on different subjects or purposes into different rooms.

Next is a matter of cluster size and the resulting inefficiencies in use of the disk space. If you have a logical volume that holds more than 512MB, its cluster size must be at least 16KB. Go over 1GB and the cluster will double to 32KB. Every file uses some number of clusters. If most of your files are much smaller than a cluster, you will be wasting most of the space on your hard disk. (The best way to get around this is to convert all of your large drives to FAT32, which I discussed in the previous chapter.)

What about the option of making each volume very small and using a lot of volumes? This might be a good idea, but there are some drawbacks. First, remember that nearly every Windows application will put some data onto the drive that holds your Windows directory, even if you install the application to some other drive letter. Second, enlarging a logical volume once you realize you've made it too small can be tough. Be sure you allow enough room for growth in every volume, and especially in the one into which you install Windows. Additionally, you could easily end up running out of alphabet for your disk drives! DOS can only assign letters to a maximum of 26 drives, including the floppies that get A: and B:. (Adding even more pressure in this regard, if you want to map some network drives to local drive letters, you will have to reserve some portion of the alphabet for that use.)

What about the opposite extreme? Suppose your files are, on the average, pretty large, so you don't worry much about cluster size. Can you make a single volume as large as you like? DOS and Windows 95 OSR1 will not work well with any volume over 1 or 2GB. Windows 95 OSR2 and Windows 98 have no such limitations if you use FAT32. (Additionally, as I've said elsewhere, FAT32 uses much smaller clusters, so even very small files are stored with great efficiency.)

SMART Drives and RAID Are Other Good Ideas

Before leaving the topic of hard disks, I will mention two fairly recent developments that are technologies to watch for in your next PC. The first is the SMART hard drives. The second is RAID arrays.

SMART Hard Drives Tell You When to Fix Them

SMART is an acronym that stands for Self-Monitoring And Reporting Technology. Hard drive manufacturers are starting to ship more drives with this feature. These drives monitor their internal "health" and report on it to the PC's system BIOS. External utility programs, like Norton System Doctor, in the Norton Utilities can monitor the BIOS for SMART messages and advise you to act accordingly.

RAID Finally Makes Sense for Most of Us

Redundant Arrays of Inexpensive Disks (RAID) is an idea for enhancing the reliability of a PC by having it store data on more than one disk, in a fashion that lets you avoid or minimize downtime and the risk of data loss when one of those disks fails.

Five levels of RAID are formally defined. They range in complexity and in the degree of safety they offer. The highest level stores data and ECCs across several disks in a way that lets you replace any disk at any time with almost no chance of losing any of your data.

Some RAID implementations also allow you to exchange, or *hot swap*, disk drives or power supplies whenever they seem about to fail or have failed, all without shutting off your PC system. This is especially critical for large companies that are running their mission-critical applications on such a PC.

Formerly, RAID was used only on mainframe computers and large servers for networks because, despite the name, implementing RAID is more expensive than just buying a hard drive or set of hard drives with the same total capacity. But now, with hard drive prices plummeting, it might be time for you to consider adding RAID to your desktop PC.

Variations on the Theme of PC Storage

Until fairly recently, floppy diskette drives and hard disks were probably the only widely used data storage hardware for a PC. It doesn't appear likely that either floppies or hard disks will totally disappear from PCs any time soon, but a plethora of new products for PC storage have become quite popular. These products use many different technologies, some new, some new versions of old. I would like to give you a broad overview and enough depth on the most important of these products so that you can understand where each one fits into the picture. That understanding will be critical in guiding your future PC storage purchase decisions.

The Multiple Dimensions of PC Storage Technologies

All PC storage technologies can be classified in one of several dimensions: speed (performance), capacity, whether a device can write as well as read data, and the technology behind the technology (or, what makes it go). Keep these dimensions in mind as you read what follows. I will organize my presentation around the last dimension I named: the technologies behind the technologies. Thus, I will talk first about magnetic data storage devices (other than the hard disks and floppies that I have already discussed), followed by optical, magneto-optical, and electronic PC data storage devices, respectively.

Primary Versus Secondary Data Storage

Almost all of these devices are used most often for what we call secondary data storage—as opposed to primary data storage, usually represented by your PC's hard disk. When you use your PC, the program you run usually comes from your hard disk. The data comes from your hard disk, usually, and the data that is generated goes to your hard disk almost always. Thus, hard disks are our primary storage devices.

Secondary storage devices are the ones to which you copy data from the primary device (or from which you copy it onto the primary device). A floppy diskette is one of the most common secondary storage devices. A tape drive, ZIP drive, or most any other data storage device you can name is most often treated as a secondary storage device.

A CD-ROM is a good example of a PC storage device that is most often used as secondary storage, with some exceptions. You probably use CD-ROMs to install programs, but you may also use them to run those programs if you don't want to give up the hard disk space the program would require. You definitely use CD-ROMs as primary data storage when you use a CD-ROM reference disc (an encyclopedia, atlas, and so on).

Going the other way, some people actually use hard disks as secondary data storage. They'll remove a hard disk from one PC and carry it to another, or store one that is loaded with archival data in a closet. Such things are, or were, common for large companies; less so for individual users.

Alternative Magnetic PC Data Storage Devices

The same basic magnetic recording technology used in hard drives has also been used in several alternative PC data storage devices. The most common are tape drives. Others include removable hard disks, hard disk drives with interchangeable media, and various types of super-floppy diskette drives.

Figure 10.3 shows a number of different removable magnetic media used with PCs. In addition to the original 5 $\frac{1}{4}$-inch and 3 $\frac{1}{2}$-inch floppy diskettes, this figure shows the LS120 super-floppy, a 100MB ZIP disk, and a SyQuest 270MB cartridge.

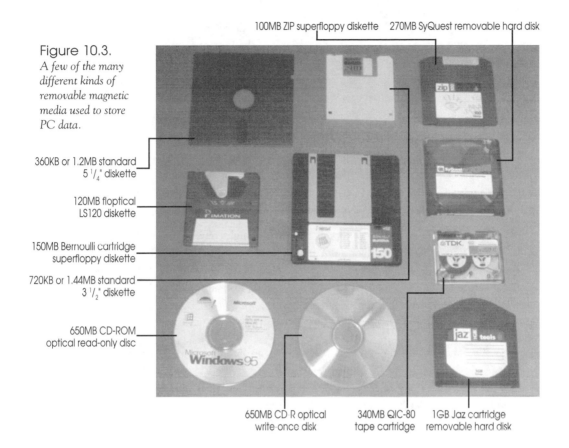

Figure 10.3.
A few of the many different kinds of removable magnetic media used to store PC data.

100MB ZIP superfloppy diskette   270MB SyQuest removable hard disk

360KB or 1.2MB standard
5 1/4" diskette

120MB floptical
LS120 diskette

150MB Bernoulli cartridge
superfloppy diskette

720KB or 1.44MB standard
3 1/2" diskette

650MB CD-ROM
optical read-only disc

650MB CD-R optical   340MB QIC-80   1GB Jaz cartridge
write-once disk   tape cartridge   removable hard disk

Tape Drives

The one magnetic storage device, besides floppy and hard disks, that has been used for PCs from the beginning—actually, from before the beginning—is the magnetic tape drive. One option for the earliest PCs was to hook up an audio cassette tape drive and use it to store data. Audio cassette recorders were designed to record audible sound—analog signals. In order to make it suitable for digital data recording, the data must be encoded as tones. (This is what is done by a modem to encode data for transmission over the voice telephone network, for the very same reason.) This worked, but not well. It was slow beyond belief, and not much data would fit on a standard audio cassette.

Soon those tape drives were supplanted by special-purpose drives meant just for digital data recording, which worked much better. They use another form of data encoding, storing the information as magnetized regions on the tape, and reading that information back as the tape passes over the read head. These drives have gone through many generations of improvements, with special Digital Audio Tape (DAT) drives representing the present state of the art.

One thing is constant here. All the different types of tape drive are sequential access devices. That simply means that to read something from a tape, all of the tape must pass the read head from the beginning of the reel or cassette to wherever the data is that you want to read. When you want to write to a tape, you must again scroll past all the previously recorded information before you can start recording more (unless, of course, you want to tape over the previously recorded information with the new data).

Because tape drives are sequential devices, they are best suited for situations in which you want to read or write a great deal of information at once, but won't need to retrieve it repeatedly or instantly. Backing up your hard drive's data is a perfect example. If the tape controller, tape drive, and PC are all matched properly, data can flow continuously, or "stream," off the hard drive and onto the tape without ever having to stop the tape movement until the entire task is complete.

If, however, the whole system isn't properly tuned, you might have to move the tape a short distance, then stop it while you wait for more data to be prepared for writing. To keep from having a gap on the tape, you might even have to back up the tape and let it take a running start before resuming recording where you left off. Such a lack of streaming performance can turn an otherwise relatively speedy tape drive into a real sluggard.

Generally, tape is the cheapest form of data storage available for your PC, but it also is the slowest. Unfortunately, it is not always as reliable as you might wish. Every good tape system comes with software that includes an option to verify the tape. Whatever that option does, it doesn't catch all the mistakes the tape drives make. So my personal recommendation to you is this: If you use tape as a critical backup medium, please verify your backups on your own, by restoring a sample backup set to a different drive letter and checking that every file made that round trip (hard disk to tape and back to hard disk) flawlessly. Then repeat this test occasionally on at least a random sampling of your backed up files.

Because their operating characteristics are so different, the software that operated tape drives initially was totally different from that used for disk drives. More recently, some manufacturers have created device drivers (the software that handles talking to the tape drive) for their products that make them emulate a disk drive. If you use one of these products, you might think you are performing random access to some DOS logical drive that acts just like all the others in your PC—except that it will be horribly slow.

Removable Hard Disks

At the opposite extreme, in terms of speed and cost, from a tape drive is a removable hard disk. You could, of course, use any ordinary IDE or SCSI hard disk, and (after turning off your PC) remove it and take it to another PC or store it away as archival storage. It is much more convenient, however, to add a docking bay to your PC. This is simply a box that goes into a space in a PC that is meant for a floppy diskette drive, with an opening in the front into which you may plug suitably designed swappable drives. The docking bay connects internally to the PC's power supply and also to either an IDE channel or a SCSI host adapter.

With this type of device, you can swap drives in the bay while the PC is turned on although you might have to reboot the PC before it will recognize what you have done. A PC with full plug-and-play support, on the other hand, may be able to see that the device has been swapped and immediately recognize the new device and use it properly.

Aside from the mechanics of the docking bay, these devices are just like a normal hard disk you might install inside your PC or via an external SCSI cable.

An alternative approach is to make a hard drive subsystem that can be attached to a PC's parallel port. This works, but it has an inherently lower performance than a drive that is attached directly to the PC's I/O bus either via an IDE channel or a SCSI host adapter.

Hard Disks with Interchangeable Media

You can gain most of the benefits of a removable hard disk at much lower cost by using a special kind of hard drive that can accept interchangeable platters. It isn't easy to make this approach work well—primarily because even tiny dust particles can foul up a hard drive, and keeping a removable cartridge clean is hard—but with good design, it can be done. SyQuest has been the leader in this approach, but now Iomega and others offer this type of drive and cartridge also. The SyQuest SyJet 1.5GB and EZFlyer 230MB system are two examples. The Iomega Jaz (1GB and 2GB) drive is another. Figure 10.3 shows several removable media.

These devices are most commonly attached to your PC via a SCSI bus, and they provide a performance level (rate of data transfer and speed of initial access to randomly chosen data) that approaches or equals that of a good internal hard drive, while offering the potential for unlimited amounts of storage. The capacity per cartridge varies currently from around 100MB up to over 2GB.

Super-Floppy Diskette Drives

The super-floppy diskette category can cover several different technologies. All of them differ from the simpler technologies used in standard floppy diskette drives. Ordinary floppy diskette drives position the head using a stepper motor. Any system that aspires to store a much greater amount of data cannot afford to do this because the stepper-motor cannot be made to support the necessarily higher data density. Thus, all super-floppies use the same type of advanced head positioning mechanism as is used in hard drives.

Another difference is in how the head is positioned relative to the surface of the medium. A normal floppy diskette drive presses its two heads against one another, with the floppy disc in between. This means that these drives are actually dragging the heads across the surfaces of the disc. To keep wear to an acceptably low level, the drives cannot turn the disc quickly. Again, to get high capacity and higher performance out of a super-floppy, these issues must be addressed.

Iomega's Bernoulli Drives

An early solution was that used by Iomega in its line of Bernoulli disks. These used special cartridges with two discs mounted a short distance from one another on a single shaft inside. They recorded data on only one side of each disc. The two heads were positioned on the outside of the disc sandwich.

But the discs don't actually touch the heads because of a physical phenomenon called the *Bernoulli effect*, after the Italian scientist who discovered it. It causes the discs to fly a short and nearly constant distance off the surface of the heads, held in place by the pressure of the air that is entrained by the discs as they turn. This technology stored up to 230MB per cartridge.

ZIP Drives

Iomega brought this technology down in size to something just a bit larger than the now-standard 3 $1/_2$-inch floppy diskette. This new standard is their ZIP drive and its new ZipPlus successor. This has proven to be a hugely successful product line, with over 10 million sold in under two years. It comes in both internal and external SCSI interface models for both PCs and Macs, and in an external model that attaches to any PC's parallel port. When a device driver program (called GUEST.EXE) is run on that PC (or under Windows 95 and 98, which both natively support ZIP drives), the drive will appear as an additional DOS logical drive. This is a great way to carry relatively large amounts of data from PC to PC when a LAN is not available.

The performance of a ZIP drive over a parallel port is not very high. Over a SCSI port, however, it approaches the performance of a moderately slow internal hard drive. The new SCSI-based ZipPlus drives, according to Iomega, have an accelerated performance of up to 50 times that of a standard floppy disk under Windows 95.

PC Card Hard Disks, Magnetic Stripe Cards, and Other Similar Devices

There is a constant push from consumers for smaller devices for their PCs. In part, this trend is driven by the increasing power of portable PCs and folks' natural reluctance to lug along lots of heavy add-on gadgets for what is getting to be a rather light and compact computer.

The removable magnetic data storage industry continues to create more and better gadgets to serve this market. In addition to creating adapters that let PCs read magnetic stripe credit cards, there are devices that read special-purpose cards. These cards have magnetic stripes that hold more data than a normal credit card.

The memory suppliers to both the PC and the game machine world created a standard some years ago for small cards to carry add-on RAM. This was first called the PCMCIA card (for PC Memory Card International Association, the name of the trade group that published the standard). Now we call these PC Cards. They come in one size, but three thicknesses, and are called Type I, Type II, and Type III, depending on how thick they are. Type III PC Cards are thick enough that some clever manufacturers managed to fit tiny hard drives inside them—a good trick, but not one that has proven terribly popular. So it became another technically interesting product that failed to meet market requirements, and is now just a historical footnote.

That doesn't mean that there are no magnetic data storage options for miniature computers. For example, Iomega is preparing to introduce a super-small storage device they call *clik!*, which is just slightly larger than a mounted 35mm slide (about 2×3×$^1/_2$ inches). Each of these minidisks will hold 40MB of data. At first, its primary market will be for digital cameras, personal digital assistants (PDAs), and the like, but, if they catch on, we surely will find them being used in PCs as well. At the least, adapters will let you transfer data to and from your PC.

Other miniature magnetic recording options include magnetic strip cards. These are similar to credit cards, but they can have a larger data storage capacity, achieved by using more of the card's area for recording data. At this point, these are hardly mainstream products, but they do exist, and if you really want a small, rugged, yet magnetic data storage device, this is one candidate.

All these devices are proprietary. None are interchangeable with their competitors, but those that manage to achieve sufficient market penetration (such as the ZIP drive) become new standards. Will the *clik!* device manage this? Only time will tell.

Optical PC Data Storage Devices

The most common optical PC data storage device is the CD-ROM (Compact Disc, Read-Only Memory). As the name suggests, this is a form of read-only storage. That is, a CD-ROM comes from the factory with its content already in place; you cannot alter that content later.

To explain how CD-ROM drives work, and also to explain the many alternatives to them now on the market, I must first start the story where it actually began, with music CDs.

Music CDs Set the Standard

In the old days, when someone made a new audio recording, the electrical signal from a microphone was used to vibrate a needle while it dug a spiral groove into a master vinyl record. Next, this master record was duplicated in two steps. The first step is to cast a mold of the master. The next step is to stamp out huge numbers of identical copies of the master using this mold.

CDs Are Made Almost the Way Vinyl Records Were

The process for making music CDs shares much in common with their predecessors, the vinyl records, with one tremendous difference. The master discs for music CDs are made in a different way.

The first step in making a music CD is to convert the analog signals from the microphone (or from synthesizers and other sources) that represent the audio information to be recorded into a string of numbers. This analog-to-digital conversion step captures the music into a form that can be reproduced over and over again without any alteration (which is very much unlike analog music recordings on tape or vinyl records).

The binary digital data is recorded on the master disc in a manner I will describe in a moment. From this master, molds are made and multiple copies stamped out much in the manner in which vinyl records are made. The differences are these: Only one side of a CD is available for use, while the opposite side is silk-screen with the disc's identifying label. Additionally, the binary data is read optically, instead of mechanically (by passing the data under a beam of light instead of dragging a needle across it), and the data bits are stored more densely on the CD's surface than the wiggles in the grooves of a vinyl record.

Because of the second difference, the surface of the CD that has the data impressed into it is coated with a mirror-like metal film (aluminum or gold). That surface is then protected by an overcoating of clear plastic. Because of the third difference, that mirror-like surface is broken up with tiny spots that might appear to be imperfections but are actually the data, arranged in a spiral, and this spiral has its turns so closely wound that the resulting disc acts like a diffraction grating, breaking white light into a rainbow.

How CDs Store Digital Information

The way in which music CDs store information digitally is both simple and stunningly clever. It uses the fact that lasers produce highly directional light beams of a single, pure wavelength. You can focus such a beam onto a small spot. If that spot has a mirror-like surface, the beam will bounce back essentially unchanged. If, however, that spot has a pit of exactly—or almost exactly—the right size and depth in the mirror, the light bouncing from the bottom of the pit will be out of phase with the light bouncing off the surface around the pit. These two out-of-phase components will interfere with each other, and the resulting reflected beam of light will be noticeably different from the original.

Manufacturers have developed a way to use a moderately high-powered laser to burn these pits in a spiral on the master disc. Your CD player has a (relatively low-powered) diode laser that tracks this spiral as the disc turns, shining a tiny spot of infrared light on the spiral to detect the data stored there. It then converts the digital information it reads into analog signals that can drive your headphones or be routed to your stereo system.

The pits serve two purposes in this scheme. First, of course, they encode the digital data. Second, their presence signals where the spiral track goes. The read head follows the pits like a trail of bread crumbs and reads the data encoded in the exact placement of those pits.

Technical Note: In the previous chapter, I mentioned that in magnetic data storage it is necessary to encode the digital zeros and ones into patterns of zeros and ones to be able to read them back reliably. The same thing is true for optical digital data storage, for essentially the same reasons.

CD-ROMs Aren't So Different; CD-ROM Drives Are

The data CD-ROM emerged when someone realized that if an audio CD player didn't convert the information it read from digital to analog form, this could be a wonderful way to store huge amounts of digital information.

Data CD-ROMs are made in the same way as music CDs. That is, they are stamped out as exact copies of a master disc (subsequently coated with metal and then protected with a plastic overcoat), and they contain purely digital information. The only difference is that the CD-ROM drives don't convert that information to another form; it remains digital. These drives simply present the data they read to your computer and let it decide what to do from there. (CD-ROM drives can also play music CDs and for that purpose they have the digital-to-analog conversion circuits built in.)

Partly because of the demands of the huge music industry for music CD players, manufacturers have learned how to make CD-ROM drives inexpensively. (This same technology is also used as a part of the new super-floppy drive technology known as a floptical drive. I'll tell you more about that later in the section, "The Floptical: A New Kind of MO Drive.")

Key to this success is the fact that all CDs (including CD-ROMs and the CD-R and CD-RW disc I will describe next) and their drives are built to a set of exacting specifications. These standards (variously called Red, Orange, Yellow, Green, White, and Blue Book) guarantee that these different styles of discs share many properties in common. This allows for the sharing of designs and even some parts among the different kinds of CD drive.

Having a CD-ROM drive, or more than one, is a great boon to the PC user, and an even bigger boon for software companies. With a maximum storage capacity of around 650MB per CD, it is possible to provide huge amounts of data and some large programs on a single disc. This disc can be used directly at modest access speeds, or the PC user can load those programs (and perhaps some or all of the data) onto their PC's hard drive for even quicker subsequent accesses.

However, there is still one major limitation to CD-ROMs: They can't be used to store data, only to read data that was stored on them by the manufacturer.

Recordable CDs (CD-R) Are Really Different

Naturally, so inviting a prospect as a CD to which you could write was a challenge to inventors. After some missteps, the inventors have come through. The resulting device is now called a

Compact Disc, Recordable (or CD-R for short). Expensive at first, at the time of this writing these blank disks cost only about $2.99 for 670MB of storage. Incomparable!

A CD-R disc looks largely like a CD. While pressed CDs are silver, CD-R discs are usually gold on their label side and a deep green on their recordable side. They act like a CD-ROM (in that you can read the contents of a CD-R in any normal CD-ROM drive). Put one in a special CD-R drive, however, and you can also write to it.

This trick is achieved by making both the CD-R disc (blank) and the CD-R drives a little more complicated than their ancestors. The CD-R disc has four layers instead of three for a CD (see Figure 10.4). The CD-R drive's laser operates at three or more power levels. At the lowest level, the laser light suffices to detect the presence or absence of pits or marks on the recording surface—to read the disc. At the higher level, it can actually burn marks into that surface.

Figure 10.4.
A CD-R disc has one, special extra layer and a slightly wobbly spiral pregroove.

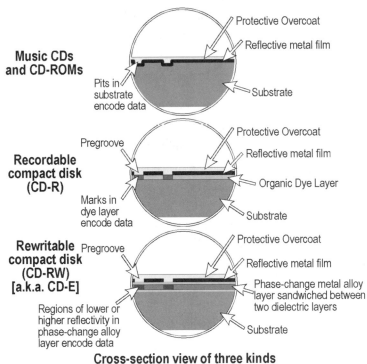

Cross-section view of three kinds
of compact optical disk (not to scale)

You might not have thought about it, but the machines used to make a master CD have one complexity that the corresponding players don't need. The recorders must be capable of creating—not merely tracking—the spiral pit pattern. They do this by having a carefully machined mechanism that moves the burning head out away from the center by a fixed amount each time the disc makes one revolution.

To keep from having to build that type of mechanical complexity into all CD-R drives, the designers of this new medium added a slightly wobbly spiral pregroove to the disks. The laser light that will be used to read or write information to this disc can sense this groove and follow it. The wobbly bit about that groove means that the light reflected from it will vary in time, giving the tracking mechanism an always changing signal to grab hold of and lock onto. This helps not only with following the pregroove, it also helps keep the disc turning at just the right speed. (Some disks have information modulated onto that pregroove signal to tell the drive about the optimal power level for recording, and so on.)

Technical Note: Until recently most CD drives turned their disks at a speed that varied depending on how far the portion of the spiral they are currently reading is from the center. The purpose is to keep the head moving over the surface at a constant linear velocity (CLV). This is in contrast to the way a hard disk turns at a constant angular velocity (CAV)—a pattern that is also referred to as a constant number of revolutions per minute (rpm).

The newest high-speed CD-ROM drives (above 12X) use a mix of CAV and CLV, but there are no new standards for doing this so far.

The main way this affects users today is that manufacturers are free to call a CD drive (of any variety) a 12X drive (for example, if at its peak speed it passes the head over the surface 12 times faster than is standard for music CDs). If the disc turns with CAV, that means its top linear velocity occurs only for the outermost turns of its spiral track. And because CDs record from the inside out, only a full CD will completely benefit from the advertised speed of the drive, and then only when reading from its outermost portion of the spiral track.

By the nature of the process used to record data on a CD-R, recordable discs are write-once objects. You can burn marks into the surface, but you cannot remove them later. This makes a CD-R best suited for archival storage of information. It is not a candidate for day-to-day temporary and reusable storage, like a floppy diskette. The fact is, however, that most floppies are recorded on once, most paper is written on just once, and there are many situations in which a CD-R is an almost ideal recording medium.

CD-RW Adds Erasability and Reusability

As nice as CD-R disks are, you can't reuse them. Folks turn out to value that property in a disk, so inventors and engineers toiled and came up with a more complex version of the CD. A CD-RW disc contains two more layers than a CD-R. What really matters is that the recordable layer is made of a special material, an alloy of several metals. As it comes from the factory, this layer is formed of some highly reflective crystals (refer to Figure 10.4).

Instead of burning marks into it with a high-power laser, a CD-RW drive uses its highest power to melt a small region of the recording layer. After it is melted, that material freezes into an amorphous form that doesn't reflect light nearly as well as its crystalline form. The laser's middle power level is used to warm the layer to something less than its melting point, but a high enough temperature to anneal those spots back from the amorphous to the highly reflective crystalline form.

This strategy allows the CD-RW media to be written to and erased many thousands of times. The erasing can happen as new data is written, unlike the earlier recordable optical disc technology we now call MO (magneto-optical). One downside to this technology is that the marks created on a CD-RW disc are not quite as good at light scattering as the marks on a CD-R disc or the pits on a CD or CD-ROM, so they are not readable in all CD drives. Only drives with automatic gain control circuitry can handle them correctly, and so far this feature is far from ubiquitous.

CD-RW is a brand-new technology. Its market acceptance, therefore, is still in doubt, but it seems to be a winner. Some heavy hitters are betting that consumers will choose to use lots of these new disks.

Digital Versatile Disc (DVD) Ups the Ante

Also in the wings waiting for its entrance is the next, much higher-capacity version of optical disks. This is the Digital Versatile Disc (DVD), which is essentially a pair of ultra-high density CDs back to back. A DVD can be used to store up to 4.7GB currently and close to 20GB in future versions.

A DVD disc is, like a CD or a CD-ROM, a read-only medium. It is a great way to distribute feature-length movies, complicated computer games, and huge computer databases. However, only information that can be put on the disc by a manufacturer and distributed in large quantities will show up on DVDs for the next few years. As of this writing, DVDs are enjoying great success in the consumer electronics market as the technology to replace pre-recorded videotapes. Indeed, DVD originally stood for Digital Video Disc. The stand-alone players sold for this purpose work consistently; this is not true of the first generation of DVD players designed for use with PCs. Indeed, in a recent magazine article, not one of the currently available PC-DVD drives was capable of successfully reading all of the 41 DVD discs that the testers randomly selected. Until better standards are defined and the technology perfected, PC-DVD remains a questionable investment.

DVD-R and DVD-RAM Are Technologies to Watch

We are promised that DVDs will be followed by recordable and erasable-rewritable versions to be called DVD-R and DVD-RAM, respectively. But they are not likely to hit the store shelves for another couple of years, if not longer.

One fly in the ointment regarding DVDs is that the specifications for them do not require full backward compatibility. In particular, all DVD drives will probably be able to play music CDs and normal data CD-ROMs, but they needn't necessarily be able to play CD-R and are even less likely to be able to play CD-RW disks. Those drives that do read CD-ROMs do so only at a slower speed than is today's state of the art. Keep this in mind when you decide whether to commit to CD-RW technology between now and whenever DVD-RAM arrives.

Magneto-Optical PC Data Storage Devices

In addition to devices that use either a purely magnetic or a purely optical technology for data storage are two quite different techniques that use a blend of the magnetic and optical phenomena. The oldest kind of MO disk uses both a laser light beam and a magnetic field to write information; just the laser beam is used to read it back. The newer kind uses a pure optical technology to position the head and a purely magnetic one to write and read data. I will follow the industry standard and call the older technology MO, and the latter, the floptical.

Basics of Magneto-Optical Data Storage

When I wrote about how hard disks work, I skipped over many of the more arcane details. You must understand one, in particular, in order to realize how MO recording is both almost the same and at the same time, different from all the other magnetic data recording technologies.

The detail you must understand is how the physical characteristics of the magnetic recording medium dictate the design of the recording device. Three properties of the magnetic recording medium are used in MO recording: two for recording and another one for reading back the recorded data.

MO Recording

All magnetic storage devices, and this includes MO, use as their medium a material that can be permanently magnetized in either of two directions. The material is never *not* magnetized at every place in the medium it merely is sometimes magnetized in one direction and sometimes in the opposite direction. There are several key properties of any such magnetizable medium. The most important one, for our purposes, is how easily you can switch the magnetization from one orientation to the other. The name for this property is the medium's *coercivity*.

If the material's coercivity is low, magnetizing it is easy. This helps when you are trying to design a tiny write head for a miniature disk drive. The small head can generate only a fairly modest level of magnetic field. However, a low value for coercivity also means that it is relatively easy for the magnetization of the medium to get reversed accidentally. If you have ever damaged data on a floppy diskette by inadvertently passing it near a magnet, you have seen a vivid demonstration that the coercivity of the magnetic material used in floppy diskettes (and, as it happens, also used in most hard disks) is not very high.

Magneto-optical disks, in contrast, use a medium whose coercivity is over 10 times higher. This means that after you record something on an MO disk, it is almost invulnerable to any passing stray magnetic field. That higher coercivity also means that MO disks require recording magnets that can generate fields that are over 10 times stronger than those used in other magnetic data storage devices. Those fields just can't practically be made in the tiny sizes needed to pack lots of data into a small space.

The solution to this dilemma is a clever one. It takes advantage of a second important physical characteristic of the magnetic recording medium. This time, the property to focus on is called the Curie temperature. All permanently magnetizable materials have a coercivity that falls as the temperature rises. In fact, after a critical temperature is reached (called, as you might now have guessed, the Curie temperature), the material stops being a permanent magnet. After you cool it off below that critical temperature, however, its permanent magnetic properties return.

So if you use a laser to heat the surface of an MO disk hot enough, you can easily set the orientation of its magnetization with a small magnetic write head. A blast of light from a focused laser of a suitable power quickly heats the magnetizable material in just one tiny spot almost to its Curie temperature. Simultaneously, the write head generates the field necessary to change the magnetization of this spot. Soon after, as the spot cools off, that new magnetization will be locked in place.

Reading Data from an MO Disk

Reading data back from an MO disk uses the third curious property of the magnetic recording medium: its capability to twist the polarization of light. A laser beam consists of light of a single wavelength, moving in a single direction. It can also be strongly polarized, which means that the magnetic fields for each quantum of light (each photon) are parallel to one another (and at right angles to the direction the beam is traveling). Bounce such a beam off a magnetized surface and the angle of all those photons' magnetic fields will rotate a small amount in a direction that depends on which way the magnetic field points in the surface from which the light beam bounced.

The returning light beam passes through a linear polarizer. (You can think of this device as being like a comb that only passes photons whose magnetic fields are aligned so that they can slip through the teeth of the comb.) If the polarizer is set just right, it will pass many or most of the photons bouncing off places on the surface that are magnetized in one orientation and almost none of the ones bouncing off places where the magnetization is oppositely oriented. Detect this change in light amplitude, and you have, in effect, read the orientation of the magnetic field on the surface of the medium.

There are two standard sizes for modern MO media: approximately 5 $\frac{1}{4}$-inch and approximately 3 $\frac{1}{2}$-inch. The larger ones can hold about as much as a CD-ROM. MO disks come permanently housed in much thicker and sturdier cartridges than even the smaller floppy diskettes. This is important because they are often used to store valuable data, and keeping the surface of the media clean and undamaged can be key to giving data a long life.

The Floptical: A New Kind of MO Drive

The MO drives I have discussed use the same technology that is incompatible with any of the traditional magnetic recording devices. The floptical, in contrast, combines optical and magnetic technologies in a way that is both familiar and innovative.

A floptical drive is basically an ordinary floppy diskette drive with optical positioning hardware added. There are two heads: One is the traditional floppy diskette read-write head, which is used to read and write all the usual formats of 3 $1/_2$-inch floppy diskettes. The other head is much smaller, originally developed for hard disk use. The optical components are all taken from standard CD drives. This ensures that they are well-engineered, have been tested thoroughly, and are quite inexpensive. They come into play only when the drive is reading or writing to a special floptical diskette.

This approach has been around for a few years. The early implementations offered only modest capacity gains over standard floppies, and they weren't able to be used as the boot drive of a PC. Now, the LS120 technology, named for the media it uses for high-capacity recording, can store up to 120MB on a single 3 $1/_2$-inch diskette that looks and feels just like a normal 1.44MB floppy. Although these drives attach to the IDE chain (for greater speed than is possible over the traditional floppy diskette drive interface), thanks to advances in the EIDE standard, they can be bootable devices and can be made to appear in your PC as your A: drive.

In order for your PC to support an LS120 drive in all these ways, it must have a BIOS that supports all the latest enhancements to the IDE standard. If not, you must use an add-in card (and Promise Technology makes one, called the Floppy Max), which carries a BIOS upgrade and an EIDE interface to attach to the drives. One advantage of using the Floppy Max card is that its IDE interface is positioned as the quaternary (fourth) IDE channel. Therefore, you can have four other drives on your PC's normal primary and secondary IDE chains and still have two LS120 drives attached to the Floppy Max card.

Therefore, an LS120 drive can serve as your PC's main floppy disk for booting from a safety boot disk or from a system disk, when your hard disk dies, and can be used to install programs from A: or B:. It also can be used for backups; with 120MB per diskette, it won't take too many of them to back up all the files you have changed recently for all but the most active PC user.

With all these features and an aggressive price, this drive is quite an attractive replacement for the floppy drive that is standard in most modern PCs. So far, the developers haven't come out with a version small enough to fit into a laptop computer, but they promise that one will be available soon.

Electronic PC Data Storage Devices

One other group of electronic data storage devices is used in or with PCs. This group uses totally electronic means for data storage. They look like disk drives, but they really aren't. Therein lie both their strengths and weaknesses. Ordinarily, electronic memory is volatile, but there are several ways to make nonvolatile electronic data storage devices.

RAMDRIVE and Its Cousins

The non-disk disk that is most familiar is probably the one created by running the RAMDRIVE program. This is an electronic disk simulator. Essentially, RAMDRIVE adds a block device driver to DOS, and thereby creates the illusion of a disk drive. Whenever DOS (or Windows) writes information to that drive, the RAMDRIVE block device places the information into a region of RAM that it has blocked for its exclusive use. Whenever you read from that disk, the block driver retrieves the information as it would from any other kind of disk drive. While access to this pseudo-disk is phenomenally fast, this type of electronic drive is still volatile; turn off your PC and RAM gets zapped.

PC Card Flash RAM

Portable computers need storage, just as much as desktop PCs, but they can't always accommodate the same kinds of storage devices. One solution to this need is to use PC Card Flash RAM. These are PC Cards, formerly known as PCMCIA cards, that have nonvolatile RAM in them. This can be electrically programmable read-only memory chips (EPROMs), ferro-electric random access memory chips (FRAMs), or simple DRAMs with a small battery attached to preserve their contents.

Whatever their technology, PC Cards let you permanently (or close to permanently) and rapidly store information, and they let you read it back even more quickly. The only drawbacks they have are that their capacity is small and their cost is high. Still, if you have a PDA, you might find that PC Card Flash Memory is your best option. This is especially so if you treat your PDA roughly, because a flash memory card with its lack of moving parts is inherently more rugged than any kind of hard drive, and even more rugged than most floppies.

Miniature Cards

PC Cards are small, but not small enough for some. So an industry consortium of Intel, AMD, Compaq, Hewlett-Packard, and Philips Electronics, among others, has come up with something they have rather unimaginatively called simply *Miniature Cards*. They are flash memory cards that are approximately a quarter the size of a PC Card. SCM Microsystems has made a name for itself as the principal supplier of adapters to let you use PC Cards with PCs. It also has announced that it will offer similar adapters for these new Miniature Cards to let them be used in PC Card slots either in a notebook computer or in one of its adapters for a desktop PC.

Smart Cards

The Smart Card is actually quite a complex device. It looks and acts a lot like a simple credit card, but it contains a microprocessor and some nonvolatile RAM. In short, it is a full computer hidden inside a credit card. With a suitable interface, you can read and write to these cards from a PC. Their principle market is for use in ATMs and Point of Sales terminals as the digital equivalent of actual money. They may, however, also find a role in the PC world for general data storage if their prices fall sufficiently.

Disk Utilities

What a wonderful and wild world of PC data storage devices we have and what a terrifyingly diverse set of technologies on which to manage our data. There two saving graces in this situation. First, the manufacturers of most of these devices—and certainly of all those that have been blessed with market success—have managed to design them in a way that lets them appear to be more-or-less-normal rotating hard or floppy disks. Second, there are many quite useful (and some simply wonderful) tools you can use to manage your data on all these diverse devices.

The disk emulations provided for some of these devices are nearly perfect. The RAMdisk is a good example of this. Others, hampered by what is inherently a different technology, only manage a halting emulation of a hard disk, and using them as if they were a disk drive turns into an exercise in patience. Tape drives are a good example of this. The utilities you can use on these devices include some that are shipped with DOS or Windows and some that are sold separately.

Disk Utilities That Come with DOS Versus Third-Party Programs

Unless you have given it some thought, you might not be aware that DOS and Windows 95 and 98—the products—are much more than just operating systems. The essential operating system in DOS is contained in just three files: two have hidden and system attributes (usually called either `IO.SYS` and `MSDOS.SYS` or `IBMBIO.COM` and `IBMDOS.COM`), and the third has a familiar command interpreter called `COMMAND.COM`. The essential operating system in Windows 95 and 98 is contained in just two files: `IO.SYS` and `COMMAND.COM`.

What I mean by this is that you can boot a PC to either DOS or Windows 95 with a floppy diskette that contains only those files (and a DOS boot record that will load them). If you prepare a DOS system diskette (using, for example, the DOS `SYS` command), you will get a disk with either just those essential files, or perhaps it will include one other optional file. If you prepare a startup diskette under Windows 95, you are actually creating an emergency startup disk, and Windows puts nearly a score of files on that diskette, hopefully providing you with tools to emerge from an emergency situation. However, only the two files I mentioned above are truly essential to booting to a command prompt.

At the resulting DOS or Windows 95 command prompt, you can issue any DOS command you like. However, only the DOS commands that are "internal" commands (and thus whose programs are built into `COMMAND.COM`) will work. All the other commands you normally are able to use depend on the presence of additional components, many of which are the files you will find stored on a Windows 95 or 98 emergency startup diskette.

So what are the several dozens of files that come in DOS or Windows 95, the product? Why do these products come either on a CD-ROM or on a whole stack of diskettes?

There are two answers. First, some of the files you get in either of those products are modules you can use to extend the basic operating system. These include the data compression driver (DBLSPACE.BIN or DRVSPACE.BIN) and various device drivers and terminate-and-stay resident (TSR) programs that augment what the OS can do. For Windows 95, these modules also include device drivers to enable Windows 95 and 98 to support a vast array of diverse hardware, and all of the graphical user interface, which most users associate with the operating system, but which is merely a way to make manipulating the operating system easier).

I will talk more about the whole subject of data compression in just a moment. First, I want to look briefly at the other parts of DOS you might want to use to help you manage the files you have stored on your disk drives.

The DOS (or Windows 95) Disk Utilities

All the other files included in the DOS and Windows product packages are add-on utility programs. These programs are, as far as the operating system is concerned, just like any other DOS or Windows application program. They are loaded and executed to accomplish some specific task. The FORMAT command is a good example. You run it only when you want to format a disk. Other important DOS commands for dealing with storage devices include FDISK (which is used to partition disks), SYS (which is used to copy the operating system to a formatted disk), and SCANDISK (which is used to check the integrity of the file system—which is to say, the consistency between the information stored in the FAT and the various directory entries).

If you want to learn more about what each of these DOS commands does and how to use it, you can ask the program in question. That is, issue the command FORMAT /? at the command prompt and the FORMAT program will tell you, very concisely, what it can do and how to get it to do each of those things. Every other DOS command will provide you with similar additional help.

If you want more help than you can get from DOS or Windows Help, refer to *Peter Norton's Complete Guide to Windows 95* or *Peter Norton's Guide to DOS 6.22*, both from Sams Publishing. Both of these books will tell you all that you want to know about each of these operating systems' commands. Space limitations prevent me from going into any more detail about those commands in this book.

Third-Party Disk Utilities

I've already mentioned the Norton Utilities several times, and in particular, the Norton Disk Editor. You can use it in its read-only mode to learn about disks, and when you are ready, you can turn on its capability to change things, then actually use it to alter a disk's contents.

I strongly suggest that you try this first on a disk whose contents you don't care about. Like any tool, this one can be dangerous if it is misused. Practice is the best way to ensure that you understand its job and how to get it to do what you want it to do.

The Norton Utilities product also includes several other utility programs that can help you deal with PC storage devices. The most important is Norton Disk Doctor. This program can diagnose many disk drive ailments (and often those in disk-like devices as well). For most of those ailments, the Norton Disk Doctor has a solution.

Norton Disk Doctor is also capable of undoing whatever it does. So if you ask it to fix some problem, and then you change your mind, you can usually get NDD to reverse its actions.

Another type of disk utility program is known as a disk defragmenter. In the Norton Utilities suite, this is called Norton SpeedDisk; in Windows 95 and 98 it is creatively called Disk Defragmenter. I'll tell you about these next.

Optimizing (Defragmenting) Your Disk Drives

You might be saying to yourself, "All this sounds great. But what, exactly, is this disk defragmentation all about?" I told you earlier in this and the previous chapter how DOS allocates units of space in the disk's data area (called clusters), and how it links them by entries in the File Allocation Table (FAT). And I pointed out in that discussion that if you add information to an existing file, after some other file(s) have been written to the disk, you will almost certainly end up with a fragmented file.

DOS (and Windows 95) usually do a splendid job of hiding all this from you and of getting your data for you whenever you want it. But they can sometimes get confused by a disk with too many fragmented files, especially when it comes to undeleting the ones you have inadvertently deleted. Also, very fragmented files can trash your PC's performance.

So, for performance reasons as well as for an extra measure of safety, I and most other experts recommend that you defragment the files on your disk periodically. How often you do it is a personal decision. Your PC is, after all, your *personal* computer. I'd certainly do this at least several times a year. Some folks do it every day.

There are many ways to optimize the placement of files on a disk. Having them unfragmented is only the beginning. You also can choose to put the files that contain programs you use a lot near the beginning. That will let DOS find and load them just a tad faster. You might want to put frequently referenced data files relatively near the front as well. Most disk optimizers (including Microsoft's Disk Defragmenter and Norton Speed Disk) suggest that the ultimate in disk optimization is achieved when all your files are unfragmented and pushed up as close to the beginning of the disk as possible. Under Windows 98 and the Norton Utilities for Windows 95, v.3, you can have your PC automatically track which files you use the most. With that information, your drives can be optimized for you, personally, and not merely in accordance with what "most optimizers" suggest.

> **Warning:** Whenever you use a low-level tool to make alterations on a disk drive, you are putting your data at risk. You can minimize this risk by making sure that your tool has been designed with a full knowledge of the operating system version you are using.
>
> Check with the vendor to be sure the version you have is the correct one for your operating system version and also see if there are any patches or upgrades available. Each time you upgrade your operating system, double-check with the makers of all your low-level tool programs to see if you should also upgrade them. Not much will make you unhappier than learning that you just damaged your files unnecessarily simply because your tools were out of date.

Data Compression

One of the most confusing areas in disk management is the notion of compressed disks. This name, for one thing, is a total misnomer. Disks aren't compressed—data is.

The compression being referred to in this context can also be called "squeezing out redundancy." Chapter 3, "Understanding Bits, Nybbles, and Bytes," discusses that ordinary speech contains a lot of redundancy, so do most PC program and data files. If you could create from one file another, smaller file that contained the same information as the source, and from which the source could be exactly reproduced, you could store only the nonredundant form of that file and save space on your disk drive. In fact, you can do this.

There are two complementary strategies for doing this. One uses a utility program to compress individual files or groups of files whenever you choose. The other strategy builds the data compression (and decompression) engine into the PC's operating system so that every file is compressed when it goes to the disk and decompressed when it returns from the disk. This way takes no thought on your part, and so is much more convenient.

A downside to using a separate compression utility program is that you must consciously use it twice on each file or group of files for which you want to save disk space. You use it once to compress the file and another time to decompress it back to its original form. If you don't do the second step, you will find that the nonredundant form of your file looks like gibberish. The advantages of this approach include these: You can compress only certain files that you know will compress well. You can combine compressed versions of multiple files into one file called an *archive*. That file can then be sent over a modem in less time than the collection of uncompressed files, and you have the advantage that all the different, related pieces can be kept together.

The downside to using operating system compression is that when you have your PC compress or decompress a file, some time is required for the PC to do that work. If you do this for every file going to or from a disk drive, you may slow down your computer.

The advantage to the integrated OS approach is simply that you don't have to think about it. It works automatically for every file you copy to the compressed drive, and it works just as automatically to decompress those files when you read them from that drive. So, there is a place in our world for both programs to do compression of files on demand, and also for an operating system-level data compression engine. Fortunately, both kinds of data compression are available for our PCs. Even more fortunately, the plummeting cost of long-term storage is making compression all but unnecessary. (It is still very useful to reduce the size of files you want to move over the Internet.)

Stand-Alone PC File Compression Programs

Many programs that can scrunch files down to a fraction of their original size are now available. These programs come in two basic flavors. One flavor is the loss-less compression programs. The other is the lossy compression programs.

Lossy Compression

Lossy compression programs are useful for making an approximate representation of an original file. That is fine if the file is an image and you don't mind a slight degradation of the image when you reconstitute it from the compressed file. Lossy compression programs usually can be made to compress files by differing amounts, depending on how you want to trade off degradation versus space saved on the disk. Often you can compress an image (or a video clip, and so on) by a factor of 10 without much noticeable degradation. But, if you compress it by a factor of 100, you almost certainly will notice that the reconstituted images are not the same as the originals. Examples of this type of compression are used to create GIF or JPEG image files and MPEG movie files.

Loss-Less Compression

The more interesting programs for most uses are those that can create a nonredundant version of a file and then, upon demand, can re-create the original file *exactly*. Make no mistake: When you are compressing a program file, you must be able to get it back again exactly as it was, right down to the very last bit; otherwise, it is worse than useless. A program that is incorrectly reconstituted might simply not run—but it also might do something horribly different from what the original would have done.

Typical compression ratios achievable with program files are a little less than two to one—that is, the non-redundant form of the file may be only a little more than half the size of the original. Some spreadsheet and other data files can be compressed by much more than that, with the nonredundant copy sometimes taking only a tenth of the space needed for the original file.

A couple of the most popular DOS-based loss-less compression programs are Phil Katz' PKZIP (and its companion PKUNZIP), and Haruyasu Yoshizaki's LHA. PKZIP is a shareware program. LHA is freeware. You can get more information on PKZIP and the other PKWare products at their Web site:

http://www.pkware.com

You can also download either PKZIP or LHA from many shareware program sites or local electronic bulletin boards.

Data Compression Integrated into the Operating System

If all that mess about compressing and decompressing files sounds like too much to think about, perhaps you'd prefer to use the hands-off way to do data compression. This is the concept behind the DoubleSpace and DriveSpace programs offered by Microsoft as a part of DOS 6.x and Windows 95.

This idea, like many in the PC world, was first developed by third-party utility companies, and only later was included in the OS package. In this case, the prime developer was Stac Electronics. Their Stacker program was sold as an operating system enhancement long before DoubleSpace showed up as an integrated part of DOS 6.0.

My description of data compression being integrated into the operating system might sound nice, but it is, so far, rather vague. You should know more in detail what the data compression engine does to the appearance of your disk drives in order to manage your data properly.

If you choose to use this type of automatic data compression, the operating system will load at boot time an extra device driver that does the data compression and decompression. This driver works in such a way that what appears to be the space on the compressed drive is actually the content of a huge file on your hard drive. (That file will have the hidden and read-only bits set so you won't normally see it if you do a DIR on the disk, and you won't be likely to erase it inadvertently.)

This means that if you choose to create a compressed drive E: (and I remind you that the drive isn't what is getting compressed—the data that you store there is), the compression engine will create a large file on, perhaps, your C drive. When you think you are writing information to the E drive, you actually are sending it to the compression engine, which compresses it and stores it away inside that special file on the C drive. When you look at E: (for example, with Windows Explorer), you will see what appear to be the uncompressed files. When you copy them off of E:, they will come out just as you sent them in. What really happens, though, is that the nonredundant form of that information is read from within that special file on your C drive, decompressed, and then handed to you as if it had come from the phantom E drive.

The jargon term for the drive that contains the file whose contents are made to look like another, compressed disk drive is the *host volume*. So in this case, C is the host of E. The jargon term for the file whose contents appear to be the E drive's contents is the *Compressed Volume File, or CVF*.

Where this gets really strange is that C can be the host of a compressed version of itself. When you compress your C drive, the utility program that sets this up first creates an empty file in the free space on C. Then it compresses several files from C and puts the compressed versions of those files inside the special CVF (and its size will, in that process, grow somewhat, but not by as much as the size of the files whose information it now contains).

Next, the compression engine erases the originals of those files, freeing up more space on the disk than the space occupied by the CVF. It repeats this process with most of the other files on C. When it is finished, almost all the files that were on C are now gone, but the compressed versions of them are stored away safely inside the CVF.

Now when you boot your computer, it will start loading the operating system off of the uncompressed part of C. Of course, in order to do this, the essential operating system files must still be outside the container and not compressed. After they have been loaded into memory (and the data compression driver is one of those essential files), then the system makes the real C drive appear to be some higher-lettered drive (for example, H:) and makes the contents of the CVF appear to be C instead. The actual C drive must remain visible, but it may be relocated to whatever drive letter you choose.

At this point, the story can develop in two ways, depending on which integrated compression engine you are using and just how you invoke it. You may compress any or all of the DOS logical volumes you originally had. That is, for each one you may create a new container file that will show up eventually as the original volume's drive letter. The original volume (other than the boot volume, C:), can be made to show up at some higher drive letter or—and this is where I get a bit boggled— it can be made to disappear totally!

Warning: These on-the-fly, integrated data-compression schemes have been developed and tested over several years and by lots of people. Still, things happen. Nonredundant files leave no room for mistakes. (This is not to say that the disk drives that store those files don't still use ECC to protect the information. They do, but even with that, things happen.) So, test your system before you trust your data to it, and, in any event, keep good backups—periodically tested backups—of all your valuable files. Then when things happen, you can just say, "Oh, well," and head for your backups to restore the glitched files.

Some Things to Think About and Try

How many disk drives do you have in your PC? How many logical volumes? Do you know which ones are in what partitions? Go to a DOS command prompt and enter this command:

```
FDISK /MBR
```

(This undocumented command-line switch to FDISK has been valid since version DOS 4.0, and it is the quickest way to see what drive letters have been assigned to which logical drives in what partitions.)

Explore your system. If you have the Norton Utilities, use its System Information program to explore your System. If you don't, use the My Computer icon and the Control Panel | System Applet | Device Manager tab.

Whatever method you use, find out what kinds of hard drive and what kinds of removable storage devices you have. Then, in light of what you have learned here, decide whether you need to upgrade or add some new ones.

11

Bigger Is Better in Ballrooms and in a PC's Memory

Peter Norton

In the last two chapters I told you all about storage in a PC. This chapter focuses on PC memory, which is where all of the required elements are temporarily held while the actual computing happens.

Understanding PC Memory

Many new PC users become very confused by the difference between storage and memory. And keeping these two clearly separate in your mind is crucial to developing a sound picture of how a PC is built and how it works. So I will say it for you once more: Memory and storage are two entirely different things. Many folks who are new to the PC business get them confused. If you do, you will have no end of trouble trying to understand how your PC is built and how it works. So repeat this until you get it clearly in your mind: Memory is the fast information holding place (made up of RAM and ROM). Storage is the long-term information holding place (often made up of magnetic or optical disks or tapes).

Typically, a PC will have tens or hundreds of times as much capacity in storage as in memory. For example, a pretty good system these days might have between 16 and 64 megabytes (MB) of RAM (and a small fraction of that much ROM), and it might have several gigabytes (GB) of disk storage. One GB is the same as 1024MB.

The CPU's Essential Playground

The PC's main memory is the collection of all the fast information holding places in a PC that can be "seen" by the CPU. That is, those places into which it can place information—or from which it can retrieve information—directly, without needing to have that information pass through any other holding places along the way. And it is only in these places that programs can execute or data can get processed.

Note: Well, if your PC has a memory cache, that is a temporary holding place for information on its way into or out of the CPU. We normally don't think much about this memory area when discussing PC memory because it is more or less a part of the CPU subsystem. I discuss this topic in more detail in Chapter 7, "Understanding PC Processors," and Chapter 8, "How Your PC 'Thinks.'"

Most of these fast information holding places are contained in the memory modules (DIMMs or SIMMs) that are most likely plugged into special slots on the motherboard. Those modules are small printed circuit cards that carry several integrated circuit (IC) memory chips that are the actual holding places for information. Figure 11.1 shows a close-up of the motherboard for our featured desktop system, with the location of the main memory modules (which in this system are DIMMs) and the memory cache module (which is a COASt module) indicated. I'll explain just what DIMMs and COASt modules are in the next few pages.

Figure 11.1.
Main memory modules and memory cache modules on a Dell XPS motherboard.

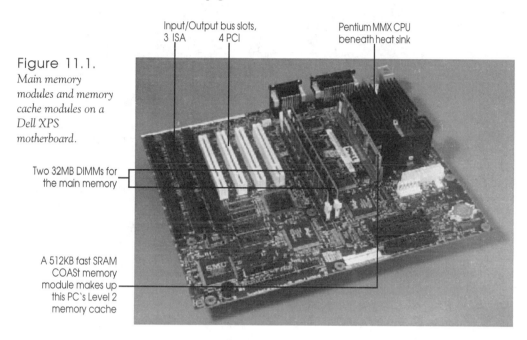

Input/Output bus slots,
3 ISA   4 PCI

Pentium MMX CPU
beneath heat sink

Two 32MB DIMMs for the main memory

A 512KB fast SRAM COASt memory module makes up this PC's Level 2 memory cache

Some of these places can be in similar memory chips located on plug-in cards inserted into one of the input-output bus slots on the motherboard. For example, Figure 11.2 shows the video card from our desktop system with its memory chip locations indicated. These memory chips are examples of surface-mounted flat packs. This is another kind of memory chip I will discuss in the next few pages. In Figure 11.2, the two connectors accept a plug-in memory card to let you add 4MB of additional video RAM. The four 1MB memory chips are the built-in (minimum) video memory for this particular Matrox Millenium PCI graphics card.

It is important to realize that the physical location of these holding places is not nearly as important to your understanding as knowing their logical location. They are all at some address in the CPU's memory address space. (The notion of the CPU's memory address space is discussed in some detail in Chapter 7. You might want to return there and review that discussion if what you read here isn't making a lot of sense.)

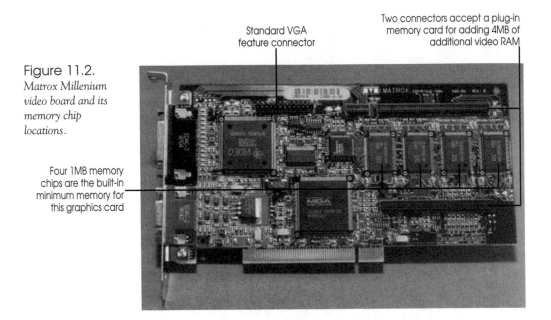

Standard VGA
feature connector

Two connectors accept a plug-in
memory card for adding 4MB of
additional video RAM

Figure 11.2.
*Matrox Millenium
video board and its
memory chip
locations.*

Four 1MB memory
chips are the built-in
minimum memory for
this graphics card

Why Memory Is "Where the Action Is"

The reason why storage is where information is kept and memory is where it is processed is quite simple: Storage devices are good at holding information for a very long time. Some of them hold it essentially forever (but those are what we call read-only devices, and can't be used to store changing information). Others are capable of accepting alterations to their contents, yet hold those contents very well between times they are told to change them. That is unlike the behavior of memory chips which, with a few exceptions, "forget" whatever they are holding the instant the power fails or your PC is reset.

Almost every type of storage device is much slower than the memory chips used in a PC's main memory. And this speed difference is why the memory, and only the memory, is the CPU's essential playground. It must have all the information it is going to use readily available at electronic speeds. As a matter of fact, even the fastest of today's main memory modules aren't capable of keeping up with the fastest central processors used in PCs, which is why memory caching is so important in enhancing a system's performance.

Having the CPU constantly fetch all its information from a disk drive and store intermediate values there while it was computing some result would be extremely impractical. The only practical approach is to bring your information (both data and the programs that specify how that data is to be processed) into the PC's main memory. Then, and only then, can the CPU be asked to process it (to run the programs and thereby alter the data values before they are stored back on the disk once more for safekeeping).

What You Must Know About Memory Chips and Modules

There are at least three reasons to know some details about memory chips and modules. Each of them is valid, and all of them may apply to you. One is simple intellectual curiosity. They are, after all, some of the most intricate devices designed and built by human beings. And there almost certainly are more memory "bit cells" manufactured and sold each year than any other product. (This is virtually guaranteed by the fact that most memory modules now sold contain literally millions of bit cells. And many millions of those modules are sold annually.)

A second reason is that understanding memory at the chip level and at the module level helps you understand the overall design of a PC. This includes such key ideas as the notion of banks of memory and what parity memory is and how it is used.

Third, you must know what the key parameters that describe memory chips or modules are if you are going to buy more and insert them into your PC. (And knowing what they look like is also handy when it comes to finding them, and perhaps removing or inserting them, if appropriate.)

First I'll tell you a little bit about the many ways memory has been packaged for use in PCs. Then I'll go into some of the different "flavors" of RAM now available, and describe which kinds you might be using in your PC.

Recognizing the Different Ways Memory Gets Packaged

Electronic memory is made in integrated circuit (IC) chips. These are tiny, tremendously complex creations crafted from very pure silicon, some trace impurities, and a little bit of metal, built in super-clean (and super-expensive) factories.

Each chip can hold up to several tens of millions of bit cells, and each bit cell, as the name implies, can hold one bit of information. These chips are made on large hyper-pure single crystal silicon wafers; each wafer holds perhaps a dozen to as many as a hundred chips. Only after all the chips on the wafer have been completely manufactured and tested are the chips cut apart. The good ones are used and the bad ones discarded. (A bit of jargon: A naked chip is often referred to as a *die*. A collection of them are, therefore, called *dice*.)

IC memory chips come in two main types and, within each type, in many flavors. The two types are read-only, or non-volatile, memory chips and random-access, or volatile, memory chips.

The non-volatile memory chips either have their data permanently manufactured (ROM chips) or they are relatively rarely reprogrammed with new data (NVRAM, or non-volatile random-access memory). In either case, they hold whatever data is put in them essentially forever, even when you turn off your PC. The volatile memory chips (RAM)—which are by far the more numerous in almost every PC—are meant only for holding information temporarily. They can be written to as easily as they can be read from, but they forget whatever information they were holding when power is turned off (or whenever you reset your PC).

There are many subtly different ways of making either of these two basic types of memory chips. I will come back to these technological differences shortly, but first I want to explain why you very likely have never seen any of the actual integrated circuit memory dice. (And I'll explain what you have seen if you've looked inside your PC.)

Memory Chip Packages

Memory chips generally are sealed inside small ceramic or plastic packages before they leave the factory. This is done to protect the delicate die, which is quite vulnerable in its unpackaged state. Often before you get to them, several of those packages will have been mounted on a small printed circuit board (PCB) called a memory module.

Figure 11.3 shows the relative size and shapes of several memory chips and modules that you might have in your PC. (Ordinarily, a given PC will use only a few of these designs, but different PCs use different ones.) Some of these forms are intended for use in sockets. These you can plug in and—if they fail, or if you want to replace them with more capacious chips—remove them relatively easily. Other packages are intended only for use by manufacturers who will solder them onto a printed circuit board. You won't want to try removing or replacing these. The drawings in Figure 11.3 are all to the same scale, so you can easily see how the different package sizes compare to one another.

The names of the different styles of chip package reflect their physical forms. DIPs, for example, are small rectangular blocks of plastic or ceramic with a row of metal leads (electrical contacts) poking out of two opposite sides, and then bent down parallel to each other. The name DIP stands for Dual Inline Package, which refers to the arrangement of leads on those devices.

Some memory chips have been mounted in SIPs (Single Inline Packages), which are like DIPs but with leads on only one side. ZIPs (Zig-zag Inline Packages) have leads on only one side, like a SIP, but those leads are alternatively bent to one side or the other to form two staggered rows of contacts.

Each of the chip forms just described can be mounted in sockets, or they can be soldered in place in a printed circuit board with suitably located through-holes. Figure 11.3 shows a cross-sectional view of each of these methods of chip mounting.

Miniflat chips look like DIPs with the leads bent flat so they can be easily soldered down onto a circuit card with no holes in it. Quad Flat Packs (QFPs) are similar, but they have leads coming out all four sides. These so-called "surface-mount chips" are one of the more popular forms of chip for manufacturers to solder in place permanently (and this also is shown in cross-section in Figure 11.3).

Figure 11.3.

Some of the many forms in which memory chips and modules are made, the three ways they are mounted on circuit boards.

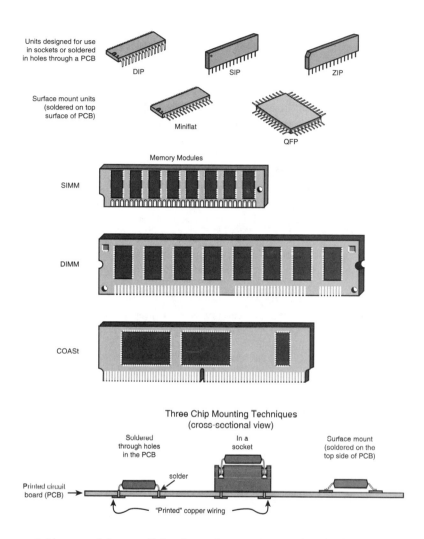

Cache memory is now available in modules as well. Intel is pushing its COASt (Cache On A Stick) module design. This is the type of cache memory used in our desktop system (refer to Figure 11.1) and I have included a drawing of a COASt module in Figure 11.3.

The chips you plug in to sockets individually (DIPs, SIPs, and ZIPs) have their leads spaced one-tenth of an inch from center to center. The surface-mount chips usually have their leads only half this far apart. SIMMs, like the plug-in chips, have contacts on one-tenth inch centers; DIMMs and COASt modules, like surface mount chips, have contacts on one-twentieth inch spacing.

What Is Parity, and Why Might I Want It to Be Used in My PC?

IBM's original specification for the PC indicated that all RAM used in the main memory would have a *parity bit*. This means that in addition to storing the eight bits' values (ones or zeros), a ninth bit is also stored. The value of this bit is chosen so that counting all nine locations there will be an odd number of one bit.

According to this strategy, before each time a PC writes to memory a special circuit on the motherboard will calculate the correct parity bit value for that byte and then all nine bits will be sent to the main memory location. And correspondingly, whenever such a PC reads a memory location it again computes what the parity bit should be from the eight data bits it finds there, and then it compares that to the parity bit it also read. Only if they are the same value (one or zero) will the PC let you go on. Otherwise, it comes to a complete halt with a message on the screen announcing this parity error.

IBM's decision to use parity bit protection for all data stored in a PC's main memory reflects its belief (which I agree with) that data integrity is of the highest importance. IBM felt it was the best plan simply to prevent you from computing with any known-to-be-incorrect data.

Modern RAM is very reliable. And modern PCs are commodity items, often sold on the basis that a particular one will cost less than its competitors. Therefore, many makers of PCs have decided to forego the protections of parity RAM (with eight data bits and one parity bit per byte-wide memory location). They use non-parity memory (collections of chips or modules that hold just the eight data bits for each byte location) instead. This works almost all the time, but it is a little riskier than using parity RAM.

Warning: Some unscrupulous memory module makers use a clever dodge to save themselves a bit of money. They sell what purport to be parity memory modules, but in fact they use memory chips that hold only the eight data bits for each byte location. Then they include on the module an extra chip called a parity generator.

Any time your PC goes to read a byte of information from this module, that parity generator chip looks at the data that has been read from its memory chips, and from that data it simply computes what the parity bit should have been and offers that as if it were a reading of a parity value it had been holding in memory. This cheat saves very little money, and it completely defeats the whole purpose of parity memory. Unfortunately, detecting memory modules that use this cheat isn't easy. Buying from a reputable vendor is about the only practical defense you can have against being "taken" in this way.

At the opposite extreme, some makers of very powerful PCs actually use error correction codes (ECC) to protect the contents of RAM, just as is done on hard disks. This can be done by using several non-parity RAM modules (by having some extra modules in which the ECC data will be stored), or by using parity RAM (and using all the parity bits in a bank in combination to store ECC bits instead).

Peter's Principle

Do I recommend that you pay extra to get parity memory in your PC? Not necessarily. It is a good thing to have, but it might not be worth what it will cost you. The same can be said about ECC memory. Probably the deciding factor will be just how much memory your PC has (the more it has the more likely you are to encounter an error someday) and just how critical you feel your data's integrity is. The more costly your PC, and the more RAM it has installed, the more likely you will want to have parity or even ECC protection for the data. (But don't even think about this until after you have protected your data by installing an uninterruptible power supply for your PC. This protection is much more likely to be called upon to save the day—and if it is too expensive for you, then so is parity RAM.)

How Memory Chips Are Organized Internally

Many ROM (read-only memory) chips and some NVRAM (non-volatile random-access memory) chips have their bit cells arranged in groups of eight. These groups are always accessed as a unit. This means these chips must have eight wires for data to flow out of those locations (and for an NVRAM chip that is able to be reprogrammed, another eight wires for data to flow into them) in parallel. In addition, they must have several "address" wires over which the chip can be informed which of its many groups of eight bits is being accessed at this time. This type of a chip is called a *byte-wide memory chip*.

This strategy is not commonly used for (usually very much larger capacity) RAM memory chips, simply because a large capacity means more address wires are needed to point to the desired memory location, and the chip designers would rather have only a pair of data in/out wires instead of 16 of them. So RAM chips most often have their bit cells individually addressed. Or, at most, you can address groups of four bits at a time. The former kind of chip is called a *bit-wide* memory chip, and the latter is a *nybble-wide* memory chip.

How might these chips be combined into a usable amount of RAM? That depends on the number of parallel data wires in the memory bus (from the CPU to the main memory). If your PC has 16 (bi-directional) data wires, then you'd need to use 16 bit-wide memory chips (or 18 if you want to also be able to hold parity information), or else you might use four nybble-wide memory chips (plus a pair of bit-wide chips for parity). Each of those memory chips would hold its one (or four) bit of information for each of some large number of locations—and for the same number of locations in each chip, of course. This collection of memory chips is referred to as a *bank* of memory for that PC.

Modern PCs have many more data wires, and so their memory banks must be correspondingly wider. A Pentium, for example, has 64 data wires. Its banks of memory must, therefore, store 64 bits of data (and perhaps also eight bits of parity information) for each of some large number of locations.

If you use memory chips that are all bit-wide and each can hold 1,048,576 bits (1MB), then you would be able to hold a total of 8MB of data in one memory bank. This arrangement of 72 chips would take up a lot of room, and any time you wanted to change those chips it would be quite an arduous task. Fortunately, we now have a better way to do this, which is the topic of the next section.

How Memory Modules (SIMMs and DIMMs) Are Organized Internally

The first memory modules used in PCs were called SIMMs (for Single Inline Memory Modules). These simply are small printed circuit cards with anywhere from three to nine memory chips soldered in place on one side of the card. The complete module typically was organized as a byte-wide memory module. That is, it had enough contacts on it to allow one to load or recall one byte (all eight bits, plus perhaps a parity bit) at once. These contacts are located all along one edge of the card, which slips into a socket at an angle and is then tipped upright to lock into place.

You can plug one of these SIMMs into a socket much more easily than you could plug in all of the chips it contains, and the manufacturer that assembles them can guarantee that the several memory chips on that SIMM are compatible with one another. These features account for the great popularity enjoyed by SIMMs from almost the moment they were introduced, and for the near-total disappearance of individual plug-in memory chips from modern PCs.

SIMMs proved very popular, but they too have been replaced, for the most part, by DIMMs. The reasons for this are not hard to find.

As I explained earlier, a bank of memory is enough memory chips or modules to hold or supply in parallel as many data bits as there are data lines on the PC's CPU. Having all the memory chips in a single bank fairly well matched is important. In particular, they must all be able to hold the same number of bits of information. And furthermore, they should all respond to requests to hold or recall data in about the same time and should need similar signals to do so. These things can be readily guaranteed if you use identical memory chips or modules in all the sockets that make up one bank. But doing that takes conscious action on the part of whoever puts in those memory chips or modules.

Note: It isn't obvious, but many PC motherboards are built in a way that enables you to fill up each bank of memory sockets with any of several different sizes of memory modules or chips. That is, all the chips or modules in one bank must hold the same number of bits as every other chip or module in that bank, but the ones in the next bank over might hold a different amount.

One simple way to guarantee that each bank will be properly filled with matched memory chips is to make up larger memory modules. These can have 32 or 64 data lines (depending on the type of CPU your PC has) and so a single one of them will serve as an entire bank of memory. Of course, such a memory will need to have many more contacts than a byte-wide SIMM where it plugs into its socket. And to fit all of those contacts without making the module unduly large, the manufacturers put contacts on both sides of the printed circuit card that carries the memory modules. (They also can put the memory chips themselves on both sides.) These modules are called DIMMs (Dual Inline Memory Modules).

Plug in a DIMM and you have plugged in an entire bank of memory for your PC. Everything in that bank is automatically matched, with no further effort on your part. (Furthermore, these modules come with notches that "key" them in a way that prevents you from plugging a DIMM designed to work at 3.3 volts into a socket meant for a 5 volt DIMM, and vice versa. Also, DIMMs have many more ground wires than a SIMM, which is becoming crucial as we begin to run our memory modules at ever higher speeds.)

Warning: Every PC motherboard or system comes with a manual that specifies, among other things, just which types of memory chips or modules it can accept. Please read this document carefully before you go out and buy additional memory for your PC. You must follow the manufacturer's recommendations or your PC might malfunction.

This also means that there might be some pretty severe limits on how much (or how little) RAM memory any particular PC can have. If you want to upgrade your PC, you might be able simply to get and plug in a new DIMM, or you might end up having to remove and replace all the memory chips or modules it now contains with new, more capacious ones. And which course you must follow will naturally affect the cost of the upgrade.

Another aspect to this is the question of parity versus non-parity memory. If your PC uses parity memory, then you must supply it with memory chips in groups storing nine bits at each location. Similarly, if it uses memory modules, you must have ones that store and return that ninth bit for every byte location.

However way your PC is built, that is how it is built. You cannot change this aspect of its design without replacing the motherboard. So, again, know what you have, and know what it uses. Then, if you want to upgrade your PC's RAM you will know what you must buy.

Well, things aren't always quite as simple as I might have made it sound so far. You might also have a choice among different flavors of RAM modules. I discuss that choice and the reasons for it in the next few pages.

The Many Ways Memory Chips Are Made

Memory chips are more than just ubiquitous. They also have been made in a startling number of different ways. You don't need to know all the intricacies of each one, but a general understanding of the different approaches used will help you understand how memory chips operate and why some behaviors are easy for one kind and impossible for another kind.

Integrated Circuit Chip Construction (Quick Overview)

Integrated circuits (ICs) are made in a multi-step process. The different kinds of chip just differ in some of the process details. But then, as they say, "It's all in the details."

The base for virtually all memory chips used in PCs is a thin slice of a single crystal of silicon, called a wafer. This initially thoroughly homogenous material has an intricate structure crafted in its upper surface through a combination of many steps.

First, the surface is oxidized. This creates a tough coating of silicon dioxide (which is the silicon equivalent of iron oxide, known to us as rust). A pattern of openings (holes or channels) are created in this coating by a process quite similar to that used to create a printed circuit board. The main difference is that the pattern details are just about 1,000 times smaller.

Of course, having such fine patterns means that the place in which these devices are made must be super clean. The tiniest speck of dust that one can hardly see floating as a mote in a sunbeam would dwarf the details on most ICs.

Carefully chosen impurities are then made to sink into the surface of the silicon through those holes, creating regions of altered electrical properties underneath each one. Depending on the impurities chosen, these regions become *p-type* or *n-type* (having positive or negative electrical properties). Eventually, by a repetition of up to a few dozen similar steps, many millions of transistors are formed in the silicon wafer's surface.

This circuit fabrication process is done inside a vacuum chamber, at high temperatures and using some very nasty chemicals plus, at times, vaporized metal. If this sounds like a difficult environment to create and maintain, you have an inkling of why integrated circuit manufacturing plants are so very expensive to build.

Each transistor is essentially a sandwich of regions with differing electrical properties. That is true of all the different kinds of transistor one can make—the differences all come in the details of just how these sandwiches are built.

Typically on one wafer (which can be as much as eight inches across), there will be anywhere from a few to a few hundred repetitions of the exact same circuit. Each of those circuits will become one chip die.

At the end of the wafer processing, each of the dice it contains is tested, and then the wafer is cut apart; the dice that work are mounted in packages such as those I described earlier, and the bad ones are discarded. (Intel and the other IC makers now offer "bare" dice mounted on a reel of tape. This is an option only for manufacturers that are capable of building those dice into adequately protected multi-component modules. That requires a pretty sophisticated manufacturing line, and so this is done only when it is truly necessary. Some of the most modern laptop computers use this procedure to keep the size and weight of these PCs down, but doing this also makes those machines more expensive than would otherwise be the case.)

Bipolar, Field Effect, and CMOS Transistor Circuits

Transistors are, in essence, electrically controllable switches for electricity. This means that by using a transistor, a small electrical signal can be made to control a larger one. Some of these transistors are controlled by the *flow* of electricity, which is simply a continuing supply of electric charges. These so-called "bipolar" transistors, therefore, require a source of electric current to operate.

Other transistor construction techniques produce devices (called *field effect transistors*) that are controlled by the mere presence of electric charges. These devices can be operated by a one-time introduction (or removal) of some electrons. They don't need the ongoing electric current required by the other type.

Both bipolar and field effect transistors can be made in either a p-type or an n-type manner. This refers to the polarity of the overall behavior of the sandwich, and it is controlled mostly by the sequence in which p-type and n-type regions are put together. Some wafers are built with circuits that are composed of collections of transistors of opposite polarities. If those transistors are all field effect transistors, then the resulting circuits are called Complementary Metal Oxide Semiconductor Field Effect Transistor arrays. You've probably heard of them by their nickname, CMOS.

Initially a rather expensive process, the CMOS technology is now the dominant way in which integrated circuits for PCs are fabricated. These circuits can do more computing with less power than any of their competitors—which is what has endeared them so to the makers of PCs.

Various Flavors of ROM or NVRAM

All integrated circuits are simply arrays of transistors that are wired together in a particular pattern to do a specified job. The wiring used is actually created by etching that pattern in the last (or last few) metal layers put on the wafer.

When a CPU (or other part of a PC) reads data from a ROM chip or collection of memory chips, it supplies an address and then waits for the binary values to show up on the data pins. Internally the chip activates a particular subcircuit specified by the address values on its input address lines, then causes the output from that subcircuit to show up on the data output lines.

Mask Programmed ROM

The earliest read-only memory chips, called *mask programmed ROM*, were wired at the factory in a way that forced them to produce the binary data corresponding to the information they were supposed to contain. This hard-wired information content is, clearly, permanent. This was a simple and effective means of making ROMs, and it is still used whenever one needs many chips that each contain exactly the same information.

The Oxymoron Chips: EPROMs

The makers of mask-programmed ROM chips knew that some of their customers wanted to have different information permanently held in different chips, and they wanted to have only a relatively few chips with each set of information. This is not something that is economically feasible by the mask-programming method simply because creating the mask used in the fabrication process typically costs many thousands of dollars, which is affordable only if one needs many thousands of chips created using that mask.

The first solution to this problem was an insightful use of one of the ways a ROM chip can fail. The wiring that connects the circuits is composed of extremely fine traces of metal. If you run too much current through one of them, it will melt or vaporize.

So, someone realized, if only you make the points of failure in predictable places (by thinning the traces at those points), you'll have made a circuit that has some initially manufactured-in set of data, but in which you can alter that data simply by overloading selected points. In essence, these chips are manufactured to hold data that consists of all one-bits. You can "blow out a fuse" to convert a one to a zero wherever you need a zero in the data in a particular chip. Manufacturing in the one-bits is done at the factory. Blowing some of them to zeros can be done anywhere and any time you like.

Thus was born the electrically programmable read-only memory (EPROM) chip. Think about it. This name is surely an oxymoron. If you can program it, then you are, in effect, writing data to it. But it is true that almost all the time you can only read data from these chips. You must use a special, over-voltage circuit in a special fashion to program these chips.

Battery Backed Up RAM

When PCs were young, one could easily buy mask-programmed ROM (and even EPROMs) or RAM. What one couldn't buy was any kind of simple, inexpensive devices that would act like a ROM most of the time, yet enable one easily to change the contents from time to time. But that is exactly what PC makers wanted for one special role in their machines.

In the IBM PC and PC/XT (and clones of those machines) switches on the motherboard were used to store configuration information. This was awkward, and meant that any time the PC configuration was changed, someone had to open up the PC and alter some switch settings.

IBM decided in its PC/AT to include more configuration information than in an XT, some of which might change at times when you didn't otherwise want to have to open up the case. IBM also wanted to include a "real-time clock" circuit, so you wouldn't have to tell your PC what time and date it was each time you turned it on.

IBM's solution was to include in the PC/AT's motherboard a special integrated circuit chip that held both a clock circuit and some RAM to store the current time and the configuration data. Near this circuit was a battery to keep it working even when the rest of the PC was turned off. To keep the demand for power from the battery low (so it would last a long time), IBM chose to use then-relatively expensive CMOS technology for that chip.

This is what soon got the name of "the BIOS Setup CMOS," or simply "the PC's CMOS." Now, even though virtually all the circuits in our PCs are made using the CMOS technology, we still often refer to the subsystem of CMOS chip plus battery used for the real-time clock and configuration storage as the PC's CMOS. (Recently some manufacturers have begun using a more general, and more precise term by calling this the PC's NVRAM, which stands for Non-Volatile RAM.)

This combination is such an attractive one that some manufacturers now sell modules that look just like any other integrated circuit package, but which actually have a long-life battery built into it along with the semiconductor integrated circuit chip.

EEPROMs, Flash RAM, FERAM and other NVRAM Technologies

Now we have some better solutions to these problems. Clever engineers found several different ways to make a chip that acts like a ROM most of the time, yet which can have its data altered on demand. Generally these chips can have any specified collection of one-bits changed to zeros, but they can have the zeros changed back to ones only in a mass operation that affects all locations on the chip, or all of the locations in one block on the chip.

These chips carry many different names. Electrically Erasable Programmable Read-Only Memory (EEPROM) chips was an early name. Accurate, but cumbersome. These chips use a newer strategy than the fusible-link EPROMs. In an EEPROM each bit cell stores its data as an electric charge on a capacitor. And by one of several strategies the manufacturer makes it possible for one to alter that charge with a suitable electrical signal. A yet-newer design uses a ferro-electric effect bit-cell. These FERAM (or FEROM) chips act pretty much just like RAM, except that they don't forget the information they hold when you remove power.

All of these devices can accurately be called non-volatile random access memory (NVRAM) chips, and because the PC user really doesn't have any reason to care which technology is used, this name is coming into vogue for referring to the function, and not to the technology by which it is achieved.

Various Flavors of RAM

Not only NVRAM comes in many different technologies; so too does the ordinary, volatile kind of RAM. One distinction separates all (volatile) RAM chips into two main groups. One group is called *static* RAM (SRAM), and the other group is called *dynamic* RAM (DRAM). The DRAM group is further broken down into several additional categories.

Static RAM (SRAM)

The earliest electronic memory chips used at least two (and sometimes as many as four) transistors per bit cell. In this design, one transistor—let's call it transistor A—is *on* (carrying current) when the cell holds a one, and another transistor—let's call it transistor B—is on when the cell holds a zero. The circuit is arranged so that when one of these two transistors is on, the other one is forced to be off. This arrangement has two stable states: A on and B off, or A off and B on. The additional transistors, if they are used, are there to help one switch the circuit from one of its stable states to the other.

This works very well, and SRAM chips can be very fast. But it isn't the best way to make really massive amounts of memory. The reason is simply that dynamic RAM (DRAM) chips can have as much as four times as many bit cells formed in a given amount of silicon, and by the economics of IC manufacturing that means DRAM can be about one-fourth as expensive for a given data-holding capacity.

Still, when you need the very fastest possible RAM, for example in a PC's L2 memory cache, or any time you need only a modest amount of RAM, SRAM is the way to go.

Dynamic RAM

A constant pressure is on the makers of RAM chips to come up with newer designs that will hold more bits of information. One way to do this is to reduce the number of transistors required to hold each one.

In dynamic RAM chips only a single transistor is used to hold each bit. This must be a field effect transistor, and its "gate" electrode must be enlarged a little in order to serve as a *capacitor*, which is an electrical device that can hold an electrical charge. Because a field effect transistor needs no input current to control its output, it is possible for this capacitor, when it is charged or discharged, to control whether the transistor is on or off for a (relatively) long time. And using techniques similar to those used in EEPROMs it is possible to put charges onto those gate capacitors or remove charges from them whenever you want.

There is only one fly in this ointment. Nothing in this world is perfect; in particular, the capacitor formed on the gate of the field effect transistor isn't perfect. It will, over time, leak away its charge. Does this mean DRAMs can't be made to work? Clearly not. The computer on which I am writing this has hundreds of millions of bits of DRAM information storage, and it works very well.

I can best explain how this happens by using an analogy. Suppose you have a team of people who are going to help you remember some numbers. Suppose you arrange those people into an array with some number of rows and columns (also known as ranks and files—which is the source of the term *rank and file* for referring to a mass of workers).

Now tell each person what number he or she is to remember. If you don't let these people write down their numbers, and if you engage them all in small talk, within just a few minutes many if not all of the people will have forgotten the number they were told to remember. However, if you do one special thing they will all be able to remember their number essentially forever. Here is what you do:

Have a helper go to each row in the array of people and have that person call out just to that row, "All right, people. Listen up. Get ready to tell my buddy your special number if he asks." And have another helper go to one of the columns and call down that column, "Okay, if you are in the active row, tell me your number."

Only one person will call out his number. But every person in that row will bring it into the forefront of his mind and thus "refresh" his memory. Do this to every row often enough and no one will forget the number he was told to remember.

This is a very good analogy to how a DRAM chip works. If it contains, for example, one megabit of information, those 1,048,576 bit cells are arranged into 1,024 rows with 1,024 cells in each row.

When you read from this chip, you tell it which cell to read by activating one *row address* and one *column address*. (This could take 20 wires, but more often it is done by using the same 10 wires in two steps.) Every cell on the selected row is activated. Doing this means that if its voltage is high, it makes its voltage higher. If its voltage is low, it makes it even lower. In that way, all the information content of these cells is refreshed, and they place that output value on the corresponding column output line. Only the one selected column line's value is reported to the data-out line of the chip.

So if you will only remember to read some cell from each row in every DRAM chip often enough, your PC's DRAM memory will work, but if you fail to do this for too long (and it turns out that *too long* in this context means for more than about a thousandth of a second), some of those bit cells will drift to a voltage where it isn't clear whether they are high or low, and thus they cannot be refreshed accurately.

You say you don't remember doing this with your PC? You might not even touch the keyboard for many minutes, and still it keeps remembering information in its RAM. How does it do this? It has a special "DRAM refresh" process going on all the time, in the background. This happens no matter what else the PC is doing. In fact, it is the very highest priority task performed by your PC, because keeping those DRAM cells working properly is crucial to everything else it will be asked to do.

This DRAM refresh process takes some effort and time, but not much. If you had only a small number of DRAM bit cells to refresh, it wouldn't be worth all the overhead. That is one reason why for a small amount of memory (as in an L2 cache, for example) SRAM is often used instead of DRAM. The other reason is that SRAM is often faster than DRAM, and its premium price can be affordable if you use only a little bit of it.

If you have hundreds of millions of bit cells to refresh (as is the case in a modern PC with tens of millions of bytes of RAM), it is most assuredly worth the overhead in time and cost of special circuitry for the savings in the cost of all that RAM. This is why we use DRAM exclusively in the main memory of our PCs.

When Is EDO, FPM, RDRAM, SDRAM, SGRAM, VRAM, or WRAM the Best?

Now for the confusing part: all the many different subflavors of DRAMs. This is where the alphabet soup comes in. In an effort to make DRAM chips that work ever faster, manufacturers have enhanced them in many ways. Each one carries its own fancy name and some special advantages.

One way, called *fast page mode* DRAM, concerns itself with the fact that normally DRAM chips have only half the number of address lines they need. They use the same wires for row and column addresses, distinguishing between the different values on those wires for a row and a column address by when those values are placed there. To speed things up, if the processor is accessing several memory locations in successive, or even nearly adjacent, locations, it need only tell one of these chips a row address once, then it can go ahead and access all the columns it wants. Only when it must move to a new row will it have to reissue the (new) row address.

Another strategy (used in EDO DRAM) is to have the data produced by the chip linger awhile on the output. This *extended data out* design allows you to access a location, and then while you are still busy reading the information you just accessed, the chip will be getting ready to supply the next bit of data.

Dual-ported DRAM chips enable you to access two locations at once. They do this by having two complete sets of circuitry for reading data from locations in the bit-cell array. When millions of bit cells are on a single chip, this additional overhead can be built in for a minor additional cost. These devices are not symmetrical. That is, whereas one of the input/output ports lets you access any place you like at random (and it also has the input circuitry for writing data to those locations), the other port is used just for reading data out, and then only an entire row at a time. These dual-ported DRAM chips, also sometimes called video RAM (VRAM) are especially useful for video frame buffers because those are inherently used for random-access writing and reading by the CPU and linear readout (by the video display circuitry). I'll tell you more about this in Chapter 13, "Seeing the Results: PC Displays."

Windows RAM (WRAM) is a special version of VRAM that is optimized for the types of access that are common in PCs running Windows and Windows applications. These include such things as filling in all of a region's bits devoted to a single color with a constant value, and easy ways to move a block of data from one region to another ("bit blitting").

Synchronous DRAM (SDRAM) and Synchronous Graphics RAM (SGRAM) are some other popular variations on the same themes. Both of these types are single-ported and thus a little cheaper than the VRAM or WRAM designs. SDRAM and SGRAM have an advantage over regular DRAM (or dual-ported DRAM) that these synchronous memory chips use the same clock signal as the CPU. This means these memory chips are ready to transfer data when the CPU expects them to be ready. With other types of memory the CPU must allow more time to be sure the chips have transferred the data, thus slowing everything down.

Rambus DRAM (RDRAM) is perhaps the most different memory design now available, requiring as it does a whole new memory architecture. Also, of all the technologies developed to date, it is the one with the greatest speed potential. But that promise comes at a price. RDRAM must be connected to the CPU over a very special bus, and that bus cannot be very long.

It will be some time before we should expect to see RDRAM as our PC's main memory. Still, Intel has committed itself to RDRAM as the solution for PC memory needs in the not distant future, and because Intel is the major maker of PC motherboards, we can expect its vision to become a reality— as soon as it figures out how to achieve that vision at a price we will be willing to pay.

It appears right now that SDRAM will soon become the mainstream mass memory choice, WRAM or SGRAM the high-end graphics memory choice, and eventually, RDRAM might supplant both.

This is a never-ending story. All I can hope to do is give you a glimpse of what it looks like at the moment. In another few years, no doubt, we will have moved on down the road and a new memory chip landscape will confront us. All we can be sure of is that it will be one of faster, larger capacity and cheaper memory, which will make our PCs all the more delightful to buy and use. Of course, the programs of the future very likely will demand all the additional space and speed we can possibly give them.

Addressing Memory: Intel's Segments

I mentioned earlier that the contents of memory chips are addressed by voltages on the wires that attach to them. That is the physical level at which the circuitry actually works. From the programmer's point of view, the important issue is how memory is addressed from a logical perspective. I explain in Chapter 8 in the section titled "Calculating Addresses" that in real mode (which is how every PC starts working when it is first turned on) memory is addressed in a peculiar way called segment:offset addressing. (Refer to that chapter, please, if you are unclear on the difference between real mode and the several protected modes that PCs can use.)

The segment:offset addressing strategy simply means that every reference in a program to a memory location uses two 16-bit numbers. One is called the *segment value* and the other the *offset*. The segment number, multiplied by 16, is added to the offset to get the actual physical address.

One consequence of this design is that in real mode a PC can address only about 1MB of memory. That is the size of its real-mode memory address space. When this design was first created, this seemed to many people a generous amount. And it was, compared to the mere 64KB address space in all the previous microcomputers. Now it is positively stifling. Of course, our PCs are now programmed to go into protected mode early in their boot process, and when they are there they can access as much RAM (and ROM) as you have installed.

> **Technical Note:** By a "trick" it is possible to address 17/16ths of a megabyte in every PC that has some extended memory. This extra 64KB is what we call the High Memory Area. But for most purposes it is adequate to say that a PC can address only 1MB in real mode.
>
> There is one other trick that can be used to let PCs with a 286 or 386 CPU access up to 32GB of memory—the full amount it can access in protected mode—even in real mode. But this involves cheating in that it uses an undocumented command to manipulate the contents of the page descriptors in a way that Intel never intended and does not sanction. This isn't often done, but for completeness (and only for the very techy among my readers) I thought I should mention it here.

In the late 1970s Intel chose to make its first x86 CPUs access memory in this two-step fashion (using segments and offsets) so that converting programs originally written for the previous generation of microprocessors to run on these (at that time) new CPUs would be easier. And we have been stuck with this design ever since.

In protected mode, conversion of a logical address to a physical one is more complicated. Several steps are required to combine the selector value (which is the protected-mode name for what was the segment value in real mode) with the offset and pass that address through the page translation tables before finally coming out with a physical address. You'll find all the messy details described in Chapter 8, and I will recap them for you briefly in this chapter in just a moment.

The important point of this section is that when any PC starts booting, it has only about 1MB of memory address space. This implies some things that are critical to memory design and usage in PCs even when they aren't running in real mode.

IBM's and Intel's Limiting Choices

Intel made some other choices that force the hand of any PC designer. It made all its x86 family of CPUs automatically go to a particular address (FFFF0h) that is just 16 bytes shy of 1MB above the bottom of memory address space immediately after they "wake up." Whatever number the CPU finds there is presumed to be the first instruction it is to execute (see Figure 11.4).

Figure 11.4.
The special memory addresses for every Intel x86 CPU.

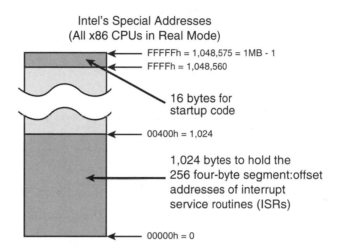

Intel's Special Addresses
(All x86 CPUs in Real Mode)

FFFFFh = 1,048,575 = 1MB - 1
FFFF0h = 1,048,560

16 bytes for
startup code

00400h = 1,024

1,024 bytes to hold the
256 four-byte segment:offset
addresses of interrupt
service routines (ISRs)

00000h = 0

Note: I should point out that this diagram shows memory addresses increasing from the bottom up. That seems a perfectly normal thing for a graph to do, but it is not the only way to represent memory. In fact, nearly as many authors use exactly the opposite tack as there are who use the approach I do. One justification for those who use an "upside down" way of presenting memory diagrams is that the MEM command does that as well. But that is done simply because of the way text scrolls on a video screen, not because the author of the MEM program thought that was the right way to display such a diagram. So all the memory diagrams in this book will be "right side up." Just be aware when comparing them to what you see elsewhere that other authors do not always create their memory maps in the same way.

This means that you absolutely need ROM located at this defined (FFFF0h) address. If you don't, the CPU won't find any instructions and it won't be able to boot itself.

At the other end of the memory address space, Intel put the interrupt vector table. Again, this is only a real-mode issue, but because all PCs start out in real mode, it affects memory design for every one of them.

In this case, RAM is required. This lets the PC store numbers that point to interrupt service routines and to change those numbers when new ISRs are loaded. (If you aren't clear on these concepts, please refer to the discussion in the section titled "Interrupts: The Driving Force" in Chapter 8.

ROM at the top, RAM at the bottom; it's actually a pretty simple picture. Then IBM went on to make some more decisions that slightly complicate this picture. IBM had, in its previous mainframe computers, reserved half of the memory address space for "system uses" and left the other half for "users" to use however they wanted. That is, the operating system and hardware had exclusive use of half the memory address space. Any application program got to use some portion of the other half.

IBM apparently realized that Intel's 1MB of memory address space wasn't all that generous, so it reserved only $^3/_8$ of it for system use and left the remainder for application programs to use. And $^5/_8$ of 1MB is 640KB, which is where the infamous "640KB barrier"—which I talk about at the end of this chapter—comes from.

Figure 11.5 shows how the real-mode memory address space of a PC is divided according to these choices by Intel and IBM. This figure shows some of the details of how the system space was to be used according to IBM's initial plans.

Figure 11.5.
IBM's plan for PC real-mode memory usage.

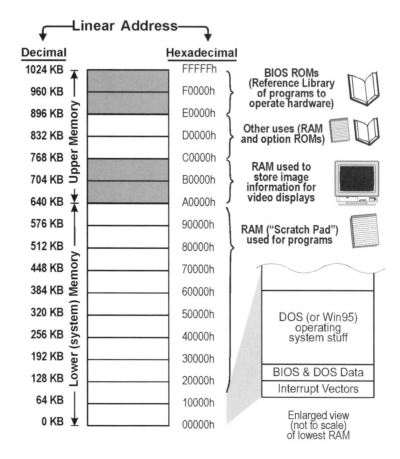

The Newer, Flatter Memory Model

Doubtless you have run into the jargon phrase "32-bit access" or perhaps "32-bit program," and you might have wondered just what these phrases mean. Unfortunately, their meanings are not always the same. You also might recall having run across some reference to a "flat memory model" and wondered what that is. This section explains all these things.

When a PC is running in real mode it can access only about 1MB of memory address locations. This means it needs only a 20-bit (or perhaps a 21-bit) address—if you include access to the High Memory Area—to point to any place in its memory address space. That is true even for the latest and greatest Pentium II machine—when it is operating in real mode.

DOS is a real-mode operating system. Over the years it has been gussied up with protected mode extensions, and now it comes dressed up in a new interface, as Windows 95. But at its core, it is a real-mode operating system. This shows up in the fact that quite often a PC running DOS or Windows (including Windows 95) will have to switch out of protected mode, back into real mode, to do some task. Then it will switch back to protected mode to continue its work.

This fact has two important implications. First, when in real mode, the PC can access memory only in the first megabyte. So that space is always going to be special and precious as long as our PC operating systems must go back to real mode for any purpose. (And to maintain backward compatibility it is almost a given that they will have to do so for a very long time.) Second, while in real mode, all the protections that give protected mode its name aren't there. So whatever program is running at that time must be a very trusted one if you are not to have your PC be vulnerable to all sorts of unexpected crashes.

Technical Note: There is one kind of exception to this last problem. One of the several protected modes of operation of an x86 CPU is called *virtual 86 mode* (v86), and another in the most recent models is called *extended virtual 86 mode* (Ev86). In these modes the CPU acts as though it is in real mode, for most purposes, but actually it still implements all the protections. And if the program running in this mode attempts to do something prohibited, the CPU automatically transfers control back to a portion of the operating system called the *v86 monitor program*, and that program decides what to do next.

This is how a "DOS box" (or DOS window) inside Windows 3.x or Windows 95 works. And for those programs that can run in that environment, this mechanism offers a lot of protection between that program and all the others running on that PC at the same time. Unfortunately, not all real-mode programs can run in a DOS window, which is why Windows 95 provides its MS-DOS mode. And in that mode, the CPU really is operating in real mode with no protections at all. (Of course, the real-mode program can't access extended memory and no other programs are operating at the same time, so at worst you'll simply have to reboot your PC to recover from whatever crashes may occur.)

For both these reasons, PC operating system designers have been eager to get us past DOS and on to something better. The most common jargon term for this newer, better world is *32-bit*. That gets stuck on the front of all kinds of references, and mostly what it implies is that the reference is to some program that runs in protected mode. Indeed, when a PC is running in protected mode (provided it has a CPU that is at least a 386-compatible chip) it has access to a full 4GB of memory address space, for which 32 bits of address are a necessity.

At the beginning of the section "Addressing Memory: Intel's Segments" earlier in this chapter I pointed out that in real mode a program refers to an address in segment:offset form. In protected mode the same form is used; the segment number (still a 16-bit number) is termed a selector, and the offset now is expanded from a 16-bit number to a 32-bit number.

The selector's value is not itself a part of the memory address. It is, instead, a pointer to a data table called a segment descriptor table. (There is one for all the programs running in the PC at a given moment, called the Global Descriptor Table, or GDT, and there is another one for each program, called its Local Descriptor Table, or LDT.) Part of the information in that descriptor table is the base address for this segment, which can be anywhere in the CPU's 4GB memory address range.

Another part of the segment descriptor specifies its size, and that includes a bit called the granularity bit. If that bit is turned off, the maximum segment size is 1MB. It can be of any size up to that large. If this bit is turned on, the size number (which is 20 bits long) is multiplied by 4,096. In this case the maximum segment size is equal to the total memory address space (4GB), and the size must be some integer multiple of 4KB.

It is possible, but by no means necessary, for a protected-mode operating system to set the granularity bit to a one and the segment base address to zero for all segments. If this were to be done, every program would see the full 32-bit address space. That is the ultimate in what a programmer would call a flat address model. In this case only the (32-bit) offset portion of the address would have any significance.

However, PC operating systems don't do this, and for some very good reasons. The best way to protect one program from another is simply to ensure that each cannot see the other's memory address space. And that requires that each of those programs uses segments that are smaller than the total memory address space. (There are other considerations also, but this makes my point.)

Not All Memory Is Equal

Most of the time, whenever you hear a reference to memory in a PC it refers to some portion of the main memory that is the view of the CPU. But not always. I want in this section to remind you of some memory areas that are not a part of main memory and also of some of the jargon terms used in reference to memory.

Even before that, I will remind you of another very important fact: Not every physical memory address has memory at it. Some addresses will be locations in ROM. More are locations in RAM. But in almost every modern PC, most (quantitatively) of the memory addresses the CPU can address simply point to nothingness. Not even to an empty socket where you could plug in a memory module. Just to nowhere at all.

This means, of course, that the CPU better not address those locations. And it doesn't. But it still gets to use the full range of memory address in its internal workings, because of the "magic" of page mapping.

Logical, Segmented, Virtual, Linear, and Physical Memory Addresses

I want to bring together some concepts I have scattered around various other places in this book, and flesh them out a little more. Four terms are used to describe a memory address, and they mean quite different things.

Logical Memory Addresses

Logical memory addresses are the addresses used in programs. This term can be applied no matter whether the program is running in real or protected mode. It simply means the numbers that specify where a program is pointing in the PC's main memory.

Segmented Memory Addresses

A segmented memory address means an address in a real-mode program. It is specified by a pair of 16-bit numbers joined by a colon, for example 1A35:0043. (Both numbers are assumed to be in hexadecimal notation whenever you see an address written in this way, even though there is no trailing h or leading 0x on either number.) The first number is the segment, and its value multiplied by 16 is added to the second number (called the offset) to get the actual, physical memory address.

Virtual Memory Addresses

In protected mode, what was called a segmented address is now referred to as a virtual memory address. This is still a pair of (hexadecimal) numbers separated by a colon. Now, however, the first one (still a 16-bit number) is called the selector and it points out which segment is to be used by reference to a segment descriptor table. The second number is the offset and now is allowed to be up to a 32-bit number. If you want to see the details of the descriptor table elements, please refer to Figure 8.4.

Linear Memory Addresses

Both segmented and virtual memory addresses are translated from two numbers into one. This single memory pointer is called the *linear memory address*. Its maximum size in PCs so far is also a 32-bit number. (Well, in the Pentium Pro and Pentium II it could be a 36-bit number, but so far that possibility has not been supported in any PC operating system.)

Physical Memory Addresses

Beginning with the 386, all Intel's x86 processors and all their clone CPU chips have had a memory paging mechanism built in. This paging mechanism can either be enabled or disabled, under software control. If it is disabled, then the linear address is put on the CPU's address lines, and as such it becomes the *physical memory address*.

If, on the other hand, paging is enabled then the linear memory address is further translated into a (generally different) physical memory address by reference to a pair of tables in main memory. These tables are called the page directory table and the page table.

The most significant 10 bits of the linear address (bits 22–31) pick out a line in the page directory table. That line contains a number that points to the location in RAM where the relevant page table can be found. The next set of 10 bits in the linear address (bits 12–21) select a row in the page table. A number found there points to a page frame, which is a 4KB-long region of physical memory address space. The bottom 12 bits of the linear address (bits 0–11) point to an actual memory location within that page frame. The page table and the page directory table entries also hold some additional information the CPU must know about the page frame and page table to which they point (respectively). If this paragraph was confusing, you might want to refer to Figure 8.5, which shows this process graphically.

Some Ways the CPU Saves Time When It Does Memory Address Calculations

All this translation from segmented or virtual address to linear address and linear address to physical address could take up a lot of the CPU's time. This is especially so because each translation requires reference to some table or tables in RAM. However, starting with the 386, Intel has included some special, hidden registers inside the CPU to cache the relevant information.

Each time a new selector is loaded into a segment register, the segment descriptor information from the corresponding Global or Local Descriptor Table (GDT or LDT) is loaded into an invisible portion of the segment register (called the descriptor cache register). That lets the CPU use it for address validation and translation without repeatedly rereading the GDT or LDT.

Similarly, whenever a page table is read, its contents are cached in the Translation Lookaside Buffer (TLB) in the CPU. Therefore, linear to physical memory translations can also be accomplished without a constant need to reread that table from RAM.

> **Note:** All of this caching for the purpose of speeding up memory address calculations is in addition to the L1 (and perhaps L2) memory caching that is being used to speed up access to data and instructions. This combination of techniques is a substantial part of what accounts for the very much faster operation of PCs using 386 or better CPUs over their predecessors, even when the CPU clock speeds were comparable.

Finally, when the CPU wants to send data out or pull data in it puts the physical memory address on its address lines as low and high voltages (standing for the zeros and ones of the binary number that is the physical memory address value). From there, the external circuitry must route this memory reference to the correct memory chips or module (refer to Figure 8.2).

Memory the CPU Can't See (At Least Not Always)

Not all memory in your PC is a part of its main memory. The following is a quick rundown of some of the other kinds of memory you can have in a PC.

Cache Memory

In effect, the CPU doesn't "see" the memory that is actually closest to it, physically. That is, it doesn't really see the cache memory. It uses it, looking through the cache to see the main memory beyond.

Video Memory

The video subsystem needs some memory in which to build the images it will display on your monitor. This memory is referred to as the *video frame buffer*. (And if you have two monitors, each will likely have its own frame buffer.) Because memory always comes in powers of two, and because most frame buffers need some different amount of memory, it is quite common for the video subsystem to have some other memory under its control, in addition to the frame buffer.

When PCs were young and their video displays primitive, the entire video frame buffer showed up in the CPU's memory address space. That was fine for a 16KB, 32KB, or even a 128KB video frame buffer in a 1MB PC. But now, with high resolution and large color depth displays, a 4MB frame buffer is common, with even larger ones being used in high-end machines. In real mode, in particular, it just isn't possible to fit all that frame buffer into the CPU's meager 1MB of memory address space. This is dealt with by making at most 128KB of it show up at once. The CPU can command the video subsystem, via some I/O ports, to reveal whatever portion of the frame buffer the CPU must access. The rest of the time that memory is kept out of the CPU's direct field of view.

This means that different portions of the very large frame buffer will occupy the same region of the CPU's memory address space, but at different times. When such a portion is not occupying that portion of the CPU's memory address space, it is, so far as the CPU is concerned, simply nonexistent.

In protected mode, with the full 4GB of memory address space available, this need no longer be a problem. It is perfectly possible to have the full 4MB or more of frame buffer show up somewhere in the CPU's 4GB memory address space. But often this is not done, for simplicity and compatibility with the real-mode way of doing things.

Finally, the video subsystem might have some uses for memory that don't involve the CPU. The video subsystem's main use of the frame buffer is simply to store there the image that is currently on the screen, and to pump out the pixels to the monitor repeatedly so it will continue to redraw that image. But it also might need to have some font bit-patterns cached somewhere, or might need some scratchpad space for doing various graphics acceleration actions. Often that space is taken from the portion of the frame buffer memory that isn't being used for the actual frame image.

Expanded Memory

This isn't common anymore, but if you have a very old PC, you might have an expanded memory card in it. This was a way to make a large amount of memory (relatively speaking) available even in a mere PC or PC/XT. Up to 32MB of RAM on a special add-in card could be made to show up in the CPU's memory address space just 16KB at a time, in a manner quite analogous to that used by modern video subsystems to reveal just a portion of their frame buffer at a time.

Today, if you have a program that wants to use some EMS memory, that resource is simulated by the operating system. DOS users will know the parts that do this by the names `HIMEM.SYS` and `EMM386.EXE`. These are device drivers that augment what DOS alone can do. `HIMEM.SYS` takes some or all of the extended memory in the PC (memory at addresses above 1MB) and converts it into something called XMS memory. EMM386 then converts as much of that XMS memory into what appears to a program to be EMS memory as that program requests.

Windows 95 automatically provides proper memory emulation on an as-needed basis to any DOS programs that you launch from within Windows—either in a DOS box or full-screen mode. Because of this, you need not specify `EMM386.EXE` in your `CONFIG.SYS` file, and you should not specify `HIMEM.SYS`—both of these will actually diminish Windows 95's capability to internally manage memory. If you have an old DOS program that will not run under Windows 95, even in DOS mode, then you must boot from a system boot diskette made under an earlier version of DOS, and you will, in that case, need to load HIMEM or EMM386 in the diskette's `CONFIG.SYS` file if your old DOS program requires them.

Several third-party programs do this job, and in many ways do it better than these OS-included device drivers do. The most popular have been Quarterdeck's QEMM and the Qualitas program first called 386Max, and now just called Max.

Disk Controller Card Memory

Some hard disk controllers have cache memory built onto them. This is a way to speed disk accesses that doesn't use any of your PC's main memory. It has some advantages over using SmartDrive (or some other disk caching program that does the same thing, but uses a portion of main RAM for the purpose), but they aren't usually compelling enough to justify the added cost. So again, this is a relatively rare kind of CPU-invisible memory, but you might have some of it in your PC.

Network Interface Card Memory

Some Network Interface Cards (NICs) use a small amount of onboard memory to cache information on its way into or out of your PC via the network. This is another kind of memory your PC's CPU knows nothing about and cannot directly access.

Memory On an Add-In Slave PC Board

You can buy a PC these days in many forms. One form is an entire PC on a plug-in card meant to be inserted into another PC. That way you can have multiple keyboard, mouse, and screen setups attached to your PC. Each one has its own CPU and those CPUs each have their own main memory. Naturally, the host CPU can't see any of this. It just communicates with the slave PCs through input/output ports via its input/output bus.

Printer Memory

You might have as much as several MB of memory in your printer. If it is a page printer (such as a laser printer) it probably has a buffer internally that is sufficient to let it compose at least most of an entire page image before it begins printing that page. And this is also memory that the CPU doesn't see.

External RAM Disk Memory

You can create a fictitious "RAM disk" inside your PC by running a program that uses a portion of your PC's main RAM to emulate a disk drive. That RAM is fully in the view of the CPU, and indeed the CPU—under the direction of the RAMdisk program—causes that RAM to act like a disk drive.

But you also can buy external RAM disks. These simply are boxes that contain a large amount of RAM, a power supply (probably with battery backup to keep them running when power fails), and a small computer that causes this RAM to look to your PC just like any other (very fast) disk drive. Because it looks just like a disk drive, it doesn't look like RAM to your CPU.

Your PC's Memory Needs Managing

Memory is one of the main resources in a PC, and all of the PC's resources (memory, input/output ports, DMA channels, IRQ lines, drives, and so on) must be managed. That is, in fact, one of the defining characteristics of any computer's operating system. It is a means of scheduling and managing the resources in that computer for the benefit of the computer's users and the programs that they run on that computer.

DOS and Windows are mainly systems for managing the PC's resources. They make these resources available to your programs as those programs require—and they arbitrate between competing requests for resources. DOS and Windows don't exist in a vacuum, however, and you might discover great benefits in actively helping the operating system manage your PC's uses of its memory. I'm going to talk about active participation now.

How DOS and Windows 95 Allocate Memory

First, you must understand how memory is assigned for various uses in a PC. I have already told you most of the story for protected mode. Now I will tell you the real-mode portion of the story, and then finish the protected-mode story.

Real-Mode Memory Allocation

In real mode DOS manages memory by using a chain of *memory allocation blocks* (MCBs), also known as memory arena headers. Because in real mode no protections are operative, DOS cannot really manage memory in the same aggressive fashion that is possible in protected mode. It can, at best, control what programs get loaded where, and then trust that each of them will only do safe things. Each program is capable of doing anything it wants after it is loaded and given control of the machine.

How the OS Core Gains Control of Physical Memory

When a PC first boots, the BIOS POST program has absolute control over everything. At that point, no memory is allocated to any use—except that by Intel's fiat the first 1KB is reserved for the interrupt vector table (IVT) and the top of the first megabyte better contain a ROM with some suitable boot program code in it.

During the POST process some IVT entries are filled in with pointers to interrupt service routines (ISRs) located in the motherboard BIOS. Also, some data is placed in the BIOS and DOS data area, which is a three-quarters of a kilobyte region immediately following the IVT.

When the BIOS POST completes its work, it loads the operating system. Well, actually, it loads the boot sector program from the boot disk. That program is loaded into memory at physical address 700h (immediately after the BIOS and DOS data area). Control is then passed to that program to do whatever it was written to do.

If it is a DOS boot sector (and both DOS and Windows 95 use what amounts to a standard DOS boot sector), it will load the operating system files and let them prepare the in-RAM, ready-to-run version of the operating system. (It takes some initialization steps, and the program code to do those steps is discarded when they have been done.) At the end of that process more of the IVT has been filled in, and the operating system core has been loaded into RAM, also starting at 700h (overlaying the boot sector program).

How the OS Core Builds the Memory Arena Chain

Now the operating system core starts to process the startup files (CONFIG.SYS and AUTOEXEC.BAT, or the Windows 95 registry and then those files). At this point some memory management becomes both possible and necessary.

Deep inside the operating system core, at a location that is both officially undocumented and quite widely known (and also has been very stable from version to version of DOS) lies a special table of pointers called the *list of lists*. One entry in that table points to the beginning of the first memory control block (MCB), which is located just above the operating system core. Each MCB is "owned" by some program. The first one is owned by DOS, and so is every other block that "controls" an unallocated region of memory.

Any memory region (memory arena) that contains a program is owned by that program. Also, any other memory regions that are used by that program for data will be owned by that program. (One program might end up having half a dozen MCBs that it owns—or only one if that is all it needs.)

The first MCB DOS creates starts out including all the rest of lower memory (from where it is up to the infamous 640KB boundary). DOS loads programs into an empty memory arena (the area controlled by an MCB that belongs to DOS). Ordinarily it will load any program into the first such block which it finds that is large enough to accommodate that program. Then, control of the PC is passed to that program.

Some programs (all application programs, for example) will do their thing and then exit, turning back to DOS all the memory they were using. DOS then reuses that memory to load the next program.

Some programs (device drivers, for example) will do some initialization work, then return control of the PC to DOS but ask that they be allowed to keep some portion of the memory they were using. Another name for such a program is one that *terminates and stays resident* (they are often referred to as a *TSR program*). In those cases, DOS shrinks the memory arena to whatever size that program declares it must keep, and creates a new MCB to control the memory that it reclaimed from that program.

After this process goes on for awhile, a chain of MCBs will develop. Each one says how large the memory arena it controls is, and because that arena always starts right after the MCB, figuring out where it ends is pretty easy. The next MCB in the chain comes right after that.

After you learn how to decode the contents of an MCB, stepping through the MCB chain yourself is pretty easy. Just use the DEBUG program to display the contents of one MCB. Now figure out the length of the memory arena it controls and add that length to the address of this MCB (and don't forget to add in the length of the MCB itself) using hexadecimal arithmetic. This will give you the address of the next MCB in the chain. Use DEBUG to display its contents. Repeat until you find a chain with a block type of Z, which indicates the end of the chain.

Alternatively, you can get much of the same information, but not see the form in which it is held in memory, by using the MEM command with its optional /d command-line switch. I describe this more later in this chapter.

Secondary Chains of MCBs

One main chain of MCBs starts with the first one just above the operating system core and typically ends just below 640KB. There can be one or more secondary chains. One type of secondary chain is more commonly called a subchain. This is a chain of MCBs within one memory arena controlled by another MCB. Figure 11.6, later in the chapter, shows two examples of this.

The other type of secondary chain is found in upper memory (at a physical memory address above 640KB, but below 1MB). Such a chain can be formed by a third-party memory manager, by any XMS-aware program, or by DOS if you use its memory managers and declare DOS=UMB in your CONFIG.SYS file.

Structure of a Memory Control Block

A memory control block occupies exactly 16 bytes. It always starts at a physical memory address that is an integer multiple of 16.

Table 11.1 shows the structure of an MCB. Figure 11.6 shows a typical chain of MCBs on a particular PC running Windows 95 (in this case a Dell Latitude XPi CD M166ST portable). I created this figure by running a small DOS program to "walk the MCB chain" inside a DOS window running under Windows 95. This program doesn't report the Process ID field of the MCBs directly. Instead, it attempts to give the name of the program that owns each one.

Table 11.1. The structure of a memory control block (MCB).

Byte Position	Contents
0	Block type [*]
1 and 2	Process ID [**]

Byte Position	Contents
3 and 4	Size/16
5 to 7	Reserved
8 to 15	Owner name [***]

[*]   Z for end of chain, M for all others except in device subchain, where

D = Device driver (from `Device=` line in `CONFIG.SYS`)

E = Device driver appendage

I = Installable file system (not currently used)

F = Storage area (if `FILES > 5` in `CONFIG.SYS`)

X = File Control Blocks (FCBS) storage area

B = Buffers (from `BUFFERS=` line in `CONFIG.SYS`)

L = Drive information table (from `LASTDRIVE=` line in `CONFIG.SYS`)

S = Code and data area for DOS stacks (from `STACKS=` line in `CONFIG.SYS`)

[**]   The Process ID is 0000 for free space, 0008 for blocks owned by the operating system, and it is the segment value of the Program Segment Prefix of the owning program for all other MCBs.

[***]   Only those MCBs whose Process ID is one greater than the segment value of that MCB (and thus is a block controlling the PSP of its owner) and only for DOS versions 4 or later, this area may contain the name of the owning program, either null terminated or padded with spaces.

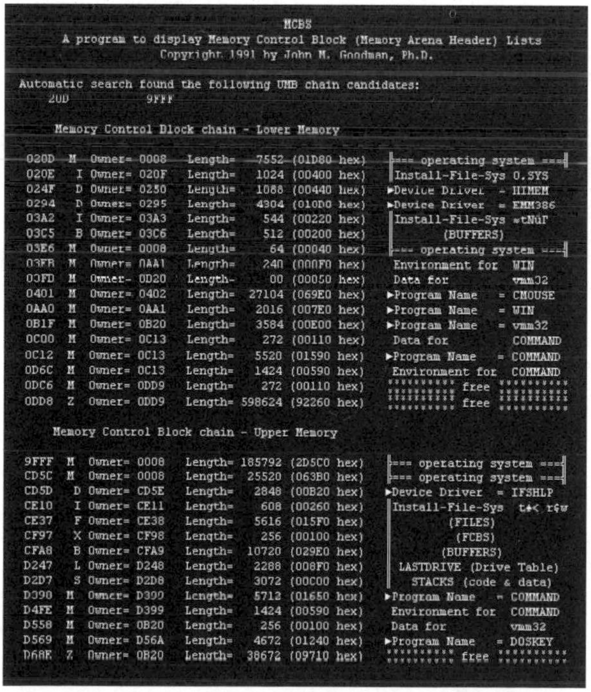

Figure 11.6.
Sample MCB chain on a Windows 95 machine.

This particular PC has a small CONFIG.SYS and AUTOEXEC.BAT file in which I load the necessary real-mode device drivers to support memory management and a contour design mouse. The program used to display this particular list of MCBs is one I wrote a few years ago for another project. You can get the same information for yourself by stepping through the chain, using DEBUG, and manually doing all the translations from the numbers you find.

Notice in Figure 11.6 that installable file system devices (which are block devices) have very odd "names." Typically the name field in their MCB is nonsense. That only occurs for block device drivers (ordinarily); all the other MCBs that control a region in which there is a program will have a sensible name.

If you use a third-party memory manager, you might find that some of the MCBs will have very odd Process ID values. These programs use their own, proprietary values in that location to signal something special to themselves. And they typically don't tell users what those special values are or mean.

IBM's PC DOS 7 also has added some new block types for the device subchains. And it, too, has declined to publish what these block types mean.

What Real-Mode Memory Management Is—And Isn't

Remember, in real mode there is no way for the operating system to force a program to stay within any particular memory boundaries. (Nor can it prevent that program from doing anything it likes at any of the input/output port addresses.) After control of the PC is passed to a program, that program reigns supreme. It can do anything at all. So memory management in real mode is more accurately described as cooperative memory allocation and use. Everything is "on the honor system." Protected-mode memory management is altogether different from this.

Protected-Mode Memory Allocation

I have already told you a lot about how memory addresses are specified in protected mode. You know that the segment portion of a logical address is replaced by something called a selector in a virtual address (which is what logical addresses become in protected-mode programs). And you know that selectors designate one segment descriptor in either the global descriptor table or in a local descriptor table. That descriptor contains an actual linear memory address for the beginning of the specified segment, and it also contains a length for that segment.

What I haven't yet told you is about the protection mechanisms that get involved in all this. There are several, so bear with me, please.

Actually, the entire story is too much to tell here. It would take up far too many pages. And, unless you are a budding CPU designer or operating system programmer, it would put your eyes in jeopardy of semi-permanently glazing over! So I'll just give you the short version of the story. That's enough to let you see, at least roughly, how memory is allocated and protected in protected mode, and what that means for programs running in that mode.

Intel's Rings

Intel defined four levels of privilege for programs running on any x86 CPU in protected mode. It pictures this with a diagram that looks like an archery target. Ring zero is at the center, surrounded by rings one and two with ring three on the outside.

Programs running at ring zero have full access to the entire machine. They are every bit as powerful as real-mode programs. In fact, they are a little more powerful because they can set the boundaries on what other programs, running at lower permission levels, can do.

In each ring outside ring zero programs have less access to the hardware and more restrictions on their behavior. Programs in ring three are the least powerful. Still, with some help from some ring-zero programs, even a ring-three program can accomplish any task it must do, provided that some ring-zero program is willing to do the hardware accesses for it.

This model is splendid. In principle you would have a very small operating system core, consisting only of modules that had been extensively tested and were highly trustworthy, running in ring zero. Ring one would contain other parts of the operating system. Ring two might contain helper programs—applets, and that sort of thing. Ring three would be reserved for your application programs.

As it happens, this model is too much. All the mainstream PC operating systems use only rings zero and three, which turns out to be sufficient. More than that is too much sophistication (and complexity) or else using that many levels would cost too much in terms of performance (because it takes at least a little bit of time to effect a switch in operating level).

Therefore, most of the operating system, portions of many third-party device drivers, and certain other kinds of modules run in ring zero. Everything else runs in ring three. This works, but it also helps explain why even after extensive testing, Windows and Windows applications manage to crash every once in awhile.

Protected-Mode Segments Are Special

In real mode, a segment (any segment) is just a region of memory that is exactly 64KB in size and starts at some memory address that is an integer multiple of 16. That's all. Protected-mode segments are much more than this. A protected-mode segment can start at any memory address. It can have any length it must have, and it will ordinarily not be any larger than it must be. But most importantly, protected-mode segments have *properties*.

There are two main types of segment, and some subtypes for one of these. The main two types are *code segments* and *data segments*. These names suggest something of their purpose, and imply some of their properties. Data segments can be further subdivided into *stack* segments (which can be identified as either 16-bit or 32-bit stack segments) and other data segments.

Code segments are meant to hold pieces of a program (which is necessarily held there in the form of machine code, so it can be directly used by the CPU). Because of that, these segments—and only segments of this type—are segments from which the CPU is permitted to withdraw its instructions. And it is not possible to alter the contents of a code segment. (Well, it isn't possible to alter its contents as that. But if you define another segment of a different type that just happens to cover the same stretch of linear memory, then you can modify its contents, which are the same contents as those in the code segment. This sounds convoluted, but that is exactly how one must go about modifying a program in memory and also being able to execute it.)

Stack segments are places that hold information temporarily. A program normally directs the CPU to "push" the contents of some or all of its registers onto the stack before beginning a new task. At the end of that task, those values can be "popped" back from the stack into the registers from which they came. (This must be done in just the right way. Otherwise, a value might get put back into the wrong register, and that could lead to much mischief.)

Necessarily, therefore, a stack segment must be a region in which it is both possible to write and read information. But it won't be used to hold instructions, so being able to execute the information held there as CPU instructions is not necessary. These rules are enforced by the CPU after it discerns that a particular segment is of the type "stack segment."

Stack segments also come in two sizes, but in this context that size does not refer to how large a region of memory the segment contains, but rather to the assumption the CPU will make about what size numbers it is to push on and pop off the stack. The two sizes are, as you might have guessed, 16-bit and 32-bit.

Data segments comprise the remainder of the existing segments. These can be given a variety of properties. Like stack segments, data segments cannot have their contents executed as instructions. (Unless, of course, a code segment is defined that just happens to contain those same contents, because its memory region happens to coincide with or overlap that of this particular data segment.) But they can be set to be read-only segments, write-only segments, or read-write segments.

Segment Descriptor Table Entries

Back in Chapter 8 I told you about selectors and the segment descriptors to which they point. These descriptors contain a linear address that indicates where the segment starts, another number that specifies how large a region of memory this segment contains, and several more fields that specify what kind of segment it is, and more.

Figure 8.3 shows the "access rights" portion of a segment descriptor and of the "requestor privilege level" bits in the selector. Figure 8.4 shows the details, but I didn't discuss them there. Nor will I discuss them here any more than I just have. You can get a sense of what they do from what I just told you and by studying that figure. But if you *really* want to know more, I suggest you refer to any of the many specialized books on the subject. One of my favorites is Robert L. Hummel's *The Processor and Coprocessor*, (Ziff-Davis Press, 1992).

The main thing to know is that a combination of the requestor privilege level of the selector and the access rights bits in the segment descriptor pointed to by that selector determine most of what it is possible for a program to do with the contents of that segment. And these descriptors are entries in either the Global Descriptor Table (GDT) or a Local Descriptor Table (LDT).

The contents of the GDT (of which there is only one for the entire PC) and of the particular LDT that a particular program accesses totally controls which portions of memory that program can see and use. (There are also similar ways the operating system and CPU cooperate to protect the other resources such as interrupts and ports from misuse by errant programs, but those topics are outside the scope of this chapter.)

The CPU contains some special registers that point to the GDT and the LDT. Normally, only the operating system is allowed to change the contents of these registers, which is another aspect of how it can keep control over different tasks.

When One Program Calls Another

Where things get really complicated is when one program wants to ask another program to do something. This happens all the time. If the calling program and the called program both reside in the ring of privilege there is no special problem. But if they are in different rings, then some very special care must be taken to ensure that the more privileged program isn't effectively conned into doing something it shouldn't, and that it doesn't in the process confer more privileges on the calling program when it returns control.

These matters are taken care of by some very clever and intricate features of the x86 processors. To understand them you must learn all about Task Switch Segments (TSSs) and gates—all very arcane stuff, and too much off track for this discussion. Just know that Intel's engineers figured all this out correctly. So if the operating system is also crafted correctly (as seems to be the case with all the popular PC protected-mode operating systems), the right things will happen and the wrong ones will be prevented.

The Bottom Line

Protected-mode memory management enables the operating system, with a lot of help from the CPU's protection hardware, to rigidly enforce limits on programs. It can keep them completely separate, or it can let them share some resources, but not others. The particular decisions on these matters differ from operating system to operating system, and are, in fact, the source of some of the most critical differences between, for example, Windows 95 and Windows NT.

Understanding the MEM Command

DOS and Windows 95 provide a command that lets you look at how memory is being used on your PC. This isn't a book about DOS commands, so I won't go into any detail on how this MEM command works, but I want to point out that it is there, and it will also let you see much of what I have just been discussing.

If you just execute the command, you'll only get a summary of the types of memory your PC has and how much of each one is in use. If you add a command-line switch of /? (a slash character followed by a question mark), you'll get a help screen that shows you what other switches you could use.

The /c switch is very useful for seeing which programs are loaded into lower or upper memory and how much memory each one uses. The /d switch essentially presents the information one can get by "walking the MCB chain." The form of this display has changed with different DOS (and Windows) versions. Earlier ones used only hexadecimal values in the /d display, which discouraged most folks from using it (though it was wonderful for programmers). The latest versions only use decimal values except for the segment addresses in the left-most column. That is more people-friendly, in general, but it does mean you might have to do some translations from decimal to hexadecimal if, for example, you want to add the size of one memory arena to its address to get the address for the next one.

The Infamous 640KB Barrier and How to Break Past It

Let's return for a moment to the relatively simple (if uncontrolled) world of real-mode PC operation. Here is where memory management (in the sense of something a PC's user could do to make it work better) all began.

I have told you how DOS loads one program after another and lets each one keep some or all of its memory if it needs to. After awhile you can accumulate quite a stack of programs in your PC. Normally you want to do this because those programs are the very necessary pieces that extend the operating system so you can access your CD-ROM drive, a network, a mouse, and other things that you must use. But it is also very possible to have all these bits and pieces use up so much memory that there isn't enough room left over for that big application program you must run. That's when memory management comes into play.

The first 640KB of physical memory is what IBM decreed programs could use. IBM reserved the rest of the 1MB of real-mode memory address space for system uses. Only a fairly small part of that reserved space is actually being used by the video adapter and motherboard BIOS ROM in most PCs. This suggests an opportunity: If only we could use some of that extra, unused space in lieu of a portion of the lower memory region, then we might leave enough room down there for our big DOS program.

I won't go over the many ways in which folks devised to take advantage of this unused space. But I will tell you briefly about the one we mostly use today.

By putting a 386 (or later model x86-compatible) CPU into its virtual 86 (v86 or Ev86) operating mode, you can make it act as though it is in real mode, and yet take advantage of extended memory and the CPU's paging mechanism. This is precisely what HIMEM.SYS and EMM386.EXE do and what Windows 95 and 98 do for DOS applications: They take control of the PC, put it into protected mode, and remap some of the extended memory so it appears to be located at physical addresses in upper memory (between 640KB and 1024KB). Then it runs your DOS programs in v86 mode, so they think they are running in real mode. They don't actually make the memory move to a new physical address, but any program running in v86 mode thinks that the linear addresses it generates are actually physical ones, but the paging mechanism can make any correspondence between the two that it has been told to make.

That creates some available RAM in upper memory. The next step is to move some of the real-mode programs cluttering up lower memory into this newly available RAM. Starting with version 5, DOS enables you to do this quite easily. Just put the line DOS=UMB in your CONFIG.SYS file and then use the LOADHIGH, DEVICEHIGH, and (in DOS 6.x) INSTALLHIGH directives to put your resident programs up there. (The DOS=HIGH directive also helps because it moves some of the core of the OS up into the High Memory Area, just past the end of the first megabyte.)

If you find yourself needing to run lots of TSR programs and real-mode device drivers, and if you then run low on available lower memory, this is the best approach to use to get more free lower memory.

If you are running Windows 95, it will take care of much of this problem. Mainly it does this by substituting protected-mode drivers for most of those real-mode drivers and TSR programs. Also, it solves some memory usage problems that Windows 3.x has that were another reason many folks had to use DOS-level memory management on their PCs.

Understanding Windows Memory Use

DOS plus Windows 3.x or Windows 95 is in many ways just DOS in a pretty dress. So whatever DOS does with memory before Windows is started is something that Windows simply must deal with. And then Windows goes on to do more with memory on its own.

Most of the time, Windows does an admirable job of using memory for its needs and those of the programs it is called upon to run. But when it doesn't, you will get an out of memory message. That doesn't mean that all your PC's RAM is in use. It just means Windows needs some more of some part of it than it is able to get right now. That is when memory management (in the sense of your involvement in the issue) makes sense for Windows users.

The most important point to remember is that Windows (either version 3.x or Windows 95) is a protected-mode environment. That means that after you start Windows, your PC is running in protected mode until you shut Windows down. Well, it will revert to real mode from time to time to do some low-level DOS system actions, but then it immediately springs back into protected mode. (Windows 95 goes back to real mode much less than Windows 3.x, but it still will go back sometimes.) This means that Windows will allocate memory for programs from the entire pool of RAM on your PC. It can access all the RAM you can give it. (And it would probably benefit from having more!) It uses memory from every range of available addresses, both in the first megabyte and beyond.

Some of its uses are for system-level things, such as a disk cache to speed up access to your disk drives. Other uses are for pieces of programs and portions of the data with which they are working. Windows is quite clever about swapping out to disk chunks of data and overlaying chunks of programs with other program chunks whenever it starts to run low on free memory. But it still isn't always capable of running programs you'd think it could. The reason sometimes is that Windows is running low on some specialized pool of memory it needs.

Windows Has Some Special Memory Needs

Whenever Windows loads a Windows application (or a Windows applet—any program that is a Windows program), it must use a small amount of the first 1MB of real, physical RAM to hold some information about that program. This special region that is normally called *lower memory plus upper memory*, or *conventional memory* when we are talking just about DOS, is now called *global DOS memory*. This is one of the precious memory regions Windows must use. And especially if you have a lot of TSR programs and device drivers cluttering up your global DOS memory, Windows might find it hasn't enough room there for its needs. In that case you will get a "not enough memory, close some applications and try again" message.

Also, Windows uses some other and much smaller special memory regions called *heaps*. These are places in which it stores the elements of the dialog boxes, windows, and other things you see on the screen. These also are places Windows programs store some of the many small data structures they use. They are most often described as the GDI and User resource heaps, but in fact, several heaps are being referred to by each label.

Different versions of Windows use different numbers of heaps, and their sizes can also differ between versions. Under Windows 3.x there were clearly too few heaps and they were too small. Running out of heap space (which in Windows jargon became running out of *Windows resources*) was an all-too-common way of finding yourself simply unable to run the programs you wanted to run.

Windows 95 has essentially solved this problem also. In principle, you could run out of resources still, but it is very much less likely. The only time that it might occur is when you run programs that have *resource leaks*. That is, programs that ask for portions of the heap space, then when they are finished with it, forget to tell Windows it is okay now to take that memory back. Run enough of these guys and you are sure to run out of resources.

DOS Virtual Machines Under Windows

Whenever you run a DOS program under Windows 3.x or Windows 95, you are actually running it in a special environment called a *DOS Virtual Machine* (DVM). Another name for this is a "DOS box" or a "DOS window." This is true whether you see the DOS application running literally in a window smaller than your whole screen or you see it running in full-screen mode.

The only exception to this rule is that if you run a DOS application under Windows 95 that must run in MS-DOS mode, then Windows 95 will first shut down all the other programs that are running, shut itself down, and then run your DOS program in actual real mode. (You may, if you want, run that program from a batch file which could load a memory manager and then run your DOS program not in real mode, but this isn't commonly done. The point of MS-DOS mode is to let you run DOS programs that just can't tolerate the protected-mode environment created by Windows.)

Under Windows 3.x and Windows 95 you can have as many DVMs running at once as you want. Well, each one of them can use up just a little more than 1MB of your RAM, so how much RAM your PC has will limit the number of DVMs you can have running at once. And don't forget, Windows still needs some memory for itself.

Each DVM is actually an instance of v86 protected mode. It gets what it sees as a megabyte (or with the HMA $^{17}/_{16}$ of a megabyte) of what it thinks is physical memory address space starting at address zero. Indeed, the interrupt vector table appears at the bottom of this space and the BIOS ROM near the top. But actually this is some remapped RAM (courtesy of the CPU's paging mechanism) into which Windows has copied these portions of the real first megabyte's contents. This allows each DOS program to do whatever it likes in that megabyte of memory with utterly no impact on any other program running on the PC at the same time, whether it's a Windows program or another DOS program in a different DVM.

Any time this DOS program tries to access the screen or keyboard, or some I/O port, or other similar action, the Windows v86 monitor program will intervene. It "virtualizes" the screen memory (the frame buffer) so the DOS program thinks it is writing to the real screen. Windows then copies over that portion of the frame buffer's contents that it needs to make the appropriate window appear on the screen to show you what that DOS program is doing. (Of course, if the DOS program is minimized, Windows won't show you any of its frame buffer.)

Similarly, the DOS program only gets to see the real keystrokes when that DVM has the focus. The rest of the time Windows gets the keystrokes and uses them for itself or passes them to some other program.

Almost all DOS programs can be run this way, and this is the best way to run them on a Windows machine because they are protected in this fashion from one another. This is *real* memory management.

The Windows Virtual Machine

Curiously, Windows doesn't do nearly as good a job of protecting Windows programs from one another, for a simple reason. Only one Windows virtual machine exists. All Windows programs share that one simulated PC.

Another way in which Windows fails to fully protect one application from another is that it uses a message-passing model that allows one ill-behaved program to stop all the rest from working. Windows 95 sort of solves this problem by making it relatively easy to use a local reboot (Ctrl+Alt+Del key combination) to halt that errant program.

Some Ways to Help Windows Manage Memory

You can do several things to help Windows use memory more successfully. Undoubtedly the most important one is to buy and install all the RAM you possibly can. And you can do some other things as well. If you are getting any out-of-memory messages from Windows, the first thing you must do is figure out which kind of memory is in short supply. The most probable kinds are global DOS memory and heap space (resources).

The first stop should be the information that Windows itself offers on the topic. Look at the Help/About dialog box in Windows Explorer (Windows 95) or File Manager (Windows 3.*x*), or in almost any other Microsoft program. They all will tell you something about the program, but they also will tell you about the available memory and available resources. Just one number for each one.

That might be enough. If the free resource percentage gets low, that can well be the problem. Sometimes something as simple as not loading a huge wallpaper image will free up enough of the heap space to let you get on with your work. If that doesn't do the trick, however, you might have to dig a little deeper.

Another way to find out what is going on is to use a system monitor program. One is built into Windows 95, and Windows 3.*x* has one included in the resource kits you can buy for them. But these Microsoft tools require resources of their own, and don't quite do the job when it comes to finding out about the amount of free global DOS memory.

The Norton Utilities for Windows 95 has Norton System Doctor among its many tools. And among the many "sensors" this provides are ones for (global) DOS memory and separate ones for User and

GDI memory. In NSD, you can configure various gauges or sensors to display many details about your system.

If you determine that you are running low on global DOS memory, go back to the section in this chapter titled "The Infamous 640KB Barrier and How to Break Past It." Once you have done what you can at the DOS level there will be at least one more thing you can do.

If you are running Windows 95, make sure you aren't loading any real-mode device drivers that you can avoid using. (This is a good idea in any case, because the protected-mode drivers that come with Windows 95 generally work better and faster than their real-mode counterparts.)

So How Much RAM Do I Need, Really?

I'd like to close this chapter with the one question I get asked most about memory in PCs: "How much RAM do I need, really?" My favorite answer is, "It depends."

And it does. You must look at what you are doing with your PC (or perhaps what you are attempting to do, or wish you could do, if low RAM is preventing you). Also look at how much RAM your PC can accept and what it now has in it. Finally, look at your budget, and think about your plans for possibly getting a newer, bigger, better PC someday soon. After you have looked all those issues, you are ready to address head-on the question of how much RAM to have.

Let me make a few remarks about some of those questions. First, about what you are trying or wanting to do. If you want to run several large Windows applications at once, and especially if you will be manipulating large graphic files or video presentations, then you almost can't have too much RAM. For Windows 3.x I'd start with 32MB. For Windows 95, start with 64MB. And for Windows NT start with 128MB. If those sound like impossibly large numbers, your understanding is outdated. Fortunately, RAM prices have been coming down recently. Adding lots of RAM to your PC has never been less costly. (Memory for portables is still pretty pricey, however.)

When you are considering the cost of adding RAM, also remember to think about what *not* adding it is costing you. Every time your PC must use the swap file (also known as virtual memory), it and most likely you are being slowed down. Add more RAM and that won't happen nearly as often.

Of course, if all you want to do is run one rather modest-sized Windows application, or if you are only running DOS applications and don't use Windows at all, then you can get away with a whole lot less memory in your PC. In that case I might settle for as little as 8MB if you never use Windows and 16MB if you use Windows moderately. But no less—there just isn't any good reason not to have that much.

Some Things to Think About and Try

Use the MEM command, first without any command-line switches, and then with the /c and the /d switches. (You might also want to use the /p switch to keep from having the output scroll off the screen.) You can capture the output to a file with redirection by putting the greater-than symbol (>) and a filename after the command.

Now use DEBUG to explore memory. See the discussion in Chapter 6, "Enhancing Your Understanding by Messing Around (Exploring and Tinkering)," for some suggestions on how to do this. Try to find the MCBs in your PC. Use the segment address information you get from the output of the MEM command with the /d option to guide you.

Use any system monitoring tools you have available to see how much you can learn about what kinds of memory you have and how they are being used. If you have Microsoft Word, or any of a number of other large Windows applications, you may find a System Information button in the Help/About dialog box. Try it out and see what it will tell you. These and similar explorations are among the very best ways to learn about your PC in particular, and in the process about how PCs work in general.

12

Getting Your PC's Attention: Input Devices

Peter Norton®

Your PC is valuable only because it does what you want it to do. And it can do that only if you tell it what you want it to do. So, having a means of sending messages to your PC is vital. Furthermore, you want to be able to enter data for the PC to work on. For example, right now I am doing that by typing on a keyboard the words I want it to put into this chapter.

The keyboard is the means of information input that we use with our PCs most often, but it is hardly the only one. In this chapter I will explain how keyboards work, and also discuss many of the other technologies used for information input to PCs.

Note: You don't actually need to have a keyboard or a mouse attached to a PC. It can run quite happily without either—if it is set up appropriately. Of course, this isn't something you are likely to do unless the PC is being used essentially as an embedded computer (running a fixed program) or you have attached to it some alternative input device such as a touch screen.

The focus here is on the devices that capture information from external sources (people or other things), and not on the means by which that information is conveyed from the input devices into the PC. That latter topic is just one aspect of a more general question that I treat in great detail in Chapter 15, "Understanding Standard PC Input and Output," and Chapter 16, "Faster Ways to Get Information Into and Out of Your PC."

There is one other aspect to PC input I feel is important to cover, at least briefly. I'd hate to see you hurt yourself—especially unnecessarily. Although most things about PCs are quite harmless, some of the things we often do when putting information into them can do real damage to our bodies. I call this topic the "dark side" of PC computing. PCs have empowered many office workers in unprecedented ways. They also have helped make office work into much more of a hazardous occupation than ever before.

One name for these problems is Repetitive Strain Injury (RSI). This is not just a PC-specific problem. It also strikes many musicians, meat packers, and even grocery clerks (now that package scanners have become ubiquitous). We PC users can thank our lucky stars that we aren't the only group of affected workers. Because these problems have been around and recognized in other industries for many years, there is a body of research on RSI. The results of this research have been applied to PC-caused RSI, and now we have both an understanding of the problem and several useful aids toward solving it.

RSI is not something to make light of. Ignoring the symptoms is never the cure. Fortunately, an awareness of the problem and of some of the ways to prevent or mitigate that problem can go a long way toward preventing a minor case of RSI from becoming a truly disabling injury, with repercussions far beyond just what one can do with a PC. I close this chapter with some pointers to resources where you can learn about this very serious problem and how you can minimize your likelihood of being damaged in this way (or how to find help if you already have an RSI condition).

The Keyboard Is "Key"

PCs began as character manipulating devices. Now, of course, we also routinely use our PCs to create and modify images, and even when we use them for "simple" character-oriented tasks, such as letter writing, we concern ourselves with much more than just which letters, numerals, or symbols our documents contain. But before you can think about fonts, formatting, and fancy file manipulations, usually you must first enter the words themselves. And for that the keyboard is, so far, the unequaled champion.

Keyboard Basics

Computer keyboards descended from typewriters, which is the reason for the general placement of the keys (including the QWERTY key layout). This way, people who learned to "type" (in the olden days we used to refer to it this way) now can "keyboard" (in the modern usage) equally easily. Of course, computer keyboards must do more than typewriter keyboards. So your PC keyboard has more keys than most typewriters do. Also, there quite probably are more on the keyboard you are using than there were on earlier PC keyboard models.

The keys on a typical PC keyboard that are in addition to those found on any typewriter are there to allow you to perform some control functions. These include navigation keys (Up, Down, Left, and Right arrow keys, PgUp, PgDn, Home, and End), and the Delete and Insert keys. Furthermore, like any typewriter, this keyboard has two Shift keys, two Control (Ctrl) keys, and two Alternate (Alt) keys. These keys, like the Shift keys, are used to modify the meanings of other keystrokes.

These facts apply to every PC keyboard, but PC keyboards are quite a diverse lot in many other ways. Next I'll tell you some of the details about how an actual keyboard works. Then I'll tell you how they sometimes differ in how they convey information to (and perhaps from) the PC to which they are attached.

Different Keyboard Technologies

The purpose of a PC keyboard at its lowest level is to tell the PC each time a key is pressed or released. Knowing about the key releases is just as important as knowing about the key presses. This is especially so for the Shift keys (which modify the meanings of other key presses for as long as the Shift keys are held down), but it also can matter for keys that can be used together sometimes in sets (called "chords").

Some Different Kinds of Keyboard Key Switches

Any way in which you can sense when the person using the keyboard presses or stops pressing a key will do. And many different ways have been used for keyboards intended for different kinds of use.

The "Best" Snap-Action Key Switches

The initial IBM keyboards used special, miniature snap-action switches. If you press on the key very gradually, you will notice that the key presses back with a force that increases as you press it down farther and farther. But then, at some point ("the break-over point") the force with which the key pushes back decreases precipitously, for just an instant. The key will lunge forward a short distance and then once again resume pressing back on your finger. Shortly after that you will reach a point at which the key simply cannot be moved any farther, no matter how hard you push.

As you then slowly reduce the pressure of your finger on the key, you will notice that at first the key moves slowly back up. Then, at some point the pressure on your finger falls briefly to almost nothing, and the key lunges upward. After that it continues to follow your finger until it returns to the full-up position. The fact that the break-over points on the push and release occur at different points in the key's motion is called *hysteresis*.

Figure 12.1 shows this force-versus-distance curve. Notice the two dashed lines across the figure. These indicate the points at which the key switch notices a key depression (indicated by the downward pointing triangle with a D inside) and a key release (indicated by the upward pointing triangle with an R inside).

Figure 12.1.
Force-distance curve for a typical PC keyboard's key switch.

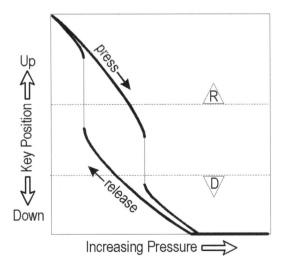

Hysteresis is built into many electric switches. This is especially true for those that carry substantial electric currents, such as the toggle switch you might use to turn on and off your room lights. The snap action in these switches guarantees that their contacts will snap together rapidly and decisively when they are turned on, and also snap apart very rapidly when they are turned off. This helps keep the switches from burning out from arcing that otherwise would happen for as long as the switch contacts were nearly, but not quite closed.

This is a non-issue for switches used in PC keyboards. And making switches this way can cost much more than almost any alternative method. So why did IBM choose to use this type of switch in the original PC keyboards? When you press a key on the keyboard, your purpose is to send a message to the computer. But you also must get one back. You must know when you have pressed enough to signal the computer. At that point you can stop pressing harder. Also, knowing when the key-release signal goes to the computer lets you stop lifting your finger.

You might think that you could simply watch the screen and in that way see whenever the computer noticed you pressing a key. That sometimes works, but not always. The computer might not do anything you can see for some time after it has noticed a key press or release—if it ever does. And in any event, there are better and more direct ways to learn when the keyboard notices those events.

When you press a key such as the one whose force-distance curve is shown in the first graph in Figure 12.1, you will feel the key lunge down and, on release, lunge back up. This gives you valuable "tactile feedback." At the same instant that the key is lunging up or down you will hear a click. That gives you "auditory feedback." For the type of keyswitch I've been describing, these three events (the computer sensing the key action, the feeling of the key lunging, and the noise) occur at precisely the same time. They must, by the very nature of how the switch is built.

IBM did tests and discovered that typists were more accurate when they got both tactile and auditory feedback for every keystroke. Therefore, they chose to use these more expensive, but in this respect, better quality, snap-action switches in their initial PC keyboard.

Inexpensive "Dry-Contact" Key Switches

The most common alternative way to build switches for a PC keyboard is what is sometimes called a *dry-contact switch*. This is a switch designed for use in circuits that carry very little electrical current. Because they don't carry much current, these switches will never arc. Therefore, their contacts don't have to snap together and snap apart.

At its simplest, a dry-contact switch might be just a spring wire that the key presses against another wire. When they touch, the switch is closed. When they come apart the switch is opened. Nothing snaps, no sudden movements occur, and there is no noise. Nothing about this type of switch actually lets you know when the computer sensed your key press or release.

Some PC makers include in their BIOS setup an option to have the PC beep or click every time you press a key. That feature is included in case you are using a keyboard with no other means of giving you feedback.

Membrane Key Switches

PC keyboards that are intended for use in very hazardous environments often are sealed and use membrane or simple capacitive switches. This is a switch similar to those often used on microwave ovens or office building elevator controls. Instead of keys that move, these keyboards have sensitive regions called keypads. Push on one, and they notice it. Stop pushing and they notice that also.

Again, you get no direct feedback from the switch when it closes or opens. Even if your PC beeps or clicks for each key stroke, you'll find that you simply cannot type as quickly, nor will your typing be as accurate with this type of keyboard as with either of the preceding two.

Domed Elastomer Key Switches

Perhaps the most common key switch design in use today is one made with a sheet of an elastomeric substance (an artificial rubber) placed between the keys and a printed circuit board. This rubber sheet has a dome formed in it directly beneath each key. When you press a key, it pushes down on the dome. When it is pushed far enough, the dome buckles and the key pushes the rubber sheet into contact with the circuit board below. A conductive spot on the inside of the dome completes a circuit on the printed circuit board, signaling the computer that the key has been pressed.

Correctly designed, this type of keyboard has an action very much like the "good" snap-action key switch designs, and it can be made at a much lower cost. These two facts combined are why this is now a very popular way to make PC keyboards.

Key Matrices and the Keyboard's Own Computer

When you press and release a key, that action only closes and opens an electrical contact (and perhaps makes some noise and gives you some tactile feedback). It doesn't directly cause any messages to go to the PC. Those messages come from some electronics that is built into the keyboard. In fact, an entire computer exists within every PC keyboard. This is an example of what we term an *embedded computer*. It runs a single program all the time. That program causes this keyboard computer to watch all the keys to see which are pressed or released and to send appropriate messages to the PC to inform it about those events.

Ordinarily, the keys on a PC keyboard are arranged in five or six rows. The keys in each row are offset to the right from the ones in the row just above. Internally, the keyboard has a wire that goes to each row of keys and other wires that go to each (angled) column of keys. This forms a matrix, with each key at the intersection of one row and one column wire. The keyboard electronics activates one column at a time and looks briefly at the signal on each of the row wires (or vice versa). In that way it can examine the state of each switch in the entire matrix. It does this scanning so rapidly that it can examine every switch on the keyboard many times each second.

Besides noticing the switch closings and openings, the keyboard's computer creates and sends appropriate messages to the PC. Also, it turns on and off the lights that indicate to you whether the Shift Lock, Num Lock, or Caps Lock states are in effect.

PC-to-Keyboard Conversations

PC keyboards talk to the PC to which they are attached. Most of them also listen for some return messages. Some are "bi-lingual"; most are not. Some PCs are also bi-lingual, but again, most are not. However, virtually all modern PCs and their keyboards share the same language.

Many Designs, Only Two Languages

Despite all the different forms in which keyboards for PCs have been built, there are only two "languages" spoken by them in their conversations with a PC. The 83-key keyboards used with the original IBM PC and PC/XT (and all clones of those two computer models) were output-only keyboards. The language they used was different from that used by all subsequent PC keyboards. Starting with the IBM PC/AT, the PC keyboard gained the capability to listen as well as speak to its host PC. And the language for its messages back and forth was changed.

Some clone PCs "know" both the XT and AT keyboard languages, and they detect which kind of keyboard is attached each time they boot up. Some clone PC keyboards know both languages, and you can tell them which one to use by flipping a small switch on the back or bottom of the keyboard. But mostly today, we only have and use the newer, "AT-style" keyboards (that speak and listen), and our PCs assume that this is the kind of keyboard that is attached to them.

Details of What the Keyboard Computer Does

The conversations between keyboard and PC are very simple and boring. At the time of boot, the PC tells the keyboard to reset itself, thus restarting its internal program from the beginning. (XT keyboards reset each time power is applied.) Later, the keyboard sends a message to the PC every time any key is pressed and every time any key is released. The PC tells the keyboard any time the shift state changes (so it can update the little lights on the keyboard). The PC also tells the keyboard computer what time delay and repetition rate to use for its *typematic action*.

The typematic action is what happens when you hold down any key other than a shift key. The keyboard's internal computer notices when you first press a particular key (and sends a corresponding message to the PC). Later, if it notices that you have been holding down that key for more than a set time—which by default is one-half second—the keyboard computer will start spitting out multiple messages to the PC—10 times each second by default—each of those messages saying that this key has just been pressed again. When you finally release the key, the keyboard computer sends a final message saying that key has been released (and, of course, it stops its typematic action with respect to that key).

Scan Codes and the System Unit's Keyboard Controller

The messages from the keyboard to the PC's system unit enter that box through a special dedicated keyboard serial port. For more details on just what that means, please see Chapter 15, "Understanding Standard PC Input and Output." From there, the messages go to what we term the *keyboard controller*. The PC system unit's keyboard controller can be another tiny embedded computer with its own microprocessor, ROM with a fixed program, and some RAM. Or, that functionality can be included as a part of the VLSI motherboard chip set.

The keyboard controller gets from the keyboard messages about which keys have been pressed or released. Every time it gets such a message, the keyboard controller takes two actions. Its first action is to place into a buffer (a small region of RAM), normally located at a very low address in main memory, a scan code that stands for the keystroke. The second step is to trigger a hardware interrupt of type 09h. (Interrupts are discussed in detail in Chapter 8, "How Your PC 'Thinks.'")

One very important fact to understand is that the scan codes indicate which key has been pressed rather than what symbol you intended to type. Thus, the scan code for "a" and that for "A" are identical. The scan code must be interpreted in the light of the present state of each of the three kinds of "shift" (letter and numbers, control, and alternate) and the three kinds of shift-lock (caps, numbers, and scroll) to determine what the person typing intended that keystroke to mean.

The original PC keyboards sent out one byte scan code. All modern PC keyboards do that for the keys they have in common with those earlier keyboards, and they send modified forms of some of them (indicated by a prefix byte or bytes) for keys that have been added to that layout. This includes, for example, the second Ctrl and Alt keys. The scan code for a key release is identical to the scan code for that same key being pressed, except that the most significant bit is turned on. This is equivalent to adding 80h to the scan code value.

The interrupt handler for Int 09h retrieves the scan code from the buffer, and also the state of the shift and shift-locks from location 0417h and 0418h in the BIOS data area. It then converts this information into an ASCII or extended ASCII character code, or if the key pressed was a shift or shift-lock key, it alters the data on them stored in locations 0417h and 0418h in the BIOS data area.

How Application Programs Learn About Keystrokes

I hope by now that you are thoroughly disabused of the notion many people have that whenever they press a key on the PC's keyboard, that directly causes a character to appear on their PC's screen. Clearly, things are much more indirect than that. Indeed, many times you will be typing away and nothing appears on the screen for awhile. Then suddenly a burst of characters appears. Other times, the keystrokes get swallowed up or sent somewhere else, and you never see them on the screen.

The only way any program finds out that a keystroke has arrived at the keyboard is by "hooking Int 09h" if it is a DOS program or by looking for an appropriate message from the Windows kernel if it is a Windows application. These concepts are described in more detail in Chapter 8, "How Your PC 'Thinks'," and Chapter 17, "Understanding PC Operating Systems." For now, though, I just want to make the point that when keystrokes happen, two embedded computers (one each in the keyboard and the system unit) have a conversation, and then one of the PC's CPU interrupts is triggered. What happens from there is strictly determined, not by the hardware, but by whatever software is running in the PC at the time. For example, the keystroke might result in a character appearing on the PC's screen, but often it does not.

A Trip to the Keyboard "Zoo"

Keyboards for PCs come in a variety of sizes and styles. The plain keyboard that comes with most PCs is merely the most basic design in common use. Here's a brief description of some other designs.

Ergonomic Keyboards

Figure 12.2 shows the Microsoft Natural Keyboard. This is a very popular ergonomic design. Instead of a flat keyboard or one that slopes up toward the top row, this design actually has the top row of keys closer to the desktop than the bottom row. Furthermore, the keys are arranged in three groups. The left and center groups where your left and right hands spend most of their time are turned slightly in toward one another. The right group has the dedicated navigation keys and the numeric keypad, and it is oriented in the same way as a non-ergonomic keyboard.

Figure 12.2.
Microsoft Natural Keyboard is a popular ergonomic alternative PC keyboard design.

Foot raises front edge of keyboard to ergonomically correct angle

This is referred to as an ergonomic design because research has shown that using this type of keyboard tends to keep your hands in a more neutral position, and that reduces the likelihood that you will develop a repetitive strain injury.

Cirque makes a variation on this design that it calls its WaveKeyboard2. It looks very much like the Microsoft Natural Keyboard, but it also has a Cirque trackpad and a few small buttons associated with that trackpad embedded in it, just below the navigation keys. This provides an alternative way to point that many people find preferable to using a mouse.

Many other ergonomic PC keyboard designs exist, including ones that fold the keyboard in half so that the palms of your hands are facing one another when you type. However, none of these designs has achieved more than a minor penetration into the market.

Keyboards and Laptops

Laptop computers present many design challenges, not least of which is how to fit in a full-size keyboard. Most present laptops use a compromise keyboard. It isn't quite full size, nor does it have all the keys you will find on a normal PC keyboard. But it is still large enough for touch typing and has some means for simulating all the missing keys. You will learn more about the special challenges faced by laptop designers in Chapter 23, "Why Mobile PCs Must Be Different."

Keyboards for Handheld PCs and PDAs

When a PC is too small, there simply isn't room for a normal keyboard. Still, that functionality has proven to be essential. Devices such as the Palm Pilot use a touch screen for most of their input. In one mode, that screen displays a miniaturized keyboard, and you can point with its stylus at keys there, one at a time. The fact that the designers of this popular personal digital assistant felt it necessary to include some type of keyboard shows how vital an input device it is.

The Point Is Pointing (Mousing Around)

Your mother might have taught you that it is impolite to point. And it is, for humans, in public. But when running a Windows program on a PC, you almost can't avoid having to point at and select various items. The "point" is, some type of pointing device is an essential complement to a keyboard. The most common pointing device is, of course, the mouse. But whatever pointing device you use, remember that its only function is to indicate (by pointing) some item and then select or act upon that item (usually by clicking or double-clicking a button on the mouse).

Many Kinds of Mouse

Compared to a keyboard, a mouse is a very simple device—as it should be, for it has a very much simpler job to do. Essentially, a mouse is an object that you move around on your desktop (or some other surface). As you do so it reports to the PC its motion. The mouse software in the PC uses these signals to move a pointer around the screen. When that *mouse cursor* points to some object of interest to you, one way you can signal your interest in that object is by pressing a button on the mouse.

Mechanical Mice

The original mouse was a box with a small rubber ball sticking out of the bottom. Pushing the box around on the desk caused the ball to roll, and that in turn made some shafts turn and switches close to indicate the amount of motion in each of two perpendicular directions. This mouse design has been copied and refined in many ways.

On the left in Figure 12.3 is the present standard-bearer of mice, the Microsoft Intellimouse with wheel. On the right is one of the few mice that comes in multiple models for left- or right-handed users, and in several sizes to better fit your hand. Each company makes claims that theirs is the most ergonomic mouse on the market (as do several other mouse or mouse-alternative makers).

Figure 12.3.
A Microsoft mouse and a Countour Design large, right-hander's mouse.

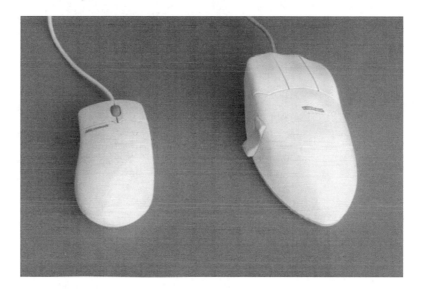

Figure 12.4 shows the Microsoft mouse from the bottom, with its rubber ball removed, as one does to clean the mouse. The two shafts inside detect the rolling of the ball in the X and Y directions.

Purely Optical Mice

A strictly mechanical mouse is prone to many problems, and one of the worst is picking up dirt. That can interfere with the mechanism that converts the ball's rolling motion into X- and Y-displacement signals. An early solution to this problem was a design for a ball-less mouse that shines light of two colors downward. You moved this optical mouse over a smooth, reflective pad that had many parallel lines printed on it, one color going in the X-direction and a different color going in the Y-direction. The mouse detected its passage over these lines by changes in the light that reflected back into it from the pad. This design worked very well, but it was too limited, requiring as it did that one use only their special mouse pad. So that design has fallen from favor.

Figure 12.4.
Microsoft mouse from below, with ball removed.

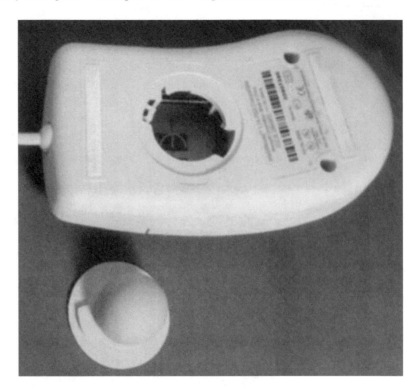

Opto-Mechanical Mice

The best mouse designs today use a combination of optical and mechanical mechanisms. Most of them have a ball that rolls on two shafts which turn optical shaft-angle encoders to convert those motions into electrical signals for the PC. These mice get dirty, but they are much easier to clean than the original, purely mechanical models.

Key Tronic sells a different type of opto-mechanical mouse. This one has small plastic wheels attached directly to the two optical shaft-angle encoders. When you move this mouse on the desktop, these wheels roll directly on the mouse pad or desktop, converting the mouse's X- and Y-motions into signals for the PC.

Mice That "Fly"

The Logitech Magellan 3D Controller is one of the first mice for a PC that provide information about motion in three-dimensional space. Not only does this device signal movement in the X-, Y-, and Z-directions, it also signals rotations around three mutually perpendicular axes (usually referred to as yaw, pitch, and roll).

As PC users start using more 3D simulations and business applications, I expect that this type of input device will become more and more common. And, of course, that means more companies will make competing models, and the design will be further refined.

Mice That Lie on Their Backs

What is a mouse that is lying on its back? It isn't a dead mouse or one that wants to be tickled. It could be a mouse you are about to clean (as shown in Figure 12.4), but sometimes it is a device we use like a mouse, but that goes by the name *trackball*. With a trackball, you roll the ball with your fingers or hand. That means you don't need to have an open space on your desk for a mouse to roam. And it can provide a means for much more precise pointing than is easy with an ordinary mouse.

Many different companies have made a wide variety of trackballs. The balls themselves range in size from less than half an inch in diameter to one that is four inches in diameter. That last one is Microsoft's EasyBall, and it is shown in Figure 12.5. Although Microsoft intended it for children, I find it one of the most comfortable trackballs I have ever used. Unfortunately, it has only one button, and many PC applications require the use of more than a single button.

Figure 12.5.
Microsoft EasyBall trackball.

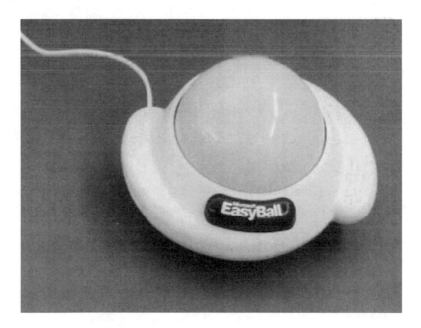

Possibly the most interestingly different trackballs are those made by ITAC Systems. Their top-of-the line Evolution Trackball has six, symmetrically placed switches and an internal microprocessor programmed to make all setup operations possible without use of a specialized mouse software driver in your PC. It also has some well-supported claims to a very high degree of ergonomic effectiveness. In my experience, your hand must be the right size (neither too large nor too small) for this to work well, but it can be wonderful.

Mice That Don't Look at all Like Mice

Trackpads and pointing sticks are some of the latest innovations in the pointing device marketplace. I already mentioned the Cirque WaveKeyboard2 with its embedded trackpad. This looks like a small, gray window, just over two inches wide. You merely slide your finger tip across the window and the mouse cursor moves. You tap the window and it is like clicking the primary mouse button.

Cirque also makes a larger trackpad it calls the Power Cat. The "window" on this device is about three inches wide. It has a special region on it where a finger tap produces the effect of a secondary mouse button click, and some which you can use to scroll up, down, left, or right in a document. It also has two places for triggering the effect of the Forward and Back buttons in a Web browser.

Some people with severe RSI conditions are simply unable to use any mice, or even most trackpads. One of them has reported learning to use a Power Cat with a stylus held between his toes as an alternative.

The pointing stick is a force transducer. It is a small post in a keyboard that usually sticks up between the F and G keys. When you push on it with your finger tip, it doesn't bend appreciably, But it does signal the computer as to the direction and pressure with which you are pushing. That gets translated by software into the equivalent of a mouse motion, with more pressure corresponding to higher speed.

Absolute (Versus Relative) Pointing

You use a mouse to indicate displacement; but from what? That is, by intent, not clearly determined. Their purpose is to move a mouse cursor from wherever it is, in your chosen direction and at your chosen speed. Alternative pointing devices exist in which one points to a place, not just a displacement from wherever one happens to have been. Many of these devices can also be used in a "mouse mode" in which they send displacement information to the PC just like a mouse, rather than their usual practice of telling the PC an absolute location.

Graphics Tablets

Graphics tablets are flat, rectangular devices. Each point within some defined inner rectangle corresponds directly to a point on the PC's screen. They come with a stylus, or a puck, or both. The stylus is like a pen with one or two buttons on the side and a pressure switch in the tip. The puck looks a lot like a mouse, but it might have a paddle sticking out with cross-hairs engraved on it for very precise following of a drawing or map placed on top of the tablet, and it may have anywhere from just 2 to 16 buttons.

Point to a spot on the tablet with a puck or stylus and, without even a button press, the mouse cursor immediately jumps from wherever it was to the corresponding place on the PC's screen. This is what is meant by absolute coordinate pointing. Pressing down with the stylus is like pressing the primary mouse button (which is usually the left one, except for left-handed mice, or for any mouse that has been reprogrammed to act as a left-handed one).

Graphics tablets use any of several different technologies. Most have a grid of wires buried in the surface of the tablet. The tablet's electronics puts signals on those wires and the stylus or puck acts as an antenna to receive them. The signal returned by the stylus or puck (either over a wire or over a radio link) to tablet electronics enables it to determine over which intersection of wires the pointer was positioned.

Other technologies include ones based on sonar and magneto-strictive effects. To keep this discussion reasonably brief, I won't describe those in detail here.

Graphics tablets are made in many different sizes, ranging from small, handheld ones, up to ones as large as a drafting table. One primary use for a tablet is to allow tracing over an existing drawing, photograph, or other two-dimensional piece of artwork. Naturally, you are best served by a tablet that is just a little larger than the largest such art you must trace.

Other Digitizers

There are many other two-dimensional and even some three-dimensional digitizers made for use with PCs. These devices come in a wide variety of forms, but in all cases their purpose is to facilitate entering absolute 2D or 3D coordinates into a computer.

What Mice (and Other Pointing Devices) Say to PCs

Most mice, trackballs, trackpads, pointing sticks, and graphics tablets connect to a PC via either a standard serial port or a special bus mouse or PS/2 mouse port. The messages they send in are received and acted upon by a software program called a mouse driver. (You can learn all about serial ports in Chapter 15. You can learn more about device drivers in Chapter 8.)

What do mice say to a PC? Ordinary mice, trackballs, and the like, or graphics tables operating in mouse mode send a message every time the mouse (or other, equivalent device) moves by a specified unit of distance in either the X or Y direction. (I'm going to limit my discussion to the more common, 2D mice and graphics tablets.) The jargon name for this minimum unit of displacement is the *Mickey*. Originally, a Mickey was 0.01 inch. Now it can be whatever the maker of the device wants it to be, and often is as small as one-third to one-quarter the original size. The only other thing a mouse must tell the PC is whenever one of its buttons is pressed or released.

> **Tip:** The mouse software in the PC is responsible for all the rest of what a mouse does. A very important point to realize is that a mouse driver includes some software that writes to the video display subsystem so it can create and move the mouse cursor. This is important because if you are having trouble with your video display, not only must you make sure your video display driver is up to date, you also must do the same for your mouse driver.

Graphics tablets can act as if they were mice. If they do, then their conversations with the PC are just like those of a mouse. But when they are operating in their native, absolute position mode, they do something different. In this mode they send messages at regular intervals saying either the pointer (stylus or puck) is out of range, or at which coordinates it is now pointing. And, of course, information about any button presses or releases.

There are a variety of protocols ("languages") in which these conversations can take place. But the industry standard methods are those Microsoft developed for its mouse, or the ones that were developed by Calcomp, Summagraphics, or Wacom for their graphic digitizers.

One Button, Two Button, Three Button, Wheel

"One Button, Two Button, Three Button, Wheel"—this sounds like the start of a child's rhyme. This also describes the number of buttons you are likely to find on a PC's mouse or other pointing device. (Well, graphic tablet pucks sometimes have as many as 16 buttons, but that is a special case.)

Mostly one-button mice (or other pointing devices) are used on Apple Macintosh computers, and not on PCs. One exception is the EasyBall trackball shown in Figure 12.5. When there are two buttons, one is designated as the primary button, and the other is the secondary button. This is the most common arrangement (see the Microsoft mouse in Figure 12.3).

Other mice have three buttons. Because most PC mice have only two buttons, most PC software ignores the third button. And whenever a software package does respond to the third button it often is also capable of responding in the same way to a *chording* of both buttons on a two-button mouse. (Chording means simply that one presses more than one button or key at a time.)

Microsoft's Intellimouse includes a novel feature: a wheel located between the two buttons. This can be rolled forward or back, and you will feel it click from position to position as you do so. If you are using a software program that supports this new mouse (and mostly those are only programs from Microsoft, such as Internet Explorer and Office) this wheel motion can scroll a document you are looking at up or down the screen. (This is different from moving your insertion point up or down, which is what the arrow keys do.) The wheel also has a switch that is activated when you press on it. This serves as a normal third mouse button, or with software that is specially programmed to use this feature, it can activate an automatic scrolling mode.

Some Other PC Input Devices

A keyboard and a pointing device are the most common and most often used PC input devices. But many others sometimes are just the ticket for what you must do.

Scanners

Perhaps the most common other input device is a scanner. These come in several forms. Originally, most were black-and-white-only devices, just capable of seeing lightness or darkness at each point on the scanned document or object. Now, however, color scanners are available for very little more money, and they are fast becoming the most common kind. After all, you can still scan black-and-white objects or documents with a color scanner.

The other big difference in types of scanner has to do with whether they can scan only flat sheets of paper or if they can scan bulkier objects, such as a page in a book. And then there is the size dimension. Many scanners accommodate full letter (8.5×11-inch) or legal (8.5×14-inch) pages. Others can scan objects no larger than a business card or a snapshot, or they can accept very much larger objects. Finally, some scanners are designed to be held in your hand and rolled across a document manually, while most will either move the document through themselves for you, or they will scan a document or object while it sits stationary on a window. (These last resemble a full-size office copier and work in a very similar manner, except that they digitize their output instead of creating a printed copy.)

In all cases, the output of the scanner and its associated software is a bitmapped image file representing the appearance of the document or object that was scanned. This later can be converted in any of several ways, but this is the essential form that scanner output always come in, first.

Figure 12.6 shows an inexpensive yet very capable scanner that accepts photographs up to five by seven inches in size. (The active width is, however, just 4.1 inches.) This Storm product was used to scan all the photographs used in this book. The software that comes with it was used to do some preliminary photo manipulation of those images as well. That software stores the completed scans as relatively high-quality JPEG compressed files, to save disk space.

Figure 12.6.
*Storm EasyPhoto
Reader is a small
scanner for use with
color snapshots.*

Optical Character Recognition

The output of a scanner is a bitmapped image file, usually in a PCX or JPG format. If you scanned a page of text, it would be nice if the output were an editable text file (either pure ASCII text or a formatted word processor document).

Converting scanned text into editable text is the job of *optical character recognition* (OCR) software. Several OCR packages now on the market do a very creditable job. Some will even recognize columns of text and ignore figures and will create fully formatted word processor documents in approximately the right fonts and sizes to match the original.

As with all "artificial intelligence" computer applications, OCR programs require real, human supervision. They make mistakes, and you must go in and fix up the file after they finish. Still, if you have many pages of text to enter, this can be the fastest way to get the job done. And it certainly is less stressful than typing all that text yourself.

Facsimile (Fax) Machines

An office copier and a facsimile machine both are combinations of a document scanner and a printer. The difference is that the office copier keeps the document information it scans in analog form until it prints the copies. A facsimile machine, in contrast, scans the document into a digital bitmapped image file. That image file is then sent out either across a telephone line to a remote fax machine or directly to the printer in the originating fax machine.

If you have a fax modem in your PC, then any fax machine anywhere on the planet can become an input device to your PC. Just save the file the modem creates from an incoming fax message to your disk.

> **Tip:** This suggests an easy way to get a copy of your company's logo into your PC. Just fax a copy of your letterhead into your PC. Of course, this will only be as good a copy as your fax machine can scan, but it may do for your intended purposes, or you then can "clean up" the image with an image processing program.

Less Common PC Input Devices

Anything that can generate information and supply it to a PC is potentially a PC input device. These include digital cameras, video capture cards, touch screens, and GPS (Global Positioning Satellite) receivers, among others. In Chapter 19, "Some PCs Can Understand Speech and Talk to Us," I tell you about the state of the art in voice input to PCs. In Chapter 22, "Immersive PC Experiences," I tell you about some additional input devices, including ones that you push on and that can push back on you.

The "Dark Side" of PC Input

The worst thing about PC input devices is that using them can hurt you—badly. Every PC user must be aware of this danger, and learn how to minimize it. If you ignore the problem, you can end up disabled in a way that prevents you not only from using your PC normally, but also impacts the entire rest of your life. Many sad stories abound of people who no longer can even hold a knife and fork to eat their meals, all because they ignored the warning pain and let a full-blown case of RSI develop.

There Is Light on the Other Side

The good news is, we understand this problem quite well now. The sequence that causes RSI goes like this: An environmental stress (such as using a non-optimally configured workstation too many hours at a time) combined with bad habits leads to tension in your body, which over time leads to injury. One way to address this is to make sure your workstation is as ergonomically correct as possible. Another is to become aware of your bad habits (incorrect posture, for example). And it helps a lot to know that "working hard" can be a euphemism for being tense as you work—which almost certainly will lead you into pain and, eventually, injury.

I cannot go into much more detail about RSI and its prevention in this book. Instead, I suggest that you look at the following Internet Web sites (plus the links you will find at each). I particularly like the approach represented by the information you will find at the first URL. It speaks to what you can and must do to yourself, apart from whatever you are able to do to make your workstation more ergonomic, in order to protect yourself from RSI.

```
http://www.somatic.com/
```

```
http://www.engr.unl.edu/eeshop/rsi.html
```

```
http://www.engr.unl.edu/ee/eeshop/findadoc.html
```

```
http://www.eecs.harvard.edu/RSI/
```

```
http://www-engr.sjsu.edu/~svei/tifaq/
```

The following pages offer information on some products that might be of interest as well:

```
http://www.ergodyne.com/
```

```
http://www.bambach.com.au/
```

```
http://saturn.vision.net.au/~macsol/equip.htm
```

```
http://www.mousetrak.com/
```

Summary

In this chapter I have told you about some aspects of the most common PC input device technologies. Far more could be said about even the ones I did explain, let alone the many I had to omit. Still, with the information you found here, you should now know pretty much what any PC input device does, in a general sense, and you have a fairly solid knowledge about the most important characteristics of several "key" ones (not to make a pun—unless that's what you want).

13

Seeing the Results: PC Displays

Peter Norton®

One of the five key parts of any computer is its mechanism for information output. In almost all PCs, the principal means of information output is the video display, also known as the monitor or the screen. This chapter will introduce you to most of the technologies that now are in use, or might soon become important, in PC display subsystems. Although my goal is primarily to help you understand these different technologies, you will find that such an understanding will come in very handy when you evaluate different options for the display on your next PC, or if you are considering upgrading the display on your present PC. You can find a more in-depth look at some of these issues in Part V, "Splendiferous Multimedia PCs."

It's Just No Good If You Can't Get the Information Out

What good is a computer that can process information, but that cannot display the results of that processing? Not much, which is why your PC has a video display screen, or monitor, attached to it. And that's why you spend most of your time while you are using your PC looking at that screen.

What Is the Display Subsystem?

Every PC's display subsystem consists of three parts. One part creates and holds the image information; this is the video display adapter. Another part displays that information; this is the monitor. The remaining part is the cable that goes between the other two parts.

The video adapter can be either some specialized circuitry on the motherboard, or it can be a plug-in card. In the latter case it is often referred to as the PC's *video card*. The monitor consists of a display device (the hardware that actually creates the image you see) and some electronics that activate that display. Often, though, people use the terms *monitor* and *display* interchangeably.

You can change your video subsystem's capabilities by changing the video hardware. Mainly, this means changing your video card. However, the monitor to which that card is attached (and the cable used for the attachment) must meet the minimum requirements of the video card or it will not be capable of displaying the images the video card creates. Some video monitors can, however, display images produced by any of several video cards, and even a single video card often is capable of forming images with a variety of resolutions, thus requiring a monitor with flexible capabilities.

Fundamental Notions to Keep in Mind

There are several extremely fundamental notions about images and how humans see, plus some critical jargon, all of which you must understand in order to make sense of any discussion of PC image display technologies. I'll define each one here briefly, then go back and describe some of them in more detail as I tell you more about how they are used.

Pixels

Digital computers make images one "picture element" (or *pixel*) at a time. These pixels are simply small regions of the overall picture. The color and brightness in each one are fixed. The neighboring pixels can have some other values of color and brightness, but each of them also will have a constant color and brightness throughout its portion of the image. The assemblage of some very large number of pixels, placed so close together that we see them as touching, makes up the image we see.

The computer computes and holds in its memory somewhere a number, or a small group of numbers, that specifies the color and brightness of each pixel in the image. Said this way, it is clear that the number of pixels in an image is fixed by the program that creates that image (and might be limited by the amount of video image memory in the PC). It is not set by the hardware used to display it. A related concept, which I will cover in just a moment, describes the minimum size of adjacent, visibly different parts of the picture. That size is a property of the display hardware, and it commonly goes by the name *dot pitch*.

Resolution

The *resolution* of a computer-generated image refers to the minimum distance over which the color (or brightness) of the image changes. This is the distance from one pixel to the next. Image resolution is often described as some number of pixels per inch. For example, a typical PC monitor displays screen images with a resolution of somewhere between about 25 pixels per inch up to 80 pixels per inch.

The most fundamental meaning to image resolution is this question of pixel spacing. But often the term in used in another way. In this alternative version, the *resolution* of an image refers to the total number of pixels in the entire width or height of the image. Thus, we often speak of images that have a resolution of 800×600 pixels.

The pixel spacing gives you the *image resolution*. The monitor also has an *inherent resolution*. This is the minimum distance between points at which it could display dots with different colors or brightness. This is not at all the same thing as the image resolution.

Don't feel bad if you find this all a bit confusing. You'd hardly be the first person to be confused. One way to help straighten out the confusion is to limit the use of the term *resolution* to the properties of the image—which is to say, compute the resolution from the spacing of the pixels. And instead of speaking of the inherent resolution limit of the monitor, we usually speak about its minimum dot pitch, and perhaps also its beam spot size.

Dot Pitch and Beam Spot Size

Dot pitch and *spot size* are properties of the monitor hardware. You can change the resolution of the image you are asking it to display, but these physical properties of the display device won't change.

Imagine that you want the monitor to display an isolated dot of light surrounded by blackness. How small a dot can it create? This depends wholly upon how the monitor causes dots to appear. The most common type of monitor, a cathode ray tube (CRT), squirts a beam of electrons at a phosphor. Wherever the electrons hit, the phosphor light is emitted. So the minimum size spot the monitor can create is set by the diameter of the beam of electrons.

Typically, a CRT's spot size is smaller in the center of the screen than it is near the corners or edges. Often we care a great deal about the details of our screen images in every part of the screen. This means that what matters to a PC user is not the smallest spot the monitor can create in any one place, but rather the smallest that it can create in all parts of the screen.

Now imagine that you ask the monitor to create two dots, side by side, with different colors. How closely can they be spaced and still be seen to be two distinct dots with different colors? (You are allowed to use a magnifying glass for this test. This is not a test of your eyes.) There are two different ways to look at this question. If you try to place the dots closer together than the diameter of either one, they will end up overlapping and you won't really have two distinct dots. This means that the minimum space between distinguishable dots must be at least as large as the beam spot size.

This is not, however, the whole story, in particular for color monitors. All modern computer color monitors cheat. They don't really make spots of arbitrary colors. Instead, the monitor makes triplets of what I will call "sub-pel spots," each of which glows with a single pure color (red, green, or blue). By controlling the relative brightness of the different colored sub-pel spots the computer is capable of creating what to our eyes appears as a small spot of almost any color you want. But this trick works only if the minimum size spot of color you want to create is at least large enough to include one each of all three different color of sub-pel spots.

Standards: Like pixel, *pel* is a shorthand name for a picture element. The term pel is used exclusively to refer to the minimum possible size dot of full color that a particular display device can produce. (This usage began with printers, but I find it a very useful one for any display device.) In color monitors (both CRTs and LCD panels), each pel will have three sub-pels—one each for emitting red, green, and blue light. By using this term I can now reserve the word *pixel* for exclusive use as the name for the minimum size chunk of an image. This distinction is not made by all authors. Too bad, because it really helps keep things clear.

The distance from a red sub-pel spot to the next red sub-pel spot (or green to green, or blue to blue) is, therefore, another important limitation on the minimum spacing of distinguishable spots in the image. This one we call the dot pitch of the monitor. A monitor's dot pitch is commonly quoted as some decimal fraction of a millimeter. (A pretty good 14-inch [diagonal measurement] monitor can have a dot pitch of 0.25mm.)

No necessary connection exists between the beam spot size and the dot pitch for a CRT monitor. In an effort to make computer monitors that are capable of displaying images with the maximum possible detail and with the maximum possible brightness, manufacturers typically try to make the dot pitch and the beam spot size about the same size. Because the dot pitch is clearly set by how the monitor is manufactured, that number is usually what is quoted. You just expect and hope that the beam spot size is not much larger than that.

Most of this discussion has assumed that the monitor uses a CRT as its display device. What about Liquid Crystal Display (LCD) panels? They also are built with triplets of single-color sub-pel spots that can each glow with an adjustable brightness. So the concept of dot pitch is exactly the same for them as for CRTs. What is different is that LCD panels activate each sub-pel individually. So, in effect, they have a beam spot size that is exactly equal to the dot pitch, and this is true in every part of the screen.

Image Resolution Versus Dot Pitch

What happens if the image resolution is different from the inherent resolution of the display device? There are two cases to consider. If you try to display an image that has many more pixels than there are pels on the screen, each pel will end up showing a color and brightness that is an average of several adjacent pixels. The effective resolution of the image will be reduced to what the monitor is capable of displaying.

Because what matters to us most of the time is the content of our images, clearly the second situation is preferable. Don't try to display a 1024×768 pixel image on a monitor that has only about 700 pels per line. The image will look blurry, and you'll lose some of the information that it is supposed to be showing you. Naturally, when the number of pels and pixels per line is identical, the image is displayed perfectly, and the monitor is being used to its maximum capacity.

Most of the time you can get away with displaying images that have fewer pixels almost as well as ones with the optimum number of pixels for a given monitor. The only case in which this really doesn't work out well is when you try to display an image on an LCD display with just the wrong number of pixels. Some pixels will be properly displayed while others will fall in the cracks between pels and will appear drastically fainter than they should. This is one reason why you are normally better off using an LCD display panel to display images that match its nominal resolution, or ones that have half as many pixels per line, but not two-thirds as many, just to name one example where trouble might arise.

Color Models

I said each pixel in an image has a particular color and brightness. We use several different *color models* to describe the visual appearance of the pixels. The most common model for PC video displays is referred to as the *Red-Green-Blue* (RGB) model. This says that you can describe any color of light coming from a spot within an image by saying how much red, blue, and green light it contains. This is an *additive color model*, in that the total light that hits your eye from that spot is the sum of the amounts of red, green, and blue light. Because of the way in which most PC displays create their images, this is the most natural way to describe them.

In the RGB model you can specify a pixel's color by giving three numbers representing the amount of R, G, and B light the screen emits on some suitable scale. Thus, a color of (0, 0, 0) would be black (no light of any color is emitted). A color of (255, 0, 0) would be a pure red at maximum brightness (assuming a scale of 0 to 255, which is the most commonly used scale). A color of (255, 0, 101) turns out to be a lovely rose, the color (162, 240, 0) is a vivid new-leaf green, and (0, 142, 61) is a dark forest green.

However, certain types of displays, in particular LCD panels, don't emit light at all. Instead, they modify the light that is reflected from them or that passes through them. Some make color images by passing light through a clear liquid crystal that is covered with an array of colored dots. This results in an effect very much like the three-color emitting dot groups on a color CRT. Other LCD panels pass light through three layers of colored liquid crystals. Each layer subtracts an adjustable portion of one color only of the light that falls on it.

This latter behavior is very nearly the same as what happens when you look at a printed image on paper. Colored images are formed from layers of color-absorbing dyes. The color you see is determined by what other colors are absorbed by those dyes. From this description you will understand why this is referred to as a *subtractive* color model. The primary colors—normally red, blue and yellow—get slightly skewed in this model, into cyan, magenta, and yellow, so this model is called the CMY model. When black is added, we call this the CMYK model (the "K" standing for black, to avoid using "B," which might imply blue). This is the model used by every modern PC inkjet printer and some color laser printers.

A third model for expressing color—one that is of very limited interest to us here—is termed the Hue-Saturation-Brightness (HSB) color model. This model forms the basis for understanding color television signals. And, as you may know, many PCs now include the capability to display television images in a window on the PC's display or to overlay PC-generated graphics on top of a television signal.

Figure 13.1 shows these three color models. In all cases the left portion of the model shows a range of colors, and the bar on the right indicates the brightness. In each drawing, the circled numbers 1 through 4 show where the colors I mentioned above would appear on those schematic color solids. Number 1 is the pure, bright red, number 2 is the rose, number 3 is the new-leaf green, and number 4 is the forest green.

Figure 13.1.
Three common color models.

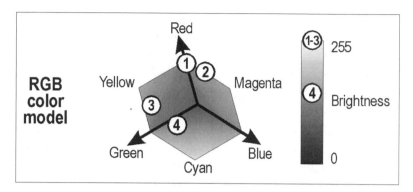

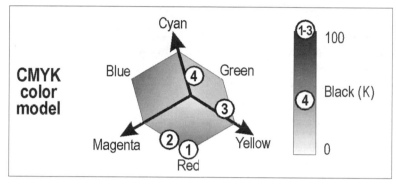

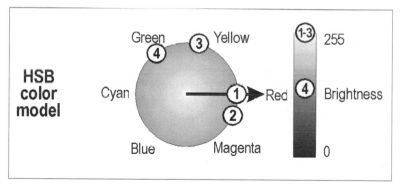

How Images Are Painted on the Screen (Overview)

The pixels that make up an image are "painted" on the screen. I think you'll find that the following analogy to this process will make some important facts about this process clearer.

Imagine that you are holding a hose and directing a stream of water at the side of a building. The wall surface is rough, and it reflects a lot of sunlight. But where the water hits the wall, the reflectivity of the wall drops markedly. This means that you can "paint" darkness on a region of the wall simply by directing your stream of water there. As long as any place on the wall stays wet, it will also stay dark, and you'll be able to see that you had pointed your hose there. But suppose that it is a very hot day and the water evaporates from the wall quickly. Now you can see only the places you have most recently played your stream of water. Finally, suppose that you modulate the amount of water that is flowing out of the hose as you sweep it across the building. This makes some places it passes get very wet, and others get hardly wet at all.

This method of "painting" water on a wall is very much like the way most PC display technologies make images. In CRTs the water stream is replaced by a beam of electrons hitting a phosphor. Where the beam is intense, with many electrons hitting the phosphor each microsecond, the spot will glow brightly. Where the beam is weaker, it will produce less light. In an LCD panel the pixels are addressed one after another, each one being set to the appropriate color and brightness in its turn, thus achieving a similar effect.

What does the notion that each spot on the wall will dry up shortly after the water stream leaves it say about PC displays? Two things. First, CRTs and some other display technologies have images that naturally die after some short period of time. These devices need the PC to "refresh" the images many times per second. If they aren't refreshed often enough, you'll experience a flickering image, and it might also be too dim to see clearly. The number of times each second that the image gets refreshed is called the *refresh rate*. Typical PC CRT-based displays have their images refreshed at least 60 times each second, and sometimes more than 100 times per second.

LCD panels, on the other hand, are capable of holding images indefinitely. Their weakness is that they cannot change those images arbitrarily rapidly. (In our analogy, the humidity isn't low enough, and so the water doesn't evaporate quickly enough.) This makes these displays fine for static images, but unsuitable for video clips (movies). If you try to refresh (and alter) an image on an LCD screen too quickly, you either will see a smeared version of the image, or you might not see an image at all. In the former case it is as if the wall got wet all over and until it dries up, you won't be able to see the image. In the latter case you are trying to turn on pixels and then turn them back off again so fast that they never really get turned on at all. (In our analogy, the stream of water is so weak the wall doesn't have time to get properly wetted.)

Raster-Scan Versus Vector Displays

How do you move the water stream to paint an image on a building? If the image is a circle, for example, you could just swing the hose in a circle, painting only those parts of the wall that needed to be painted. Some CRT displays do something very similar. They move their electron beam across the screen in a pattern that is similar to how one might move a pen or pencil over a piece of paper. In effect, they print each character and symbol by drawing it as a number of curves or lines. This is called a *vector-scan* display. This type of technology has found some niche applications (laser light shows are one), but it is not commonly used for PC displays.

The alternative to a vector-scan display, and the one used in virtually every PC display subsystem, is a *raster-scan display*. Some raster-scan displays use a cathode ray tube (CRT); others use an LCD panel. I will describe the details of how each type is built later in the "Raster-Scan CRT Images" and the "LCD Panel Images" sections, respectively. For now, I just want to focus on the nature of the images being displayed.

How this applies to a CRT display is that the electron beam is played across the screen from left to right in essentially a straight, horizontal line. Then it is moved back to the left edge and down a little, after which it again is moved smoothly across the screen. This continues until the lines have been painted in succession all the way down the screen. (Actually, the beam drifts slowly downward the whole time, so each line is very slightly tilted down to the right. The right end of each line is essentially at the same level as the left end of the next line.)

In a vector-scan display, the path of the beam forms the image, one stroke at a time. (When the beam must be moved from the end of one stroke to the beginning of the next, the intensity is simply turned down to zero.) Raster-scan displays, in contrast to this, use an unchanging pattern of sweeping the beam to draw any image. The image is drawn while the beam sweeps by modulating the beam intensity very rapidly in an appropriate pattern.

Figure 13.2 shows how both types of display might draw a triangle. The top of the figure (a) shows the strokes that make up the triangle using the vector-scan approach. The middle portion (b) shows how a raster scan can accomplish the same thing. The bottom section (c) shows graphs of the raster-scan beam's horizontal and vertical position, each as a function of time.

Scanning Frequencies and Refresh Rates

Your PC display subsystem draws and redraws the screen image constantly, and at very frequent intervals. It must do this. If it didn't then when the information to be displayed changed, you wouldn't know about it.

How often must it redraw the screen image? That depends on what type of image it is. In all cases you want to have the feeling that you aren't waiting to see the new information. That requirement alone means that you must have the screen refreshed at least 10 times per second. If you are looking at a movie, it will appear jumpy unless you see at least 25–30 new images each second. And if the scene has any objects that change their brightness significantly from one screen image to the next, then those images better be painted on the screen at a rate of at least 60 per second. Otherwise you will see a flickering and soon you will get a headache.

So, to be sure that your PC display works well for all purposes, manufacturers usually try for a refresh rate of at least 60 times per second. Indeed, many of the better video cards and CRT monitors are capable of operating at refresh rates in excess of 60Hz, all the way up to 120Hz in a few cases.

Here I want to point out some of the requirements that this imposes on the display mechanisms. First I'll treat the case of the CRT displays, then that for LCD displays. Most other display technologies will closely resemble either one or the other of these two principal categories.

Figure 13.2.
How vector-scan and raster-scan displays form images.

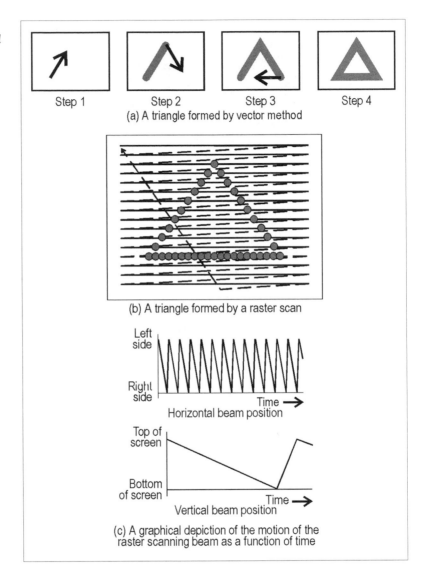

(a) A triangle formed by vector method

(b) A triangle formed by a raster scan

(c) A graphical depiction of the motion of the raster scanning beam as a function of time

To simplify this discussion, I will go through just one example numerically. You can generalize this to any other case you might want to consider. The case I'm going to use is that of a graphic screen image with a resolution of 1024×768. That means an image with 768 lines of information, each line containing 1024 pixels.

Raster-Scan CRT Images

A raster-scan image on a CRT is painted one pixel at a time, and the display must paint all of those pixels 60 or more times per second. This implies some pretty tough requirements on the speed of the display system. PC displays form raster-scan images in what is called a *progressive* manner. That means they sweep down the screen from top to bottom once per image. And they must do this in a 60th of a second, or less. So the minimum "vertical sweep rate" is 60Hz.

To get all of the 768 lines of pixels drawn 60 times each second, the lines must be drawn at a rate of 46,080 lines per second. Actually, the required rate is a little bit higher than this, because there must be some time equivalent to that required to draw several lines for what is called the *vertical retrace blanking interval*. During this time the electron beam is shut off and the beam steering mechanism moves it up from the bottom of the screen to the top. So, the actual rate at which lines are drawn horizontally is probably at least 48kHz (48,000 lines per second). We call this the *horizontal sweep rate*.

As it is drawing a single line, the display mechanism in a CRT must be capable of turning the electron beam on or off (or to some intermediate level) rapidly enough to set the correct brightness for each pixel, independently of the brightness for its neighbors. Because it is sweeping the lines at least 48,000 times per second and must paint 1024 pixels on each one, that means it is painting individual pixels at a rate of around 48 million per second. Again, to account for what is termed the horizontal retrace blanking interval—the time during which the electron beam is shut off and the beam steering mechanism moves back from the right side of the screen to the left—we must add something to the 1024 before multiplying by the 48kHz. When this is taken into account, the actual rate of pixel drawing might be around 50 million per second. This means that the electronics in the monitor (and those on the video display adapter) must have a bandwidth in excess of 50MHz.

The CRT display must, therefore, be capable of synchronizing its electron beam sweeping to the vertical and horizontal drive signals that are, in this case, coming to it at around 60Hz and 48kHz, respectively. And its video bandwidth must be at least 50MHz. These are the numbers to look for if you want to have a CRT that is capable of displaying good, clear, 1024×768 graphic screen images.

LCD Panel Images

LCD panels come in several types. The different types create their images in quite different ways. All of them use a raster scanning procedure, but some allow the individual pixels much more time to be set to the correct brightness than is the case with the others. And that is a good thing, because LCD panel pixels cannot be turned on or off at anywhere near the rate at which pixels are painted on a CRT's screen.

The simplest LCD panels paint an entire line of pels at one time. Then they move to the next line, and the next line, until they complete the entire screen image. Once set, these pels stay at a fixed brightness until the next time they are reset. (Remember, a pel is a physical picture element within the display device, as opposed to the screen image elements that are termed pixels. And also remember that we must have at least as many pels as pixels if we are going to display the entire image in full detail.)

This time required to set a single pel's brightness can be as much as a few hundred microseconds. But spending that much time on each line, for our sample image with 768 lines, means that refreshing the screen more than a few times per second just isn't possible.

Double-scan LCD panels paint the top and bottom halves of the screen in parallel. This strategy just doubles the effective refresh rate. Active matrix LCD panels put a transistor at each pixel. (Actually they use one for each sub-pel, or three per pel in a color screen.) The raster-scanning mechanism goes rapidly over the whole array, setting brightness values into each transistor on the entire screen. Those transistors then have the entire time until the next refreshing of the screen to set their pel's brightness. This strategy allows refresh rates that are as high as one might desire.

This analysis explains why LCD panels, other than active matrix, have trouble displaying movies, yet are quite capable for simple static graphics or text screens. It also explains why a portable computer with a non-active-matrix LCD panel isn't capable of driving both its internal screen and an external CRT monitor simultaneously. The video display circuitry must operate at radically different refresh rates to properly drive the two different kinds of display.

Character Versus "APA" (Bitmapped) Images

The original IBM PC display subsystem that most people bought was what IBM called its Monochrome Display Adapter and Monitor. This monitor was a simple green screen cathode ray tube. The video adapter that drove it created images that consisted solely of letters, numbers, and a few graphic symbols. The screen image was divided into 25 lines with 80 character positions on each line. Any one symbol could be placed in each of those 2000 character positions, and each of those symbols could be either bright or dim, or it could blink. This was a pure character display system.

An early alternative to this green screen, character display was the IBM Color Graphics Adapter (CGA) and its monitor. This display system took quite a different approach to forming its images. Instead of putting character symbols into character cells on the screen, the CGA display painted 64,000 individual pixels. Each one could be made to glow in any one of four colors. Far less detail exists in an image formed this way, but what detail there is can be specified more arbitrarily. IBM dubbed this type of display an All-Points-Addressable (APA) display. Today we usually call it a bitmapped display, because one or more bits in the video image memory are assigned to each pixel on the screen.

Today, most PC users see only bitmapped screen images almost all the time. If you are running Windows 95, for example, the only character screens you ever see are those you get when you first boot the machine, when you go to MS-DOS mode, or in an MS-DOS window. If, on the other hand, you are running plain old DOS on your PC, then you will see a character screen whenever you are at the DOS command prompt, and often when you are in other programs, as well.

Where and How Is the Image Formed and Held?

As I just explained, screen images for PCs come in two forms: character images and graphic (APA, or bitmapped) images. Each of these forms requires storing the image information in memory in a different form. For a character image, all you must store in RAM is two bytes of information for each character position on the screen. One of these bytes holds the extended ASCII code for the character to be displayed in this position. The other byte holds attribute information. (These attributes specify such things as the color for this character, how bright is it, and whether it is supposed to be blinking or underlined.)

If, on the other hand, the image is to be a graphic, then much more detail must be stored. The color of every pixel must be described. Just how that is done depends on what *color depth* this image is to have.

Bit Planes and Color Depth

Color depth refers, indirectly, to the number of possible colors for each pixel in a graphic screen image. If all the pixels are either black or white, then you need only one bit to specify in which of these two colors a particular pixel is to be shown. If the image allows each pixel to have any one of four colors, then you need two bits per pixel to define which of those four colors is to be used. By similar reasoning you can see that four bits suffice to select any one of 16 colors. Eight bits can specify any one of 256 colors. The color depth is simply the number of bits needed to specify the color of each pixel.

The most commonly used color depths in PC images have been 2, 4, 8, 15, 16, and 24. Some special-purpose video cards use 32 bits per pixel, but in this case only 24 are used to specify the color. The remaining eight bits are used for what is called *alpha channel information*. This includes such things as information that specifies a degree of transparency to let an underlying image (perhaps from some external video source) show through.

A *bit plane* is simply an organization of the bits used to store an image in a three-dimensional array. First you form a planar array of bits, with one bit for each pixel on each line of the raster-scan image. Then you replicate this plane as many times as there are bits per pixel, placing each bit plane behind its predecessor. The result for N-bits per pixel is a collection of N planes.

To put some numbers to this, consider a common VGA graphic display. The resolution of the entire image is 640 pixels per line and 480 lines. This says there are 307,200 total pixels. Normal VGA specifies that each pixel can be given any one of a specified set of 16 colors. That means that the color depth is four bits. So, for each pixel you must have half a byte of video image RAM, for a total of 153,600 bytes (exactly 150KB). Because RAM chips always hold a number of bits that is some integer power of two, this means that normally VGA video cards carry 256KB of video image RAM.

Where, Physically and Logically, Is the Video Image RAM?

I just said that the video image RAM is typically on the video card. Is that always true? Why? Screen images for a PC must be held in some very special memory locations. These locations must be accessible to the CPU, but they also must be accessible to the video image output circuitry. The CPU needs rapid access to them, but the video output circuitry needs even more rapid access. This dictates where the chips that make up that memory can be placed, physically.

If you have a plug-in video card, because the video image output circuitry is on the card, it only makes sense to put the video image RAM there also. Or, if your PC has its video display adapter circuitry located on the motherboard, you will find the video image RAM somewhere very near it. In any event, the video image RAM consists of a totally separate set of chips from those that make up the PC's main memory that is used by the CPU for all other purposes. That is because of the special qualities this memory must possess and to enable it to be placed right next to the video image output circuitry.

That is where this RAM is located physically. But logically, things seem quite different. By that I mean that from the perspective of the CPU, this block of RAM is just more RAM like any other it can see in its memory address space. This block of memory in 386 and higher CPUs can have its physical memory addresses remapped to any location within the CPU's logical address space. (To learn more about the difference between physical and logical memory addresses, and about memory mapping, see Chapter 11, "Bigger Is Better in Ballrooms and in a PC's Memory.")

Forming PC Images the Old-Fashioned Way

Character-based images are prepared by the CPU. It stores the ASCII values for the characters to be displayed, along with an attribute byte for each one, into the display adapter's video RAM. These are the simple images. Much harder to create are graphic images, simply because they have so much more information in them. One way to do this job, and the only way it was done in early PCs, is to again have the CPU compute the correct color value (a number with however many bits the color depth for this image requires) for each pixel and then store those numbers in the video display adapter's video image RAM. This works, but it uses a lot of the CPU computing power.

Accelerated Video Cards

A better solution is to have a *graphics coprocessor* as a part of the video display adapter. This is a small computer within the PC whose sole job is computing pixel color values for graphic images. Now the program that is creating the image can describe that image in fairly broad, high-level terms. For example, it might specify that a triangle is to be drawn and give the coordinates of the corners, the width, and color of the line to be used, and perhaps a color to use to fill the interior of the triangle after it has been drawn.

If your PC has a graphics coprocessor, most of the time the CPU won't compute the pixel information for the images to be displayed, but it will instead pass instructions at this high level off to the graphics coprocessor. That device will then compute which pixels in the image must be set to the color of the border, and which are to be set to the fill color. And it will load all those pixel values into the video image RAM.

Figure 13.3 schematically shows these two different approaches to graphic image generation. The first panel shows a block diagram of how images are created and then displayed when a graphics coprocessor is not involved. The second panel shows how this changes with a graphics coprocessor. This figure doesn't show any details for the video image readout hardware. That is something I will cover shortly.

Figure 13.3.
Two ways to generate a graphics image.

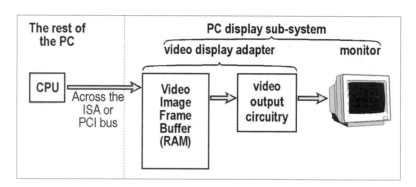

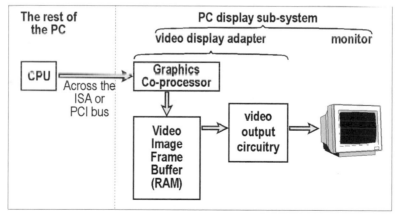

Perhaps the most significant point to make here is that the speed of data flow from graphics coprocessor to video image RAM and the flow from there to the screen are controlled only by the details of how the video card is built. If you have a high-end video card it might use a very fast clock speed and a very wide data bus (up to 128 bits flowing in parallel) between the graphics coprocessor and the video image RAM. Furthermore, whenever the images being formed are very detailed (high-image resolution) and with a lot of color depth, then the data flow from that RAM to the screen must also be tremendously fast. Naturally, the high-end video cards can support whatever rate they must to handle the images they are designed to create.

What Paints the Image on the Screen and How?

I have mentioned many times now, but up to now not explained, the video output circuitry that makes up one essential part of any video display adapter. Now it is time to remedy that.

Modern display adapters can operate in a huge number of different video modes. The particular mode you are using determines three things. First, it specifies whether the image you are creating is composed solely of characters, like a DOS-mode screen, or whether it is a bitmapped graphic. Second, it specifies the resolution of the image (how many pixels per line and how many lines). And third, it specifies the color depth (how many bits per pixel are stored in the video image RAM). The video output circuitry has anywhere from one to three separate jobs to perform. Which ones it does are determined by the video mode in which the video display adapter is operating.

I am going to limit my discussion here to the most common kinds of video monitor, a VGA or better analog display. These monitors connect to the video display adapter through a cable with 15-pin connectors. Inside that cable are three analog signals carrying brightness information in parallel for the three color components of each pixel. The cable also has two digital signal lines for the video and horizontal drive signals, and up to three digital signal lines by which the monitor can inform the video display adapter about its capabilities. (The H-drive and V-drive signals are also used by a PC's power-management circuitry when it determines that it should tell the monitor to go into some lower power state.)

The video modes in which the video output circuitry has the simplest job turns out to be, curiously enough, for the most complex images. These are the ones that are crafted in full-pixel detail in the video image RAM (frame buffer) by the CPU and graphics coprocessor, and for which the frame buffer holds at least 15 bits of color value per pixel. In this case, all the video output circuitry must do is generate the horizontal and vertical drive signals (so the monitor can sweep its beam across the screen in synchrony with the read-out circuitry's sweep through the frame buffer), and at the same time pump out each pixel's three color brightnesses on the three analog output wires going to the monitor.

One step in this process is worth noting. The video output circuitry reads a color value (a binary number) from the frame buffer, but what it must put on the output lines are three analog voltages between zero and one volt. The output circuitry does this by breaking up the color value into three parts and sending each part to a separate digital-to-analog converter (DAC).

If the color values are only eight-bit or four-bit numbers, then another step is added to the video output circuitry's job. In these cases, the color number doesn't directly specify the color of the pixel. Instead, it is used as a pointer into what is called a palette or color look-up table. For example, if the color number from the frame buffer is four, then the actual amounts of red, green, and blue to be displayed for that pixel will be found at the fourth line of the palette. Figure 13.4 is a block diagram of this with a sample palette table for default 16-color standard VGA images.

Figure 13.5 shows a typical, modern super-VGA (SVGA) video card. In this case it is the Matrox Millennium 4MB accelerated video card from our sample desktop system. This card has hardware support for fast 2D and 3D image rendering. It doesn't do 3D texture mapping in hardware, so that aspect of some images must be computed by the CPU using the Matrox or third-party supplied driver programs.

This particular card is capable of creating and displaying images with up to 1024×758 pixels with photo-realistic color (24 bits per pixel), or up to 1600×1200 pixels with high color (16 bits per pixel). The DAC modules on this card are capable of running at a pixel clock rate of up to 220MHz, which implies that it can pump out all the pixels in a VGA (640×480-pixel) image quickly enough to refresh the entire screen up to 200 times per second, or up to half that fast for its highest-resolution modes. (The actual speed it uses is set in the driver software.) This card can accept an additional memory module to allow even higher color depth at the highest resolution, and a proprietary Media XL connector for sound and television signal input and output.

Getting the Colors (Almost) Right

Including color in an image makes a huge difference. Color displays convey information more compactly than monochrome ones, because colors can be used to convey subtext to various items on the screen. (For example, warning messages often appear inside a red box.) And because color printers now are becoming quite affordable and capable, and thus more commonly found on PC systems, preparing documents in color is becoming more important.

But colors are slippery things. People don't see them the same way on paper and on a monitor, nor are all color display devices (monitors or printers) properly adjusted when they come from the factory. These things combine to make it difficult to be sure when you look at a screen image whether its colors are the same as what you will see when you print it.

You can take two approaches to get the colors in an image just right. One is to tweak how the monitor displays colors, and the other is to alter the stored information in the image until the monitor colors look however you want them to.

Figure 13.4.
How a VGA display creates colored pixels through translating numbers from the frame buffer.

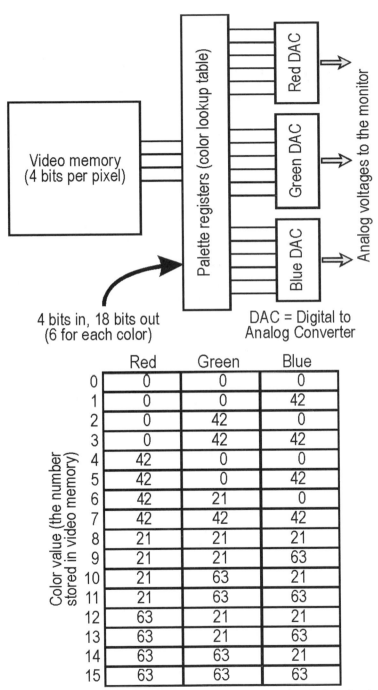

4 bits in, 18 bits out
(6 for each color)

DAC = Digital to
Analog Converter

	Red	Green	Blue
0	0	0	0
1	0	0	42
2	0	42	0
3	0	42	42
4	42	0	0
5	42	0	42
6	42	21	0
7	42	42	42
8	21	21	21
9	21	21	63
10	21	63	21
11	21	63	63
12	63	21	21
13	63	21	63
14	63	63	21
15	63	63	63

Color value (the number stored in video memory)

Contents of palette registers for default 16 color VGA display
(0 = None of that color, 63 = Full brightness of that color.)

Figure 13.5.
Matrox Millennium 4MB PCI-accelerated super VGA video card.

Adjusting the Monitor

If you plan to print some computer-generated color images, or intend them to be viewed on more than just your PC, then you probably will want to adjust your monitor until each color appears at least very nearly correct. That is, white pages should look white, and red should look red.

The first level of accomplishing this is called aligning the monitor. This is simply making sure that the electron beam that carries information for the red sub-pixels in the image is hitting only the dots or stripes of phosphor that glow red. (And, of course, doing the same for the other two colors of sub-pixels.) When that is done, any field of pure color will appear to be the same hue and saturation. But this color might or might not be right. The reason that this is so has to do with some details of both how humans see color and how display devices create colored images.

Suffice it to say that you can make some useful adjustments to an image that can make its colors appear more nearly correct. Figure 13.6 shows the Color tab on the Display Properties dialog box from the Windows 95 driver for the Matrox video card shown in Figure 13.5. Notice the adjustment slider for color temperature at the bottom left. This is used to make a white page seem white rather than bluish or yellowish. At the right are three sliders to adjust individually the "transfer curves" shown at the left for the three color signals. In essence, these enable you to emphasize or de-emphasize mid-level brightness pixels for a given color relative to the brightest ones. Normally you set these sliders until a test image displayed on your monitor looks as much like a printed copy of that image as you can manage.

Figure 13.6.
*Color adjustment
software for the
Matrox video card
enables you to tweak
images for proper
appearance.*

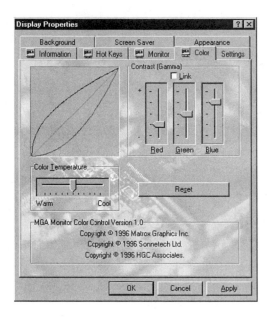

Adjusting the Image Information

The alternative way to adjust the color appearance of images is simply to alter the color values that are stored in the image itself or in its palette table. This is the only way to go if your video display adapter and its driver software don't provide the type of color compensation program just described. And it also it the best way to go if the images you are creating are to be viewed onscreen only on this one PC.

Understanding Display Technologies

Up to this point I have told you a great deal about color vision and color images, but not actually very much about exactly how the display devices we use create images we can see. There are two principal categories of display devices for PCs. The most common for desktop PCs are cathode ray tubes (CRTs). Virtually all laptops use LCD panels of one or another type. Projection display devices (for use in showing PC presentations to large audiences) can be built using either type of technology.

Cathode Ray Tubes (CRTs)

A CRT is a big glass bottle with a vacuum inside. It also contains three electron guns that squirt out focused beams of electrons, some deflection apparatus (either magnetic or electrostatic) that deflects these beams both up and down and side-to-side, and a phosphor screen upon which these beams impinge. The vacuum is necessary to let those electron beams travel across the tube without running into air molecules that could absorb them or scatter them off course.

Color CRTs also have one more essential part, either a *shadow mask* or an *aperture grill*. In these tubes the phosphor is not a continuous sheet of material, but instead consists of dots or stripes of three different materials. All three materials will glow when they are hit by an electron beam, but each glows in its own color (red, green, or blue).

In the first kind of color CRT, a shadow mask is located a short distance away from the phosphor. This mask is simply a metal sheet with a regular array of holes punched in it. The electron guns are arranged in a triangle at the back of the tube, and the phosphor has a triangle of dots of different color phosphors in front of each hole in the shadow mask. Because of this geometrical arrangement, each of the electron guns can only "see" the dots it is supposed to illuminate. The beam deflection apparatus deflects all three beams together to form the raster scan pattern. As the set of three beams sweeps across the shadow mask, the holes guarantee that each beam lights up only phosphor dots that glow in the correct color for that beam.

The alternative arrangement uses an aperture grill. In these CRTs the electron guns are placed side-by-side, just as you see in Figure 13.7. The aperture grill is simply an array of parallel wires, shown in this figure as the dashes in the dashed line near the phosphor. The gaps between those wires let the beams from the three electron guns illuminate three adjacent stripes on the tube surface. And at just those locations behind each gap are three stripes of the corresponding phosphors.

Sony patented this technology under the name Trinitron. That patent has now expired, and many manufacturers use it. Figure 13.7 shows a simplified diagram of how such a tube is constructed.

The industry standard for TV sets, and now for monitors as well, is to state as the size the diagonal dimension of the tube. Some portion of the edge of the tube is covered by the case, of course. TV images are normally adjusted so that you don't see the edges of them. But we must be able to see all the way to the edge of our PC images. So, in our system's 20-inch monitor, for example, the actual viewable (usable) portion of the front of the tube measures only 19 inches from corner to corner. Like most standard TV sets and computer monitors, the height is about three-quarters of the width. Thus, in our case the image width is about 15 inches and the height is about 11 inches. For a 1024×768 image, this implies the pixel spacing is about 0.37 millimeters (to convert to metric measure, as is commonly used for dot pitch specifications). This monitor has a dot pitch such that it can support images of up to 1600×1200 pixels.

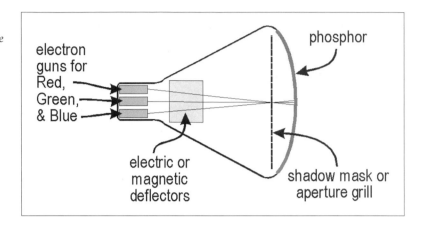

Figure 13.7.
Color CRTs use three electron guns and a shadow mask or aperture grill to illuminate triplets of phosphor dots or stripes.

Thin CRTs

Some people want a big monitor without taking up a whole lot of desk space. There are currently several ways you can achieve this. The least expensive is to use a thin CRT; the other options are to use an LCD panel, a plasma display panel, or an LED panel.

The thin CRT is quite an impressive technical achievement. Essentially, the normal CRT is bent in the middle. The deflection apparatus is modified so it can steer the electron beams and at the same time bend them through 90 degrees at a height that can be moved up and down the screen. Figure 13.8 shows such a CRT schematically.

Liquid Crystal Displays (LCDs)

The other major category of PC display devices are Liquid Crystal Display (LCD) panels. These devices come in many different variations, but the fundamental method of operation is the same for all of them.

Figure 13.9 shows a simple LCD panel. Here a light source shines through a linear polarizer. This sheet only passes photons (quanta of light) with their electric fields aligned parallel to the polarizing direction of that sheet (here shown as horizontal). Next, this light travels into a container filled with a special liquid crystal fluid. The property of the molecules in this container will rotate the plane of polarization of the light quanta by an amount that can be altered by an electric field imposed parallel to the path of the light. The last element is another linear polarizer, which will preferentially pass the photons that are aligned in its preferred orientation, in this case shown as vertical.

The container of liquid crystal fluid has several horizontal (x) transparent electrodes on one surface and a similar set of vertical (y) ones on the opposite surface. A voltage applied between one of the x-electrodes and one of the y-electrodes will impose an electric field on the liquid crystal material where they cross, and that will alter the light transmitted through that spot on the panel. By applying a voltage to one x-electrode and driving each y-electrode independently, it is possible to adjust the transparency of each pel on that row at the same time. Repeat this for every row (all the different x-electrodes) and you will have scanned the entire image.

Figure 13.8.
A thin CRT is a bent version of a standard CRT.

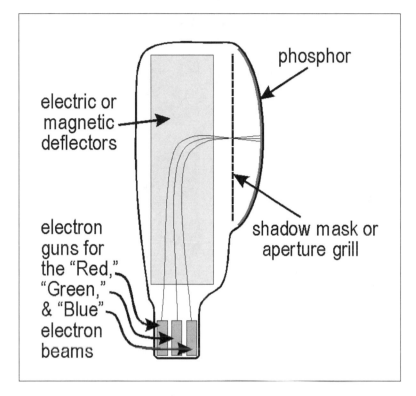

There are two ways to modify this design to make a color LCD panel. One way uses three times as many intersections as the number of pels to be formed in the final image. Each sub-pel is covered with a colored plastic filter. Then the signals applied to each intersection adjust the brightness of each sub-pel. This creates a color image in a manner that is essentially identical to that used by color CRTs.

The other way to modify the design is to layer three liquid crystal panels on top of one another. Each one is filled with a colored liquid crystal. Each one has its own set of x- and y-electrodes, this time just one intersection per pel. Each layer absorbs just an adjustable portion of just one color of the light passing through it. This is similar to the way printed color images are created. The principal advantage to this design is that it lets one create as many pels as intersections, thus making higher-resolution LCD panels possible. The principal disadvantage is that the light must pass through three layers, and so the resulting image is fainter, or you must use a stronger back light.

Figure 13.9.
The key elements of a typical LCD panel.

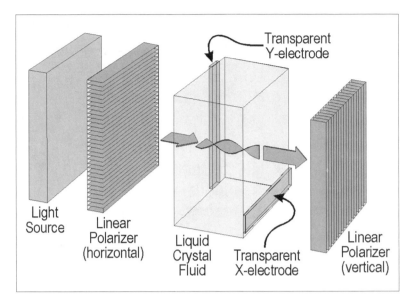

The main problem with LCD panels is the time it takes to set the brightness of all the pels. That takes so long that you cannot afford to set them one at a time. Instead, as I mentioned in the section "Scanning Frequencies and Refresh Rates," earlier in this chapter, only by driving all the columns in parallel can acceptable refresh rates be achieved. Even then, a simple LCD panel can be refreshed only a few times to perhaps a dozen times per second.

Double Scanning Helps

One simple way to get double the refresh rate is to break each column wire at its midpoint. Then put a separate amplifier at the top and bottom ends. Now you can scan information into two rows at once, one in the upper half and one in the lower half of the panel. This is what we call a double-scan LCD panel. Such a display works much better than a single-scan LCD, but still not well enough for video.

Active Matrix Thin Film Transistor (TFT) Displays

The best LCD panels (and, of course, the most expensive) are what are termed Thin Film Transistor (TFT) LCD panels. In this design a separate amplifier exists for each intersection (each pel) in the entire panel. This can be done only by building those amplifiers right onto the surface of the LCD panel rather than on semiconductor chips that are placed around the edges.

At first this was very difficult to do. Now, however, manufacturers have become so good at this that the price for TFT panels is fairly low. And if you can afford it, you will enjoy the resulting images a lot more—especially if you want to watch video clips on your laptop PC (or your desktop PC if you opt for one of the new ultra-thin desktop displays made using an LCD panel).

By having an amplifier per pel, you can refresh the entire screen essentially as fast as you can set the brightness for a single pel. With a TFT LCD panel, refresh rates of hundreds of times per second are practical.

Other Display Technologies

CRT and LCD monitors account for almost all the displays used in and with PCs. But a few other technologies have been tried at one time or another. Perhaps the most important are plasma displays. These are very large neon bulbs with fancy electrodes and internal partitions to form effectively one lamp per pel. You drive them in a manner similar to that used for LCD panels, but the voltages involved are much higher. The result is to cause a small section of the gas inside the panel to form a glowing plasma. If you do it right, this plasma won't spread to neighboring cells, and it will die out promptly when you turn off power to that cell. These plasma displays are most often used for very large panels that must be viewable in relatively high ambient light situations. Making color plasma displays is much harder than making monochrome ones, and thus it is not done very often.

I describe several other special-purpose PC display technologies in the section of Chapter 22, "Immersive PC Experiences," on "'Real' 3D." That discussion includes mention of head-mounted displays, direct retinal projectors, and other exotic technologies, some of which are only on the drawing boards, and others of which are available now in your local computer store.

This Story Is Incomplete

As you can imagine, more developments in PC displays will occur as time goes on. None of the ones we use now are perfect, so there is ample room for improvements. But for now, CRTs and LCDs are the primary display technologies in use. In addition to CRTs and LCD panels meant for direct viewing, there are products that use displays of either of those types in a projection mode. These projectors can fill a large screen with a PC-generated image, and they might seem quite exotic compared to a simple desktop or laptop PC's usual monitor. Actually, though, they are merely the same types of display made super bright and imaged on a screen.

Running the Display System Backward

The PC display system is all about showing you output from your PC. Well, that is mostly true. But sometimes a PC input device uses the display as part of its hardware. One example is a light pen. This is essentially a fast-acting photocell in a pen. You hold it up to the screen of a CRT, and it will "see" the scanning beam go by. Electronics in the PC can detect this pulse and correlate it with what part of the screen was being scanned at that moment. In this way you can point to things on the screen and the PC will know just where you are pointing.

The most common other example of this approach is a touch-screen display. These are monitors (usually CRTs) in a case that adds some means of detecting any time someone touches a spot on the screen. One method uses both a horizontal and a vertical grid of invisible light beams and photo-cells to see your finger approach the screen. Another method uses a transparent sensing membrane applied to the face of the CRT. Whatever the means, the effect is the same: You can point and the PC knows when and where you pointed. These pointing devices aren't suitable for very fine work, but they work well to let a user pick out one among several choices without needing to use a keyboard. This means that the most common application for this type of display system is in information kiosks rather than in general-purpose PCs.

Summary

When it comes to PC display subsystems, you have a lot of choices. Many different technologies exist, as well as many implementations of each one. Armed with the information in this chapter (and the additional information in Chapters 21, "Special Storage Hardware Needs for Multimedia," and 22, "Immersive PC Experiences," you will be able to understand each new PC display product. You will know why it works as it does, and therefore which ones will be of interest to you and which you can quickly pass by.

And now that you understand how PCs display information on a screen, it is time to turn to the other most common method of getting information out of your computer: printers. That is the subject of the next chapter.

14

Getting It All Down on Paper: Printers

Peter Norton®

Most PC information input comes via the keyboard (or is loaded in bulk from a disk or over a connection to a remote computer). Most PC output goes to the screen. The second most important information output path is to some type of printer. Screen images can be very rich in information, and when animated or video images are combined with sound they can be very compelling. However, they are inherently transient displays, and they can't be carried away from the display device.

The Purpose and Power of PC Printers

A page of printed output can display considerably more information than can a single screen image, and it clearly is much more permanent and portable. Thus, PC printers are one of the most used peripheral devices. As such, they have attracted a lot of development effort, and we now have a wide variety of printer technologies to choose from.

The point of a printer is to make marks on paper or some similar medium. In this chapter I will first explain the five principal mechanisms that are used in PC printers to make those marks. Then I will explain the difference between character printers and page printers, and give you a brief description of the principal kinds of each. Finally, I will mention some of the special issues surrounding printing images in color.

Printing Technologies—An Overview

No PC printers use chisels to carve marks in stone tablets. That is almost the only method of "printing" ever devised that hasn't been adapted to use in a printer for a PC. All the printers in common use with PCs use one of five basic methods to make their marks on the paper or other media on which they print. Each of them comes in many forms, some of which are different enough from one another that I will discuss those details below. But first, an overview of these five ways to "make your mark."

Making an Impression: Impact Printers

The first computer printers were simply computer-controlled typewriters. In these machines a ribbon soaked with ink is positioned in front of a piece of paper, then banged upon with a shaped hammer. The impact drives ink out of the ribbon and onto the page. Many modern computer printers do much the same thing. We call them *impact printers*.

Impact printers can be further subdivided into two classes: Those that use shaped hammers to produce an entire symbol in a single blow (called *character printers*), and those that form images one dot at a time, in a manner reminiscent of the way in which PC displays form their images. These latter devices are commonly called *dot-matrix impact printers.*

Xerographic (Laser, LCS, and LED) Printers

Having a laser printer for your PC has been one of the ultimate status symbols (as well as a very practical thing to do) ever since Chester Carlson's 1938 invention of xerographic printing—which was turned into the wonderfully convenient Xerox 914 office copiers (in 1959)—was further transformed into the Hewlett-Packard LaserJet family of PC printers (starting in 1984). The correct name for what most folks refer to as a *laser printer* is a xerographic printer. That is, its basic process is xerography: the printing process that Chester Carlson invented.

Three physical facts underlie xerographic printing:

- Photoconductive materials exist that are very good electrical insulators as long as they are kept in the dark, but which become good electrical conductors whenever light shines on them.

- Materials that have opposite electrostatic charges are attracted to one another.

- You can bond particles of one material to another material by melting and re-freezing some bonding agent. If, instead of simply melting the bonding agent, you also produce some chemical cross-linking, the resulting solid bond will be relatively immune to being softened by heat later.

A xerographic printer is built around a photosensitive transfer surface. This surface is usually built either in the form of a rigid cylinder of metal with a thin coating of the photoconductor on its outer surface, or in the form of an electrically conducting closed-loop belt with similar coating on one side. Xerographic printing proceeds in six steps:

1. The photoconductive surface (which is in a darkened space) is cleaned of any residual toner and then charged to a high electrostatic potential.

2. This charge is selectively drained off by shining light onto only selected regions of the photoconductive surface.

3. The surface is flooded with toner particles. These are a mixture of tiny specks of some highly colored material and equally tiny chunks of a plastic bonding material. The toner particles stick only to the portions of the photoconductor that are still carrying a large electrostatic charge.

4. An oppositely electrically charged piece of paper (or other medium on which printing is to occur) is pressed against the tone-coated photoconductive surface.

5. The paper is then separated from the photoconductive surface. In this step most of the toner comes along with the paper, held there by electrostatic attraction.

6. The toner-laden paper is heated, thus fusing the ink particles to the paper.

The image being printed is formed at the second step. In an office copier this is accomplished by imaging a document onto the surface. The dark places on the document show up as the regions that don't get discharged on the photoconductor. That means they stay charged electrostatically, and therefore they attract toner, which is later transferred to the paper and fused to make dark places on the copy.

Computer printers create images that start with information in a file. There is no pre-existing dark and light image to be projected onto the photoconductor. So, instead of imaging a pre-existing image, a xerographic computer printer builds the image one pel at a time, just as a computer display shows graphic images by building them up one pel at a time on the monitor's screen.

Standards: As I did with PC display technologies, I'll call the minimum size dot you can print a *pel*. This is in contrast to the notion of *pixel*, which is the minimum element you can specify in a computer-generated image file. Pels refer to the least size printable (or displayable) dot. You can print one pixel to a pel, or you can spread a pixel over several adjacent pels, but you cannot print two different pixels within the space of one pel. (At best, you can print an average value for all the pixels that contribute to a pel; but the pel itself is the indivisible unit of what gets printed.)

This story can become confusing when you try to understand how a xerographic printer causes light to fall on the photoconductor wherever the resulting image is to lack color and not fall on it wherever color (which could include black) is to appear in the final image? The reason for the confusion is that there is no one, simple answer.

The computer printers that truly deserve the name "laser printer" (and the HP LaserJet family are examples of this type) have a laser light source inside them. A set of moving mirrors causes the beam to scan across the photoconductive surface in a raster, just like the raster drawn on the screen of your PC's monitor. The major difference is that the laser beam draws a much smaller spot.

Early laser printers turned the beam off to print a pel and on to discharge a spot and thus not print that pel. Modern laser printers often can modulate the beam intensity in more subtle ways, modifying the size and sometimes even the location of the spots that get printed within the region described as a single pel.

Other xerographic printers use a variety of means to accomplish what the laser does in a laser printer, but in different ways. For example, one version uses a row of *light-emitting diodes* (LEDs). Each LED corresponds to a single column of pels on the page. Very similar to those printers are ones that use a single, very bright light that shines on a row of *liquid-crystal shutters* (an LCS array). Each LCS works in a manner very similar to the individual pels in an LCD display panel. (See Figure 13.11 and the discussion of it in the previous chapter, "Seeing the Results: PC Displays," for details on how this works.)

Both LED and LCS xerographic printers are able to print an entire row of pels across the drum simultaneously, and they do this without any moving parts. In these printers only the paper moves (and, of course, the rollers that force the paper along its path). In contrast, a laser printer must also have a complex optical arrangement with moving mirrors to scan the page one pel at a time.

Squirting Ink Printers

Another traditional way to make marks on a surface is by painting them. That means, in its essence, putting a colored liquid on the surface and letting it dry. This is the basic technology behind what we term *ink-jet printers*. These printers spray a liquid ink onto the page. Most of them are descended from the dot-matrix impact printers, and so the design of much of their internal mechanisms are quite similar to those earlier generation printers. (For example, most ink-jet printers have multiple jets vertically aligned on a carriage that moves horizontally across the page.)

Pass the Crayons: Hot Wax Printers

Crayons are sticks of colored wax. Heat a crayon just to where it begins to melt, then touch it briefly to a piece of paper. You will leave a small amount of colored wax stuck to the paper where you touched it. This is the basis of several different kinds of hot wax printers.

One kind of hot wax printer can best be described as an ink-jet printer that uses a solid ink that is melted before it enters the ink jets. A very different design uses a ribbon that carries the wax and that is as wide as the paper. While this ribbon is in close contact with the paper along a line across the page, individual spots (pels) on that line are heated briefly. This melts the wax, which, as it cools, tends to stick more to the paper than to the slick surface of the ribbon's base material.

In the latter kind of hot wax printer the individual spots can be heated in any of a really large number of ways. Electric sparks, tiny electrically heated wires, piezo-electric emitters of sound energy, lasers—you name it, somebody has probably used it to build this type of printer.

The Sublime Printers: Dye Sublimation

Some solid materials don't melt when you heat them. Instead, they turn directly into a gas. (So-called "dry ice," which is solid CO_2, is an example of such a material.) We term this process *sublimation*. In dye-sublimation printers a ribbon carrying a special colored material that can be sublimed is placed in close proximity to a specially treated paper. A spot on that ribbon is heated briefly. The dye there sublimes, and the resulting tiny gas cloud partially re-solidifies on the paper. This is the basic process used in dye-sublimation printers.

An important point to notice is that the amount of dye that is transferred to any one pel can be controlled by monitoring how much energy is dumped into the corresponding spot on the ribbon. Thus, this process inherently allows printing in a sort-of grayscale fashion—something many of the other processes are inherently incapable of supporting.

The list of methods that have been used to produce the spot heating of each pel in this class of printers is essentially identical to the list for the hot wax printers that use a page-wide ribbon. In fact, some printers can be used for either hot-wax printing or for dye-sublimation printing with just a change of ribbons and paper, and perhaps a resetting of some parameters used in the spot-heating mechanism by the driver software.

Impact Printers for PCs

As I told you earlier, impact printers for PCs can either be formed-character printers or dot-matrix printers. That might surprise you, because formed character printers are rarely used with PCs today. Still, for historical accuracy, I want to mention them. And indeed, if you get a computer-printed paycheck or utility bill, it very possibly was printed by a formed-character printer attached, typically, to a computer that is larger than a PC.

Character Printers

Formed-character impact printers use shaped hammers to drive ink out of a ribbon in the shape of the letter or other symbol you want to print. Their chief advantage is that you can print very complex symbols in this way, without having to specify that shape anywhere inside the computer that is driving the printer. The principal disadvantage of this type of printer is exactly the converse of that statement. Because the shapes of the characters are fixed by the shapes of the hammers, the computer cannot alter them, even when you might want it to.

The only way to change fonts in such a printer, for example, is to remove and replace the entire set of hammers. Ordinarily this is done by stopping the entire printing process and having some human being open the printer and change an object that carries all the hammers. And that is certainly not something you want to have to do many times per page of printed output.

Daisy Wheel Printers

When PCs were young, however, the only affordable technology for printing really good-looking text was a computer-driven typewriter. The most common of these used an electromagnetically driven solenoid to pound a shaped hammer tip against the ribbon and drive the ink onto the page. These hammer tips were formed out of plastic and placed at the ends of narrow strips of plastic radiating from a central hub.

This wheel-like arrangement of spokes around a central hub looks a little like a daisy flower, hence the name *daisy-wheel printers*. Before a character can be printed, the computer must turn the daisy wheel to the correct orientation, so the properly shaped hammer tip is in front of the solenoid. The daisy wheel, its electromagnetically driven solenoid, and the ribbon mechanism travel together on a carrier from left to right and back again, and between passes the paper is advanced vertically by a rolling action of a platen, just as has been standard for typewriters for many years. Naturally, this arrangement prints only one character at a time, just like a typewriter.

The daisy wheel can easily be swapped for a different one in order to change the font. But "easily," here, is a relative term. Even though a person could do it in a few seconds (with practice), that takes enough time and enough human effort, that normally it just isn't done—certainly not several times on each page.

Standards: I want to make one thing very clear here. A font, in the way I am using it here (which is the formally correct usage) means a particular *style* of a particular *typeface* in a particular *size*. For example, it might be 12-point Courier bold italic. In this example, Courier is the typeface, bold italic is the style, and 12-point is the size.

Many people call *Times Roman* (just to name one common example) a font. But that is incorrect, because the size and style have not been specified. All this name really tells you is the typeface, which is the family name for a family of fonts. True enough, when you get a "font file" for your PC, it is a single file that can be used to print any size letters, and often in any one of several styles. But this usage of the term *font* is actually a misnomer.

Because a single daisy wheel can hold hammers for only a single font (in the narrowly restricted usage of that term), with these printers you couldn't italicize a single word on a line or use boldface to emphasize a single sentence—well, you could do so, but only at the very substantial cost of making someone stop the printer and change wheels to and back from that alternative font possibly several times within the printing of a single page. (A pseudo-bold was possible by overprinting a group of characters, sometimes with a small horizontal offset, but that in no way is true boldface printing as typographers understand the term.)

Using daisy-wheel printers also has two other drawbacks. One is that they are slow. They are faster than a human typist, but compared to almost any other computer-driven printing technology, they are very slow. The second drawback is that they are noisy; not a lot noisier than an ordinary electric typewriter, but that isn't saying much.

When laser printers became inexpensive enough to compete with the other low-cost printers for PCs, daisy-wheel printers headed straight for the museums and attics of the land, never to be heard from again.

Line Printers

The other principal kind of formed-character impact printer is the line printer. These are still in use in many large computer installations. They have never, however, been very popular as PC printers.

A line printer has a solenoid-driven hammer for each column of type on the page. In one variation, each hammer has a vertical strip of metal raised and lowered between it and the ribbon. On that strip are formed all the different character shapes it can print. When the strip is raised to the correct height, the hammer strikes it and the character is printed. This can be going on simultaneously for every column on the page, and in that fashion, an entire line of type can be printed at once.

An alternative design for a line printer uses a ribbon or chain of hammers. The set of character shapes is repeated on this chain many times. The chain is in continuous motion in a loop around all the hammers for all the columns. Each hammer strikes out at just the right time to imprint the correct character in its column position. In this kind of printer not all the columns on a line are printed simultaneously, so it is somewhat slower than the design described a moment ago. On the other hand, only one set of hammers is needed, so this can be a somewhat less expensive kind of printer to manufacture.

You can tell which kind of line printer was used to print a document by noticing the minor misalignments of the characters. If all the characters fall accurately underneath the one above, but they wander slightly up or down from the level of the characters on either side, then the first type of line printer I described was probably used. If they seem to wander a little from side to side while remaining on the same level, then the second type (a chain printer) was used.

The advantage to either kind of line printer is speed. The disadvantages are inflexibility (changing fonts in these machines really is hard), noise, cost, weight, and size. These are more than enough reasons for their unpopularity as a printer for PCs.

Non-Character (Dot-Matrix) Impact Printers

The first non-character impact printers for PCs were again based on the design of a typewriter. Only the hammer design was changed. Now, instead of a single hammer that drives a formed shape onto the ribbon, these printers have a vertical column of closely spaced round wires that strike the ribbon. Each one is driven by its own solenoid and is capable of printing a single dot on the page with each stroke. But by moving the carriage horizontally only about one dot's width and striking the page again and again, this mechanism can use a single wire hammer to "draw" a horizontal line on the page. It is, of course, actually a row of dots, but if they touch one another, it will look like a line.

And while that is happening for one wire, similar things are happening for all the others above and below it. This means that in one pass across the page this mechanism can print, or not print, all the dots within a rectangle whose height is the distance from the top wire to the bottom wire and whose width is the width of the page.

Note: The name *dot-matrix printer* comes from the notion that these printers form characters out of a rectangular array of dots. That array is called the matrix. The particular dots in that array that get printed defines the character's shape. A dot-matrix printer normally prints an entire row of characters each time it passes the head across the page. Each pass, therefore, corresponds to a line of "type" just as was the case with the predecessor technology, the typewriter.

Because there is no need to wait for a character daisy wheel to turn into the right position for each character, these printers can be quite a bit faster than daisy-wheel printers. However, they are not nearly as fast as good laser printers.

After the hammer finishes its first pass across the page, the printer rolls the paper up just as far as the height of that rectangle, then the head passes back across the page, again printing as it goes. Repeating this enough times will allow you to print dots on the page anywhere and everywhere you want.

I pointed out in Chapter 13, "Seeing the Results: PC Displays," that if you can control, one by one, all the spots in an image, you can form any image you want. Similarly, a dot-matrix printer can print virtually any image you want. With at least seven wires you can make a dot-matrix printer that can print readable text with a single pass per line of type. It isn't pretty, but it is legible. That is what the original, inexpensive dot-matrix printers were made to do.

They also could operate in a "near letter quality" mode in which they would make two passes across each line at slightly different vertical positions to allow putting in more dots for each character. That helped a lot, but it still didn't produce letters nearly as nice looking as those printed by daisy-wheel printers. On the other hand, this technology does enable you to change fonts on the fly. Because the computer is dictating each and every pel that is to be printed, it can change the shapes or sizes of letters arbitrarily and often within a page.

Warning: This flexibility, combined with the power to control every step of the process of preparing documents, from creating the text to formatting the output, has led some PC users into some very bad habits. They go hog wild putting multiple fonts on a page. This is excusable. After all, they never had any training as typographers or graphic designers. But it is regrettable, nonetheless.

Pages like that look ugly. With modern PC printers you have even more power to create documents that are absolutely stunningly beautiful, or ones that could qualify for the "Document Hall of Shame." Generally, what are considered good graphic design rules will allow you to use on any one document at most several sizes of a single typeface (or maybe two faces), and in differing styles (italic or not). But more in this case is definitely not better—at least most of the time.

Modern dot-matrix impact printers have many more wires in the print head. This lets them print better-quality documents, but still not nearly as nice as almost any laser printer can. Dot-matrix impact printers continue to be used, despite their noise and relatively low print quality, because they are fairly cheap and they will print multi-part forms. Only impact printers have that latter capability. So, as long as there are multi-part forms to be printed, impact printers of some kind will continue to be used. (Of course, the alternative to printing on a multi-part form is to print each page of that form separately. And that is precisely what more and more businesses are now doing.)

Non-Impact Printers for PCs

All non-impact printers for PCs are, in a sense, dot-matrix printers. That is, they all control the printed image pel by pel. Some of them even do so in groups of pel-rows, just as the stacked-wire impact dot matrix printers do. Others in this class print an entire page one row of pels at a time.

Ways to Describe Images to be Printed

If a page to be printed contains only text, and especially if all of that text is to be printed in a single font, then all you must tell the printer is which characters go where. A simple ASCII text file can be used to do this very nicely. If, on the other hand, you want to print highly formatted pages, possibly including some graphic images as well as type in various fonts, then you must tell the printer what it is to do in a great deal more detail.

Bitmapped Page Images

The simplest solution is to tell the printer about each and every pel it is to print. This means sending the printer a bitmapped image of the page. And in some cases, this is the only available means of telling a particular printer how to do its job.

Pure ASCII Text Pages

A printer that uses a formed character mechanism obviously must be told only which characters to print in each column of each row. That is, after all, the limit of what it can do. But practically every PC printer in use today is capable of printing bitmapped images; and yet, most of the time we don't give them information in that form.

With the sole exception of some PostScript printers, every PC printer has built into it the necessary capability to convert a stream of ASCII characters into a corresponding stream of printed characters (in some default font) onto successive lines on the page, as if it were a formed character printer. If you don't do something special, then it will interpret any arriving ASCII text as something it is to print in just this fashion.

Plotter Languages

Before we had any kind of PC printer other than computer-driven typewriters, it was possible to make drawings by using a computer-driven plotter. This is a machine that essentially has a robotic arm of some type that holds a pen and can press that pen down or raise it up while moving around on the page in a prescribed manner.

Plotters are like the vector display devices discussed in the section "Raster-Scan Versus Vector Displays" in Chapter 13. Because they draw images a stroke at a time rather than a pel at a time, you must command them in a different way. (Plotters have now been all but replaced by large page-size ink-jet printers.)

Several different languages were devised for sending commands to a computer-driven plotter. Hewlett-Packard's HPGL is perhaps the best known. Later, an industry standard graphic file format was developed for holding descriptions of computer images of all kinds, including those for plotters. This file format is called Computer Graphics Metafile (CGM). These languages are still sometimes used with PCs, but mostly they matter to us now because they led the way to the page description languages that are what we more commonly use today.

Page Description Languages

When Hewlett-Packard introduced the LaserJet, it also introduced a new way to specify how a computer-generated page should look. Its new *Printer Control Language* (PCL) was primarily intended to control the font, size, style, and placement of letters on a page. It had some provisions for other, more graphic elements, but those clearly were not its main focus.

Not long after that, Apple Computer introduced its LaserWriter printer. And with it Apple bundled another new page description language. This one had been developed at Adobe, and its name was *PostScript*. A major difference between PostScript and PCL is that PostScript is intended to be a totally general-purpose page description language. Indeed, with suitable hardware, a computer running PostScript can become a general-purpose computer. It has provisions for handling disk storage of information and many other things that the makers of PCL apparently never contemplated including in a page description language. (Observers at the time noted that it was ironic that the most powerful computer being marketed by Apple—and it was more powerful by a large margin than the Lisa, which was Apple's best other computer—was the one contained in their LaserWriter.)

Historical Aside: Much has been made of how the Apple Macintosh's graphical user interface and "ease of use" won the hearts and minds of the graphics arts community. Even today, more Macs than PCs are used in that industry, while they are a tiny minority of the personal-scale computers used in most other industries. But very likely the real reason for that bias was first and foremost the great graphic design power that PostScript gave to designers who used the Apple LaserWriter.

Both of these general page description languages have been substantially improved and extended over the dozen or so years since their introduction. PostScript, as the more fully fleshed-out concept initially, has needed much less in the way of extension. The current version of PostScript is 2. HP's PCL has undergone many more revisions and a much larger expansion of its scope. It now is quite comparable to PostScript in its graphic power, control, and flexibility. The most recent release of PCL is 6XL.

"Smart" Page Printers

When HP introduced the LaserJet and Apple introduced the LaserWriter, the common personal computers of the day to which these printers were to serve as peripherals were simply not very powerful. They were not nearly powerful enough to do all the computing needed to *rasterize* pages described in PCL or PostScript in a reasonably short time. (To rasterize a page is to compute the color for each of the pels on the entire page. The name comes from the notion that those pels can be organized into rows just like the pels on a raster-scan video display.) This is why those companies made their printers with a very powerful computer built into each one. Those computers were dedicated to just the one job of rasterizing pages.

This makes them what I call "smart page printers." You send such a printer a description of the page in either PCL or PostScript, it will figure out what the page is to look like, and then print it. Not only does that mean that these printers need a lot of computing power, it also means that they must have quite a lot of RAM in which to hold the page image they are computing. Only after the entire file has been processed can they be sure it is safe to begin printing any portion of it. This is so because both PCL and PostScript describe pages in a way that is somewhat like the way a vector art file describes an image. They use the display list concept. That means that the very last item in the file might be telling the printer about a header line that is to go at the very top of the page.

Back when these printers first came on the market, enough RAM for a full page frame buffer could cost a small fortune—more than the rest of the printer's parts put together. So a strategy was devised to let one print the page in pieces, called bands. In this strategy one might have a RAM buffer that is only large enough to hold, suppose, one-tenth of a page. The computer that is rasterizing the image will pretend that it has a full page buffer to work with. It then merrily rasterizes the entire image and deposits that information into that imaginary frame buffer. Only one-tenth of those locations have actual RAM; in the rest of the locations the information "written" is actually simply discarded. If that real RAM is located at the top of the page image, that top one-tenth of the page can be printed when the computer has completed rasterizing the entire page. Next, the RAM is cleared, and its addresses reassigned to the next tenth of the frame buffer. The computer then must redo the entire process of rasterizing the file, from the beginning to the end. When it finishes, the next tenth of the page can be printed. This continues, with the paper advancing through the printer in spurts, until the entire page has been printed.

That strategy works, and it saves on the cost of RAM, but it obviously also makes printing pages take much longer. Now that RAM is (relatively) cheap, it makes more sense to be sure your page printer has enough RAM so it can rasterize the entire page image just once and then print it as a whole. (Furthermore, this will ensure that you don't get lines across the page where the bands end, which can happen if the paper-moving mechanism cannot be stopped and restarted gracefully.)

All of these smart page printer ideas have been applied to page printers using each of the principal printing technologies. Thus, you can have an ink-jet page printer, a xerographic page printer (using a laser, an array of LEDs or an LCS array), or a hot wax or dye-sublimation page printer. In all cases, the most common way those printers are supplied is with a very powerful computer inside of them to rasterize the page images. Some of these printers come equipped to interpret PCL files; some "understand" PostScript files; a few can do either; and all of them also can accept a pure bitmapped image of the entire page, or of any portion of a page, if that is what you want to send it.

One advantage to PCL as a language for controlling a printer is that if you just send some ASCII text to a PCL printer, it will print what you send it in some default font. (You must be sure to include the Form Feed character to tell it when to print and eject the page.) A pure PostScript printer can print an ASCII text file only if you first wrap the text inside a short PostScript program.

Dumb Page Printers

PCs are much more powerful now than they were a dozen years ago, and pages of text or even of images aren't all that much more complex than they were back then. So now our PCs are capable of doing the rasterizing job every bit as well as the computers in our printers.

Some companies have capitalized on this fact. They point out that if you buy a very fast computer, you can then buy (from them) a very inexpensive printer that can print images that are just as good as those from a very much more expensive printer. This will work because these inexpensive, "dumb" printers don't have any computer inside. They depend instead on a software program running in your PC to do all that work, and then ship out just the pels to be printed to the printer. And all it can do is print a bitmapped image from that string of pels.

These companies also point out that the money you are investing in your PC can be put to good use when you are printing and also when you are not, whereas the investment you make in a computer that is built into a printer can do you some good only when you are actually printing something. This argument has merit, and it certainly has convinced some PC owners to get a much more graphically capable printer than they otherwise would have afforded. But of course, there is a downside to this approach. If all your PC's power is going to be consumed in the rasterizing task for the next hour, then during that time you aren't going to be doing much of anything else with it. And it also means that you must have a lot of free RAM and free disk space on your PC for this strategy to work.

To cite just one example, I have a tabloid (20×12-inch page size) dumb page printer that can use either the hot wax or the dye sublimation printing process to print page images in full color at 300 dots per inch resolution. This means that there are 20×12×300×300 pels per page. That is 21.6 million pels. And for full color I must store three bytes for each pel. This isn't possible unless I can give the software rasterizing program at least 62MB for its frame buffer in which it will create the image. In practice, the program spools most of that information to a disk file, so I can get away with merely a few megabytes of free RAM. But I find that unless I have a couple of hundred megabytes of free disk space, the printer simply fails to print the page at all!

Getting the Color (Almost) Right

I haven't said much about color printers up to now, but nearly everything I have said applies to them just as much as it does to black-and-white printers.

Color Models

Monochrome (black-and-white, or any single color and white) printed pages require knowing for each pel just how black (or colored) it shall be. Many printers only allow each pel to be fully black or fully white. Some permit gray values as well. To print images in color, first you must understand how we see colors, and how we can be fooled by the clever use of just a few colors of ink into thinking we are seeing a much wider range of colors. This is an area of psychophysics and technology that I already explained in connection with PC displays. So, if you skipped Chapter 13 I suggest you turn to it now and read at least the section on color models.

Printed images on paper (or on a transparency for use in an overhead projector) are subtractive images. That is, you shine nominally white light on them and the inks on the page subtract out some of that light before it is bounced back to your eyes. To create the appearance of a red pel you must subtract most of the non-red color in the light that is reflected from it. That is usually done in printing by the use of a suitable combination of cyan and yellow inks, with possibly some black thrown in to lower the overall brightness of that pel.

Note: There is another way to print colors, called in the printing industry *spot color*. Here you use inks in each of the colors you care about. This can require the use of up to a dozen separate inks, and it is the only way to print documents with convincing golds and silvers, for example. But all common color printers for PCs do not use this approach. Instead, they use the more common four-color printing model with inks that are cyan (C), yellow (Y), magenta (M), and black (K).

Whichever mark-making technology is used (impact, xerographic, ink-jet, hot wax, or dye sublimation) it can be done in color just as well as in black and white. Color printers are more complex, so they generally cost more to make and to buy. Likewise, they use more expensive *consumables*. This is the jargon term for the paper and "ink" you use when you print documents. In some printers the ink comes on a ribbon; in others it comes in another form.

Ribbons or Cartridges

Impact printers normally use a fabric ribbon that is soaked in ink. If they are color printers, commonly that ribbon will have four parallel stripes of different colors (CYMK). You can exchange that ribbon for a single-color one when you want to print documents just in black (or any single color) and white. Doing so will save your expensive four-color ribbon for when you must print in color. When any one of the four stripes of color wears out, you must replace the entire four-color ribbon.

Color xerographic printers must have four supplies of toner (the "ink" for this type of printer). Some models will have each color in a separate container. Others will combine all four and perhaps even include the photosensitive drum unit as well. How much of the printer you end up replacing when you run out of a single color of ink (and the cost to do so) will vary, depending on which way your printer is constructed.

Ink-jet printers can come with a unified ink supply or with separate containers for each color of ink. Naturally, when any one color runs dry in the unified supply version, you must replace (or refill) the entire unit. Hot wax printers that use solid sticks of colored wax are very much like ink-jet printers with separate ink reservoirs. They can be re-inked one color at a time rather easily. Hot wax printers that use a paper-wide ribbon must have their entire ribbon, with all four colors on it, replaced when it gets used up. This also applies to all dye-sublimation printers.

Color Correction Programs and Printer Profiles

Just as with color displays, color printers won't always print images that look exactly alike. Our eyes can be very sensitive to even minor variations in color in an image. And some companies are extraordinarily concerned that their logos, for example, be printed in exactly the "right" colors.

For these reasons, color printers often are supplied with a special "printer profile" file. This file contains information on just how much of each of the four colors it must be commanded to print to achieve certain standard, blended colors. Such a profile might be prepared separately for each individual printer, or it might be one that applies, in an average way, to all printers of a given model.

The printer driver that sends color images to the printer will often allow installation of this printer profile, to inform that driver how to shade the colors in the image it sends out in order to make the resulting printed colors more accurate representations of the image creator's intentions. Programs to create color images often also incorporate tools to compensate for the characteristics of your particular color printer.

By using some combination of all these tools (printer profile, driver adjustments, and image creation program adjustments) creating images both on your PC's screen and printed on paper that look very nearly alike should be possible, and in the case of ones that reproduce the appearance of some real objects, very nearly like those actual objects.

Summary

You now know the five basic mark-making methods used in PC printers. Each of the hundreds of models on the market uses only one or two of these five, and none of them uses anything else. You know that printers often have a default font (and you know that this means a prescribed typeface, style, and size) in which they will print ASCII text. And you know that most are also capable of being commanded to print much more complex page images.

I have explained to you the difference between a formed-character printer and a dot-matrix printer, as well as the difference between printers that print a single character at a time, a line at a time, or a page at a time. And you have at least been introduced to some of the issues that are special to color printers.

I pointed out that most PC printers have some pretty powerful computers inside, and that the printers that do not contain such a computer will in effect need to borrow the power of your PC in order to get their jobs done. Armed with all this knowledge, you can now analyze any printer you come across and understand both what it is likely to be capable of doing, and also what it will require in the way of support by your PC and by you to keep it doing those things.

15

Understanding Standard PC Input and Output

Peter Norton®

Computers are useful only if information can get into them and back out of them. In this chapter you'll learn several of the most important technologies used to get information into and out of PCs.

Note: In Chapter 7, "Understanding PC Processors," you learned how the CPU can send data to or receive data from either memory address locations or input/output (I/O) ports. Those ports are the logical interfaces for the CPU to everything external to it (other than memory). In this chapter you will learn more about input/output ports, but focusing on the interfaces between the PC system unit and the world beyond it. Please try not to let the similarity of name and description confuse you, but if it does, you can be assured that you are hardly the first person to be confused in this way.

Some Special-Purpose I/O Interfaces

The keyboard is one input device that is so much a standard part of a PC that it has, from the beginning, had its own special-purpose interface. Our modern PCs often have several other obviously dedicated, special-purpose input or output interfaces. Figure 15.1 shows the rear panel of a desktop PC.

Figure 15.1.
The rear panel of a typical desktop PC has several special-purpose inputs and outputs.

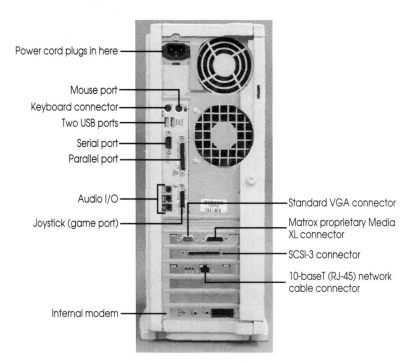

Power cord plugs in here

Mouse port
Keyboard connector
Two USB ports
Serial port
Parallel port

Audio I/O
Joystick (game port)

Standard VGA connector
Matrox proprietary Media XL connector
SCSI-3 connector
10-baseT (RJ-45) network cable connector

Internal modem

At the top you see two fans and the place where the power cord connects. The top fan is inside the power supply. The lower fan is an extra one included to promote excellent air flow inside the case. Just below the power cord connector, in the middle of the rear panel, is a section that contains several special-purpose inputs and outputs as well as some more general-purpose ones. The keyboard, mouse, and sound connections can be used only for those particular purposes.

Universal Serial Bus (USB) ports, serial ports, and parallel ports can be connected to any of several possible peripheral devices. But each of these port connectors represents a particular way to access the PC. These are multi-purpose I/O interfaces (but not fully general-purpose ones).

The bottom section has slots through which you can see the rear brackets of the plug-in cards. Many of those hold additional I/O connectors. This section of the system unit provides the most general access to the PC's input and output capabilities. These I/O slots are the main general-purpose I/O connection points, and I'll discuss them in more detail in the next chapter, "Faster Ways to Get Information Into and Out of Your PC."

In Figure 15.1 you see that this PC has four cards with external connectors plugged into those slots. The top one holds the video subsystem. Below the video card is a SCSI (Small Computer System Interface) host adapter and below that a network interface card with a 10-baseT connector. At the bottom is an internal modem with three connectors for the telephone line, a local telephone, and an audio output that can be connected to one of the sound inputs in the middle section of the rear panel.

Figure 15.2 shows a view of this motherboard from the rear, without the case and without any plug-in cards installed. It also shows a close-up view of the rear panel that contains the special-purpose and multi-purpose I/O interface connectors.

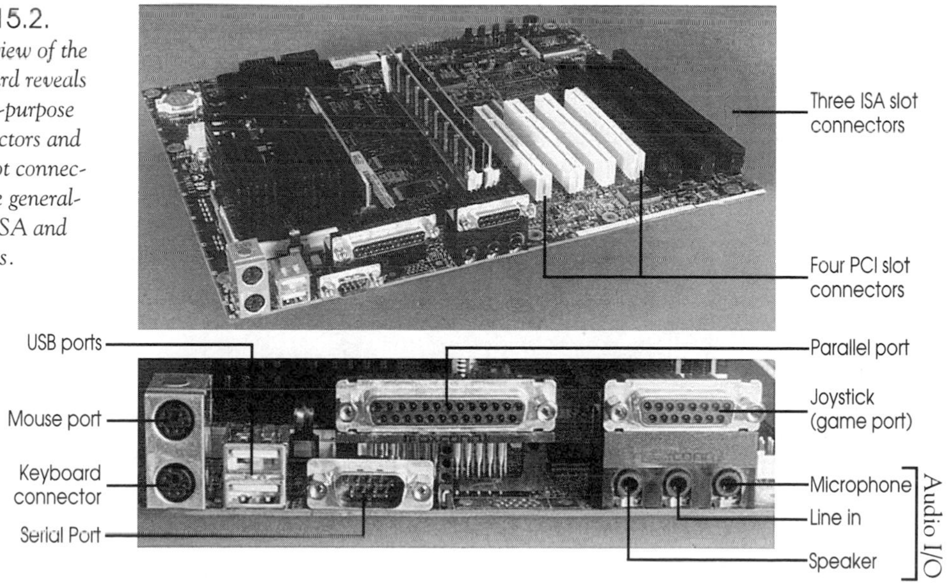

Figure 15.2.
The rear view of the motherboard reveals the special-purpose I/O connectors and also the slot connectors for the general-purpose (ISA and PCI) buses.

Three ISA slot connectors

Four PCI slot connectors

USB ports

Mouse port

Keyboard connector

Serial Port

Parallel port

Joystick (game port)

Microphone

Line in

Speaker

Audio I/O

At the right side of the motherboard are seven slot connectors. Each of these can accept a plug-in option card. (The white and black connectors next to one another share a single rear-panel slot. You can use at most three of the white slots plus the three black slots, or all four white slots and only two of the black slots.)

These connectors provide the most general-purpose way to access the PC's I/O capabilities. The connectors you see in Figure 15.2 represent two different ways to accomplish PC I/O. The larger, black slot connectors are connected to what we call the Industry Standard Architecture (ISA) bus; the smaller, white connectors connect to a newer, higher speed bus called a Peripheral Component Interconnect (PCI).

In Chapter 12, "Getting Your PC's Attention: Input Devices," you learned how keyboards and mice function as information inputs to your PC. You didn't learn about the hardware interface these devices use at that point because the interfaces used for the keyboard and mouse resemble in many ways one of the multi-purpose I/O interfaces (the serial port). Later in this chapter you'll learn about the serial, parallel, and USB ports. The discussion of the sound inputs and outputs appears in Chapter 20, "How to 'Wow' a Human." You'll learn about the video output interface later in this chapter; the details of what passes over that interface are discussed in Chapter 13, "Seeing the Results: PC Displays."

Talking Through a Tiny Pipe: Serial Ports

PCs move information around internally either a byte at a time (on eight parallel wires), or several bytes at a time (using even more wires). This is practical inside the system unit, and valuable because all the bits of a byte arrive at their destination together, and the maximum possible number of bytes are transferred each second.

This is not so practical outside the system unit. Or at least, it isn't always the best way to go. If you are sending information a relatively short distance—say to your monitor or perhaps even to a printer nearby—you can use a multi-wire cable to carry data in many parallel bit paths similar to those inside the system unit. But if you want to send information a longer distance, and especially if you aren't concerned with achieving the ultimate in speed of communication, it's often more practical to use a totally different strategy called *serial communication*.

This approach is often used where a parallel cable would work, just because there is no pressing need for speed. Your mouse and keyboard are examples of this. Some older printers also used serial connections to a PC. That is still an option on many modern printers, although most printers are now connected to PCs via a parallel port (and usually they need the fastest possible data link).

The serial approach becomes much more than just a measure of convenience when you want to send data for many miles. The cost of the wire alone argues against using a parallel cable for such a distance. A modem that connects your PC to the telephone line expects data in serial form because that's what it must send (and receive) across the phone line—an example of a single-wire pair communications link.

Naturally, sending data a single bit at a time is slower than pumping it across a multi-wire bus. Choosing a serial link is almost always a compromise between cost and speed. Modern PCs can send and receive data over a serial link at rates of up to 115,200 bits per second (bps). For reasons that will become clear in the next section, this corresponds to a maximum throughput of about 11.5 kilobytes per second (kBps) without parity, or 10.5kBps with parity.

Serial Communications Basics

The idea behind serial communication is quite simple: Just send one bit at a time. To send a byte, send each of its eight bits, one after another. If you want some insurance that the byte gets where it's going without any of the bits being changed, you can have the serial link also send along a ninth (parity) bit.

Technical Note: Usually, PC serial communications links don't use the parity bit. One reason for this is that data integrity can be assured at a higher level of the communication. For example, if you download a ZIP file and you can unzip it, that's a good indication that it arrived at your PC undamaged.

When these links do use parity, they can use either even or odd parity. To compute the value for the parity bit, you add all the values of the preceding eight bits in the byte. This number will either be even or odd. For even parity, set the parity bit to a 0 value if the sum of the other bits is even, and to a 1 value if that sum is odd. For odd parity, do exactly the opposite. This strategy ensures that, counting all nine bits together, you will have an even number of 1 bits for even parity or an odd number of 1 bits for odd parity.

When the byte plus its parity bit is reassembled at the destination, the receiver counts the number of bits whose value is 1, and if the count's even-or-oddness matches the kind of parity protocol being used, then the receiver can safely assume that the byte arrived okay. If the parity does not match, the receiver will alert the host PC and the communication program running in it will usually ask the sender to resend that byte.

In principle, you should need only a single wire—or actually a single pair of wires because you need a "ground" wire over which the electric currents you send out can return—for serial communications. In practice, separate wires are normally used for the outbound and the inbound data, making a minimum of three wires in a serial communication cable (send, receive, and ground). Often, several more wires are added. These extra wires are used to signal things such as whether the receivers at each end are ready for incoming data.

Two common connector styles are used for serial ports on PCs. One is the male DB9 connector shown previously in Figures 15.1 and 15.2. The other is a male DB25, which is essentially the same except that it has 25 pins instead of 9.

What's a UART and What Does It Do?

People needed devices to convert data from several parallel wires into a succession of bits on a single wire and back again, long before there were such things as PCs. Several decades ago, engineers designed some integrated circuits to handle this task that are rudimentary by today's standards. The module that does this task is a *Universal Asynchronous Receiver/Transmitter*, or *UART* for short.

There have been several generations of UART. The first popular model was called an 8250. This integrated circuit module could convert a single byte into serial bits and back again, and it could do this at a maximum rate of 9,600bps. (That is the maximum *guaranteed* rate; many individual chips could do much better than this.) This model was soon replaced by a 16450, which could convert a single byte at a maximum (guaranteed) rate of 115kbps. It also was capable of working reliably with a faster bus on the parallel side, which was necessary as PCs began to run faster than the original 4.77MHz. Because of the overhead inherent in an asynchronous serial link, a data rate of 115kbps translates to a top data transfer rate of about 11.5kBps.

Standards: Notice that a small letter "b" usually stands for a bit and the capital letter "B" stands for a byte in these discussions.

An even later model of UART, the 16550, could transfer data at rates up to around 400kbps, and it had some other even more important advantages. Those added advantages are explained in the "How the 16550C Buffered UART Can Save the Day" section later in this chapter.

How Serial Data Is Sent

The serial data-sending process occurs like this: The CPU addresses the UART at one of the CPU's (internal) port addresses. It sends a byte of information to the UART over the system's (internal) I/O data bus. The UART picks up the data and stores it temporarily in a register inside the UART. At that point, the CPU is free to use the system bus for other purposes.

> **Technical Note:** The CPU actually uses eight consecutive I/O port addresses for its conversations with each serial port's circuitry. The first one (with the smallest address) is called the port's *base address*, and is used for the actual data transfers. The other ports are used for various control functions including the means for setting the *serial communications parameters* for that serial port.

Now the UART serializes the data bits, sending them out one at a time over the serial communications link's outbound data wire. Because this is an asynchronous device, it can start this process at any time. (The other kind of serial communication device is a synchronous link device, which means that it will always operate in lock-step to the clock of the receiving system at the other end of the link.)

To get the attention of the receiving device at the other end, the UART first sends out a *start bit* by changing the output voltage from the *Mark* state to the *Space* state. It holds the output voltage at that level for one *bit-time*. Then, it sends the least-significant bit of the byte (also holding its level for one bit-time), followed by the next-to-least significant bit, and so on. For each bit the level of the output is set to the Mark level for a 1 and to the Space level for a 0. It is possible to program a UART to send 5, 6, 7, or 8 bits per character. In most PC communications situations, you either send 7 data bits plus a parity bit or 8 data bits and no parity bit. If you send fewer than 8 data bits per byte, the highest order bit(s) of each byte will simply be ignored. And, the receiver will pad the received byte with 0 bits at the most significant end if it is receiving fewer than 8 data bits per byte.

If a parity bit is to be sent, it will be sent out just after the most significant data bit. Finally, the UART will wait (with the output line held at the Mark level) 1, 1 ½, or 2 bit-times before it begins to send the next byte. That waiting time is referred to as the *stop bit* (or bits).

The UART incorporates an internal clock that tells it when to send out the next bit of data. One cycle of this clock is a *bit-time*. You can program this clock to run at different rates. When you tell the UART what clock speed to use, how many data bits to send, whether to use parity (and, if so, which kind), and how many stop bits to use, you are setting the *serial communications parameters*.

It is vital that the UART at each end of the serial link be programmed in the same way. If not, the receiving UART will be unable to make sense of the signals it receives, and the overall link will fail.

Physical Characteristics of Serial Communications Signals

The actual voltages and currents sent on the serial link wires are not the same as the electrical voltages used in the system bus. Inside the PC's system unit, any voltage that is nearly 0 is seen as representing a binary 0 value. And, any voltage that is over about 2 volts is seen as representing a binary

1 value. But on the serial link, 0s are represented as Space values, which means by a positive voltage (greater than 3 volts, but less than 12 volts) or a positive current. Binary 1s are represented by a Mark level that is a similar size negative voltage or current. Figure 15.3 shows these details. One advantage to this approach is that a broken wire is readily detectable, as it will result in a lack of any voltage or current, which the receiver knows is not legal for either 0s or 1s.

Figure 15.3.

Asynchronous serial data communications protocol.

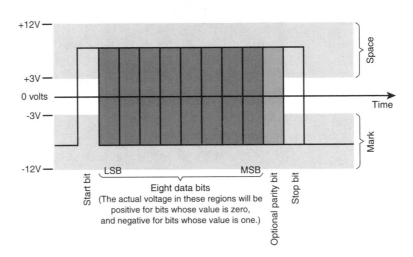

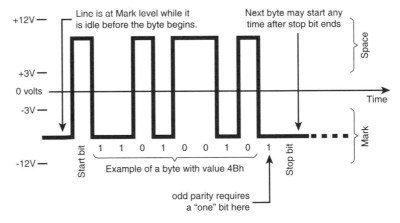

How Serial Data Is Received

At the other end of the line is another UART. Its job is to undo what the first UART did. That is, it must notice each incoming packet (which it does when the transition from a Mark level to a Space level occurs, marking the beginning of a start bit). Then, it must look at the right times for each bit of the data byte to arrive, and store those values in a register. After it has received the entire byte (plus its parity bit if it has one) and checked the parity (if that is the mode in which it is operating), the UART is ready to present the complete byte at its parallel output port.

Once the UART has the data byte ready, it "rings the CPU's doorbell." That is, it asserts an interrupt request. After the CPU acknowledges that request, the UART is free to dump its data byte onto the system's internal I/O bus, from which the CPU will read it. Notice that the CPU is not required to accept the byte immediately because this is an asynchronous serial communication. The CPU normally waits at least until it is finished with the current instruction it is processing, and it might wait much longer than that.

But also notice something else: If the CPU waits too long, it might lose some of the incoming data. Most of the time the first few bits of the next byte arriving across the serial link will already be coming into the UART while the UART is waiting for the CPU to pick up the just-received byte. If the CPU fails to pick up that received byte in time, the UART simply discards it and replaces it with the next byte it received. (It also signals the CPU that a byte of received data has been lost—an event referred to as a *data overrun*.)

How the 16550C Buffered UART Can Save the Day

Keeping up with the UART can be quite a burden on the CPU, especially at the higher rates of data transmission commonly used in PCs today. Every time a byte is received or a byte has been sent out, the CPU must go through a fairly convoluted process of saving its place in whatever task it is performing, switching to the communications program that handles the data sending and receiving, sending or receiving the next byte, then saving the state of that program and switching back to the original task.

To help reduce this burden, an improved version of the 16450 called the 16550 was created. The most significant difference—and it is significant—is that this version includes two 16-byte FIFO buffers inside the UART. (The 16550 is also guaranteed to run at data rates faster than what is guaranteed to work on the 16450 or 8250, but in most PC applications they are not called upon to do so.) A *FIFO* buffer is simply a fancy name for a queue. The name stands for First In First Out, meaning that bytes are pushed in one end and pop out the other end in the same order.

Consider what this means for data transmission: It is now possible for the CPU to dump up to 16 bytes of data in a block into the UART for it to send out, then the CPU can go away and do other things until the UART has completed that task. Only then must the CPU stop its other work to dump another 16 bytes in the UART. Thus, even without constant attention from the CPU, the UART will keep busy sending out the bytes (as serialized bits) just as fast as it can.

The effect of buffering is even more important for data reception. Now the UART can accumulate up to 16 bytes of received data before the CPU must get them to prevent the UART from losing any of the incoming information. Normally you set up the UART so it will signal the CPU after its receive buffer is almost full—typically when it has 14 bytes in it—to give the CPU some time to respond before that buffer is totally filled. If you experience lots of data overruns when downloading files, you might want to set this number to something less than 14.

Both for incoming and outgoing data, the buffering of data on the UART saves a lot of overhead time that the CPU would otherwise have to waste as it constantly jumps between servicing the UART and whatever else it was doing.

What You Must Know and Do About Serial Communications

Modern PCs often have the serial port interface electronics included in the motherboard chip set. In today's systems with their large-scale integrated circuits, you probably won't actually have a 16550, or other UART chip on the motherboard. You will probably have the functionality of one or more such chips hidden away inside a Very Large-Scale Integrated Circuit (VLSI) chip that is part of the motherboard chip set. The UART circuitry is there, but it might not be activated, or might be only partially activated, until you take some specific actions. This statement also applies to many of the plug-in cards you can purchase to add extra serial or parallel ports to your PC.

The motherboard BIOS setup program often includes entries to enable or disable the serial ports. It might also enable you to set the default communications parameters for those ports. Even though the UART circuitry has buffers, they can do nothing unless you explicitly instruct that circuitry to enable buffering. Some BIOS setup programs enable you to do this; most will not.

Windows 95 handles all this for you. Windows 3.x can do it, but you must edit the SYSTEM.INI file to include lines that turn on buffering and set the communications parameters. If you are running bare DOS, your communications program can probably do what you need, although many of the DOS communication programs lack the capability to turn UART buffering on. (If you are using such a program, you can find a freeware program to enable 16550 FIFO buffering on the Internet and on most electronic remote bulletin boards.)

The essential step that you still must perform is to set the communications speed for your serial ports to match the expectations of the device at the other end of that cable. The only exception is that some especially clever serial devices (and this includes many modern modems) are able to infer the communications rate from the first byte they receive. With them you can just choose any suitable rate within their operating range for the PC's UART, and they'll adapt to it.

Serial Links Without the Wires

Serial links usually include a serial port interface on the PC, a cable from the PC to some peripheral device, and a serial port interface on that peripheral device. Sometimes you can have the effect of all that without using a cable. This is the growing field of wireless connectivity. Several physical technologies are used in lieu of passing an electrical current down a copper wire.

One technique uses infrared light. This is essentially the same technology used in most TV and VCR remote controls. In desktop PCs, this is simply an attachment to a standard serial port that converts the electrical signals into light signals and back again. The form of those light signals is a modulation on a carrier wave imposed on the light beam. This type of wireless serial port is particularly popular on laptop computers.

The Infra-red Data Association (IrDA) has defined a standard called, appropriately, *IrDA*. Devices that are compliant with this standard are capable of linking two standard serial ports at any data rate up to the normal maximum for such ports of 115kbps. Special high-speed versions of these infrared links can achieve data rates of up to 4Mbps. Those higher-speed devices are used to link network interface adapters instead of normal serial ports. You'll learn more about network interface adapters in Chapter 25, "The PC Reaches Out, Part Two: Through the NIC Node."

The Keyboard Interface

The keyboard connects to the PC system unit via a special connector that can be used only for that specific purpose. But in fact, it is just another serial interface, much like the more general-purpose serial ports I described in the last section.

The keyboard port's UART is a part of the *keyboard controller*. One key difference of this port from the standard serial port is that the buffer for the keyboard port is located in the PC's main memory, instead of being inside the keyboard controller circuitry. This means, among other things, that its contents are available for any program to pick up in any order that the program needs. The bytes stored there aren't just available in the order they were placed there. Also, that buffer can be relocated and enlarged if it turns out to be too small.

There are two commonly used connectors for keyboards on PCs. The most common connector used for older desktop machines is the five-pin DIN. (The name comes from the acronym for the German standards agency that published the specifications for this connector family.) The male connector (the plug) goes on the keyboard cable; the female connector (the jack) is mounted on the PC's motherboard.

The other common design is a 6-pin mini-DIN connector. IBM pioneered the use of this connector for keyboards and mice in its PS/2 line of computers, and it has become the favored connector for both keyboards and bus mice in most modern PCs. (Bus mice are discussed in the next section.) The 6-pin mini-DIN is virtually the only kind of keyboard connector used on portable or laptop PCs.

Figure 15.4 shows the 6-pin mini-DIN plug on the end of the cable from the keyboard of our sample desktop system. Next to it you see an adapter that accepts that plug on its far end and has the 5-pin DIN connector on the near end. With such an adapter you can use a modern keyboard on an older PC. A reversed version of this adapter allows you to use older keyboards with newer systems.

Figure 15.4.
The 6-pin DIN on the left is the most popular connector for modern PC keyboards. The adapter on the right allows use of such a keyboard with older PCs that have a 5-pin DIN keyboard port.

6-pin PS/2 female connector accepts cable from keyboard

6-pin PS/2-style keyboard cable plug

5-pin DIN keyboard cable plug

Bus Mice Versus Serial Mice

Mice can come with any of four kinds of plugs at the end of their cables. One kind is the PS/2 6-pin mini-DIN mentioned earlier; another looks similar to the PS/2 6-pin mini-DIN but is electrically and physically different. It is used by a variety called *bus mice*. The others use female DB9 and DB25 connectors and are called *serial mice*. They are for use with standard serial port connectors on a PC. Many PCs now come with a PS/2 mouse port. Others can have a bus or PS/2 mouse port added by use of a plug-in option card.

Some laptop computers come with a single 6-pin mini-DIN connector that can be used either for an external keyboard or for an external mouse, but not for both at once. These computers typically have both a keyboard and a pointing device internally, so you wouldn't need to use this port at all, or you could use it for a keyboard or a pointing device—whichever internal device you most want to replace with an external one.

There are only a few differences between a bus mouse port and a standard serial port. Both work in the same manner. However, commonly the bus mouse ports (the ones with the mini-DIN connector) use an IRQ value in the upper range (8–15), whereas the standard serial ports (with DB9 or DB25 connectors) usually can be set only to use one of the lower IRQ values (most often 3, 4, 5, or 7). The only other difference between the dedicated mouse ports and standard serial ports is in the CPU port addresses over which they communicate with the internal system I/O bus.

Mice typically communicate at a fairly low data rate. The most common speed is a mere 1200bps, but they will adapt to whatever speed the serial port is set to, up to some limit. Even the low default data rate is plenty, as all a mouse must do is tell the PC each time it moves a unit distance (usually one one-hundredth of an inch) in either the X or Y direction and each time one of its buttons is pressed or released. If you are jerking your mouse around faster than this data rate allows, you aren't really mousing properly. Slow down, or you'll damage your body, if nothing else.

There are several reasons to be concerned about the difference between serial and bus mice. One is if you have too few serial ports on your PC, then using a bus mouse can free up one of the serial ports for some other use. But, of course, you can do this only if you have a bus mouse connector available.

The second reason for paying attention to the bus versus serial mouse issue is much like the first: If you are running out of available interrupt request lines for your serial ports, then switching to a bus (or PS/2) mouse (which usually uses one of the upper eight IRQ lines) might help. Most serial ports can use only one of the lower seven IRQs, and mostly those are taken for system uses, so the remaining few can't do all the things you'd like them to do.

This discussion has only described how the mice connect to your PC. The discussion in Chapter 12 covers what they say to the PC (mouse protocols).

Combining the Keyboard and a Pointing Device

Some keyboards now come with a pointing device built in (usually either a trackpad or pointing stick). Other keyboards sport a mouse port on the side or back, so you can plug in a standard mouse there instead of into your PC's system unit. Mostly this is just a matter of packaging. At the end of the cable from such a keyboard you will typically find that it splits into two cables, ending in two separate plugs. One goes into the special keyboard connector on the back of the PC system unit, and the other connector goes into either a mouse port or a standard serial port near the keyboard connector.

The Faster Output Path That Can Work Both Ways

When IBM introduced the PC, it offered an optional printer interface card and printer. Breaking with what had been customary for small computer makers up to that time, IBM used a parallel interface on its printer port. Such an interface uses a separate wire for each bit of the bytes of data being sent to the printer. Thus, an entire byte can go to the printer at once. This approach enabled IBM's printer adapter to pump characters to the printer much faster than would have been possible with a serial communications link.

The Original IBM PC Unidirectional Printer Port

Clearly you need at least eight data wires (one for each bit in a byte) for a parallel port. But, in fact, many more than just eight wires are needed for this type of parallel-data-transfer interface. In the IBM printer port design, 17 wires are used for signals plus several more "ground" wires. Why so many signal lines? That is an important question with an interesting answer.

The printer port sends data to the printer by first putting the data bits on the eight data lines. Then, it sends a pulse called a *strobe* signal on another line to tell the printer that the byte to be sent is ready to go. After it receives the strobe signal, the printer reads that byte and, after it has finished, sends back an *acknowledge* signal on yet another wire to the PC. This tells the printer port circuitry that it's okay to prepare the next byte for transmission. Because of this tightly interlocked handshaking protocol, the printer port can send data to the printer just as fast as the printer can accept it (and it won't send it any faster than that). This data flow is not synchronized to any clock signal; it just goes as fast as it can.

Five status wires allow the printer to ask the PC to wait if it is busy processing the data it has already received, or it can tell the PC when it is out of paper, or when some error (such as a paper jam) has occurred. Four control wires allow the PC to tell the printer, for example, to reset itself or to move to the top of the next page. This is how IBM intended this interface to function originally. As you will see, just because IBM said these lines would have these uses doesn't actually limit them from being used in some other interesting ways.

It takes four separate operations (and thus at least four clock cycles of the system I/O bus) for the CPU to send out even one byte to a printer, using this type of parallel port. Making parallel ports more automatic is a major way in which the enhanced parallel ports manage to achieve higher data throughputs. (You'll learn more about that point shortly.)

A standard parallel port interface is capable of data transfer rates of around 50 to 150kBps. This speed is limited mainly by how much work the CPU must do for each character it sends out and the speed of the internal I/O bus. Still, this speed is noticeably faster than the rate at which most standard PC serial ports can be operated reliably.

Now, with all the changes in printers, and with the many other uses for printer ports, this simple picture has become considerably more complex. In Chapter 14, "Getting It All Down On Paper: Printers," you learned how page printers differ from character or line printers in the kinds of information they are designed to accept and process. But no matter what the bytes that the PC sends to the printer are intended to mean, from the perspective of the printer interface, they are just bytes. It doesn't care what their content is, let alone their meanings.

PC and Printer Connectors and Cables

IBM did not originate the parallel printer interface that it used on its PCs. This interface, originally developed by Centronics, was changed by IBM in one respect. The 36-pin Amphenol-brand connector Centronics chose for the printer (and which appeared on the printers sold by IBM for use with its PCs) is a bulky one. In fact, it looks a lot like the SCSI-1 connectors you will encounter later in this chapter. It was simply too large to fit on the rear bracket of a PC plug-in card. So IBM chose to use a female DB25 on the parallel port card instead. Most printer and PC manufacturers to this day follow IBM's lead in this respect.

> **Technical Note:** You must use a special 25-pin to 36-pin cable to connect the PC to the printer, and therein lies the potential for a problem. Centronics specified that nearly half of the 36 pins in its printer input connectors were for signal grounds. This meant that nearly every signal line could have its own ground wire. That design is especially useful for fairly long printer cables because it enables the printer input circuitry to cancel out much of the electrical noise such a long cable inevitably picks up.
>
> However, the industry standard for PC-to-printer cables cuts some corners to save costs. Only eight of the pins on the 25-pin connector are connected to ground. And, often only a few of those get connected to just a few of the 17 ground pins in the 36-pin connector. For many printers this causes no problems, but with some it can be disastrous, causing badly corrupted output. If you experience this problem, the solution is simple. Just modify a standard PC-to-printer cable so *every* ground pin on the 25-pin side (pin numbers 18–25) is connected to *every* ground pin on the 36-pin side (pin numbers 19–30 and 33), and the cable will work flawlessly.

Bi-Directional Printer Ports

The intent of the original IBM PC printer port was simply, as its name suggests, to pump data to a printer. There were a few wires over which the printer could send signals back to the PC, but only a few and only ones that were essential for controlling the data transfers from PC to printer.

Soon it became clear that there were times when it was highly desirable for the parallel port to be capable of receiving data as well as sending it out. IBM included this capability in its next generation of computer, the PC/AT, but many people were unaware of it. IBM did publicize the bi-directional capability of the parallel port when it introduced its PS/2 line, and because of that, this type of parallel port is now often referred to as a PS/2 parallel port.

In fact, there are two ways to make a standard PC parallel port function in reverse. The method used by IBM in the PS/2 computers is to modify the circuitry so the data wires can be driven either by the port or by the peripheral device to which it is attached. This method, sometimes referred to as *byte-mode reverse operation*, enables data input rates that are comparable to those achievable on data output.

There is also a much simpler way to accomplish reverse operation of a standard parallel port, albeit at a lower data rate for input than for output. This technique, which works on even the original PC, is sometimes called *nibble-mode reverse operation*.

This method comes down to simply a creative "misuse" of the control and status lines. In this technique, the eight data lines are simply ignored. Four of the status lines (which had been intended only for sending status information from the printer to the PC) are now used to carry half a byte from the peripheral device back in to the PC. The control lines are used to control the process. This requires suitable software at the PC to manage the process and a peripheral device that has the smarts to recognize what the PC wants and follow its dictates. So the essence of *nibble-mode reverse operation* of a parallel port lies both in the printer driver program that is running in the PC and in the hardware in the peripheral device. The hardware in the PC's parallel port doesn't have to be modified at all.

However, because the data coming into the PC is transferred in a process much like that used for sending data out, and only half a byte comes in for each transaction, the inbound data rate in this technique is just about half that of the outbound rate—fast enough to be useful, but not as fast as you might want.

Enhanced Printer Ports

Despite the limitations of parallel ports, they have in the past been the fastest standard I/O hardware available on just about any PC. For this reason, lots of additional uses for them have been developed beyond simply spewing out characters to be printed.

There are two classes of use for parallel ports that go beyond its original purpose. Because these two kinds of use involve different patterns of data transmission, they have led to the development of two different, improved standards for parallel ports.

One of these classes involves a fairly well-balanced use of both input and output, with data transfers in both directions needing to go as fast as possible. These uses include hooking up a CD-ROM drive, external hard drive, ZIP drive, or other mass storage medium to the parallel port. This strategy always runs slower than if these devices were directly connected to the PC's general-purpose I/O bus via a plug-in card with interface circuitry that has been optimized for that use. On the other hand, it's convenient to be able to hook up such an external peripheral device to a PC parallel port, perhaps load a driver program off a disk, and then use the device. For one example, this makes doing backups a breeze and also enables easy transfers of rather substantial amounts of data between PCs that are otherwise not connected. These two possibilities help explain why the ZIP drive has been such a smashing success.

The other class of extended use is for printers that must get much more data for each page they print than just the characters you might see there. (In particular this describes page printers, especially those printing large bitmapped graphic images.) These printers might occasionally need to send data back to the PC—sometimes even a fairly substantial amount of data—but those occasions are fairly rare compared to the times they need huge amounts of data shipped out to them.

The two new designs for "super parallel ports" have been combined with the two methods for using standard parallel port hardware bi-directionally into an official standard published by the Institute for Electrical and Electronic Engineers (IEEE) in 1994. They named this the IEEE 1284 standard.

Any peripheral device that conforms to the IEEE 1284 standard connected to a parallel port that also conforms to that standard is capable of operating in any of five modes. The first is the original mode of operation of a PC parallel port, now called *Compatibility* (or Centronics) *mode*. The second is the nibble-mode reverse operation. The third is the byte-reverse operation. The two new, "advanced" modes are referred to as EPP (Enhanced Parallel Port) and ECP (Extended Capability Port). However, even the right combination of peripheral and port interface hardware won't work without being told to do so by a suitable software driver or being put into the correct mode by the PC motherboard BIOS setup program.

EPP Ports

The EPP super-parallel port design was developed first by Intel, Xircom, and Zenith Data Systems. Their focus was on creating a port that would support fast data transfers both in and out and also enable easy switching between the two directions of data flow. The initial group of companies supporting this approach soon swelled to around 80 members. That level of industry support was instrumental in getting IEEE to include the EPP design/protocol as a part of its 1284 standard.

The original PC parallel port design was so simple that instead of the eight CPU I/O port addresses needed to operate a serial port, IBM originally only used three. One was for data transfer. The other two were for status and control.

After the parallel port hardware has been told to operate in EPP mode, up to five additional CPU port addresses become active. (All these I/O ports are at the addresses immediately above the nominal "base address" for this parallel port. Using a block of eight addresses in the CPU's I/O port address space is thus identical to the way serial ports use CPU I/O ports.)

If the software driver program that must transfer data over the parallel port only accesses the traditional three CPU I/O ports, then the port operates in compatibility mode. If, however, that driver sends the appropriate commands to the other five registers (and if the peripheral hardware attached to the port can respond suitably), then the port will function at a much faster rate. The main reason it can do this is because the hardware of the parallel port has been enhanced so it is now able to handle all the separate steps for a single byte transfer by itself. Now the CPU can execute just one command and the byte transfer happens, without it having to be involved in each of the negotiation steps in the interlocked handshaking.

Right away this means that EPP data transfers can go as much as four times faster than compatibility mode transfers. If the interface hardware also enables transfers of multiple bytes in one cycle, which is the case for some EPP port hardware designs, this top speed can be boosted to nearly 2MBps. This is over 10 times faster than the compatibility mode.

Additionally, the EPP design enables block transfers of data as well as arbitrary intermixing of reads and writes (data reception and data transmission) with no additional setup delays. This is the ideal mode for use with a ZIP drive or similar peripheral device.

ECP Ports

Hewlett-Packard and Microsoft were interested in a different kind of parallel port improvement. They focused on speeding up huge block data transfer rates and lowering the demands on the software driver and CPU even below those needed for EPP operation. The result of their work is now a part of the IEEE 1284 standard and is called the Extended Capability Port (ECP).

Among other features, ECP includes provision for data compression using Run Length Encoding (RLE). This is a data compression scheme that is particularly effective if the data being sent has long runs of a single value. For example, if you are sending a bitmapped image of a page and there are big areas of white, RLE encoding will just say, in effect, "Okay now, white goes here for the next thus-and-so-many pels." That is much more efficient than sending a white pel over and over again. Combining this efficiency improvement with the high data rates (comparable to EPP) yields the highest possible data transfer rates for large blocks of data all going in one direction.

ECP is a more loosely coupled mode of operation than any of the other 1284 modes. Unlike standard compatibility mode and EPP operation, the handshaking is not tightly interlocked. This makes the ECP protocol suitable for systems with large FIFO buffers at either end and also supports the goal of achieving maximum speed at single-direction data transfers. This capability is even further enhanced—and in particular the CPU demands dramatically lowered—by ECP's support of Direct Memory Access (DMA) data transfers. This means that the CPU can tell the DMA controller to transfer a block of data via an ECP port with a single command. The DMA controller and the ECP port do the rest.

ECP can accomplish data transfers in either direction, but the channel must be "turned around" before it can be used in a direction opposite to its most recent use. This turnaround requires several steps of time-consuming negotiation. Perhaps the greatest delay involved is that the turnaround cannot happen until after the current DMA transfer is complete and the FIFO buffers have been flushed. This restriction makes ECP port mode less suitable than EPP for external mass storage devices in which reads and writes are often intermixed.

ECP also has the drawback that it requires the exclusive use of a DMA channel. If you have one to spare, then go ahead and assign it to this use. But if you are running short of DMA channels (as seems pretty often to be the case in a modern, fully equipped PC), you might have to forgo the advantages of ECP and fall back to EPP operation instead.

Finally, there is one other way in which an ECP port can be used that goes well beyond what is possible with a parallel port used in any other mode. This involves the use of *ECP channels*. In effect, ECP channels are subdevices within the peripheral device attached to the ECP port. By designating different data transfers as going to or from different channels, it is possible to communicate with one channel over an ECP port even when another channel in that same peripheral device is busy. For example, in a combined printer/fax/scanner device it would be possible to receive a fax while the printer was busy printing a separate document. You'll see this same idea in Chapter 16,

"Faster Ways to Get Information Into and Out of Your PC," when the SCSI interface and its idea of logical units within a SCSI device is discussed.

"Printer" Ports Aren't Just For Printers Any More

As noted before, what were first called printer ports (and now are referred to more generically as parallel ports) are often used for much more than just shoveling data out to a printer. Indeed, these ports have become one of the most-used means of connecting external peripherals to a PC for some good reasons.

It's so easy to get a peripheral to work when it is plugged into a PC's parallel port, that this is now the preferred way to hook up almost any device for which you want a substantial data transfer rate, as long as you are willing to put up with not getting the absolute ultimate in data transfer rates. (But with an ECP or even an EPP port you can approach the maximum possible transfer rates of any other channel available on a PC today.)

Circumventing the Limits on Numbers of Parallel Ports

It's nice that you can hook so many things to a parallel port on a PC. But remember, PCs can have at most only three parallel ports, and most PCs have only one. So how are all these different devices attached?

One of the answers used to be by the use of printer port switches. You'd hook up several printers, and perhaps some other devices to this Hydra-headed box, and simply flip the switch to the one you wanted to use at the moment. Later, electrically switchable boxes were developed that could flip their own switches as needed. These devices enabled the user to have multiple peripheral devices and to send messages to or request messages from any of them. That works—sort of. But it was at best a clever kludge.

A far better solution is to use an ECP port and have the hardware for each peripheral device set to respond to a different channel. That way, no switching of the parallel port connection is needed. Each device sees all the messages, but it only responds to the ones for its channel. (This is much like an old-fashioned party-line telephone hookup.) Still, this solution leaves something to be desired. It requires modifying all the attached devices to make them respond to only one ECP channel, and then it requires all uses of that parallel port to be made in ECP mode. That is just too much to ask, especially if you want to combine different gadgets from different manufacturers.

Therefore, the stackable parallel port device was invented. Using this device, you connect one device to the parallel port. On its backside are two connectors. One hooks the cable to the PC, and the other is an additional parallel port. You can now plug in a printer here. The first device—for example, a ZIP drive—communicates with its software driver over the parallel port. But whenever the printer driver sends some information to the printer, the ZIP drive is smart enough to know that it must pass that data along to its pass-through port instead of acting on it. Figure 15.5 shows the rear view of just such a parallel port ZIP drive.

Figure 15.5.
A parallel port ZIP drive has two ports. One connects to the PC and the other (pass-through port) can accept a cable to a printer.

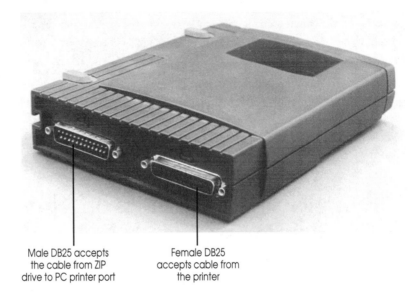

Male DB25 accepts
the cable from ZIP
drive to PC printer port

Female DB25
accepts cable from
the printer

Can you stack up many such devices? Maybe. It depends. (Those are two of my favorite, all-purpose answers to questions in the PC field—and they almost always apply.) If the devices have been built by different manufacturers, you cannot be sure they will work in a stacked fashion. You just have to try them. If they don't work stacked in one order, try reversing that order. Don't be surprised if one or both devices fails to work properly. That often happens simply because there is no industry standard for how these pass-through parallel ports function, and in particular no standard way to make several of them cooperate. Will there ever be such a standard? Unlikely. Instead, you'll probably see PCs moving to the newer I/O standards called USB and IEEE 1394.

Serial and Parallel Port Addresses and Their Names

Parallel ports are addressed by the CPU at certain of its I/O port addresses. The address you mostly see mentioned in descriptions of these ports or that is displayed by diagnostic programs, such as

Microsoft Diagnostics (MSD.EXE), is the port's *base address*. The CPU uses this address to send and receive data, and it also uses several additional ports (at the immediately higher port addresses) to read the port's status and send it control commands.

If you have multiple ports (either serial or parallel), it's important that none of them tries to use the same CPU I/O port addresses as any of the others. If you break this rule, the CPU will end up sending messages to one port, and it will be received (and acted upon) by both that port and some other one with a conflicting address. Worse, when the CPU is "listening" for input from that port, it will "hear" what both ports have to say at once, and that will at least be confusing and, at worst, will damage your PC's port hardware.

So far, what you've learned about a parallel port applies equally to serial ports. But there are some significant differences as well.

- Serial ports all use a block of eight consecutive CPU I/O port addresses. Standard parallel ports use only blocks of three port addresses (but enhanced parallel ports use more, and often as many as eight just like the serial ports).

- Serial ports have names, and there is a fixed association between the names and the base port address for each one. Thus, COM1 is always at 3F8h and COM2 at 2F8h. Similarly, COM3 is at 3E8h and COM4 is at 2E8h.

However, while PCs can have up to three parallel ports, called LPT1, LPT2, and LPT3, there is no necessary association between these names and the base port addresses.

When IBM first introduced the PC, it offered printer ports two ways: on a stand-alone option card or as an additional feature on a monochrome character video display adapter (MDA). The parallel port on a video adapter had the port address 3BCh. The parallel port on a plug-in card of its own could be set to either 378h or 278h.

Later, IBM used the port address 3BCh for the standard parallel port on its PS/2 models with the MCA bus because those machines couldn't accept the MDA video card (so no conflict could occur). Most clone PC makers have simply not used this address for a parallel port, just in case you might want to plug in an MDA video card.

The motherboard BIOS program looks for these ports during the PC's Power-On Self Test (POST) in the order 3BCh, 378h, and then 278h. The name LPT1 is assigned by the BIOS to the first parallel port it finds, LPT2 to the second one, and LPT3 to the third one. If it finds only one parallel port, that one gets the name LPT1, no matter which port address it might happen to use.

Another Way to Get More Than the Allowed Number of Serial (or Parallel) Ports

The design of PC serial and parallel ports imposes some severe limits on how many ports you can have. You can have up to four serial ports, although finding enough free IRQ values to support all of them is often a problem. You can have up to three parallel ports, but again an IRQ shortage may limit you to fewer than that. How do you get past these limits if you really need more ports? There have been several ways to do so in the past, and soon there should be several more.

Two situations were prevalent in which people needed a lot of ports on their PC: when there was a need to attach a lot of terminals (each terminal having a keyboard, a monitor, and perhaps a mouse), or when there was a need to support a large number of modems (or other serial peripheral devices such as data acquisition stations). A need for many parallel ports on a PC is less common.

The usual solution to the need for many more than four serial ports on one PC has been to fit a plug-in card with a micro-controller that can handle many (up to 64) serial ports into one of the ISA bus slots. This board comes with a specialized software driver that runs in your PC and communicates with the on-board micro-controller to cause it to route messages to and from all these different ports appropriately.

Essentially, that solution involves putting another computer inside your PC. This is the essential idea behind the Intel-sponsored I2O (Intelligent I/O) Initiative. By using for the serial port co-processor an Intel i960 (which is about as powerful as a Pentium), this allows a PC to have nearly the I/O channel capacity of a mainframe computer.

An alternative is to put one or more other computers outside your PC. Connect them via a local area network (LAN) of some sort, and then use all the serial (or parallel) ports you want as long as you use no more than four serial and three parallel ports per PC on the network. You'll learn more about LANs in Chapter 25.

Soon we'll have another option. Two other high-performance serial buses will be on PCs: USB and IEEE 1394. With those (and peripheral devices that are built to work with these interfaces) it will be possible to have all the serial devices you could ever want (and many of them performing faster than the fastest of today's parallel devices). Then the issue of getting more than three parallel or more than four serial ports on a PC just won't be urgent any more.

The Video Output Port

The last of the standard special-purpose ports on a PC is the video output port. If you have a monitor to display images on your PC, then you have a video output port to which that monitor is attached. (Some PCs have two monitors and two video output ports. For the purposes of this discussion, they just have two each of all the pieces discussed here.)

The original PC offered two video options: monochrome character display or color graphics display. Both of them used the same female DB9 connector for the video output, so that became the standard video output connector for PCs for the next several generations of video displays.

In this original nine-wire design, all the signals are digital. This worked okay for the early monochrome and color display systems, but as explained in Chapter 13, this didn't allow for the subtlety we expect of modern PC display systems. For that you need analog signals for the three colors. Only in that way is it possible for the PC to tell the monitor exactly how much red, green, and blue to put into a particular pixel on the screen. The horizontal and vertical signals, on the other hand, can still be essentially digital because all they must do is signal when a new line or a new scan is to begin.

When IBM introduced VGA video (just one more of the innovations included in its PS/2 offerings), it defined a new video output connector standard. This is a female high-density DB15 connector with three rows of holes to accept the pins of the mating male connector. Three of the pins are used to send the three analog signals telling how much red, blue, and green is needed at this time. To keep down noise, there is a special *analog ground* connection for each of them. That accounts for 6 of the 15 pins.

The H-sync and V-sync signals use two more pins, and there are two digital ground pins. The seven pins still not accounted for are used for some different purposes. One is plugged, so you can only insert a male high-density DB15 plug that has the corresponding pin removed. This helps to keep the user from plugging in a cable from something other than a video monitor.

The remaining four pins were initially just "reserved." Now they are used for communications from the monitor to the video display. (Yes, even though this is called a video output connector, it also accepts some input signals.) This enables the monitor to inform the video display what range of frequencies it can handle for the H-sync and V-sync signals, for example, and thus helps to keep the video display adapter from sending inappropriate signals that might harm the monitor. It also enables a monochrome VGA monitor to tell the adapter to send only grayscale signals, as such a monitor cannot display color in any case. The Video Equipment Standards Association (VESA) hammered out several standards that address the proper use of these (digital) signal lines. Those standards have helped ensure that all the different brands of monitor and video display adapters will use the signal lines for the same purposes, and thus can be connected without concern for what those lines mean to a particular brand.

Some high-end video display adapters use a different kind of output connector. The video display in the sample desktop system, a Matrox Millenium, has two output connectors: one is the standard VGA connector, and the other is intended for connection to a companion "Media" board that Matrox also makes.

Some of the better monitors were designed to work with specialized video systems (not necessarily in a PC). They require five separate shielded cables ending in BNC connectors to convey the red, green, and blue analog signals and the horizontal and vertical drive signals. Some monitors can accept input over either a standard VGA connector or these five separate cables. Figure 15.6 shows the rear panel of the monitor for our sample desktop system, which happens to be one that can accept input either over five shielded cables with BNC connectors or via the standard VGA cable.

Figure 15.6.
Some video displays accept a VGA cable, and others accept only five separate shielded cables with BNC connectors. This Dell Ultrascan 20TX accepts either.

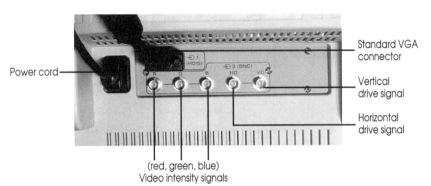

Summary

I've now told you about the basic set of I/O ports (serial, parallel, keyboard, and video) that have been around since the dawn of IBM's PC. You have seen some of the improvements made to each as the PC's design has matured, but wholly new protocols are on the horizon. Chapter 16, "Faster Ways to Get Information Into and Out of Your PC," will cover in detail the standard I/O bus (where option cards are plugged in) and some of the exotic new I/O options appearing on today's systems.

16

Faster Ways to Get Information Into and Out Of Your PC

Peter Norton®

In Chapter 15, "Understanding Standard Input and Output," I told you all about the dedicated purpose I/O connectors most PCs have for transferring data to and from their keyboards, mouse, or other pointing device, modem, printer, and so on. What I deferred to in this chapter is a discussion of those mysteriously general-purpose input/output slots on the motherboard and the various things that might plug into them to facilitate faster input and output of information.

The Most General I/O Interfaces: The PC I/O Bus(es)

In Chapter 4, "Understanding Your PC's Parts," you learned that information is frequently carried within a PC, and also in or out of a PC, on a *bus*. So most of this chapter is going to be the story of PC buses. As explained in Chapter 4, a bus is a definition of how one part of a computer communicates with another. It defines a pathway for signals to flow between functional elements of the computer. If it's a full bus definition, it will be sufficient for different manufacturers to make those different parts, safe in the assumption that their separately designed and manufactured products will work together properly when they are connected.

The remainder of this chapter is also a description of many of the important standards that have defined PC hardware and architecture. True, the design of the CPU has been the driving force in the evolving design of PCs, but the bus definitions have played an important supporting role.

The Original (ISA) PC I/O Bus

When IBM introduced the original PC, it used a CPU that had only eight data lines and 20 address lines. The CPU was connected to every other part of the PC over a bus that carried those lines (and some other wires for control signals). Data moved on this bus at the speed set by the CPU's internal clock. Everything worked in synchrony, and it was all simple.

This simplicity was both intentional and necessary. At that time it wasn't possible to put all the memory necessary on the motherboard. Often, some of the PC's main memory would end up on plug-in option cards. Certainly most of the other functions that required much in the way of integrated circuit support also had to be put on plug-in cards. That was true of the controllers for the floppy disk drives (and later for the hard drives introduced with the PC/XT). It also was true for the video subsystem and for the serial and parallel ports. Every one of these parts ran initially at a speed of 4.77MHz. Later, with the introduction of the PC/AT, that clock speed was increased first to 6MHz and later to 8MHz. But that is as far as it went.

Before CPUs started running significantly faster than this, the Input/Output (I/O) bus was divided from the other functions in a PC. But before I explain that development, you must learn more about the I/O bus in the early models of the IBM PC, and the clones of those computers.

An Industry Standard Is Born

IBM not only created the first PCs, it also published the details of how they were designed. This was done so others could know enough to build plug-in cards that would work with the PC. That was a very wise decision on IBM's part, because it lead directly to the huge success of the PC in the marketplace. In the long run, this openness about the design of the PC also lead to the development of the clone PC market. That development nearly put IBM out of the PC business altogether.

Because the original PC used a CPU with only eight data lines, that is all that were needed in the I/O bus. Likewise, the bus only needed to have 20 address lines in order to address the full 1MB that was the maximum memory such a PC could use. By adding lines necessary to carry power, ground, clock signal, and an assortment of control lines (such as interrupt request lines, and so on), the total I/O bus in a PC or PC/XT had 62 wires.

When IBM introduced the PC/AT, which used the 80286 CPU chip with its 16 data lines and 24-bit addresses, they needed to widen the I/O bus accordingly. But they didn't want to make all the plug-in cards they and other manufacturers had created for PCs obsolete, so they added a new connector behind the original PC I/O bus connector. The original connector was referred to as the 8-bit section and the new connector as the 16-bit section for the overall PC I/O bus. This new section carries the additional eight data lines, the additional four address lines, and some additional control signal, power, and ground lines. This 16-bit section has 36 connectors in it.

Cards designed to only plug into the 8-bit section still worked fine. And, the newer cards had an extra tongue on them to plug into the new, 16-bit section and let them access the newly included lines in this expanded PC I/O bus. Figure 16.1 shows how the ISA bus is used to connect the CPU to various PC peripheral devices both inside and outside the system unit. This figure shows how it was used initially, before some of the more recent advances in I/O buses for PCs.

In Figure 16.1 the keyboard is shown connecting directly to the motherboard chip set. In fact, it connects to the keyboard controller. Originally, this was a separate chip (one of perhaps 50 in the original PC). Still, this is a part of the overall motherboard chip set's function, and it now is built into the (now usually only one or two) large-scale integrated circuits that make up your PC's motherboard chip set.

The serial and parallel port interface circuits and the floppy and hard disk controllers are shown as residing on plug-in cards. That is how it was done in early PCs. A more modern PC includes most of that functionality as a part of the motherboard chip set.

IBM's decision to augment, rather than replace, the PC I/O bus design was the first sign that this was becoming a real standard—what we now know as the Industry Standard Architecture (ISA) I/O bus. This name reflects the market reality that although IBM created this design, they no longer "owned" it in the sense that even they couldn't ignore it, but needed to respect it in their next generation of PCs.

Figure 16.1.
The Industry Standard Architecture (ISA) bus is the main means of connecting to PC peripherals.

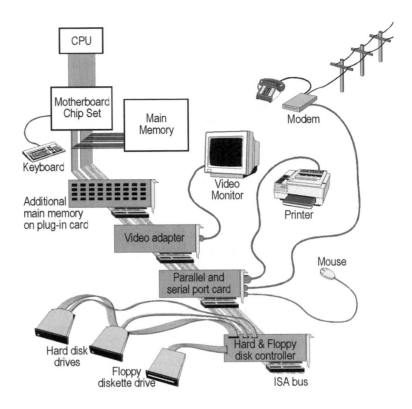

And still today, we have connectors on our PC motherboards that are identical to those found on an original IBM PC/AT. You can see the connectors on the sample desktop system's motherboard in Figure 15.2. They are the long black connectors at the far right in that figure. Figure 16.2 shows a closer view of all the slot connectors on this motherboard viewed from above. This figure clearly shows the two different sections in the ISA connectors. There is a close-up view of both the ISA connectors and the newer-style PCI connectors that are found on the sample desktop system's motherboard.

Not only are we still using the same connector (with all the same definitions of the purpose for each contact), we also are using this I/O bus at the original speed, or very nearly so. The first PCs and PC/XTs ran the CPU and the I/O bus at 4.77MHz. The first PC/ATs ran them at 6MHz, and later AT models ran them at 8MHz. Some clone XTs and ATs ran their I/O buses and CPUs at speeds up to 15MHz, but they didn't always work correctly at the highest speeds.

When the industry came out with the Extended Industry Standard Architecture (EISA) version of this bus, the designers of that standard specified that no matter how fast the CPU, the I/O bus should not be clocked any faster than 8.33MHz. This was done to ensure that all the plug-in cards ever designed for this connector, no matter how antiquated, would work in any PC no matter how modern and zippy it might be. And indeed, no PC that is properly configured will have any signals in these connectors that change any more often than 8.33 million times per second.

Toward rear of
PC system unit

Four PCI-bus
I/O slot connectors

Toward front of
PC system unit

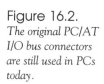

Figure 16.2.
*The original PC/AT
I/O bus connectors
are still used in PCs
today.*

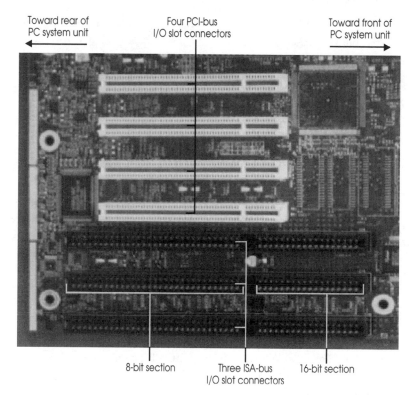

8-bit section

Three ISA-bus
I/O slot connectors

16-bit section

Extending the Standard

The ISA bus served the PC/AT well. But soon, clone computers that ran faster came on the market. And soon after that, IBM came out with an entire new set of machines, supposedly to replace the PC, which it called its PS/2 family of computers. Examined closely, the low-end members of the PS/2 family were nothing more than PCs in new boxes. They used the ISA bus inside and had many other features in common with the PC/AT and similar machines. And, virtually any good-old ISA plug-in card could be used in one of those low-end PS/2 computers.

The higher-end models really were different. In particular, they had a whole new I/O bus structure. IBM termed this the Micro-Channel Architecture (MCA) bus, and they promised that it would be used across their entire line of computers from PCs (well, PS/2s) to mainframes.

The Micro-Channel Architecture (MCA) Bus

The MCA bus was indisputably a technically better bus than the ISA bus. But it was different. You couldn't use an old ISA card in an MCA slot. It just wouldn't fit, and if it had, it wouldn't have worked. The MCA bus had nearly twice as many wires (and connections in each slot connector) as the ISA bus (even including both its 8-bit and 16-bit sections). Curiously, even though there never were any 8-bit PS/2 computers, IBM divided the MCA connector into an 8-bit section, a 16-bit section, and a 32-bit section. Then it defined two different extensions beyond that—one for use by special *matched memory cards*, and the other for use with cards that offered extended video processing. (The main video subsystem for these PS/2 models was included on the motherboard.)

The Extended Industry Standard Architecture (EISA) Bus

At the same time that IBM brought out this new line of PS/2 computers, it decided it was time to crack down on some of the clone PC makers. To accomplish this, IBM put a very punitive precondition on the license agreement for the MCA bus technology that would have required the clone makers to pay back royalties on years of PC sales. None of the large clone PC makers could possibly have agreed to that deal. Instead, several of them responded by forming a committee (sometimes referred to as the Gang of Nine) to develop an answer to the MCA challenge. Their final result, the Extended Industry Standard Architecture (EISA) bus is technically a tour-de-force solution, but it has not turned out to be much of a winner in the marketplace. Both MCA and EISA bus slots can be found in some PCs today (mainly those intended for use as file servers), but not in large numbers. The bulk of the PC marketplace stuck with the old tried-and-true ISA bus design until something more compelling came along.

Proprietary Memory (and Video) Buses

One of the driving forces behind both the MCA and EISA buses was the increasing clock speeds and wider data paths available in the CPU chips. As soon as CPU chips became available with clock speeds well in excess of 8MHz and with 32-bit data paths, PC makers decided to divide the bus from the CPU into two paths. One path would go to the motherboard memory and if it had one, the motherboard video subsystem. The other path went to the I/O bus slots.

The path to main memory was as wide as the CPU could support (16 bits or 32 bits) and it operated at the same speed as the CPU. But the path to the I/O bus slots was limited to 16 data lines, with those lines (and all the others in this bus) switching no more rapidly than 8.33MHz.

The bus that carries the full number of data bits that the CPU can accept or generate and at the maximum speed is now called the *system bus* or *host bus*. For several generations of CPU, this bus was clocked at the same rate as the CPU, but now it has maxed out at 66MHz, while CPU rates have already gone up to 300MHz and are reaching beyond that.

These differences meant that if you plugged a memory card into an I/O slot, it would run much slower than the memory on the motherboard. This is a very good reason to have all the PC's main memory on the motherboard. Unfortunately, that just wasn't always feasible. Furthermore, PC video subsystems were getting faster and faster. If a user chose to use a plug-in video card, it couldn't exchange data with the CPU any faster than the I/O bus would let it.

Both these pressures led several companies to create an additional, proprietary bus with slots into which one could plug special, proprietary memory or video cards. These worked well, but they suffered the disadvantage of being proprietary. If you bought one of these PCs you couldn't simply upgrade it by replacing the cards in it with newer, better cards from some other manufacturer. Those cards wouldn't fit. The marketplace has resoundingly rejected these not-quite-compatible "clone" PCs.

The Video Equipment Standards Association (VESA) Solution

That situation was intolerable; it was clear that a new standard for the PC I/O bus was necessary. Actually, two new standards appeared at almost the same time. The VESA Local (VL) bus was simple to implement, and it arrived in the marketplace first. The PCI (Peripheral Component Interconnect) bus was more technically ambitious, and it took almost two years longer before it was truly available. Since its arrival, the PCI bus has essentially driven the VESA bus (and all previous PC I/O buses except the ISA bus) out of the marketplace.

You've learned that the CPU chip has pins where it presents address information and other pins through which it sends or receives data. You've also learned that those signals are sent out from the CPU to memory and to I/O bus slots. But, to really understand the VESA bus, you must know the manner of that connection.

> **Note:** The signals from the CPU chip are not powerful enough to travel great distances or to activate a large number of receiving devices. But the I/O bus potentially might have to send those signals along to many simultaneous recipients. It can do this only by buffering (also called amplifying) those signals. Amplifying makes those signals arbitrarily strong, but it also slightly delays those signals.

If you can be sure the signals from some of the CPU output pins will go to only a few receiving circuits, and that they will be located close to the CPU chip, then it's permissible to make that connection directly. The VESA bus does just that. It takes a few critical pins on the PC and connects them directly to special slot connectors on just two or three slots.

The CPU now talks to two entities. One is the motherboard chip set (with its signal buffers) and the other is the VESA slot connectors. Also, the motherboard chip set now talks to the main memory (and the L2 cache if present) over a separate bus from the one that goes to the ISA bus, enabling the CPU to transfer data to and from main memory locations much faster than it could over the ISA bus. Although signals on the ISA bus slot connectors are limited to 8.33MHz, those on the VL bus connector are allowed to go up to four times faster. And, the VL bus connector permits the transfer of information from all 32 of the CPU's data lines in parallel. For these reasons, the rate of transfer of information from the CPU to a VL bus card can be increased by about a factor of eight over an otherwise equivalent 16-bit ISA card.

When VESA motherboards and VESA video cards became available, they were instant successes. Nothing else you could do would give such a dramatic boost to your PC's performance.

Unfortunately, the VL bus solution has several low-level implementation problems and works with only two or maybe three slots. What if you wanted more than three fast bus slots? You were simply out of luck. The real solution to the high-speed bus quandary was to replace the VL bus plus ISA bus combination with a different high-performance bus altogether: The PCI bus. Before I tell you about the PCI bus, I want to describe another bus that has been available in PCs for many years and became prominent around the same time as the VL bus.

The Really Good Bus With the Really Bad Name (SCSI)

The Small Computer System Interface (SCSI) bus, pronounced "scuzzy," is a relative old-timer in the industry. But it didn't achieve much popularity in PCs until fairly recently. There were several good reasons for this, among them the perceived difficulty in setting up a SCSI bus on a PC and making it work correctly.

In contrast, a SCSI bus has always been built into every Macintosh computer, so Apple aficionados have had the advantages of this bus available to them for much longer. But now, after some years of struggle, the SCSI bus host adapters and supporting software for PCs are all in place and well tested. So, for those situations in which the SCSI bus outperforms all the alternatives, PC owners can take advantage of it easily.

The SCSI bus is the preferred way to connect hard disk drives with the largest capacity and highest data transfer rates (although this preeminence is constantly being challenged by developments in EIDE drives). It also provides a convenient way to attach several different types of external PC peripherals (such as CD-ROM, ZIP, and other removable media storage devices) and get maximum performance from them. These advantages are offset to a degree by a slightly higher price for SCSI-enabled versions of all these devices, and by some added complexity in the setup of your PC.

The SCSI Architecture

Fundamentally, the SCSI architecture is simply two buses connected by a bridge. Figure 16.3 shows this relationship graphically. Here you see how the SCSI host adapter sits on the ISA bus and connects on its other side to the SCSI bus, extending both inward toward an internal hard drive (as an example) and outward to external SCSI devices.

Figure 16.3.
The SCSI bus architecture.

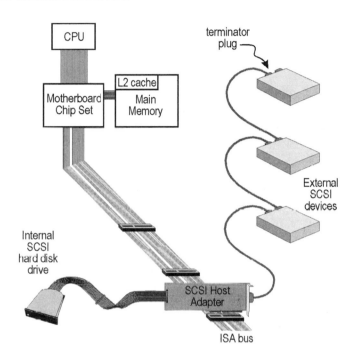

In a sense, you can think of a SCSI bus as a small local area network. The main difference between the SCSI bus and the ordinary LAN is that rather than being a means of communications between multiple PCs (and perhaps a file server), the PC to which the SCSI bus is attached is the only general-purpose computer on this bus. Each SCSI device has, in fact, a small special-purpose computer in its SCSI interface portion. But that computer has only one task to perform, and that is to manage communications on behalf of the peripheral device to which it is attached with the host adapter and perhaps with other devices on the SCSI bus.

The term "the SCSI bus architecture" has been used in this discussion as if it were a singular thing. But as with most standards that have been around awhile, it has grown and changed over time. So there are, in fact, several versions of what SCSI means. By now it has evolved into several distinct "flavors" of bus. The overall architecture has not changed, but the details of the bus design have, and along with those changes have come a range of performance possibilities.

The Several Flavors of SCSI

The original source of the SCSI standard was a proprietary protocol developed by Shugart Associates (an early maker of hard drives) and the NCR Corporation at just about the same time as IBM's introduction of the first PC. A short time later this standard was adopted (and somewhat modified) by the American National Standards Committee, giving it at that time the name Small Computer Systems Interface (SCSI).

SCSI-1

The original version of SCSI, now called SCSI-1, called for a cable with eight data wires (or 16 pairs in the preferred, differential signaling mode) plus one for parity. This cable was to be connected from the host adapter to any SCSI peripherals inside the system unit in parallel, and to SCSI devices outside the system unit in a *daisy-chain* fashion. (You can see such a daisy chain of cables in Figure 16.3. On the internal cable you see the hard disk at the end of the cable, and an extra connector in the middle that could be connected to a second internal SCSI device.)

The SCSI bus operates as a synchronous bus. All the SCSI devices attached to that bus operate independently. Each has its own, unique SCSI ID number (from 0 to 7). Any of them can put a message on the bus requesting permission to transfer data from itself to a specified other device on that bus, or to receive data from a specified other device. If the bus is not otherwise occupied, these two devices "have a conversation" all on their own, without any intervention on the part of the SCSI host adapter. The host adapter is involved only when it is the target (or source) of such a conversation.

It is vital that each device on the SCSI bus have its own unique ID, because that is the only way they know when they are being "spoken to." Normally, the host adapter is given the SCSI ID of 7. The other devices can usually have their ID set by the user. There are two common ways this is done.

Most external SCSI devices have a switch of some kind on their back panel to let you set their SCSI ID. Some will enable you to choose any value you like; others will only let you choose from among a few pre-selected options. Figure 16.4 shows a rear view of a SyQuest 270MB removable hard disk drive in an external SCSI box. Notice the small switch by the power cord and on/off switch. If you press in on the center of what appears to be a post above or below the visible number with a piece of wire (an unrolled paper clip works nicely), the switch will move to the next higher or next lower number. Other SCSI boxes use a switch that looks like a miniature clock face, with a pointer you turn with a small screwdriver, or a switch with numbers like the one shown in Figure 16.4, but with a thumbwheel beside them to let you turn the switch by hand.

Figure 16.4.
A SyQuest external SCSI removable hard disk has SCSI-1 connectors and a typical switch for selecting the SCSI ID.

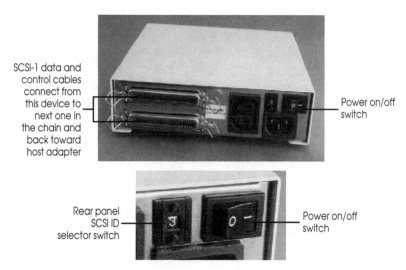

SCSI-1 data and control cables connect from this device to next one in the chain and back toward host adapter

Power on/off switch

Rear panel SCSI ID selector switch

Power on/off switch

The cable to this device from the host adapter, or the next device on the bus toward the host adapter, plugs into one of the large connectors on the left. Another, similar cable goes into the other one and connects this device to the next one. If this is the last device on the external SCSI bus, then a terminator plug must be inserted into the otherwise unused SCSI connector.

It takes three bits to designate a number between zero and seven. So another way to designate a device's SCSI ID is to use three jumpers. Putting shorting plugs on just the appropriate jumpers will set the SCSI ID for that device. (Think of the shorted jumper pairs as representing 1 bits and the open ones representing 0 bits.) This method is most commonly used for internal SCSI devices.

The original version of the SCSI bus allowed data transfers at rates of up to 5MBps (one byte on each clock cycle, with a 5MHz clock frequency). That is faster than the ISA bus could support, and so was thought to be amply fast for the time when it was introduced. The cables and connectors used with this standard are discussed in more detail in the "SCSI Cables and Connectors" section, later in this chapter.

SCSI-2

In 1991, ANSI came out with an update called SCSI-2. This newer version of SCSI includes everything in the older version with some additions. First, it endorsed a new, more compact cable-end connector. Second, it allowed the use of multiple cables to support 16- or even 32-bit data transfers in parallel. And, it established a complete software-control system for SCSI, called the *Common Command Set* (CCS).

SCSI-2 also provided support for doubling the clock speed on the SCSI bus. This variation was called "Fast SCSI." With Fast and Wide SCSI (16 bits in parallel over two separate cables) it now became possible to carry out data transfers at rates up to 20MB per second.

SCSI-3

As soon as SCSI-2 was officially approved, the committee began work on SCSI-3. This update made several significant changes in the standard. First, it decoupled the CSS (software) definition from the hardware definition. That means it is now possible to have several different hardware connection schemes that are all a form of SCSI simply because they use the same command set.

In fact, the SCSI-3 standard is a whole collection of standards documents, each covering one "layer" of the interface. The lowest level is called the physical layer and defines the cables and connectors to be used. The next layer, referred to as the protocol layer, describes how the signals are organized to send packets of information. The third layer is called the architecture, and it covers how command requests are organized, queued, and responded to. Primary commands are the top-level set of commands that all SCSI devices must support. Device-specific commands are optional ones used by particular classes of device (for example, CD-ROMs or hard drives).

The second major change in SCSI-3 is the endorsement of a new kind of cable-end connector, this time with more contacts to enable supporting 16-bit data transfers over a single cable. Today this style of cable is referred to as a Wide-SCSI connection.

Third, SCSI-3 adds one bit to the SCSI ID, thus allowing up to 16 devices on a SCSI bus. The host adapter is still given the SCSI ID of 7 by default, but now other devices may be given any ID from 0 to 15.

Finally, SCSI-3 enables the use of a variety of physical layer media. These can be anything from a serial link (sending only a single bit at a time) all the way up to a parallel link that conveys data 32 or even 64 bits at a time, and the link can use wire, infrared beams, or optical fibers. Along with this new catholicity about what type of hardware link is used is the capability to support even more rapid data transfers than any previous version of SCSI. With Fast-40 Wide SCSI, it is possible to transfer 80MB of data per second on a single SCSI (wire) cable. Use of an optical fiber link enables even higher data rates.

The serial SCSI link became the basis of what is now called the IEEE 1394 standard. You'll learn more about that topic in the section, "The Wonderful, New, High-Speed Serial Buses (USB and IEEE 1394)," near the end of this chapter.

The SCSI Host Adapter

The SCSI *host adapter* is interface circuitry that sits between the internal system bus of the PC and the SCSI bus. Its job is to send and receive messages in the SCSI fashion on the SCSI bus and simultaneously to send and receive messages on the PC system I/O bus in its native protocol.

Some PCs have a SCSI host adapter built onto the motherboard (as has been the case for all Macintosh computers), but most use a separate plug-in host adapter. If it's on a plug-in card, the host adapter could be on an ISA card, a VESA VL bus card, or a PCI card. To get the highest performance out of SCSI devices, it is important that the data transfers not be limited by the slow ISA bus. So mostly, the good SCSI host adapters sold today are PCI cards.

Because SCSI functionality has not been built into PCs from the beginning, the motherboard BIOS does not contain software support for that function. This means that to operate a SCSI bus, the host adapter must either have an on-board BIOS ROM chip, or else you must load a suitable software driver from a non-SCSI hard disk before using the SCSI bus at all.

Furthermore, the software in the BIOS ROM on a SCSI card (or in the lowest-level software driver that might have been provided on a disk with the host adapter) is probably only barely adequate to set up the SCSI host adapter for minimal operation. To get the full benefit of the SCSI bus, and in particular to support multiple devices hooked to it, you probably must load at least one more driver program. This might be a CAM (Common Access Method) driver, or it might be an ASPI (Advanced SCSI Programming Interface) driver. You must use whatever your SCSI host adapter and the devices attached to it requires.

You can have more than one SCSI host adapter in your PC. However, if you have many of them, you likely will find yourself running out of IRQ levels to assign to them. The practical limit is probably two.

Tip: Another job the host adapter has is to check at power up and see which SCSI devices are at which SCSI IDs on the SCSI bus. For this to work, all those devices must be powered on when you boot your PC. If you plug everything into one power strip or power controller, you can easily ensure that this is so by having the entire system turn on with one switch. Otherwise, just get in the habit of turning on the external SCSI devices before you power up your PC.

Some SCSI Host Adapters to Avoid (or Use Sparingly)

Some SCSI host adapters have been built onto sound cards. Others are shipped with external removable media drives (for example, ZIP drives). Most of these host adapters only support 8-bit data transfers, and they usually use the ISA bus or an IDE interface, neither of which is capable of the highest data transfer rates. The intent of these interfaces, typically, is to support just a slow SCSI device, not to also support a hard disk. For these reasons, I don't recommend that you attach a SCSI hard drive to such a host adapter. In practice, many such adapters will not function properly if any other SCSI device (other than the one they came with) is attached to them.

Any host adapter sold today that is intended for use with SCSI hard drives will likely be a PCI card, and it probably will have a BIOS ROM on it to let you boot your PC from a SCSI hard disk if there is one attached to that SCSI bus (and if that disk is suitably formatted and has an operating system installed). If you don't have one of these and you want to use a SCSI hard disk, then get one. They are worth the cost.

SCSI Devices

What, exactly, is a SCSI device? It can be almost anything: hard disks, CD-ROM drives, ZIP drives, recordable CD drives, printers, mice, tape drives, image scanners, and graphics tablets. Really, just about any PC peripheral device can be given a SCSI interface. The defining characteristic of all SCSI devices is that they have a SCSI interface. This is a small computer that "speaks SCSI" out of one side of itself (across the SCSI bus) and that understands how to operate the peripheral device(s) to which it is attached out of the other side of itself.

Because of this "intelligent" aspect to SCSI devices, and because the SCSI standard allows multiple, independent conversations between SCSI devices to be going on simultaneously across a single SCSI bus, it is possible to have a high degree of multi-processing in a PC with a SCSI bus and a suitable array of SCSI devices. This won't happen automatically, but it can happen, with suitable software support.

SCSI Logical Units

The SCSI standard only contemplated up to eight devices (including the host adapter) on a single SCSI bus prior to the advent of SCSI-3, and 16 on a SCSI-3 bus. However, as mentioned previously, you can have more than one SCSI bus in a single PC by installing more than one SCSI host adapter. That works, but it uses up IRQ lines (each host adapter will need its own IRQ).

Another solution is to put more than just seven devices, plus one host adapter, on a single SCSI bus. Although you can have only seven (or 15) SCSI devices on the bus (in addition to the host adapter), it is perfectly possible for each of them to be a mini-manager of multiple (up to 8 or 16) "logical units."

This is a very complex process and it is not something that you should "try at home"—but it is perfectly possible, and is supported in the SCSI standard. Many custom systems houses have built such systems for their customers.

SCSI Cables and Connectors

Many of the problems involved in SCSI installations originate with the necessary cables and connectors. Knowing the differences between SCSI cable and connector types and the factors involved in proper termination can keep a simple SCSI installation job from turning into a challenge to your patience.

External SCSI Device Connectors and Cables

Most SCSI-1 devices use a 50-pin Centronics-style connector. This has enough wires to support eight pairs of data wires plus all the needed control, status, and ground wires. That means it is possible to do differential data transfers over this type of cable and connector. A *differential mode* of operation simply means that when the signal on a data wire goes up, the voltage on its paired companion wire goes down. The receiver doesn't actually care what voltage is on either wire; it looks only at the difference of the two voltages. This strategy is very useful for canceling out inevitable noise signals that will be picked up on any long cable, because adjacent wires commonly pick up approximately equal noise voltages.

However, the SCSI-1 standard also contemplates the use of single-ended cable (with only a single wire per data or parity bit, and with receivers that simply compare the voltage on those wires with ground). This reduces the needed number of wires enough that a 25-pin connector can be used, but it requires limiting the sum of the lengths of the SCSI cables attached to such an interface to about 20 feet. (With differential signals it is possible to extend a SCSI bus to around 80 feet from the PC.)

Warning: Macintosh computers use female DB25 connectors on their SCSI bus interfaces. This is the same connector used on PCs for the parallel port (printer) interface.

Until PCs had SCSI host adapters this was not a problem. Now, it can be. If you have a SCSI host adapter that uses the Macintosh-style female DB25 connector for the SCSI bus, you might inadvertently plug your printer into it. Not only will this not work, it very likely will burn out some of the interface circuitry in the printer, and it could damage the SCSI host adapter as well. The reverse is also true of plugging a SCSI device into a printer parallel port. If your PC has both kinds of female DB25 on it, please mark them prominently so you never make this mistake.

If your PC SCSI host adapter has the more conventional 50-pin connector, you won't have that problem. But there are other issues to attend to.

You can get a SCSI cable with any of several different combinations of connectors on its ends. The original standard cable has a 50-pin Centronics-style male connector at both ends. And many SCSI devices have two female Centronics 50-pin connectors. But some have 25-pin female DB connectors instead. You can buy adapter cables that have a 50-pin connector on one end and a 25-pin connector on the other. If you do this, and if your SCSI host adapter has a 50-pin connector, be sure to put all the SCSI devices with 50-pin connectors closer to the host adapter than any of the 25-pin ones. You do this because after you make the transition from 50-pin down to 25-pin (going out across the SCSI bus from the host adapter), you are also going from differential operation to single-ended. That means you will lose the noise canceling benefits of differential operation beyond that point. Going back up to 50-pin connections beyond there doesn't help.

And, it gets worse. There are two other kinds of connectors to be concerned with. The SCSI-2 standard introduced a miniature 50-pin DB connector, which has its pins spaced 1/20 inch apart (instead of the 1/10 inch used in the DB25 connector and a somewhat larger spacing in the Centronics-style connectors). Except for the style of the connector, and the fact that it is small enough to fit on the rear panel of a PC plug-in card, this is electrically the same as the 50-pin Centronics connector.

The really different connector is the *P connector* introduced with SCSI-3. This 68-pin connector has enough pins to support differential data transfers 16 bits at a time. If you have any SCSI devices with this type of connector, you'd better have a host adapter with one, also.

You must have a full 16-bit data path from a 16-bit SCSI device to a 16-bit SCSI host adapter. That can only be done with a single 68-wire cable, or with two 50-wire (or 25-wire) cables. You may at any point on the SCSI bus convert from a 16-bit connection down to an 8-bit connection (using a single 50-wire or 25-wire cable with a special 68-pin connector on one end). But you won't be able to support a 16-bit SCSI device at any point beyond there (going away from the host adapter) on the SCSI bus.

Internal SCSI Device Cables and Connectors

On the SCSI host adapter card, in addition to the external data cable connector mounted on the rear panel, you will likely find one or two post and header connectors. If there is only one, it will probably have 50 pins. If there are two, one will have 50 pins and the other will have 68 pins. The 50-pin header is for 8-bit data transfers, and the 68-pin header is for 16-bit transfers.

From either of these connectors you will run a ribbon cable (with the correct number of conductors) from the host adapter to the SCSI devices that are mounted inside your PC's system unit. If you have only one, be sure to put it at the end of that cable, even if some connectors are on that cable midway. Those other connectors are only for use when you have more than one internal SCSI device to hook up.

The Issue of SCSI Terminations

If you have a cable and you launch a rapidly changing signal onto it, that signal moves down the cable as a wave traveling at very nearly the speed of light from where you launched it to both ends of the cable. (If you are launching it from one end, you will only notice the wave going away from you to the other end.) At either end of the cable, unless something absorbs the energy in this wave, it will bounce and return back toward its source.

If this is a SCSI bus and a device is monitoring its signals, it will see two waves instead of just one. If this is a hard disk that is recording data, it might record too many instances of the data. Worse, if a new chunk of data follows the first (as is usually the case), the bounced copy of the first batch of data can overlap the new data and confuse the hard drive about what data value it is to record. Follow this reasoning even a little bit and you can see why signals that bounce back and forth on a cable can cause data loss.

So how can you stop this from happening? The obvious solution is to absorb all the wave's energy at the end of the cable. That is precisely what a *cable terminator* does. A cable terminator takes away the signal's energy so nothing is left to bounce. However, if you do this in the wrong place—like in the middle of the cable—you could keep the signal from ever reaching some of the devices on the cable. So, it is necessary to properly terminate cables that carry fast signals over any distances greater than a few inches.

On a SCSI cable, the usual practice is to terminate the cable at both ends, and nowhere else. This means one of two things: Either the devices at the ends of the cable must incorporate some suitable termination network (some resistors attached to each data wire), or a terminator must be added to the end of the cable.

Both strategies are used for external SCSI devices. If the device has two SCSI connectors, one will be used for the cable going toward the host adapter. The other will either be used for a cable going to another SCSI device, or else it may have plugged into it a special terminator plug.

Alternatively, there might be a switch on the device to enable it to terminate the cable internally. If it has such a switch, that is generally a preferable way to do SCSI cable termination. Just be sure you don't have the internal termination turned on in any devices before the end of the cable, and use only the internal terminator *or* the external terminator on the device at the end of the cable. Two termination devices at the end of a SCSI chain can cause erratic operation of the devices attached to it. You may also purchase active termination devices that will sense the presence or absence of proper termination on a SCSI bus and provide only what is necessary.

What about the other end of the cable, back at the host adapter? Some host adapters are clever enough to always provide the right termination at that point. Others are not. If you have both an internal and an external SCSI cable attached to the SCSI host adapter, depending on exactly how its internal circuitry is built, the host adapter might have to provide termination to the cables going out in both directions, or it might have to avoid terminating what amounts to one long cable that passes through the host adapter. You must consult the manual that comes with your host adapter to know which way it is built.

Finally, for the ribbon cable that extends inside the system unit, you have only one option. Turn off (or remove) the terminator resistor packs or other termination means on each SCSI device before the end of the ribbon cable and be sure the cable ends on a device that has a terminator.

Some Special Considerations for SCSI Hard Disks

The SCSI host adapter "lies" to the PC about any hard disks it has attached to it across the SCSI bus. It must lie because SCSI has no concept of a three-dimensional disk drive (with some number of heads, cylinders, and sectors per track). On the other hand, the PC BIOS is built assuming that all disk drives have that type of structure.

So most, if not all, SCSI host adapters do something like this: They treat the actual hard disk simply as a long string of logical blocks. Then they turn those block addresses into head, cylinder, and sector numbers on some fictitious 3D hard drive, and they tell the BIOS about the data's location in those terms. (Conversely, when the BIOS asks the SCSI host adapter to put or retrieve some data at a particular head, cylinder, and sector location, the host adapter converts that set of numbers to a single logical block address and puts or gets the data from that block.)

All this works very well. That is, right up until you change which SCSI host adapter a particular hard drive is attached to. You can freely move many kinds of SCSI device from host adapter to host adapter and never have a problem, but if you move a formatted hard disk with data on it, you stand a very good chance of finding that the new system you attach it to sees this hard disk as unformatted and without any data at all. You haven't really lost anything—yet. But if you actually go ahead and use this hard disk on the new system you will be destroying the data it contains as you reformat it to the new system's view of how it should have its logical blocks arranged.

Removable hard disks (like a SyQuest disk or an Iomega Jaz disk) and CD-ROMs or CD-R discs don't have this problem. The device driver software that supports their use handles all these geometry conversions in a universal manner—or it doesn't do them at all.

Bottom line: Don't move a hard disk from one SCSI host adapter to another unless you plan to reformat it and start over as if it were a brand new disk immediately after you move it. If you must move it while it is full of important data (say, if your SCSI host adapter dies), be sure to use a new host adapter of the same brand, and preferably the same model, as the original one.

Mixing IDE and SCSI Disk Drives

The most common kind of hard disk in a modern PC is one that connects to an IDE bus. You can have up to four IDE devices (hard disks, CD-ROM drives, and so on) in most PCs, and with the use of special plug-in cards you can add up to four additional IDE devices.

You also can use SCSI hard disks in a PC. There are two advantages to using SCSI hard disks. One is that at least the best of them are capable of higher data transfer rates than even the best of the IDE drives, and the other is that you can have more SCSI hard disks than you can IDE drives. (You can easily put on seven hard disks (or 15 on a SCSI-3 host adapter), and with the use of logical units you can push that as high as 56 (or 240 with SCSI-3). This latter advantage might be of little interest to you unless the operating system you are running is capable of supporting that many hard disks—which certainly rules out DOS and Windows 95 or 98.

What if you want to use both IDE and SCSI hard disks in your PC? In that case, you must know some special things. First, unless your motherboard BIOS has been specially enhanced, you must boot your PC from one of the IDE devices. (That could be a hard drive or it could be an EIDE CD-ROM.) The only other alternative supported by most PCs is to boot from a floppy disk. The very newest BIOS revisions sometimes incorporate support for booting from any EIDE or SCSI drive.

Understanding How ISA Grew Into IDE, ATAPI, and More

If you want to understand, in a general way, what all this IDE, ATA, and ATAPI stuff is about, then a simple telling of the tale will do. The IDE bus is that part of the ISA bus that is needed to support disk drives and the like, redirected to a special connector to save on the use of ISA slots. The ATA standard describes how to deal with hard disks over this IDE channel. The ATAPI standard extends ATA to allow dealing with CD-ROM and certain other types of devices on that same channel. You say that's too brief? Okay, then here is a little more detail.

For perspective, note that the IDE "channel" (to give it the technically correct descriptor) is intended only for use inside a PC's system unit. Any devices hooked to this channel will be internal ones, unlike what is possible with the SCSI expansion bus. The one exception to this comes via the IDE channel enhancement called the *PC Card* (and now, in one of its versions, going by the name *Card Bus*).

The Early Days

When PCs were young, electronics could not be nearly as densely integrated as they can be today. It took a lot of room to fit in all the chips one needed to do useful tasks. This meant that hard disks had a lot of electronics built on them and still required a controller card plugged into an expansion slot and connected to the drives by multiple ribbon cables.

Electronics evolved. Eventually all that was needed to operate and interface a PC with a hard drive was put onto the drive itself. The first version in which this showed up were products such as the HardCard. That was Plus Development's trademarked name for a hard disk controller card with the hard disk itself actually mounted on the card. These cards were large. They completely filled an ISA slot and physically obstructed another. But, when you plugged one of them into your PC, voila! You had just installed a working hard drive. No more having to match up a controller, cables and a drive. No more having to low-level format the drive. Just add DOS and go.

Early IDE Drives

The next stage was closer to what we have today. The electronics were further reduced in size, to the point that it all was put on the hard drive itself. This drive didn't need a separate controller. Because all the electronics are on the drive, this was called an *Integrated Device Electronics* (IDE) hard drive, and was the first of the breed of today's most popular hard drives.

These IDE hard drives didn't need any external controllers, but they did need to connect to the ISA bus. So we got things called "IDE paddle cards," "IDE host interface cards," and so on. These looked a lot like the old hard disk controller cards. They plugged into an ISA slot and had a 40-pin post and header connector that accepted a ribbon cable from the IDE hard drive. But instead of a lot of interface electronics, these cards essentially enabled you to plug a ribbon cable into the ISA bus. Most of the time these cards—like the hard disk controller cards that preceded them—also had a floppy disk controller on them, and that meant having at least a little bit of circuitry including one or a few integrated circuit chips.

The next move was pretty obvious. Makers of motherboards knew their customers were going to want to plug in a floppy disk drive or two, and also one or two hard drives. So they moved the floppy disk controller to the motherboard chip set. They connected it to a 34-pin post and header connector for the cable to the floppy disk drives. And next to that, they put a 40-pin connector that carried all the signals from just those wires in the ISA bus that an IDE hard drive needed to see. Plug in your floppies to one connector, plug in your IDE hard drives to the other, and you were off and running.

EIDE, ATA, and ATAPI

Next, motherboard manufacturers started including two IDE connectors. These were connected separately to the ISA bus lines, and now each of these connectors could support one or two IDE devices. (Besides adding a second IDE cable connector, accomplishing this required some changes to the motherboard BIOS both to add the necessary four-drive support and to add the appropriate entries to the Setup program.)

Then they speeded up first one of the IDE channels and then both of the channels by using Fast PIO support. They added logical block addressing as well as some other extensions to the Interrupt 13h BIOS calls (the primary way that application programs ask DOS to help them move information on and off a hard disk and to various other parts of DOS). Overall, the result was to make it possible to have the four IDE devices be any mixture of slow CD-ROMs and fast hard drives you liked, with the hard drives being allowed to be as large as you wanted (for now, anyway).

That is where we are today. Figure 16.5 shows the IDE and floppy disk connectors on the motherboard of the sample desktop system. (As is the case with most systems today, this motherboard offers two IDE channels. It is possible to add up to two more, but for now that must be done by adding one or two plug-in cards on the ISA bus.)

Of course, speeding up the support for IDE drives wouldn't have been helpful if the drives themselves hadn't also been speeded up. Which they were. Many minor and a few more major changes were made in the specifications for those drives and in the ways they were used and controlled. Overall we call these new, improved IDE drives Enhanced IDE drives, or EIDE drives for short.

Figure 16.5.
Floppy disk drives and IDE (or EIDE) drive cables plug directly into connectors on the motherboard.

Two 40-pin ribbon cable connectors for two IDE channels, each able to support two devices

34-pin connector for ribbon cable to one or two floppy diskette drives

Front edge of motherboard

Most of the details of just how EIDE drives are "better" than plain old, ordinary IDE drives are not all that important. All those details are contained in a specifications document called the AT Attachment (ATA) specification and its extension the AT Attachment Packet Interface (ATAPI), published by the Small Form Factor (SFF) Committee.

Hooking Up Multiple IDE or EIDE Devices

One detail about IDE and EIDE devices probably deserves a little more careful treatment. Each IDE channel can have one master device and one slave. As mentioned in Chapter 10, "Digging Deeper Into Disks," when you install these devices, you must take care to have only one of them set to be a master device and the second one, if it is present, set to be a slave. It doesn't matter which one (master or slave) is at the end of the ribbon cable (and thank goodness you don't have to worry about terminating this cable).

If you are particularly lucky, you might have a BIOS that supports the "Cable Select" setting of the master/slave role for each drive. In that case the system will make that assignment on its own, during its plug-and-play setup. Of course, if it does something other than you expect, you could find your nominal C drive suddenly becoming your D drive. But if your system is set up appropriately, that shouldn't happen.

You once had to put only fast IDE devices on the primary IDE channel and all your slower IDE devices on the secondary channel, or else everything would run at the speed of the slowest device.

While improvements in the ATA and ATAPI specification have made that worry mainly of historical interest now, it is still good practice to put your fast devices on one channel and any very much slower ones on the other.

Furthermore, the newest version of the standard allows one to have up to four EIDE channels. No commercial motherboards support more than two, but you can add plug-in cards to support one or both of the others. Promise Technology's FloppyMAX card is an example of this. It is an ISA bus card that can be used, as one example, to put one or two LS-120 drives on the fourth ("quarternary") EIDE channel.

PCMCIA Becomes PC Card and Now We Have the Card Bus and Zoomed Video

Next, I will talk about the technical essentials you must know to understand what PC Cards are all about, and to anticipate what is likely to show up in this corner of our industry in the near future.

It All Began as Memory, and Not Just for PCs

Memory chips (RAM and ROM) are useful in many devices. We may focus on PCs, but the makers of those chips are well aware that automobiles, game machines, and other products also use up lots and lots of their output. Several of the major memory chip makers got together and decided to create a standard specification for how to package some small add-on memory modules for use in game machines and other applications. Because they were interested in memory cards and were an international group of companies (and because PCs are one of the major target uses of the products they met to discuss), it is perhaps not surprising that they named their group the *PC Memory Card International Association* (PCMCIA).

They settled on a form factor (size and shape) for these modules that is roughly that of a calling card (business card) and a third of a centimeter (which is about an eighth of an inch) thick. And they published a standards document (that is a lot fatter than the cards it describes) detailing many arcane details about these cards.

Broadening the Range of Uses

One especially important group to adopt this new standard module for memory add-ons was the laptop PC makers. They received this new form factor gratefully, because it fit well with their goal of making laptop computers ever smaller while still providing the amount of memory that their customers wanted.

Type I cards are the original size, about 85×54×3.3 mm (which in English units is about 3.3 inch×2.1 inch×0.13 inch). Type II cards are 5mm thick. Type III cards are 10.5mm thick. Allowing something for the space between cards, this works out to say that one can build a card bay that will hold one Type II or one Type I card, or a larger card bay that will hold one Type III, or two of any mix of Type I and Type II cards.

The thinnest cards (Type I) work well for RAM or ROM (or Flash RAM), and very clever manufacturers have even managed to put a modem or a network interface card into this size PC Card. The thickest (Type III) cards have been used for such relatively bulky items as a miniature hard disk. Figure 16.6 shows two different PC Cards. At the right you see the cards lying next to our sample laptop computer (a Dell Latitude Xpi CD M166ST). On the left you see them fully inserted into the PC Card bay in the laptop.

Figure 16.6.
Two PC Cards (Type I) are shown both inserted into the bay in a laptop computer and separately.

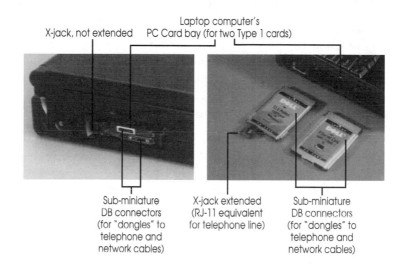

X-jack, not extended

Laptop computer's PC Card bay (for two Type 1 cards)

Sub-miniature DB connectors (for "dongles" to telephone and network cables)

X-jack extended (RJ-11 equivalent for telephone line)

Sub-miniature DB connectors (for "dongles" to telephone and network cables)

The modem card (on the bottom in the right picture and on the left in the left picture) has two alternative ways to connect it to a telephone line. The pop-out X-jack accepts a standard telephone modular plug (RJ-11). This card also has on its end a really tiny sub-miniature DB connector (like the standard serial port connector, only much, much smaller). This PC Card comes with a short cable that can plug into this DB connector on one end and has an RJ-11 jack on the other end. The 10/100Mbps Ethernet NIC card (on the top in the lower picture and on the right in the upper picture) has on its end a similar sub-miniature DB connector, and it comes with a short cable that plugs into it and that has an RJ-45 jack for a 10BaseT cable on the other end.

These are typical PC Cards, but many other models are available from multiple manufacturers, with different functionalities and different connector styles. Some of them include multiple functions (for example, a modem and a NIC) on a single PC Card.

Connecting PCMCIA Cards to a PC

To use these cards it is necessary to provide a bay in which they will fit, and appropriate additional connection circuitry and software. What the committee evolved was a standard that essentially specifies that the socket for a PCMCIA card shall present what amounts to an ISA slot in a smaller space. That lets those cards do anything, functionally, that an ISA card can do—provided one is clever enough to fit that functionality in such a tiny space.

Originally, whatever was on a PCMCIA Card was supposed to show up in the CPU's memory address space in a single 64kB region of upper memory (between 640kB and 1MB). Soon this restriction was relaxed, to accommodate the wide range of devices being put on these cards. And, ultimately, the PCMCIA Card jaw breaker of a name was shortened to PC Card.

What's a Card Bus and What Is Zoomed Video?

The original PC Card interface was, like the ISA bus, a 16-bit interface. As PCs evolved, it became clear that it would have been nice if the interface had been designed to support 32-bit data transfers. So the committee went back to the drawing board, and came up with just such a variation on the original plan. It named this new interface design the *Card Bus*, mainly to distinguish it from the earlier PC Card (just 16-bit) interface. Having twice the number of data lines meant, of course, that the new Card Bus interface could transfer data twice as fast as the original PC Card interface.

Even that wasn't fast enough for some, so the committee came up with one more innovation. This is a special new system bus that goes directly from a Card Bus slot to the frame buffer of the video subsystem. That lets the video accelerator use the memory (or other resources) on a PC Card without the delays of going through the slow ISA bus. The folks at PCMCIA gave this new bus the fancy name of *Zoomed Video Port*. (I suppose that this refers more to the zippy way data can move from PC Card to video frame buffer, rather than anything about actually "zooming" a video image, per se.)

The Card Information Structure (CIS), Card Services, Socket Services, and More

Every PC Card carries some information on it in a standard location and format to identify just what type of card it is and what it can do. This *metaformat* information is contained in something called the Card Information Structure (CIS).

The software support for PC Cards includes some additions to the operating system. At the lowest level these pieces are called the *Socket Services*. These deal directly with talking to the socket in which the PC Card sits. The logically next higher level operating system enhancements are called the *Card Services*. They include the software that responds to calls from application programs that need to use the capabilities offered by the PC Cards plugged into a given PC. Some varieties of Card and Socket Services software use the CIS information to decide how the PC Card should be connected to and serviced by the operating system.

Other parts of the evolving standard that describes PC Cards include the *Media Storage Formats* (describing how a Flash RAM card can be made to look as if it were a hard disk, among other things), the *PC Card ATA* (details on how to use the now-customary ATA protocol to access hard disks, and how to modify it for use with PC Cards), and the *eXecute in Place* (Xip) standard for running programs stored in ROM on a PC Card without having first to load them into the PC's main RAM.

This is a vital and fast developing area of PC technology. It is being pressed by developments in storage devices such as the Miniature Card and Smart Card. So we very likely will see yet more developments in this area in the very near future.

The PCI Bus

The VESA bus and PCI bus development projects were started simultaneously, over a period of many months. The makers of video cards pushed the former new standard. Intel pushed the PCI standard. At that time Intel was not only far-and-away the primary supplier of CPU chips for PCs, it also was becoming one of the major players in the market for motherboard chip sets. These are the very large-scale integrated circuits (VLSI) chips that include the memory address decoders, data buffers, and other interface logic circuits needed to interconnect all the different functional parts on a PC motherboard.

So, it was a natural extension of that role for Intel to develop an improved I/O bus and the chips necessary to support it. Intel labeled its design the Peripheral Component Interconnect (or PCI) bus, and it targeted it for more than just use in IBM-compatible PCs.

PCI Basics

Fundamentally, PCI is a rethinking of the way the parts of a PC are interconnected. Initially this only included those parts that were internal to the system unit, but in later versions of the PCI design it also encompasses ways of connecting to pieces that are outside that box.

PCI began as a means of interconnecting the chips that surround the CPU more efficiently, and to make those interconnections less dependent upon just which CPU chip one might be using. Later, as Intel explicitly added a PCI bus connector, this became a viable replacement for (and vast improvement upon) the ISA bus.

Because it was a fresh rethinking of the problems that the ISA bus had been designed to solve (and some that the ISA bus had evolved to solve), the PCI bus could be made as good as the technology of that time would enable, without having to carry along all the "baggage" that the ISA bus carries even to this day. However, when the PCI bus was defined and widely adopted, it quickly acquired new baggage of its own.

PCI Is an Efficient Bus

A PCI bus has only about half as many active lines as the ISA bus, yet those include twice as many data lines and can operate four times faster. To make the PCI bus work reliably at this speed, the connectors have a few more connections (124), with most of them being connected either to "ground" or one of the power supply voltages.

Also to enhance reliability, both address values and data are supplied with a parity bit. The PCI bus will notice if either addresses or data get messed up. If that happens, the bus controller will notify the devices involved in the transfer, but it leaves up to those devices just what type of error recovery procedure to take.

The PCI bus is designed to operate without termination (unlike a SCSI bus). This makes it easier for users because they don't have to think about termination issues. But it also limits the length of a PCI bus segment to just a few inches. (A somewhat longer bus can be achieved by using bridge chips between segments.)

PCI Supports Plug-and-Play Automation

Like the EISA and MCA buses and some of the later ISA cards, PCI supports automatic (plug-and-play) system configuration. Each board plugged into a PCI slot (and each device connected to the bus on the motherboard) must have a local configuration data storage unit. The system reads and writes the data stored in them as it configures the system.

The PCI Bus Is Called a Mezzanine Bus— What's That?

PCI was designed to replace the ISA bus, but it is in fact a little different. Like the ISA bus it routes signals between the CPU, various other chips on the motherboard, and cards that are plugged into its bus slot connectors. To do this it must buffer those signals and, in some cases, alter their timing.

But unlike the ISA bus, the PCI bus definition is not tied to any particular CPU chip or even to a chip family. It can be, and has been, used with many different CPUs in the Intel x86 family (and their clones), and also with PowerPC chips, and others. The advantage to having a bus (or as Intel prefers to call it, an interconnection standard) that is processor-independent is that now many manufacturers can build PCI cards and potentially have them be usable in a much wider variety of microcomputer-based systems.

PCI and Speed Issues

The PCI bus was designed to run at what was, at the time, the full motherboard system bus's speed and to support full motherboard system bus-width parallel data transfers. Given the year it was introduced, this means PCI is clocked at 33MHz and has 32 data lines. That makes this bus four times faster and twice as wide as the ISA bus it replaces. (Because some people will continue to use old, slow ISA cards, the PCI bus hasn't totally replaced it—yet. PC makers hope we will stop using those older, now fairly obsolete cards soon, so they can indeed stop putting ISA slots in PCs. But although the marketplace is quick to adopt new beneficial technologies, it is quite slow to discard totally the older, less capable but more familiar technologies.)

PCI was widely adopted very soon after its introduction. It was such a clearly better idea than its predecessors in the PC bus arena that all the PC makers wanted to include it in their new products, and their customers were happy to buy these new products. Many companies started making PCI cards to go into these new slot connectors. (Most of them were video cards, hard disk interface cards, and network interface cards because those are the only kinds of card for which the higher speed of PCI is really crucial.)

And after this happened, the standard got boxed in, unable to be improved still further without causing too much grief in the industry. So although PCI has gotten away from the baggage of ISA, it now has generated its own, new baggage that will limit how much and how quickly it can be further improved.

When motherboard speeds jumped to 66MHz, the PCI bus stayed at 33MHz, and when CPUs starting handling data 64 bits at a time, the PCI bus stayed with 32 bits. A lot of pressure is on the various players in this industry to make the PCI bus work faster despite the issues this raises about backward compatibility. And two different ways of making it capable of moving more data per second have been proposed. One is to double the number of data bits. The other is to double the bus clock speed. With sufficient care these things can be done, but it won't be easy.

Furthermore, because making the PCI bus wider (64 bits is the next logical width) costs makers of motherboards and PCI cards a fair amount in redesign, more printed wires to run, more complexity on the PCI cards, more pins on the motherboard chip set modules, and so on, it is probable that the first step will be to make the PCI bus run at double its present speed—however, it won't do even that for awhile yet.

Thus, although we can expect to see motherboard bus speeds jump from the present maximum of 66MHz to 100MHz, most industry analysts expect the PCI bus to stay around its present 33MHz. The width of the motherboard system bus may soon be doubled from 64 bits to 128 bits (because it only goes a few places) but the PCI bus will most likely stay at 32 bits.

A few manufacturers of motherboards run at 75MHz or 83MHz now, but those are not major players in the marketplace. Very likely they will try to trump Intel by going to something more than 100MHz, but they might find that hard to do because Intel has decided to keep a firm proprietary grip on its new "Slot 1" socket that it is using for its Pentium II and intend to use in future CPU designs. The older, "Socket 7" motherboards might simply be unable to go any faster than 83MHz reliably.

PCI As the "North-South" Axis In a PC

PCI is a very capable means of interconnecting different parts of a PC, both within the system unit and outside that box. Intel has taken advantage of this to separate the different functions of a motherboard chip set into two groups. It has integrated one group of functions into a chip that it calls the *Northbridge* chip. The other group of functions has been integrated (both by Intel and some of its competitors) into what it calls a *Southbridge* chip. The connection between the two chips is made using PCI. This (and a lot more) is shown in Figure 16.7.

Figure 16.7.
The near-term future of the PC architecture.

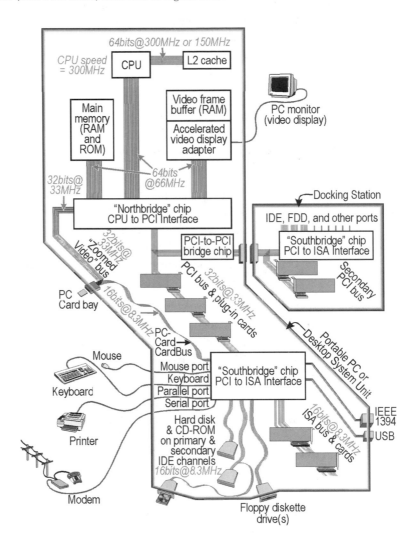

Figure 16.7 is complex. It summarizes a lot of what I have been explaining up to now and adds this latest feature of the Northbridge and Southbridge chips. Careful study of this figure will give you a deeper understanding of the architecture that is developing for modern PCs.

I have shown here a hypothetical, state-of-the-art PC (either a desktop or a laptop computer) connected to a "docking station." The notion is that when the docking station is disconnected, the PC is a perfectly usable machine, but when it is "docked," the PC becomes potentially much more powerful. I'll give you a guided tour to all the things the figure contains, starting with a description of the Northbridge chip and of a newest way to hook up the video subsystem to the CPU.

The Northbridge Chip

The CPU in all modern PCs connects to main memory via a faster and wider data path than it uses to connect to the PCI bus. This faster bus is what we term the *system* or *host* bus. The CPU is not capable of connecting directly to the memory modules. Some buffers and some memory address decoders are needed, at the least. And likewise, it cannot connect directly to the wires in the PCI bus. (All the signals needed to communicate with any of the other parts of a PC are included in those that go to the PCI bus, so Intel decided to let all those other parts simply attach to the PCI bus rather than to the Northbridge chip directly.)

The needed interface electronics to do these tasks (sometimes called a part of the *motherboard glue logic*) has been integrated into one very large integrated circuit chip (nearly as complex as the CPU). Intel calls this chip the Northbridge chip. And while they were at it, they also threw in support for another special-purpose, very high-speed data bus. They called this the Advanced Graphics Port.

> **Note:** What I am describing here is essentially Intel's latest design for a PC motherboard chip set. There are other makers of motherboard chip sets, and no doubt they will make some that are comparable to the Intel offerings. And Intel offers many different chip sets, optimized for different uses. In this discussion, though, I am going to gloss over those differences and describe a hypothetical chip set that includes all the latest and greatest features—even though there might never be any single chip set that does all of these things.

AGP: The Side Trip to Better Video

The Advanced Graphics Bus (AGP) is a new bus that operates at the full system (host) bus speed and width (currently a maximum of 32 bits in parallel, clocked at 66MHz) and it connects from the Northbridge chip to the video accelerator. The video accelerator could be mounted on the motherboard (as I have suggested it is in Figure 16.7), or it could be mounted on a plug-in card to go into a special AGP connector.

The video accelerator in this design has a local pool of memory that only it can access, in addition to the video frame buffer which still is logically located at a range of main memory addresses. In addition, it can access main memory at high speed via the AGP bus, Northbridge chip, and main memory bus. The video accelerator can talk to its local memory on as wide a bus as the manufacturer of the video card wishes to use (and many of the high-end PC video cards today do use an up to 128-bit wide private bus on the video card for just this purpose), but all transfers over the AGP will be limited to 32 bits in parallel for now.

The L2 Bus: The Side Trip to Better CPU Performance

Figure 16.7 shows another way in which PCs can be made faster. This is by the use of a private bus from the CPU to the Level 2 cache memory. This is already a feature of the Pentium Pro and Pentium II CPU chips. In the Pentium Pro, that private L2 cache runs at the full clock speed of the CPU chip. In the Pentium II it runs at only half the CPU clock speed. In either case, it is running a lot faster than the main system bus, the AGP bus, or the main memory bus. (I have shown in Figure 16.7 a CPU whose clock speed is 233MHz. There are already faster Pentium II chips, but so far there aren't any faster Pentium Pros.)

Not only does this private L2 bus run faster than the main bus from CPU to the Northbridge chip, it also runs independently of that bus. This means that different data can be transferred over each bus at the same time. So the CPU can be fetching information from the L2 cache while the cache controller is updating main memory at some other location.

There Can Be More Than One PCI Bus

Figure 16.7 also shows a configuration with more than one PCI bus. The main PCI bus is shown as connecting to the Northbridge chip and has three PCI cards shown plugged into slot connectors on that bus. At the other end of that bus is the Southbridge chip, which I will discuss in a moment.

Also notice that the PCI bus has a branch going off to the right. This branch goes through a "PCI-to-PCI bridge chip" to a special connector designed for use with a docking port. The docking port has a mating connector, and it carries the main PCI bus into the docking port a short way. There it goes two ways: One way enters another Southbridge chip; the other supports more PCI slot connectors.

The Southbridge

At the "south" end of the PCI bus is a Southbridge chip. This chip contains all the needed interface logic to convey the signals from the PCI bus to the much slower ISA bus and other interfaces that a PC may have. The ISA bus shown here has just a couple of slots, partly because so many of the things that once where done with plug-in ISA cards are now done with dedicated ports or with PCI cards.

The floppy diskette drives connect to the Southbridge chip. That chip also supports two Enhanced IDE channels (primary and secondary) with up to two EIDE devices on each one. And it has a separate bus for keyboard, a bus mouse, a standard (possibly ECP or EPP) parallel port, and one or more standard serial ports. And it can have yet another bus interface for some Universal Serial Bus (USB) connectors as well as some IEEE 1394 (Firewire) connectors. Finally, the Southbridge chip will probably have an interface for a PC Card bay, in this case shown as a Card Bus (32-bit) interface with a Zoomed Video bus connecting directly to the video subsystem.

The ISA, IDE, and PC Card interfaces run at 8.33 MHz (exactly one-quarter of the PCI bus rate). The other ports run at some slower speed.

What We Gain From Intel's North-South Division

By establishing a standard way to divide the electronics needed in a PC between what it calls the Northbridge and the Southbridge, Intel has made it possible to do many interesting things. One is, as shown in Figure 16.7, to have a docking station to which a (perhaps portable) PC could be connected. That docking station has its own set of peripheral devices that can augment the functionality contained in the PC. Another possibility is that the Southbridge chip can be made by a different vendor than the Northbridge chip. As long as each properly interfaces to a PCI bus, they will work together flawlessly.

Finally, by having multiple Southbridge chips in a PC (and only one Northbridge chip), it would be possible to have multiple pointing devices, each supported by its own port, and multiple other ports as well. Of course, supporting all that hardware in one PC could be a software nightmare. But I won't get into that just now.

The Future of PC-to-Peripheral Interconnections

There have been several major trends in the PC world in the past decade, and if they keep on going as they have been, there will be a collision between them. The rest of this chapter is about what folks who've noticed this are doing to avoid that collision.

Learning From the Past

Certainly the major story about PCs in the past decade has been how very rapidly they have become more powerful, more complex, and less costly for what they do. One obvious consequence of this is that as these little boxes have become more capable and more affordable, more and more people want to have them. That is why PCs are now a mass-market item. And it is very much in the interests of all of us in this industry for PCs to become even more of a mass-market commodity, used by even more people for more of what they do.

But a problem is brewing. Right now PCs sport close to a dozen special-purpose I/O interfaces. Every one is different from all the rest. And you must have most, if not all of them on your PC to hook up all the pieces of hardware you want to have connected to your PC.

It appears that it is going to get worse before it gets better. We are beginning to see the much-touted "convergence" of PCs with telephones and other "commodity appliances" such as VCRs, televisions, radios, washing machines, ovens, toasters—you name it. And probably in the not-too-distant future, you will be able to buy one that is ready to be controlled by your PC or to report to your PC. We can't go on adding special-purpose interfaces for each and every one of these gadgets, nor can we hook them all up to the I/O interfaces we have today. Something radically different is needed.

We must make PCs simpler: They must be made simpler to buy, simpler to set up and use, simpler to maintain, and simpler to upgrade. And their cost must be reduced as far as possible. Only then can they reach their true potential as ubiquitous computing devices, helping out in nearly every area of daily life.

The New Direction for PC Input and Output

The solution, some very clever people have decided, is to replace all the present-day special-purpose I/O interfaces with just one or two truly general-purpose ones. Well, that is one or two *types* of truly general-purpose interfaces. You might need more than one of a given type to get enough data transfer bandwidth for all your needs.

These interfaces must be simple to set up and dirt cheap. This argues for an interface that uses a small, simple, and inexpensive connector with a thin, highly flexible cable. You'd like to be able simply to plug in a gadget and have your PC notice it, recognize it, and respond appropriately. No powering down the PC. No opening up the box. No setting jumpers, switches, or even software options to select an IRQ level, a DMA channel, an I/O port address, or a memory address. No fussing with terminators.

But is such a dream interface workable? Could it possibly be fast enough if it were so simple and easy to use? Surprisingly, the answer seems to be "yes"—or at least that is the message we are hearing from the development laboratories and the meeting rooms of some of our industry standards committees. We will need two types of interface, but only two. And they will be just as simple and elegant as I have described.

The Wonderful, New, High-Speed Serial Buses (USB and IEEE 1394)

The groundwork for these developments was laid some time ago. As I told you earlier in this chapter, the SCSI bus has many of the properties we want. The PCI bus has some others. Combining the best of each and using what they've learned, engineers have come up with some better-than-ever options. These are new developments, just now coming into the marketplace.

One is the *Universal Serial Bus* (USB). The other is a similar standard, but optimized for faster data transfers, currently called by its standard committee's name, *IEEE 1394*. (Apple Computer helped develop this latter standard and they gave it the much more mellifluous name "Firewire," but they have trademarked that name and so far are not allowing anyone else to use it.)

They Have More in Common Than Not

There are probably more ways in which these two standards resemble one another than there are differences. So I'll first describe those common features, then I'll point out some of the differences.

First, both are serial standards. That is, they send data over a link just one bit at a time. That sounds slow, until you realize that at the very slowest, $1^1/_2$ million bits move over the link every second. At the fastest, more than a thousand million bits will pass each second. Even though it takes approximately 10 of those bits to send each byte, these are some pretty seriously impressive data transfer rates.

Next, each bus can accept a whole flock of different peripheral devices ranging from a keyboard, a mouse, a "smart" loudspeaker, or a "smart" microphone, all the way up to a video camera, DVD player, or a hard disk. In fact, you can hook up all those things at once.

Here is where we first come to a difference between these buses. The USB is specifically designed for low- and medium-speed peripherals. A keyboard, for example, must send very few bits per second to the PC and it receives even fewer of them back. That is a typical low-speed device. A *smart* loudspeaker (and by that I mean a device that can receive digital data and convert it into sounds) will need to receive a lot more bits per second. But a few hundred thousand would be enough. That is a typical medium-speed peripheral device.

The USB can handle these devices in two modes. In low-speed mode, it enables communication at a rate of 1.5Mbps ($1^1/_2$ million bits per second). At medium speed it goes eight times as fast, 12Mbps. Converting those into bytes per second you come up with something like 150–200kBps (which is around the top speed of a standard serial port) up to a little more than 1MBps (close to the maximum speed of an EPP parallel port).

In contrast, an IEEE 1394 connection is meant for high-speed, serious capacity data transfer work. The starting speed for this bus is around eight times faster than the top speed of a USB bus. And projected developments (still in the laboratory, but likely to reach the desktop in the next few years) will stretch up past the speed of the fastest SCSI bus.

Back to something these buses have in common: They handle bandwidth intelligently. That is, they will let any device have as much data transfer capacity as it can use—up to a point. But they will reserve enough of their overall capacity to let them also service the other devices on the bus. A device, like a video camera, that simply *must* have all its data passed down the bus because it has nowhere to store them, can request and be assured of receiving enough data transfer capacity to keep the frames of the image flowing down the wire as they are taken. Other devices that can afford to wait might be forced to do so, but their data transfer needs will ultimately be accommodated, so long as the total bandwidth (bits per second capacity) of the bus is sufficient.

Transfers like those needed for a video camera are called *isochronous*, meaning that uniform amounts of data must be transferred every second, and that fixed amounts of that data must be transferred in chunks on a regular schedule. In this type of data transfer late data is useless, and if there is some error, there is no point in trying to resend the data because then it would be late (and thus of no value).

The other kind of data transfer these buses support is called *asynchronous*. This type of transfer emphasizes reliability. The data *will* get through—eventually, and retries are not only permissible, they are mandated if errors occur. The host PC and the software running in it has the job of managing the available bandwidth and parceling it out to all the requesting devices, keeping a good balance between the needs of all. Only when there simply isn't enough total bandwidth will some problem occur, and then some device must be denied its request for bandwidth. (In that case the PC might direct you to unplug that device and plug it into another bus that has some available bandwidth.)

Both USB and IEEE 1394 are capable of supporting multiple devices because each of them assigns an address to each device. These addresses function very much like SCSI IDs, but with the very important difference that they aren't set by hardware switches on the devices, but rather are assigned by the host when the device is plugged into the bus.

Also, both buses enable devices to talk to one another, without having to involve the host in the conversation. That is, after the host has assigned addresses to everyone on the cable, any device can ask the host about who else is on the cable, and subsequently can address messages directly to a desired target device. The host might be carrying on a separate conversation at the same time with some other device. (In detailed fact, the packets of data are interleaved. Only one voltage can be on a wire at a single instant. But it will appear to all the devices as if the conversations are simultaneous.)

The commands supported on these buses are modeled after those used in the SCSI-3 standard. This is explicitly so for IEEE 1394, and certainly the lessons learned in the SCSI development have influenced how USB's commands work.

Furthermore, both buses allow power to travel alongside data. Each cable design (and USB and IEEE 1394 use different cables) includes power wires separate from the data wires. That allows devices such as a keyboard or mouse that need only a little bit of power to get it from the data cable, just as they do in present-day PCs. Any device that needs massive amounts of power (for example, a big loudspeaker) must have a local power supply, but again this is no different from our present situation.

With both USB and IEEE 1394 a device may serve as a link to other devices. The details differ some, but in essence, it will be possible to plug in some devices to the PC and then plug other devices into the ones you connected first. In this way you can extend the cable reach for either bus more-or-less as far as you are likely to want to extend it. (Not surprisingly, the faster IEEE 1394 bus is limited to shorter distances than the slower USB bus—especially if the IEEE 1394 bus is running at one of its higher data rates.)

The resulting chain of cables may branch at some devices and just be extended at others. But logically the system will treat all the devices on the chain, no matter which branch they may be on, as equals. It is as if they were all connected in series, or as if they all were connected directly at the PC host.

OK, You've Convinced Me; Now How Do I Get Them?

Here we come to one more place where USB and IEEE 1394 are different. USB is a completed standard. That is not to say it won't be extended and modified, but an adopted standard is out there for manufacturers to use. And some PC makers have already started shipping PCs with USB ports in them. Our sample desktop system is one such system.

The state of IEEE 1394 is a bit more confusing. The IEEE organization has approved a version of this standard (1394-1995) and is considering several extensions to it (called things like P1394.1, P1394.2, P1394A, and P1394B). The reason for these different, in effect competing, "standards" is that different groups of would-be users of this bus have different needs. Hard disk vendors want one thing, video camera makers are concerned with something else, and each group wants the standard "bent" toward their concerns.

But we are clearly well on the way to having a real, usable 1394 standard. With all the advantages it offers, we can expect to see at least one of the competing versions of IEEE 1394 be approved and compliant hardware be built and sold. Just not right away.

There *Will* Be More I/O Bus Standards

This has been a long and involved story covering many different I/O standards. It ended with what appears to be a new, and more wonderfully simple age that is dawning. Is this story then about to end? No way.

As experience is gained with USB and IEEE 1394 we can expect those standards to go through additional generations. And as PCs move further into the convergence with all the other electronics in your life, new needs are likely to pop up. Some of those might necessitate the devising of wholly new standards. Finally, some of the old war horses aren't likely to die any time soon. We will have EIDE interfaces inside our PCs for quite some time to come. Parallel cable SCSI buses might last even longer. USB and IEEE 1394 aren't *that* much better than everything that went before.

So you can rest assured that the I/O bus standards committees will have plenty of work to do for a very long time to come. And you'll just have to stay tuned, if you want to know how all those future buses will function. But the basics I have given you here should stand you in very good stead as you attempt to understand whatever innovations the future may bring.

17

Understanding
PC Operating
Systems

Peter Norton®

The topics covered in this chapter are a substantial departure from those in the other chapters in this part of the book. Those emphasized hardware. This one is all about software. But it's not about all kinds of PC software, just one very special kind that all of us use every day.

In fact, this chapter is about the most popular computer program ever created—and one that most of its users normally don't even think about as a software program—and about some alternatives to that program. I am referring here to DOS. This is the operating system that is used most or all of the time in nearly all PCs ever made.

If your PC is turned on right now, then it probably is running DOS, and you might not even know it. Furthermore, DOS is a software program of great complexity and power.

Most people who use PCs think of the software they use in terms of the application programs: Word, Excel, or Netscape Navigator. But you couldn't run any of those programs unless you first ran the program that creates the environment in which they are designed to operate. For the three programs I just mentioned that is some version of Windows. And Windows cannot run unless DOS is loaded first. (Yes, that is true even if you are running Windows 95, despite Microsoft's many public comments to the contrary.)

You might be running some other PC operating system. If so, you probably know it. Popular choices include OS/2, Windows NT, and Linux or some other version of UNIX. I'll discuss these options in the section of this chapter near the end titled, "Understanding Your Choices for Your PC's Operating System." But my initial statement is still true: DOS clearly is far and away the world champion best-selling computer program of all time.

What Is an Operating System, and Why Do I Need One?

For something that has been purchased in more copies than any other program, DOS is very much misunderstood. It is a computer operating system. But that sentence doesn't mean a lot to many people. What is a computer operating system and why must you have one? Those are important questions with non-obvious answers. I will make the answers to those questions clear.

The formal definition of a computer operating system is something that "manages and schedules the resources" of the computer. Unless you are different from most people I have talked to, reading that doesn't help increase your understanding very much at all.

Let me put it this way: Think of your computer as a business, and you are the owner. You have some tasks you want accomplished. You hire workers who have specialized skills to do some of those tasks, but they need a good work environment. When they pick up the phones on their desks, they had better be connected to dial tones. When they want some supplies, somebody had better have them in stock and be prepared to deliver them. In an office, these tasks are done by the office manager and sometimes a whole staff of helpers. That is very much like what DOS (or any other computer operating system) is. It is a manager of the environment in which other programs work, and it also is a bunch of grunt laborers ready to do particular subtasks whenever they are directed to do them.

How You Can Avoid Having an OS—And Why That Is a Bad Idea

It is perfectly possible to avoid having an operating system for your PC, in the sense of a separate program you run first before you run your application programs. But doing that would be a very bad idea.

The way to avoid having a separate OS is simply to build into each application program all the instruction code necessary to accomplish all the things an operating system normally does. That is, if you are going to be doing some word processing, your word processor program also would have in it the necessary detailed instructions to accomplish reading characters from the keyboard (and knowing when to do so), writing them to the video display, and accessing the disk drives to store your work in files and manage those files appropriately.

One reason doing this is a terrible idea is that it requires the authors of all the application programs to know intimately how your particular PC's hardware works and is configured. That's really not their jobs. They must know how to write the word processor (or other application) and shouldn't be bothered with the nitty-gritty details of making a PC work.

The second reason this is a terrible idea is that each application would be very much larger than it now is, because each one would have to incorporate much of the same set of instructions for operating the PC hardware. Putting those common instructions into a separate program you run first (and that keeps on running "underneath" your application programs) is a much better plan.

Finally, if you did put all that operating stuff into each application, the only way you could shift from one task to another would be to reboot your PC with a new boot disk containing the next application you wanted to run. Major awkwardness! And what about multitasking? Under this scenario, the only answer would have to be "forgetaboutit."

No, this is not a viable solution. There are just too many compelling reasons to have and use an operating system. And that is why DOS has sold so very well.

What Is DOS? Hasn't It Gone Bye-Bye?

The name *DOS* stands for Disk Operating System. This means that DOS is an operating system that is particularly concerned with how to deal with disk drives.

Back in Chapter 5, "How to Get Your PC to Understand You," I told you that the motherboard BIOS ROM contained some small programs to activate the normal PC hardware pieces. Those mostly are interrupt service routines to deal with the keyboard, the original PC video display options, the floppy diskette drive(s), and some elemental actions on the hard disk drive(s). DOS uses all these programs. But it also does much more. (If you are unclear about what an "interrupt service routine" is, please go back and review Chapter 8, "How Your PC 'Thinks.'")

DOS is mainly concerned with how the disk drives are used at a higher logical level. DOS worries about files and how you store and access them. The BIOS routines, by contrast, deal only with disk information storage in terms of sectors of data at some absolute physical address (specified by a head number, cylinder number, and sector number within the single track at that head and cylinder location).

Furthermore, DOS is a full operating system, and as such it is concerned with much more than just disk management. It has the job of allocating memory (RAM), scheduling tasks, and resolving competing demands for the PC's other resources. Thus, you use DOS to launch programs, which use DOS to access various features of your PC. DOS was originally intended to be a single-user, singletasking operating system, but it has been stretched to the point where it sometimes can (and must) function as if it were a true multitasking system. This is especially so when it is augmented by the addition of Microsoft Windows. (I discuss this combination more fully in the section, "Dressing Up DOS: What Microsoft's Windows Adds to the Game," later in this chapter.)

How Does DOS Work?

DOS provides an environment for the user and for other programs. Its job is to keep track of what is using which portions of memory, which spaces on the disk drives, and so on. It also has the job of coordinating the work of all those lower-level programs that respond to interrupts. These include the ones in the motherboard BIOS ROM, ones that come bundled with DOS, and ones that are added to your system by various "device driver" or "TSR" programs.

What Are the Essential Pieces of DOS?

DOS as a product comes on many disks or on a CD-ROM. It contains a huge number of modules, each in its own file. But this collection is a great deal more than what I would consider the essence of DOS. The essence of DOS is a "kernel" and a "command processor." All the rest of DOS, the product, is a collection of useful utility programs called, collectively, the DOS "external commands."

The DOS Kernel

The *kernel* means the fundamental, central part of the operating system. (Think of a nut, like a walnut or cashew, that has a shell on the outside and a kernel in the center.) For DOS this kernel consists of two or—in recent versions if you are using OS-level (on-the-fly) data compression—three components, each of which comes in its own file on the DOS disks.

The filenames for these components vary with the brand of DOS you buy. Most clone computers come with Microsoft's MS-DOS installed on them. IBM's PC comes with its version, called PC DOS. And a few other companies make so-called third-party versions of DOS. The most visible of these used to be Digital Research's DR-DOS, which later was purchased by Novell and is still sold as Novell DOS.

Microsoft's names for the kernel files are IO.SYS, MSDOS.SYS, and DBLSPACE.BIN or DRVSPACE.BIN. These are all files with the file attributes of "hidden," "system," and "read-only." (Please do not confuse these DOS files with the Windows 95 files of the same names. Those are different, though IO.SYS in Windows 95 contains most of the content of both the files IO.SYS and MSDOS.SYS in MS-DOS version 6.22. The Windows 95 MSDOS.SYS file is a totally different animal, more akin to a CONFIG.SYS file than to any of these kernel files.)

IBM's names for the files corresponding to Microsoft's IO.SYS and MSDOS.SYS are IBMBIO.COM and IBMDOS.COM. Its on-the-fly data compression in PC DOS version 7 is provided by a different version of DBLSPACE.BIN created by Stac Electronics.

The DOS Command Processor

The only visible (not hidden) file on a DOS disk that qualifies for the description "an essential part of DOS" is the command processor. This is the file called COMMAND.COM (in virtually all versions of DOS).

I mentioned previously that you can think of the kernel of DOS as being like the kernel of a nut, namely the portion at the core that is hidden from view but which carries most of the value of the nut. Following this analogy, the command processor often is referred to as the "shell" program for the operating system. (This usage is universal in references to UNIX, and it is not uncommon in discussions of DOS written for programmers.)

What the Essential Parts of DOS Do

The kernel is, as its name suggests, at the core of the operating system, and as such it is involved in nearly everything DOS does and much of what is done by other programs running in your PC "on top of DOS." The kernel presents a uniform "application program interface" (API) by which other programs can ask it for services. And it supports the rest of the programs (including other parts of DOS) in doing their jobs.

Generally, a program that wants some help from DOS will cause a *software interrupt*. This causes the CPU to stop what it is doing within that program and go instead to an external program called an interrupt service routine (ISR). In the case I am describing here, that ISR program will be somewhere within DOS. That program does whatever it was designed to do, and then it returns from the interrupt. At that point the CPU resumes executing the instructions in the original program. All of this happens very rapidly, and normally it does so totally without the PC user's awareness.

The command processor is not only the only essential part that is contained in a visible disk file, it also is the most visible portion of DOS when you are running it. This program presents the DOS command prompt, and it accepts and processes commands for you.

The command processor also includes several useful built-in command functions. These include the DIR command to display a directory listing, the VER command to report the DOS version, and several others, referred to collectively as "the DOS internal commands." But most of what you know as DOS commands, such as FORMAT and FDISK, are not among them. Those are the external DOS commands, which are just a bunch of useful utility programs that were bundled with DOS.

What Does DOS Do for Me?

DOS works for you in several different ways. Some of these are apparent to you; others are fully hidden from you. If you run DOS programs from a DOS command prompt, you will see more of what DOS does for you than if you run Windows on top of DOS and then launch all your programs from within Windows. But even then, DOS is working on your behalf behind the scene.

What COMMAND.COM Does for You

Do you ever do any work at a DOS prompt (which often looks something like the following line)?

```
C:\>
```

If so, then you are using DOS directly to control what your PC does. You type a command and press the Enter key; you expect your PC to do what you just told it to do.

It sounds simple, doesn't it? Let me assure you, it is not nearly as simple as it appears. (If you run programs by clicking on their names or icons in Windows, you are causing a very similar chain of events, with a few differences that I will go into more later on.)

The first thing for which the DOS component called the command processor (COMMAND.COM) is responsible is presenting you with a DOS command prompt and then watching the keyboard and noticing every keystroke you type. As you type each one, COMMAND.COM takes that keystroke, converts it to the appropriate ASCII character, and sends that character to the screen for display. If it didn't do this, you'd never see what you typed show up there. COMMAND.COM also keeps track in an internal buffer of all the keystrokes you have pressed so far in the current command (and, in a separate buffer, of the last command you issued).

If you type a backspace, COMMAND.COM has a more complex job to do. First, it must send a backspace to the screen. That moves the cursor back one space (unless it is already back as far as it can go). Then COMMAND.COM sends a space character to wipe out the character that was at that position on the screen. As is the case with any other character it "prints" on the screen, this moves the cursor forward one space. Then COMMAND.COM sends a second backspace to the screen to move the cursor back again. Finally, it must adjust back one space the pointer in its internal buffer that tells it where to store the next character you type.

If you press one of the function keys F1 through F6, COMMAND.COM must take some other special actions. Mostly these involve copying one or more characters from the last command buffer into the
current command buffer and putting them on the screen.

But all of this activity's complexity pales by comparison to what COMMAND.COM must do when you press
the Enter key. Now it must switch roles from assisting you in typing a command to trying to figure
out what your command means, and then doing that job.

First COMMAND.COM must *parse* your command line. Parse is a fancy word that means to figure out where
the "words" are that make up this "sentence." Any valid DOS command must begin with a verb (an
action word), and it then can go on to add an object or a subject plus an object or some qualifying
adjectives or adverbs.

COMMAND.COM is mainly concerned with finding out what the verb is, and it assumes that will be the
first "word" on the command line. After it has found the verb, it checks this word against its list of
DOS internal commands. If there is a match, COMMAND.COM launches the mini-program of that name
that it contains as a part of itself, and as a part of that process it sends the rest of the command line
to that program. This is, for example, how the program that does the work of the DIR command gets
to run and do its job.

If the verb doesn't match any of the entries in COMMAND.COM's list of internal DOS commands, then it
will assume that this verb is the name of a program that you want to run. It now turns to the task of
finding that program.

COMMAND.COM will look first for that program in what is referred to as the *current directory* on the current disk drive. (DOS, in a portion of the kernel, maintains a pointer to the current disk drive and
another pointer to the current directory on that disk drive. What Windows 95 calls a "folder" is the
same as what DOS calls a directory.)

COMMAND.COM will assume that the name specified by the verb is to be followed by .COM, .EXE, or .BAT
unless it already has an explicit extension attached to it. And so it looks for files with the verb name
as the filename and with one of these three extensions in the current directory.

If it finds such a file, it opens the file and reads it into memory. If it is a COM file, the contents of
the file are simply copied into a region of RAM. If it is an EXE file, just the first 256 bytes of the file
are read into memory initially. COMMAND.COM examines the contents of that "EXE header" to determine where in memory to put which portions of the rest of that file's contents. Finally, if the file is
a BAT file, COMMAND.COM reads in just one line of that file at a time, each time treating that line as if
it were typed at a new DOS command prompt.

When COMMAND.COM loads a COM or EXE program into memory, it also puts the remainder of the
command line you typed (or that it found in a batch file) into a small block of memory it provides
for the program's use located just below the program in memory (RAM). Then it passes control of
the PC to that program.

After that program is finished, it will turn control of the PC back to COMMAND.COM, which then normally asks DOS to deallocate the memory that program was using (unless that program asks for some of its memory not to be deallocated, as device drivers and TSR programs do). After it has done this, COMMAND.COM presents another DOS command prompt and goes back into the mode in which it helps you compose the next command.

If COMMAND.COM doesn't find a matching file in the current directory (with an appropriate filename extension), it must look elsewhere. To do this, COMMAND.COM refers to a region of memory called the DOS environment and from that region reads an ASCII character string called the *PATH*. This is a collection of locations on your PC's disk drives that are specified in terms of disk volume letters and subdirectory names separated by semicolons. It parses this path statement into its elements. For each of those locations, COMMAND.COM repeats the search it performed in the current directory until it finds a program to run, or until it runs out of places to look. In the latter case it will put up the message Bad command or file name and again present you with a new DOS command prompt.

Other Things DOS Does for You

Many of the things I just described as actions COMMAND.COM takes involve it asking the underlying kernel portions of DOS to do some task. For example, the kernel becomes involved in allocating memory regions into which a program can be loaded. DOS also must be called upon to access the files that contain the programs COMMAND.COM loads, and before that, DOS kernel services are used to get the directory contents so COMMAND.COM can figure out what program to load.

What Does DOS Do for My Programs?

I have given you a summary of the things DOS does for you, the PC user, more or less directly. But DOS is much more important to you than even that list suggests. This is because virtually every program you run will call upon DOS for the help it needs to do whatever it was designed to do.

In particular, every program that must use some of the memory in your computer will ask DOS for it. (As I explained in Chapter 11, "Bigger Is Better in Ballrooms and in a PC's Memory," DOS allocates all the memory blocks in the first 640KB and often in upper memory as well. I also pointed out that other memory managers can be called upon to allocate memory in the upper memory region—640KB to 1MB—or beyond that in the High Memory Area or Extended Memory.)

Likewise, if an application program must access a data file, it must have DOS help it find the file and then either open the file and read the contents of it or put new or additional contents into it. And there are a whole bunch of other things that DOS can do for a program, ranging from the relatively trivial, such as telling it the time of day or the date, to fairly complex actions, such as launching another program and then returning control to the original program after that program has completed its work.

Does DOS Have a Future?

You might be getting the idea that DOS is still a pretty essential part of our PC landscape. That is certainly correct today. But will it be true tomorrow?

Microsoft has worked diligently to make people believe that DOS is dead. Dead and gone forever, and aren't we all glad of that? But Microsoft is being most disingenuous.

Trade reports indicate that a sizable majority of PC users today run DOS, some with Windows 3.x on top of it. A very substantial minority are running Windows 95. And only tiny minorities run Windows NT, OS/2, Linux, or some other PC operating system. Those same reports indicate that in another year or two, probably Windows 95 (and Windows 98) will have gained the upper hand, with DOS and Windows 3.x moving into the substantial minority position.

But please realize that Windows 95 (and 98) are based firmly on DOS. Microsoft really had little choice in the matter if it was going to maintain full backward compatibility with the installed base of DOS and Windows 3.x programs—and that backward compatibility was *the* key focus in the development of Windows 95 and Windows 98.

So I think that some version of DOS will be with us for quite a few years. Indeed, I expect that literally millions of PCs will be running DOS alone, or DOS plus Windows 3.x, well into the next century. (Just not quite as many millions as will be running something else by then.)

Dressing Up DOS: What Microsoft's Windows Adds to the Game

Windows is simply DOS in a dress. How's that for a catchy phrase that lets you in on what Microsoft has tried so hard to hide?

Originally, Windows was designed and marketed as an add-on "operating environment." That phrase was supposed to clarify its relationship to the underlying operating system. Windows used DOS to manage most of the resources in the machine; the only job for Windows was to manage the appearance that the user saw and the appearance that Windows applications "saw." Users got a graphical user interface (GUI); programs got a new and much richer collection of application program interface (API) calls they could issue to ask Windows, or DOS, to do something for them.

Each new version of Windows pushed the boundary between it and DOS down a little, as Windows took over more of the tasks that DOS had handled for the previous versions. With Windows 95 many—perhaps even most—of the things that DOS once did are now done with 32-bit (protected mode) modules within Windows 95. But under it all there still is good old DOS. And at times, even the latest version of Windows must go all the way back to real mode and back to DOS, or even to the motherboard BIOS, to do some tasks.

Variations on Windows Now in Common Use

Windows is not a singular thing. Microsoft has brought out many versions of it, and even some third-party versions have achieved a significant market share. The earliest versions of Microsoft Windows are only of historical interest at this point. They were very limited functionally, and they have been rendered almost totally obsolete by the later versions.

So for this book I shall just recap briefly the different versions of Windows that are still being used in significant quantities on PCs. (If you haven't yet upgraded to Windows 3.x or a later version, please do so as soon as you can. You won't be sorry you did.)

Windows 3.0, 3.1, and 3.11

By the time Microsoft released Windows 3.0, most observers agreed that it had finally gotten that program just about right. It finally worked the way we all had been told it would—at least most of the time.

Windows offered users two big advantages over plain old DOS. One was that it allowed users to run Windows-specific application programs, and soon quite a few very good programs were Windows-specific. The other was that it allowed users to run multiple programs at once, shifting easily among them. This was true not only of Windows-specific applications, but also of most DOS applications. Windows managed the extended memory on a PC and thus augmented what DOS alone was able to do. And as PCs became more and more powerful and had more and more RAM added to them, this was something we desperately needed.

Windows 3.1 and the final version of Windows before Windows 95—3.11—just added a few relatively small additions to the functionality of 3.0. The notorious Unexplained Application Error (UAE) of Windows 3.0 had become the equally frustrating General Protection Fault (GPF). Technically they are slightly different, and with GPFs it is possible (sometimes) to recover more or less gracefully, whereas a UAE almost always meant it was time to reboot your PC. But probably the most significant single change these versions brought is that, beginning with version 3.1, they finally did away with Real Mode Windows altogether. Which was just as well, because that had always been a very crippled version of Windows, included only to let Microsoft make the claim that Windows could run (albeit only in this crippled "real mode") on even a mere 8086-based, original PC.

Windows for Workgroups 3.1 and 3.11

At about the same time Windows 3.1 was being readied for market, Microsoft came out with a variation on that product it called Windows for Workgroups, version 3.1. This was a significantly different product than ordinary Windows. Mostly the difference lay in the fact that Windows now had the capability to connect multiple PCs via a network, with all the needed network operating software (NOS) having been built into Windows for Workgroups. The particular kind of networking this program supported natively is what we term peer-to-peer networking, but it also could be used on a workstation that was hooked to a network running some other network programs, including Novell's Netware, which is a server-based network. (I'll tell you more about the different kinds of networks in Chapter 25, "The PC Reaches Out, Part Two: Through the NIC Node.")

The purpose of this network support was simply to allow users of any PC in the network to choose to share some or all of their disk directories and any printers that were attached to their PCs. Then other users on the network could access those files and printers remotely. This is basic networking, but it certainly filled most of the needs for a simple network in many small workgroups.

Another innovation in this version was support for a concept Microsoft called *Local Reboot*. This meant that Windows now would trap the "three-fingered-salute" (the Ctrl+Alt+Del key combination) that was previously used only to reboot a PC when it got hopelessly stuck. Windows then would present the user with a dialog box allowing the user to choose whether to reboot the PC or simply to terminate the process that was in control of the PC at the moment the Ctrl+Alt+Del key combination was struck. This gave us a way to end errant applications without having to give up altogether and restart Windows and DOS.

Enhancements to Windows 3.x

A steady trend throughout the successive versions of Windows (and only accelerated as Microsoft moved on into Window 95 and Windows NT) is the push to move more and more of the operating system functions out of real mode into protected mode and to make the protected mode programs that serve those functions operate in extended memory.

Some of this was done with Windows 3.x, but later still more was found to be possible. So Microsoft released a Win32s upgrade kit for developers to use with Windows 3.x. This would give them the capability of using most of the Windows 95 or Windows NT kinds of functionality on a smaller-scale machine running the older version of Windows. Many of the more advanced Windows-specific applications were modified to use this support, and they shipped with a copy of the necessary library programs for Win32s.

From a user perspective, these changes are not revolutionary, but they do add up to some pretty important improvements in the convenience and reliability of PCs running Windows.

Windows NT

The next version of Windows was a really different animal. It was never intended to be anything less. This was Windows NT and it was more Microsoft's answer to IBM's newly improved OS/2 than it was an upgrade to Windows 3.x. It also was Microsoft's attempt to displace Novell and Netware as the *de facto* industry standard of PC networking.

Windows NT truly is a new operating system. Compatibility was much less of an issue for its developers, whereas stability was much more of one. So Windows NT is among the most reliable PC operating systems. It is fully 32-bit code, and although it makes some attempt to be able to run older 16-bit Windows applications and DOS applications, it has some very stringent requirements on those it will accept. Many, or most, of the older programs just won't run on NT at all—certainly none that attempt to access the PC hardware directly (as many did to improve their performance). But then, that is the price of its far greater stability and security.

Windows NT comes in two flavors (and several versions). The two flavors are NT Server and NT Workstation. (The current version is 4, with version 5 promised for sometime in 1998.) The idea is that Windows NT is for serious networking, with one or more central file servers that also can run "back-end" application programs, including some database servers. For this you use Windows NT Server as the operating system. Then the workstations connected to it can run either Windows 3.x (or Windows 95 or 98) or Windows NT Workstation. Using NT for both the server and the workstation provides the best stability and security.

Windows 95

At last, after a long period of development, Microsoft introduced Windows 95. This version was meant for ordinary desktop PC users, and it is a direct upgrade from Windows 3.11. (If you look deeply inside Windows 95, it will identify itself as Windows version 4.)

Microsoft intended that everyone using Windows 3.x and almost all new PC users would use Windows 95. (It continued to say Windows NT was best for servers, but now it said Windows 95 was a perfectly fine operating system for a client workstation. The opinion of veteran NT users can differ on this point.) Windows 95 was hugely different from Windows 3.x in many ways. Or at least that is what we were told, and it certainly *looked* like a major change.

A more accurate assessment is that Windows 95 represented two things. One is that it exemplifies a very substantial re-thinking of the user interface. The other is that it nearly is the end product of the process of moving all the operating system support functions that could be moved from real mode to protected mode. Now, according to Microsoft, almost nothing a Windows-specific application needs is likely to require switching the machine from protected mode to real mode and back again. Or at least this can be true, if you don't have to run any real-mode driver programs to support your hardware devices. (The Windows 95 library of device drivers is pretty extensive, so only some rather rare, antiquated, or newly introduced hardware devices are likely to need real-mode drivers.)

But remember, this is what we have been told to believe about Windows 95. Actually, a little more of Windows and its drivers than you might expect still haven't been upgraded fully. For example, many of the printer drivers that ship with Windows 95 are still running real-mode (16-bit) code. Does this matter? It might. Any time you are running your PC in real mode, it is much more vulnerable than when it is running in protected mode. So you are more likely to crash your machine if you use any of these not-yet-upgraded pieces. Unfortunately, the crash might well occur some time later, after you have stopped using that piece, so figuring out which piece was to blame isn't always easy.

Whatever the true balance of 16-bit and 32-bit code in Windows 95, it generally is a more stable operating environment than Windows 3.x. And it has support for a very wide range of hardware and software, which goes a long way to explain why it is becoming the desktop PC operating system of choice for at least a very sizable minority of PC users. And with its next version, Windows 98, it might well become the operating system of choice for the majority of PC users.

Microsoft has also loudly and frequently proclaimed that Windows 95 replaced DOS. This is simply not true. There still is a DOS underneath Windows 95. True enough, Windows 95 now does more of what DOS used to do, but still, for certain purposes you'll need to have DOS, and Window 95 does still have it built in. They've just hidden it a little better.

What DOS is it? Microsoft won't tell you, but in fact it is almost exactly MS-DOS 6.22. About the only changes are that this new "version 7.0" of MS-DOS "understands" Windows 95 long filenames and it has had several of the external commands (in particular those that pose some danger to data when run in a multitasking environment) removed, with their functionality moved into protected mode (32-bit code) modules within Windows 95.

I'll describe some more details about Windows 95 in a moment. First, though, I want to mention some other versions that are now common, or that soon will be.

Windows 98

As I write this, Windows 98 is being readied for market. It isn't here yet, and anything I might say based on the existing beta versions is subject to substantial change between now and its release.

But there are some things we can be pretty sure of. First is that the underlying program is only slightly different from Windows 95. Microsoft calls the DOS under Windows 95 version 7.0. It calls the DOS under Windows 98 version 7.1. This new version of DOS "understands" FAT32 formatted partitions (which were introduced in the "OSR 2" release of Windows 95, also known as Windows 95b). This ability to access and store files in a FAT32 volume is necessary to let you boot from a DOS disk and then access any disk volume you have formatted in that way. And it is necessary if you want to boot to DOS and then run Windows 98.

Most of the changes from Windows 95 to Windows 98 in a functional sense have been anticipated in the steady stream of updates and upgrades that Microsoft has made available on its Internet Web site. Most of those upgrades were also bundled into the Windows 95a Service Pack upgrade and then into the Windows 95b (or OSR2) version it has supplied to original equipment manufacturers (OEMs) to put on new PCs since late 1996.

The one area in which there is a very obvious and striking difference in Windows 98 is in the appearance of the user interface. This has been redone almost totally. Well, this is true if you use the default interface for Windows 98. Microsoft is saying now that it will ship the product configured for an interface based on its current version of the Internet Explorer Web browser. But an alternative interface will be available that is essentially the "classic" Windows 95 interface, and users will be able to revert to that if they want.

One two-word phrase can explain the reason for this change: The Internet. The importance of the Internet has grown so much that Microsoft decided that to keep its dominant position over our PC computing experience it essentially had to expand its next-generation operating systems in a fashion that allowed it to build the Internet into them in an apparently seamless manner. The notion Microsoft has is that all resources you want to access—whether they are on a disk drive on your PC, on another PC across the room, connected to yours via a LAN, or on some PC clear across the globe connected via the Internet—should look to you just like more folders on your PC. So the distinction between the Windows Explorer and the Internet Explorer are now meant to seem trivial. And the way Microsoft did this was to make the new interface for Windows 98 almost exactly like that for Internet Explorer, version 4.

Of course, the difference between what you have on your own PC's hard disk or on a disk attached to a PC on your local area network and what you might be able to access on some remote computer halfway around the globe is not trivial. And this new interface has, therefore, the potential for creating a great deal of mischief before all is said and done. After all, you can count on the files on your hard disk in ways you simply cannot trust files on some distant machine belonging to total strangers. But the intentional blurring of the line between what is local and what is remote will make it more difficult to keep those different levels of trustworthiness clearly in mind.

Another new feature of Windows 98 might cause similar unexpected misery. This is the intent that Microsoft has announced of having the operating system update itself automatically by downloading and installing patches (possibly from the Internet, or perhaps in another manner I will describe in a moment)—very possibly without notifying the PC's user of these actions. Because no software as complex as a PC's operating system, or even any significant module within that system, is likely to be totally bug-free, this means your system might be importing new and unknown bugs in an effort to expunge the older, more familiar ones. That is not necessarily a trade that most PC users would happily make—if only they were consulted on the matter.

One of the "coolest" features in Windows 98 is its capability to work with up to nine PCI video cards attached to a like number of monitors. You can spread the "desktop" over all the attached monitors, and then you can put an application's window in whichever visible portion of the overall desktop you want. You might think of this as the "Windows 98 video wall" concept.

This is undoubtedly a "cool" achievement. But I also would argue that except for the very fortunate few who can afford several of the very highest-priced monitors and video cards, this feature is not actually practical.

My analysis goes like this: Consider the cost of a video card and monitor. For low-end units you can get VGA resolution in 13-inch monitors for relatively modest costs. However, multiply that modest cost by nine and you will find that you are contemplating spending much more than you would have to spend on one very large monitor (say a 35-inch unit) with super-high resolution and driven by a very high-resolution video card. Also, in the high-end card and monitor combination you are likely to get some wonderful video acceleration hardware features, including perhaps 3D acceleration and MPEG decompression, that just aren't going to be included on the low-end video cards.

Therefore, the only case in which this feature is actually worth going out and purchasing hardware to exploit is if you can afford to buy several (ideally nine) of the 35-inch monitors and associated top-level video cards. Then you'd have a video wall seven feet wide and five feet high with a resolution that far exceeds anything available today on a single monitor. Now that would be *really* cool; also *way* too expensive for most of us.

In a related development, you can expect to see new Windows 98 machines come with a built-in TV tuner. This will let you see a TV show on your PC monitor, perhaps in a window within the desktop. Why would you want to do this? Well, it is possible that you will have a TV channel listing program that lets you choose all the shows you'd like to see and record for the next week. And you then would be able to order the recording of them on your USB-attached VCR and view the shows in progress while you did other things. This really is not such a fantastic extension of what you might be doing now with a TV in the corner of the room where you can glance at it from time to time.

Where this technology becomes really interesting—and more than a little scary—is when you find out that the TV shows you are watching may be sending digital data out in the *blanking* periods. These are the small intervals of time that occur at the end of each line of the image and a somewhat longer time that occurs at the end of each frame, while the electron beam in your TV is being sent back to the beginning of the next line or frame. Microsoft hopes to use these times to broadcast updates to software and other information. So you might think you were just watching a TV show, when in fact you were having your PC's operating system covertly upgraded while you watched. This way Microsoft wouldn't even have to get you to sign onto the Internet in order to muck around with your PC. Again, this is not something that I, for one, will welcome with open arms.

Finally, I shall mention one promise Microsoft has loudly made for Windows 98 that I, and most other observers, fervently hope will be kept. That is its intention to replace all the device drivers (the programs that activate peripheral hardware devices) in Window 95 with new ones that are compatible with Windows NT. Windows 98 has been changed to use this new unified model of device drivers (what Microsoft calls the WDM, for Windows Device driver Model) instead of the ones it used before that were not compatible with NT. The benefit this represents to device manufacturers is that they would need to write only one device driver for each device they make. The benefit to users is that NT will at last get as broad a range of device drivers as Windows 95.

However, this is a promise yet to be kept or broken. Only when the product is released will we know how close Microsoft has come to converting all the device drivers to the new, NT-compatible model.

Windows CE

Windows on your washing machine? Maybe so, in just a few years. Microsoft's plan is to have Windows become the ubiquitous computing interface. It wants to see Windows (Microsoft's Windows, in some version) on virtually every electrical device in our lives.

Windows CE is the version of Windows that Microsoft devised for use on smaller, less capable hardware. Initially targeted at the Hand-held PC (HPC) or the Personal Digital Assistant (PDA), it will in time (Microsoft hopes) also be made a part of many other consumer electronic devices, and eventually of other appliances. So yes, in time, you might use a Windows GUI to set your washing machine clothes cleaning cycle. (Or, even better, you might be able to schedule it to run at a predetermined time and using your choice of cycles, with all of this being set from your desktop PC, which will be linked to the washing machine over a Universal Serial Bus [USB] link.)

Microsoft has just released version 2.0 of Windows CE, and this version supports many more kinds of hardware platforms than the first version of CE. The original version worked on only a few specific RISC microcomputers, but the new version can also work on low-end x86 processor-based systems. Therefore, the CPU chip that was the new hot thing for the desktop PC of a "power user" soon might become the so-cheap-one-might-as-well-use-it CPU in a major appliance. And after that happens, you will be able to reprogram that appliance to your heart's content—assuming you ever craved the ability to do that in the first place.

The first generation of Windows CE devices weren't very popular. But then Windows, version 1.0, wasn't either. So it simply is too early to tell how much of Microsoft's vision for Windows CE will come to pass. But given Microsoft's past track record, I wouldn't bet against it.

Other Windows

Before I leave this subject I certainly want to at least tell you a little bit about the program that claims to be "a better DOS than DOS and a better Windows than Windows": IBM's OS/2 Warp operating system. Because IBM once was Microsoft's partner in the development of both DOS and Windows, its programmers understand those programs very well. And they crafted OS/2 with the explicit notion that it would enable DOS programs and Windows programs to run every bit as well as if they were running on top of real DOS or real Windows. Yet, OS/2 is at its core something very different.

Like Windows NT, OS/2 is a totally protected-mode operating system. It has stability, reliability, and security comparable to Windows NT. Yet it can run virtually all DOS and (16-bit) Windows applications as well as or better than a DOS-plus-Windows 3.*x* machine. (It isn't yet able to run all the very latest 32-bit Windows software—and it might never be, because Microsoft no longer cooperates with IBM on operating system development.)

OS/2 can do as much as it does because it does a very good job of *virtualizing* the hardware pieces of the PC. This means that whenever a program thinks it is talking to some part of the PC hardware, it really is just sending a message to the V86 monitor portion of OS/2 that is supervising the virtual DOS machine within which the DOS or Windows program is running.

Every version of Windows runs each DOS program in its own virtual machine. Every version of Microsoft Windows runs all the Windows applications in a single virtual machine. (Another way to say this is that they all share a single Local Descriptor Table and the other data structures that define the virtual machine.) This means that although multiple DOS applications running simultaneously under Windows are fully protected from messing up one another or the overall operating system, multiple Windows applications are not at all well protected from one another. As long as all the Windows applications are "good citizens," there is nothing wrong with this. But if any Windows program happens to be a rogue, or if its programmer simply made some bad mistake, you could find that it will not only crash itself, it will bring your whole PC to its knees. That is, in fact, the source of many of the remaining instabilities in Windows 95.

OS/2 does things a little differently. It opens a virtual machine for Windows, loads a copy of the IBM clone of Windows into it, and then runs a Windows application. The next time you want to start another Windows application you have a choice. You can set things up so it will run the second Windows application in the same virtual machine as the first one—which means it will be doing the same thing Microsoft Windows does—or you can have OS/2 open up a fresh virtual machine and load another copy of its Windows program into that, and then run your second Windows application there, totally protected from the first Windows application. Doing things in this more secure fashion will cost you. Launching all but the first application this way takes longer. It also uses up much more RAM. But if you have enough RAM in your PC (and with the steadily falling price of RAM, I hope you do, or soon will), then you may well desire the security that can come from this approach. But you can get it only by switching from Microsoft Windows to OS/2. (In Windows NT you can get this protection of a separate virtual Windows machine for 16-bit applications, but only if you select that feature in the properties dialog for those applications.)

The Future of Windows

What can we expect from Microsoft in the future? More versions of Windows, that is for sure. But what can we say now about what these new versions are likely to be? Well, if you believe what Microsoft is telling us, there won't be any more generations of Windows in the model of Windows 95 and Windows 98. The next step beyond Windows 98 for the desktop PC user will be a new, kinder, gentler version of Windows NT. At that point Windows NT will come not just in two versions (Server and Workstation) but probably in at least four versions (Enterprise, Server, Workstation, and Consumer).

And at that point, MS-DOS might actually truly be dead and gone. I think IBM will still be selling PC DOS. Caldera bought Novell's DOS in 1996, and Caldera now has upgraded it and markets it under the name OpenDOS in a manner similar to the marketing of Linux (which I describe later). And maybe someday Microsoft will find that the millions of PCs still running DOS deserve to have a source of upgrades and will therefore still market some version of MS-DOS. Again, this is an imponderable at this time.

When we get to the point that Windows 9x is history, we will still have Windows CE as well as Windows NT. In fact, I expect to see Windows CE expand both up and down in capabilities to fit into a broader range of appliances. These will include, no doubt, the "smart" washing machine. These also will include "Windows terminals," which will be fairly dumb or "thin" clients attached to a Windows NT Server and running applications on that server, rather than in the terminal's own hardware, or perhaps some applications in which a portion runs on the server and a portion runs in the Windows terminal.

Will OS/2 continue to track the new generations of Windows (albeit one or two generations behind Microsoft), as well? Now that is truly an imponderable. I doubt any observers of IBM can predict what it will be able to do or what it will decide to do in this area. We'll just have to wait and see on that one.

Windows Is an Event-Driven Environment

So far in this chapter I have pointed out that DOS and Windows are the dominant operating systems for PCs. And I have described the various versions of Windows that are in common use today, or are likely to come into use soon. (I didn't describe the different DOS versions, because their differences are for the most part less dramatic, and because almost everyone has upgraded at least to DOS 5, which has almost all the features you would get with any modern DOS.)

I also told you a little bit about how DOS works, both in terms of what you see it do for you, and what it is doing behind the scenes both directly for you and also for the benefit of the application programs you choose to run.

Now I want to go into one of the most important ways that Windows as a programming environment differs from DOS. Understanding this is crucial to understanding how any Windows program works.

When a programmer sits down to write a DOS program, he or she will start with a procedure it is to perform. Then the programmer writes instructions that follow each step of the desired procedure. This is called, not surprisingly, "procedural programming."

Windows is different. The programmer first must think about the appearance of the program. The next concern is to define all the events that might occur; for example, a mouse pointer being moved across a certain region or a mouse button being pressed while that pointer was at that location. Then, for each event, a separate procedure is written. The collection of all these event handlers is the Windows application.

Windows must send notice of all these events to all the programs that might need to react to them. After all, only one mouse pointer is on the screen, and many programs can be running. So the underlying Windows program will notice where the mouse moves, when the mouse's buttons are clicked, when keystrokes occur, and so on. For each such event, Windows sends out a message. This is routed to every Windows program much in the manner of a magazine making the rounds at a company with a check-off list of readers stapled to the front cover.

Each Windows program must receive the message, decide whether it is supposed to act on it, and if not (or perhaps anyway), pass it along to the next program.

If any one of the Windows programs becomes stuck, messages can't be passed around this loop—and that can stop Windows as a whole. Well, there can be several loops going, and some of them might still continue to work. This is why often even when your PC seems to be, and in fact is, quite solidly stuck, you still are able to move the mouse pointer all around the screen as freely as you like.

For these reasons Windows programming is not referred to generally as being procedural in character (even though Windows programs are full of procedures). Instead, it is called "event-driven" or "message-based."

Cooperative Versus Preemptive Multitasking

Now I have set the stage so that you are ready to learn one more important aspect of how Windows works, and also how this aspect has changed from version to version of Windows. I am referring here to what is called cooperative multitasking versus preemptive multitasking.

Multitasking means running several programs at once. In fact, it means having the CPU spend some time running one program, stop that and spend some time running another program, stop that and go on running a third program, and so on. If all those times add up to a very short time, so that the CPU gets back to each program many times each second, it will seem to the user as though all the programs are running simultaneously. But actually they are simply doing what is called "time sharing," "time slicing," or "time domain multiplexing."

There are two ways this can be accomplished. In both cases, you need some supervisor program that handles the context switching for the CPU from one program to the next. (Each time a context switch is about to occur, the CPU must be instructed to save enough information about the task it has been doing to be able to resume that work later on, and then it must reload the previously saved information about the task on which it is about to resume its work.)

The two strategies for multitasking differ in how they figure out when it is time to make a switch to the next program. *Preemptive multitasking* means having the supervisor program set strict time limits on each program. At the end of its "time slice" that program simply gets cut off, no matter where it was in its process. This is okay, because the CPU will complete the current instruction, and it will save enough information for it to be able to resume exactly where it left off, as soon as it gets to return to running this program.

Cooperative multitasking, on the other hand, means that each program is asked to relinquish control on its own. Windows programming guidelines suggest a maximum time that any Windows program should be allowed to hold control before it relinquishes it, but it is up to the programmer who writes that program to be sure that those guidelines are not violated.

DOS programs have no notion of multitasking. Each one assumes that it "owns" the entire PC for the duration. So the only possible way to multitask DOS programs is by a preemptive multitasking supervisor program that pulls the rug out from under the DOS program on a strict time schedule. And that works just fine.

I suppose the Microsoft programmers who created Windows felt that not only was their new operating environment (as it was termed back then) special, so too were any programs written especially for it. So they treated Windows applications very differently. And true enough, it was possible to ask the programmers who wrote Windows programs to include code that would let it relinquish control to Windows, and thus to other Windows programs, on a regular basis. But trusting that they would always do so has proven, in retrospect, to be a bit naïve.

Anyone who has run any number of Windows programs in the past has seen many of them share the machine most of the time, yet on occasions grab the machine in a vise-like grip and not let go until they are good and ready. Worse yet, sometimes a Windows program would get "hung" and couldn't let go of control, at which point you had no choice but to reboot your PC. I'd cite an example, but I hesitate to tar one good program with a brush that could as well be applied to almost any number of other (and otherwise, fine) programs.

Even Microsoft has seen this behavior, as is obvious from some changes it made in how later versions of Windows handle things. Whereas Windows 3.x used only cooperative multitasking for all Windows applications (and preemptive multitasking for DOS applications), Windows 95 uses cooperative multitasking only for the older, "legacy" 16-bit Windows applications. All newer, 32-bit programs are preemptively multitasked, as are all DOS applications.

Windows NT goes even further, using only a preemptive multitasking model. That prevents any one program, no matter how badly (or maliciously) written, from taking control of your PC and not letting go. To achieve its goals of stability and reliability for Windows NT, Microsoft could do no less.

Understanding Your Choices for Your PC's Operating System

For most of this book I have acted as though you are running DOS, DOS plus Windows 3.x, or Windows 95. I have done this because, statistically speaking, you are. But, of course, you might not be. You aren't, after all, a statistic.

And there are many fine choices for your PC operating system. This section briefly lists some of the more popular options and tells you a little bit about why you might want to choose each one.

Sticking with DOS

I must say it: DOS is fine for many purposes. If you have an older computer, and especially if you do some not very demanding things with it, DOS still is an excellent choice for its operating system. You don't even need to add Windows unless you must run some Windows application, want to multitask DOS applications, or simply love that GUI.

DOS is one of the smallest PC operating systems. It has been around "forever," and thus it is very well understood. Its bugs, features, and limitations are out in the open, so you can plan your way around them. Therefore, its limited stability and its various limitations are often quite acceptable.

DOS Plus Windows 3.*x*

Still, many more PC users have decided that DOS plus Windows 3.*x* is the way to go. They value its capability to use all the RAM they can give it. They also like it for letting them run many DOS applications at once (and, with version 3.1, being able to use the local reboot feature to end one errant DOS application without having to shut down and restart the machine).

And it has been around "almost forever," so its flaws and blemishes also are pretty well-known, as are the workarounds that will let you get on with your business despite them. So if your PC is sufficiently powerful for this, and if you have no compelling need to run a very recent version of some software package that otherwise would force you to upgrade to Windows 95, you might as well stay where you are with DOS plus Windows 3.*x*. Maybe when Windows NT, version 5 comes along, then you will want to think about upgrading.

Windows 95 and Windows 98

Windows 95 has been until very recently the focus of almost all the hype. It was the hot new thing. But moving up to it often meant having to add to or upgrade your hardware. (Naturally, the makers of new PCs and PC add-on pieces loved this aspect of Windows 95.) And it does give developers some new features to exploit. So the very latest and presumably greatest versions of all the top-of-the-line PC products have been rewritten to run exclusively on Windows 95.

Windows 98 isn't going to cause another, similar revolution. Anything that runs on Windows 95 also will run on Windows 98, and probably almost anything that runs on Windows 98 also will run on Windows 95. That isn't really the point of Windows 98. The shift from a desktop focus to an Internet-centric focus is more of Windows 98's thrust, along with its increased support for the integration of television with PCs.

Both these versions of Windows are all about compatibility: Compatibility with the past and with the present, bleeding edge of technology. They support nearly any DOS or Windows program ever written, including some pretty funky game programs, and they also support the very latest efforts from the mainstream PC software publishers. Plus, they offer built-in support for more odd-ball hardware than any other PC operating system. Occasionally you still must go to the hardware gadget's manufacturer for a suitable device driver (and more often you'd benefit if you did so), but out of the box, Windows 95 (and presumably Windows 98) support so much stuff—and with their plug-and-play aspects even recognize the stuff—that many people never need to concern themselves with a search for or the process of installing third-party drivers.

About the only other thing I must tell you about this option is that I hope you will not starve it for RAM. Please give all your Windows 95 machines *at least* 32MB of RAM apiece, and preferably 64MB. (If you are running Windows 95 on a laptop, you might have to settle for less RAM than this, but it definitely will be settling—and in the long run you might not enjoy the experience.)

Windows NT

Windows NT is Microsoft's crown jewel. It has bet the farm on this one, and its bet seems to be winning over the hearts, minds, and dollars of most of the larger companies.

Windows NT is stable and it is secure, so it is a safe choice. But it also is the most finicky Windows version. You simply will be unable to run that old, funky DOS game program. And you might be unpleasantly surprised to find out that some other, what you thought to be fairly ordinary, Windows or DOS programs also have problems. So before you commit to this operating system, be sure it will not complain about some program that you simply *must* be able to run. Or else, check out the last part of this section where I explain how you can have your cake and eat it too, running your PC both with and without Windows NT.

OS/2 Warp

IBM's OS/2 Warp is its answer to Microsoft Windows in all its flavors. Warp has the stability and most of the security of NT, yet it can run virtually any DOS or older Windows program.

Since Microsoft and IBM ended their joint development agreement several years ago, IBM has struggled mightily to keep up with the moving target presented by Microsoft Windows. And it has done an admirable job of it. But it isn't able to keep up altogether.

This means that OS/2 is the best choice if you find that there are some OS/2 applications that do what you mostly want to do, and if the only Windows-only programs you must run happen to be compatible with the Windows clone inside OS/2. You are pretty safe running any DOS programs under OS/2—probably at least as safe as if you used Windows 95. But Windows 95-specific applications, and even some of the later Windows 3.*x*-specific applications, might be unable to run under

OS/2. Again, remember that you always have the option of using OS/2 plus some other OS as a way around this limitation.

Linux

Linux is a marvelous program and an unbeatable value: It is free! Linux is a version of UNIX that first was crafted as a work of love by one programmer and then augmented by many others. You can get the whole operating system, source code and all, for nothing more than the price of a download. Or you can buy it on a CD-ROM for the cost of the disc.

Or, you can buy versions of Linux that are supported by several reputable companies. This is probably a better option if you aren't at heart a "hacker" and would rather ask questions than figure things out for yourself.

Given its heritage (UNIX), it is not surprising that Linux is a very suitable choice for a PC operating system for a PC that is to serve as a Web server. In fact, this or some other flavor of UNIX is the best choice for any system that must be extremely reliable and flexible or any that must do a lot of *real-time* work. (That is, where the PC must respond in a time-critical fashion to events in the outside world.)

Most computers that host World Wide Web sites are UNIX-based machines. Among the other computers that make up the Internet, probably there are more Macintosh computers than PCs running Windows, but PCs running Linux might well have the Macs on the run.

QNX or Some Other UNIX

If your task is to set up a PC to do a critical real-time job (for example, a numerical controller for a machine tool), where it simply must keep working at all times and must be able to respond in a timely manner to even a lot of very fast external events, then DOS is a bad choice of OS; so is Windows. Windows NT or OS/2 might do the job, but almost any flavor of UNIX would be better.

QNX Software is one of the leading contenders for this task. Its real-time optimized UNIX clone has one of the smallest kernels (under 32KB). All the other modules in this system run at a lower level of privilege than the kernel, and thus PCs running QNX are protected against even the programming errors in the operating system (outside the kernel) by the CPU's built-in protection features.

QNX also offers a rich assortment of modules and programmers' tools. With it, you can build a highly sophisticated, full-featured GUI-based system to do almost anything. Or, if buying is more your style than programming, a lot of companies specialize in building custom or semi-custom QNX systems.

Furthermore, QNX offers a module that will let you run DOS programs on top of QNX. This might let you have the best of both the DOS and UNIX worlds.

How You Can Avoid Making a Choice

Finally, I must point out that you really don't have to choose. You can have them all. Yes, really, you can run one PC with all the operating systems I have mentioned loaded onto it. Naturally, you will be running only one of these operating systems at a time, but you will be able to change which one it is running simply by rebooting your PC.

Several strategies exist for doing this. Windows 95, Windows NT, and OS/2 all come with a version of *dual-booting* built in. This strategy lets you choose between their native operation or booting to another OS, usually DOS. Usually this involves some batch files that replace critical system files for one operating system with the corresponding files for the other system.

OS/2 and version 3 of Partition Magic offer another way to go. They include IBM's Boot Manager. You install this program into its own, private 1MB partition on your hard disk, and you mark this partition in the Master Boot Record (partition table) as the one bootable partition. Thus, whenever you reboot your PC, the motherboard BIOS loads the operating system from the Boot Manager partition.

The Boot Manager program presents a menu of choices, and after you have selected one (or after some time-out if you want to accept the default choice and aren't in a hurry about it), Boot Manager simply reaches over and acts like the motherboard BIOS, but this time reading the boot sector from the location you have just selected. In effect, you have booted from a different partition, even though in fact you booted from the Boot Manager one. Using this strategy, Boot Manager will let you choose from up to four different operating systems.

Partition Magic also offers yet another way to go. Its program enables you to hide and unhide partitions. So you can have multiple C: drives on a single hard disk, with only one of them being visible at a time. Which one is visible is the one from which you will boot.

Finally, a very fine program from V Communications, System Commander, uses a variation on the Boot Manager approach to let you boot from any of up to 100 different PC operating systems. Its approach is to replace the master boot record (MBR) program in the very first sector on your hard disk with its special program. It presents a menu and then boots into the OS of your choice. In some cases it does this by swapping some files, in a manner similar to the dual-boot strategy used by Windows and OS/2. In other cases it can boot from another disk drive than the C: drive.

Warning: I'd be remiss if I didn't end this discussion with a cautionary note. Some of these PC operating system choices use the good-old DOS FAT12 and FAT16 formats for their file systems. All of them are able to read those file systems (and almost all of them can write to them, as well). But many of these operating systems also support some alternative file systems.

Windows 95b and Windows 98 support the new FAT32 file system, but none of the other operating systems can make any sense out of disks formatted in that way. OS/2 has its High Performance File System (HPFS), which DOS and Windows aren't able to understand. (Well, the original version of Windows NT could, but it lost that capability some time ago and the other versions of Windows never had it.) Windows NT also supports a file system that only it can access, called NTFS.

Linux normally uses several different disk volumes, some with their own proprietary format and others with a DOS-like format. Many other UNIX flavors do something similar.

If you choose to load several different operating systems on your PC you must have enough disk space for all of them. Each one wants some space for its files—and in modern versions those are some pretty substantial amounts. And the only shared spaces will be those that use a commonly accessible file system. Any non-shared spaces are in addition to that. Thus, you'll need a pretty large hard drive to make this strategy practical. (Fortunately, these days, that doesn't have to cost you very much money.)

Therefore, the bottom line is this: If you want to be able to boot your PC into any of a number of different operating systems, you will have to give some careful thought to what file systems you will be using under each one. And be sure that each OS will be able to access the files you want it to see (and perhaps also assure yourself that it won't be able to access the files you want it not to touch). You can do this, with sufficient care, but it does take some careful thought and planning. The documentation that comes with Partition Magic and System Commander lay out several different scenarios to help you in this planning.

Summary

This chapter has told you a lot about a topic you might never have realized you would want to understand. I hope you found it interesting as well as illuminating reading. And after you have made your decision as to which operating system to use, you will be able to go back to ignoring your PC's operating system much of the time. Still, knowing what you now do about how it works will serve you well whenever you find that your PC's OS isn't working quite the way you want it to work.

This chapter completed the task I set for myself in this part of the book; namely, explaining how all the basic hardware and the fundamental (operating system) software in an isolated PC function.

Armed with that understanding you now are ready to learn how people program PCs to do useful things. That is the focus of the next part of the book.

IV

Peter Norton

PC Programs: From Machine Language Bytes to Natural Human Speech

18

Understanding How Humans Instruct PCs

Peter Norton®

This chapter is all about the many ways in which we can tell our PCs what to do. That covers a broad range of subjects, from the careful crafting of assembly-language programs and the ins and outs of object-oriented computer languages to simple macro definitions that customize how some application works. Chapter 19, "Some PCs Can Understand Speech and Talk to Us," continues the story with how you can instruct some PCs simply by talking to them, as well as how those and other PCs are now sometimes talking back to us.

Harnessing the PC's Power to Help Mere Humans

The first digital computers were programmed in a very laborious manner. The only "language" they understood was an appropriate collection of binary numbers, so their human makers had to insert these numbers by hand. In those days, every time a computer operator turned on a computer for the first time (or had to restart it for some reason), he or she would have to set a group of switches to represent the ones and zeros of a binary instruction word. He would have to do this repeatedly, just in order to prepare the computer to read in and then run a longer program from some punched cards or a tape drive.

Fortunately, we no longer have to worry about all that. Our PCs know how to start themselves, and modern methods of program generation enable us to create computer programs in a much easier way. There are, in fact, several quite different ways people program computers. The rest of this chapter describes the most popular ones.

Assembly Language Saves Mental Effort

People are good at different things than computers are good at. Computers excel at keeping track of details. People excel at seeing the big picture or, in general, at seeing patterns.

Using assembly language is a strategy for using the computer to do what it does well, in ways that make it easier for humans to do the work of building computer programs. This strategy is the closest to the original method of computer programming of all the ones I will describe for you. It also was the first strategy devised. But it still is extremely useful, because it is in certain ways the most powerful way to program a computer. And because it shows most of the characteristics of all the other ways to program computers, I will spend more time describing this kind of language than on any of the others.

The General Characteristics of All Computer Programs

A computer program is simply a long list of instructions, perhaps with some data values mixed in. The CPU reads the instructions and performs the indicated actions. If some data is mixed into the program, then there must be some instructions in that program which tell the CPU when and how to use those data values, and some other instructions that will cause it to skip over the data values as it is reading the program so it can find the next instruction it is to perform.

Some instructions contain data within themselves. Others reference data the CPU will find in a specified register or at some designated memory location. Some instructions are simple, taking only one byte to state. Others are much more complicated, and expressing them might require more than a dozen bytes of program code.

That means that a list of the binary numbers that make up a computer program will almost certainly make little sense at a glance to any human. We see the meaning a whole lot more easily when the program is broken down into its individual instructions. And if each instruction is further broken down into the action to be done and the data to be acted upon (or an indication of where that data may be found), the intent of those instructions is much easier to see.

The next section goes into an example in great detail. If you already know how an assembly-language program is structured and how it corresponds to the machine language program it represents, or if you simply can't be bothered, you can skip the next section. However, if you want to understand how assembly language works, in at least this very simple case, please take some time to study this example.

A Very Simple Sample Program

Figure 18.1 shows a very short (15-byte long) program as the CPU would see it. You and I see numbers here. The CPU sees this as what we term "code," by which we mean that these numbers encode the actions we want the CPU to perform. Every pair of hexadecimal values in this figure specifies the value of one byte of the program code. So, for example, the hexadecimal values 8E (for the fourth byte) imply a byte whose binary content is 10001110 (8h = 1000, Eh = 1110). Go back and review the section in Chapter 3, "Understanding Bits, Nybbles, and Bytes," on hexadecimal numbers and especially Table 3.3 if you are confused by this.

Figure 18.1.
A very short program as it is seen by the CPU.

BA 00 00 8E C2 26 80 36-17 04 20 B4 4C CD 21

Now I will show you how that short program would look as an assembly-language program (see Figure 18.2). All the numbers in this figure are, like those in Figure 18.1, hexadecimal values, even though I didn't put a letter h after each one. That is simply the assumption you must make whenever you read any assembly language program, at least in the form in which they usually are presented.

Note: Sometimes authors put a suffix letter b for binary numbers, o for octal, h for hexadecimal, and t or d for tens or decimal. Other times you are simply expected to know from context the number base that is being used.

Figure 18.2.
That same information expressed in assembly language.

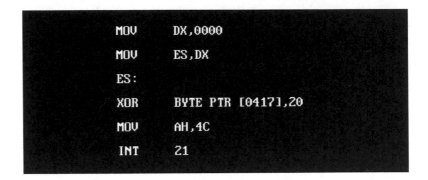

```
MOV     DX,0000
MOV     ES,DX
ES:
XOR     BYTE PTR [0417],20
MOV     AH,4C
INT     21
```

This is, as it happens, a small real-mode program. You could run it at the DOS prompt. But before you do, it would be nice to know what it would do to your PC if you did. And I will explain that in some detail right now.

The first instruction (MOV DX,0000) "moves" (copies) the explicitly stated value of zero into the 16-bit wide data register (DX). The second instruction (MOV ES,DX) copies the contents of the DX register (which we now know is zero) into the extra segment register (ES).

Notice that the structure (syntax) for a line of assembly code like this is that the first "word" is the verb, specifying the action to be taken. The next word is the destination, and the last word is the source of the data to be used in this action—or in the case of the first line, it is the actual data value to be used in the action.

Then comes a line that asserts that the currently active segment (for purposes of reaching out into main memory) shall now be the extra segment. This assertion applies until it is countermanded by another, similar assertion, or until the program ends.

The line that begins with XOR (XOR BYTE PTR [0417],20) is an "exclusive or" statement that compares the values of two bytes. Just what this statement tells the CPU to do takes a little bit of explaining.

First, you must know what an "exclusive or" (XOR) of two bits means. If either of the bits is a one, but not both of them, then the result is a one; otherwise, it is a zero.

Another way to look at this is to notice that if one of the bits is a zero, the result is going to be the same as the value of the other bit being compared. But if the first bit is a one, then the resulting bit will be the exact opposite of the other bit you are comparing.

And when you do an XOR of two bytes, you just go through each position in the two bytes. First you compare the least significant bit in each byte and put the XOR result into the least significant bit of the result byte. Next, you move to the second bit in each byte, and then on to the third, fourth, and finally the eighth, or most-significant, bit in each byte.

The part of the assembly language line that says BYTE PTR [0417] indicates that one of the bytes to be compared is located at address 0:0417, where I am giving the address in segment:offset form—which always means I am using hexadecimal numbers before and after the colon. (You might wonder why the number before the colon is zero. Remember, the segment value was set to be whatever value is in ES in the line just before this one, and we just loaded it with a zero value in the lines before that.)

The final portion of this assembly language line gives an explicit value to the other byte in our comparison. That value is 20h, which is the same as the binary number 00100000b.

There is one more not-so-obvious thing you must know about this assembly language instruction: The result of the comparison of the two bytes will be put into the memory location from which the first byte value being compared was taken. That means that this instruction reads into the CPU the value that was stored at 0:0417 in main memory, XORs that 8-bit value with the 8-bit value 20h, and then puts the resulting byte back into main memory location 0:0417.

Now, from what I just told you about what the XOR operation does and the fact that one of the bytes being compared is 20h, you can now see that this instruction just reverses the value of the sixth bit in the byte at main memory location 0:0417, leaving all the other bits in that byte unchanged.

As it happens, this particular memory location has a special significance. It is the byte in which the BIOS stores the current state of the shift keys on the keyboard as well as the "shift state" of the system corresponding to each shift key. The first (least significant) bit has the binary value "one" if, and only if, the right-hand shift key is pressed. The next bit is a one if, and only if, the left-hand shift key is pressed. The next bit tells if either Ctrl key is pressed (one=yes; zero=no), and the fourth bit does the same for the Alt keys.

The upper four bits show whether the system is in the ScrollLock, NumLock, CapsLock, or Insert states. That is, a one in any of these positions corresponds to that state being on.

Aha! Remember that our program is going to change only one bit, the bit in the sixth position. Now you know enough to see that when you run this program it will reverse the value of the bit that says whether the NumLock state is on. Thus, running this program will set the NumLock state off if it is on, and on if it is off. That is just what pressing the NumLock key does. So this program is a way to press the NumLock key without touching the keyboard.

But the program does something more. The next line (MOV AH,4C) says that it moves the byte value 4Ch into the upper half of the AX register (which is also known as the AH register, meaning the higher portion of the A register). The last line (INT 21) produces a software interrupt of type 21h.

This is perhaps the most commonly used DOS interrupt service. It tells DOS that this program is finished with its work, and for DOS to return control back to whatever program had it before this program got loaded. Normally, that means to let COMMAND.COM put up another DOS prompt and wait for you to tell it what you want to have your PC do next.

This was just a simple sample program. It is actually a useful one (in case you want a way to achieve the effect of pushing the NumLock key in a batch file), but by no means does it show you the range of things one can do with an assembly-language program.

In particular, many assembly-language programs let the programmer refer to locations in memory or locations within the program by symbolic names. The assembler keeps track of where these locations are (actual RAM address or offset from the beginning of the code segment and actual line of code). The programmer then can use meaningful names for each block of code, based on what it is supposed to do. And when an instruction tells the computer to jump to a new block of code to do some new task, that instruction will read something like "JMP CloseFile" instead of "JMP 0A35" or some other arbitrary numerical address.

The Power of Assembly-Language Programs

What you can see from this example is how very detailed and "close to the hardware" an assembly-language program really is. It actually must specify each and every byte of *machine-language code* (the binary numbers the CPU will read) that is going to become a part of the final program. That is in marked contrast to what a programmer does when using what we call a "high-level" programming language, as I will explain in more detail in a moment.

This low-level characteristic of assembly-language programming means that a person who writes a program in assembly language has total control over what the PC will do. It is logically exactly equivalent to writing down the exact bytes of machine code the program is to contain. But writing assembly language instead of machine language code is much easier for humans to do.

The main reason that one writes in assembly language instead of in actual machine language bytes is that it is so much more mnemonic (which means suggestive and memorable) to write down MOV DX instead of writing down simply BAh, which is the actual byte that means that action to the CPU. If one had to remember only a few instructions, memorizing them all might not be too tough. But when there are as many instructions as there are for a modern x86 processor, plus a large number of possible modifications to those instructions, it all becomes a bit much for mere humans to memorize.

After an assembly-language program is completed, the programmer will *assemble* it. This means running a special "assembler" program that takes the assembly-language statements as input data and generates the actual machine-language bytes that the CPU must see in order to know what it is supposed to do as its output.

Let me repeat that thought in several sentences: A programmer writes assembly-language statements. An assembler program converts them into machine-language bytes and stores them in a file. That file is the final program the programmer set out to create. When it is run, the CPU reads those bytes and does what they direct it to do.

The Problem with Assembly-Language Programs

The power of assembly-language programming is the ability one has to specify exactly everything that is going to happen and exactly where and how it will happen. This is also the problem with assembly-language programming.

It is a problem simply because humans are not very good at keeping huge amounts of detail in their minds at once. You can keep track of which numbers are where in a short program, but when the program becomes really large, there simply is too much to keep track of. Or, at least, doing so without making mistakes from time to time becomes very hard.

It would be so much nicer if you could somehow let the computer keep track of the details and just focus your attention on the bigger picture. So, for example, you might not want to have to decide which numbers would be put into which registers, or when to put a number into a memory location instead of into a register. And when writing information to a disk you certainly don't want to have to be concerned with all the things DOS must do to manage files. That's why we have DOS.

And indeed, we can let the computer do more of the work. But as always, there is a price to be paid when we do so. Still, most programmers, most of the time, are more than happy to pay that price, in exchange for what they get from using a higher-level programming language.

Working at a Higher Level: Letting the PC Do More of the Work

A popular piece of advice to managers is "Don't micromanage." That means, tell your workers what results you want, but don't tell them exactly how to do their jobs. Assume they know what they are doing, unless you have a pretty good reason to think that they don't.

The Notion of a High(er)-Level Language

This also describes the goal of higher-level programming languages, which embody a lot of detailed programming knowledge. They are like workers who know how to do a job. We call them tools, because they help us do jobs with less effort.

The programmer who uses one of these tools is acting like a manager, specifying a desired result without having to go into the details of just how that result will be achieved. The program then figures out a means of accomplishing the specified result, and generates a machine-language code sequence that will do that.

In effect, this notion enables one to break up the work of writing a complex computer program into two steps. One is the step of deciding what overall actions are to be performed, in what order, and so on. That is the job of the programmer at the higher level. The other job is deciding how each of the specified actions will be carried out. That is the job of the author of the programming tool that the first programmer is going to use.

After a program is completed, if it is going to be used a lot, a good programmer will examine how the tool did its job in at least those areas of the program that are used most extensively. Then, depending on the programmer's judgment about how well the tool constructed that portion, he or she may redo it using a lower-level tool that gives the programmer more control over just how that task is carried out. In this way the portions of the program that get executed most often can be made as efficient and speedy as possible, without the programmer having to spend an equal amount of effort on all the other parts of the program that only rarely get invoked.

Higher- and Lower-Level Programming Languages

Many different "higher-level" programming tools have been constructed. They differ in a number of ways. Some are barely higher-level than machine language. That is, they make it pretty easy to specify almost exactly what the machine is going to do at every step of the way, yet they manage to remove at least a little of the grunt work off programmers' hands.

Other high-level programming tools are much farther away from what actually will happen. They let the programmer who uses them specify actions in much more general terms, and then they do those specified actions in whatever way the author of the tool deemed best. Using one of these tools makes writing complex programs easier, but it also makes those programs less predictable in terms of exactly how they will do whatever it is they are to do. Generally, even the best of the programs written using the higher-level languages are less efficient and run more slowly than equivalent programs with equivalent functionality that have been carefully crafted in a lower-level language.

Classifying Computer Languages by Generations

Observers of the industry have come up with a classification of computer languages according to how low- or high-level they are. These levels are called *generations* (which partly reflects the fact that it was not very feasible to develop a yet higher-level language until the immediately preceding generation of programming tools was available). Many different computer languages exist in each generation, each optimized for a certain kind of programming task.

The lowest-level, or *first-generation* languages are simply the actual binary machine languages "understood" by the various CPUs. Each different kind (or model) of CPU has its own machine language. (The machine languages used for all the models in Intel's x86 family of CPUs are sufficiently similar to one another that rather than refer to each one as a completely new language, you can think of them as simply different dialects of a common tongue.)

The *second-generation* languages are assemblers. This includes both the very basic assemblers, such as the one built into the program DEBUG, and much more powerful macro assemblers that enable one to use symbolic names and also to name whole blocks of code as macros and invoke them simply by using their names. Generally one needs a different assembler for each new kind of CPU with its own new machine language. Each assembler typically is upgraded when new *models* of that kind of CPU come out, so it can understand and assemble correctly the new dialect of machine language understood by the newest model of the target CPU and still be able to handle assembly-language programs written for earlier models in that CPU family.

The *third-generation* languages enable a programmer to create programs without having to know much about the details of how the particular computer on which it will run is constructed. In particular, you don't have to know how many registers the CPU has (let alone their specific names or sizes), whether there is a memory cache, and so on. Typically each of these languages is available in several dialects, each dialect being designed for use in generating machine language code for a particular kind of machine. The programmer may well be able to write the program once and then compile it several times, using different dialects of the same programming language to create versions of the program to run on each of several different kinds of computers.

An enormous number of third-generation computer programming languages has been created. Some that are commonly used on PCs include FORTRAN (*Formula Translator*), COBOL (*Common Business Oriented Language*), BASIC (*Beginners All-purpose Symbolic Instruction Code*, to give it the original full name), Pascal, Lisp, APL, C, Ada, C++, and so forth. (I have listed these names roughly in the historical order in which these languages were developed.)

The most popular third-generation languages for writing commercial software today are probably C, COBOL, BASIC, and FORTRAN in descending order of popularity. There are so many different languages and so many in widespread use because each different language has its own strengths and limitations.

FORTRAN was originally created to help scientists program computers for technical calculations. COBOL was developed by a committee as the best all-purpose computer language for business programs. It is widely used for accounting programs and other financial applications in large corporations.

BASIC was developed as an instructional language for students at Dartmouth University, so it stresses ease of program crafting with minimal need to remember arcane details. C is intended as a very powerful language for writing operating systems and other incredibly complex software. Because it is intended for use mainly by professional programmers, it has a lot of arcane detail that must be mastered in order to become an expert C programmer. Also, it has enough low-level manipulation possibilities that it almost could be described as both a third- and a second-generation computer language bundled together.

The *fourth-generation* computer languages are designed to minimize the effort necessary to create a program. Often these are intended for use by non-professional programmers. Examples of fourth-generation languages (or 4GL languages as they are sometimes denoted) include dBASE, Forth, Perl, SQL, Clipper, and Visual Basic.

Finally, a *fifth-generation* computer language incorporates knowledge-based expert systems, inference engines, natural language processors, or other kinds of "artificial intelligence." These are only now being developed, and so not many good ones are in widespread use on PCs yet.

Choosing a Computer Language Requires Compromise

From all this diversity, you might be getting a notion that there are some trade-offs one must make—and that would be exactly right. Sometimes a programmer wants nearly total control. Other times programmers must relinquish some of their control in order to focus their attentions on larger issues and leave the lower-level work to others. Some applications involve lots of higher mathematics. Others simply do an enormous amount of simple arithmetic. Still others are primarily concerned with organizing and managing large databases. Choosing the right programming language for a particular task is, therefore, an exercise in balance and compromise.

Often, a high-level language must inefficiently accomplish particular tasks. This is because a tool's authors cannot know exactly which tasks you will be using it to perform, so they build in the flexibility to let it do any that you might want to have it do. But that means carrying along some options you might have no use for, and that can mean the final program it produces is inefficient.

Sometimes the right choice is to first work in some very high-level language to get a working program no matter how inefficient it may be. Then you can go in and redo portions of that program using a lower-level tool to create greater efficiency. This sort of strategy is closely related to the reasons why there are both interpreters and compilers for many of the higher-level programming languages. But to explain that, I must first tell you what those things are.

Interpreters

I have told you that after you have written a program in a higher-level language (anything above the first generation), it must be translated into actual machine language (binary number) code before the CPU can understand and use it. But this translation step can be done in any of several ways.

One way that has a lot of utility is to run a program that will translate one line of the program, and then ask the CPU to execute that line (in its translated form, of course). Only after that is done will it go on to translate the next line. Such a program is called an *interpreter*.

Think of it as acting in a sense like a human language interpreter who is assisting two people in having a conversation. The first person says something. The interpreter translates it. The other person responds, and that response is interpreted back to the first person. This cycle repeats throughout the conversation.

The advantage to this approach is simplicity for the user. I write a program and then run it immediately, and see exactly what each line of the program causes the computer to do. If I must alter a line or two, I can do so and immediately rerun the program, reinterpreting it each time I do so. But when I finally finish the program and then intend to run it many, many times, this is not the optimum way to do the translation.

Compilers

Think of the human language parallel: I am writing this book in English. Suppose the publisher wants to sell many copies in certain foreign countries; the sensible plan for the publisher is to hire interpreters to translate the whole book one time into each target language, and then print and sell copies of each translation. (The alternative, which would resemble the use of a computer language interpreter, would be to let customers rent only the English language book accompanied by a skilled human translator and have that translator read it to the foreign language-speaking customer. Obviously, this isn't the least expensive or most efficient way for the publisher to distribute the work.)

So people have crafted *compiler* programs. After a program is completely written out in the high-level language, the compiler reads it, generates a machine-language program, and saves it in a file. Then, as a totally independent step, that file (the executable program) can be run once or as many times as one wishes.

Almost all commercial programs are created this way, and usually only the executable (translated) program is shipped to the customer. The programmer and publishing company keep the *source code* (the high-level language version of the program) to themselves, in part to keep others from seeing just how they wrote it and perhaps writing a competing program more easily. (One prominent exception to this rule is OpenDOS from Caldera. They have chosen to market it in a fashion similar to the usual way Linux is marketed. That is, they offer the full source code and the compiled program over the Internet for free. But if you want the convenience of having their support, then you can buy a copy of the program from them.)

The advantages of doing this are clear. But the disadvantage to this approach is also clear: If you must alter even one byte of the higher-level language program, then you must recompile the entire program before you can test it. Again, there is an important exception to this: Many commercial programs support some sort of "macro" capability, and/or the use of plug-ins. The macro strategy means that you can embed in the file that the program is designed to process some instructions that effectively augment what the program knows how to do. The plug-in strategy effectively lets third-party developers create small programs that just add some functionality to the main program. I'll tell you more about one kind of plug-in program in my discussion of Web browsers in Chapter 27, "You Can Touch the World, and It May Touch You, Too!"

P-Code

In an attempt to get the best of both worlds, some tool builders came up with what they term *p-code* (or pseudo code). In this approach you write the program in a high-level language, and it is immediately processed into an intermediate form that is close to machine language, but not actually machine language. Then, when you want to run the program (to test it, for example), a p-code interpreter is invoked to do the final step in the translation.

The advantage to this approach is that the p-code translator has a relatively simple job to do, and thus it can be much faster than a full interpreter. But it can enable you to alter just a portion of the program (and recompile just that portion to its p-code equivalent), and then quickly test the whole program once more.

This approach was used for Pascal when it was first introduced for the PC as one of the initial programming languages offered by IBM. BASIC, on the other hand, was introduced only in a fully interpreted (and relatively slow) version. Later, various companies (including Microsoft) came out with compilers for BASIC. And eventually Microsoft introduced QuickBasic, which is a p-code interpreter and editing/compiling environment for BASIC that functions in much the way the early Pascal tools did.

Virtual Machines

In another variation on this same theme, some high-level language developers have built special-purpose computers whose machine language instructions are essentially identical to the constructs in their particular "high-level" language. Then the programmer can write the program and directly execute it on this special kind of computer. No interpretation or compilation is needed.

This special kind of computer (one that has as its basic instruction set the instructions that form a particular high-level computer language) can be, and occasionally is, actually built in a hardware form. The most recent example of this is Sun Microelectronics' microJava 701. This is a new CPU chip that essentially has Java as its native language.

More commonly this type of special computer is merely simulated by running a special program on a more general-purpose computer. For example, you can run a program called Pick on a PC or on a mainframe computer. Either way, the result is to make the computer act as though it were built in some different way as a "Pick machine." Then you run Pick programs on this "virtual Pick machine." Pick machines are special database engines, and they are optimized for that task. Pick programs access databases, using the special qualities of a virtual Pick machine. A very important point to notice is that this strategy enables a user to run the same program on any virtual Pick machine, no matter what kind of computer hardware is actually doing the work.

Similarly, although it now is possible to build a computer with a CPU that executes Java directly, the more common approach, and what is now universally done in PCs, is to simply simulate the Java virtual machine in software running on the PC's normal CPU. I have more to say about this language in my discussion of the Internet in Chapter 27, but for now I just want to point out that Java is meant to be run on either a virtual (simulated) Java machine or on an actual hardware Java computer. And the main virtue of Java is exactly this relative "hardware independence."

Supposedly, a 100 percent pure Java program will run in exactly the same way (although at perhaps different speeds) on any computer, be it a Macintosh, a PC, or Sun workstation. It won't need to be rewritten or recompiled for each different type of computer.

Dividing Up the Work

I have mentioned several times already the notion that programming a computer can be quite complex, and that often the best strategy to follow is to divide the overall task to be accomplished into several subtasks, letting specialists work on each separate subtask. Now I want to go back over that notion in a little more detail and explain the distinction between BIOS programs, the operating system, application programs, and applets.

BIOS-Level Programming

The BIOS (Basic Input-Output System) is the name given to the programs in your PC that are designed to activate the various pieces of hardware. Someone must know exactly how each chunk of hardware works, and therefore exactly what instructions the CPU must process in order to get that chunk of hardware to do some useful task. And there is no need for everyone who writes any other type of PC program to have this detailed knowledge.

Instead, we let BIOS programmers write those very low-level, right-next-to-the-hardware programs to activate each gadget within our PCs. And no matter how this particular keyboard (or video screen, or modem, or whatever) operates, any other program can ask for it to be operated by using a standardized protocol called an Application Program Interface (API).

The motherboard BIOS includes hardware driver programs for all the standard pieces of PC hardware. Any added, non-standard, hardware must either have as a part of itself another BIOS ROM containing its driver programs, or you must load the appropriate programs off a disk into memory before the PC can utilize that non-standard hardware.

But no matter how non-standard the hardware may be, the application programmers don't need to know anything about how it really works. They can just write their programs to ask for standard "services" from that hardware and trust the BIOS driver to handle the details.

On the other hand, many modern operating systems (notably Windows NT and most variants of UNIX) tend not to use the BIOS programs for much of anything. One major reason for this are concerns about security coupled with a need to make sure the operating system works in the same way independent of the machine on which it is running. Instead of executable BIOS code these operating systems incorporate either the equivalent programs, or in the case of Windows NT, a p-code language called ACPI Source Language (ASL) which was developed as a byproduct of the Microsoft-Intel-Toshiba Advanced Configuration and Power Interface (ACPI) initiative.

Application Programs

Application programs do whatever it is you bought your PC to do. At least, I don't know of many people who bought a PC just to watch the DOS prompt or read directory listings. Most of us want to write things, keep track of our money, or communicate using our PCs. And we need application programs to accomplish those tasks.

The Operating System as Middleware

In between the BIOS and the application programs is the realm of the operating system. So, in a way, it could be termed *middleware*. (There is another use for this term that I will explain in Chapter 25, "The PC Reaches Out, Part Two: Through the NIC Node," when I discuss what is termed "client/server" computing.)

The operating system does many things, including, as I mentioned previously, scheduling application programs, resolving conflicts among applications that want access to the same resources, and so on. And it has the task of handing off service requests from the application programs to the hardware device drivers in the BIOS that do the actual work.

Sometimes in the handing off, the operating system also must amplify those requests for service. For example, an application program can ask the operating system to open a file named `C:\MyDocs\Alice` and leave the task of finding that file up to the operating system. But the BIOS can't do that task, described in that way. It must know the exact head, cylinder, and sector numbers where the contents of that file are stored. So the intervening layers of the operating system have to do some work to prepare the request for the BIOS routines.

In this example, the operating system must ask the BIOS to do several subtasks before it can proceed to the main task. The OS must find out, by using the services of the BIOS, which files are stored in which locations so it can figure out from which locations to ask the BIOS to retrieve the required data.

And there are many other instances in which the API used by the application program is stated in more general terms than the API understood by the BIOS routines. Each time, the operating system must do any necessary translation and amplification in order to get the BIOS routines to do whatever is needed to satisfy the application program's requests.

I have stated all this in very general terms. I didn't say whether the operating system were DOS or Windows, or perhaps OS/2 or Linux. It doesn't matter. All of them work in conceptually the same fashion, which is the point I wanted to make.

The Role of Applets

Some programs we run aren't the point of our having a PC. They just make our lives easier along the way. These are the programs we call *applets* (for little applications).

Some applets are utility programs that do such things as format a disk or compare the contents of two files. You run them when you need them. The rest of the time, they just sit peacefully on your disk drive waiting for you to use them next. Other applets are programs you run to alter how the operating system works. In effect, these applets become a part of the operating system. This includes any program you run that doesn't just do a task and exit, but which stays in memory, in a sense running "in the background" while you use your PC to run your major applications.

These programs are generally called "Terminate and Stay Resident" (TSR) programs. This is because they do some initial work when they are first loaded, and then they tell the operating system that they are finished (in computereze, they "terminate" their execution), but that they don't want to give up their memory (thus, they stay resident in that memory). The specific interrupt call these programs use to convey that intention to the operating system has as its name "Terminate and Stay Resident."

Some of these are pop-up programs. You press some hotkey combination of keystrokes (such as Alt+Shift+M), and up pops some little program window in which you can do some side task or look something up.

Other applet programs modify how some device driver works. For example, I have a Microsoft mouse that comes with some special software called Intellipoint. I don't need to use it, but if I do load this software into memory it lets me make the mouse behave quite differently than is possible with the simple Microsoft mouse driver alone.

With the Intellipoint software active, I can make the mouse cursor jump to the default button in any dialog box, or I can make it "wrap around" from one side of the screen to the other. Some other brands of mouse come with different applet software that lets them do different things, such as magnify a portion of the screen around the mouse cursor.

These are just a few things I can do to my mouse driver. Many different applets are loaded each time I boot my computer. You probably do as well—possibly many more than you know.

A special kind of applet that is much talked about these days is the Java applet. Java applets are small programs that are downloaded from some site you are visiting on the World Wide Web (on the Internet). You might not notice that this is happening, but suddenly your Web browser program (Internet Explorer or Netscape Navigator, for example) will start doing something that it simply couldn't do on its own or by using any applets you have stored on your local hard disk.

Mainly this is wonderful. It means that the Web site creator can augment the capabilities of the programs on your PC so you can better interact with that site. Of course, it also has a possibly grim downside: The Java applet could possibly do some damage to your PC. A part of the design of the Java language and virtual machines within the browser in which it runs is supposed to protect you from any rogue Java applets. This works at least most of the time, but it might not work every time. (Most modern Web browsers allow the user to turn off their capability to execute JavaScript or their capability to load and run Java applets. Thus, if you are afraid your data might be damaged by either form of Java, you can protect yourself and still browse the Web—although not all the wonders that are out there will be available to you if you use a Java-disabled browser.) This too, is something I will return to in Chapter 27.

How Not to Keep On Reinventing the Wheel

Programming is detailed, picky, hard work. Programmers are no less lazy than the rest of us, so they have devised some clever ways to avoid the avoidable portions of their work. This section describes briefly some of those strategies. And in the process I also will help you understand one of the most misunderstood jargon terms of our time: Object-oriented programming.

Programming Libraries

Almost all application programs must handle the same jobs, such as getting input from the keyboard and mouse, putting information on the screen, and opening files. By the division of labor described earlier, all the picky details of these tasks are handled by low-level driver programs. But even with that help, the application program must have at least a few lines of code to ask for that help, and those lines will be repeated over and over again in program after program.

To save time and effort, the obvious thing to do is save those lines of code in some form that lets them be reused as needed. This is the essential idea behind a *programming library*.

Such a library can be as simple as a single file that contains many lines of code, with the idea that the programmer will cut and paste sections from this file into the program currently under construction. Or it can be somewhat more sophisticated, with a directory portion that describes all the blocks of code it contains so that the cutting and pasting can be automated.

Program Linkages and Modular Programs

The next step beyond this is to build a mechanism for assembling programs out of building blocks. Those building blocks are pretested blocks of code in a library. But now, instead of cutting out each little program fragment he or she wishes to use and then pasting it into your main program, the programmer can simply include in the main program a pointer to that block. Then, when the program is compiled, the compiler can know enough to open up the library file, read the relevant blocks, and act as though they were a part of the main program.

This action is called *linking*. The compiler translates the main program into machine code (putting it in a file called an *object module*), with a description included of where routines from the library must be inserted. Then a separate program, called a *linker*, will read the object module and extract from the library the appropriate machine language routines to complete the program. Notice that now the library will not contain blocks of high-level language code. Instead, each of those blocks must have been precompiled and ready for use.

There is another way to use a library of this type. You don't have to have the compiler actually include the machine language code fragments inside the compiled application program. Instead, you can have the program reach out and execute those code fragments from within the library program each time it needs them whenever that application program is itself executed. In order for this to work, of course, the library in question must be available to that running application program. Such a memory-loaded, instantly available, run-time library of code fragments is called a *dynamic link library*, or DLL.

Yet another variation on the same idea is the use of a plug-in applet. This is a small program that can add functionality to an application. In effect, the application must be built to, at various points, call a routine in an external DLL. That routine does nothing. But if you load the plug-in, it is capable of insinuating itself in a way that makes the main application run it instead of the do-nothing routine in the DLL. Mechanisms of this type in an application are referred to as *hooks*, and without them, no plug-in programs could possibly be added to the application.

Object-Oriented Programming

Finally we come to that wonderful and frustrating phrase, object-oriented programming (OOP). This once meant something very precise. Now, however, it sometimes seems to mean whatever the speaker wants it to mean. If a company says its tools really support OOP, it means the tools support what the company wants you to think OOP is. And each company's tool is likely to do slightly (or greatly) different things.

I won't go into all the variations on this idea that are currently in use. Instead, I shall try to give you a sense of the overall concept. It is a very powerful concept, even though the tools to put it into practice are still being refined in an attempt to make all the promise of this approach at last become real.

Before I can define OOP, I must describe the old style of programming in a slightly different way than I have up to now. In most older programming languages, the programmer crafts some lines of code designed to perform a procedure on some data. The data is thought of as being the object acted upon by the program—something that is outside the procedure.

If you were to create a new program based on an existing program, you would read over the details of the existing program, copy unchanged what you wanted to use, and write the new parts from scratch. Then, after compiling it, you would introduce this program to the data on which it is to work.

The essence of OOP is to create new kinds of programs. They are functional blocks that contain procedures and even some data, and you are supposed to view these blocks as being *black*. That is, you can activate a block (have it do one of the things it "knows" how to do) and yet have utterly no notion of how it works or what it contains.

This all sound quite abstract, and it is. So, let me get a little more explicit, and in the process introduce some of the OOP jargon.

Objects, Classes, Instances, and Libraries

In OOP programming a key concept is a *class*. This is a type of a something. For example, you might define a class as a button in a dialog box on a computer screen. You can do something with this button (in particular, you can "press it" by clicking on it with your mouse or other pointing device), and it will react somehow. The "class" in this case would be simply all possible buttons that you can make appear on a computer screen and that could then be pressed.

When you have a class, you can define subclasses with some additional particulars. For example, you might define a subclass of buttons called "rectangular buttons." Or green ones. Or ones with labels. Each of these is a particular subset of all possible buttons. And of course you could have among the rectangular buttons a subclass of those that also have labels, and within them a subclass that are red but turn green when pressed.

A particular button is an *instance* of a particular subclass of the class of all buttons. An instance of a button is also referred to as an *object*.

The definitions of various classes of objects (and also of some subclasses) can be referred to in the aggregate as a *class library*.

Attributes, Behaviors, and Methods

Each class (or subclass) will have some set of properties. Some of these are best called attributes. For example, a particular instance of the button class will have a particular size, shape, color, and value (content) for its label.

The attributes are stored in variables. The values in those variables are the attributes for this particular instance of this class; the variables themselves are the attributes of the class.

Other properties tell how the button behaves. For example, when it is pressed (by a mouse click) it will do something. Perhaps it will send a particular message to some other object. Behaviors are defined by *methods*. That is, you write a procedure to spell out just what a certain behavior shall be, and that procedure is now one of the methods for this class of object.

Notice that methods within a class can act upon objects outside that class. Thus, in our example, the button can send a message to some other kind of object (perhaps a window that is supposed to open or close when that button is pressed). This behavior is specified by a method within this class definition, even though it implies an action on an outside object.

Inheritance, Interfaces, and Packages

The payoff to all this begins with the concept of inheritance. After you have defined some classes, you can define a new subclass by naming the class of which it is a subclass and then spelling out only those attributes and methods that this subclass has but its parent class doesn't also have.

By the act of saying that a new object is an instance of a subclass of a certain class you automatically imply that it has all the attributes and methods that characterize the objects in that class, plus the new ones that you are explicitly defining for this subclass. (If you don't want some subset of the attributes and methods in the class of objects you referred to, you can simply redefine those attributes or those methods in your new subclass definition.)

The jargon language for this goes thus: A subclass *inherits* the attributes and behaviors of its parent class of objects. The way this helps is that you don't now have to copy the sections of older programs that you like. Just name your new objects as subclasses of those older program's classes (with specified differences), and you will get the full attribute and behavior set you want. The older program is in a sense included by reference. (And you must build into your OOP program a pointer to that older program, which is to say to its class library.)

The *interface* to an object is just a list of the methods it contains (without the details of what those methods actually do). This list doesn't include the methods that are defined in the parent classes above this one in the hierarchy; only the ones defined in this class definition are listed in its interface.

Finally, *packages* are groups of related classes and interfaces that are bundled together, so you can imply all of them by referring to the package name or some of them by referring to the package name and the class name within that package. This lets different objects have the same name and yet be different, simply by being contained in different packages.

Putting It All Together

Whew. That was a quick one. I hope I didn't confuse you any more than necessary. And in case I did, let me try to recap what I just described. Object-oriented programming simply is a formally defined way to access the capabilities of previously written programs within a new program. This strategy means that when you have a useful package of classes and interfaces, you can use it without needing to know the details of its contents. And yet you can override any of the attributes or behaviors of any of the individual classes within that package any time you need to do so.

There is nothing magic about OOP, nor is it necessarily a "better" way to program than the older style with its libraries and linking. Modular programming in some manner is almost a necessity, and certainly adds efficiency to the programming task. But which kind of modularity one uses is less critical.

Helping Ordinary People "Program" Their PCs Easily

Now for the last section of this chapter. The one that tells you how you, whoever you are, can and probably do engage in programming your PC. Often it is so easy that you won't even be aware that what you are doing is programming—but it is.

If you have ever written a DOS batch file, which is a list of commands you don't want to have to type over and over again at the DOS prompt, you were programming. So you put them into a file, give it a name (with the extension .BAT), and thereafter you simply type its name at the DOS prompt and COMMAND.COM does the rest. COMMAND.COM is, in this instance, acting as an interpreter of the DOS batch programming language.

If you use PC DOS 7 or OS/2, another kind of programming language is available that is similar to the DOS batch language but a good deal more powerful: That is what IBM calls its REXX language.

Similarly, if you use a spreadsheet program and write some macros to perform useful calculations for you, then you are programming. The spreadsheet program is interpreting them, which is to say that, among other things, it is an interpreter for that macro programming language.

Early versions of Microsoft Word had a macro language (Word Basic). That was modeled upon QuickBasic, which is one of the older computer programming languages (well, at least in its earlier, interpreted form, usually referred to as BASIC). With this language you can write macros to do all manner of things within your word processor. More recently, Microsoft has phased out Word Basic, but that functionality has been transferred to a more general language, subsets of which are available in all the Office applications. This universal language is now based on the more GUI-oriented version of Basic known as Visual Basic, and the form in which it appears in Office is known as Visual Basic for Applications.

With the growth of the power of these batch and macro languages, many people who never thought they would be programmers are writing some pretty serious PC programs. And now we have yet another kind of programming that "ordinary" folks may find themselves doing: HTML programming for Web or intranet publishing.

If you run a Web page editor or word processor that can save your work as hypertext, you will seem only to be typing and formatting a page of text. Then you will highlight some phrases or words and indicate that they are links to some other pages. The program you are running will use that information to construct for you a HyperText Markup Language (HTML) document, which is a kind of program. You can see this when someone viewing that page clicks on a link, and some action results (the display of a new link usually, but it also could be the downloading and running of a Java applet or a JavaScript program). In this context, your word processor or Web page editor is actually a fourth-generation computer language programming tool.

Summary

In this chapter I have explained a wide variety of ways that people write programs for PCs. I also have shown you some of the distinguishing features of different generations of computer programming languages and of different ways that these high-level language programs can be translated into machine-language instructions that the PC's CPU can understand and act upon.

Finally, I explained what OOP means (and a lot of associated jargon), what Java applets are, and how creating a Web page, which is some serious programming, can be done as easily as writing a letter.

In the next chapter I will carry this story on to the next stage: how PCs can literally talk to you, and how you may be able to fix up your PC so that when you talk to it, it will understand you and act on what you tell it to do.

19

Some PCs Can Understand Speech and Talk to Us

Peter Norton®

For many years after the invention of the digital electronic computer, virtually all the information that was put into computers came via a keyboard.

Historical Aside: For the first several decades of their existence, electronic computers ran most of the time in what was referred to as *batch mode*. This meant that the programs and data were prepared offline by people typing on keypunch machines to create several reams of punched cards. Then, when an entire job's worth of cards were readied, they were submitted for online processing.

When the computer—which was time-shared among hundreds of users—next became available, a computer operator had to run that deck of cards through the computer's punched card reader. The computer would read the cards and do the actions indicated thereon. The output would mostly be printed on paper or punched on additional cards. The operator would gather up the output, bundle it with the deck of input cards, and place them in some convenient place where they could be retrieved later by the user.

Starting in the late 1960s, computers began to be operated in a more direct manner. It became common to enter information on the keyboard of a terminal that was attached directly to the computer. Some of the output (about the job's status, or in a few cases its actual output) would show up on the user's terminal screen more or less immediately. The rest of it would be sent to paper, punched cards, or magnetic tape, which the user would not get until later.

The era of mainly characters-in-and-characters-out computing persisted until after the PC was introduced in 1981. In the mid 1980s, computer interactivity took on a new aspect. We became concerned for the first time with the *graphical form* of the information being put into and coming out of our computers.

Most input was still done by means of characters typed on a keyboard, but we supplemented that with the use of a mouse, trackball, or graphics tablet. The output, on screen or on paper, began to take on a much richer graphical form. Letters were set in various fonts, and pictures were often added. (Color had been an option for screen output for a long time. Soon, adding color to output printed on paper became another common option.)

More recently, another new dimension has been added to computer input and output. This time it involves hearing. The new dimension is that of sounds—sounds generated by our PCs and sounds we make that it "hears" and responds to.

This and the next several chapters tell you the story of how sound has been added to the PC's repertoire. This chapter focuses on the ways in which sounds are used to enter information that otherwise would have to be typed on a keyboard or input by using a mouse, and as an alternative means of output for information that in the past could only have been printed (on screen or paper) in character form.

Making Conversational PCs: Breaking Down the Overall Job

The notion of being able to converse with a computer is not new: *Star Trek* is famous for having used this idea very effectively for over 30 years. But when manufacturers tried actually making a computer that was capable of conversing with users, they found that the task was much, much harder than they had expected. (I can recall reading the predictions of "experts" that speech recognition would be common to computers "within the next five to ten years" many times over the past 25 years.)

You can divide the things a PC must do in order to converse with a user into four subtasks. It was obvious to researchers early on that these were the tasks to be performed, although just how each one could be performed by a computer turned out to be not quite so obvious.

First—and by far the easiest—the PC must speak. By this I mean it must be able to produce sounds that resemble what one human might say to another.

Second, the PC must be able to listen and to recognize what it hears. By this I mean that if you speak into a microphone, the PC must be able to convert the electronic signals from the microphone into a stream of data which it can manipulate. This has proven to be one of the most difficult parts of the overall job.

Third, the PC must be able to understand the speech it has heard. This means taking the sentences it recognized and figuring out how to respond. The sentences might be commands it is to perform, or they might be data it is to process. Combinations of these two are also possible—even likely. You might say to your computer "Find Joe Jones' phone number." The PC must understand that this sentence is both a command (find a phone number and display it, recite it, or perhaps offer to dial it) and data (the name of the person whose number is being sought).

Finally, the PC must be able to compose relevant responses, in a human language form. Then it can use its speaking capability to deliver that response.

Making PCs Speak

Most natural human languages are expressed in two ways: orally and in writing. Either way, an expression in a language can be broken down into its constituent parts. There is a virtually unlimited number of possible expressions, but only a limited number of basic elements are needed to construct these.

For written language, we all know the rules: Anything we write will be composed of paragraphs, each containing sentences, with each of those containing words, and each word being written as a string of letters. Letters are the basic symbols; words, sentences, and paragraphs are larger units in which those basic symbols are organized.

Spoken languages have a similar, yet different, structure. You can think of a spoken sentence as being composed of words, but if you consider it in terms of the sounds that make it up, it pretty clearly isn't made up of words—or at least not of clearly separated chunks that can easily be recognized as words. Realizing this was the first step to making PCs that could speak (or hear).

Phonemes

The actual building blocks of speech are called *phonemes*. These are the elemental sounds any human being can make. You can utter only some fairly limited number of possible sounds.

The sounds that any particular person learns to utter are determined largely by the language(s) spoken around that person early in life. You normally learn to speak as your parents and others near you speak. So if you grow up in Japan hearing only Japanese, you will learn a different set of common sounds than if you grow up in France hearing only French.

Anyone who has learned a foreign language as an adult can testify to the difficulty of learning the sounds that are used in that language but not in any you learned early in life. Still, it is possible to learn to utter just about any sounds that any other human can utter. And the whole collection of those sounds makes up the universe of human phonemes.

After you understand the relationship between phonemes and speech, the next step is to relate the strings of characters we call words in the written form of a language to the corresponding phonemes as those words are spoken by a native speaker of that language. If we can make that connection, we can teach a computer to speak. This isn't, as it turns out, a trivially easy task. But doing a pretty good job is possible.

Pronouncing Dictionaries Are Necessary, But Not Enough

The first step in the association of text and sound is simple. Associate a most commonly used phoneme or set of phonemes with each letter used in the language you want the computer to speak. Next, consider all the special-case combinations. In English, the combination *ph* carries the same pronunciation as the letter *f* (most of the time). Similarly, the letter combination *tion* usually is pronounced like the word *shun*.

Some words are special cases in themselves. They simply don't have the pronunciation you would expect from the way they are spelled. For these, you must have a dictionary that spells out the *phoneme sequence* needed to pronounce that word correctly.

Even that isn't quite enough. Sometimes a word's pronunciation depends upon how it is being used. In that case you also must have some way to figure out what part of speech it is from the structure of the sentence containing it and then apply the correct pronunciation for that context. Or, the context might be determined by the subject matter. In either case, more global analysis of the sentences is needed to decide which pronunciation to use.

Gender, Inflection, and Emotion Are Other Issues

With a combination of all these strategies, it is possible for a computer to analyze a text string and then produce a phoneme string representing that text string. If those phonemes are pronounced correctly, a spoken sentence will be generated.

Correct pronunciation opens a whole new can of worms. Who is speaking? What gender is the speaker? What age? With what accent does that speaker say things in this language? And what is the emotional content of the sentence? Some of these issues are relatively easy to deal with. Others have only been approximated, so far.

The first step is to decide how the phonemes will be generated. There are basically two choices: one is to synthesize them, and the other is to play back a pre-recorded sample of a person saying that phoneme.

If you use a synthesis technique, many parameters can be applied to influence how the phoneme will sound. These parameters enable you to simulate either gender and to adjust for apparent age of the speaker. They also will allow some rough simulation of dialect.

But the approach that will yield the best-sounding speech is simply to record actual human beings (of a range of ages and other characteristics) speaking. Then break down those recordings into their phonemes. If you do this and store them in a cataloged fashion, it is possible (although hardly easy) for the computer to stitch the sampled pieces together to pronounce the sentences.

All this tends to produce fairly flat, emotional-less speech. So far, computers are not very good at generating the correct emotional flavor for a speech. Still, this is good enough for many purposes. The raw information in a sentence is usually discernible by human beings, if only they can hear each word. The emotional embellishments add a lot to human conversation, but mostly they are used to convey an emotional subtext and we aren't yet in a position to ask our computers to do this for us.

PCs, or even mainframe computers, aren't yet up to analyzing a textual passage and then giving an emotionally compelling rendition of that passage. But then, many people aren't able to do this either. That is one reason why we pay actors to do this for us. So asking computers to do the job of translating text into speech better than most ordinary people can do that job is probably asking too much, at least for now.

What Is the Current State of This Art?

The many steps I have just described sound rather complicated. They are, but not unmanageably so. People who care have figured out how to do this job fairly well.

Not everyone needs or wants a talking PC. However, if you are blind (or even nearly blind), it can be crucial. For this reason, most of the text-to-speech tools were initially developed for the sight-impaired.

In other contexts, having a PC that talks—especially if it also can listen and understand human speech—can be more than just convenient. That combination, what I call a conversational PC, can be used to support someone who is doing a task that requires the use of their hands and eyes.

One example of this is an aircraft mechanic doing a routine maintenance inspection of an airplane. Having a computer that can record messages about what the mechanic is finding and also prompt the mechanic for what parts must be replaced can greatly enhance the mechanic's productivity. In fact, some airlines (and also some railroads) have been doing this for the past several decades using minicomputers. Now it is practical to do the same thing using PCs.

As the PC's capability to analyze speech input increases, and as this gets applied to performing increasingly sophisticated database accesses, having a talking PC as a surgeon's assistant in every hospital might become standard procedure. We aren't there yet, but it is certainly coming—and yes, these things will probably be commonplace "within the next five to ten years."

Teaching PCs to Listen and Understand

This, of course, brings us right back to the other side of the equation: Having PCs that are capable of listening to humans and understanding. This involves two tasks: Hearing the words and sentences, and then figuring out what those sentences mean.

Hearing and Understanding Is Hard Work

You probably haven't given much thought to how you understand what people say to you. If you have, you realize just how complex that operation is.

First, realize that you don't hear words. You don't even hear phonemes. You hear sounds. Sometimes it is hard to distinguish the wail of a cat from some sounds people make. So you really ought to have sympathy for the designers who have endeavored to make PCs understand speech.

There are, it turns out, two very different ways to speak to a computer. One is the natural way people talk. The other is a highly artificial way to talk that is much easier for a computer to understand.

After I explain this distinction, I will also address briefly the issue of having a computer that understands one particular person versus one that can understand a wide range of people.

Natural Speech Versus Interrupted Speech

If you have tried to learn a foreign language, you have no doubt noticed that one of the very hardest things to learn is to hear what a person speaking that language is saying. That is, what exactly are the words being spoken. Leave aside their meaning for a moment, just try to recognize what words the sounds represent.

The reason this is hard is that usually we speak rapidly. It seems much more rapid if you aren't familiar with the language. We do this because we seek to convey content as quickly as we can. So we speak essentially as rapidly as a trained listener can comprehend our speech. And if you aren't yet a well-trained listener in that language, you will have difficulty discerning the words being spoken.

This suggests that the most difficult aspect of understanding is just this task of deciphering the words from the stream of sounds. This is precisely what the research into making a PC that hears has also told us.

Breaking It Up Makes Hearing It So Much Simpler

Think about what foreigners do when they want to be understood. No, I don't mean that they shout. They slow down. They speak each word clearly and distinctly. That is essentially what we had to do until very recently to get a computer to understand speech. Separate each word by short bits of silence—in effect, make the speaker pronounce each interword space.

This is called *interrupted speech*. With this strategy the computer's task is made very much simpler. Each burst of speech can be counted on to represent one word. So the computer can compare that burst of sound with a stored sample of all the words it understands and pick the one that matches most closely.

Flowing Speech Is Much More Natural

Speaking for an extended period in an interrupted fashion is rather tiring, however, and most unnatural. Clearly the goal must be to have PCs that can listen to a human speaking as humans normally do, and still be able to pick out the words and the meaning. For many years this was only a holy grail out there somewhere to be yearned for and sought but never found.

Now, finally, we have arrived. Sort of. In some fairly limited situations it is now possible to use natural, connected speech in speaking to a PC and have the PC able to discern what words are being spoken. This only works (so far) for single-speaker recognition, although the best of today's speech recognition programs are capable of storing speech and expressive-style profiles for many different individuals. Each user of the program has his or her own profile, which the program uses to aid in the interpretation of that user's words. Group conversational recognition remains elusive, but individual recognition can approach 97%. That is already quite an achievement.

Phonemes and Context Are Key

Whether you are attempting to make a PC program to recognize interrupted or connected speech, the first step is to attempt to identify the phonemes from the sounds the PC receives. Interrupted speech helps, mainly because the program knows where at least some of the phonemes start (right after each pause). With continuous speech, just the problem of deciding when a new phoneme begins is a fairly tough one.

All natural human languages are redundant. We say quite a few more words than we need to say, just to minimally represent our thoughts. One reason we do this is to give some contextual clues to our listeners to help them identify the words we are speaking from the sounds they are hearing. Naturally, this suggests that a PC program for hearing should also be looking for these same contextual clues. Fortunately, all the good ones do.

In fact, they take this notion somewhat further—and often a bit more rigidly—than we do. The PC program will have a dictionary of all the words you might say (with their pronunciations), but it doesn't assume that every word is equally likely. Instead, it takes careful note of what you have just said to make predictions about what you will likely say next.

This means that a speech recognition program has at every moment a fairly fixed notion of what you are about to say, based on what it has already recognized. If you suddenly change topics, you can expect that the recognition accuracy will fall until the PC figures out once more what the relevant context is.

If you think about it, this is not very different from what happens to people. If you suddenly jump to a wholly new topic, you can expect your listeners to ask you to repeat yourself. People have the same problems as PC speech recognition programs—although mostly we are much better than those programs at hearing an unexpected word correctly the first time. Still we are likely to be unsure, and to ask for clarification.

Most speech recognition programs aren't that conversational yet. They simply make their best stab at recognizing whatever you say, and let any mistakes simply enter their generated text. You must go back later and clean up those messes manually. (Some of these programs will flag the words it is pretty sure it didn't get right—perhaps by displaying them in a different color—to help you find them when you are in the correction phase.)

Trained Recognition Versus Universal Recognition

People and PC programs both can only recognize a word by what it sounds like, and it certainly helps both people and PCs if the same word always sounds the same. This is much more likely to happen if the words are spoken by the same person all the time.

Thus, one way to make a PC speech recognition program work much more accurately is simply to limit it to recognizing a particular person's speech. This strategy has been used for a long time, and whenever it can be applied, it certainly makes the PC program's job much easier.

Single-Speaker Recognition Is Relatively Easy and Reliable

With the single-speaker approach, you first "train" the recognition program by reading some sentences that the program displays. This lets the program analyze how you say each of those words. Later on, it can apply that knowledge to figure out what words you are most likely saying as you dictate.

You can let other people train the program also, but you must first tell the program each time you change to a new speaker, and let it store each person's pronunciations in a separate profile. When you begin dictating, you first identify yourself to the PC so it will recognize your speech accurately.

Using this single-speaker, trained recognition strategy—and assuming you are using a very proficient context analyzer—it is possible to get over 90 percent accuracy in recognizing the words spoken, even when the total vocabulary of possible words is many tens of thousands.

Nobody's Perfect

Whether your recognition program has been trained or not, you must realize that mistakes will be made. So some means of correcting errors is important. If you are using the speech recognition program to enter a block of text, you might choose to enter it all without regard to errors. Later, you can find and correct all the errors. That interrupts the dictation process minimally. But if you are using the speech recognition program to control a process by voice commands, you must catch and correct each error as it occurs. The best way to do this is to have the PC tell you what it thinks you said and have you confirm that before it takes any significant action based on what it heard. If it got the command wrong, you can simply tell it to ignore that command, and then try again to get it to recognize what you want it to do.

Understanding What You Have Heard

Now that it is possible for a PC to recognize what a person says to it, what's the next task? Understanding what those spoken words, phrases, or sentences are telling the PC to do (and then doing it).

The level of difficulty this job has will depend on the context in which you are doing it. If you plan to let your PC listen and then take actions based on what you said to it, you might be able to limit the possible actions enough that you can recognize each command with a very high probability.

But what if you want to have the PC able to engage in a normal, flowing human conversation—with all the interrupted sentence fragments, sudden changes of subject, "ums" and "ahs," and other extraneous noises that this implies? You'll have to accept a lot less reliability in the recognition you'll get, and you will probably have to build in a lot of confirmation loops to check on how accurately the speaker has been heard. Even worse, you won't have many clues to let you know whether the speaker's utterances are commands or simply data to be stored.

Indeed, this latter task—making a robot that can hold a normal conversation with a human being in a fashion that is indistinguishable from talking to another human—is the benchmark for a true "artificial intelligence," and so far it is another holy grail out there somewhere, but certainly not within our immediate reach.

Generating Useful and Relevant Responses

The last task in making a conversational PC is enabling it to generate meaningful verbal responses. If your PC program has understood the oral input, it probably can generate relevant output. This task seems likely to be the least difficult of our four.

In fact, for some limited contexts, this task is being done right now and very well. Seeing-impaired folks can get their PCs to talk to them, giving them prompts as to what they are to do next, and also speaking all the error messages, and so on. This works just fine. The talking PC has been invaluable to people with other types of physical disabilities as well. Stephen Hawking, the brilliant quantum physicist, has been able to give lectures and express ideas which have redefined our very understanding of the universe around us through the use of a talking PC which is built into his wheelchair.

However, if you want really general conversations from your PC, you will find that doing this well is harder than anything we are able to do with our PCs today.

How Far Along Are We Now?

What is the current state of the art in this whole area of creating a conversational PC? The answer you will get to this question will depend a good deal on the person you ask and the assumptions that person makes about what you are seeking.

Converting Text to Speech

Many companies have made products that are pretty good at converting text to speech—provided you don't mind that the speech has little or no emotional embellishment. Some companies let the user add special emotion tags in the text and then their products can do a fair job of adding appropriate inflections to their output—although nothing you would mistake for a real human being. Most of the time, text-to-speech programs are used to read prepared text files or simple canned messages rather than to speak some complex response the PC generated in reaction to an event input. IBM's voice recognition program ViaVoice can speak any text you give it. You even can tweak it to let your PC sound more or less like a man, woman, or child, and to speak your text with at least some emotional embellishments.

Speech Recognition

The progress in speech recognition in the past few years has been quite dramatic. We have had some fairly single-speaker (trained) recognition programs for interrupted speech for several years. There are also some very successful applications in which untrained recognition of (some very limited) oral input has been possible.

But for the more general problem, it is only this year that I can say that it is possible to buy a reasonably good continuous speech recognition program. Those programs work best when trained properly by the speaker and when the program has had a chance to "read" a lot of text either spoken or written by that speaker to learn that speaker's habits in terms of how he or she puts words together.

IBM's ViaVoice program is one very good example of a product that can do this job acceptably. It requires a pretty hefty assemblage of PC hardware. You better not try using it on anything less than a 200MHz Pentium with MMX, and you'll do best if you give it lots of RAM to work with (at least 32MB for Windows 95 or 48MB for Windows NT), as well as sufficient disk space to hold all your utterances as well as the text into which they get translated.

But with these restrictions, it is possible for ViaVoice to do a decent job as a dictation assistant with an internal vocabulary of up to 64,000 words or phrases. (A single phrase that is always spoken as a single burst of sound is, so far as any speech recognition program is concerned, a single word.) Words which are not part of ViaVoice's default vocabulary can be added by each user on an as-you-use-them basis.

Dragon Systems has a similar product called Naturally Speaking. Its hardware requirements and performance are comparable to those of ViaVoice.

"Understanding" Oral Input

Both ViaVoice and Naturally Speaking are intended primarily as tools to let you enter text without typing. They aren't really set up to accept lots of commands and have your PC act on them.

Microsoft's product, Voice Pilot, lets you command your PC orally. It isn't intended for extended textual input. In order to make the program work satisfactorily, the user must create a structured file of acceptable responses at each stage of operation of the PC. Because of design limitations in that program, this file structure cannot be very complex. Still, it will work, and if you are unable to operate either the keyboard or mouse, being able to run your PC orally can be a godsend.

Generating Relevant Oral Output

As I mentioned earlier, the task of generating relevant outputs to be spoken by a text-to-speech program to create a conversational PC is either pretty simple (if you don't want many alternative spoken utterances) or far too complex for the state of the art (if you want a fully natural conversational capability). So there is no generally applicable answer to where we are in accomplishing this task, other than to say that substantially more work is needed.

What's Next?

Will your PC ever be capable of holding a conversation with you that is as smooth and natural sounding as the ones with the android "Data" on the TV show *Star Trek, The Next Generation*? Ever is a long time. That show is set in the twenty-fourth century, and by then, we might have that kind of capability. But for now, it doesn't look like it's going to be any time soon.

It is already relatively easy to make PCs speak error messages, instead of beeping at you and putting a dialog box on the screen. It's easy, but do you want your PC to nag you? I predict that having a PC that can nag you will not be very popular—except with the seeing-impaired for whom it is nothing short of wonderful.

You should now have a good sense of what the problems are with oral PC input and output and know roughly where we are in solving those problems. Next, I explain other ways that sound (and video) is being used to enrich the computing experience, and to integrate the personal computer with the rest of a person's consumer electronic devices.

V

Splendiferous Multimedia PCs

20

How to "Wow" a Human

Peter Norton®

Initially, the "killer application" for PCs was Lotus 1-2-3. By this I mean that once we had that program, its popularity made it quite obvious that PCs were here to stay. This one program made a PC so useful to so many people in business that nothing more was needed to ensure the success of PCs in a business setting.

For most of the next five years, almost every PC user used his PC exclusively to manipulate numbers and words. This meant that displays that could do more than show numbers and words (as simple, monospaced text) were almost superfluous. Likewise, the capability to make sounds other than a beep was just not a priority for most PC users.

Now, however, multimedia PCs are all the rage. Purchase-packages today are such that you may actually pay more to get less. The manufacturers of PCs are suggesting that the "killer" reasons for buying multimedia PCs are our growing need to use the Internet and the coming convergence between computers and television.

What is all the fuss about, and is it really an important issue? What, in fact, makes a PC a multimedia PC? Those are some of the questions I'll answer for you in this chapter.

What Is a Multimedia PC?

In general, PCs handle information. We put information in and get that information out. They are, therefore, acting also as communication devices—they convey information. In the past, the principal medium of communication for PCs was numbers and words. Now we have added to that still images, moving pictures, and sounds, including voices and music. (Even touch is sometimes used for communication. When you wear gloves to play a game and they give you the tactile feeling of touching something, that is the PC communicating to you via your sense of touch, which makes that PC an even more multi- type of multimedia machine. So far, we haven't extended the range of PC's multiple media into smells, but can that development be far off?!)

All these different modalities of communication also can be viewed as different mediums of communication. A multimedia PC is simply one that can use more than one of these media. Strictly speaking, this means all our PCs have always had enough capabilities to justify the descriptor "multimedia," although only barely in some cases. But clearly the current notion of a multimedia PC (MPC) means something much more than simply a PC that can show you words, numbers, and still images, and possibly also make some sounds.

Indeed, there is a formal definition of an MPC. Actually there are, so far, three of them. These definitions were first agreed upon by an industry consortium called the Multimedia PC Marketing Council. That group has now been absorbed into the Software Publishers Association, where it is referred to as the Multimedia PC Working Group (MPCWG).

A Moving Target

Near the end of the PC's first decade, when a 386-based PC was a pretty hot machine and when CD-ROM drives were just beginning to show up in computer stores (mostly single-speed, with a few double-speed ones available at a premium price), it dawned on several people that soon PCs would be capable of doing some pretty serious multimedia work. That wasn't going to happen, however, unless some standards were in place—some agreed-upon definition of what capabilities a multimedia PC would have, and therefore some guidelines for developers as to what their programs could expect to find in the way of features they could utilize.

Unfortunately, getting some international standards body to promulgate a new standard would have taken too long, so a group of manufacturers banded together and called themselves the Multimedia PC Marketing Council. They applied for a trademark for an MPC and told all the manufacturers of PCs and PC add-in devices that if they'd like to have the benefits of using this trademark on their products, those products would have to at least have this particular specified set of capabilities.

The MPC Council wanted manufacturers to agree to build machines to this new standard and wanted multimedia program authors to tailor their programs to use just those guaranteed features. In order for this to happen, the designers of the new standard had to make that standard something that could be built and sold at not too high a cost. That meant that they couldn't specify a dream machine; they could only specify a pretty good PC configuration that could be built affordably using available parts and that would be at least minimally capable of presenting multimedia materials.

MPC1 and MPC2

As created by the Multimedia PC Marketing Council, the first version of the MPC definition was called MPC1. To qualify for the MPC trademark, a PC must, at a minimum, have had a small variety of characteristics—386SX processor or better, 2MB of RAM, VGA display, and so on—all of which are already ancient by even today's low-end standards.

Just two years later, the Multimedia PC Marketing Council came out with an upgraded version of the MPC definition. This one they referred to as the MPC Level 2 specifications, or MPC2. The council also upgraded its requirements of the manufacturers in another, significant way. It made eligibility for displaying the MPC trademark depend not only on the features included in a system, but also on having that system pass some qualifying tests that would verify compliance with the newly toughened standard.

To qualify as an MPC2 machine, a PC must at least have these things:

- 25MHz or faster, 486SX or better CPU
- 4MB of RAM (with 8MB being recommended)
- 3.5-inch floppy diskette drive

- 160MB hard disk drive
- Video display capable of 640×480 pixel resolution and at least 16-bit color graphics
- Two-button mouse
- 101-key keyboard (or functional equivalent)
- CD-ROM drive (at least double-speed)
- Audio board
- Serial and parallel ports
- MIDI input-output port
- Joystick port
- Headphones and/or loud speakers
- Capability to run Windows 3.0 with its Multimedia Extensions, or Windows 3.1

In addition, the council specified in some detail what features the CD-ROM and audio boards must support. None of the things it specified are now anything less than standard, and again in most respects, our modern equivalents far surpass these requirements.

Finally, of course, an MPC2 machine must pass the MPC2 test suite. That test suite is available on a CD-ROM. With it you can load the CD and run its program to exercise your PC's multimedia features and thus determine if it really does qualify for an MPC Level 2 certification.

Historical Aside: Because multimedia applications for PCs generally produce images on the screen and sounds from the speakers, it is quite clear that an MPC must have at least fairly good video and audio capabilities. Less obvious is why it must have a CD-ROM drive.

Back when the first MPC standard was promulgated, hard disks were relatively expensive. Very few people had many hundreds of megabytes of free hard disk space on their PCs, but multimedia applications often require enormous amounts of data—which must be stored someplace. So the obvious solution, given the market realities of that time, was to require a CD-ROM drive.

Now we can afford much larger hard disks, but still, the most affordable way to deliver a multihundred megabyte software package is on a CD-ROM; until recently some companies even charged up to $50 less for their software if you bought it on CD-ROM. That is why all levels of MPC specification require a CD-ROM drive, and why the higher levels demand even greater speed performance from those drives.

MPC3

MPC1 and MPC2 are system specifications. In 1995 MPC3 was announced. It differed from the former two standards in that it was called a "minimum system functionality, but not a recommendation for any particular system configuration." Furthermore, the MPCWG explicitly said that MPC3 does not replace either MPC1 or MPC2. It merely updates the list of desirable properties for a multimedia PC.

Among other changes, MPC3 specifies at least a 75MHz Pentium with hardware-assisted MPEG1 capability, but it also explicitly endorses brands other than Intel-brand CPUs as long as the PCs using them can pass the MPC3 test suite. It ups the minimum acceptable RAM to 8MB and the available hard disk space to 500MB.

The floppy diskette drive is now optional for laptop computers. (When the MPC1 and MPC2 definitions were introduced, laptop computers that could do any multimedia work were rarities. Now, in contrast, most of the ones on the market qualify for MPC3, but still many do not have floppy diskette drives as standard equipment.)

The MPC3 standard goes into great detail on just how fast the hard disk must be and how little of the CPU's time must be needed to transfer data to and from the hard disk. Likewise, it lists the CD-ROM drive capabilities in far more detail than either MPC1 or MPC2. Because caching can increase the apparent speed of any CD-ROM drive, MPC3 specifies a minimum cache speed level as well as a basic, underlying CD-ROM speed (of at least 500KB/sec transfer rate, about equivalent to a triple-speed CD-ROM drive).

The MPC3 audio subsystem description is similarly enhanced. Now stereo speakers are required, with a subwoofer option described but not mandated, and the graphics performance of the video display is detailed in ways not previously mentioned, including mandated support for the VESA Display Power Management System (DPMS) standard.

Video playback capability is now a must. The minimum capability that will earn MPC3 approval includes MPEG1-decoding support with its output being able to drive at least a 320×240 pixel video window, with at least 15-bit color numbers for each pixel, and a full 30 frames per second. All of the I/O ports have their minimum performance specified, and if there is a modem, it must support faxing and at least 28.8kbps data transfers, plus have TAPI support for both inbound and outbound call control.

An MPC3 system must be one that is running DOS version 6.0 or higher and Windows 3.11 or Windows 95 or 98. It must be capable of running one of these software platforms and have that installed on it. Nothing says you can't also have other operating environments installed, with some multiboot capability letting you choose which one to run at any given time.

Finally, the MPC3 standard includes specifications for upgrade kits to enable owners of older PCs to upgrade at least their CD-ROM drive and audio subsystems to full MPC3 performance. However, the resulting PC wouldn't qualify as an MPC3 PC unless it could pass the test suite, which wouldn't be possible if it had a slower, older CPU.

We can all be happy that the industry has adopted these standards, because now we can be quite certain that an MPC2- or MPC3-compliant PC will run any multimedia software we might want to use.

Although the MPC1 standard is now pretty much obsolete, the MPC3 specification is still ahead of most of the market. Our sample desktop system, the Dell XPS M200s, is one of the very few systems that has achieved formal MPC3 certification, so far. The architect of this system said, "It took quite a deal of work to get the certification" (like needing special audio drivers that used Type F DMA to drop the CPU utilization below the requirement; also EDO [memory] would not pass the test but SDRAM memory did).

Do I Need an Intel CPU with MMX to Have a Multimedia PC?

Do you need to have an Intel CPU with MMX to have a multimedia PC? The short answer is no. First of all, remember that MMX is now an industry-wide standard. Intel helped develop it, but they don't own it. So CPU chips from Cyrix and AMD, for example, can and do support MMX. More importantly, however, there is no mention of MMX in the MPC3 standard. So many perfectly good multimedia PCs that are in current use don't have MMX support and don't really need it.

When Intel first started making Pentium CPUs that included support for the so-called multimedia extensions (now known as the MMX instructions), they sought to convince everyone that this capability was vital to good multimedia performance. The truth is, though, that MMX only helps out if the programmer who wrote a particular program decided to use those special instructions. And so far, not many programs use them—and even those often include alternative routines that will be invoked if the CPU doesn't support the MMX instructions.

So unless you run certain game programs or some other program that really needs MMX for speed, you aren't likely to notice the benefits of this technology. That will change in time, as more and more CPUs ship with MMX capability included. (Intel has now stopped making anything but MMX-capable CPU chips, and essentially all of its competitors include MMX support in all of their products as well.)

Understanding the Multimedia PC Technologies

In order to understand what is special about multimedia PCs, you must first understand the technologies that are special to those MPCs. Mostly that means understanding how PCs can produce compelling images (both still and moving) and how PCs can produce impressive sounds.

Screen Output Versus Printer Output

An important point to remember is that most multimedia applications are concerned with presenting information on the PC's video screen (or on some attached video display device, including perhaps a large-screen projection TV) and with offering the user associated sounds via the PC's speakers. (Those audio signals can also be routed to an external sound system to support a large-screen presentation.) You will appreciate the significance of this fact more if you reflect on what is special about the screen output as opposed to, for example, output to a printer.

Most printers are limited to black-and-white pages, although many color printers for PCs are now making their way into both homes and offices. Images on paper and those on screen differ in many ways, of which these are the two most important: First, the printed page images are, of course, static, whereas the onscreen ones can be animated or can even be full-motion video. Second, all PC printers are capable of creating more detailed images than any PC video display. The best video displays offer no more than about 100 pixels per inch. More commonly a PC's screen display presents 40 to 75 pixels per inch. In addition, the screen sizes are often smaller than, and only rarely very much larger than, the pages that PC printers can accommodate. Printers have resolutions that range from a low of 200 dots per inch (dpi) up to a high of 1200 dpi. When you combine their much higher dot resolution with their generally larger page size, you see that you can have much more detail in printed images than you have onscreen.

This difference means that applications that send their output to printers are likely to emphasize the creation of very detailed static images. On the other hand, applications that are mainly intended for use onscreen (as is the case for most multimedia applications for PCs) are likely to emphasize animated or video images of only modest resolution, probably in color.

Vector Versus Bitmapped Images— Rasterizing and Rendering

Images can be generated and stored inside a PC in two radically different ways: One is called vector art and the other is referred to as bitmapped. A piece of vector art is a file that contains descriptions of how to generate the image but not the actual image itself. Such a file must be rasterized before it can be presented as an actual image either onscreen or on paper.

Technical Note: *Rasterizing* an image means converting instructions for what an image is to contain into the actual pixels that can be displayed on the video screen. A *raster* is a name given to the way in which our PC displays (and television sets) make their images. The display device sweeps across each line of the image, working its way down the screen

continues

from line to line. Eventually all the picture elements (pixels) on each line are drawn, which completes the raster. (The word raster comes from the Latin word for a fork. Think of a fork being dragged from side to side of a region of dirt. It will leave lines in the ground similar to the raster image lines on a video display.) The rasterizing engine is a software program or a piece of hardware that takes in the vector art descriptions and produces all the pixels needed to paint the raster.

Another kind of vector image specifies the contents in full, three-dimensional form. Here the objects are not what gets drawn in the image. Instead, a view of those objects is drawn. This substantially more complex process is called *3D-rendering*. The file in this case must specify the actual sizes of all the objects and their positions in 3D space, plus their surface textures and the positions of all the light sources in the "scene" and the point of view from which it is being viewed. The 3D scene-rendering engine then must use all those facts about the objects to construct an image that corresponds to what you would see if you were looking from the specified point of view, at the prescribed objects, under the prescribed set of lights.

Technical Note: With both rasterizing and rendering, the work proceeds from the background toward the viewer. Objects that are behind other objects may be partially or wholly obscured. In rasterizing this is handled by simply drawing them in place, then allowing nearer objects to replace those pixels with their own, thus overwriting the hidden portions of farther-away objects. In 3D-rendering an attempt is made to decide before actually rendering an object if it will be obscured or outside the field of view. It is only worth spending the effort of rendering on objects that are at least partially visible.

There are many different ways to render 3D images, each with its own set of limitations and advantages. And there are several different languages in which an application program can specify the work a rendering engine is to do. When you see phrases on a video card's box such as "supports OpenGL" or "with hardware Z-buffer," these are merely mentions of some of the tricks hardware and software developers have used to facilitate 3D rendering. The particular features you will want your hardware to have are whatever ones your software (games, presentation packages, or whatever) will use. And you must also have the appropriate set of driver software to tie the two together. Some of that software will come with the video hardware. Some will come bundled with the operating system, and some you must acquire from another source and then install. Carefully follow the directions that come with your hardware and you will likely get this right. Also check the Web sites for all the vendors involved to see if they have some later updates to the software that you should be using.

A *bitmapped* image, in contrast, has in the file the actual pixel image data. Your PC's video display adapter simply must pump those pixels to the screen display or printer to have them show up as a visible image. Some bitmapped images are stored in a compressed form, which means that by any of several means, much or all of the redundancy in that image has been removed. Naturally, you must reverse that process to recover the original pixel data before the image can be presented to the user.

There are several advantages to each kind of image file. Bitmapped files are simple and can easily be displayed onscreen or printed. Vector art tends to be much more compact—at least usually—and because it has only mathematical descriptions of the objects that make up the final image, such a file can generally be used to create images at any desired resolution. Thus, the same vector art file can be turned into a modest-resolution screen image or a very high-resolution printed page. Full 3D scene files go way beyond either form of 2D image file, because they contain much more information than you will see in any one image rendered from them. Appropriate programs can take such a scene file and modify it to produce not just an image, but many different images, or even an actual movie of what you would see if you were to walk or "fly" through the scene in some specified manner.

The rasterization process for 2D vector art requires a lot of computer power. Much of that work can be done by a graphics coprocessor on an accelerated video card, but some can be done by the PC's CPU. Some printers contain their own rasterizing engine; they can rasterize at least certain kinds of vector art by themselves. Other printers depend on the PC to do all the image rasterizing, before the images are sent to the printer. Even these "smart" printers, with their own rasterizers, need help from the PC's CPU to rasterize vector art that is contained in files of any kind other than the few they understand. (For example, Hewlett-Packard's LaserJet and DeskJet printers can rasterize PCL image files, and in some models can also handle PostScript (EPS) files. Images stored in Computer Graph- ics Metafile (CGM) format or Windows Metafile (WMF) images must be rasterized in the PC be- fore they are sent to those printers if any sense is to be made of them.)

Bitmapped files are ready to show. Just send the pixel data to the video screen or printer, and the image will appear. Generally these images appear only at the resolution at which they were prepared. (Some printers and image display programs can scale these images, but unless they are specifically directed to do so, they will display bitmapped images pixel-for-pixel as they receive them.)

These facts have some profound implications for multimedia applications. If you are always going to be showing your images on a PC's screen, and only at some set resolution (commonly 640×480 or 800×600), you can store them all as bitmapped images. This relieves the PC of the work of rasterizing, but it does mean that the PC must pump lots of bytes of data from wherever the images are stored to the video display device.

If you know your images are always going to be displayed on a PC running Windows (and especially if you know which version of Windows), you can speed up the data transfers and the image genera- tion by using a particular kind of vector art. In these image files, you store image object descriptions in the native language of a standard Windows graphics device or one of the new Graphic API sets that amount to a simulated special-purpose graphics device. This is especially helpful if the PC has an accelerated video card that understands how to deal with and interpret those Windows graphics API calls (or calls to some other graphics API such as DirectDraw/DirectVideo/Direct3D or Open GL) directly.

If, on the other hand, you know that you are going to be showing either many different views of a single scene, or a movie that takes place within that scene, then storing the scene information in a full 3D scene file often makes the most sense.

The upshot of all these considerations is that many PC multimedia applications handle their images mostly as bitmapped or as Windows metafile (WMF) vector art. They aren't designed to create high-resolution printed images, and they often emphasize animation or video over static imagery. Some fancier multimedia applications will handle their images by using one of the specialized graphics APIs, or as full 3D scenes.

How PCs Create Compelling Visual Images

In order to understand the technical tricks used to make the most compelling PC images, you must know how PCs present images on their screens in some detail, and you must understand some things about how people see. The first of those I discussed at length in Chapter 13, "Seeing the Results: PC Displays."

However, some of the issues of how people see images are so fundamental that most people have never even thought about them.

You Never See Any Thing!

You probably think that when you look at something you see it, but you don't. *No one ever sees any objects.* We see, at the literal level, (by which I mean our retinas receive) a constantly changing pattern of light and color. Hidden in this pattern are clues from which we can learn about the world "out there." Those clues are almost always ambiguous. We cannot infer with certainty what is "really" out there just from those clues, but we can and do make reasonable guesses. Indeed, we must do that for without a pretty clear notion of what probably is out there, we wouldn't be able to function.

So, if the video display shows us a pattern of light and color that resembles something that would come to us from some arrangement of objects, we are likely to interpret that "scene" as if it actually contained those objects. The more accurately the PC display simulates the light patterns of nature, the more realistic we say it is, and the more we "believe" what we see. In terms of multimedia PCs, this mostly means that we need enough total pixels, with enough possible colors per pixel, and the capability to change those pixel colors quickly enough for moving images.

Images Persist in Our Minds

If you see something and soon thereafter see a modified version of that same thing, you are likely to interpret what you have seen as movement or change in a single object. You don't have to see every stage of the movement or change—just seeing several successive stages in the process is sufficient. This fact is what makes it possible for motion pictures to work.

Early developers of movies experimented with frame rates until they found a number of images per second that would let most people see a continuous motion instead of a succession of snapshots. For the first few decades after the invention of motion pictures, all of them used just 16 frames per second, whereas modern movies use at least 24 frames per second. Television uses 30 frames per second. All of these schemes work, with the higher frame rates producing smoother illusions of motion.

Using Facts About Perception to Fool the Eyes

Why is all this important? Because it suggests how to fool the brain into thinking you are seeing things that aren't actually there. An early digital artist, John Whitney, once said, "He who controls the pixels controls the image." He meant simply that if you could digitally compute and control each pixel in every frame of a moving picture, you could control the viewer's illusions about what they were seeing. At the time he said this, back in the early 1980s, computers weren't powerful enough to do that for more than a very rudimentary type of image. Now they are powerful enough, and we see evidence daily of just how much image manipulation is thereby made possible. (It used to be said, "Seeing is believing." That is simply no longer true, as you are probably well-aware.)

We See Light in Two Dimensions, But Perceive the World in Three Dimensions

The patterns of light that fall on each of your retinas are 2D patterns, but the world we invent to explain those patterns is in 3D. How do we get the extra dimensionality? We can do this in many ways. The most obvious one is by using our two eyes. The patterns on the retina differ between our two eyes in ways that hint at the 3D quality of the world at which we are looking. But we don't really need those clues to see the world in 3D. Just cover one eye and look around. Do you have any trouble picking out which objects are nearer and which are farther away? Probably not.

We infer depth from a single eye's view by using what are called monocular depth cues. These include such things as noticing which objects block the view of portions of other objects. The blocking objects are clearly in front of those they block from our view. Another clue is the relative size of objects. The farther away an object is, the smaller it will appear to be.

You might wonder why this matters. After all, you don't normally cover one eye when you look at your PC. Ah, but both your eyes see the same image on the surface of the PC's video display. Yet, with appropriate use of monocular depth cues in that image, you can become convinced that you are looking through the screen at some 3D scene.

It turns out that these monocular depth cues are more important than the stereoscopic (two-eye) ones. This is why a flat photograph of a scene can still give the illusion that you are looking at a 3D scene. Of course, adding stereoscopic information helps add to the sense of reality. That is why virtual reality systems often include a means of creating two independent images and sending each to just one of the viewer's eyes, as I will explain in more detail in Chapter 22, "Immersive PC Experiences." Still, we can create some pretty compelling visual experiences—which is what we often seek to do with an ordinary multimedia PC—using only a single video display monitor presenting the same image to both eyes.

Making Images with Visual Pizzazz

The simplest images are static ones, and if those images are sufficiently bold and detailed, they can be quite compelling. Adding even a small amount of apparent movement to an image, however, can add a great deal of excitement. For this reason, animation has become commonplace, especially in multimedia PC applications.

Attractive Visuals Are Complex and Changing Them Is Hard Work

An image on an MPC display screen can involve a lot of information. At a minimum it will have the standard VGA resolution image (640 pixels per line and 480 lines per image), with each pixel having 1 of 16 possible colors. Such an image has 204,800 pixels and for each one, half a byte of information is needed to specify its color. This means that if you want to replace one image with another, you must move about 100,000 bytes of information into the video frame buffer.

Many modern PCs have SVGA displays with higher resolutions and higher color depth. To specify this type of image, you must have 3 bytes, or 24 bits, of color information for each of 786,432 pixels. That is 2 $1/4$ megabytes of data just to specify one static image.

Images with this many simultaneous colors are called *photorealistic*, because they can reproduce almost anything that you can capture on a photograph. Resolution is not nearly as important to the illusion of photorealism as is the number of different colors. You can realize this by simply noticing that the resolution of normal TV images is relatively modest. At best, a TV can display about 548 pixels per line, and most TV sets don't really resolve more than about 300 to 400 lines in each image. If you want to animate a scene with images this complex—and in particular if you try doing it by creating a new image for each sixtieth of a second—the video subsystem of your PC has a tough job cut out for it. Also, the CPU and main bus may be taxed in the extreme, shoveling new data to the video display system quickly enough to update that image this often.

There are several ways to cut this task down to size. One way is to use less-detailed images (ones with either fewer pixels or with fewer colors per pixel). That works, but it often means settling for a less-compelling visual experience. Another way is to change the image less often or to change only part of the image at a time. One trick, called palette animation, sometimes can be used to cut the work down to less than two one-thousandths of the original amount. I'll describe next some of these ways that animated or video images can be generated more economically.

Alternative Frame Buffer Animation

For just the price of a bit more RAM in the video image frame buffer and a little bit of added switching hardware, you can make the creation of animated imagery a lot simpler. To prevent flicker, the video card will normally redraw the entire screen image at least 60 times per second, but you must change that image only about 10 times per second to simulate convincing, if jerky, motion. At 30 image changes per second, the effect is as smooth as normal television.

Suppose you have enough frame buffer RAM to hold two complete images. First, draw a complete screen image in one region, and then, while the video output circuitry is scanning through that region 60 times each second, displaying that image on the screen, the CPU can be using the other region of the frame buffer RAM to create the next image. When that next image is ready, the CPU directs the video output circuitry to switch its focus to that new region, and the new image will instantly appear onscreen. Meanwhile, the CPU can go back to work in the original region of the frame buffer generating the next image.

If the images are so complex that the CPU must spend a second or more on each one, you will get the effect of a slide show. If it can create wholly new images in less than about one fifteenth of a second, the result will appear to be a movie. Giving the CPU a whole fifteenth of a second to create an image, however, means cutting the required rate of data pumping from CPU to video frame buffer by four over that which would be required to keep up with the full 60 frame per second rate used by the video output circuits. Thus, a mere 34MB per second will suffice, even for a 1024×768 photorealistic (24-bit per pixel) movie.

Using a Palette Can Greatly Reduce the Image Data You Need

For many purposes, you don't need photorealistic images. That is, you often can get away with many fewer colors. This certainly is true for graphs and other business graphics where 16 well-chosen colors can be plenty. Even photographs can look quite good with as few as 256 colors—if they are the right 256 colors for that particular photograph. The most important trick to making really good images with not very many colors is to include some means of choosing the best few colors to use.

The original VGA standard for video cards required them to display images of up to 640×480 pixels, with up to 16 different colors simultaneously onscreen. It further specified a palette by which those colors could be any 16 you wanted, chosen from a much larger set of possible colors. That set of all possible colors for any VGA image includes 262,144 possibilities. That's more than enough for most normal uses, although it's not quite good enough for full photorealism. (I described this palette mechanism in detail in Chapter 13.)

This type of standard VGA image requires storing and manipulating 153,600 bytes of information, which is half a byte per pixel for the full 307,200 pixels in the image. This only permits you to have 16 different colors in any single image, but by using the palette, you can have any 16 you like from over 250,000 possibilities. The palette table just takes an additional 36 bytes (or 288 bits, organized as 16 lines and each carrying 18 bits of color intensity information). Thus, the total data for a standard VGA image takes up precisely 153,636 bytes.

VGA displays had only this resolution and color depth for a simple reason: Making a video display with more resolution or more color depth requires more video RAM than could be included in an affordable display at the time VGA was first introduced.

Of course, RAM prices soon fell. SVGA video display systems became common, and now are the norm. This means that now we can build and display much more complex images. Doing so, however, means that we also must manipulate and store much more information for each one.

When Images Must Change More Rapidly Than Your PC Can Draw Them

The output from some multimedia programs includes actual video. That is, those programs attempt to show portions of what amounts to a television program. This potentially involves an utterly huge amount of data being pumped into the video card. In many cases, the amount required is more than the card can accommodate. When you can do the full job, we say you are displaying "full-screen, full-motion video." That is the goal for much of our multimedia, but often it is just that, a goal, and not a reality for the present time.

There are at least three ways in which you can deal with the problem of having too much data to display on your PC. First, you can choose to display the video image in a window that is smaller than the entire screen. Often a window that is 160 pixels wide by 120 pixels high is used. Other times the window will be 320×240 pixels. The first of these sizes has only $1/16$ as many pixels as a standard VGA screen. The latter has $1/4$ as many pixels as a full VGA screen. Naturally, this means you can get away with pumping in $1/16$ or $1/4$ as many bytes of video information as you would have if you were trying to create full-screen, full-motion video.

The second commonly used way to deal with a too-large incoming flow of video data is simply to drop out some of the frames. If you use only every other frame, you cut in half the number of bytes you must transmit to the video card. (Remember, the video output circuitry is copying the full contents of the frame buffer to the screen 60 or more times each second. That keeps on happening no matter what, so you don't get flickering images if you drop frames. You just get a more choppy or jerky-looking video.)

The third way to deal with this problem is to compress the data. If you "squeeze" out some of the redundancy in the image data, you might be able to get the required flow of (compressed) data down in size to something your PC can handle. Of course, before the images can appear onscreen, they must be decompressed. That can be done in specialized hardware added to the video card's circuitry if your PC's CPU isn't very fast, or in a very fast PC, it can be done by a software driver.

Static images are often compressed to reduce the file sizes and thus to save some disk space and shorten the time it takes to transfer those files over a communications link. The most common ways used to compress static image files are by using the GIF, PCX, or JPEG algorithms. GIF stands for Graphics Image Format. JPEG stands for the Joint Photographic Experts Group, which is the standards body that has promulgated this standard.

GIFs and PCX files have been compressed in a *lossless* fashion. That is, only truly redundant bits are squeezed out, and they all can be returned exactly as they were when the file is decompressed. None of the original image's data is deleted in the compression process.

JPEG, on the other hand, is an example of a way to compress a file that is inherently *lossy*—data from the original image which is deemed to be redundant is thrown away in the compression process. (And, as you would expect, lossy compression yields smaller compressed files than does lossless compression.) This means that the image resulting from the decompressed files will differ from the originals to some degree. The tricky part of these algorithms is their attempt to lose only "unimportant" features of the images. That is, they are designed to make the kinds of "mistakes" when reconstructing the images that people are least likely to notice, and they do a pretty good job of that. (All lossy compression techniques have a parameter that can be adjusted to control how much compression they will achieve, which implies how much real information they will lose. You can set this parameter to a value that makes the "damage" to your images acceptable, or you might need to set it higher to achieve adequate reduction in file size and thus in your required data flow rates.)

JPEG compression still might not be sufficient to let you achieve full-screen, full-motion video. In fact, it usually is not sufficient. Fortunately, a generally acceptable solution has been found.

The secret to this solution is a key fact about video: Most of the time a frame of video is very much like the frame that preceded it. So if you can somehow record only the changes from one frame to the next, you can lower the required data rate significantly.

The MPEG process of movie compression does just that. There are several MPEG standards (MPEG1, MPEG2, with MPEG4 under development; MPEG3 was abandoned shortly after work on it began). Each higher-numbered one is more aggressive, and more capable of yielding higher quality images and accompanying audio with a smaller data flow. Each higher-numbered one also requires more computing power to do the compression and the decompression.

MPEG1, which is currently the most widely supported standard in PC software, starts by degrading the original video image to something equivalent to a 352×240 pixel frame. The audio signal is retained at its original, CD-quality level. The next step in MPEG1 encoding is to convert the video signal from the original RGB (red-green-blue) signals captured by the camera into a color space called YUV. This is the set of signals transmitted over the air and used by modern television receivers. One of these signals carries intensity information only. The other two modify that signal with color information. (Chapter 13 has an explanation of RGB, YUV, and other common color models.)

The MPEG1 standard drops about half of the color information's resolution, which is okay because our eyes are quite tolerant in this regard. It then compresses the signals in a complex manner.

MPEG1 encoding splits up the frames into two or three categories. Some frames, called I frames, are simply sent as-is (or with a compression that is comparable to JPEG for static images). Other frames, called P frames, are sent as the difference of this frame from the frame just before it. When the third type, called B frames, is used, it becomes the bulk of the frames. These B frames are sent as a difference signal, relating them to both the frame before and the frame after. In order to reconstruct the original video, it is necessary to have all the frames since the last I frame. For B frames, you must also have the next frame. (This is true whether that next frame is a B, a P, or an I frame.)

By sending I frames every once in awhile, you are protected against losing track of the whole picture. Even if you lose some intermediate frames, when another I frame comes along you can get back on track. Any loss between I frames, however, will probably mess up the picture until the next I frame. Because I frames come more often than one per second, and because most of the time no frames are lost, this degradation is usually quite acceptable. Because the B frames in particular (and also the P frames to a lesser extent) are greatly compressed compared to the I frames, the overall effect is a reduction of the digital data rate to an acceptable value.

The MPEG algorithms are very much asymmetrical. Doing the compression takes a lot more computing than doing the decompression. By design, this was built in at the outset to make it as easy as possible to build affordable hardware or software MPEG decompressing engines—even at the cost of making the compression job hugely more difficult. A movie must be compressed only once, but it will end up being decompressed by each and every viewer's PC (or digital television) every time it is shown. Clearly it makes sense to unbalance the work load in the way the MPEG designers have chosen.

So far, several video cards or add-on boards for video cards can do MPEG2 decompression in hardware. As hardware speeds and capabilities continue to rise, there's no doubt that in a few years we will have affordable hardware MPEG compression engines that can work in real time available for desktop PCs. But for now, the compression job is done offline on larger, more powerful computers, and compressing a movie still takes far longer than the time the movie will run when it is displayed, in part because to get acceptable quality results, considerable human intervention and tweaking of the process is necessary.

PC Image Manipulation Programs

The last topic about PC image creation I want to cover has to do with the latest developments in image manipulation programs. I mentioned earlier in this chapter that PC images come in two broad categories: vector art and bitmapped art. Not surprisingly, the programs to manipulate those files also come in the same two broad categories.

The programs that manipulate vector art are called, generically, drawing programs. The programs that manipulate bitmapped images are called, generically, paint programs. (And just as vector art can be divided into 2D and 3D, we also have 2D and 3D drawing programs. Often the later come with specialized 3D rendering programs as well.)

You will want to know some key facts about each kind of program. For example, a vector art (drawing) program creates a file that is simply a list of instructions to the drawing engine. This type of list is often referred to as a *display list*. For example, the list might contain a section that specifies that the program should draw a rectangle at a certain location, with a certain width and height; rotated by a certain angle; with a particular line width, color, and style along the edges; and with another particular color and style filling in the interior.

When the drawing program draws an image from such a display list, the first items in the list end up on the page "behind" the later items. Usually the later items will obscure any items that they lie on top of. This can be very useful, because it lets you create, for example, a picture of pie with a slice cut out by first making a whole pie, then laying on top of it a "missing slice" image. You can also first draw the pie pan, then the pie, and only the edges of the pan will show around the pie. At all times, however, all the items in the display list are still there in the file, so if you remove one of them, the image will change to reveal whatever was hidden by that item.

Paint programs and their bitmapped image files work in quite a different manner. Normally a bitmapped file simply holds the color numbers for each pixel (and, perhaps, a palette table to help in interpreting those color numbers). The paint programs usually alter those files not by adding new items, but by altering the pixel values. This means that adding a new item to a bitmapped image file actually destroys a portion of the image that had been in that file. If you later erase the newly added item, you will simply leave behind a hole in the image. This strategy keeps these bitmapped files as small as possible, but it also makes editing them a sometimes terrifying job. You can so easily mess up the whole file by making a simple mistake.

Perhaps that shouldn't be so frightening. After all, painters have been doing this for centuries. If you paint over something, you can't easily remove that paint to get back the image you had before. With computers, you can at least save your work from time to time into newly named files to keep many versions of your image.

Whatever your feelings on the matter, the makers of paint programs have taken pity on hapless users. Now, many of the paint programs offer *layers* and *checkpointing*. The first innovation, layers, lets you place new objects on a separate layer from your current image until you are satisfied that it really does belong where you placed it. Then you can send it to the background layer, at which point it becomes an inseparable part of the final image. Checkpointing is simply a means of automatically saving interim versions of your picture, and then recovering the last saved version if you decide what you did since then was a mistake.

This is enough to say about PC images. We have still to talk about PC sounds, and they are more important than you might have realized.

Making Socko PC Sounds

In the beginning, the PC could make only beeping sounds. Now it can sing, shout, growl, and play symphonies. Almost any sound you can imagine can be produced on a modern multimedia PC. This development is a lot more significant than many people realize. They think that images are much more important than sounds, but in certain ways they are wrong. Sounds convey emotions far more powerfully. You can thrill or horrify someone with an image, but you'll induce deeper feelings of pleasure or send chills up the spine even more easily with the appropriate sounds. Movie makers know this very well, which is why so much money has been spent on developing and installing the very latest in sound technology at movie theaters. Now PCs are catching up.

The sounds from early multimedia PCs were a lot more interesting than the beeps and clicks that were characteristic of the earliest PCs, but the most recent high-end MPCs are even more impressive—with their five-channel surround sound and powerful subwoofers, they can make watching a movie on your PC seem acceptable. Break out the popcorn and enjoy!

But, before you stop reading and reach for the popcorn, I have a little bit more to explain. In order to appreciate fully the changes in technology that have occurred in the process of evolving our modern multimedia PC, you must look at some of the details about how sounds are reproduced and about how people hear.

How People Hear

Sounds are variations in air pressure. We hear them mostly with our ears, but also to a degree with our whole bodies. Although we can sense only light with our eyes, we can sense air pressure variations (sounds) with our ears and also—and this is especially true for loud, low frequency sounds—with our bellies, our chests, and our feet, among other parts of our bodies.

Perhaps the most important difference between visual and auditory information has to do with the dimensionality of the experience. We receive visual information (on the retina of each of our eyes) in an inherently 2D form, and from that we build up a perception of a 3D world around us. Auditory information, however, is inherently 1D. The air pressure in the auditory canal inside each of your ears has only one value at any given instant.

You can tell pretty well, by using both ears and sometimes also perceptions of sound waves hitting other parts of your body, whether a sound is coming from the left or the right. You even can tell, usually, if it comes from in front of you or behind. However, you are much less capable of telling whether a sound comes from a source that is on your level, above you, or below you. In a sense, we use our ears to expand the 1D sounds we hear into a mostly 2D soundscape around us.

The designers of sound reproduction systems have used their knowledge of these and other more arcane facts about human hearing to create a wide range of audio systems. The earliest PCs used some of the most primitive. Modern PCs use some of the most sophisticated ones yet invented.

Evolving Speaker Technologies

Any loudspeaker works by moving air. It pushes on air to squeeze it and then pulls back to create a region of lowered pressure. These low and high pressure regions travel away from the loudspeaker at about 1,000 feet a second, in the form of a compressional wave in the air.

The first PCs used a cheap speaker, but that isn't really what made their sound capabilities so limited. The circuitry that drove that speaker was of sufficiently limited capability that it could only produce a tone with a fairly harsh timbre and fixed volume. This quality of tone was sufficient to alert the user to an error condition but was good for little else.

A small speaker can produce only significantly loud sounds in the upper portion of the audible range — that is, high-pitched sounds but no really low ones. To make a low-pitched sound, you need a big speaker, capable of moving a lot of air. That is why the best sound systems have a relatively big, heavy woofer or subwoofer. Because the lowest frequency sounds aren't very directional, one such speaker is enough. All the directional information in the sounds can come from two or more much smaller speakers. Starting with the MPC2 specification, our multimedia PCs have had sound systems with stereo speakers for the higher tones, and—if they included a subwoofer at all—they would have only one. The audio electronics in these PCs would appropriately mix the low end of the audio spectrum from the left and right channels and send that mixed signal to their subwoofer.

The fanciest surround sound systems today include five speakers for the upper frequency ranges and one subwoofer. The five speakers serve to bring you sounds from straight in front of you (but probably above or below your line of sight), from the left and right in front, and from the left and right behind you. All of these channels route their lowest-frequency sounds to the one subwoofer, whose position you usually cannot discern just by listening to the sounds it creates.

Creating Beautiful Sounds

Almost any way you make the audio signals that are sent to the speakers will be better than what the earliest PCs used. A pure tone must have a smooth waveform (much like a gentle ripple on a pond). The height of the ripples determines the volume; the time between crests determines the pitch. Absolutely any sound can be made from an appropriate mixture of pure tones. So if you make a sound system that is capable of reproducing all frequencies of pure tones, each one at any arbitrary loudness, and all of them at once with no interaction among those tones, you have made a system that can reproduce any sounds you want.

After you have such a sound reproduction system, you need a way to drive it with digital signals. In an MPC this is most often done with numbers stored in what are called wave files (and most often are given the file extension WAV). These numbers simply represent instantaneous samples of the sound pressure at one or two microphones (one microphone for monaural sounds and two for stereo). These samples are taken at equal time intervals, and the exact interval used is set by the quality of the sound you want to record and play back. Also, these sounds can be sampled—digitized— with any of several different degrees of accuracy. That accuracy is typically specified in terms of the number of bits used in each number that represents an instantaneous sound pressure.

If you sample 22,000 times per second and use 16-bit numbers, you'll get a pretty decent representation of the original sounds. If you double that sampling rate and also use two microphones, you'll get a fairly high-fidelity sound recording, but at the cost of four times as many bytes of data storage.

That's a fine way to capture sounds and play them back. In fact, it is probably the most commonly used method—it is essentially how every audio CD is made—but it has several drawbacks. One is that the only sounds you can play are ones you have captured with a microphone. That leaves out playing new sounds that have never before been heard anywhere. The other drawback is that these WAV files can become quite large if you record a long segment of sounds.

Synthetic Sound Is Superior

One solution to both these problems, and the one required for a PC (in addition to the capability to play WAV file sounds) in order for it to be able to earn an MPC designation, is to build in the capability to synthesize sounds. This is usually done by analyzing what sounds each of a large number of instruments makes for each note that it can play. Then, using several pure-tone generators (called oscillators) in a specialized FM-synthesis microprocessor chip, it is possible to produce any musical note you might imagine, nearly the way it would sound if it had been played on one of those instruments. At least, that is the idea.

By this strategy, all you need to store in a file of sounds to be generated is to list the instruments that will be playing the sounds and then list the notes each one will play, indicating for each one how loud it is, what pitch, and how long it will last. That is most of what gets stored in a Musical Instrument Device Interface (MIDI) file.

Standards: The MIDI standard was first developed to help professional musicians create quality music using electronic instruments. It is a standard for conveying control messages among different electronic musical instruments. In a professional setup, a keyboard will generate MIDI signals that then are sent to a synthesizer where the actual sounds are created. (This is just one example of how such a system might function.)

The MIDI standard allows for several kinds of signals that a typical MPC audio system cannot recognize or use. By taking advantage of a pre-existing standard, however, the MPC specification has the benefit of turning every PC that meets the specification into a (somewhat limited) MIDI musical device. You can use an MPC to capture MIDI signals from a MIDI keyboard or to send MIDI signals to a more capable MIDI synthesizer.

Eventually, the best multimedia PCs will contain synthesizers as capable as the best professional ones, and they might also come with full piano-style keyboards (in addition to the typewriter-like keyboards all PCs use). But for now, they are very much junior members of the MIDI world.

A very close analogy exists between this synthetic sound approach and the vector art approach to storing an image. In both cases, what gets stored are the directions for creating the sound or image, rather than the actual details of the sound or image. In this analogy, a vector art file is to a bitmapped image file as a MIDI sound file is to a WAV file.

Every MPC entitled to the trademark has—at least—a frequency modulation (FM) MIDI synthesizer built in, ready to play the sounds indicated by such a file. MPCs also come with rudimentary software that interprets the MIDI commands and turns them into appropriate commands to the built-in FM synthesizer. This works, but unfortunately, the results are often disappointing.

Mainly, the results disappoint listeners because the analysis of instruments used in creating these FM synthesizers is inadequate. No instrument creates every note in the exact same way. The analysis used for FM synthesis also ignores the very subtle ways in which the tones die off differently or in which the resonances of the instrument impact the tones they produce.

The upshot is that FM synthesis still produces a rather harsh, if tolerable, *representation* of the sounds of traditional instruments. However, it isn't one that anyone would confuse with the real thing.

Tables of Waves Are Even Better

The next step in the progression of PC music-generating technologies is referred to as *wave sound*. This means capturing a sample of an actual musical instrument playing a given note, then saving all those samples for all the instruments you are interested in (and perhaps for many, if not all of the notes each one can play). The notes are not broken down into individual pure tones, but instead are simply stored in their messy entirety as mini-WAV files.

When presented with a MIDI file, a wave sound synthesizer will select appropriate combinations of these prerecorded instrumental sounds and play them back together to generate the desired music. The result can be substantially better than even the best of the FM synthesis machines. Still, it isn't quite as good as listening to the real thing.

And You Can Do Even Better Still

Now we are beginning to have even better musical synthesizers in the best high-end PCs. The brand of synthesizer that has set most of the standards in this area is produced by Creative Labs. Its basic Sound Blaster is the sample audio subsystem that defines an MPC-compliant audio system. It is the presumed sound system for many multimedia PC programs.

Creative Labs has enhanced its Sound Blaster technology in a several ways. The first was its introduction of what it called its Advanced WaveEffect (AWE) Sound Blaster. This adds a wave sound synthesizer—another microprocessor, separate from the FM synthesizer. The AWE add-on carries the sound samples for all the known instruments in a ROM chip and then plays back mixtures of them as indicated by a MIDI file's contents. Some of these AWE cards also have some RAM into which a user can download additional wave samples in groups Creative Labs calls Sound Fonts.

Having the capability to store and use user-defined samples allows you to make a MIDI machine that can play more different kinds of instruments. In fact, you can substitute the sounds of a person speaking or singing, of a whole chorus singing, of banging on a pipe, of an explosion, or of a car crash, and so on in place of an ordinary musical instrument.

Most recently, Creative Labs has brought out a further refinement to its AWE line of Sound Blaster cards. This refinement is referred to as the Sondius WaveGuide Synthesis approach. Essentially, this is a method of generating the sounds of certain solo instruments by a far more complex synthetic approach than simple FM synthesis, using a lot of what is known about how those particular instruments make sounds. This approach is useful only when it is applied to well-understood instruments and in a fashion that has been carefully tweaked by experts. But when it is applied, the result is a marked increase in the smoothness and richness of the sounds that are created. It also gives musicians more control of the sounds they create than is possible with either conventional FM synthesis or the use of wave samples.

Creative Labs is, of course, far from being the only company working on advanced PC sound synthesis and sound reproduction technologies. One area that has seen a lot of activity is the attempt to add 3D realism, which is sometimes referred to as expanded stereo or surround sound, to an otherwise simple stereophonic sound system. Dolby is one of the leading names in this field, and its Dolby Digital surround sound–encoding strategy is now the industry standard. SRS Labs is another leader in this area; Intel has proposed a version of this idea that it refers to as its Realistic Sound Experience (RSX); Microsoft is pushing new sound protocols that go by the names DirectSound and DirectSound3D. All of these companies claim to understand how sounds we hear are modified by the way those sound waves interact with our head and ears. They have applied that knowledge in unique ways to improve the listening experience, both for stereo sound (two speakers) and "surround sound" (with five or six speakers).

This discussion of MIDI sound generation on a PC has necessarily been abbreviated. There are many additional subtle effects that you can use, and these are documented in the literature that comes with the sound cards or MPC systems. You can get an entire book devoted simply to making and capturing music with your PC. One such book is *The MIDI Manual* by David Miles Huber (Sams Publishing, ISBN 0-672-22757-6). Another brilliant resource for the topic of computer music—and a dandy doorstop—is Curtis Roads', *The Computer Music Tutorial* (1996, MIT Press, ISBN 0-262-68082-3). It discusses just about every aspect of computer-based sound, including MIDI and digital (WAV) audio.

Sound File Formats

I have already told you a little bit about the two most popular sound file formats. WAV files just store samples of the actual sound pressure, sampled at some fixed rate (commonly 22KHz or 44KHz), with each sample being converted to a 16-bit binary number. Stereo wave files store two sound pressure numbers for each sample time, corresponding to the sound pressures at the two microphones (or to a left and right input signal, if you are creating a WAV file from some other stereo sound source).

MIDI files (the extension is most commonly shortened to MID) store descriptions that a MIDI synthesizer can use to generate sounds. These descriptions must conform to the official standard for MIDI messages. As such, they can be played on or generated by any MIDI musical instrument, which includes a very wide range of objects from keyboards to synthesizers to PCs.

Audio files on the Internet are often in the AU format. This is like a WAV file, but has a different internal format. Real Networks has created a standard for streaming audio files. These RM or RA files can be played back as they are being received by the Real Player programs. Otherwise, they are like WAV files (with sometimes video information as well as audio).

One of the newest, and in some ways most different, sound file formats is that used by the Koan sound generation program from SSEYO. This program doesn't just play a set of predefined sounds, it generates sounds with some randomness, but it does so according to some fairly tight constraints indicated by parameters in its input file. Thus, you can send a very short Koan sound file to one of their player programs, and the program will output many hours of music in a set style. Your file also can specify that the style change from time to time.

SSEYO is pushing this as a way to get new, constantly changing music to accompany World Wide Web browsing, or stand-alone PC usage, without having to create, store, or send huge sound files. You can learn more about this interesting new development by pointing your Web browser to this URL:

```
http://www.sseyo.com/
```

Will Your PCs Play Your Radio or VCR?

Will your PC soon be playing your radio and your VCR? Sure—or at least it will be able to do those things soon. When the Universal Serial Bus (USB) becomes a little more established, and when most of the inevitable bugs are shaken out of it, I expect to see a lot of USB-enabled appliances of all kinds. When you are able to buy them, if you simply cable one (or many) of them up to your PC (and load suitable software in the PC), your PC can converse with that other device, both interrogating it and commanding it. For a radio, that means finding out if it is available (plugged in and whatever else it needs), then commanding it to set itself to the station and the volume that you want to have it play.

This is just the tip of the iceberg! I believe we are right on the edge of a major shift in how multimedia PCs are built and operated. The USB bus (and also the 1394 bus) are just one part of the story.

What an MPC Is Now, and What It May Become

Right now a multimedia PC is mostly a system for displaying information on the screen (including static images, animations, and full-motion video) and through the PC's loudspeakers or earphones. These systems also respond to user input—mainly via the keyboard and pointing device. The principal sources of the information that is displayed are multimedia application programs that reside either on our hard disks or on CD-ROMs we load into CD-ROM drives attached to our PCs.

Ubiquitous Multimedia PCs

With the continuing integration of our PCs with the Internet, and with improved connectivity to nearby "appliances" via the USB and 1394 buses, I expect that our MPCs will soon turn into much more than mere delivery mechanisms for information. They also will become control centers for our lives. At least, they will if we let them. (Not everyone is thrilled by the prospect of having a PC mediate between them and their washing machine, just to pick one example.) Furthermore, they might become gateways to new virtual environments in which we will work and play for a good deal of the time, each day of our lives. That will truly be a PC as a multimedia system.

Why We Need Digital Audio and What It Will Be Like

Even before all that happens, I expect some rather dramatic new developments in the audio side of multimedia systems. Goodness knows that they need some help, and at last a viable solution to many of the PC audio problems is in sight. Its name is digital audio.

So far in this chapter, I have spent a good deal more space on describing the video aspects of multimedia technology than on the audio ones. I did this because there is, at present, more to say about video than about audio. With the advent of true digital audio, however, that might soon change. I will close this chapter with a brief overview of why this is important and what it might look like, once it really gets here.

Doing Brain Surgery in a Bumper Car

Honestly, making high-fidelity music inside a PC is like doing brain surgery in a bumper car. The audio subsystem in a modern PC ought to be pitied. It is trying to do the impossible. Audio electronics, at present, are analog circuits that create and change millivolt signals in subtle ways. In a PC this is happening alongside digital circuits that are constantly switching voltages by (relatively) huge amounts at very high speed. This makes the environment for those audio circuits quite hostile. Noise doesn't just creep into them; it crashes in wholesale.

Every time my PC's screen display changes substantially, I hear a thump, or a boom, or at least a click from my PC's speakers. This is normal. Sure, shielding helps, but what will really help is getting all those low-level analog signals outside the PC system unit entirely.

How Digital Audio Will Save the Day (and Your Ears)

I hope you remember that one of the greatest virtues of digital electronics was that it could reject noise signals totally. At every stage in the processing of digital signals, they are reconstituted at full strength, and any noise that might have piggy-backed onto the signal is removed. This is why you can make copies of copies of a digital file any number of times and still be certain that the contents of that file are exactly the same as the contents of the original. Perfection of this sort is possible only in a wholly digital world.

Sound systems must use analog signals, at least at their inputs and outputs. So how can we avoid noise when we are processing audio? The answer is as near as the CDs that have almost totally re-placed vinyl records and audio cassette tapes as media for storing music. Convert the audio inputs from analog signals to strings of binary numbers just as soon as you can. Do all the processing of the audio information in its digital form. Convert it back to analog for output only at the very last moment.

Don't our PCs do this already? Not really. Here is what a much more purely digital audio system might look like: Imagine a microphone that has a preamplifier and analog-to-digital converter built in, along with a microprocessor. This encapsulated subsystem is connected via a USB cable to your PC (perhaps in many jumps from one USB-enabled device to another until finally the signals reach the PC). Because of the marvelous noise-ignoring properties of digital signal processing, we can be quite sure that the binary numbers received by the PC are exactly those sent by the microphone.

The PC accepts these digital representations of the audio signals and does whatever processing, stor-age, or output we want. Ultimately, it might send these binary numbers out over another USB link to a "smart" speaker system. There, actually inside the speaker box, is where the digital signals will be converted back into analog form, just inches away from where those analog signals are to be trans-formed into sound pressure waves that you'll hear as sound.

This type of segregation of all the low-level analog electronics within the microphone and within the speakers keeps all that vulnerable stuff far, far away from the "hotbox" cacophony of the digital system unit. As the audio information passes through that system unit, it is protected from any al-teration or degradation by its being expressed totally in a digital form.

I can hardly wait until this truly high-fidelity version of PC audio becomes available. Fortunately, neither you nor I will have to wait for very much longer.

The essence of a multimedia PC lies in its diverse inputs and outputs. In order to work well, how-ever, it must also have some very special internal parts. In the next chapter I will tell you about some of those special hardware concerns and how they are being addressed.

21

Special Storage Hardware Needs for Multimedia

Peter Norton®

The essence of multimedia PCs lies in their support for excellent input and output, mainly in the areas of video and audio. Naturally, this means multimedia PCs need the kind of good video and audio hardware and software discussed in Chapter 20, "How to 'Wow' a Human."

But data always must be able to linger somewhere within any computer. So that means that with the very large amounts of data used in high-quality visual and audio files, some pretty fierce demands are placed upon the storage components of a PC as well.

The demand on the storage components isn't just for space for these large files—although sometimes that is an issue. What is often a tougher demand to meet is the speed with which the data must flow into or out of the storage device. If you are recording live video or trying to play back some prerecorded video, you must move the data from the camera or to the screen at the proper rate. And if your PC's storage mechanisms can't keep up—then, oops, you have either just lost some of the incoming data from the camera or forced the user to experience a pause on the output as the storage device catches up to the demands of that output device.

This chapter discusses how hardware manufacturers have responded to those demands, primarily in the areas of improved storage devices and, to a lesser extent, the most recently improved input-output options. Chapter 22, "Immersive PC Experiences," extends that discussion to cover the latest developments in immersive PC experiences. Both chapters also cover some hints on what to look for when you are selecting pieces for your next PC.

Multimedia Issues in PC Storage

Everyone who uses a PC wants the storage components of that PC to work as swiftly as possible. But users of multimedia programs have some particular concerns that make it especially important that the hard drive, in particular, performs splendidly. To meet these needs, the hard drive must be able to stream data out of a file at a very high and steady rate.

Two Ways Storage Devices May Disappoint You

Notice that there are two ways a hard drive, or other storage device, can perform inadequately with respect to multimedia. One is simply to be too slow overall. The other is that the drive might be able to stream the data out rapidly enough most of the time, but every once in awhile it might pause before resuming that speedy streaming action.

Maximum Streaming Speed Issues

The basic speed question comes down to this: What is the fastest speed at which the drive can pump out data? The answer to this depends on which one of several possible bottlenecks limits speed the most.

The most fundamental limitation is how rapidly the data on the disk's surface passes under the head. That is the absolute maximum rate at which this particular hard disk can deliver up its stored data. This speed is a combination of two factors. One is the rotation rate of the disk, and the other is the number of bits of data that are stored on a single track.

Modern hard disks turn at a fixed rate. Originally, they all turned at 3,600 revolutions per minute (rpm). More recently, manufacturers have upped this number on at least some of their better hard drives. They first went to 4,500rpm, then 7,200rpm, and now drives from several manufacturers spin at an amazing 10,000rpm.

The other number—the data bits per track—is a little trickier to understand. Modern hard drives use *zone bit recording*, which simply means that they take advantage of the fact that the outer tracks on the disk platter are longer than the inner ones. They break up the disk into several zones: The outermost tracks in a zone have the maximum number of sectors per track, and those in the innermost zone have a minimum number of sectors per track. Unfortunately, there is no industry standard for how many zones drives use, or how many sectors per track are in each one. What is standard, however, is that each sector contains exactly 512 bytes of data.

If you are unclear on these concepts of sectors, tracks, heads, and cylinders, please review the discussion in Chapter 9, "You Can Never Have Too Much Closet (or Data Storage) Space." In particular, look at Figures 9.1 and 9.4.

Because the original design of hard drives for PCs used only a single zone, our PCs expect a hard drive to have a single well-defined number of sectors per track. Modern hard drives simply lie to the PC about their construction to give the appearance of having only a single number of sectors per track, and sometimes in order to appear to have fewer cylinders (and more heads) than they really have. But, of course, the real number of sectors per track on the particular tracks that you must read is going to be what sets the absolute maximum rate at which data can stream off your hard drive.

Another bottleneck can occur in the disk controller electronics on the drive. Normally, however, this isn't a problem. The next important bottleneck is likely to be the bus that is used to connect the hard drive to the rest of your PC. If your hard disk is connected to an old-style IDE cable and the interface is connected to the motherboard, it just won't be able to pump out data very quickly. If it uses a modern EIDE channel, it might go fast enough, but for the best performance, most hard-drive makers recommend using a very fast PCI-to-Ultra Wide SCSI host adapter capable of moving up to 40MB of data per second, with an Ultra Wide SCSI interface on the hard drive and a full, 68-pin SCSI-3 cable connecting them together.

Once the 1394 (FireWire) high-speed serial bus is widely available, this may be an even better way to connect up a hard drive for multimedia use. But until there are real products to evaluate, we cannot be sure of this. (You'll find more technical information about FireWire in Chapter 16, "Faster Ways to Get Information Into and Out of Your PC.")

Whichever bus you are using, there may be a question as to what else that bus is being asked to do at the same time. If it is congested, even the most speedy bus will fail to carry your streaming video data fast enough—just as a very wide freeway can slow to a crawl at rush hour.

So, depending on where the narrowest bottleneck occurs, your hard drive's maximum streaming rate may be set either by the bus you are using or by the rate at which data flows under the heads. Notice that which one of these is the limiting factor may change, depending upon where the file you are reading is located on the disk drive. If it is in an inner zone, as I discussed earlier, the disk drive itself might be the more important limitation. For files at the outer edge (which means nearer to the "front" of the drive), the bus speed is more likely to be the limiting bottleneck.

"Burps" Along the Way

Even if your hard drive and the bus by which it delivers data to your PC are up to the task of streaming video from file to screen, you might experience some very annoying pauses in the video display from time to time. Why is this, and is there anything you can do about it? As usual, there are several reasons why these "burps" occur.

First, if the hard drive is barely capable of keeping up with the required data rate, then anything that makes it work a little harder will cause delays. Fragmented files, for example, can make the disk work a lot harder to get at your data.

In a fragmented file, the data is scattered across the disk surface in several fragments. Each fragment is a group of clusters, and all the fragments together make up the total file. In each group, the clusters are adjacent to one another, but each group is somewhat, or perhaps very much, removed from its neighboring groups. As the disk is reading data from one group, it will pump those data bits out pretty much as fast as possible. But when it must move the heads to a new cylinder and wait for the disk to turn around enough to present the beginning sector of a new group of clusters, it must pause in that data streaming for at least a little while.

Even with totally unfragmented files, there will be some momentary pauses in the data flow. These will occur either each time the disk must switch from one track to another or when it must switch from one cylinder to another. Moving the heads to another cylinder takes a significant amount of time, possibly enough to show up as a minor glitch on screen.

A much more serious source of delays can happen if the disk encounters an error in reading a sector. Each time this happens, the disk most likely will wait for that sector to come around again and try to re-read it. It may do this up to 10 times—or in some cases up to 100 times—before giving up. If it finally succeeds in reading the sector (but only after many retries), there will, of course, have been some delay while it was doing that re-reading. You won't get any messages about what happened. You'll just experience a short pause in the video stream.

Finally, delays can be introduced by episodic congestion on the input-output bus. Between congested moments, the data flows freely. When something else takes over the bus, the video data might have to wait.

What's an AV Hard Disk?

A few years ago, hard drives for PCs just weren't up to this task. More recently, many, but not all of them, have gotten fast enough that they can do the job quite adequately. When only some of the available hard drives were capable of meeting this need, their makers often labeled those particularly speedy models as *AV hard drives*.

In this context, AV stands for audio-visual. These hard-drive makers were simply saying that these models of hard drive would be capable of streaming data from files sufficiently rapidly and smoothly for real-time video display purposes.

One key way in which these hard drives differ from their less-capable peers is that they turn very rapidly. No mere 3,600rpm drives need apply for this designation. They also have a high number of bits per square inch (described in industry literature as a high *areal density*) of data storage. This translates into many more sectors per track, even in the innermost zones.

Yet another way they can differ is in the interface they use. SCSI is the most popular, but some EIDE interface drives can also make the grade, at least in some PCs.

One of the best ways to make a hard drive capable of the needed high and steady rate of data streaming is to build in a large RAM cache on the drive. That temporary holding area for data can be used to buffer data streaming off the disk surface while it waits its turn to go out over the bus, and to accumulate extra data that has been read so its flowing out can cover up any small pauses in the flow of data from the disk surface.

Now that hard drives and their interfaces to PCs are so much faster, is there still a need for AV drives? Some manufacturers think so. Western Digital and Microsoft collaborated on a new specification for what an AV hard drive should be. For example, among other things, it must be a drive that can be set to do few or no retries when it fails to read a sector correctly on the first pass. That is vital for good streaming video performance.

Warning: Perhaps you noticed. There is a possibility lurking here for some serious data integrity problems if you mistakenly think an AV hard drive is just another name for an excellent hard drive. The very thing that makes an AV hard drive best for streaming video (its tendency simply to keep on going in the face of errors) would make it horrible for storing and retrieving binary executable (program) files. So, buy an AV drive if that is what you need. Stick to ordinary hard drives for other, more customary uses (for which data integrity will trump streaming-data–flow speed every time).

How Fast Must My CD-ROM Drive Go? Can I Make It Go Even Faster?

Hard disks keep on getting faster and faster, but their makers don't normally tell us about that progress in nearly as blatant terms as those used by CD-ROM drive makers. I'm not sure why this is so. Perhaps it has been true because up until very recently, CD-ROM drives were so very much slower than even the slowest hard drive.

The makers of CD-ROM drives are always trying to outdo their competition with ever larger "X-numbers." And there are some pretty good reasons why they do this. However, you must be careful comparing those numbers; they don't always tell you what you might think they do.

X-Numbers and CAV Versus CLV Operation

The original CD-ROM drives were nothing more than audio CD players with a digital interface. After all, audio CDs store musical information in digital form. At first, manufacturers just omitted the digital-to-analog portion of those drives and added appropriate interface circuitry to allow connecting these drives to a SCSI host adapter. Voila! They had a CD-ROM drive. (CD-ROM drives that connect to an IDE channel came along a short time later.) Actually, they didn't take out the audio interface. It simply is ignored when you use the drive for digital data. If you want, you always can play music CDs in a CD-ROM drive with the audio output showing up in an earphone connector and perhaps some other output terminals.

Those first CD-ROM drives were what we now call a 1X CD-ROM drive. They turned the discs in the same fashion as a normal audio CD player. Notice, please, that this is not to say that they turned those discs in the same manner as a hard disk turns. CD discs are normally played at constant linear velocity (CLV) instead of the constant angular velocity (CAV) that is used for hard disks. In CLV operation, the disc turns relatively fewer revolutions per second when it is reading the outer tracks and at a higher rpm when it reads the inner tracks. What stays constant is the number of bits read each second.

A single-speed (1X) CD-ROM drive pumps out data at 150kBps (kilobytes per second). A double-speed (2X) drive supplies data at 300kBps. Naturally, a quad-speed (4X) drive supplies data at 600kBps. Curiously, CD-ROM drive makers that advertise more than 12X operation often aren't being totally honest about what they do. These super-high-speed CD-ROM drives (and some are now bragging about 30X operation) actually are operating more like a hard drive. They turn at a constant angular velocity (CAV). Then the manufacturers rate these drives by the *maximum* data rate they achieve—which is, of course, when they are reading the outermost track—and fail to mention that on the inner tracks the effective speed may be around half the advertised rate. (What makes this practice particularly reprehensible is the fact that CDs start at the inside and spiral out. So, unless the CD-ROM disc you are reading is completely filled up with data, you may find that *none* of it gets read at the drive's "nominal" speed.)

Why is the speed of a CD-ROM drive such an issue? Because that speed is hardly blazing, even at best. It is definitely faster than reading a stack of floppy disks, of course—especially when you factor in the time to swap disks. So this makes CD-ROMs a wonderful way to deliver software to a customer. However, keep in mind that the speed at which you can read data from a CD-ROM is still far below that for data coming off a hard disk, which has become our standard of comparison for speed of PC storage media.

Caching Helps

So, what is the answer to our insatiable demand for ever-faster performance? The makers of CD-ROM drives hope your answer will be to upgrade to a new model every five or six months. But, for most of us, they are merely dreaming.

Still, there are some options you might want to consider (all of which cost less than buying a new CD-ROM drive every six months). When CD-ROMs were new, their approximately 650MB capacity was a good deal bigger than the total hard-drive capacity of a typical PC. However, now that multi-gigabyte hard drives have come down in price, it is quite common to have more free hard-disk space than the total capacity of any single CD-ROM.

This suggests that one option is to partition your hard drive so you have one otherwise empty partition with at least 650MB of space available. Now you can copy the contents of an entire CD-ROM to that partition, and then install and run the application programs it contains from that hard disk image of the original CD-ROM. The main advantage to this is speed. The main disadvantage is inflexibility. You must take the time to load up this partition before you can use that program, and then you have committed all that hard-disk space to just one CD-ROM. If you often switch among a number of different CD-ROMs, this solution might not be very practical, unless you buy a really large hard disk for the purpose.

A variation on this is to install the program that comes on a CD-ROM to your hard disk, letting it copy over some of its data files as well. Often these applications offer several levels of hard-drive installation, ranging from just a small file to point to the CD-ROM, to loading the program but no data files, to loading the program and all its overlays plus some index files, to loading the entire application. All but the last one still require you to have the CD-ROM in the CD-ROM drive when you run the application, but each of these options will speed up the operation of the program somewhat more than the preceding option.

A more flexible way to speed up all your CD-ROM–based applications would be to set aside some of your hard disk to serve as a cache for data on its way from whatever is the current CD-ROM in the CD-ROM drive. You'll need a special CD-caching program to implement this strategy. One Taiwanese manufacturer, the Elitegroup, has introduced a product it calls the Smart 100X CD-ROM drive that uses very nearly this strategy. They stress, however, that theirs is really a read-ahead buffering technique—not really caching, per se.

When you insert a CD-ROM into Elitegroup's drive, their special software automatically starts loading the contents onto a pre-selected, otherwise unused, region of your hard drive. Thereafter, any time there is a request for data from the CD-ROM, this software will attempt to satisfy the request from data it now has in this hard-drive buffer.

If the region is large enough, and if enough time elapses first, all the contents of the CD-ROM will be copied there. But even a much smaller space can speed up things a lot. First of all, most CD-ROMs have less than half their capacity actually used for data. So, a buffer that holds 200–300MB may suffice to hold all the contents of most of your CD-ROMs. Also, any accesses you make to the data that is stored near the "front" (which is to say, the inside) of the CD-ROM will be satisfied from the buffer.

The process that copies data from the CD-ROM to the buffer is a low-priority one, and thus will be interrupted any time any other process attempts to access either the hard disk or the CD-ROM. This ensures that this program won't slow down anything in your PC, but it might greatly speed up almost all your CD-ROM accesses.

Finally, and this is the method most commonly in use now, you can do a lot to speed up your CD-ROM–based applications simply by using a general-purpose disk-caching program, giving it enough RAM to work with, and making sure that it supports caching of accesses to your CD-ROM drives as well as to all your hard-disk drives. With DOS this means loading your MSCDEX driver before you load Smartdrive (or whatever other disk-caching program you may be using). Windows 95 does this automatically, and allows you to adjust the amount of caching that it provides, depending on your PC's performance needs.

Multimedia Issues for PC Input and Output

I've made the point several times in this chapter that data flowing off a storage device must make its way to the video subsystem before it can be displayed there (and the audio portion must get to the sound subsystem). The paths that connect the various subsystems in your PC can, therefore, become bottlenecks.

Also, whenever you send multimedia data in or out of your PC (for example, from a camera or over a network), the data paths leading to the outside world come into play. These, too, can become serious bottlenecks.

One means of mitigating most of these bottlenecks is to have the multimedia data compressed. Removing redundancy is the first step. Dropping out real information—but, you hope, not information whose absence will be noticed—is the next step. Many multimedia applications do this; some do it quite aggressively.

Compression always helps when you are sending data out from your PC or receiving it from a distant source via some network link or modem link that is less rapid than you want. It also can help even when shuffling data inside your PC. The main thing that will determine how much help it can be is whether you have hardware support for the needed decompression in the display subsystem, and for compression in any source devices. If so, the compressed data is all that the internal buses must handle, and the compression will help a lot. If not, the CPU must do some additional work of compression or decompression, and the internal bus will, at some point, have to carry the uncompressed data. In that scenario, compression helps only by saving on disk space, and perhaps by letting you get the data to or from the disk more rapidly.

New, higher-speed buses are, of course, one good way to deal with this problem. And the emergence of new, higher-speed versions of venerable buses (such as UltraWide SCSI), plus the appearance of other new, high-speed buses (in particular IEEE-1394, also referred to as "FireWire") are other good ways.

Summary

Any PC that is running multimedia software will work its hardware pretty much to its performance limits. You are most likely to find those limits evident in the audio, video, and storage subsystems. I described many of the ways PC makers are improving the audio and video subsystems in Chapter 20. In this chapter I have pointed out why the storage subsystem also needs improving, and then described some of the industry attempts to address this need.

In the next chapter, "Immersive PC Experiences," I will carry the discussion on into the specialized hardware and software needs (and their solutions) for some of the most difficult tasks PCs are currently being asked to perform. This includes enhancements to PC video for true 3D imagery and adding the sense of touch to the media your multimedia can handle.

22

Immersive PC Experiences

Peter Norton®

This chapter completes my discussion of PC technologies for stand-alone desktop and workstation units. It also covers some applications for those PCs when they are connected to other, similar machines. To end this part of the book with a bang, so to speak, I have saved for this chapter the very latest and greatest innovations in what are now sometimes collectively referred to as "immersive PC experiences."

Just looking at the words in this phrase, you can see that this could refer to any experience using a PC in which you could become fully absorbed. Therefore, even a simple word processor could qualify, if you were able to "get into" using it sufficiently. But as the term is more typically used, immersive PC experiences refers to the types of PC systems and applications that are more likely to engage any user fully—especially ones that address most of our senses. One general category that might fit this description is PC game programs. Another is any that use a real 3D display system. Also, anything that deserves the name *virtual reality*—if there is any such—might qualify. As you will soon see, there are at least a few others besides these.

A key to any immersive PC experience is that the PC should be providing most of the important sensory input stimuli to the user. I say the important ones because humans have a notable characteristic: We tend to ignore any unchanging sensations. This means that the PC can dominate our sensory experience just by dominating the sensations that change. The fact that you are perhaps sitting in a chair or that there might be a pervasive odor in the room might not distract you from the time-varying interaction you are having with your PC.

This subject is a large and complex one, so first I'll describe some of the technologies that are being used in these immersive PC experiences, and then the principal applications that have been found for those technologies.

Immersive Technologies

By their nature, all the immersive PC experiences tend to be heavily multimedia in character. As such, most of them use more than a single technology. But to understand these technologies, it's best to look at them one at a time.

You have already read about most of the technologies that are used in these experiences. This chapter, therefore, will explore the few, fairly far-out ones that remain. For example, a superior sound system can be assumed to be part of any immersive system. Video, on the other hand, is one area in which a PC might need to be enhanced for some of the experiences that follow. In particular, the PC might need to be able to create 3D scenes.

Simulated 3D

As you read in Chapter 13, "Seeing the Results: PC Displays," any PC that can present photo-realistic images can give a strong illusion of three-dimensionality to the scenes it displays. This is because the monocular depth cues in those scenes are normally more important than their lack of binocular depth cues. This is fine for a great many purposes. Lately, though, people have come up with some really interesting applications that require an even more realistic 3D view of something.

There are two levels at which this can be done. The first level is to create a scene with strong depth illusions. So strong, in fact, that you could easily use this scene to discern the true, 3D locations of all the objects in it. This can be done quite effectively using stereoscopic or binocular images.

At the other level, a scene doesn't just appear to be 3D; it really is. You can move your head and look around some of the front objects, bringing objects into view that were formerly hidden. Now that's really 3D!

Fortunately, we don't always need scenes to be *that* 3D. Often it is sufficient to be able to rotate the scene in front of your view. To think of this in another way, if the view on your PC's screen is a 2D image of what is seen by a camera, it might be enough to move the camera around the scene, looking from whatever perspective you want. You also might want to fly the camera *into* the scene, and once there, turn around and look at the back of some objects the camera had passed.

3D Modeling Programs and More

I don't want to suggest that having this type of 2D flying-camera view of a 3D scene is an easy thing to accomplish—far from it—but at least it can be done with some powerful software. The video display itself doesn't need to be anything particularly special.

The first programs that could create true 3D models of objects were computer-aided design (CAD) programs. They were used by designers and by architects to help them visualize their more difficult constructions. (Most simple architecture and design is still done with 2D drawings of various views of the imagined, but never imaged, 3D reality.)

The hardest part of using one of these CAD programs is constructing all the parts and pieces that go into making up the whole object or scene. This is much harder than the traditional 2D drafting techniques—or at least it is a lot more tedious. (Which is, of course, why this technique is not used unless it is really needed.) If, for example, you are drawing an idealized brick (to name something that is very geometrically simple) in a 2D program, you just draw some rectangles and parallelograms by pointing out where each corner of each visible surface goes.

However, in a 3D program, you must not only define each corner's location (and do so for every surface—not just the ones that are visible from a certain point of view), you also must define those corners in the right order. This matters because the program determines which side of each rectangle is "inside" the object by the order in which you describe its corners and sides. And, of course, you want the notion of where inside the brick is to be consistent for each of its six surfaces. Fortunately, these programs now come with libraries of prebuilt parts and objects. For many purposes you can simply assemble a lot of these building block pieces, perhaps modify some of them, and create your scene or your complex object in far less time than was previously possible.

After you have specified the basic geometry, you also must deal with how each surface is going to look. That is, you must specify a texture and reflectivity for each one. And, if you are going to see anything in the scene, you must specify the type and location of all the light sources.

When you are finished, you can view your creation from any desired place and look at it in any desired direction and with any desired degree of "zoom." Furthermore, you can alter the lighting and the camera view dynamically to create a "fly-by" view of the scene. If you really want to get fancy, you might have some of the objects in the scene change their shape, color, or texture as the fly-by takes place.

You're likely already thinking that these programs are complex and need all the computing power you can give them. Often, computing the full appearance of each view of the final 3D scene (a process known as *rendering the scene*)—especially a fly-through view of a scene—takes many times as long as the fly-by itself will last. Sometimes graphics design firms use rooms full of very powerful PCs 24 hours a day for many days just to render a short, animated 3D scene.

If you want to get some hands-on experience with this type of program, one relatively powerful, yet modestly priced one is trueSpace3 from Caligari Corporation, based in Mountain View, California (www.caligari.com). There are many others, but this one is a good compromise between power and ease of use, and is relatively affordable.

In another use of the same technology, this type of program can be used to create the actual, physical objects that you have designed. In order to do this, the PC on which the design is created is linked to one or more fabrication tools. Then, under the direction of the PC, these tools will either carve up a block of metal or plastic or perhaps build a solid object from a liquid material.

This approach is called computer-aided manufacturing (CAM). It is often used to create the prototype of something, which later can be mass produced by other means. For some items that aren't needed in large numbers, however, this can even be the best way to make all of them.

A related development has been the creation of devices that can take an existing 3D object, scan it, and generate the computer model for it automatically. There are several ways to do this, the most complex of which use cameras and are fully automated, and others which use a 3D pointing device to do this task in a much less automated way.

Virtual Reality Modeling Language (VRML)

The Internet has brought us a new variation on 3D modeling. Most of the time when people on the Internet are using a browser to view World Wide Web pages, those pages are actually documents created in a language called Hypertext Markup Language (HTML). In Chapter 27, "You Can Touch the World, and It May Touch You, Too!" I will tell you more about HTML and its many kin. Here I want to focus on just one of those related languages. It is called Virtual Reality Modeling Language (VRML).

Web sites that use VRML can be viewed with any browser that has a VRML plug-in loaded into it. This enables the browser to do a rendering task similar to that done by one of the 3D design programs like trueSpace3. The design itself is contained in the VRML code of the Web page.

This means that you can download into your PC the VRML code that describes this scene, then view the scene from any defined vantage point. The characteristics of the objects in the scene and their lighting are fixed by the scene designer, but you, the user, choose the places from which you want to see it, as well as the directions in which you will look at it.

This allows the presentation of information in wholly new ways. If the scene you are viewing is an accurate copy of some actual real-world place, you can have something of a tourist experience without ever leaving your desk. If the scene is an imaginary one, you can go there when there really isn't any real, physical "there" to go to. The latest twist on this notion is to allow the PC user to insert an *avatar* (a modeled representation of a person, animal, or other entity, possibly with your actual face superimposed on it) to be in the scene and interact with the avatars of other users also currently viewing the scene.

"Real" 3D

Good as it is, sometimes a simulated 3D view is not enough. This is especially true if you want to be able to have several different people view something from his or her own vantage point. This is now possible for computer-generated scenes. However, the PC's video system must first be altered in some fairly dramatic ways.

What almost all approaches to creating "real 3D" share is that they manage somehow to present a different image of the scene to each of the viewer's eyes. The differences between these left and right views are computed to be just what you would see if you were actually looking at the reality that the computer-generated scene is emulating. (Near the end of this section I'll mention two true 3D scene generators that don't use stereoscopic images.)

One fairly obvious approach is to create two small monitors and mount them, one in front of each eye. You must add some optics to this to make them appear to be large and located at infinity, so that the viewer's eyes will blend the two 2D views into a single 3D one. The only real problem with this approach is getting sufficiently high-resolution display panels small enough to mount in a pair of comfortable glasses. So far this technology is only able to support VGA resolution in monochrome or a reduced resolution in color, and it has yet to be commercially successful.

A variation on this has recently been announced by a new company, Microvision, in Seattle (www.mvis.com). It has a technology it calls its Virtual Retinal Display (VRD). Essentially, Microvision proposes to mount two miniature projectors in a hand-held or head-mounted device that would project images through the pupils and directly onto the retinas of your eyes. You wouldn't be looking at any object outside your eye—the apparatus would simply create the illusion that you were.

Microvision doesn't yet sell an end-user product, but its VRD technology might become the basis of a whole family of quite exciting ones some day soon. Keep your eyes peeled for this one.

More common than any two-display approach is a method of producing stereoscopic images using only a single monitor. This is accomplished by running the video display at double the normal frame rate and arranging to show only every other one of those frames to each eye. This lets each eye see a normal frame rate video image, and the two images will differ in just the right way to cause a stereo image to be seen.

The standard version of this approach in the workstation market is the CrystalEyes product from StereoGraphics Corporation (www.stereographics.com). They also have a lower-priced version for PCs called SimulEyes. Another vendor with a very similar product, called Knowledgevision, is Neotek Automation (www.neotek.com). Their Web site has a well-written discussion of the science behind 3D vision; if that interests you, point to www.neotek.com/3dtheory.htm.

The systems from both of these companies include special glasses you must wear to see the stereoscopic images their systems create. These glasses have electrically driven shutters that alternately open and close to let first one eye and then the other see the screen. The glasses can be connected to the PC by a wire, or they can be wireless and receive a synchronizing pulse of light or radio energy from a transmitter on top of the PC monitor. If you've ever seen one of the large-screen format IMAX 3D movies, you've already worn the IMAX PSE glasses, an advanced implementation of this technology.

Still other companies—3DTV for one—offer projection systems that let you put both the left and right eye images on a screen, with each one reaching only the proper eye. This is accomplished by linearly polarizing the light for each eye at right angles to that for the other eye and then having the viewers all wear special polarizing eye glasses to let each eye see only the image meant for it. This also requires a special type of screen, so the polarization of the light in each image will not be appreciably diminished as it is reflected from the screen. This technology, originally developed in 1981 jointly by The Walt Disney Company and Kodak, can be experienced on a theatrical scale at EPCOT Center, at Walt Disney World.

These are by no means the only technologies that have been devised to give a viewer the perception of a true 3D scene. However, they are the most commonly used ones to date. Still in development are several very different approaches. One is already a product; the other only a technological approach toward a future product. In both cases, the goal is to create a "real image" (in the technical sense in which that term is used by optical engineers and physicists) of the 3D scene that will hover in space where you can walk around it and see it from different perspectives.

The first method, which has already been demonstrated as an actual product, uses a spherical mirror whose focal length can be rapidly altered to image the surface of a monitor at a variety of positions throughout a 3D region. At each position at which the monitor is imaged, it presents just that portion of the final image that belongs in that plane. Because of persistence of vision, you see the full, 3D object apparently just hanging there in space over the vibrating mirror.

Additionally, Fraunhofer-Gesellschaft, a company in Germany, is developing what it refers to as computer-generated hologram (CGH) displays. The company claims that its technology will give not merely a stereoscopic simulation of a 3D scene, but will make a real image of that scene that will force your eyes to focus differently on different objects depending on how far they are from your eyes. You can contact this group by sending e-mail to researcher Haimo Fritz at `fritz@egd.fhg.de` or you can visit their English Web site at `www.fhg.de/english.html`.

Force Transducers

Innovative video displays and superb audio are enough to create some very powerful immersive PC experiences. If you add to this a means of stimulating the user's sense of touch, and of using the user's kinematic senses, however, the experiences can be made even more powerful. Most ordinary joysticks accept your forces and translate them into PC inputs, but they don't give feedback other than in the sense of a spring return to the neutral position. The devices I am about to mention go well beyond that.

This is the land of the Nintendo Rumble Pak, reactive joysticks like Microsoft's SideWinder Force Feedback Pro, and similar technologies. Some of these devices let you point in three dimensions. Others let you push, pull, or squeeze objects, and in the process feel them resist your force. Still others are more like Sens-o-Round sound in movie theaters in the 1970s. The first kind of mechanism is simply special-purpose input devices. The second group is quite a lot more complex, serving as both input and output devices.

The actual variety of these devices and the technologies behind them is tremendous. You can get anything from a simple, inexpensive glove that lets you control a program by waving your hand, up to a full body suit that will sense every motion of any part of your body, and also will push back on the appropriate parts to simulate what you would experience if you actually moved around in an object-filled scene that, in fact, exists only inside the computer's memory. Combine this last with a helmet that lets you see that scene (and your own body in that scene), and you have the makings of a really convincing virtual reality experience.

High Data-Rate Communications

One common characteristic of all these immersive experiences is that they involve huge amounts of information. The input and display devices must move those huge amounts of information in and out of the PC at a very high rate, if the user is to have a smooth and compelling experience. This is not very hard to do if all the hardware is in one place. But sometimes, the application involves people interacting in two or more locations. Then the demands on the data communications channels can become truly frightening.

No special technologies are used for these high data-rate communications, just some good, old standards like T1 and T3 telephone lines, or fiber optic lines and so on. I only mention them here to remind you that this might be an important technical issue to deal with for some of the applications I will be discussing in the following sections.

There is one caveat: You probably don't want to use a communications link that uses geosynchronous satellites. Those satellites are so far out in space that the round-trip travel time of the signals, even at the speed of light, is long enough to introduce noticeable and possibly very annoying delays in the interactions between the several participants in your virtual world.

Immersive Applications

What are the uses to which people are putting all of these technologies? You'll not be surprised, I suspect, to learn that games were some of the first, and continue to be some of the most, popular ways these technologies get used. We are, however, also beginning to find some other valuable ways they can be applied.

Games

Single-user and multi-user games have been popular applications for computers from nearly the very beginning. Even before it was feasible to generate complex graphics, we had Adventure and Star Trek. These early games used only keyboard input and simple, character output, so they could be played even on computer terminals that could display only text.

As soon as more visually compelling experiences became possible, computer game designers eagerly exploited those new capabilities. Their customers reacted to these new developments with great enthusiasm, and they pressed the developers of hardware and software for ever more reality and even greater speed in those games. Doom and Myst are two of the most popular examples of how far we have come from the old days of Adventure on a "glass teletype."

Letting a user play against the computer presents one set of challenges for the game designer. Supporting multiple players who vie against one another in the same game from different locations presents a set of challenges that include all those for the single-user games and a great deal more. Here, for example, is one place where the issue of high-bandwidth data communication comes into play.

Gamers push the technology, and their enthusiasm has paid for a lot of the new developments. Military "gamers" also have paid for a big share of them and continue to do so. Computer weapons training systems are now turning out to be good models for advanced game systems—so as the cold war winds down, many of the former military hardware and software companies are turning to the game market for replacement income. When these new technologies exist, and especially as they begin to be mass-market items at a correspondingly modest price, many folks beyond the gaming community will find valuable uses for them as well.

Collaborations

Remember the multi-player games? We also are seeing that model extended into business applications. Once again, we are using many of the same technologies that gamers have used, but for completely serious business purposes.

Video Conferencing

A major expense for any large corporation is travel. Usually, the reason for having employees travel is so they can attend some meeting. However, with virtual reality technologies, we can make that meeting happen without any two of the participants ever being in the same city. If the meeting is just that—a chance to talk to one another and to see and hear presentations—it can be accomplished in this remote fashion by using a form of video conferencing.

Virtual Whiteboards

Going one step further, you can now buy *electronic whiteboards*. These are devices that look much like a normal blackboard (or whiteboard) on which you draw or write things with markers. When you do so, however, these same drawings can appear simultaneously on a PC monitor in the same room or in a room halfway around the world.

Moving on to the next step, you can dispense with the whiteboard itself and just use a portion of your PC's screen as a shared whiteboard. Then everyone who sees this "board" on his or her PC screen could also be enabled to draw on it things that would be seen by all the others, or to erase something that someone else had drawn.

This will enable the type of meeting in which the participants brainstorm together and take collective notes on the board—again without the participants having to be in the same room, or even on the same continent. At the end, each participant would have a permanent copy of the final result and, if they wanted, a record of all the steps that the group took to get to that result. Microsoft NetMeeting, which is part of Windows 98, is a strong first try of this type.

Virtual Worlds

A good example of this process can be found in the area of virtual worlds. At first, the capability to have a computer generate a purely illusory virtual world in which you could move around and perhaps even affect the actions going on in that world was used almost entirely for games.

Architectural Applications

Architects soon realized that they could use this approach to build a building in a virtual world long before it could be built in the real world. Then they could take their clients for a walk through the project. If either the architect or the client decided that a window was in the wrong place or a wall should be a different color, those things could be changed quickly and at very little cost. Thus, architects became some of the primary users of virtual reality as a means of testing their ideas and getting them approved by clients before any final construction plans were ever drawn up.

Educational Applications

The capability to build a virtual building doesn't just apply to ones that have been designed but not yet built. It can also be applied to buildings that are already constructed—including ones that were built long ago and have long since fallen down or been demolished. Some educators are now in the process of constructing a virtual Rome and a virtual Athens. Several other places are being created as well. This company is CyberSites, Inc. (`www.ancientsites.com/as/`).

Another group, SIMLAB (`http://demios.rec.ri.cmu.edu/`), is re-creating Pompeii. This project is apparently intended to be a full re-creation of the entire city as it is known from the excavations to date. Naturally, such an ambitious project will likely take several years. When they finish, it will be possible for students who cannot travel to Italy to nonetheless explore Pompeii for themselves. In fact, this will be quite a significant opportunity for anyone. The Pompeii that is being built in virtual space is Pompeii as it was in its ancient heyday—a place that no one can go for any amount of money in other than a virtual way.

Data Mining

All the applications I have spoken of so far are fairly straightforward uses of the notion that you can build virtual worlds that mimic our own. However, some of the most interesting applications of this technology are for building virtual worlds that are totally different from our own.

Imagine, if you will, a world in which abstract databases become buildings. Records within those databases become rooms. Then imagine that you can walk or fly through these structures, looking for something you want. Something like this was in Michael Crichton's mind when he wrote his 1994 novel, *Disclosure*. (This was made into a movie later that same year, staring Michael Douglas and Demi Moore. In the movie you can see one visual representation of what this idea might look like.)

Still, I think the most significant virtual worlds of data will be ones that don't use an architectural model at all. They will, instead, be structured in some fashion that directly reflects the relationships inherent in the data. This will be significant because human beings have an innate ability to perceive patterns. We are, in fact, much better at this task than any computer yet built.

So if you could make a virtual world out of a large mass of data, with the patterns in that world meaningful in terms of some real relationships among that data (even though the computer that builds this world does not know or understand what those patterns are), then putting a human observer into that world might be the most efficient way to discover those patterns.

In a real sense, this could be called data mining. Current efforts go by that name, but are in fact not much more than standard computer-assisted methods of searching through large databases.

No Longer Just for Gamers

I hope you have discovered in this chapter why I think it is very likely that we will be using more and more of these multimedia-enhanced, virtual-world types of immersive PC experiences not only in our leisure time, but also on the job. What was once dismissed as merely for gamers is now becoming vital for business.

This means that the types of PCs we will be buying for all purposes are in many ways going to be getting more and more alike. Certainly at the very high end this will be true. I think that at the low end there will still be a place for simple, character-only terminals and PCs in many organizations for quite some time to come. But even there, eventually, I think we will see voice-responsive speech-enabled, highly graphic PCs replace those character terminals—and when that happens, we'll have some much more people-friendly ways to use computers to do even the most mundane of data access tasks.

In the remaining three parts of this book, I will address the special requirements for mobile PCs and talk about how PCs get connected to one another and to the outside world. Chapter 26 discusses PCs that serve as if they were mainframe computers. The final part explores briefly some of the technological underpinning of the Internet and wraps things up.

VI

PCs Are Frequent Fliers, Too

Peter Norton®

23

Why Mobile PCs Must Be Different

Peter Norton®

People who work in more than one location or who must work on the go need something special if they are going to be able to use PCs conveniently and effectively in their jobs. Taking a PC from one location to another has always been possible—after all, the pieces that make up a PC aren't all *that* large or heavy—but it certainly isn't a convenient thing to do. You can use an ordinary desktop PC only when it is set up somewhere, with all the pieces attached, and with its power cord plugged into a live wall socket supplying power at an appropriate AC voltage and frequency.

As a result, there is a need for a special PC—one that can be moved from one place to another conveniently, and for some uses, it must also be able to operate wherever it is located, without needing any outside source of power. We call these *mobile PCs*.

From Luggables to Laptops and Beyond

The first PCs were exclusively desktop machines. They had at least three parts: a system unit, a keyboard, and a monitor. Early PC users who absolutely had to have the use of a PC in more than one location either got more than one machine (and carried their data back and forth on floppy diskettes) or they went through the inconvenience of taking their PC with them from location to location, which involved the effort of setting up the PC in each new place.

Luggables

Some manufacturers, including IBM, soon realized that there was a niche market they could serve by providing a portable PC. The first so-called portables were single-box units, which included the keyboard, the display, and all the system unit pieces in one handle-equipped case. Although they were about the size and weight of a sewing machine, they could be lifted by a single (strong) person. After you set it on a desk, all you had to do to get it working was open the lid, which often contained the keyboard, and plug in the power.

Those early manufacturers called these machines *portable*, but we now refer to them as *luggable* to emphasize their lack of battery power and the fact that you certainly wouldn't choose to carry this type of load around if there was any easier way to get the job done.

True Portables

The reason we had only desktop PCs and luggables for many years was simply that the state-of-the-art of manufacturing electronic circuitry was insufficiently developed. When people knew how to make really compact circuitry that contained all the necessary functionality for a PC, making a true portable PC became possible.

At first, even portables were rather heavy and bulky by today's standards. I remember, about 15 years ago, my first portable weighed about 12 pounds. I particularly remember how I felt one day when my plane had been set to depart from one gate at Chicago's O'Hare airport, and then suddenly was changed to another gate in an entirely different part of the airport. Carrying that portable all day was no fun. But I did it, like many other people, because that was the best available way to get PC computing capability on the go.

These portable machines had one important thing that the luggable PCs never had: a rechargeable battery. This meant that not only could you take your PC to your destination and plug it in and use it there, you could even use your portable PC en route—for a short time, at least.

Early battery-powered PCs were only able to operate for a short time before their batteries needed recharging. Later models got better and better, but even today, the issue of battery life between charges is often a troublesome one.

Laptop PCs

The progress in miniaturization did not stop; indeed, it has not stopped, and it shows no signs of letting up any time soon. Not too long after I bought that 12-pound portable, manufacturers began making even smaller and lighter machines. These machines were small enough to operate on your lap. So, of course, they were given the new designation, *laptop* PC.

Now this is the most common type of mobile PC. These machines are small enough and light enough (about three pounds) to carry around quite easily, yet they essentially can be as powerful as a good desktop PC. (They aren't so small or light that you can just stuff them into a purse or pocket, but they will fit inside a briefcase or attaché case, or a similar size computer case.)

These machines are typically about the size of a piece of letterhead (8.5 by 11 inches), and perhaps one to two inches thick. There are several reasons why this size has evolved as the more-or-less standard size for a laptop PC.

Probably the original reason for designing a mobile PC at this size was that it would allow you to put it into a standard attaché case. The designers believed that people would want to carry around their laptop PC along with their office reports and other similar sized objects. In fact, this is often done. Because laptop PCs are rather fragile, however, the laptop and those other papers now get shoved into a specially built, padded, and shock-resistant computer carrying case.

There are two other good reasons for not making the machine any smaller than this size. One is to ensure that the keyboard is large enough to type on comfortably. The other is to have the screen nearly the same size as a desktop monitor.

One interesting exception to the obvious fact that a laptop's keyboard can't be any bigger than its case was a novel portable PC design introduced a few years ago by IBM and referred to as the "butterfly laptop." The keyboard in this machine is split into two parts. It folds in a clever manner when you close the case to make it narrower, and it opens to its full width almost like a flower unfolding its petals when you open the case. All the other laptop PCs have simply had their keyboards fit within the boundaries of their cases.

Thus, we have the size that has worked out to be the best compromise between an adequate-size keyboard and as large a screen as possible, while still fitting it into a case that is small enough to carry easily. Still smaller PCs are being made. I'll describe them in a moment.

Figure 23.1 shows a Dell Latitude XPi M166ST portable computer. This is a mid-range example of the genre today. It has a 166MHz Pentium with MMX as its processor, an 800×600 pixel active matrix screen, 32MB of RAM, 2GB of disk space, a floppy diskette drive, and a CD-ROM drive—all that and battery power, too! It has built-in serial, parallel, and IrDA ports and a connector for attaching an external keyboard or screen, and a proprietary connector for attaching this machine to a "docking station" to access even more peripheral devices than would fit this modest-sized case.

Figure 23.1.
A Dell XPi M166ST portable computer.

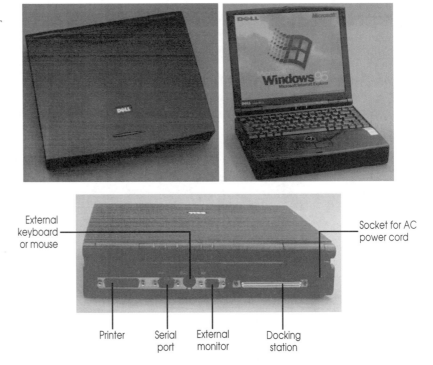

The bottom panel of Figure 23.1 shows this mobile PC from the rear. The connectors for a printer, serial port, external keyboard or mouse, and external monitor are indicated, as is the connector for the docking station. Not indicated is the small oval window above the external monitor connector. That is the rear panel IrDA infrared port. Another one on the front panel is indicated in Figure 23.3 (although again the window itself is not shown in the photo).

Fitting everything into this case was something of a tour de force for the engineers. The only way it could be done was by using both the very smallest standard parts, and in many instances, custom-designed parts. Also, these designs leave out some things that are standard on desktop PCs. For example, there are no slots into which you can plug a standard ISA or PCI option card.

After they put all the pieces in place, the manufacturers do not encourage end users to open up the case. This is very much unlike the situation for desktop PCs. This makes sense because the parts in a portable are often not only smaller but also more fragile than those used in desktop units. The makers of these machines often do allow for some limited amount of upgradability. For example, in this portable you can add more memory if you like. Figure 23.2 shows the small door on the bottom that you remove to do this. You see a little printed circuit card carrying memory chips that can be removed and replaced with a different card of the same size but with more or more capacious memory chips. This is the only way to upgrade this machine from the original factory configuration.

Figure 23.2.
Bottom view of the portable PC. The main memory in this portable PC can be increased by exchanging a memory module, accessible through this door on the machine's bottom surface (shown enlarged in the left panel).

Many of the parts in this computer were modified in order to save weight or space. For example, in Figure 23.3 the CD-ROM drawer is open with a CD on it, but the drawer itself has been cut away. Nearly half the bottom of the drawer is missing. The missing part of the drawer is not important either for supporting the CD or for giving the drawer sufficient strength, and so it could be omitted safely. The small amount of mass it represents could be shaved off the weight of the machine. Being concerned with such minor amounts of weight might not seem important, but if you trim away a little bit here and there, the overall weight savings can be quite significant.

Figure 23.3.
The CD-ROM drawer comes out from the front of this portable PC.

Built-in trackball

One of two buttons for trackball

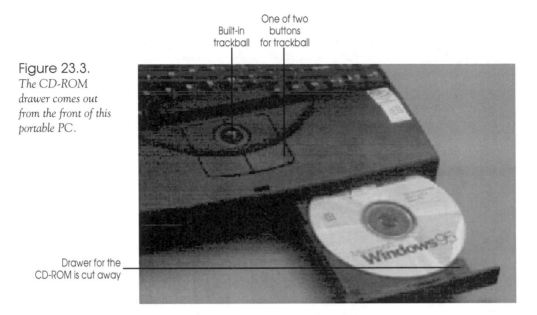

Drawer for the CD-ROM is cut away

This figure also shows the built-in pointing device, in this case a trackball, and the two buttons on either side of it that serve as mouse buttons. Some laptops use other pointing devices (most notably a tiny graphics trackpad or a pointing stick), but a trackball like this one is probably the most common pointing device for this class of machine.

The hard disk drive in this PC is an industry-standard model, but it is mounted in a custom holder that slips into the case and locks in place. Likewise, the battery is held in a custom housing for the same purpose. Figure 23.4 shows both of these parts removed from the PC. The battery goes into a hole near the back on the right side. The hard disk goes into a hole relatively high on the left side, between the audio connectors and the PC card slots.

Figure 23.4.
The hard disk (left) and the battery (right) for this portable PC, removed from their normal places in the case housing.

Just as desktop PCs are gaining in power and dropping in price every year, so are laptop PCs. These trends show no signs of abating any time soon.

In the past, it was common for laptop PCs to receive upgrades (to a new generation of CPU chip, for example) months to years after the corresponding upgrades were introduced for desktop machines. Now, however, the manufacturers are starting to introduce some new upgrades in mobile PCs first.

The one feature that laptop PCs have had for years and that is still rare on desktop machines is the PC Card slots (many of which now are the improved version referred to as CardBus slots or with Zoomed Video). Of course, the major reason why these slots are not so common in desktop machines is because those machines have I/O bus slots (mostly ISA and PCI) instead. With the growing popularity of digital cameras and other peripherals that use a PC Card slot for their interface to a PC, we will likely see the market for adapters which allow you to use PC Cards on your desktop continue to expand.

Sub-Laptop PCs

Miniaturization did not stop at the laptop phase. There are some good reasons to be very glad that it did not. After all, we now have cellular phones that fit in a shirt pocket. Why not full-fledged PCs that do so, as well? Microsoft is pushing this idea with its Windows CE operating system. With the recent introduction of version 2.0, Windows CE is starting to look pretty good, but it still has some pretty severe limitations, and it certainly has some fierce competition.

The main competition to a hand-held PC (HPC), as these sub-laptop PCs are termed, are devices referred to as personal digital assistants (PDAs). The most popular of them is the Palm Pilot from U.S. Robotics (now a division of 3Com Corporation). These devices, in general, are capable of storing a database of contact information, an appointment calendar, and often a collection of memos or a to-do list. Some also include game programs. Some PDAs enable you to enter data as handwriting that they recognize. Others use tiny keyboards. Many of them also have some means to be connected to a PC and to synchronize their data with similar data files on the PC. This allows entry of masses of data on the PC followed by a simple download to put those data into the PDA. In some cases the hardware supplied for this purpose is a cable and docking stand (this is what the Palm Pilot uses). In other cases, the link is accomplished by an infrared beam to an IrDA port on your PC.

On the other hand, some hand-held PCs (HPCs) can do significantly more than a simple PDA. For example, they can run spreadsheet programs, word processors, database programs, and communications programs. With a version of a cellular phone linkup, these machines can even be used to surf the Internet.

One of the great beauties of PDAs is that they are optimized for just the few tasks they are supposed to perform. They don't attempt to be full PCs with all the generality that implies. That means they are often cheaper and offer more functional utilities than the present generation of Windows CE hand-held PCs.

Of course, in time, as Microsoft improves Windows CE and as the hardware makers learn how to stuff ever more goodies into those little packages, we will no doubt have some pretty amazing hand-held PCs. But because they are too small to have a "real" keyboard (by which I mean one that is large enough for touch typing), they might not become a mainstream item until they have the power to understand speech. That will come, I have no doubt. Because it takes at least a 200MHz Pentium with MMX with 64MB of memory to do good voice recognition now, and because a hand-held PC with more than 2MB of memory or with a processor more powerful than a 486 are rare, I suspect it will be quite a few years before we have hand-held PCs that are up to the task of good voice recognition.

Until we get to that stage, PDAs that clearly are not PCs will have a secure niche in many of our pockets and purses. After all, they do quite well whatever limited jobs they are designed to do. Those have turned out to be things people value even when these devices cannot also be used as power word processors or for demanding graphical design work, and so on.

Lessons Are to Be Learned from Portable PCs

That was a fairly fast overview of the progress to date in mobile computing. There are, I think, some very important lessons we can learn from looking more carefully at that history.

Space Constraints Lead to Proprietary Parts

As I previously said, cramming all the power of a desktop PC into a package as small as a laptop is no easy feat. Just look at your desktop PC a moment. Think about all the space it takes up. Notice, if you will, the mass of cables and connectors it contains. Now consider what you might have to do to put all those pieces into such a tiny box.

The only way to do that (so far) is to use at least some proprietary parts and some industry-standard parts designed especially for mobile PCs. This means that it isn't possible to build your own laptop as easily as building your own desktop PC. You can't just go to the nearest computer superstore and buy a case plus a bunch of parts to go in it and end up with a laptop PC.

The biggest implication of this is that the number of each different kind of part that gets built is much smaller for those parts that are used only in a particular model of laptop or other mobile PC. This means that the cost of those items for mobile PCs is likely to be significantly higher than the equivalent items for desktop PCs.

As just one example, memory modules (SIMMs and DIMMs) for desktop PCs are a commodity item; they are made by many different companies, and for the most part, are interchangeable. There is only one size for a DIMM or for a 36-pin SIMM. However, memory modules for laptop computers come in many different shapes and sizes, and they often cost several times as much per megabyte as the standard memory modules used in desktop PCs.

This is only one example of the main reason why laptop computers cost more (for a given level of performance) than their desktop brethren. It is the direct result of their having to use proprietary designs in order to put all the pieces a particular manufacturer wants to include into such a cramped space.

Space Constraints Limit Upgrade Possibilities

There is another lesson we can learn from the history of mobile PCs. When you build a desktop PC, you put its "guts" into a system unit case. Normally that case is noticeably larger than it absolutely must be. This is done so it can have unused slots and bays for optional cards and drives, making upgrading that desktop PC pretty easy.

The only upgrades that are possible for a typical mobile computer are those that were contemplated by the manufacturer and allowed for in that particular model's design. Other than functionality that can be added via PC Cards, there are no option slots here for additional technologies and no spare drive bays. You may be able to swap the floppy diskette drive for another hard drive, a CD-ROM drive, or another battery, if the manufacturer of your laptop PC chose to give you those options. Some do, but many don't.

The main way mobile PC makers have addressed this limitation is by offering *docking stations*. These are boxes into which you can plug your entire mobile PC. They have some I/O slots and drive bays, plus some additional connector spaces on the rear panel for additional I/O connectors.

There is one big drawback to using a docking station. They take up enough room and are sufficiently nonportable that you likely will use one only at a desktop location. So really, the docking station is a way to convert your mobile PC into a desk-bound PC temporarily.

Docking stations are a little like the expansion chassis that were offered for desktop PCs 15 years ago. Back then, PCs were cramped inside, and you couldn't add much in the way of upgrades without running out of slots or bays. So, if you wanted, you could buy a second system unit without a CPU and hook it to the main system unit. Then you could put any additional plug-in option cards or drives into that expansion chassis.

This strategy soon disappeared from the desktop marketplace for the simple reason that it was expensive and cumbersome, and with the improvements in electronic miniaturization it became possible to put almost anything one might want within a normal-sized system unit. Something similar might very well happen in the mobile computing field. Only this time, the driving force will be the rise in popularity of the Universal Serial Bus and the IEEE 1394 bus. When those bus designs are sufficiently well established, I expect to see laptop PCs that have only those types of connectors (plus perhaps PC Card slots) for attaching peripherals or upgrading system memory, and so on. If this comes to pass (as the proponents of those two standards are passionately sure will happen), we might come to a point where upgrading a mobile PC is as easy and inexpensive as upgrading a desktop machine.

Space Constraints Mean Greater Control

A flip side to all these limitations in the design of mobile PCs is that the manufacturer has much more control over what they contain and how they work, because they are mostly fixed in their features by the manufacturer and because they use proprietary parts.

Therefore, mobile PCs aren't subject to nearly as many weird problems as desktop PCs. They just don't have nearly the chaotic mix of parts from different manufacturers tucked inside, so the makers can feasibly test almost all the possible variations of each of their models before shipping them to customers. This is simply impossible for a general-purpose desktop PC that can have any of several thousand different add-on pieces put in it by the customer after it is shipped from the factory.

For this reason, mobile PC makers have been much more successful in getting their products to work well with energy-saving features than have the desktop PC makers. Of course, the fact that battery power is such a precious resource has also impelled the mobile PC makers to work harder on this goal.

Power Is Precious on the Road

Speaking of power and how precious it can be leads me right into my next topic: Battery power for PCs on the road. The main reason you have a battery in a mobile PC is to let you compute when you aren't near a wall outlet. Other advantages include being untethered so you can use your PC as you wander around the office, although you might be close to power outlets. You can also keep your PC going during a brief power outage when it is running on AC power. That last advantage points out something that many people might not realize: Virtually every mobile PC has a built-in uninterruptible power supply, or UPS.

That's why batteries are important. Understanding how they work and how to help them do their job well and not let you down at some inopportune time is important as well.

Standard-Sized Batteries

At present, more than 150 different types of batteries are being used in the approximately 15 million portable computers and 25 million cellular phones; this is too many different models. Manufacturing and stocking them all at distributors is inefficient and leads to increased cost. An industry standard has been developed (largely through pressure by one of the major battery makers, Duracell).

This standard specifies just five standard models of battery for this class of service. Any battery that is built to one of these five models' specifications will have the same size, shape, and nominal terminal voltage, and their terminals will be in the same places. Therefore, these batteries will be as interchangeable as today's C flashlight batteries are. Any of the different chemistry models (lead-acid, Nicad, NiMH, LiIon, and so on) can be used to make these batteries, which means their weight and electrical capacity will vary. (You'll find this same situation for flashlight batteries. You can buy them in carbon or alkaline primary batteries, or in Nicad rechargables.)

The first of the five models is Duracell's DR36 or Motorola's EP36 (and similar model numbers by other makers). You can get batteries that conform to this specification in NiMH, LiIon, and also now Masti's alkaline-air.

"Smart" Batteries

Any time you use battery power for a computer, you must face a serious problem: How do you know when it is time to recharge or replace the battery? When must you stop and save your work or risk losing it when the battery voltage falls too low to keep the computer running normally?

Laptop computers commonly come with a battery gauge applet. This little program claims to report how much battery life remains. How can it do that, and can it really do that job accurately?

Typically, these programs depend on a manufacturer's experience with certain batteries of a given type. They also must make assumptions about the probable power load that the computer represents, based on which parts of it are powered up. Each second one of these programs will decide what fraction of the total battery life must have been used, and will reduce its report of remaining battery life accordingly.

What this procedure doesn't do is actually monitor the battery itself, so it is quite possible (especially for an older battery that is nearly worn out) for the battery to run out of juice before the battery gauge thought it would. Conversely, you might be prompted to shut down your PC unnecessarily, just because the battery gauge applet thinks your battery is nearly exhausted when in fact it still has plenty of power to continue for quite awhile longer.

Clearly, the right way to go about all this is to put more "smarts" into the battery—build into it some monitoring circuitry that can watch the actual condition of each cell in the battery independently, and then have it report to the computer how it is doing. A side benefit is that such a smart battery can not only tell the computer that it needs to be recharged, it also can specify what recharging current should be used and when to stop that recharging.

With such a smart battery, and with a PC that knows enough to use that battery's smarts, you could interchange types of batteries freely. Pop in an alkaline-air smart battery today and run your PC until that battery is dead. Put in a LiIon smart rechargeable tomorrow and recharge it as necessary.

If you have a PC that has the hardware and software support (system management bus and appropriate additions to the system BIOS), by all means you should use smart batteries. Then you can really believe what that PC's battery gauge tells you.

Extending Your PC's Battery Life

Whatever type of battery your portable PC uses, and no matter how long it lets your computing sessions last between recharges or battery replacement, you probably wouldn't mind if it lasted a little while longer. At the very least you could save some hassle and money. So, you must learn some steps you can take to extend your battery's life and also learn when not to use those steps that might compromise your efficiency. Not every power-saving idea that you find touted in some computer magazine makes good sense for the way you use your computer.

Use AC Power Whenever Possible

Use AC power whenever you can. Shouldn't that be obvious? No, it really isn't. What isn't obvious is a caution I must give you about doing this. Almost every PC that can run on rechargeable battery power includes a battery charger. That is true even when you might think it isn't. If your PC has a battery eliminator or any other way to power it off the AC line instead of off its internal battery, most likely the power supply inside it (or in the box in the middle of the cord or in a cube at the end of the power cord that goes into the wall) is really a battery charger.

Does this make a difference? Yes. First, this means that while you are running on AC power, you are at least trickle charging your PC's internal battery. Most of these power supply designs will charge up a depleted rechargeable battery and then, when your PC is full of charge, they will not shut themselves off completely; they will cut back to supplying a slight trickle of current to keep the battery topped up. This is done because rechargeable batteries lose some of their charge over time just sitting there. You may think of it as if there were a small load on the battery inside its case. Even if you don't pull any current out of its external terminals, the battery will slowly die on its own.

Most of these power supplies assume that your PC has its battery in place (and that the battery isn't *really* dead—by which I mean that the battery is still capable of accepting a charge even if it doesn't currently have much of one in it).

Normal power supplies for PCs convert AC power from the wall into DC power. This involves taking the alternating current (AC), which is simply alternating positive and negative waves of electric power, and turning them into a steady supply of direct current (DC). To do this, however, they must store some electrical energy internally to bridge over the times when the wall socket isn't supplying any voltage or current at all. Those are, of course, the times in between the waves of positive and negative voltage. Normal power supplies store this energy in capacitors. Because these capacitors allow those supplies to filter out the pulses inherent in AC power and thus provide a steady DC output, they are called filter capacitors.

Power supplies for PCs with internal batteries can let the internal battery do most of this energy storage task. In effect, they let the battery run the PC for short periods of time: 120 times each second. After each one of these intervals, the power supply replaces the charge that was withdrawn from the battery.

Warning: Here's the point of all this: You must have your PC's battery in place (and it must not be dead) if you are going to run your portable PC on AC line power. That is true for almost every PC with a rechargeable battery. It is not true for a mobile PC that doesn't have a charger type of power supply—its AC power supply won't be depending on the battery to help it do its job.

One big benefit you get from the strategy I have just described (and that is used in almost all rechargeable battery–powered PCs) is that when you run this type of PC from the AC power line, you are in effect running it on an uninterruptible power supply (UPS). Thus, you are automatically protected against brownouts, surges, spikes, and power failures.

Don't Recharge Inappropriately

Clearly, if you run your PC on battery power for very long, you will have to recharge that battery at some point. Most manufacturers recommend that you discharge the battery all the way, then recharge it fully. They don't approve of partial discharge and recharge cycles.

This is most important if you have a Nicad battery in your PC because partial discharge and recharge cycles cause the battery to lose capacity through the "memory" effect. It also is a good idea to use a full discharge and recharge cycle even on batteries that are built using one of the other popular chemistries.

Having a spare (and fully charged) battery with you if you are using your PC away from AC power is a good idea. That way when the first battery is depleted, you can swap batteries and keep on computing. Then at the next convenient time, you can recharge the depleted battery, making it ready for use when the swapped battery becomes depleted.

I must make another point about appropriate and inappropriate recharging. Every battery chemistry implies a different terminal voltage and a different optimum charging scheme (in terms of how much current to use and how to taper it down to the trickle-charge value as the battery approaches full charge).

Because this is so, the designers of PCs that use rechargeable batteries design their power supplies with a knowledge of which kind of rechargeable battery their PC is going to use. The one exception to this are the newest PCs that are designed to use smart batteries. The newest PCs include chargers capable of charging up any kind of rechargeable battery, and they listen to the battery first to find out what kind it is and how they should charge it optimally.

Naturally, for this latter approach to work, any battery you use in such a PC must be a smart battery. An ordinary battery, without those smarts, can't tell the PC what kind it is or what its needs are.

> **Warning:** If your mobile PC doesn't support smart batteries, don't ever replace its battery with one that uses a different chemistry scheme. Doing that could damage the new battery, the PC's power supply, or both.

Use Power-Saving Settings

The battery in your mobile PC supplies power so your PC can do its job. If your PC can be configured to require less power, the battery will be capable of supplying it with adequate power for a longer time. This fairly obvious insight behind various strategies has been implemented in most mobile PCs; you can make the PC use less power whenever you don't really need it to be using the maximum.

In practice, this means that if you aren't currently accessing your PC's hard disk, there is no reason for it to be spinning; this is also true for your CD-ROM drive. Also, if you aren't doing anything with your PC, the display can be turned off. Perhaps the most exotic approach is that you can slow down the CPU clock speed any time it is waiting for you to press a key or move your mouse. Each of these strategies will reduce the total power consumption by the PC.

However, these savings don't come without some associated costs. For example, it takes a few seconds to get a turned-off hard disk back up to speed. So if it has been shut down to save power, you will have to wait those few seconds before you can access it again.

This whole issue of power saving is one that has much broader implications than just extending the life of a mobile PC's battery, so I will continue this discussion in the next section on the ecologically sensitive PC.

The Ecologically Sensitive PC

From almost the beginning, people realized that doing everything they could to reduce a PC's power consumption was important for portable, battery-powered PCs. What is now becoming clear is that the same issue can be important for desktop units as well.

Is This Really Necessary?

When PCs were young and there weren't many of them, the total power consumption of all the PCs in the world was insignificant in the big picture. Now that there are hundreds of millions of PCs worldwide and many of those PCs are being left on all the time—sometimes for some very good reasons, such as being able to respond to incoming messages—the issue of how much power they consume is becoming a rather important one.

Overall, electrical power is one of the major ways in which modern societies use energy. Its usage contributes significantly to pollution problems. So for both economic and environmental reasons, it would be nice if we could drastically curtail our use of electrical power by our PCs.

Still, you have a PC because it enables you to accomplish some things you couldn't do without it. Therefore, you are likely to use only energy-saving strategies that don't get in your way. When saving energy and doing useful things conflict, you'll have to compromise based on your personal evaluation of the tradeoffs.

PC Power Management Overview

You can save power consumption by your PC in two ways: limit when you have it turned on and cut down on the power it uses while it is turned on.

The Ultimate Power-Saving Method

The ultimate way to save on the energy used by your PC is to turn it off. That, of course, defeats the purpose for which you got your PC. But you don't need to keep it on when you aren't using it.

There has been a debate going in this industry for a long time on just this point. Some folks have pointed out that hard disks are stressed most when they are started. Likewise, most of the electronics in a PC are stressed more by changing temperatures than by a constant temperature. So perhaps you are shortening the overall life of your PC by turning it off when you aren't using it. On the other hand, your PC clearly will last longer if it is almost always shut off, and it almost certainly will use less total energy as well.

Peter's Principle: When to Turn Off Your PC

The real question is not "Should you turn off your PC when you aren't using it?" but "For how long do you have to anticipate that you won't be using your PC before it is clearly better to turn it off rather than leave it on for your next use?"

My personal take on the matter is that any time you anticipate using your PC again within less than about eight hours it probably makes more sense to leave it on. If you are going to go away from it for longer than that, it's probably a good idea to turn it off.

continues

You should ask yourself another question before deciding: What hardware and tools are running on your PC that might help to minimize its power consumption. For example, the monitor frequently uses more energy than all the other parts of the PC put together (other than a laser printer). So if you have arranged to have the monitor shut itself off, or turn itself down to some very low level of energy usage whenever you aren't actively using the PC, you can justify leaving the system turned on more often.

Another issue to consider is whether your PC is running on a UPS. If it isn't, spikes and surges on the power line can damage it more easily (although you should have a good surge protector in place in any event). Brownouts or power failures of even a short duration can disrupt your PC more than a single simple shutting down and restarting. If you're not using a UPS or at least a good surge protector, I'd turn off your PC rather more often than otherwise.

Saving Power While Your PC Is On

I just mentioned one way you can save power without turning off your PC totally: Shut off the monitor when it isn't being used. You can do this manually, but it is even more effective if you arrange to have your PC do it automatically. You can have it do several other things automatically to save power, as well.

What Must Be Done By the Hardware

In order to be able to power down different parts of your PC selectively and under software control, the parts in question must be able to interact appropriately with that controlling software. Naturally, you can never completely turn off power to a gadget that must be able to respond to a software signal asking it to turn on, but you can let it power down all of itself but the tiny part that listens for that wakeup signal.

A common example in most homes is a television set that can be turned on using a remote control. Some part of the TV set must be listening for the infrared signals from the remote control in order to respond to them.

Modern Energy Star monitors can be commanded to go into any of several states of reduced power, from nearly all the way off (except for that tiny monitoring part) up to almost completely on but with the screen image blanked.

The reason for having several levels to which the monitor may be powered down is that it takes different amounts of time to "recover" each. The lower the power, the longer it will take to get back into full operation.

The hard disk can be turned off when it isn't needed, and modems can be powered down (with just enough circuitry left powered that they can come back to full operation when they detect an incoming call). Printers, too, almost all now have power-saving modes that drop their consumption to nearly nothing until you issue a print command. Certainly, if your printer doesn't support power-saving, it should be turned off when it's not needed.

Perhaps the most interesting of the various power-saving features is that the clock speed of the CPU may be reduced. All modern PC processor chips (and many of the other chips used in a PC) are made using the complementary metal-oxide semiconductor (CMOS) process for manufacturing integrated circuit chips. One important fact about a CMOS circuit is that it uses almost no power to sit in one state. Every time you change the state of a portion of the circuitry, however, some small chunk of electric charge will make its way through the circuit from the power lead to the ground lead. The size of the chunks of charge that fall through each time are fixed. So the average rate at which charge flows, which is to say the average current through these devices, is directly proportional to the number of state changes that are taking place within them during each second.

The power dissipated as heat in the chip is simply the average current through it multiplied by the voltage on the power lead attached to the chip. Therefore, power is also directly proportional to the number of state changes per second.

One thing CPU manufacturers have done and continue to do is work to lower the needed voltage to power their chips. Originally all the chips used 5 volts (except for a few that used 12 volts). Now most of the key circuits are designed to work at 3.3 volts, 2 volts, or in some cases as little as 1.8 volts. We very likely will see that number fall yet farther as the manufacturers learn even better ways to make their products work with minuscule power.

The lower the voltage applied to the chip, all other things being equal, the lower its power dissipation. But for a given chip, it must have some minimum voltage in order to operate. There may or may not be a minimum frequency at which it must be "clocked" in order to work correctly.

Some CPU chips can have their clock slowed down arbitrarily. They can't go any faster than the rated maximum speed without risking miscomputing, but they are capable of going as slowly as you like without any bad consequences. As you reduce the clock frequency, you also reduce the power they draw from the battery or other power source.

Other CPU chips have some minimum speed they must go. They are like a man riding a bicycle. Depending on the man's skill, it is possible to ride quite slowly, but most of us can't actually stop the forward motion of the bicycle completely without having it fall over (assuming you don't allow the rider to put his foot on the ground). The reasons are different, but many CPU chips cannot run at less than some minimum speed without failing to remember what they are doing.

Furthermore, the memory in our PCs are mostly DRAM, which, I remind you, stands for Dynamic Random Access Memory. They must be refreshed at least a few thousand times per second in order not to forget the information they are holding.

However, it is often possible to reduce the clock speed of the CPU from several hundred million cycles per second to perhaps one million. Doing so will reduce the power of the CPU chip, the memory chips, and all the other CMOS chips that are running at the same frequency by the ratio of the normal operating clock speed to the slowed down clock speed.

Reducing the clock speed of the CPU can save you up to 99% of the energy drain in those chips when you aren't actually using them. Really sophisticated energy-saving circuits can apply this strategy not only when you walk away from your PC, but any time that it is waiting for you to do something.

So if you are doing some word processing, each time you type a key the PC must do something with that. If it finishes its work before you press the next key, it can slow down its clock until you do press the next key. In effect, you make the PC run just fast enough that it is always working, but never faster than necessary. This clever trick works with virtually no downside to it because you can slow or speed the clock any amount you like in almost no time, and the circuitry needed to do this is minimal.

On the other hand, powering down the monitor or stopping the hard drive from spinning means that when you are ready to use them once more, you will have to wait up to several seconds for them to recover from their rest and get back up to speed. So you really don't want to do that every time you aren't using them for just a few seconds or a few minutes. Only when you really pause in your use of the PC for many minutes are you likely to have the screen image disappear. The hard disk may stop turning if you don't access any files on it for many minutes. If it does, you will experience a possibly quite annoying delay when you next want to save a file or load a new program, and so on.

These are some of the possible ways the hardware can reduce the average power it consumes while still letting you compute at more-or-less full speed whenever you want to do so. If your PC can take advantage of all these features, you might be able to leave it on almost all the time with very little energy wasted. However, the hardware cannot do all of this job by itself.

What Software Must Do

In order to make the hardware pieces turn off or on, slow down, or whatever else at just the right times, some program must tell them what to do and when. The programs that do this in a modern PC are a part of the motherboard BIOS that is dedicated to this purpose. Those programs are able to only activate or deactivate the hardware; they don't know when you want those strategies applied, so you need some way to tell those programs what you want.

You can do this in two different ways. One is through some entries in the motherboard BIOS setup program. (Normally you access this program with some special keystroke at a prescribed point in the boot-up process.) Here you might be able to specify, for example, whether you want the hard disk to stop spinning when it hasn't been accessed for the length of time you specified. (Usually you won't be able to enter just any time you like, but rather you must pick from among several fixed options.)

Another level at which your PC may be programmed, or configured, for more or less power savings is through an operating system applet. Thus, the operating system might monitor the programs you are running and decide, based on that, which of the energy-saving options it should invoke. Again, you can tell it (by making some choices in a setup dialog box) how you want it to do that job.

A Recommendation Regarding "Green PCs" at This Time

I have mentioned several times that there can be a cost to you when you use energy-saving strategies. I mentioned a few of these costs, such as the delay you will experience each time you access some file on the hard disk after a long period of not using the disk, if you have programmed your PC to turn off the disk drive when it hasn't recently been used.

One of the worst possible problems can happen if you have your PC turned on and connected to a phone line or network. You may be running some program that monitors the phone line or the network for incoming messages. You expect that whenever a message arrives, the PC will snatch it and do something with it. If your PC has powered itself down too far, however, it might not be able to come back to full operation in time to catch the beginning of the message. Then the cost of your power-saving strategy defeats the purpose of leaving your PC on in the first place. You might as well have saved even more energy by simply turning your PC off.

To be sure you won't get stung by a scenario such as this, you might have to run some tests. Configure your machine for power savings and then check to be sure it can respond in time to all the important stimuli you expect it to receive. If it works flawlessly, congratulations are in order; you configured it appropriately. (You might be able to save even more power by using some more aggressive settings in the power savings setup. If you try reconfiguring, repeat all your tests to be sure.)

All of what I have said to this point is mostly "a counsel of perfection." That is, it really only applies if everything works exactly as it is supposed to work. Unfortunately, not all PCs work perfectly all the time. In fact, desktop PCs are often quite unstable beasts. This is more true if you are running Windows 3.x or Windows 95 than if you are running Windows NT, OS/2, or Linux. (Well, you must configure Linux, or any flavor of UNIX, just right in order to get the stability it is capable of yielding. Once you do get the setup tweaked appropriately, it is a stable operating system.)

So if yours is a desktop PC, you may find that you must forego many of the potential power savings just because if you don't, your PC will crash even more often than it normally does. The usual crashes to be concerned about are those that happen just as the PC is attempting to recover from some power-reduced state. If it locks up then, try turning off one or more of the energy-saving strategies and see if that keeps it from crashing.

Laptops are likely to be better at using power-saving strategies without causing problems—mainly because their makers have a lot more control over the total hardware configuration. You simply cannot customize them nearly as freely as you can a desktop unit.

So for now, I suggest that you experiment with energy-saving strategies, but only if you are willing to take some time to test each one to see whether it works without any undue problems on your PC with your added hardware and software. Don't be surprised if you find you can't use all the energy-saving features you might like to use. Most of us can't—at least not on desktop PCs.

Eventually, the industry will get this all figured out and we will be able to use all those features freely. Energy-saving strategies will be a good thing—for us as PC users, as citizens in a society that is increasingly burdened by pollution, and, of course, as payers of the electric bill.

Mobile PCs at Home and in the Office

Finally, before leaving the topic of mobile PCs, I must mention a new trend: buying a laptop PC that is so powerful that you end up using it on your desktop. It becomes your only PC, but because it is a battery-powered portable one, you can use it anywhere.

What to Look for in a Multipurpose PC

The most important thing to do if you want to follow this strategy is, of course, to be sure the portable you get is powerful enough to do the computing you want to do at your desk. For a long time that would have meant buying an outlandishly expensive portable. But nowadays you can get virtually the same power in your portable as you can in a similarly priced desktop unit. You will have to pay some premium for the portability, but not very much. The main thing you will lose is the flexibility that goes with an easily reconfigured desktop unit.

The next most important thing to do, in my opinion, is to get a good keyboard and monitor for use on your desktop. You should also get a good mouse, graphics tablet, or larger trackball. Get more than one of each if you want to use your PC on several desktops. Whenever you are at any of those locations for more than a brief time, take the time to attach the external monitor, keyboard, and mouse or whatever. Laptop PCs' keyboards are sometimes okay and their screen displays are even quite nice, but a desktop PC monitor is even nicer, as is a really good keyboard. (I have yet to find a laptop whose built-in pointing device satisfied me. So far, I think of them as necessary evils to use when you can't attach a mouse or the like.)

Docking Stations Add Back Lost Flexibility

The idea of a docking station is that you can attach your external monitor and keyboard permanently to the docking station. You can also attach your office network cable, a phone line, a printer, and whatever other peripheral gadgets you might want to use when your PC is "docked."

You still have a portable PC. Just slide it out of the dock whenever you want to use it on the go. When you slide it back in, you have, once more, a fully supported desktop PC system with all the right peripheral devices. For this strategy to work well, the PC must know whether it is docked, and in each case it must do the right thing. In particular, it must load the correct device drivers to support the peripherals that are attached to it and not act as if they are still attached later when you undock your PC.

PC operating systems are not yet fully up to this task, but they are getting there. Each new generation is a little better at the job. Still, for now, you will likely want to power down your PC each time you are ready to dock it or undock it—no matter what your PC's user manual might say about its capability to safely dock with the power on.

What I have just described is how a docking station can add convenience to the use of a portable PC at an office or home desk. What it also can do is give you back the flexibility you lost when you opted for a portable instead of a desktop unit. This is because a good docking station will typically have some I/O slots (at least ISA and maybe PCI as well) and some drive bays, plus a power supply, an array of port connectors, and so on. This means that when your portable is docked, it has the potential for having more things added to its basic hardware configuration that are permissible in its ready-to-travel state. Of course, if you use this flexibility, you are on your own. In the process, be sure you don't make your nicely stable laptop into one of the all-too-typical, fragile desktop units that will crash if you look at it cross-eyed. One way to deal with this problem is to configure your PC so it doesn't use nearly as many of the energy-saving strategies if it is running on line power as it does when it is running solely on battery power.

Summary

Mobile PCs are different from other PCs intended for desktop or file server use. Mainly, the mobile PCs have been carefully designed to have the absolute minimum size and weight possible for their feature set. This means they generally are less flexible about accepting upgrades than other PCs and often are more stable in their operation as a result.

Mobile PCs use batteries. Battery technologies are complex and constantly improving. If you can get a PC that accepts standard size batteries or, even better, smart batteries (and your PC knows how to use those smarts), you will be much happier with them than with a normal, old-fashioned battery.

Whatever battery strategy you use, reducing your PC's power needs helps extend that battery's life. Modern mobile PCs are pretty good at doing this in several different ways. Many of those same strategies can be applied to desktop PCs, but for now you might want to pass on most of them because they also often bring along some additional instability.

Mobile PCs are so good now that with a docking station and an external keyboard, mouse, and monitor, they can serve very well as a desktop PC replacement. No longer is a mobile PC useful only when you are on the road.

Even smaller PCs and PDAs have their place in our computing world as well. As the technology improves, they may come to assume ever larger roles in our lives. But for now, nothing smaller than a laptop is likely to serve all the uses for we have for our PCs.

VII

The
Connected
PC

24

The PC Reaches Out, Part One: Modems and More

Peter Norton®

The previous chapters talked about an isolated PC. Some of the PCs I have discussed are loaded with features, and they might even have some of the necessary hardware to become connected with other computers, but the PC didn't have to be connected to anything outside itself. This part of the book (Chapters 24, 25, and 26) is all about how a connected PC differs from an isolated one.

In this chapter we will look at connecting PCs to other computers with simple direct connections, as terminals to large computer systems, with standard telephone modems, and across high-speed communications systems.

Reaching Out, and *Really* Reaching Out

Some PCs are connected only slightly. Others reach out a little bit, and still others reach way out—perhaps all the way across the globe—and connect to many other computers. To make this clear, we can organize them into four realms of connectedness. But before I talk about those four realms, I want to describe the very smallest ways in which a PC can reach out.

A Really Short Stretch

The shortest links from a PC are those it has to its own peripherals. But in one view, all the attached peripheral devices are really just parts of the PC itself. With modern PCs, the keyboard and screen are clearly essential parts of the PC, yet they are in separate housings and are connected to the system unit in much the same manner as many of the other "peripheral" devices like a printer, an external disk drive, a scanner, or an external modem.

So, the shortest linkages considered in this chapter are the ones that take a PC from an essentially isolated state into an interconnected state (connected to at least one other general-purpose computer). The minimal form of such a connection is when two PCs are directly linked to one another (and to no other computers) by a cable or infrared light beam.

This is probably done most often when a laptop computer is linked to a desktop computer. This is frequently done to enable easy transfers of files from one machine to the other, or to let the laptop computer print a document on a printer attached to the desktop machine.

The most common method used for this type of link is a cable that connects a serial or parallel port on one of the computers to a similar port on the other computer. You can use several different software programs with this simple type of hardware connection.

Starting with version 5.02, DOS has included two programs designed for use in exactly this situation. Running INTERSRV.EXE turns one of the two computers into a file and printer server. Running

INTERLNK.EXE on the other computer enables it to access those services across the link between the two. Windows 95 has a Direct Cable Connection facility that does much the same thing.

Before either of those programs were developed, several commercial programs that linked PCs for file transfers and printer sharing were available. These programs have been continuously improved and are still popular. Laplink is probably the most popular. (These third-party programs have been enhanced and are now capable of general remote control operation of a PC. I will tell you more about that usage for them under "Remote Control of a PC" in Chapter 25, "The PC Reaches Out, Part Two: Through the NIC Node.")

Four Realms of PC Connectivity

The first realm of connectivity covers those PCs that are each wired directly to a single central computer, which might be a mainframe or a minicomputer. When they are communicating with that central computer, these PCs are acting essentially like old-fashioned "dumb" terminals (by which I mean just a screen, keyboard, and perhaps a pointing device such as a mouse—no CPU and no local data storage capability). Later in this chapter in the section "Direct Wire Connections," I'll explain why it often makes more sense to use a PC for this task rather than the dumb terminal that once was so common.

The second realm of connectivity is when several autonomous PCs in the same general area are connected to one another (and perhaps also to one or more central computers). This is a *local area network* (LAN) and is the most common way that PCs are connected in businesses (and some homes) today.

The third realm is when several LANs are linked together into a *wide area network* (WAN). This allows all the computers in each LAN to communicate over an inter-LAN link to any of the other computers in any of the other connected LANs. Many large corporations have set up WANs to connect their far-flung offices.

Finally, we have the realm that includes PCs that are capable of establishing connections with huge numbers of remote computers, of all types and sizes. As more and more PCs are becoming connected to the Internet, this is fast becoming the most common category of connected PC.

Permanent and Transient Connections

Some PCs are permanently connected to one or more other computers. But many PCs connect to those other computers only when they need to.

Direct Wire Connections

PCs that are permanently connected to one central host computer often use a simple direct cable from the PC's serial port to a terminal server on the central computer. This is the same type of connection used by dumb terminals. But, because the PC is much more than just a keyboard and screen (plus perhaps a pointing device), it can do more than just act as a terminal. When it is acting as a terminal, we say that it is in a *host session*. The rest of the time it acts just as if it were an isolated PC.

While it is in a host session, such a PC can log the session to its local hard disk. This can serve as an audit trail, or it can be reviewed at a time the host computer is unavailable in order to analyze aspects of a previous session. When it's not in a host session, the PC can do anything any other standalone PC can do. Therefore, if a host connection is needed for only a portion of the day, the rest of the time the PC can be used to do useful work without having to rely on the host.

PCs that are connected to several other autonomous computers via a local area network can use any of several different kinds of permanent connection methods. Some names you might have heard for this type of connection include Ethernet, Token Ring, and Arcnet. These same connections can be used to access distant LANs across a WAN, if the LAN to which this PC is connected has a WAN connectivity as well. I will describe all this technology in the next chapter, "The PC Reaches Out, Part Two: Through the NIC Node."

Transient Wired Links

Although having your PC permanently connected to other computers can be very convenient, sometimes it just doesn't make sense. Portable computers are an obvious example. If you are traveling, your portable computer doesn't need to be constantly linked to the office LAN or to the Internet. And, the freedom that comes with unhooking the wire can be a very valuable one. It's possible now to keep connected without using a wire link, but that isn't yet very common for portable PC users. Even those who have these links don't use them all the time, for reasons of cost if nothing else.

Permanent interconnection is also not the best approach when computers in a home or office are remote from the computers to which they only sometimes must connect. You can save a lot of money by having that computer connected only when the link is being used.

Even if your PC is permanently connected to some other computers, there might be some types of distant connection that you occasionally want, but those needn't be available to you except when you need them. A transient link often makes sense in this situation, mainly to save money and facilitate sharing expensive resources.

The most common method of transient connection is to use a modem and a dial-up telephone line. Your PC causes the modem to dial a distant computer, and when the connection is established, you can exchange information with that distant computer just as if your PC were wired directly to it.

Wireless Links

You don't need to have a cable to link PCs to other computers. The two most common technologies for this purpose are radio links and optical links. The *radio links* are mostly used for transient connections with distant computers. These links use a modem plus a radio transceiver (possibly a cellular telephone) just as some other PCs use a modem and normal, wire-based telephone connection. In most respects these links function just the same as a modem-to-phone-line link.

Optical links are most often achieved using infrared light. Some LANs use this medium of data transmission, and the Infra-red Data Association (IrDA) standard includes a high-speed protocol for just this use. A more common example is to link a portable computer to a desktop machine via their IrDA ports. This can be done either to transfer some files or to let the portable computer use a printer that is attached to the desktop machine. Some printers have their own IrDA ports built in. They can be used by a portable PC directly, without needing any help from a desktop PC. The printer simply becomes one of the portable computer's peripheral devices, albeit one that is only sometimes connected to it.

Modems and More

I've just told you that modems are commonly used to make transient connections between PCs and other computers. You probably already knew that. Now look into what modems are and how they work.

Reaching Out and "Byte-ing" Someone

Motorola used the phrase "Reach out and byte someone" in its advertisements for modems. I've always rather enjoyed this clever play on the slogan used by the telephone company to promote voice calls: "Reach out and touch someone," because modems are how we send bytes of digital data over a normal voice-grade telephone line.

A modem is an interface device. It connects on one side to your PC, and on the other side to a telephone line (or in some cases, to a radio transceiver or to a community antenna television [CATV] cable).

The name modem stands for MOdulator and DEModulator because a modem has both a modulator and a demodulator built into it. What, you ask, are those? A good question. And why are they needed? Another good question.

"Yodeling" PCs

Most PCs sold today include a modem, either built-in or attached to it. When you use the modem to connect your PC over the phone line to a distant computer, you are likely to hear many strange sounds coming from the modem's speaker. You might have wondered what they are and why you need them.

Figure 24.1 shows an external modem and an internal modem. In this case, the external modem is a SupraFax LC144 14.4kbps data and fax modem. The internal modem is a U.S. Robotics Sportster 33.6kbps voice, data, and fax modem.

Figure 24.1.
These are typical external and internal modems for a PC.

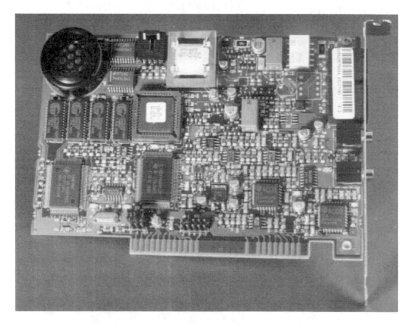

The sound you hear is essentially your modem "talking" to another modem at the other end of the phone line. The different strange tones normally go on for several seconds, and then the modem shuts up. Actually, the modems continue making their strange sounds. You just don't hear them because normally the software that operates the modem tells it to turn on its loudspeaker until the two modems have successfully "negotiated" a connection, and then to shut off its speaker for the duration of the call. This lets you hear that your modem is trying to connect—and if you understand what you are hearing you can tell how well they are doing, or if you hear a person talking at the other end you know to disconnect your PC because you haven't, in fact, reached a modem. After the connection is established properly, by shutting off its speaker, the modem saves you from having to listen to all that screeching the rest of the time your PC is connected.

Why Modems Are Needed

The standard telephone network was designed for one purpose—carrying human voices in conversation—and is now being used by many of us for a totally different purpose—carrying lots of digital data back and forth. The characteristics of the two types of signals are very different. The telephone network functions acceptably for human voices; it simply cannot carry digital data as such.

> **Note:** There are some exceptions to that last statement. I'll cover them in the "Keeping It Purely Digital" section later in this chapter. For now, let's focus on the normal kind of telephone line—called a "plain old telephone service" (POTS) line, for which this statement is true.

Why can't ordinary phone lines carry digital data directly? Human voices are sounds that cover a range of frequencies from roughly 30Hz up to about 10kHz. That is, we make vibrations in the air that fluctuate no more often than 10,000 times per second and no less than around 30 times per second. Any sounds outside that range are inaudible to most of us. We don't even need to hear all those frequencies in order to understand what someone else is saying.

Therefore, to save money and for other technical reasons, the phone companies have limited the bandwidth of their normal voice-grade lines to a maximum of about 3kHz and a minimum of around 100Hz. This lets enough of the sounds we make get through for most normal conversational purposes.

Digital data is sent over a phone line in a serial manner; that is, the data is sent one bit at a time. You can have either synchronous or asynchronous connections. A synchronous connection just pumps out the bits of each byte one after another, all in synchrony with some clock. An asynchronous connection sends out all the bits for one byte, plus some start and stop bits to tell the receiving computer where the data begins and ends (and perhaps a parity bit to verify its accuracy), and then waits a little while before sending out the next byte. There is no necessary connection between the clocks at the two ends of the link.

> **Technical Note:** Normally, in PC applications modems operate asynchronously. The main exception to that is if you are running an error-correcting protocol such as V.42, then the modems will switch to a synchronous data transfer mode. This change is invisible to the user, but it results in some improvement in data throughput (as well as a lot more assurance, thanks to the error-correcting aspects of the protocol, that your data got across the link okay). The use of error correction requires that the modems on both ends of a connection support the same protocol (V.42). This compatibility is becoming more common as computer users and connection services upgrade to newer modems.

The limit on the frequencies at the low end is no problem for people talking, but it is as much of a problem as the limit on the high end for the transmission of digital data. To see this, consider a digital message that consists of one million zero bits followed by a one bit, then another million zero bits, then a million one bits. If this message were converted into voltages in the synchronous serial manner, it would be a constant voltage almost all the time. This long time between voltage alternations constitutes a very low frequency signal and is equivalent to silence. Nothing would be happening on the link, and the receiving end wouldn't know if it were connected still or not.

One solution to this problem is simple enough: Use the data values to modulate a tone signal. The tone for a zero bit is different from the tone for a one bit, but at all times there is some tone being sounded. That way, the signal is always there for the receiver to hear.

This is how early modems worked. But this strategy doesn't allow pushing the maximum number of bits over the phone line in each second. Essentially, it uses only a few of the many frequencies the phone line is capable of carrying. By using more of those frequencies simultaneously, we can send many more bits each second—just as modern, high-speed modems do today.

In order to understand just how a modern modem does this trick, it's necessary to distinguish between two terms that are commonly confused: *bits-per-second* (bps) and *baud*.

What's a Baud?

In honor of Emile Baudot, a nineteenth-century French telegrapher who invented an early transmission code, we use the term *baud* as the unit of speed in data communications—or misuse it, as is more often the case in writings and conversation about PC communications.

Technically, one baud means one symbol per second. (Think of one change in the state of the transmission medium per second.) A symbol can represent any number of bits—the maximum number for a particular connection is set by the characteristics of the transmission medium and of the transmitting and receiving devices. At very low data rates, each symbol is normally used to represent a single bit.

In a slow modem (carrying data at 300bps or less), each bit is represented by two tones, one for a zero and the other for a one. At higher data rates, more tones are used. If you used 512 tones you could encode nine bits simultaneously. (In fact, instead of using 512 discrete frequencies, modern modems use a combination of fewer individual frequencies but delay some of those signals by a variable fraction of a cycle (phase modulates them) to convey more information. That's why your modem sounds so raspy at times during its handshaking process.)

If you are unclear on why 512 tones implies that you can carry nine bits by a single one of those tones, I invite you to go back to Chapter 3, "Understanding Bits, Nybbles, and Bytes." There you will find the relationship spelled out in great detail.

A 300-baud modem uses one symbol per bit, so the baud rate and the bits-per-second are both 300. At higher data rates, the common practice is to send signals that stand for one of a larger set of possibilities. This means that each symbol carries several bits of information. If there are 512 possible symbols (signal states), then each one carries nine bits of information. This is what is done in a V.34 (28.8kbps maximum data rate) modem when it is operating at its maximum data rate. In this case, the actual baud number is only one-ninth of the number of bits per second. Thus, a 28.8kbps (kilobits per second) modem is actually just a 3.2 kilobaud modem. But you'll never see that latter value in an advertisement for these products—it just doesn't sound impressive enough!

When Modems Talk to Each Other and to Their PCs at Different Rates

A PC that uses a modem will also be using a serial port. The serial port converts the data from parallel bytes into serial bit streams and adds the necessary start, stop, and parity bits. The modem converts these bits into tones (called "modulating the carrier with data") and sends them over the phone line. At the other end must be a similar modem that will convert the tones back into digital bit levels (called "demodulating the data"), and the serial port will convert those bit streams back into parallel bytes. (Refer to Chapter 15, "Understanding Standard PC Input and Output," for a detailed discussion of how serial ports work.)

Note: Internal modems are built on plug-in cards you put into a slot inside your PC's system unit. All the hardware for a serial port is included on the plug-in card. External modems attach to a serial port either on your PC's motherboard or on some other plug-in card. Internal modems draw their operating power from the PC's power supply. External modems use a separate power supply.

There are some important implications in these differences. If you put an internal modem into a PC, you must be sure that its serial port doesn't conflict with one that is already in the machine. Conversely, if you want to use an external modem, you must be sure your PC has a serial port available for it, and it must be one that will work fast enough to support

continues

the modem. A serial port that supports data rates of 57.6kbps or greater is preferred for 28.8kbps modems, and a minimum of 115kbps is required for 56kbps modems.

Finally, having a separate power supply means that you can turn off an external modem without turning off your PC. This is sometimes useful to reset a modem that gets "hung," and also it can be a security precaution, because if the modem is turned off there is no way anyone can "reach into your PC" via the phone line.

The data serializing and the bit-stream modulation (and the inverses of those actions) are two distinct processes. The first process (serializing the outbound data) occurs in the serial port, as does the de-serializing of the inbound data. The second process (modulating the outbound bit stream onto the carrier and demodulating the inbound tones into an inbound bit stream) occurs in the modem.

There are jargon names for each of these processes. If you read about the *DTE rate*, it is a reference to the rate at which the COM port is sending and receiving bits of data. If you read about the *DCE rate*, that is the speed at which bits of data are flowing over the telephone line. (These terms, DTE and DCE, were first used to stand for the devices. DTE is Data Terminal Equipment, and DCE is Data Communications Equipment. Now they also are used for the gender of the serial port on each, and as a reference to the processes on either side of the modem.)

These two processes might or might not run at the same rate. Often, we run the connection from our PCs to our modems (using the serial port) at one rate, and run the modems at a different rate. In order for this to work, the modem and the serial port must be able to buffer some of the information, and also to tell one another when they are ready to send or receive additional data. All modern modems and serial ports have those features.

Sometimes modems "compress" the data they send over the phone line; that is, they look at a stream of bits and figure out a way to encode that information more compactly (getting rid of redundancy) by using a standard method. The receiving modem uses the inverse of that method to reconstruct the original bit stream. This lets the modem send more data across the link (more bits per second) than the physical baud rate it is using would seem to allow. But it can do this only if the data it is receiving has redundancy in it. (I described this general concept in Chapter 3, "Understanding Bits, Nybbles, and Bytes." Please refer to that chapter if you are having trouble understanding this discussion.)

In order to keep a modem that is doing data compression busy—that is, to keep it sending "compressed" information across the link at the maximum speed of which it is capable—you must send the data to it from the PC somewhat faster than it will be going across the modem-to-modem link. And, you must take the received data away from the modem just as fast. This is why we commonly set our serial port data rate anywhere from two to four times faster than the nominal maximum bits-per-second data rate the modem can support over the telephone line.

The optimum rate multiplier to use depends on how much redundancy there is in the data you are transferring. Text typically compresses to half its original size. ZIP and GIF files don't compress at all. Some graphics, spreadsheet, and database files can compress to as little as a tenth of their original size.

Also, you should be aware that often when you see a message about how fast you are "connected," the speed refers to the number of bits per second (even if it called the "baud") at which data is flowing between your PC and your modem—it doesn't mean the speed at which the modem is sending and receiving bits on the phone line. Therefore, if the connect speed you see reported seems to be faster than you thought your modem could go, that's the reason. Nothing to worry about, but just be aware which speed you are discussing.

Standards—the More the Merrier!

In order for a modem link to work, the modems at both ends of the link must be compatible; that is, they must use the same methods for modulating and demodulating the carrier signal, compressing the data, and so on.

Over time, modems have changed a lot. Even simple, inexpensive modems today are vastly more capable than the best (and most expensive) ones were just a few years ago. This means that we have many standards for modems.

Initially in the United States, the Bell Telephone Laboratories defined all the standards used for modems. Now, however, the usual standards are set by an international standards organization. For many years, the relevant organization was the CCITT (International Telegraph and Telephone Consultative Committee). That role has now been taken over by the International Telecommunications Union (ITU), which is an organization that serves in an advisory capacity to the United Nations. Thus, the new designations for modem standards carry the prefix ITU-T (instead of CCITT).

The ITU-T standards didn't just spring up out of nothing. Usually, some company comes up with what it regards as a "breakthrough" that lets it make a modem that performs in some way very much better than any previous ones. That company will, of course, market the heck out of the idea and try to get everyone to buy its modems. But this nifty new feature will work only when one of these special modems is talking to another of the same kind of modem. Eventually, the manufacturer decides that it is in its interest to get a formal international standard to cover this new feature. Then (if it is really a nifty feature) every modem maker will put it into their products, and at that point all of those modems, no matter what brand, will be able to use that new feature when talking to any of the other modems that include support for it; that is, when an international standard develops.

Some of the commonly used data communication standards for modems include these: V.32 for 9600bps; V.32bis for 14.4kbps; V.34 for 28.8kbps; V.42 for error control; V.42bis for data compression; V.FC, a proprietary version of 28.8kbps (now superseded by V.34); MNP2-4 (various error control protocols developed by Microcom and given to the industry); MNP5 (data compression; less efficient than V.42bis); and MNP10 (data compression optimized for cellular telephony).

Modems can also be used to send and receive faxes. When they send and receive faxes, they conform to a different set of CCITT (now ITU) standards, bearing such monikers as V.17 for 14.4kbps faxing and T.30, the fax protocol itself.

A quality, modern modem will support all of the standards I have just listed (and probably several more). You can set your communications software to send a message to the modem when you begin a communications session configuring the modem. This tells it which of those standards it is to support during the present call.

Even if you ask it to work at its maximum possible speed, the modem might discover that the modem at the far end isn't capable of working that fast, or that the line in between them is too noisy or extends the signals too much. In that case, the two modems negotiate some slower speed at which they will carry on the conversation. They will, that is, unless you (or the person at the far end) have instructed your modem to accept no less than some high standard. In that case, the modems will just hang up the phone whenever they run into a problem.

Similar configuration issues apply to error correction and data compression protocols. You must tell the modem to use them, and the other modem must agree to do so.

Must you configure your modem? Probably not. Many people use communication software that is provided by their modem manufacturer, by an online service (such as America Online) or an Internet service provider, or that is built in to their PC's operating system. In any of these cases, that software is probably preconfigured to command your modem correctly for that use. Note however, that these preconfigured settings are more likely to be biased toward trouble-free modem installation rather than optimal performance.

The only time most users must ever worry about their modem configurations is if they are setting up communications programs that will use their modems for calls to local bulletin board systems or some other destinations for which no "standard" software is provided. In that case, you must look at the documentation that came with the modem, check with the manufacturer, or check with a Usenet newsgroup. Here are a couple of URLs where you can start:

```
http://users.aimnet.com/~jnavas/modem/faq.html
http://www.rosenet.net/~costmo/
```

Varieties of Fancy Modems

When you go shopping for a modem, you are likely to feel overwhelmed by all the different jargon terms and different features claimed for various models. Because this is such a rapidly changing field, it's impossible to tell you about every one of the terms you may encounter. But I can tell you about some of the more popular and important ones.

Data, Fax, or Voice?

First, you must realize that modems are frequently used for at least two and sometimes three different jobs in PCs. One is data communication. This is what you use when you surf the Internet. It also is what you need to send and receive e-mail or to transfer files. The second main use is for sending and receiving faxes. A third use is for handling voice phone calls (with the help of an additional telephone handset or other equivalent hardware). A voice-capable modem is commonly used to place inexpensive long distance calls via the Internet and can be used for simultaneous voice and data communications on a single phone line if your modem supports this mode of operation.

Knowing this, you must decide which of these tasks you want your modem to do. You don't have to buy a modem that does all three unless that is what you want. On the other hand, if all those capabilities come at an acceptable price, there's no drawback to your modem being able to do some thing you don't need or want it to do. And, someday you might change your mind.

Most modems advertise their maximum speed in big type when used for data communication. The present standards for fax transmission don't permit sending that sort of information quite as fast as the newest and fastest data modems, so the lower fax speed is not usually mentioned on the box. Be assured that if you buy a "data and fax" modem, it will support the relevant standards and will send and receive faxes at the proper speed.

One kind of data, fax, and voice modem just routes different calls to the appropriate software or hardware. That is, if this type of modem is in your PC, and if you are running the appropriate program to monitor the modem, then when a fax call comes in your fax software will be launched and the fax will be received. If a data call comes in, some data communications program will be launched. And for voice calls, a separate handset will ring.

Another, newer type of combination modem goes by either the acronym ASVD (Analog Simultaneous Voice and Data) or DSVD (Digital Simultaneous Voice and Data). These modems actually can carry data and voice information over the same line at the same time. Don't buy an ASVD modem unless it supports the new V.34Q ITU-T standard for this. These modems can transfer voice or even music at the same time a data file transfer is going on.

With suitable sound hardware (microphone, speakers, and sound card, or telephone handset or headset) attached to your PC, you'll be able to hold a conversation with a person at the other end of the link even as you are sending or receiving data. You'll very likely be able to hold "full duplex" conversations (with both people speaking at once), which is better than the usual speakerphone limitation of "half duplex" conversations (in which one person speaking cuts off the other one).

This technology can be used to collaborate between two workers who are sharing their thoughts as they work on a common document. Another use is in gaming when two players can "taunt" one another as they play. One projected use—and it might prove to be one of the most valuable—is for technical support. With this type of modem on your PC as well as on a technical support person's

PC, and if you are each running suitable remote control software, the technician might be able to ask you about your problems, then actually take control of your PC to fix them for you.

Digital Simultaneous Voice and Data (DSVD) modems conform to a different ITU-T standard (V.70). These modems digitize the voice signals and simply insert that digital data into packets that are sent along with the file transfer or other digital data being communicated across the link. These modems are a little more expensive, and they aren't up to handling music, but they may support a higher speed of overall data transfer.

As with all other modem technologies, both ASVD and DSVD require that both modems have the feature in order for it to be used.

Modem Speed

Analog modem speeds have pretty much peaked. The present standard best speed is either 33.6kbps or 56kbps. The 56kbps modems are not quite what you would expect from their name.

33.6kpbs models can transfer data simultaneously in both directions at up to 33.6kbps. This takes all the bandwidth that is commonly available on a standard (POTS) voice-grade telephone line. In fact, it requires a very good connection to get this full speed. Many times using these modems doesn't result in any faster file transfers than if you use a 28.8kbps modem, and possibly hardly any faster than a 14.4kbps mode. Still, you want a V.34-compliant modem because this standard is the most "intelligent" one. These modems are able to adapt better to changing line conditions than earlier protocols allowed. And, they can be upgraded in various ways more easily.

The so-called 56kbps modems are odd. They achieve their faster speed for downloading (data in-bound to your PC) by sending data in that direction faster than in the outbound direction. This uses more of the available voice line bandwidth for the high-speed direction, at some limitation to the speed in the reverse direction. Also, even at their very best, they cannot pump data across the line at an actual 56kbps. The telephone regulatory agencies won't allow that.

The most common application of this lopsided data rate arrangement is for connection to the Internet. In this instance, you will usually send short strings of commands and receive large image-laden re-sponses. Be aware that your Internet service provider (ISP) must dedicate specific phone lines for 56kbps service and make special arrangements with the telephone company to support them.

So, only if you are using these beasts with an optimum quality telephone line will you get anything more than 33.6kpbs throughput, and then only in one direction at a time. Furthermore, you must have a serial port that can accept the data at the appropriate rate. If data compression is being used, it's possible that the highest standard PC serial ports (running at 115kbps) will not suffice.

But worst of all, there are two competing (and *not* interoperable) standards for this speed—which in many ways means that there is no standard for it…yet. The ITU is hard at work trying to hammer out an industry standard, but it might not succeed any time soon. For now, you will be able to use the new features of this type of modem only if you are communicating with a compatible brand of modem at the other end.

U.S. Robotics (now a part of the 3Com Corporation) makes modems it calls X2 modems (because they promise twice the speed of an older-style V.34, 28.8kbps modem). Rockwell and its partners in this venture, Lucent Technologies and Motorola, calls its version K56Flex.

These two proponents have spent a lot of energy lining up support from other companies in the industry and lobbying the ITU for inclusion of their ideas into the final ITU-T standard for this speed of operation. If you buy one of these modems now, it will probably be upgradable to the ITU standard when that is settled upon. (Perhaps this will be possible at no cost to you, by using a down-loaded program to update a flash ROM in the modem).

Cable Modems and Satellite Modems

Many of the community access television (CATV) cable companies are now getting into the Internet service provider (ISP) business. They usually offer a small box that splits your TV cable in two. One branch goes to your normal television cable box for tuning channels and displaying them on your television set. The other cable goes to your PC's serial port.

These new boxes are called *cable modems*. (Some cable operators offer a combined box with both the cable modem function and the normal cable tuning function rolled into one unit.) These devices let you download information at a very high rate. They might let you upload information at a comparable rate.

The basic problem with cable modems is that the cable operator must redo all the amplifiers in the system to allow two-way communication, and then they also must do something to ensure that the bandwidth of their cable doesn't get overloaded. As long as only a few customers are using cable modems, they will very likely work. But if they are extremely fast (and they should be at least five to ten times faster than any analog modem) and also don't cost much, then lots of people will buy or lease them, and soon you might find that the cable is choked with data and the cable modem is no longer capable of running as fast as it is supposed to run. Only time will tell if this solution will be viable and in any way better than the phone-line connected options.

Another variation on this theme is coming from some of the providers of direct broadcast satellite television. These companies offer small dishes you can buy or lease that will let you receive hundreds of television channels. Some of them are now also offering the option of Internet access. (DirecPC is one trade name for this Internet access service from Hughes Network Systems, the same company that offers satellite TV service under the trade name DirecTV. It also offers a combination of the two called DirecDuo. This particular Internet access service offers up to 400kbps downloads, but all uploads are limited by your normal modem-to-ISP link.)

Mostly what this means is that some subset of the potential channels are being reserved for Internet downloads. Uploads will happen over your normal phone line. Your receiver will decode the channel it has been assigned and it will broadcast (just to you!) whatever Web page you have indicated you want by the information you uploaded over the phone line.

Again, this seems like an option that will be wonderful for the early adopters—until the word gets out and too many people want to use it. Then it might well fall flat on its face for a lack of sufficient channels to serve all the subscribers. Of course, if the provider can keep adding satellites and channels as fast as they add subscribers, then the scheme will work out just fine.

Much the same problem is faced by all Internet service providers, for they must add new dial-up lines and modems as they add subscribers in order not to give busy signals to too many callers, and also add more bandwidth on the other side to the Internet, in order not to bog down everyone. However, putting up another satellite to get more channels is a much more expensive proposition than buying a bunch of modems or even hooking up another T1 line.

Hughes Network Systems says that it has ample capacity for the near future on a dedicated satellite (its DirecTV service uses three other satellites), and that it has international agreements in place to let it place many more satellites in geosynchronous earth orbit, plus many more in low earth orbit when it needs additional capacity.

They also note in their user agreement that one is not guaranteed 400kbps download speeds. If they get too congested, they will simply throttle down all users in order to ensure fairness of access.

Is It Real, or Is It Simulated?

Most modems are complete products with all the necessary hardware in the box (or on the board). External modems are just like internal ones, except that they don't have the serial port hardware that an internal modem must have, and they do have a power supply that internal modems don't require. (External modems also offer some nifty lights. These aren't vital, however, and you can get a program to simulate them in a corner of your PC's display screen if you really want "lights" for your internal modem.)

But some modems are very different from all the rest. These special modems have hardware enough to do only a portion of the job of a modem. The rest of the job is done by your PC's CPU by running some special software. Other, nonstandard modems are different in yet another way. These "modems" are really general-purpose digital signal processors (DSPs) with a program running in them to simulate a modem. IBM's M-Wave modems are built this way.

The modems that use your PC's CPU obviously cost the manufacturers less to build, so they should cost you less money to buy. If your PC is relatively new and fast, the modem probably will work just fine. Also, upgrading them is particularly easy, because that most likely means just loading a new program onto your hard disk.

One subset of this genre to watch out for is the so-called "Windows Modem." These modems work only if you are running Windows. Of course, if that is all you run, then these can be a very economical way to go.

The idea behind the DSP-based modems (for example, IBM's M-Wave) is that the same hardware can also be programmed to do other things. Thus, one plug-in card could, in principle, serve as a modem, a sound card, a scanner interface, and more. In practice, these combinations have not proven very popular.

Do I Need a New Modem?

If all you have is an older modem, is buying a newer one necessarily a good idea? That depends on what you do with your PC and just how old your modem is. If you have a 14.4kbps modem, you will see about a tripling of speed by getting a new modem. That might be worth the cost to you if you do a lot of Web surfing on the Internet, or it might be worth very little if all you do is send or receive occasional e-mail.

If your present modem is a 28.8kbps modem, the first thing to do is check with the manufacturer. Many of them can be upgraded by "flashing" a new program into their on-board ROM. If this is possible, it certainly will be the way to go, even if there is a modest cost for the upgrade. If your modem needs a new "data pump" chip, sending it in for an upgrade still might be worthwhile.

Otherwise, this is a good time to buy a new modem. They now go about as fast as they are likely to go any time soon. There are only a couple of exceptions to this advice. If your cable TV provider is planning to introduce cable modems soon, and their prices look reasonable, you might want to wait for that. The second exception is if you think ISDN is for you. (You'll learn more about that in the "Integrated Services Digital Network (ISDN)" section, later in this chapter.)

Keeping It Purely Digital

The POTS telephone lines that you probably use in your home, and may be using in your office as well, are analog communication channels. A "wire pair"—two copper wires, separately insulated and normally twisted together in a loose helix—carries electrical signals that are an analog of the sound pressure that represents the speech signal being transmitted. When you use these lines for data transmission, you first must convert that digital data into the electrical versions of some special sounds; then, at the other end, convert them back again into digital form.

There are several ways to avoid that double conversion and get faster, more reliable data communication. But, they all cost more than a POTS line—in some cases, a lot more.

The phone companies are all converting their central offices and long-distance lines from analog to digital. When you use a POTS line for digital communication, the signals can get converted back and forth between analog and digital forms more than twice. This only strengthens the case for using a purely digital approach.

Integrated Services Digital Network (ISDN)

The simplest step up from analog to digital is to use an ISDN (Integrated Services Digital Network) line. There are several flavors of ISDN. First is the so-called Basic Rate Interface (BRI). This offers you two data channels (B-channels) and one control channel (D-channel). The combined data rate on all three channels is 128kbps. With this service you will usually get two phone numbers. You can receive a call on either number, and even do so on both at the same time. If you do this, each call will get one of the B-channels, and data can flow across this channel at 64kbps if the data channel is not in use, or at up to 56kbps if it is. If you place only one call from your computer, and if your computer software and ISDN "modem" support channel-bonding (and if the modem at the other end of the connection does also) you can get a single channel of 112kbps or 128kbps, depending on the state of the D-channel.

The interface box you must use to connect your PC to an ISDN line is called an ISDN modem. This is a bit of a misnomer because no modulation or demodulation of the digital data is involved. The only place a modem-like function happens in these boxes is when you use the extra POTS line jack they typically offer. Some offer one and some offer two POTS jacks. You can hook a normal analog phone or fax machine to such a jack and use it as if it were connected to a normal POTS line. You can even use this jack for one B-channel while using the other B-channel for a digital call placed by your PC.

A more expensive version of ISDN is the Primary Rate Interface (PRI). This offers 23 B-channels and a D-channel, with a total data transfer rate of about 1.5 million bits per second when all channels are used at once.

This sounds pretty good. And it can be, or not. There are some real advantages to an ISDN connection. First, the line is purely digital. That means it either doesn't work at all—which is relatively rare—or it works at its full speed. There are no issues of negotiation to determine an acceptable speed for the present line conditions. That means you can initiate an ISDN connection in a fraction of a second rather than in the up to 30 seconds it can take an analog modem pair to settle on how fast they are going to talk to one another.

If you can get channel-bonding to work, your data rates will be at least twice as great as the best analog modems can provide. And, ISDN lines can serve up caller-ID information even when the caller has "blocked" their end, because it uses a different technology for carrying that information.

But there are also some severe drawbacks to using ISDN. One is cost. In most places it costs anywhere from a little bit to a lot more than a POTS line to get an ISDN line. A normal analog telephone service line usually costs $20 to $30 per month. An ISDN line typically costs two to three times as much. The first-time setup charge for an ISDN line can run anywhere from free (if you get a special offer) to $500 for a remote location. Calls that are "free" local calls on your POTS line can be toll calls on an ISDN line. You can place calls over an ISDN line to any number, but if you are to realize the full digital benefits from the connection, the receiving end must also be using ISDN (or some other purely digital connection to the phone company).

Channel bonding doesn't always work. My ISP cannot guarantee that it will work for every call, though often it does. Many ISPs charge you double for calls when channel bonding happens, but only the normal rate if it fails. This variability means you can't count on getting the full 112kbps or 128kbps data rate just because you want it. Nor can you use only one B-channel for a data call without reconfiguring your modem to prevent channel bonding.

In some areas, BRI ISDN lines are available to home users for only a little more than a normal POTS line, but the only time local calls are free is during the nights and weekends. Businesses typically must pay for all ISDN calls, and their monthly fee is also larger. The PRI ISDN lines are, as you might expect, much more expensive. But, they do offer twelve times the overall bandwidth.

T1, Fractional T1, and Other Very High-Speed Connections

Before ISDN was available, the phone companies routinely leased special high-bandwidth lines to companies which needed that service. These lines, which are still available, come in several denominations. One of the most popular is called a T1 line. This line can handle 1.5 million bps, the same as a PRI ISDN line. Some companies have leased T1 lines from the phone company and then turned around and leased a fraction (some number of the 32 multiplexed "fractions" of the T1 line) of their bandwidth to other companies. That allowed companies with a smaller appetite for bandwidth to get it at a lower cost than a full T1 line.

The main difference between these options and ISDN is that whereas ISDN is a dial-up network connection (you place calls to wherever and whenever you want) a T1 or fractional T1 line is normally a leased line. You are always connected to the phone company (and always paying them for the service, whether you are using it or not). As a result, these connections cost a lot more than ISDN.

Before there was ISDN, telephone companies sought to solve this need in a different way. They offered a dial-up service called *Switched 56*. This is a dial-up connection to the Public Switched Telephone Network (PSTN) that can carry 56kbps of data.

And there are other phone company offerings such as Frame Relay and ATM (Asynchronous Transfer Mode). These are both full-time connections like T1 but, whereas T1 is a widely used means of carrying both data and voice communications, Frame Relay and ATM tend to be used exclusively for high-speed data and are much less common. Both Frame Relay and ATM are packet strategies for shipping large amouts of data quickly across a network that may be shared by many users.

Very large companies sometimes need even faster data rates. The phone companies offer something called T3 service (4.5Mbps capacity), and for the super-hungry, OC12 through OC48 (2.4gbs) services (an optical fiber channel link). If you really think you need one of these levels of data capacity, you need more information than I can put in this book. You must talk to the phone company, and you probably also want to hire a consultant to help you define your needs and the best solution to meet them.

Fibre Channel

Optical fibers can be used to carry digital data in the form of light pulses. These fibers can carry much higher data rates than any kind of metal wire. The telephone companies are now using this on their "backbone" connections. Many large companies also use optical fiber links for very high data rate communication within their facilities. Most electric power transmission companies string optical fiber cables alongside their metal power-carrying wires. (In this last case the reason is not so much the high data rate the optical cables support as it is the immunity to electrical noise signals enjoyed by any purely optical channel.)

The standard protocols for using optical cables are called FDDI (Fiber Distributed Data Interface) or Fibre Channel. The principal advantages of these LANs are high speed (starting at 100Mbps) and total immunity to electromagnetic interference. The principal disadvantage is the higher cost of hardware and the greater fragility of the connections. Because at this point most PC users aren't using fiber LANs, I won't go into any more of the details here.

Some cable TV operators are using fiber links from their "head end" equipment (where they receive the down-linked signals from the satellites and convert them into the various channels of TV signal you get on the cable to your home) to distribution points in each neighborhood. Eventually they may even put in optical fiber links to each individual home.

If your company (or home) has optical fiber cable coming to it, you can attach to that for the ultimate in high bandwidth communication; provided that someone on the other end is prepared to accept your flood of bits and send them to the right ultimate destinations, and to send back to you a similar flood of data bits from wherever you request. For now, though, this is not a commonly available option. Still, it is something to be watching for. When it comes, it will be more bandwidth than we know how to use (so far). Of course, by then, we probably will want even more!

xSDL

A new wave of technologies is coming from your local phone company. They carry names like ASDL, HSDL, and xSDL. These technologies use the traditional copper wire pair that makes up a POTS analog phone line to carry data at much higher rates. This is accomplished by changing the connection switch to a digital switch at the point where your copper wire lines reach the telephone company's central office. Some of the proposed switch types will support voice calls in a manner similar to ISDN. ASDL (Asymmetrical Subscriber Digital Link) uses the POTS line pair as a purely digital link, and it shoves much more data across the link in one direction than in the other. But, unlike the 56kbps modems, on an ASDL line the high-speed direction can be reversed whenever you want. (However, because some overhead is involved in the switch, you can't do it very often without cutting down on the overall data throughput.)

HSDL (High Speed Digital Link) is an improved version of ASDL. xSDL covers both of these and some more variations as well.

These are technologies in the laboratories and are being tested in the field in a few places. Unless you happen to live or work in one of those test areas, they are not yet options you can select. But they will be soon—or so the phone companies keep telling us.

Which Way Should You Go?

Analog or digital, which way should you go? Maybe you can have it both ways. Some Internet service providers offer both ISDN and analog modem dial-in ports. Typically, an analog dial-up account is less expensive than an ISDN dial-up account. But some will let you make ISDN calls from time to time and charge you extra only when you choose to do that. In order to take advantage of this option, you must have both an analog modem and an ISDN modem. If you only occasionally need really fast Internet access, but when you want it you really want it, this combination approach may make sense to you. Just check out what the minimum costs are and see if they are acceptable.

Summary

Connected PCs offer some capabilities that stand-alone PCs simply cannot match. In this chapter I have described the most common ways that PCs get connected to other computers through a modem link, and briefly described some of the things they can do when they are connected in that way.

In the next chapter I continue this discussion about connected PCs, but in this case discuss connections to or through a network using a network interface card (NIC).

25

The PC Reaches Out, Part Two: Through the NIC Node

Peter Norton®

In Chapter 24, "The PC Reaches Out, Part One: Modems and More," you learned about PCs that are connected to a single other PC by a direct wire (between their serial ports or between their parallel ports) or by an optical beam, and about various ways PCs can be connected to other computers using a modem of one kind or another.

I mentioned that the most common way PCs are interconnected in offices and some homes is by a local area network (LAN). This chapter focuses on LANs and the things to which they are connected, and on some of the software you need or might want to take advantage of your PC's connections to other computers.

The NIC Node

The Network Interface Card (NIC) is one of the most potent devices for expanding the capabilities of your computer. It joins your computer to a connected collection of others in such a way that all can share hard disk storage space, data files, peripherals (such as printers and modems) and messaging facilities.

A Number of Network Designs

The idea sounds simple enough. A local area network is a way to hook together many PCs so they can exchange information. But the actual practice can become pretty complicated. There are many ways to go about achieving this connectivity. Because the subject of networks is so large, I will focus on some of the enabling technologies, and those only in their more popular implementations.

This section first discusses the wiring schemes that are most commonly used. Then you learn about some popular ways to organize the exchange of information over those wires.

Many Topologies

Topology is the branch of mathematics that studies the ways things are connected to one another. It ignores the sizes and shapes of those things, and only looks at their connectivity. In reference to LANs, the term topology refers to how each PC is connected to all the others in a logical sense, without regard to the physical arrangement that accomplishes this connectivity.

Figure 25.1 shows several common LAN topologies. In each case, I have also indicated one or more of the common network cabling schemes that use that topology.

Figure 25.1.
Some common LAN topologies.

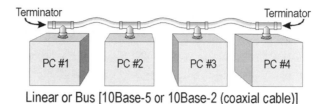

Linear or Bus [10Base-5 or 10Base-2 (coaxial cable)]

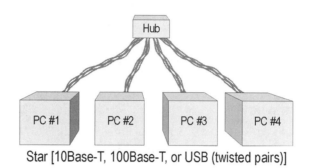

Star [10Base-T, 100Base-T, or USB (twisted pairs)]

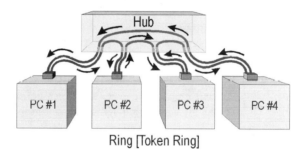

Ring [Token Ring]

Bus or Linear Networks

The top portion of Figure 25.1 shows what is sometimes referred to as a *bus topology*. The most common examples of this scheme are the 10Base-2 and 10Base-5 wiring schemes used in many Ethernet LAN installations. (Ethernet itself is a prescribed way of using the cable, as I will explain later, and doesn't require any particular form for that cable.) 10Base-2 uses a thin flexible coaxial cable. The nickname for this wiring scheme is "thinnet."

The 10Base-5 wiring scheme also uses coaxial cable, but it is a thicker, more rigid cable. This makes setting up such a network harder, but the larger cable can carry the network signals much farther than the thinnet cable without unacceptable attenuation. The 10Base part of the designation refers to the maximum data rate of the network (10Mbps). It also indicates that this rate includes transmission of the overhead information necessary to demarcate and address the data. The numbers 2 and 5 are numeric designations that identify the type of wire used for the connections.

The figure shows the taps for each PC as BNC T-connectors attached to the PCs (or actually to the network interface adapters installed in those PCs), with the cable made up of short pieces going from PC to PC. At each end of the bus, the open side of the T-connector is capped with a *terminator*. This is a device that connects an appropriate resistor between the center conductor and the shield of the coaxial cable. The result is that any electric signals arriving at the terminator are fully absorbed; none of those signals gets reflected back along the bus.

This is the common way to set up thinnet. In contrast, 10Base-5 commonly uses penetrating taps clamped onto a single, continuous backbone cable with terminators installed at the ends of the cable.

Star Networks

The middle portion of Figure 25.1 shows a star network. This is a very common way to connect multiple devices to a central one. Here you see a "hub" connected to each PC by a set of twisted-pair cables. These wires (essentially high-grade telephone lines) are inexpensive to manufacture and very easy to install, but they don't carry (or shield) the signals as well as coaxial cable.

It's important to realize that although the hub is shown as if it were at the center of the network, in a star wiring scheme all the signals that arrive at the hub on any cable are immediately sent back out on all the other cables. This means that the hub is a data interchange point. In effect, all the cables are simply wired in parallel, and thus any signal put onto one shows up on all. That makes this logically very much like the bus topology shown at the top of this figure. (This logical similarity is why this kind of wiring scheme can be used interchangeably with the bus topology for Ethernet LANs.)

Star topologies are used for many different kinds of networks (meaning different cable designs as well as different methods for using those cables). The most common use of star topologies for PC LANs is for Ethernet. This variety of Ethernet is usually called 10Base-T and each cable has four pairs of wires. Again the name, 10Base-T, implies a maximum Ethernet data rate of 10Mbps. The same wiring scheme, if it is of a high-enough quality (termed Category 5) can also be used to carry 100Mbps Ethernet-style signals. If the network is used in this way, it is called 100Base-T.

Modified Star Networks

Another star topology "network" is the Universal Serial Bus (USB). Each device that is connected to the hub can be a controlled device, another hub, or a combination of the two. The wiring in USB can be a multiple branched tree rather than a pure star network in which every device connects back to the "root" hub. USB also uses a different cable with one twisted pair of wires for data and another pair to carry power to the controlled devices. (You'll find more information on USB in Chapter 15, "Understanding Standard PC Input and Output.")

Ring Networks

The bottom portion of Figure 25.1 shows a ring network. The most common example of this is a Token Ring network. Here you see a hub (shown this time as a transparent box to make clear what is happening inside it) and a cable from it to each of the PCs with two paths for data to flow within each cable. (The arrows indicate the direction of data flow in each segment. Each data path, here shown simply as a line, is four wires twisted together in pairs and, optionally, shielded from outside signals.)

The pair of data paths shown as going from the hub to each PC is usually enclosed in a single jacket. That makes this type of network look a lot like a star, in terms of its physical cable layout. However, as I have indicated here, the separate cables from the hub to the PCs are not single data paths, and they aren't wired in parallel with the other cables. Instead, data must go into each PC and back out of it again, through the hub and on to the next PC, until the data has made a complete circuit around the ring.

The hub just connects the inbound data path from each PC to the outbound path to the next PC; it does nothing to the data as it goes by. In fact, you could build a ring network without a hub just by connecting each PC to both its neighbors. The only reason to use a hub (besides the fact that the Token Ring specification calls for one) is that it makes setting up the network easier. You have only a single cable (containing two data paths) to connect to each PC as it is added to the network.

The Token Ring specification (which is also frequently referred to by its standard organization's name, IEEE 802.5) specifies both the physical cables and connectors, and also the method in which they are used. I'll discuss the Token Ring method for handling data in the section "Token Ring," later in this chapter.

Compare this figure with Figure 16.3. Notice that the external SCSI bus shown in that figure has a "daisy chain" topology, which is very much the same as a (hub-less) ring with the return loop missing. The internal SCSI bus shown there is more like the top portion of the figure in which each device just taps the cable as it goes by.

Linking Two LANs Together

Often people want to link several LANs together to let any computer on any of the linked LANs exchange data with any other computer on those linked LANs. If you have two or more bus LANs you could simply hook them together end-to-end. (Remove the terminators from the ends you want to connect and substitute a cable from one to the other.) Then you'd have one larger bus LAN.

Similarly, if you have two or more star LANs, you can hook them together by linking their hubs. (Most star LAN hubs come with a special expansion port for just this purpose.) Two ring LANs could be combined into one larger ring. Just break each ring in one place and hook them together to form a single, larger ring.

All those ways of combining two smaller LANs into one larger LAN will work, but they usually are not a good idea. It's better to link the two LANs by an interLAN connection box (called a router or bridge) of some sort. This is particularly vital if you want to link a bus LAN to a ring or star LAN. Then you absolutely must have some type of router or bridge to pass signals from one LAN to the other.

A bridge or router is, in fact, a computer running a suitable program to examine each arriving data packet's "envelope" (the portion of the packet that specifies who sent it and where it is supposed to go), and then send it on its way to the correct attached LAN. If it just does a routing function, such a box is more commonly called a router. If it also translates the protocol (the method of handling data packets) it is a full-fledged bridge. Thus, a link between two bus topology Ethernets is called a router. But if it connects a Token Ring network and an Ethernet network, it must be a bridge.

One reason for using a bridge (or router) between two LANs rather than directly connecting them is that the bridge can isolate data traffic on one LAN from that on the other. That is, any data packets that originate on one LAN and are addressed to another computer on the same LAN have no reason to leave that LAN.

If you can keep all the "local" packets within each LAN and only exchange the "long-distance" packets, then you will keep the data traffic congestion on each LAN to the minimum possible value. For this reason, one of the most common prescriptions for speeding up a sluggish LAN is to break it up into segments and connect them to one another with routers.

Many Hardware Protocols

The wiring plan alone doesn't fully define a network. The next level of definition specifies how those wires will be used. In particular, it specifies the signals the wires will carry and how they are to be interpreted.

All networks organize data into packets. The purpose of this packaging is to enclose each message in an envelope that describes (at a minimum) who is sending it and who is supposed to be receiving it.

Ethernet

Ethernet is a strategy for exchanging data between linked computers. Every computer has an address. In some networks each computer is assigned an address by some central arbiter, or based on which segment of the network it is hooked to. Ethernet is different in this regard. Every Ethernet NIC (network interface card) ever made has its own, unique serial number. That is the address that Ethernet uses to route each packet of information that is sent to that device.

The most clever concept in the Ethernet protocol is its means of resolving an inevitable conflict that will arise whenever you have multiple "speakers" that can each start speaking at any time. On a network, this means that their signals will be mixed together and the result is a muddled mess that none of the "listeners" can understand.

Carrier Sense, Multiple Access with Collision Detection CSMA/CD takes care of this problem. First, any Ethernet device will listen to the signals on the bus to be sure no one else is talking. Then, if it wants to speak, the device will start doing so. But first each device waits for some random amount of time (all the while listening to see if any other device starts speaking in the meantime). If some other device starts speaking while the first device is waiting, then the first device won't begin speaking until the bus is quiet once more. And if, by chance, two devices do start at virtually the same instant, both will soon realize it, and they'll each stop and wait a random (and therefore probably different) amount of time before they attempt to speak once more.

Many people say that anything using this strategy is some form of Ethernet, but the inventor of the whole scheme says only the original 10Mbps design is true Ethernet. The IEEE (Institute of Electrical and Electronic Engineers) has published a standard it calls IEEE 802.3 to fully define this particular 10Mbps networking standard.

Any alternative scheme that uses CSMA/CD is perhaps best referred to as a networking scheme that uses an Ethernet-like protocol. (A version called Fast Ethernet transfers data at 100Mbps, exactly 10 times as fast as the original Ethernet. Soon we will have a 1000Mbps version referred to as Gigabit Ethernet.)

The CSMA/CD strategy works a lot like the way people talk in a polite conversation. And it works just fine—as long as there aren't too many folks trying to express themselves.

Similarly, on an Ethernet, if there isn't too much data "traffic" it all works splendidly. But if the bus is almost always busy, some devices may find it hard to "get a word in edgewise." Because the Ethernet NIC (network interface adapter) sends out data only when it has some message to convey, the size limit for an Ethernet network is set by how much total conversational content the entire collection of connected computers wants to exchange, rather than the number of connected PCs.

Ethernet has become very popular. In part this is because it can use almost any wiring scheme that can support an adequately high rate of serial bit transmission. Also, in its 10Base-T (or 100Base-T) star configurations, the fact that the failure of any one of the connected computers or of any one segment of cable will not cause the network as a whole to fail is a great advantage. Only the one computer that failed (or whose cable to the hub failed) will drop off the network. Of course, a hub failure would bring down the entire network, but because the hub is so simple, that is a much less likely event.

The main drawback to Ethernet is that there is no guarantee that every PC will "get its turn to talk." Thus, a super-congested Ethernet can simply fail to convey some of the messages it is supposed to convey, and no one will know for sure which messages will not be carried. This makes it essential that the next higher level of organization of the communication over the network use some form of error detection and correction. (That job is done by any modern network operating system that supports Ethernet.)

Token Ring

Token Ring is a very different way to handle the same problems. IBM devised Token Ring to require a ring topology network. Each device sends messages out by one port and receives messages on a different port. All the devices are hooked together by a link to a neighbor on each side, with the ends being looped back (see the bottom portion of Figure 25.1).

Only one block of information is circulating on the ring at all times. Sometimes that block is a minimal packet called the "token." At other times one or more messages is attached to it. Each device on the ring has an address. Every message starts with a header saying who is sending it and to whom it is addressed.

Whenever a PC receives a block of information, it scans the block looking for messages addressed to it. If there are any, it will remove their content but leave their headers (addressing information). These headers are now marked to say that the messages for which they were the "envelopes" have been received. If this PC has any messages to send, it will append them to the end of the information block as it sends the whole thing on to the next PC in the ring. Finally, if there are any headers in the block that were put there by this PC and marked that their data was properly received, then it removes them.

This strategy is in some ways more complex than CDMA/CS, but in other ways it is simpler. Most important, it certainly guarantees that each and every message is received by its intended recipient, and that every PC gets a chance to send a message every time the token passes by it.

However, this approach requires that every PC on the ring see and handle every message that is going to any PC on that ring. It also absolutely requires a ring topology. Any break in the ring, or the failure of any one of the connected computers, will cause total network failure.

Other Layers in the Network Strategy

The overall strategy for a network must include more than simply specifying the wiring scheme and data packet handling protocol. It also must tell about how programs within each connected computer are to communicate over that network. The OSI model is a well-defined, seven-layer model for networking.

What I've explained so far are the two lowest-level layers in the OSI model. The other layers are all components of the network operating system (NOS) software that runs on top of this enabling hardware connection. I'll tell you a little bit about them in the "Some Common NOSes" section later in this chapter.

LANs, WANs, and Virtual Private Networks

LANs can be connected to one another by the use of a router or a bridge. If the connected LANs are local to each other, the result is simply a larger LAN (but one that will operate more efficiently than if the segments were connected directly, without use of routers or bridges). If you connect several LANs that are physically spread out over a wide area, the result is called a Wide Area Network, or WAN.

Many large companies have leased high-speed phone lines to connect the LANs in each of their offices in different cities around the world into one large WAN. The benefits of doing this are very similar to those you find in linking multiple LAN segments with routers or bridges. You can get from any computer in the entire system to any other, and yet purely local data traffic is kept from clogging up the larger-scale connections.

Of course, leasing these permanent, high-speed telephone links that might span continents and even oceans can be expensive. There is now an alternative called a *virtual private network* (VPN).

The idea behind a VPN is simply this: If you can protect your data packets from snooping eyes well enough (with encryption, for example), you can ship them back and forth over the public Internet without fear. Essentially, a VPN is simply a set of software pieces that you can use at each LAN location to send and receive these encrypted data packets over the Internet. Connecting two sites in this fashion is termed *tunneling* via the Internet.

Because local Internet connections are quite inexpensive (compared to dedicated transcontinental telephone lines), this will allow you to have the effect of a WAN without its usual cost. Of course, you must make some compromises. Perhaps the most important one is that you will have to put up with the fact that Internet connections do not, so far, have a guaranteed latency or throughput capacity. That is, you never know just how long it will take to get some data from one site to another.

Some Internet service providers (ISPs) are working together to devise a higher class of service they can offer their customers in which one can be assured of a fixed, low latency (time to get the first byte of a message to its destination) and minimum throughput (guaranteed amount of data you can send per second). If these plans work out, then you will at least be able to balance the cost savings of giving up a dedicated WAN link against the speed loss you will experience by using Internet tunneling. Until that time, however, VPNs are a chancy proposition. They are okay for some purposes, and totally unacceptable for other, more critical ones.

Host Connectivity

You might get the idea from what I've said about networks to this point that they are just a means for connecting PCs. Of course, that isn't true. Networks are used to connect all kinds and sizes of computers to one another.

One use for networks is to replace the direct wiring of terminals to mainframe computers. I mentioned near the beginning of Chapter 22 that often today companies are replacing their old, "dumb" mainframe (or minicomputer) terminals with PCs. They can still use a serial cable to connect these PCs to the central host computer. Then, running host connectivity software on the PC will make it act as if it were a dumb terminal.

Replacing an inexpensive dumb terminal with a more costly PC makes sense because the PC can do so much more. Not only can you use the PC to send keystrokes to a host computer and receive screens of information back, you also can save that information to the local hard disk, and when you exit from the host session, you can use the PC to do other tasks (including, local processing of the information you just retrieved from the central computer).

If you use a LAN as the link from a PC to a host computer even more possibilities are available to you. Now, in addition to starting a host session, you can communicate from your PC to any other computer on the LAN, and you can do local processing, too. Connecting PCs in this way provides the ultimate in flexibility.

The NIC Node Needs a NOS

Whenever you add new hardware to a PC, you must also add some software to enable the PC to use that hardware. Network software is no exception. Having a BIOS ROM on a network interface card is common. That ROM contains some basic device driver programs to activate the hardware on the card. However, the job that a network does is so much larger, and so much farther abstracted from the role of mere hardware, that a simple device driver is not enough.

What Is a NOS And Why Do I Need One?

A network brings into a PC a whole new realm of resources and possibilities. To manage this new realm one needs a new operating system called a *network operating system* (NOS).

Please don't be confused by this. The NOS doesn't in any sense replace the PC's main operating system. Instead, it augments that OS, adding new capabilities to manage the new possibilities inherent in the network setup. What might confuse you about this is that some modern PC operating systems, such as Windows 95 and NT, bundle a NOS in with the main OS. UNIX is an older operating system, originally developed for mainframe computers, that also does this. In contrast, Novell NetWare adds driver software to the PC's existing operating system to facilitate network operations.

The main purpose of a network operating system is to allow the user of one computer to see some of the resources on some distant computers as if they were resources on the local computer. Think of your computer as the "local" machine and all the other computers as the remote, or foreign ones.

Using a suitable NOS and network connection you might be able to "remap" some subdirectory of a remote computer as if it were the root directory of a local drive (this will give it a local drive letter), or you might simply be able to browse that remote drive using the Windows 95 Explorer program. Either way, you can load programs from that drive or, if you have permission to do this, save files there. Some other kinds of resource that can be shared across a network include printers and modems.

Some big problems face the designers of network operating systems. First, they must be able to keep track of all the connected resources. Second, they must be able to deal with many different kinds of connected computers, and to make sense of the file systems on each one, translating filenames and path locations as necessary to make the distant computer's files look as if they are just like the local ones. Then, when a file is transferred, there might be an additional translation task to make the foreign file show up in the format expected for that type of file on the local machine.

The first of these is the directory and name problem. For small LANs it isn't too bad, but for a very large WAN it can be tough. The Internet is so large and so dynamic (and without any central control) that the directory job has in some ways proven to be beyond our present ability to solve it fully.

Technical Note: The step of translating file formats isn't always done. However, it is important if you want to give the local computer user the illusion that those foreign files are just like the ones stored on the local machine. One example is that on a UNIX computer, text files normally have only a line-feed character at the end of each line, whereas on a DOS or Windows machine text files always end each line with a two-character combination (carriage-return plus line-feed). This seemingly trivial difference has a big impact on the way the data in the file is displayed.

Some Common NOSes

Many different network operating systems are in use today, but only a few of them have a significant market share. The first to be developed for DOS-based PCs were add-ons to the PC's operating system, whether that was DOS or DOS plus Windows. Later generations of PC operating systems have included some or all of the functionality of a NOS within the basic PC OS.

Most networks can be classified into one of two categories. The first are those that use a "File Server and Workstation" model (also called "Client/Server," but a more correct use of this term is discussed in the section "Client/Server Computing," later in this chapter). The second are "Peer-to-Peer" networks. Some NOSes support just the first of these models. Some support only the other model. Some of the more recent ones support both.

File Server and Workstation Networks

The notion of a File Server and Workstation model of networking is this: All the important files reside on one or more central computers (called file servers). Each person uses a workstation, which is a computer connected to the file server(s) by the network.

Whenever you do some work on your workstation, you will get the needed data files, and perhaps some of the applications as well, from the file server. You load them into your PC and do your work with them by running application programs in your machine. When you finish, you save your data files back onto the file server.

Novell's Netware is the most popular network software used in the PC world. UNIX, with its decades-long history of supporting many different kinds of computers and its robust built-in support for networking, is the most popular network operating system for networked computers other than PCs. Both of these NOSes are primarily intended for use on a File Server and Workstation model of network.

Historical Aside: Many "flavors" of UNIX exist. Originally developed at AT&T's Bell Laboratories, UNIX was initially given away to universities. AT&T did not offer support; it just gave them the program source code. So the universities had to provide their own support. In the process, they often modified UNIX to meet their own special needs. In particular, the University of California in Berkeley, California created a flavor now known as BSD UNIX. A commercial company, SCO, markets another very popular variation. And fast becoming the favorite for UNIX users in the PC world is Linux. Linux is particularly enticing because it is available free, complete with source code. You can buy a copy (and get some technical support from your vendor), or you can download a copy or get one from a friend freely and then have at it, making any changes you want, all without any copyright violation.

There are several advantages to file server-based networking. One is that all the critical files live on just a few, central machines. Professionals can oversee these machines, keeping them running smoothly, and those professionals can be counted on to do all the prudent file management tasks, including backups. The users of the workstations needn't concern themselves with those pesky details that can be so crucial—and whose omission can be so tragic when a PC's hard disk crashes.

This arrangement also neatly separates the work of serving as librarian to many (the job of the file server) from that of working with the individual files' contents (the job of each workstation). This helps balance the workloads of the different computers in the network. The file server might have very little work to do for any one user—just retrieving a few files—but it must do that same job for many, many other users at the same time.

Another advantage is that a user can "log in" to the network from any workstation and do the same things pretty much anywhere. Because the files all live in the central repository, they can be accessed from any connected workstation just as well as another.

Of course, this is not a perfectly true statement. Some workstations might have more RAM than others. That can matter if the task you want to do requires a huge amount for manipulating large graphic files, for example. Also, to save time and network traffic, the network administrator might have installed many of the more popular applications on local hard disks in the workstations. But if the one you need hasn't been installed on all the workstations, that can limit your freedom to log in from anywhere and still do the same kinds of work. One solution to that is to have a central copy of every application that can be used if there doesn't happen to be a local copy on a particular workstation.

Peer-to-Peer Networks

The other general kind of network uses a peer-to-peer model. This means that, in principle, all the computers that are hooked together are equal. In particular, any computer on the network can be configured to share some or all of its local resources with the users of the other computers on the network. That means each computer can become a file server (or a printer or modem server). But at the same time, those computers are also workstations.

You don't have to share any resources you don't want to share in this type of network. That is, each workstation can be configured to have none, some, or all of its resources shareable. When you do share a resource, you can attach a password to it, and only those other users who know the password for that particular resource will be able to access it. Windows 95 adds a further refinement of having two kinds of access control: user-level, in which passwords are specified for specific users and groups, and share-level, in which a password is assigned to each resource. Peer networking support for PCs is now included, at no additional cost, in Windows for Workgroups, Windows 95, Windows NT, and OS/2 Warp.

One advantage to peer-to-peer networking is that users can exchange files among themselves directly. With the file server model, file sharing between workstations can happen only in a two-step fashion: First, one user uploads the file to the server. Then the second user downloads it from the server. By using passwords that are shared selectively, one can share files with only some of the other workstations. (This can also be accomplished on a file server, but it requires that the administrator of the file server set up differing access rights for different directories, and that the users be grouped according to which access rights they are to be given. This discourages an *ad hoc* decision by one user to share files with another user, yet keep them private from all the rest.)

Another important advantage to peer networking, from the user's standpoint, is that it is closer to what the PC revolution has been all about: Getting away from central control of the computing resource. There is another side to this, of course. The people in a company who are responsible for all the computing hardware and services have a much harder time keeping track of who is doing what on a peer network. And, file backups become much more the responsibility of the individual users in that scenario.

Some Networks Blur This Boundary

Windows NT and OS/2 both are marketed in two versions: One intended for file servers and one for workstations. The intention is to support the file server plus workstation type of networking and also enable you to set up peer networking if you want.

Windows NT Server not only supports workstations running Windows NT Workstation, but also workstations that are running Windows 95 or DOS plus Windows for Workgroups, version 3.x. OS/2 Warp supports all those types of workstations plus workstations that are running OS/2 Warp.

In a mixed network, some machines might be designated as file servers. They can be repositories for most of the shared files, and perhaps also for many shared applications. But the individual workstations can also be configured to share some of the files, printers, and modems that they have locally with any other workstation user. So, with the built-in NOS functionality of these operating systems, you can have the best of both worlds. (Or, from the point of view of a curmudgeonly computing services manager, the worst of both worlds!)

Protocol Differences Between Networks

Networks exchange packets of information, but they don't all format those packets in the same ways. I mentioned previously that there is a formal, seven-layer OSI model for networks. The details I told you previously dealt only with the bottom two layers. The NOS products I have mentioned all do the work of the other five layers, but in sometimes different ways.

Popular Packet Protocols

Novell Netware uses a packet protocol named IPX, UNIX uses TCP/IP, and Windows for Workgroups and Windows 95 use NetBEUI. You can have packets of more than one kind circulating on a network, but the only computers that will see each kind of packet are those that are running a NOS that understands that format of packet.

It's also possible to add support to a NOS for packets of one or more styles other than their native kind. Thus, you can add a TCP/IP protocol stack to Netware or Windows for Workgroups. Windows 95 and OS/2 include optional components to do this job.

Note: If you intend to access the Internet, you must have a TCP/IP protocol stack on your PC. Or, you must access the Internet via some "firewall" computer that will translate all the packets you send or receive across the Internet from IPX (if you are on a Netware network) to TCP/IP as they leave, and back again for the packets that come in.

An advantage to using a firewall computer with this type of translation is that outside computers on the Internet cannot see or access computers inside the firewall. That is, in fact, the main purpose of a firewall computer. The packet protocol translation is just a task it must perform in addition to its main job of blocking outsiders while letting insiders get Internet access.

There is, in principle, no problem with having any number of protocol stacks on your PC. The practical situation is often different from the ideal, however.

If you are running real-mode network drivers, they will take up some significant portion (several hundred kilobytes, typically) of your PC's precious first megabyte of main memory. If you run too many of them, they will use up too much of that space. Your PC will be connected to all manner of different network clients, but it won't be capable of doing anything useful after it connects to them.

Protected-mode operating systems, like Windows NT, OS/2, UNIX, and to an extent, Windows 95 can put their network support modules into extended memory. That helps a lot. But you still are using up memory for this purpose, so you must be sure not to scrimp on memory in your PC if you are planning to load multiple protocol networking support.

How Do You Choose Your NOS?

If you are using a PC that is running DOS plus Windows for Workgroups, Windows 95, Windows NT, or OS/2 Warp then you already have a NOS built into your PC's OS. However, that doesn't mean you must use that NOS. You may decide to add support for another NOS (most commonly for Netware). Mainly you will do this if you are going to connect your PC to an already existing Netware network. Some of these OSes have Netware client support built in; others require the addition of a device driver for that purpose.

Normally, you choose your NOS based on what you want to do with it. Or, you make your choice based on what NOS is already in use by the computers to which you want to connect.

Most file server and workstation computer networks are set up by a company's central Information Technology department. They will choose the NOS and you must simply go along. (On the other hand, they'll do most or all of the hard work of getting your workstation up and running. You only have to learn how to use it.)

If you are setting up a small network you probably will choose one of the peer networks. Setting them up is much easier than setting up UNIX, Netware, or a Windows NT Server.

Other Software for the Connected PC

In this chapter and the previous one, I've told you about network software and about communications software for accessing other computers via a modem or other, similar link. What about other software that is only useful for connected PCs?

I'll just describe briefly some broad categories of this type of software, so you will be aware of their existence. If you must get one of these programs, you'll have to assess your needs carefully and then compare the various options you have to see which one will best meet your needs.

Client/Server Computing

File server and workstation networking is often confused with another term: client/server computing. But, in fact, they are quite different concepts.

Simple file server and workstation computing usually has all the applications running on the workstations. The file server just "serves up" the files on request. Real client/server computing splits the computing work between the workstation (client machine) and the central server. A prototypical example might be a transaction processing application for, say, airline ticket reservations. The central computer maintains a database (for example, of airline seats that are available on all the flights of a particular airlines).

The workstation accesses this database by sending queries and commands to the central computer. The actual accesses to the database, either for reading a record or for updating it, are done by the server. But the client computer can also do some significant computing work. In particular, it will be responsible for drawing all the (perhaps graphically complex) screens that present the database information to the user in a pleasant manner. The client workstation might also do some cost comparisons and route optimization calculations locally. Finally, it might be accessing more than one central computer if the travel arrangements involve comparing the available seats on many different airlines.

Another example is found in the X-Windows protocol. Originally developed for UNIX machines, there are now some X-Windows applications for PCs as well. In this case, the jargon gets turned around somewhat.

An X-Windows server is a program that runs on a workstation. It receives commands from a program running on a distant machine, and in response it "serves up" some images on the workstation screen. The program running on the central machine is called the X-Windows client program. One

X-Windows server can serve many X-Windows clients, showing the images commanded by each one in a separate window on the workstation's display screen.

Finally, an Internet browser such as Internet Explorer or Netscape Navigator uses a type of client/server operation. The browser is a program that runs in your PC and its main job is to present the data it receives from the distant computer(s). Using that browser, you can run programs in those distant computers, or you can download programs from them that then run in your computer as temporary or permanent additions to your browser.

What's Middleware?

A modern innovation in client-server computing is to break up this type of work into three layers. The *front end* is the program that runs in the workstation. The *back end* program is, for example, a big mainframe database application that keeps track of lots of transactions. In between these two is a layer of *middleware* that coordinates the requests for access to perhaps several different databases (each on its own back-end computer) from the many different workstation client front-end computers.

Fat Versus Thin Client Computers

You might also have heard about *fat clients* and *thin clients*. Essentially, this distinction refers to what capabilities the workstation hardware has. If it has its own hard disk, stores most applications locally, and just requests data files from the server (and returns them when it is finished updating them), then it is a fat client workstation. (Another name for this kind of beast is simply a PC.)

If, on the other hand, it has more nearly the hardware limitations typical of an older, dumb terminal (just a screen, keyboard, and perhaps a mouse or other pointing device), then it is a very thin client. All it can do is ship commands off to the central computer to be applied there by an application running on that central computer, and then display whatever that central computer sends back.

An almost-as-thin client might have a substantial amount of computing power, and maybe a lot of RAM, but no hard disk. It must load every program, as well as all its data files, from the central computer. But it still can do the computing work with those files locally. (Any temporary files it creates will have to be created on the central machine, of course.)

What are the advantages of fat versus thin clients? Well, pretty clearly, the fat client minimizes network traffic. Only data files travel there, and those only after they have been fully massaged at the workstations. But, it is then possible for the user to save data on the local hard disk, and for any data so saved not to be backed up with the central machine backups. If that is done, and if the local PC hard disk dies, that data is lost.

Also, if an upgrade to an application is installed on the central machine, any thin clients get the benefit right away. Fat clients must be individually upgraded before they are able to receive those benefits. (Of course, it might be possible to do those upgrades more-or-less automatically, in which case this advantage becomes minimal.)

If the network fails, a thin client is useless. A fat client is a full PC, and can do anything a not-connected PC can do whenever the network is down. Although networks are fairly stable, they do crash from time to time, and this can be a significant advantage for the fat clients.

Finally, fat clients put more control and power in the hands of the individual user. This, politically, is the right thing to do—at least for well-trained users it is.

Thin clients are fine for a temporary employee or one who is relatively unskilled at using a PC. Fat clients are much preferable for most "power users."

Remote Control of a PC

Remote control programs are another category of software that has been especially designed for use on connected PCs. These programs let one person, sitting at a PC, see the screen output from, and supply keystrokes to, a program that is running on a distant PC. Usually the program on the distant PC also puts its output on that PC's screen, and it also listens to that PC's local keyboard. The remote "controller" is simply able to see and activate that program remotely at the same time the local user is doing so.

From the very beginning, DOS has provided something like this in its CTTY command. That redirects the *console* (by which DOS means the keyboard and screen) from the physical keyboard and screen to a serial port. Then, if you have a dumb terminal attached to that port, you can use the computing power of the PC on the remote screen and keyboard of the terminal.

But when you do this, you cannot also see the screen displays on the PC's own screen, nor will any keystrokes you enter on the PC's keyboard reach the running program. True remote control programs go well beyond what the CTTY command offers.

Why would you want such a program? One good reason is for training. Others are for software maintenance and telecommuting (working on the office workstation/LAN from home via dial-up access).

If you are responsible for supporting several PC users, and if you cannot easily go to the desk of each one whenever a problem arises, being able to see the screen displays and actually type commands into that PC from a remote location can be very helpful. The alternative is to ask the user at the PC to read to you what the screen display says, and then try to talk the user through the correct keystroke sequences to do whatever tests you may decide to try. Anyone who has had to do this knows that this process is at best arduous, and at worst disastrous. Many times the PC's user doesn't understand enough to know what to notice on the screen, or cannot seem to understand well enough just what to type (or not to type) in response to verbal requests over a phone line.

One potentially serious limitation to remote control software is that of the screen resolution it supports. If the local and remote PCs have screens with very different resolutions, it often is necessary to compromise on some resolution both PCs can support before the remote control software will work. Recent versions of these products (such as Norton's pcANYWHERE) are capable of adjusting to discrepancies in resolution and other screen properties relatively gracefully.

What can be worse is that these programs tend to be quite slow. If you are linking to the remote PC over a phone line, you will find that this type of link simply is not fast enough to support the full speed with which a modern PC can redraw the screen. One way some of them try to compensate is to use data compression. Another way is to send only the high-level Windows API calls instead of the actual screen information. Both help, but neither approach solves all the problems.

However, most remote control programs now come in network versions, and many networks are fast enough to draw the screen images at least reasonably fast. Therefore, I recommend that if you have a choice, you connect remote control programs to the target PCs by a network connection whenever possible.

Workgroup Computing

Finally, I must at least mention one of the hot jargon terms of the day: Workgroup Computing. This is supposed to mean some type of program or programs, commonly called GroupWare, that enables people in different locations, each equipped with a PC, to work together in some meaningful way. Lotus Notes, the most popular GroupWare, enables a group of users to set up chat databases to discuss or share work files. Notes works well equally well when executing on a local LAN, a group of LANs, or on a Wide Area Network.

Video Conferencing

One application that has been much touted is video conferencing, in which a video camera and microphone are in place at each location. Each person sees on his PC's screen images of several or all of the other participants, and hears all of them. The notion is that this will replace travel in some situations where workers must have a meeting but aren't already in the same general locale.

Shared Whiteboards

You can add to this a shared whiteboard in either a couple of ways. One is to have a portion of each PC screen set aside for a scratchpad, and then enable anyone at any of the connected PCs to write on this scratchpad with their pointing device. (You can distinguish the marks made by different users by using a different color for each user, or you could use color for another meaning—the choice is up to the group.)

Alternatively, you might get one of the recently developed commercial whiteboards with remote readout. These are devices that look rather like free-standing blackboards (except, of course, they are white). They come with special markers and when you mark on the board with one of them, your strokes are copied simultaneously to an image of the whiteboard on a nearby PC (and that image can be replicated on many PCs over a network).

Group Calendaring and Scheduling

Another groupware application is shared calendaring. This means having a calendar program for each person on which he or she can note appointment and meeting schedules. But then it is also possible, if these PCs are connected, for an authorized person at any one of them to search all (or a selected subset) of the calendars for a suitable time to hold a meeting, and then to enter that meeting on all those (selected) calendars remotely. This can shortcut a lot of "telephone tag" and greatly facilitate getting together groups of very busy people.

Shared Word Processing

Some word processors are also are group-enabled. The idea here is to let a dispersed group of people work on a document together. Everyone sees the current document on their screens. And, if they are enabled to make changes, any of them can move the cursor, type characters, cut and paste, or otherwise edit the document. This can be combined with an oral conversation if the PC-to-PC links include a voice capability (as would be the case if, for example, they were linked with Simultaneous Voice and Data modems, or if they are networked together and a suitable networked-telephone program is available to all the users).

Summary

Connected PCs offer some capabilities that stand-alone PCs simply cannot match. In this chapter I have described the most common ways that PCs are connected to other computers and briefly described some of the things they can do when they are so connected.

In the next chapter I will tell you how PCs also are moving into the realm formerly occupied only by mainframe or minicomputers. Most of these PCs are used as file servers, and thus are connected to many other PCs. But in some cases, the specialness of the PCs I will be describing comes from having more than one CPU inside their case rather than from the linking of it to other PCs, each with its own CPU.

26

PCs That Think They're Mainframes: Multiprocessor PCs and Other Servers

Peter Norton®

Interactive computing began with massive mainframe computers connected to huge numbers of terminals. The terminals were simply keyboards and screens, with no local computing power. This development began about 40 years ago.

The next stage of interactive computing saw the emergence of stand-alone PCs (less than 20 years ago). Then, those PCs became networked (mostly in the past decade). This introduced two new variations on the original mainframe-plus-terminals model: the file-server-plus-workstation networking model and the client-server model of distributed computing.

After this, elementary PCs became attached to mainframes in lieu of dumb terminals. Finally, today, we are seeing many of the central computers in those distributed computing environments being replaced by "super PCs." In this chapter, I'll describe some of those super PCs and explain what distinguishes them from ordinary desktop PCs.

Analyzing the Need

Most desktop PCs today have far more raw computing power than even the largest of the mainframe computers built 40 years ago. Because those mainframes were able to handle dozens or in some cases even hundreds of terminals, it seems reasonable to suppose that today that job could be done by a simple PC.

However, our expectations for any such central computer on a large network have grown over the years right along with the power of computers. For example, consider that 40 years ago all terminals were capable of displaying only characters. Now we expect many of our workstations to show us a richly graphical screen image. The central computer is often responsible for managing much of what we see on those screens. Thus, it would be a mistake to simply grab any old PC and put it in service as if it were a modern mainframe computer.

Context Matters: Two Prototypical Uses for a Central Computer

To successfully replace a mainframe (or a minicomputer) with a PC, the first step is to carefully analyze what the mainframe computer does and then make sure the PC is capable of doing those same things. To accomplish this, we must distinguish between two prototypical applications for which those central computers are used.

File Servers to Workstations

The least demanding use of a central computer is as a simple file server. In this scenario, the central computer is connected to a network of workstations, and it serves up files to those workstations upon request.

In this case, the central computer must have a lot of input-output capability. The actual computational task it must accomplish is quite limited, but in order to keep track of all the open files and to cache the most recently accessed ones for every user, the central PC must have a lot of RAM (and, of course, a lot of disk space).

Back-End Processor for OLTP System

A much more demanding application, and one more typical of how networks of computers are used these days, is as the back-end processor for an online transaction processing (OLTP) system. Here, the central computer must perform essentially two kinds of tasks. One is the simple serving up of files (or, more commonly, of records from within large database files). The other task involves searching those database files for appropriate sets of records. This involves all the same requirements as the file server and workstation scenario plus a substantial amount of actual computing work. So, this is a file server and workstation system, plus.

Other network configurations might require different, but similar tasks from their central computers. Client-server systems, for example, have the central computer serving up information and also running various server-end application programs. Again, this type of system looks a lot like the simple file server-plus-workstation model, but it goes well beyond that in terms of what the central computer will be expected to do.

Reliability Is Key

In all these cases, one of the most essential requirements for the central computer is reliability. After all, if a workstation computer fails, only one person is put out of business until it is fixed. But if the central computer fails (in these centralized networks), the entire network of workstations becomes nearly useless until the central computer is repaired.

Some centralized networks use multiple central computers. Failure of a single central computer might or might not take down the entire network. Or, it might knock out a segment of the network. True peer-to-peer networks, on the other hand, usually continue to run quite nicely if one or more of the workstations fails.

Of course, if you are using a workstation that is accessing files at another workstation and that remote workstation fails, you can't continue the task. But, you still have the rest of the networked resources at your disposal to do other tasks.

Steady Electrical Power Prevents Many Problems

To ensure the reliability of your central computer, power it from an uninterruptible power supply (UPS). This is essentially a box with two power supplies and a set of batteries. One power supply converts incoming electrical power from the AC line to DC power at the voltage of the battery. This electrical energy is used both to recharge the batteries and to power the secondary power supply.

The secondary power supply can work in one of two ways. An external UPS will have a secondary power supply that converts the battery voltage back into AC voltage at the same voltage and frequency as the incoming electrical power. Essentially, this box sits between your computer and the wall socket, and it makes its output look just like the wall socket's output, but without the noise spikes, brown-outs, and interruptions that are typical of the power you will get from any normal electrical outlet.

On the other hand, internal UPSs are replacements for the power supply that lives inside your PC's system unit. In these units, the secondary power supply directly converts the battery voltage into the several different, closely regulated DC voltages that the PC uses internally.

For a file server, you usually use an external UPS. Only a good-sized external UPS will be able to store enough electrical energy to keep your file server humming during a typical power outage. Good UPSs also have an output port that sends signals to the PC it is powering to alert it to power failure. A monitoring program can keep track of when and for how long the UPS has been providing power. As the UPS's batteries begin to approach failure, the monitoring program can send messages to alert the users of the attached workstations that the network will be shutting down shortly. Then, the monitoring program can automatically do an orderly shut-down process for the server before the UPS is finally unable to continue supplying power.

I recommend an internal or external UPS for all the workstations on any network (or, in fact, for most stand-alone PCs). You can get small capacity units fairly cheaply. Replacements for the internal power supply can cost little more than the supplies they replace.

Not only will these units let the user continue working at a workstation in the event of a brief power outage, they also will do a better job of filtering out noise spikes and other power-line anomalies that, if passed through, might cause computer errors.

Block Lightning and Static Electric Shocks

To protect all the portions of the network from lightning-induced power surges and spikes, you must be sure that all the workstations, printers, and other devices on the network are supplied with power from the same phase of the electrical power coming into your building. Or, do a superior job of surge protection on each of those devices. Neglect even one, and a spike could couple through it and across the network cables to all the other devices on the network, possibly destroying them.

You can get surge protectors for the network cables also. If your network is large, I recommend using surge protectors in addition to a UPS backup system. You also must surge-protect any modem phone lines or other paths by which a lightning surge might enter your network.

If your work environment has a low humidity—even just at certain times of the year—you might need to drain off static electric charges from the users before they touch the workstation keyboards or disk drives. If you don't, they might get charged up enough by simply walking to their desks to deliver potent zaps able to kill a workstation or, in the worst case, an entire network. Many companies sell simple grounding pads—often in the form of a mousepad—that you can touch before touching your PC. These pads are designed to slowly (over a second or two) drain the static electricity off your skin, so you won't feel the kind of nasty shock you experience when you instantly drain off static by, for example, touching a metal doorknob after walking across a carpet. These pads connect to your home or office's electrical ground or to the metal case of your PC, which is connected to your office's ground through its power cord.

Backing Up Data Is Even More Crucial on a Network File Server

By now, most PC users know that file backups are important. And many of them perform backups regularly. If you are in charge of a file-server-based network, this task becomes even more vital because many users' files are at risk. If you don't do backups and verify them regularly, you are running a very real risk of having a whole flock of people justifiably mad at you.

RAID Makes Sense

In Chapter 9, "You Can Never Have Too Much Closet (or Data Storage) Space," I told you a little bit about RAID mass storage systems. These redundant arrays of independent disks are arrangements of multiple hard disk drives with a special controller. Eight levels of RAID have been formally defined. Each provides some level of protection above and beyond that which you will get from the disk drives themselves.

RAID Level 1 uses simple *disk mirroring*. That is, each disk has a twin that holds exactly the same information. Every time you write anything to a disk drive A it goes to both drives A and B. If one of the two drives fails, the controller will stop using it (but continue to use the other drive as if nothing has happened), and it will notify the system administrator that this disk must be replaced. After replacement, the contents of the remaining disk drive are simply copied to the new drive. This approach works okay, but it requires buying twice as much total disk capacity as you would need if you only stored a single copy of all your data.

The most popular version, RAID Level 5, can be made to store the data on multiple disk drives (as few as two, or as many as you need). You can expect to be able to recover all of it flawlessly even if one of the disks in the array dies totally.

The best RAID implementations often enable you to *hot swap* a failed disk drive. Hot swapping means you can take out the dead drive and replace it with a good one without having to shut down the system.

After you have replaced a dead drive, you must load it with an image of the data that used to be on its predecessor. Depending on the RAID level you have implemented, this might happen automatically, or you might have to go through some steps manually.

Another benefit to some of the RAID implementations is that they let you access the information stored in the disk array more rapidly than if the disk drives were simply connected as individual drives to the PC. Also, by using an array controller, you can attach more total capacity and still give the illusion that it is a single volume. This may be a substantial benefit provided your operating system is able to handle such a large disk volume efficiently.

I won't go into all the other details of the different RAID levels. If you want more technical information, you should absolutely check out Distributed Processing Technologies' Web site at www.dpt.com/techno.html. You will find additional—though less useful—"official" discussions at the RAID Advisory Board site at www.raid-advisory.com.

Blowing By the Bottlenecks and Piloting Past the Pitfalls

The details of how to build and optimally configure the central computers for a network vary depending on what that network is to do and also on which network operating system you will be using. However, many of the issues are common to every type of network and all network operating systems (NOS). When you understand these issues you can see pretty easily how to apply that knowledge to your own situation.

The Workstation to Central Computer Connection

The first issue to be dealt with in any network is providing adequate connectivity from the workstations to the central computers. I include the possibility of multiple central computers here for several reasons.

You might want to have multiple file servers simply to have enough file storage capacity as well as the ability to access all that storage quickly. Also, using multiple file servers is an effective means of breaking up the network connecting them to the workstations into several independent segments. This is crucial for large Windows NT installations, and it can be helpful with almost any NOS. You can also provide some redundancy, so the network can keep going even if one of the central computers should fail.

Direct Serial Connections to Each Workstation

If you are setting up an OLTP application, you might connect each workstation to the central computer by its own, private serial cable. Certainly this was the original way this type of network was built. But this approach can be problematic if you want to use a PC for the central computer, especially if you have a lot of workstations to support. Fortunately, better approaches are now commonly available.

Normally a PC can have at most four serial ports. You can get plug-in port expander cards that will increase that number to a few dozen. Beyond that, you must use a separate communications processor in its own box and link it to the file server over some high-speed data path such as a SCSI bus.

Typical Network Connections

The more common way to set up OLTP systems and almost any other type of file-server-based system of workstations, is by connecting all the computers, both workstations and file servers, via a network. As I told you in Chapter 15, "Understanding Standard PC Input and Output," many alternative networks are available: The most popular are Ethernet and Token Ring. Large Ethernet networks are often implemented using 10BASE-2 or 10BASE-5 coaxial cable wiring (or 100BASE-2 and 100BASE-5 if the signals are running at 100Mbps). Smaller Ethernet networks and many Token Ring installations use unshielded twisted pair wiring—called 10BASE-T (or 100BASE-T) for Ethernet and simply UTP for Token Ring.

The simplest way to achieve this connectivity is to put a suitable network interface card (NIC) into each workstation and each file server. Then, connect all of them using a single network cable (or, if you are using a star topology, a single hub). This works, but if the network is going to carry a lot of traffic, or if many workstations are to be connected, you can do better by using a slightly more complex scheme.

You can gain a lot of throughput simply by segmenting the network. The simplest way to do this in a system that has only one file server is to put multiple NICs into that server and connect a different network cable to each. This totally separates all the data traffic that goes between the file server and the workstations on one segment from all the traffic on all the other segments. However, each NIC will use up an IRQ and some port addresses, which means you cannot have very many of them in a single PC.

Another way to segment your network is to use a high-speed backbone, perhaps using 100Base-2 Ethernet. At intervals on that backbone cable, attach a router/hub that connects a separate 10Base-T network to your individual workstations. This is a common approach, but there are many others. Whatever works well is fine.

Interconnecting Multiple Central Computers

Arguably, a better way to segment your network is to use multiple file servers and let each one serve also as a router. To implement this approach, put two NICs into each file server. Connect groups of workstations to one of the NICs on each file server and interconnect all the file servers via another network cable attached to their second NICs. (You can combine this approach with the previous one by having each file server connect to a separate high-speed cable with each one supporting multiple segments of lower-speed network cable to groups of workstations. Then, the real "back-bone" cable becomes the one interconnecting the file servers.)

Figure 26.1 shows one example of this arrangement schematically. Here you see three file servers connected by a 100Mbps backbone network. There are fifteen workstations (numbered PC #1 through PC #15) in this network, arranged into three segments of five workstations each. These segments are shown as being only 10Mbps network cable. This is about the relationship you want. In this example, it seems likely that the data traffic on any one of the segments would reach saturation of that segment's capacity before the backbone reached saturation. This is true even though file requests may have to be routed over the backbone to a more remote file server.

Figure 26.1.
One good way to arrange multiple file servers so that they segment the network that serves the workstations.

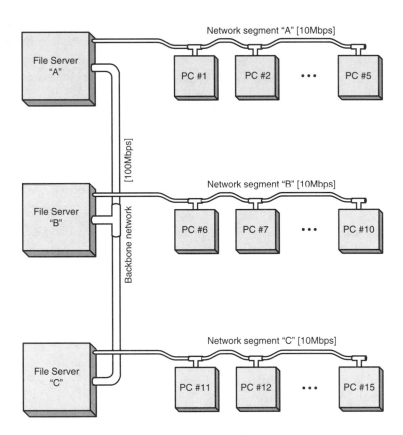

This approach also lets you divide the workload among the several file servers. Assuming the demands for data coming from the workstations is fairly evenly divided among those workstations, and if each segment has an equal number of workstations, this should balance the load across all the servers. If you know that some workstations are much more demanding than others, just put fewer of them on each segment or file server to give them the level of service they require.

Input-Output Bandwidth Issues

Connectivity is one thing. Achieving acceptable throughput is another. The NICs in your file servers, in particular, will be called upon to deliver lots of bits of data as rapidly as possible. Each file server must talk to many workstations (and also to the other file servers), whereas each workstation talks only to the file server to which it is connected.

Be sure to use a good, fast NIC and place it on a fast bus. In today's PCs, this means using an SCSI-3 fast and wide NIC on a PCI card. Also, use multiple NICs and multiple file servers as necessary to divide the workload until no one file server and no one NIC within a file server is overloaded.

For a simple file server this is the main issue. The actual CPU type and speed is much less important, although you don't want to build a network of any size these days around a file server that uses a 486 or earlier CPU.

If your file server is also running server-based applications or doing major work as an OLTP back-end processor, the CPU speed may indeed be an issue. I'll talk a little more about that point in just a moment.

Don't Put Too Many Workstations on a Single Server

If you use the file server loop with each file server supporting a number of workstations as your networking model (as I just suggested is often the best approach), then you must be careful not to overload any of the file servers. Remember, they now are serving as routers to all the other file servers, in addition to their jobs as file servers and perhaps server-based application execution engines.

Workstations, Logins, and Processes: Which Number Matters Most?

All this talk of too many workstations brings up another issue. What is the relevant number to look at? The easiest to count is the number of workstations on a given segment of your network, but that might not be an extremely important number.

Much more important is the number of users who are logged in to your network from workstations on that segment. And beyond that, the number of sessions each one might have going at once is important. Finally, each session may have multiple processes or threads that are active, and each one of these adds to the overall load as well.

In the end, the numbers you care about most are the megabytes of data traffic on the network cable and the number of independent processes each file server is expected to support. Unfortunately, those are also the hardest numbers to estimate in advance. Wise network administrators get and use good monitoring programs to give them a constantly updated picture of the load on their network segments and also on their servers. That way, a valid judgment can be made about the correct numbers of workstations to hook up to each server.

Server RAM and Disk Space

Network operating systems have to do many of the same jobs as the operating system of a stand-alone PC or workstation, but the jobs they perform are sometimes much more demanding. To do their jobs properly, they must be given plenty of RAM and plenty of disk space. How much do you need, and why is it a more serious issue for a file server or back-end OLTP processor than for a workstation or desktop PC?

The hardest challenge faced by most file servers is simply handling the input-output demand. They must be able to access a huge number of different files simultaneously.

Think about what goes on in a typical desktop PC. By design, it is a single-user computer and probably is running at most a few processes at once. Each of those processes opens a few files and reads or writes information in those files. That operating system must maintain pointers to those files, and for optimum efficiency, it must cache the most recently read or written sectors for each one in its disk cache.

Now look at the file server's perspective. It must maintain all those pointers for every user's processes, and it must cache the most recently read or written sectors in each of the files accessed by each of the processes.

A modest size disk cache that would be more than sufficient for a single-user PC will quickly be overwhelmed by the data flowing to and from the hard disk or hard disk array on a file server. That would render the disk caching virtually worthless.

Network operating system documentation may tell you about the amount of RAM you need per user. Unfortunately, the number you are most likely to find quoted tells you only about the absolute minimum amount of RAM needed to keep track of the files that each user has open, rather than the optimum amount you want to supply in your servers to let them create sufficiently large disk caches for each process. NetWare, for example, recommends (demands) about 16–32KB of RAM per user that is logged in (the actual amount varies by the version of NetWare).

A more realistic value for the optimal amount of RAM per user is at least 1MB. (The corresponding numbers for other NOSs are likely to be similar, as they all face common issues.) Those numbers should be applied per process if some of your users are running multiple processes at once. For a network with a few tens of users, this recommendation is not too hard to meet. You can put several hundred megabytes of RAM in the typical PC that is intended for use as a network file server. And you certainly should.

If your network's central computers are also expected to run server-based applications or do OLTP back-end processing, then you need even more RAM to hold those applications in addition to all the file pointers and cached data that the simple file server holds.

This recommendation becomes a problem when you have a large network (or one with lots of processes). When the number of processes passes a few hundred, it's impossible to get a PC that can hold enough RAM to do what you want it to do. The NOS might be able to address as much as 1GB of physical RAM, but the motherboard memory sockets just cannot hold that much.

In that case, you have another compelling reason to go to a network configuration that has multiple interconnected file servers. Load up each one with its maximum possible RAM and you should have enough in the total of all the file servers to support all your users' processes properly.

Sometimes More MIPS Are Needed

I made the general point earlier that simple file servers are most burdened by the amount of input and output they must do. Back-end OLTP processors and file servers that are used to run significant numbers of server-based applications, on the other hand, may actually become *compute-bound*. That is, they may be limited in what they can do not by the speed of their network attachment or their disk arrays, but rather by the speed of their CPUs.

There are only two possible solutions. You can either add file servers or beef up the processing speed of each file server. If you choose to speed up each server, you must choose to buy the fastest CPU available or use multiple CPUs within each file server. (Of course, to get the very fastest performance you can do both.)

The fastest CPUs for Windows NT file servers are the Alpha processors from Digital Equipment Corporation (DEC). However, these machines are not really PCs. For UNIX file servers, you might want to use a Sun workstation—again, not a PC. If you want to use a super PC as the central computer, then for any of the popular NOSs you should use a Pentium II with the fastest available clock speed. And in some situations, you can even increase that speed if you get a PC that contains multiple CPUs.

Can Multiple Processors Help?

Mentioning multiple CPUs within a single PC brings up a whole new topic, and one that is just beginning to get the attention it deserves. This is the field of multiprocessor PCs.

Multiprocessing Is Different than Multitasking

Multiprocessing is very different from multitasking. *Multiprocessing* refers to using more than one CPU in a single computer. *Multitasking* refers to using one CPU for more than one computing task at a time.

You most likely multitask all the time on just about any PC. If you run Windows (including Windows 3.x, Windows 95, or Windows NT), many things will be going on in the background that you are unaware of. And, you can intentionally start up several different programs and let them run at the same time. The same is true if you are running OS/2 or UNIX (including Linux) as your PC's operating system. Even a pure DOS machine can be doing some multitasking; for example, if you are doing background printing using the DOS PRINT command.

What appears as PC multitasking is actually an illusion. It is accomplished at a hardware and operating system level through "task swapping" among all the different tasks that are to be done "simultaneously." This means that the operating system directs the CPU at intervals to save all the "context" of what it is doing and then to turn its attention to a new task.

One task after another gets a little bit of the CPU's attention. Eventually, all of them have been served and the CPU is directed to resume the first one. This swapping from one to another to the next and finally back to the first task keeps on going constantly. (Windows 3.x relies on cooperative multitasking, which means that it doesn't move on to a new task until the running task tells it that it may. This can lead to very choppy multitasking or even a total failure of multitasking. For this reason all the other popular PC operating systems use preemptive multitasking. In this approach, the CPU is interrupted at fixed time intervals so that it will be sure to give some of its attention to each of the current tasks during every second of its operation.

If these "time slice" intervals are short, the user won't notice them and instead will see the PC apparently doing all those tasks at once. That is ordinary, everyday multitasking.

Multiprocessing is a whole different animal. This means having more than one CPU in a computer and somehow dividing up the work among all the CPUs. Many different schemes have been used to accomplish this, but in order for any of these schemes to work, the operating system must be able to divide the total workload into many separate tasks. Obviously, this can be done if each one is a separate program that has been launched by a separate user. But it can also be done within a single program.

When Multiprocessing Doesn't Help

Multiple processors don't always help. If you have a program that does one thing after another, a step at a time, and each step depends on the ones that have gone before, then there is no way that using more than one processor will help speed the work.

At the opposite extreme, suppose you have a program that does the exact same information processing task over and over again, each time applying it to a different set of data. And, the data to be used for all these different times of repeating the common task are all available at the beginning. You could speed up the program enormously if only you had as many processors as you had sets of data to process. Then, each one could be working on its own set of data at the same time as all the others.

Of these two examples, the first is a highly linear program, but the second one could be rewritten for massively parallel processing, with great benefit. Most things we do with our PCs fall somewhere in the middle, and the majority lean toward the linear processes. A file server is one of the least necessarily linear problems, in that we could in principle be serving each workstation's requests in parallel with all the rest. So for a file server, more than almost any other PC usage, using multiple processors can help. But it will help only if two conditions are met: The hardware must be able to perform the multiple calculations in parallel without getting confused, and the software must know how to spread the work over all the processors.

Both these conditions can be met in a properly designed file server PC. But creating those PCs has turned out to be anything but easy. Still, the potential benefits are great and many folks have given it a try—some have succeeded quite nicely.

What's Hard About Multiprocessor PCs

Managing multiple processors is not a trivial business. The operating system must be much more sophisticated than is required for properly managing the traditional, one-processor PC. The hardware also needs to be specifically tailored to take advantage of the second processor's presence. As the complexity increases of both our needs and the tools we use to address those needs, multiprocessing will become more common. Hardware and software manufacturers are already preparing for this evolution, doing the back research required to solve the unique problems such a system presents.

Hardware Issues

There are several hardware difficulties in building a multiprocessing PC. And, there are a number of different ways of dealing with them.

The first issue any multiprocessor system must deal with is how to keep the processors from conflicting with one another as they access memory and other resources in the computer. You can give each CPU its own bank of main memory. If you have a program that consists of many parts that can be run in parallel, you can simply load one part into the memory of each CPU and let them each have at the job with which they are presented.

The opposite extreme is to use only one pool of main memory, but add in some special hardware features (sometimes called gates, flags, or semaphores). These are mechanisms that can be used to tell a particular processor to wait a moment while another processor is doing whatever it must with the contents of main memory, then letting the first processor do what it wants in the same area. (If the two processors are trying to access very different addresses in main memory, there may be no conflict in letting them both do their access at the same time, but only if each has its own, independent bus connecting it to the main memory.)

Sometimes there will be only one pool of main memory, but there will be a separate Level 2 cache for each CPU. (This assumes each CPU has its own Level 1 cache on board its chip.)

Another issue that must be dealt with when there are multiple CPUs in a single computer is which of those CPUs is really in control. That is, one of the CPUs must be designated as the Master CPU. And, one program it will run (as a portion of the overall operating system) will decide which CPU will be given the other tasks it is to perform. This same program will arbitrate among the CPUs when they are about to collide in reaching for some resource.

In some multiprocessor computers, the Master CPU has been given just this one job of supervising all the others. In those computers, typically, there are many other CPUs (a dozen or perhaps a few hundred) that all perform as peers under the direction of the Master CPU.

In PCs, though, it's more common to have only a few CPUs. In fact, the most common configuration is just two CPUs; four CPUs are the next most common. In these cases, it would be a waste to let one CPU do nothing but manage the others. So, they are built to make it easy for the operating system to do the needed management and also let every CPU do some of the main work of the applications being run in the computer.

Software Issues

As you might imagine, the software to run multiprocessor computers is as diverse as the hardware configurations used in those computers. Indeed, the software must be designed with a knowledge of exactly how the hardware pieces can all work together, which means that any substantial change to the hardware configuration requires a totally new approach to the operating system's design.

The most important thing a multiprocessor OS must do is allocate the CPU resources among the processes (also called *threads*) it runs. That is, each program must have been broken up into independent threads, or chains of steps to be taken. And, for each thread there must be a set of data on which it will operate. Then the OS can send each thread with its data to a particular CPU for execution.

If the program must at some point combine the results from all the different threads, then the OS will have to choose just one CPU to do the work of combining them. At that time, it can assign the other CPU or CPUs to any other thread tasks that may be pending, perhaps for some totally different application program.

But how can the OS know if each thread is independent of all the others? This question is important, because if any two or more of the threads act on the same data, they might have to run sequentially. When these threads belong to totally separate programs, the OS knows it is safe to allocate different threads to different CPUs.

More commonly though, the different threads are parts of the same overall process. Certainly this is true of the file accesses being performed by a file server. In these situations, the only way to take advantage of multiple CPUs is for the author of the application program that is running to explicitly designate which threads can be run in parallel and which cannot. (For a file server, the relevant application is the one doing file access management on behalf of all the network users. This is actually a portion of the network operating system running on top of the basic OS for the computer.)

At this stage of development, not a lot of PC application programs have been optimized for multiple CPU PCs, but among those that have are some of the most widely-used products available. Adobe Systems, for example, has implemented multiprocessor support in their 32-bit flagship products—including FrameMaker, Illustrator, Photoshop, and Premiere—under Windows NT, Macintosh, and Sun SparcStation operating environments. You'll notice correctly that these tools are all graphics- and calculation-intensive, and Adobe began their multiprocessor support work over two years ago because the tasks this type of program performs are so suited to parallel processing.

Both DOS, with or without Windows 3.x, and Windows 95 have no notion of what to do with anything more than a single CPU. So putting in a second CPU and running the PC on any of these OSs is just a way to waste money and electricity.

Windows NT and OS/2, on the other hand, know how to use two or four CPUs simultaneously. Some flavors of UNIX know how to use even more CPUs. But in any of these cases, there remains the question of whether the applications running on top of the basic OS kernel have been written to take advantage of multiple processors whenever they are available.

Summary

PCs are now so powerful that it can be very practical to use them as if they were mainframe computers or super-powerful graphics workstations. Both of those kinds of computers used to be far beyond anything a PC could do, but that no longer is the case. (There are more powerful mainframes than any PC and more powerful workstations, but for many applications that used to require a mainframe, mini, or dedicated graphics workstation, a high-end PC is now more than adequate.)

But configuring a network and a PC to serve as its central computer requires looking at a lot of different issues that are of particular importance. The most important issues are input-output speed, providing enough central PCs to support the total load, and balancing the workload among all the central computers.

Multiprocessing PCs (those with more than one CPU) can be most helpful for graphics and digital video workstations, file servers, and other central computers in a network. The PC industry as a whole is just beginning to develop the possibilities of using multiple processors to speed up PCs. As we try to get more computing out of these boxes, though, this territory may become invaluable. There is only so much speed we can gain from wider buses and faster clock rates. At some point—barring an unforeseeable breakthrough—we also will need to use multiple CPUs working in parallel. For the plurality of tasks we perform on our PCs, however, widespread utilization of multiple processors remains where it has been for the past two years—on the horizon.

VIII

Peter Norton®

PCs,
the Internet,
the Future,
and You

27

You Can Touch the World, and It May Touch You, Too!

Peter Norton®

The Internet: Certainly, you've heard of it. Perhaps you use it daily in your work or for recreation. But do you understand what it is and how it works? The Internet is growing at a truly amazing rate. Very few things, if anything, have grown so rapidly and continued to do so for so long. Today it has changed virtually everything about the world of PCs. Tomorrow it might change virtually all aspects of our lives.

In this chapter I want to cover briefly some of the technologies that are behind the Internet and its amazing growth and impact. This won't make using the Internet any harder or easier, or more or less useful, but it might scratch an intellectual itch or two.

What Is the Internet, and How Does It Work?

The Internet is a network, in many ways just like the office LAN. It connects many different computers together for the purpose of exchanging data. What's so different about the Internet is its scope. It is an interconnection of many smaller networks. Its scope is global. The number of connected computers is almost unimaginable, and its penetration into the ways we use our PCs to work (and play) is getting deeper by the day.

Also, the Internet is—unlike every network of which it is composed—not something that is under anyone's control. No single person or organization is responsible for the Internet. Aspects to it have been entrusted to this group or that, but overall it is one of the most amazing demonstrations of a functional anarchy—quite possibly one of the few in all of human history.

The Internet Both Is and Is Not Like Any Other Network

At the technical level, the Internet is very much like any other network. It consists of computers that are connected together and exchange packets that carry information. Some of these computer-to-computer links are permanent ones; others are made temporarily to facilitate a particular data exchange and then broken once more.

One way in which the Internet is unlike many networks is its degree of massively redundant interconnectedness. For any given two locations in most networks, there are at most a few paths to get from here to there. On the Internet, however, there are usually a huge number of alternative paths. (Still, in some key places a substantial portion of the Internet can be temporarily severed from all the rest by just one mistake on the part of a backhoe operator.)

Another difference is the wide variation in the value of the data stored in the many connected computers and available to all who seek to access it. Most other networks connect computers belonging to a single company or organization, and those computers mainly store similar kinds of data with similar value to the people who make up those organizations. The Internet is, to put it bluntly, a mess in this regard.

Although you can't trust everything you find on the Internet, it is one of the most universally accessible, if not the richest, lode of information on the planet. After you learn to navigate around the Net and validate what you find there with a combination of careful consideration of the apparent source of the information and cross-checking with other sources, you may find that you turn to the Net more often than to almost any other information resource—simply because it will have proven to be the fastest way to answer most of your questions.

Furthermore, many people are now finding their natural communities of like-minded people via the Internet, without regard to their actual, physical locations. Whether this is a wonderful or a regrettable development for our society is something I will leave to sociologists to debate.

Internet Protocols

Although the Internet is, in general terms, like any other network, it also has some things about it that are special. For example, the Internet was built around a data transmission protocol that was designed just for it. Furthermore, most of the higher-level protocols used to control various kinds of network-mediated transactions were first developed for use across the Internet or its predecessors. Of course, like almost any great success in any field, these have now been adopted for use in a wide assortment of networks, including some that aren't connected to the Internet at all. (One of the hottest areas of development in many businesses now is what are termed *intranets*, which is simply copies of the Internet model on a smaller scale for use within a single organization.)

Transmission Protocols, Gateways, and Firewalls

Just about any network carries data from place to place in packages called *packets*. You can think of them as being in many ways like letters inside envelopes. The letter is the data load being carried. The envelope provides information on the source and destination of the packet. One way in which network data packets differ from most letters carried in envelopes is that the packets are too small to hold an entire message. So almost all files that are transferred over networks—and a file is what corresponds to a letter in our analogy—must be broken up into many small pieces. Each one is enclosed in its own "envelope," and includes, in addition to the addresses of source and destination, the sequence number of this particular piece of the "message" (file).

Because there are so many alternative ways for a packet to find its way from the source to the destination, and because any one of those routes can be more or less congested at any given instant, it is quite possible for the packets that make up a single message (the ones carrying all the pieces of a single file) will end up traveling from the source to the destination by different routes.

The implication is that the packets might arrive out of order. This is where the sequence number comes into play. The receiving software examines the envelopes and sorts them into the right order. It also acknowledges receipt of each one. If the sending software doesn't get an acknowledgment within a reasonably short time, it will assume the packet got lost and resend it.

One way this strategy can fail is if the link between sending and receiving programs has a high *latency*. This means simply that packets take an unusually long time to get from one point to another. That can happen even though the rate of data flow is very high, just because the overall distance to be traveled is very, very long. This is one of the salient characteristics of any link that must bounce off a geosynchronous satellite, for example. In this case the sending program may get tired of waiting and resend and resend packets ad naseum. This, of course, doesn't really help things. Instead, it just clogs up the channel.

One way around this difficulty is a strategy called *TCP Spoofing*. Here an intermediary is set up to receive and acknowledge packets midway, or just before the high latency portion of the link. The intermediary then forwards the packets over that high latency link and waits more tolerantly for the ultimate receiver to acknowledge their receipt.

Still, even with all of this protection in place, sometimes packets do get lost—permanently. No overall message-receipt assurance is built into the Internet's usual packet-handling protocols. That is a job that is left to some higher-level process.

Peter's Principle: When It Really Must Get There

If you, or any application programs you are running, want to be sure that each message sent out is received, ask the receiving person or programs for acknowledgments. Some programs do this automatically; many do not. In particular, e-mail across the Internet can be an iffy proposition. So for any important messages, I always include in the message a request to the recipient to reply immediately just so I will know that he or she has received my message.

The main protocol, itself actually a set of related protocols, that describes how the Internet shall carry packets of information is called Transmission Control Protocol/Internet Protocol (TCP/IP). Like most of the other standards that describe how aspects of the Internet work, this one was developed by a committee and then published (on the Internet, of course). The survival of the Internet as an operating medium of communication has depended upon the voluntary compliance with those standards by all the organizations, companies, and individuals whose computers make up the Internet.

Local area networks of PCs and larger computers have been built using many different wiring strategies and network operating systems (NOSs). I described several of these in Chapter 25, "The PC Reaches Out, Part Two: Through the NIC Node." Each NOS has its own native protocol for handling packets, although some are capable of supporting some other protocols as well.

Historical Aside: The reason behind this proliferation of protocols is twofold. First, companies make serious financial investments to support the development of their products. In order to protect those investments under patent law, companies devise unique, proprietary methods of doing whatever it is that their product is supposed to do. Government agencies award patents to unique processes (or devices) to enable the patent owners to better defend themselves against the theft of their work.

Of more direct benefit to us as individual users, however, is the reality that technology evolves. As it does so, better ways of doing things—better protocols—are conceived that could not have been conceived in the past. Implementing these better (more efficient, more economical, safer, or whatever) protocols often means abandoning the past. People will, of course, choose to implement these new protocols on their own time scales, so it takes a very long time, often, for old protocols to die, leaving us with a wide array of options. Of course, to maximize the appeal of a new protocol, it may be able to emulate old protocols, if necessary, thereby maintaining backward compatibility.

The most common NOS for PC LANs is Novell's NetWare. Depending on the version of NetWare, it might have either one of two native protocols: SPX or IPX. Recent versions of NetWare always support both of these. In addition, whoever sets up a NetWare network can decide whether to add support to NetWare for TCP/IP packets at his discretion. More and more network administrators are supporting TCP/IP on their organization's internal networks, as well as on links to the outside world.

Gateways connect different network segments. When the packets traveling on the different segments use different transmission protocols, the gateway is responsible for translating between them. In effect, the gateway hardware opens the "envelope" of each packet, extracts the contents, and then places it in a new envelope that is properly addressed for travel on the next network segment.

Sometimes, depending on which two protocols are involved, the gateway might not open the original envelope, but instead just places the entire incoming packet into a new envelope and sends it on its way. This works just fine and is sometimes slightly faster, although it does mean carrying some unnecessary bits around the network.

Some gateways are more than just packet shufflers; they also serve a security function. (Think of them as combination postal worker and security guard.) These gateways are called *firewalls*. They examine each packet they receive and test it against various rules. If it passes, they send the packet on to its destination.

Some of these rules might involve not passing packets coming from certain, untrusted source locations. Other rules might actually look inside the envelope and decide which packets to pass based on the data they contain. The person who configures the firewall has the responsibility to set up the correct set of rules to give the owner of that firewall the level of security he bought it to provide.

A side effect of a firewall might be to disguise the true source of packets when it forwards them. This can be both helpful and a great inconvenience. Here is one common example: A company can give the appearance to the outside of having only a few Internet addresses, but in fact have on the inside a great many more. This allows the company to better control the flow of information in and out of its networked systems. Their marketing Web site can remain easily available to the general public while their confidential financial information remains accessible to a knowledgeable few, but safe from the prying eyes of the rest of us. The gateway will set up a correspondence between the internal and external addresses for each conversation it permits to pass through its wall of safety. This correspondence will last only as long as that conversation does. Therefore, the external addresses can be reused as much as necessary while the "true" internal addresses of the users remain fixed.

This can be inconvenient when you want to carry on a conversation over the Internet with a computer that insists on knowing who you are. The firewall simply might not allow that type of conversation. The conversation you wanted to have might prove to be impossible to hold, unless you have a way of working around this roadblock. (Often such workarounds are available; you just have to ask your network administrator to learn about them.)

One way that this hiding of internal IP addresses can be extremely helpful is in dealing with the limited supply of Internet addresses. At the hardware level, each computer on any TCP/IP network, from a small office LAN to the entire Internet, must have one or more IP addresses, or 32-bit numbers. Naturally, with only 32 bits in those addresses, there can be no more than approximately four thousand million of them. (See Chapter 3, "Understanding Bits, Nybbles, and Bytes," if you aren't clear on why this is so.) Each computer's IP address must be unique in that computer's world—which is to say among all the computers that it can see directly via the TCP/IP protocol.

Technical Note: IP addresses are commonly expressed as four numbers separated by decimal points. Each of the four numbers is a decimal expression of the value of one of the four bytes that make up the total 32-bit IP address. So, for example, the IP address of 206.85.92.79 is equivalent to the 32-bit number 11001110 01010101 01011100 01001111. (This IP address happens to be the one assigned to the primary domain name server, or DNS, at Earthlink, my Internet service provider.)

Overlaid on top of—and completely independent from—the IP address scheme is a more human-friendly naming scheme for computers and their users. Thus, John's e-mail address is agoodman@earthlink.net. This says that his username is agoodman, and his mail account is accessible at the computer host named earthlink in the top-level domain net. There is a limited number of top-level domain names, and mostly they indicate either the type of computers in that domain or the country where the computer is located. The most common top-level domain name is com, which stands for some type of commercial entity. The net top-level domain refers to computers belonging to companies that provide Internet services. The gov top-level domain name includes most U.S. government entities. The edu top-level domain includes most colleges and universities.

Any time you specify a computer's domain name, as in `Symantec.com`, that name must be translated into the computer's IP address. This is done by sending a message to some Domain Name Server (DNS), which will either know the translation or will know which computer to ask. Eventually, this process brings back to the requestor an IP address that it should use in place of the host and domain name. Then, when messages for a user at a certain computer arrive there, that computer looks in its table of usernames to determine in which actual mailbox it is to put that message.

When the IP address scheme was first proposed, it seemed like four billion addresses were surely going to suffice for a long time. But with the incredible growth of the Internet, it is now proving to be a too-limited supply. The way in which those addresses were originally parceled out to organizations further limited the number that any one group could use. Hiding large numbers of internal addresses behind a firewall is one way some companies are getting around this shortage.

This is a problem now, but in the next few years we can expect a new generation of IP addresses to arrive with double the number of bits. Surely *that* number of addresses (approximately 16 million, million, million) will suffice for a long time—even if the Internet continues its exponential growth for many more decades.

Other Common Internet Protocols

The TCP/IP set of protocols handles the problems of routing packets from place to place and reassembling messages in an adequate manner. (There is still the nagging problem of ensuring that messages actually get where they are going, but that can be handled at a higher level with an acknowledgment protocol of some kind.)

Other Internet protocols deal with higher-level transactions. For example, the File Transfer Protocol (FTP) specifies how one computer can ask another computer to send it a copy of one or more files. Various mail protocols deal with how to handle e-mail. (These include protocols for addressing messages, maintaining virtual mailboxes, and attaching nontext objects to e-mail messages.) The Gopher protocol lets you access information on a remote computer arranged into a hierarchical menu. The rlogin and Telnet protocols are for remote logins; they specify a way in which you can convert your computer into a terminal to some remote computer (provided you have an account on that remote computer).

Some of the more recent additions to the family of Internet protocols are the Hypertext Transfer Protocol (HTTP) and several other protocols used in connection with the World Wide Web. Even more protocols are being proposed all the time, and no doubt some of them will be adopted as official Internet protocols at some future time.

Please keep in mind that all these protocols are voluntary standards. Someone proposes one, a committee of volunteers discusses and publishes it for additional commentary, and then it gets adopted and published as an official Internet standard. However, that doesn't ensure that anyone will actually use it. Still, this process has proven to work remarkably well. The truly useful protocols do get widely supported by hardware and software vendors soon after (or in some cases well before) their official adoption.

A Lot More Than Just Data Is Out There

The beginnings of the Internet can be found in establishment of the ARPAnet by the U.S. Defense Department's Advanced Research Projects Agency in the late 1960s. They had only a few, limited goals in mind when they set up this novel experiment.

The Early Internet Had Limited Uses

One thing the original designers of the ARPAnet hoped to accomplish was to provide a means of sharing some otherwise wasted computing resources in widely separated places. Thus, for example, if a researcher at the University of California in Los Angeles wanted to do something but his local computers were all busy, he might send his job over the ARPAnet to a computer in Upsala, Sweden. If it was the middle of the day in Los Angeles, it would be late in Upsala, and possibly their computer would be idle. If it was, his job could be sent there from Los Angeles, run there, and the results could be returned to Los Angeles sooner than the job could be run in Los Angeles (where it would have to wait for a computer to become available). To promote this goal, the ARPAnet had to support remote logins, file transfers, and a few other simple functions.

The other principle use envisioned for the ARPAnet was as a test-bed for this and other ideas about networking. These two uses compiled the expectations for their experiences.

Almost as an afterthought, the designers decided it would be handy to provide a mechanism that would allow a user at one computer to send messages to people who were near one of the other computers connected to the ARPAnet. This would allow the network researchers to talk among themselves as they did their experiments on the network. While they were at it, they made the mechanism available to anyone who wanted to use it—provided that each person had an account on some computer that was connected to the ARPAnet.

To everyone's surprise, e-mail soon turned out to be the most highly valued aspect of the ARPAnet and, later, of the Internet into which that network grew. Even today, e-mail is one of the main reasons why people start using the Internet.

Decades passed with little change in the kinds of things people did on the Internet. E-mail ruled. Throughout the 1970s, file transfers became the next most important use, and remote logins were the third. Perhaps the most appreciated of the new uses for the network were real-time chat facilities and multiperson games, the use of which exploded in the early 1980s.

The World Wide Web Brought the Internet to the Masses, and Vice Versa

Starting in 1993, the World Wide Web happened. Internet usage exploded, and it continues to explode even more daily. Some people confuse the Internet and the World Wide Web. They are definitely *not* the same thing. The World Wide Web (WWW) is simply one of many uses of the Internet.

If you liken the Internet to a system of highways, the WWW is somewhat like the practice of commuting to work. It is something that happens on the Internet. This definition tells you that it is something that lives or happens on the infrastructure that is the Internet, but it doesn't tell you much about just what the pieces are that make up the Web or how they are accessed.

What Exactly Is the World Wide Web?

The World Wide Web is the entire collection of resources that you can access, from anywhere in the world, over the Internet by use of a Uniform Resource Locator (URL). These resources take many forms, including textual documents, static graphic images, video clips, or programs.

The notion of a URL is a very flexible, powerful, and important one. Any complete URL has at least three parts. The first part of any full URL is a keyword that tells what protocol must be used to access this resource. If the URL starts out `http:`, it points to a resource that will be accessed by using the Hypertext Transfer Protocol. This is the means used to request *Web pages*, which are files that have been formatted in accordance with the Hypertext Markup Language (HTML) specification.

If a URL starts out `ftp:`, it specifies a resource to be accessed by use of the FTP. Another common keyword is `mailto:`, which specifies that this URL tells you where to send an e-mail message. Finally, the keyword `file:` specifies a resource that is a file located on your local computer.

The second part of a full URL is the name of the computer where this resource can be found (in the case of a file) or that contains the intended destination (in the case of a `mailto:` URL). The third part of a full URL is the name of the resource (or destination) on that computer.

Here is an example of a full URL:

```
http://www.w3.org/TR/WD-htm14/cover.htm
```

The first part of this URL is `http:`, so you should know that it is pointing to a resource that is to be accessed using the HTTP protocol. The second part of this URL is `//www.w3.org/`, which specifies the computer we are referencing. In this case, it is the computer that holds all the activities of the principle WWW standards group. The third part, `TR/WD-htm14/cover.htm`, specifies the particular resource on this computer, which in this case is the current specification for the HTML language.

Warning: One point that must be stressed for PC users is that at least the third part of any URL is case sensitive, which means capital letters and lowercase letters are treated differently. So in this example, if that last part were typed as TR/WD-HTML4/COVER.HTM or as tr/wd-html4/cover.htm (or any other capitalization other than what I've shown in the preceding full URL), the resulting URL wouldn't point to the HTML specification document. Most likely it wouldn't point to any resource at all. The second part of any URL (the machine name) is the only part that is guaranteed to be not case sensitive. The best plan is for you always to scrupulously follow the case you see when copying a URL. Doing so will save you from many failures to link to a resource.

This must be stressed for PC users, in particular, because most file accesses on a PC aren't case sensitive. You can pretty much ignore capitalization of all filenames (and sometimes you'll see Windows 95, in particular, change the capitalization for you spontaneously). That is totally different from how most other computers in the world treat filenames. This means that PC users might have picked up sloppy habits in this regard, which will not serve them well when accessing resources on the WWW.

The HTML standard also defines the notion of a *relative* URL and a *fragment* URL. The relative URL simply is all or a portion of the third part of a URL. The first two parts are defined implicitly by context. Thus, if an HTML document includes a reference to ./images/BigBlueCar.gif, this is a pointer to a particular Graphical Interchange Format (GIF) image file located in the images directory (a subdirectory to the current directory).

Warning: Notice that the directory separator symbol is the forward slash character (/) and not the backward slash (\) normally used on PCs because other computers, in particular those running UNIX, traditionally use the forward slash for this purpose. At present, the majority of the computers that comprise the WWW run UNIX.

A *fragment* URL is a normal URL (full or relative) that has a # character (sometimes called a hash mark, or a pound sign) at the end, followed by a name. This name refers to a region within the re-source pointed to by the URL. This form is commonly used to position your view of that resource so you can immediately start reading at the named location. Here is a sample of a fragment URL:

http://www.w3.org/TR/WD-html40/about.html#h-1.1

This points to section 1.1 of the specified document. The section name evidently is h-1.1, and the document name is about.html. That document describes the current (version 4.0) HTML specifica-tion, and this section describes how to read the document.

What Is HTML?

Web pages are essentially small files of HTML-encoded text. This is a relatively simple example of a more general class of formatted files described by an international standard that was devised many years ago, called the Standard Generalized Markup Language (SGML) specification.

You can access an HTML document by using what is called a *user agent*. This most commonly is a Web browser, such as Internet Explorer or Netscape Navigator, but it can be a text-only browser, such as Lynx, or a program that reads an HTML file and then pronounces it out loud for a blind user.

Basically, HTML files are just text files, but they contain some special words or blocks that indicate various things other than normal textual content. What I have referred to as the special HTML words or blocks are formally referred to as HTML *elements*. The beginning of an element of HTML is often indicated by a start tag. For example, <HEAD> would mark the start of the header region. The end of that element can be indicated by an end tag. For our sample case, it would be </HEAD>.

Not all elements must begin or end with a tag. Sometimes these locations are implied and don't need to be explicitly specified, although most of the time the start tag (at least) is needed.

HTML elements serve one of three general kinds of function. Some, such as HEAD, TITLE, and BODY, specify general areas within an HTML document. (The HEAD area holds general information about the document—information that your user agent, which normally is your browser program, will use but will not display. The TITLE area contains the title that will show up in your browser's title bar. The BODY contains the essential content of the page.)

The second kind of element specifies a format for some portion of the content. This could include the font, color, or location of some text, or the size of a frame to hold an image, and so on. In the latest version of the HTML specification, however, this kind of HTML element is discouraged. Instead, authors of Web pages are encouraged to use style sheets to define the appearance of various items. If that is done, this second kind of element becomes not the description of a style, but merely a pointer to a named style. Using style sheets in this way enables you to separate the content from its appearance. This lets you make many pages that resemble one another by preparing just one style sheet and referring to it in all those Web pages.

The third kind of element specifies some external resource. This might be an element that causes that resource to be included in the current page. The most common example of this are the elements that cause bitmapped images (commonly GIF or JPEG files) to show up on a Web page, or it might be an element that links to another resource. This is best exemplified by a hyperlink, which loads a new Web page when you double-click on it.

Other uses for this third category of HTML element include loading a music file and launching a program to play it, or loading and running a Java applet, and so on.

Sometimes a Browser Isn't Enough

The two main HTML user agent (browser) programs used on PCs today are Microsoft's Internet Explorer and Netscape's Navigator. Dozens of alternative browsers are available, however, plus add-on modules for many word processors to let them edit and save HTML files. All these browsers can read and display an HTML file. They mostly can also display some of the embedded graphic images. In particular, most HTML browsers understand GIF and JPG (JPEG-compressed) files. So if an HTML element in a page specifies that a GIF or JPG file should be loaded and displayed, the browser will do just that.

However, none of the browsers understands every graphics file format in common use. For example, I don't know of even one that will display EPS (PostScript graphics) files. So, while you can put in an HTML element that specifies that a certain EPS file should be loaded, when the browser reads that tag it will not be capable of complying with the instructions fully. Instead, the browser will pop up a dialog box that points out that it is being asked to load a file of a type it doesn't know about, and it will offer to go to a page of plug-ins to see if there is one there that would be helpful.

What's a Plug-In?

What are plug-ins, and how do they work? Essentially, they are small helper programs that add to the functionality of your browser. When a modern Web browser loads, in addition to loading its own program code into memory, it also loads any plug-ins that you have previously installed. Then when it is scanning Web pages, if the browser encounters an element that specifies acting on a resource of a type it doesn't understand, it will check to see whether any of its loaded plug-in programs understands this type of resource. If such a plug-in exists, the browser will hand over control to it, pointing it to the resource in question as it does so. After the plug-in has finished processing that resource in whatever way it has been programmed to handle it, the plug-in will pass control back to the Web browser.

Whenever any modern Web browser encounters an element that asks it to do something it cannot do natively and that none of its loaded plug-ins can handle, the browser is built to prompt the user and then, if the user wishes, to look for a suitable helper (plug-in) program that will be capable of handling that type of request. If a suitable plug-in can be found, you can download and install it into your Web browser for use during your next session using that browser program. (At present, you may need to close the browser before you can install a new plug-in because, until very recently, browsers load plug-ins only when they themselves load.)

Dozens of different plug-ins are now available for both Internet Explorer and Navigator. (Because the two browsers integrate with plug-ins in subtly different ways, each plug-in must be written to work with a specific browser.)

I have been using Netscape Navigator, version 4 for a fairly short time. Already I find that I have 10 plug-ins installed for it. (Two of them came with Navigator; the others I found I needed to properly view some of the Web sites I encountered.) Here is my present list, as it is presented to me by Navigator:

- Shockwave Flash 2.0
- RealPlayer LiveConnect-enabled plug-in (32-bit) 5.0 Beta 1
- QuickTime plug-in
- Microsoft NetShow Player 3.0 plug-in
- Netscape default plug-in
- SSEYO Koan Music plug-in
- Interactive Pictures Corp. IPIX plug-in v4.00 b4
- NPAVI32 Dynamic Link Library
- LiveAudio
- Shockwave for Director

Plug-ins are programs, and as such they may be written using any of the many PC programming languages. These days, they most often will be written using C, C++, or Java.

> **Warning:** This approach in creating helper programs is very general. It enables the programmer of the plug-in to make his or her program do just about anything that any other PC program could do. This means that you'll probably only want to download and use plug-ins that you get from a trusted source. Otherwise, you could be making a home for a Trojan Horse program that will do who-knows-what damage to your data at some inopportune moment.

Making Web Pages Responsive: CGI Scripts

By the very nature of the concept, HTML is mostly about displaying pages of information. Then, whenever you click on some hyperlink, your browser will summon a new HTML page to display. These pages can include not only the text that is in the file pointed to by the URL used to load the page, but also it can include graphic images, video clips, or other (HTML) text pages inside a frame.

That sounds fairly staid, but Web pages today are often dynamic and highly interactive creations. You might find that displayed pieces change when you move your mouse pointer over them. When you enter information into a form, that form could add boxes, change colors, or otherwise indicate that it had received and was acting upon your input.

How is this done? Having the HTML code on the Web page you are viewing causes some program to load and run as well. That program can be either one that runs on the Web server or one that runs in your PC.

For most of the time that the World Wide Web has existed, the dominant way of doing this job was to use CGI scripts. In fact, a recent survey of the WWW suggests that about two-thirds of the pages are just static HTML, and almost all the rest are made more active by the use of CGI scripts. Very few use any of the highly talked about new methods such as VBScript, ActiveX components, Java, JavaScript, or Java Beans. Still, with all the push those new technologies are getting, we can expect them to become much more prevalent in the next couple of years.

Common Gateway Interface (CGI) is a standard type of program on a UNIX computer, and this idea now has been ported over to Wintel machines as well. It is similar to a DOS batch file, but with considerably more power. A CGI script can be launched by an element on any Web page you may be viewing. These CGI scripts are mostly written in a language for UNIX computers called Perl. This is an interpreted language (like BASIC), although now there are also compilers for Perl (just as there are for BASIC). The variant of CGI that is used on Wintel machines can be written in VBScript, using Visual Basic as the interpreter/compiler.

Any CGI script can be interpreted on-the-fly from its source file form (much like a DOS batch file is), or it can be compiled into a binary program. Either way it will do the same thing. The advantages to the compiled version include both that it can run faster and that it will be relatively invulnerable to hacker attack. The disadvantage is that the author must go through an extra compilation step after completing and debugging the interpreted version of the script.

A general property of all CGI scripts is that they are server-side scripts, which means they are programs that execute on the Web server. You access the server with your browser by pointing to some HTML page. That page is downloaded to your PC, and its contents are displayed on your PC's screen. However, any reference it contains to a CGI script will be sent back to the Web server for execution there.

The good aspect to this, from the Web server administrator's viewpoint, is that only CGI scripts that are properly installed on her machine can be run in this fashion. That gives the administrator a chance to check all the CGI scripts that the users of this machine might want to load before they are made active.

The good thing, from your point of view, is that whatever those CGI scripts do, they do it on the distant machine. Only some response HTML-tagged text can make its way from that script into your PC.

The bad thing about this strategy, from your point of view, is that it can be quite slow. You may do something at your end that triggers a CGI script at the remote end of a long and sometimes congested link. It can be many seconds or even minutes before the intended action is taken at the remote computer and evidence of it arrives back at your PC. This is okay for some purposes for which CGI scripts are used, but it isn't really suitable for the type of quick-response interactivity that is becoming more and more popular today.

So how can one get really snappy, exciting animation and interactivity out of a Web page? Move the programs that make all that excitement happen over from the Web server to the PC (or other computer) that is viewing the Web page.

What's All This Jive About Java? And What's an ActiveX Component?

This is where ActiveX, VBScript, Java, JavaScript, and Java Beans come into the picture. The first two I just named are from Microsoft; Java and its siblings are from Sun Microsystems.

So the first question is, "What's Java?" Your second question should be, "Why should I care?" To some people, Java is just a new programming language. To others it is nearly a religion.

Actually, everyone agrees that Java is a new programming language. It is heavily object-oriented. It was devised partly by simplifying C++ and partly by looking carefully at what programmers really need in today's world of distributed, multiplatform computing.

Java has some special qualities. It is these qualities that have moved it up from merely another computer programming language to its present exalted status as the most-probable Microsoft killer and the carrier of the torch for cross-platform interoperability.

Sun's phrase for all this is "Write Once, Run Everywhere." The essential idea is that they, or someone, will create a Java Virtual Machine (JVM) for each computer platform (computer hardware plus operating system). Then anyone can write a Java program and it will run unchanged on every platform that has a JVM. This is not the first time someone has proposed something like this, but the need for cross-platform support has never before been greater, and now might be the first time that the idea has a fighting chance to succeed.

One reason for this optimism about Java is that Sun is giving it away, and many people who are nervous about Microsoft's dominance are supporting it. The pressure has, in fact, become so intense, that even Microsoft is supporting it—although Sun claims that Microsoft is doing so in a way that both violates their license agreement with Sun and jeopardizes the platform-independent nature of Java.

Java Basics

This sounds fine, but a bit abstract. Okay, let me give you a few more details and see if that will help flesh out the picture for you. Java, in its original form, is an interpreted language. The interpreter is a part of the JVM.

Microsoft wrote a JVM that became a part of its Internet Explorer (IE). Microsoft repeated this for each platform version of IE that it has released. (This means a separate JVM for the Windows 3.x and Windows 95 environments on a Wintel PC, as well as one for the Macintosh.) Netscape wrote another one for each version of Navigator or Communicator. This means all the difficult hardware and operating system–dependent details have been handled by them. Now you or anyone else can write a Java application, and so long as all the JVMs out there can interpret everything that is legal in a Java program, your program will run on all the platforms with JVMs.

This is not new. Essentially, the notion of a JVM is similar to a software simulator that runs on one platform and in the process makes it look like another platform. Thus, we have SoftPC, a program with versions for the Macintosh and NeXT computers that emulate the PC well enough that you can run almost any PC program on those "foreign" computers quite nicely. There is a problem with SoftPC and all the other emulators that use this idea, however. They are slow. Very slow.

Critics of Java said right away that it would fail simply because any Java program was bound to be ever so much slower than a well-optimized program to do the same task that had been written in a language especially devised for the platform on which the program was to run. Java proponents answer that this might be true, although they hope to narrow the performance gap soon, but the savings in programmers' time in not having to prepare a version of every program for every platform is so great that it will outweigh any performance problems.

So far that seems to be pretty much true—within some limits. There are two main uses for Java at this time. One is to create Java applets. These are little programs that run in conjunction with a Web browser, usually. The other use is to create full-scale, stand-alone applications.

Although Java applets are not all that abundant in numbers so far, they have been quite well accepted in the Internet world. Java stand-alone applications have not. The main reason is that what Java applets are doing, so far, is so simple that even with a 10-fold degradation in performance (over the comparable C program), they run fast enough. The limiting factor in most Internet-related applications is the speed with which Web pages and other resources can be downloaded—not the speed with which the applets that can be included in those downloads run when they are on your PC. When it comes to stand-alone software applications, however, such as an office suite, performance is nearly everything. Corel tried to write a Java version of its WordPerfect office suite, but it just didn't take off in the marketplace.

One way in which Java applet performance can be improved is by adding to the JVM a Just-In-Time (JIT) Java compiler. This is a program that receives the Java source code and spits out native binary code for the platform on which it is running. This binary code can be reused whenever the Java source code recycles through a given portion of its source code. With this and other careful tweaks, Java is now showing some fairly respectable performance numbers—not yet catching up to C or C++, but getting quite respectably close.

Security Issues and Java

Java's natural home is the Internet, where programs written in Java can be downloaded over the Net into different computers. This diversity of computers goes far beyond the matter of their hardware and operating systems. They are also owned by a huge diversity of people and organizations. This raises some serious security concerns. When you are Web surfing, you are reaching out and touching many different computers all over the world. Some belong to companies you have heard of; others belong to companies or individuals who are total strangers to you.

If you load a Web page that causes some CGI script to execute on the remote computer, that is surely okay—at least as far as you are concerned. No matter what the CGI script does, it isn't going to be capable of hurting the files in your computer because a CGI script is what we term *server-side* scripting.

Now consider how things change if you download a program (Java applet or whatever) into your PC and run it there. It could possibly do some severe damage to your data. You don't really want to download it unless you can trust the people who wrote it not to have a hidden agenda with a malicious twist or unless you can assure yourself that you have protected your PC against any and all rogue programs.

Generally, we don't know enough about who is behind many of the Web pages we access to extend much trust confidently. Many people worry about giving their credit card numbers to a merchant over the Internet. Actually this is no worse, in general, than handing your card to a waiter at a restaurant. (The waiter could copy down your credit card number just as easily as a snoop could take it off the Internet on its way from you to the merchant.) Furthermore, with the consumer protection laws that are in place in the United States, at least, your liability is fairly limited no matter what the waiter or Internet snoops might try to do. On the other hand, a rogue program in your PC...why, it could be worse than anything I want to contemplate!

The designers of Java were well aware of these concerns. Therefore, they made sure that their JVM design would build in as many safeguards as possible. First, any Java source code that arrives at the JVM is examined to be sure that it is valid Java source code, and that it doesn't attempt to do anything that might compromise the security of the user's PC or its data. In most Java implementations, this means it cannot do any file accesses on your disk drives, and it can only communicate with the remote computer from which it came.

Second, the JVM looks at any precompiled Java byte-codes and does similar checks on them. The name given to all of this process is "keeping the program in the sandbox." That is, confine the program to doing only innocuous things and you will keep your data safe.

This sounds like a wonderful approach, and it is pretty good, but there are two nagging problems. One is that sometimes the restrictions (such as no file access on the local disk drives) may be too severe. They just won't let you do some interesting and important things you might want to do. Second, the programmers who wrote the various JVMs are human. They make mistakes. Some of those mistakes might compromise system security.

Indeed, several security holes have been found (and patched) in the Java sandbox, and more are probably lurking out there, just waiting to be found. You can only hope that the "good guys" find these holes before the "bad guys" do. In the meantime, each user has some control over what degree of exposure she wants her PC to have; options settings in each browser allow her to restrict a variety of Java-related actions.

Microsoft's Answer to Java: ActiveX Components

Microsoft responded to Java's rapid rise to prominence with an initiative of its own. It announced and has been actively pushing the notion of *downloadable active components*. These are mini-programs that you can download to do specified tasks. In a way they act much like Java applets or Web browser plug-ins.

One big difference from Java applets is that ActiveX components can do anything any other program on your PC can do. No sandbox concept is connected to them. Microsoft instead says the right way to assure yourself that your data is safe is to download and run only ActiveX components that come from trusted sources. They have included a mechanism for putting in unchangeable digital certificates inside each ActiveX program. If you set your browser's security level sufficiently high, only those ActiveX modules that come from organizations with their own trusted certificates will be allowed to run.

In a way, Microsoft has simply proposed expanding the sandbox from a subset of the possible actions inside your PC to encompass all the programmers at all the trusted companies in your universe. Once again, this sounds pretty good. But how will it turn out in practice? It is a little too early to say.

The Java Beans Answer to the ActiveX Challenge

"Ah," say the Java devotees. "We can do just as well in a similar, yet different way." They propose writing small program pieces they call Java Beans. These are similar in their limited functionality to ActiveX components. Like ActiveX objects, Java Beans can communicate with one another, so you might have a Java Bean that presents a button for the user to press. When that happens, this Java Bean will pass a message to another Bean. That Bean may then print something. The Beans for buttons and printing are very different, and each is capable of doing only a single thing. However, by communicating and cooperating, they can add up to a whole program.

Like ActiveX components, Java Beans can live in your PC for a long time. In contrast, full Java programs (applets) are usually downloaded each time you access a Web page that offers them, and they are run in your PC until you leave that page, after which they are discarded.

JavaScript Is a Whole Different Animal

JavaScript is something else again. This is simply a syntax for putting some active programming statements in a Java-like form inside an HTML Web page. When your browser reads this Web page, it will see and execute the JavaScript lines. This will make it do what amounts to running a program on your PC, but that program needn't be downloaded separately from the Web page of HTML code. (You can store JavaScript in a file with extension .js either on the Web server or on the local PC, and then load it by a reference in a Web page. That, however, defeats much of the specialness of JavaScript.)

The nearest Microsoft relative to JavaScript is VBScript, which is mainly a language for controlling Microsoft applications. Just as Microsoft has "improved" Java to make it run more efficiently on a Windows machine (and in the process "breaking" the platform independence that was always one of Java's greatest selling points), VBScript will work only in a Microsoft world.

How will all this play out? You'll just have to stay tuned to see. As I said, the most recent survey I could find (done in Spring, 1997) showed that none of these advanced methods for controlling the presentation of Web pages and objects within them had made more than a token penetration into the Web. So it is far too soon to tell which of them, if any, will succeed in establishing themselves as well as CGI has already done.

Be Careful; It Can Be a Dangerous World Out There

I cannot leave this whole area of discussion of Internet-related dangers without mentioning computer viruses. They exist, and they *can* hurt you—or more precisely, your data. A virus cannot do any damage until it gets control of your PC. Just arriving there isn't enough.

If you should be so unlucky as to download and run a program that has been infected, you possibly will infect many other programs on your PC. Some day when one of them runs, you might discover that this particular virus has the nasty habit of wiping out some of your files, locking up your machine, or—worst of all—reformatting your hard disk.

Even worse, you can get a computer virus and infect files on your machine by downloading and then just *examining* certain types of data files. Many spreadsheet programs have an autorecalculate function. If the virus infects the program which that function actually is, then when the spreadsheet autorecalculates, it could be infecting other files at the same time.

Similarly, if you load a Microsoft Word document (or a document created for almost any other mainstream, high-end word processor), it could have some Word macro viruses in it. If one of them is attached to the Autoexecute macro, simply loading that file into Word to look at its contents could suffice to activate the virus. At which point, the virus can infect other files on your disk drives or even across your local area network.

The Connected PC Is More Vulnerable

The computer virus threat has been around for quite a long time. That goes for both viruses that infect program files (including the boot sector of your disk drives) and for those that infect spreadsheets, word processing documents, or other data files. The good news is that if you take some sensible precautions, you can avoid having any serious data loss when a virus strikes your PC. The most important of these steps is to complete incremental backups frequently of all your critical data files. Another step is to use a good virus-scanning program (with an updated set of virus signatures) to check out each new program or major application data file you receive before you run that program or load that data file.

The bad news is that it is much harder to remember to do this—and in some cases may be impossible to do—if you receive these files across the Internet. This will only become worse if Microsoft gets its way and we blur the line between the desktop and the Internet even further than it is today.

Already, if I happen to click on a URL in a word processing program, I might find that my dial-up networking program has run, I am connected to the Internet, and my Web browser has been launched and is loading up the resource indicated by the URL on which I clicked. I have done this by accident more than once. It can be unnerving to know that you might have just invoked an untested and untrusted program.

PC, NC, NetPC, or What?

I've told you what I think a PC is. But what, you may wonder, is an NC or a NetPC. How are they like or unlike a PC? Does this all matter? The reason we are hearing so much about these ideas is that two companies, Oracle and Microsoft, are pushing contrasting notions of what the ideal inexpensive computer to use the Internet might be. Oracle's notion is captured in the NC; Microsoft's is the NetPC.

Essentially, in both cases, they are stripped-down versions of a PC. The idea is that these boxes would be attached to the Internet or some other LAN pretty much all the time they were in use. They would download from this network any software they were going to use. The NC doesn't even have a local hard disk. The NetPC does, but only because large applications are going to be slow to download, so you might want to keep one you had downloaded around for awhile, until you were finished using it.

Oracle stresses that its NC will be something that cannot be messed up by a user. It is a sealed box, and all its software comes from the network. A network administrator can control what can happen on an NC.

Microsoft says its NetPC is better because it allows for some local storage. With no floppy diskette drive, the NetPC (like the NC) prevents users from "stealing" software off the network, yet lets them use that software all they like. Microsoft touts its Zero Administration Initiative as meaning that a NetPC can be administered centrally with near total control and nearly no need ever to visit the user's site.

Sound similar? They are, quite a lot, yet both are less than a full PC. The really interesting question isn't will the NC beat out the PC, or vice versa. The really critical question is will either one be popular enough to be worth the effort to the manufacturers for them to make and market these in addition to their ordinary PCs.

At present, the answer seems to be a qualified yes. Some niche markets have been identified for which a full PC is probably overkill. So if manufacturers can make an NC or NetPC with enough functionality for a low enough price, they might sell into these niches enough to justify themselves. Still, until we have these boxes around for awhile, it won't be certain if they are here to stay or if they are merely a passing fad.

What is perfectly clear is that neither the NC nor the NetPC will replace full PCs any time soon (if ever). Many folks simply want to have the local control as well as the added functionality that goes with a full PC. Also, if you are thinking of getting NCs or NetPCs for your company, realize that they will work only when your network is up. If you still can justify this type of limited, special-purpose box, by all means go ahead and get one.

Summary

The Internet has a lot to offer. Most of it is wonderful; some of it is terrifying. If you educate yourself about the dangers as well as the opportunities, however, and if you practice some simple safe computing habits, you can make sure that the balance of your Internet experiences is a good one. I hope that the information I have presented here helps you to see more clearly just how that may be done.

28

Looking Back and Looking Ahead

Peter Norton®

You've made it. We are at the end of our tour inside your PC. I expect that now you know a lot more about the technologies that can be found there. You probably also know about a lot of technologies that aren't in your PC yet, but which you will have an opportunity to add to it sometime in the near future.

Furthermore, you now can see the shape of that great tsunamic wave that is about to inundate all of us: the Internet. Its leading edge is already here, and we are all feeling its effects. When it *really* hits us in earnest, the effects will be greater still. However, because you had the good sense to buy and read this book, you will be among the lucky ones. You will be equipped with the knowledge you need to be able to surf that tsunami successfully.

Learning from the Past and Predicting the Future

We all hope to learn from our past experiences. If we are very good at it, we might even be able to discern, however dimly, what the future holds in store. In this section, I'm going to put down just a few observations I've made about our recent past and some speculations about what might be our common future—all in the context of what PCs have been, are, and seem likely to become.

The Big Story of the Recent Past: The Internet

I think few would argue with the observation that the most important development relating to PCs in the past few years has been the explosive growth of the Internet and its consequent insinuation into virtually every corner of computing on the planet. There have been a lot of other developments in the part of that world that focus on PCs, including the emergence of new generations of CPUs, new operating systems, and so on. But driving many—or perhaps even most—of those changes has been the need to adapt to the influence of the Internet.

What's the Next Big Story?

Here I'm going to go out on a limb—not very far, but a little way. If the big news of the past two years has been how the Internet has affected all of PC development, I think the next two or three years will see a similarly large impact from the coming "convergence" of PCs with telecommunications of all kinds and with the world of entertainment.

Right now, I have a telephone that includes an answering machine, some networked PCs, and a stand-alone fax machine. Will I have all those separate boxes in the future? Maybe not. Certainly, now it is possible to bring all of the functionality of each of them inside the PC. And after that is done, some new, and quite powerful, possibilities arise for synergy between the different functions. For example, if my telephone and my PC are one, then every call I make can be automatically logged, and for every incoming call, I can be shown instantly the data I recorded the last time that person called me. And those are merely two minor ways in which PCs and telephones can be made to work together usefully.

Still, just because combinations of these functions can be made now, there is no certainty that every office will take advantage of that possibility any time soon. And, in fact, I think that this type of integration of telecommunications with PCs will proceed at a fairly modest pace. But it will continue; of that I am quite sure.

Games have always been one of the first ways in which new PC hardware gets pushed to its limits. Gamers and game programmers never have too much speed or sound that is too good or nearly enough of anything else to sate their desires. So I expect gamers to push the envelope, and for that to continue to help drive developments in our industry.

However, games are hardly the only way people entertain themselves. Indeed, for many people, the thought of playing a computer game is abhorrent, or merely distastefully irrelevant to their lives. For them, entertainment is more likely to mean going to the ball game, theater, or opera—or just quietly reading a good book. Will PCs evolve in ways that change those experiences? I hope so. And I believe so.

One possibility is simply that PC hardware will evolve in ways that let you take an electronic copy of a book on a hike, to the beach, or perhaps just with you into the bathtub or bed. That would allow you to read books with a difference. When you happen to wonder when a particular character last appeared in the story, you could pause in your reading and instantly scroll back to wherever that might have been (the PC having found that place for you) and then jump back once more to where you had left off reading so you could continue the story. I know I have often wished for such a capability when reading a paperback novel and really felt I needed it when studying a textbook. This sort of non-linear reading will seem more and more natural as we spend more time on the hyperlinked World Wide Web.

Theaters might come equipped with instant translation tools to help attendees hear the dialogue in their native language. Or you might want to be able during the intermission to look up all the other plays some performer had been in and see if you can better understand the interpretation he or she is giving in tonight's show.

Television surfing is one activity that is almost certain to be affected, and very powerfully. When you get 500 channels of cable or satellite TV, finding what among that flood of offerings you want to watch can become an overwhelming task. That's something that cries out for computer-aided help. And I know we will be getting that help, in any of several forms, relatively soon.

What about the "smart clothes" I mentioned in the first chapter? What about houses that respond to voice commands. ("Jeeves, bring me my coffee, please" or "Jeeves, turn down the heat and open the kitchen window, please.") Those things may come into common use, but I certainly don't expect to see them in very many households in the next several years.

A long time ago, an astute observer pointed out to me that when new inventions come along, the time it takes for society to "digest" them, which is to say to make them integral parts of our lives, seems to depend much less on what those inventions are or the technologies behind them, and much more on various economic realities. And that usually means that this integration takes several decades for anything that really alters our lives dramatically. However, PCs have been a somewhat special case. After all, the whole notion of an IBM PC is less than 20 years old, and look how far it has come. So perhaps these PC-related societal changes will also proceed at an unprecedented pace.

I'll end this section with one safe prediction: The future of PCs and their growing impact on our lives will be anything but dull. Ours is an interesting time in which to live.

And, having said that, I must also point out that the Chinese have a curious take on that phrase. They sometimes curse a person by saying, "May you live in interesting times." I can only hope that you and I will find the interest brought to our lives by PCs in the future to be an overall benign or even beneficial one.

Our Tour Is Over, but the Journey Is Not

I must warn you: Our tour is over, but your journey most definitely is not. PC technologies are expanding and advancing constantly. Keeping current is a tough job, even for those of us who work at it full time. So don't relax totally; keep your eyes and ears open. Armed with the fundamental understandings you found here, you should be able to make more sense than most average observers of each new trend or new, fancy product.

How the Story Comes Out Depends, in Part, on You

I've told you a complex story about what our PCs are and how they got that way. It's a story that will continue, and the really good news is that how it comes out depends at least in part on you. That's right. You are able to influence your own (and others') future. You and millions of other people like you shape the future daily as you make your buying choices and as you make your views known in other ways.

Just to cite one example, a few years back a major company in the industry proposed to publish on the Internet a database of all the companies and individuals in the United States. Many people were horrified. They feared that their privacy would be intruded upon intolerably, and so they spoke up. The company in question was deluged with e-mail, conventional letters, and phone calls. The overwhelming majority of these were critical of the plan. The company backed down.

Even while explaining at great length how what they had planned to do wasn't really a threat to anyone's privacy, they reversed their course completely. They still did publish information about companies, but all the data they had on individuals was not placed on the Internet.

That's just one example of how you, acting in concert with others, can definitely affect the industry. Beyond this group power, you also must remember your personal power over your personal PC, which leads me directly to my next topic.

Remember, It's Your Personal Computer; You Are in Charge

That's right: It is your personal computer, which means you are in charge of it. Perhaps someone else paid for it. Maybe they even maintain it for you, but you have it because you are entitled to a personal computer. You have the right (and the responsibility) to decide when and how your PC gets used. Don't abdicate this responsibility to anyone else. Keep yourself informed about the possibilities. Then be vocal with your opinions.

Make and then implement your choices in whatever ways you can and need to in order to make your PC work for you in just the way you want it to. Resist the efforts of central administrators to take away this power.

The rise of PCs has meant a great leveling of many corporate power structures. It also helped end the Cold War and has contributed mightily to the massive political changes we are seeing in our world. It has brought "power to the people," many of whom were formerly quite powerless—or thought they were. It would be a shame if we let this power slip through our fingers.

Please keep on learning about PCs and everything else that interests you. This is the best way to keep yourself mentally alive and interesting both to yourself and to others. If you come across something really interesting, perhaps something you think would help others learn more about their PCs, or simply something about PCs that fascinates you, I welcome hearing about it. You may send me e-mail at agoodman@earthlink.net.

I'm pleased you have chosen to spend this time with me, and I hope to see you on our mutual journey sometime in the future.

IX

Appendixes

A

How IBM Developed the Personal Computer

Peter Norton®

Lewis C. Eggebrecht was the lead designer and architect of the original IBM PC. We asked him to contribute his personal, insider's account of how that project came to be and how it evolved. His story is not well known, it is very interesting, and it will give you some real insight into why PC's are today they way they are, both in terms of their capabilities and limitations. We hope you'll take the time to read what follows, in Lew's words.

Before the Beginning

There were many activities within IBM that preceded the start of the PC project, including the development of several early small systems marketed by IBM with very limited success. Many believe that the PC was IBM's first small computer system and the first IBM product to use Intel microprocessors. In fact, the IBM PC was preceded by no fewer than five earlier small system designs!

IBM's first small computer system was called the 5100, which was a joint project between a small IBM laboratory in Los Gatos, California and the Rochester, Minnesota development laboratory. Designed as a small scientific machine, it utilized a powerful math-intensive language called APL (Algorithmic Programming Language). The 5100 was packaged as a portable system, similar to the early Osborne portable or the original Compaq transportable PC with a small built-in CRT display and tape cartridges for mass storage. This system was based on an IBM-developed microprocessor that actually interpreted IBM 370 mainframe instructions. Because of this, it was possible to easily move the APL interpreter from the mainframe to the 5100 without having to rewrite any code. Of course, this double level of interpretation made the system very slow.

This system had one additional distinction: It was the first IBM product to use an Intel microprocessor—the 8080, an 8-bit predecessor to the 8085 and 8086. The Intel chip was not the main processor but served as a communication controller. An enhanced version of the 5100, called the 5110, supported 8-inch floppy disk drives and added an IBM BASIC language interpreter. The BASIC interpreter was moved from the IBM System 3 computer and, like APL, was implemented by interpreting the System 3 instruction set on the 5110's main processor. The last of the 5100 family was the 5120, developed in 1980. This product was actually a 5110 in a new mechanical package designed to be a nonportable desktop system. The 5100 family of computers was never as successful as IBM wished—the high cost, very low performance, and lack of compatibility with any industry software proved lethal. Nevertheless, the 5100 laid the groundwork for the next generation of IBM's small computers.

The Way Is Paved for the PC

Many at IBM felt the basic technology being used to support low-end products was not competitive with new microprocessor technology being developed by Intel, Motorola, Zilog, and others. They felt that IBM was trying to apply its mainframe technologies to small system designs, incurring a significant cost disadvantage. This view was supported by the rapid deployment of very low-cost and powerful mini-computers that threatened IBM's low-end mainframe success.

As a result of this concern, a small laboratory was informally started in Atlanta, Georgia, to investigate the use of non-IBM technologies to develop low-end IBM products. This small lab built several early prototype PCs using Intel 8085, Motorola 6800, and Zilog Z80 microprocessors. This encouraged IBM to develop a number of small systems using Intel microprocessors. As a result of this pioneering work, the IBM Displaywriter (8086), IBM 5250 Terminal (8085), and the IBM Datamaster/System 23 (8085) products were developed. IBM also selected the Intel 8048 micro controller for use in its keyboards. So, contrary to popular belief, IBM had an established relationship with Intel prior to the PC project.

The IBM Datamaster/System 23: IBM's First Attempt at a PC

In 1979, IBM was planning its next move into the small computer arena. It could continue to develop the 5100 family or develop a new system based on the latest industry microprocessor technology. In typical IBM fashion, the company decided to do both. The small group of engineers in the Atlanta lab moved south to Boca Raton, Florida, with the clear intent of building IBM's first PC. The plan was to establish an independent business unit for the purpose of developing a new small desktop system that used Intel microprocessors, an industry standard operating system, and a Basic language interpreter compatible with the industry software. The project would be done in record time and would bypass all IBM development procedures. This was the beginning of the Datamaster/System 23 project.

As the project progressed, IBM got cold feet and slowly reimposed its overly conservative and slow development methodology based on exclusive use of internal technology; for example, they began to develop their own operating system and Basic interpreter language. The project schedules slipped and the costs increased, and in the end the Datamaster was just another 5100 class system with high cost, low performance, and no software. The first attempt at an IBM PC had failed! Although this was very discouraging for the Datamaster engineers, they continued to work under the table on the true PC, developing new graphic adapters and support for 5.25-inch non-IBM disk drives. Figure A.1 shows the family of small systems that preceded the PC.

Figure A.1.
The IBM PC's lineage.

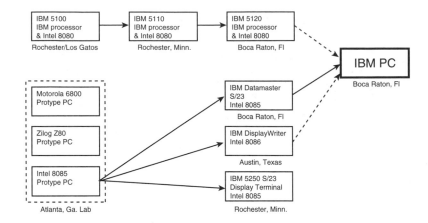

The Group of 13

In 1980, the PC project got a boost from the top at IBM. Small systems from Apple, Tandy, and others were beginning to sell in large volumes beyond the hobbyist markets. These systems were actually being used in business to perform applications that IBM felt were encroaching on its turf. IBM never viewed the new PCs as much of a direct threat to mainframes and saw no large revenue opportunity in this market. Its major concern was that "new users" were using non-IBM products, and when the need to do "real" work arose, they would not be familiar with IBM products and would select a non-IBM system in the future. IBM had seen this trend occur in the mini-computer market, where Digital Equipment had given systems to universities, and when students graduated to the business world, they selected DEC computers over IBM systems.

In May 1980, IBM Chairman Frank Cary and President John Opel concluded that IBM must have a PC offering that competed with Apple and Tandy and established the IBM name at the lowest entry point in the computer market. Bill Lowe, the systems manager for the Datamaster project and now laboratory director for the Boca Raton site, was asked to formulate a plan to develop a PC. After several weeks of study, he reported back to Frank Cary and John Opel that IBM's best strategy was to purchase an existing design from Atari and manufacture it with IBM's name. This proposal was rejected and Bill Lowe was asked to return to Boca Raton and develop a plan for an "IBM" PC design.

Bill formed a small task force of marketing and manufacturing people and included several of the engineers on the Datamaster project, including those who worked on the original PC prototypes in Atlanta. This task force included many of the group of 13 who eventually worked together at the beginning of the PC project. The Datamaster engineers already had a good idea of the PC system that they wanted to build and had secretly built many of the components in the lab. Within two weeks the task force had agreed on a system design using the Intel 8088 microprocessor, a simple metal enclosure, a keyboard from the IBM S/34 terminals, and industry 5.25-inch floppy disk drives. The plan was to use Digital Research's CP/M operating system and the BASIC 80 interpreter from Microsoft. The plan called for a total development cycle of nine months, from start to product shipments.

As word spread inside IBM that a PC project was likely to be approved at the highest levels, several competing proposals came forward. Most of these proposals involved using IBM developed microprocessors, technology, software, and development methodology. They simply could not meet the aggressive costs and schedules defined by the group of 13. Even as additional progress meetings with IBM top management were being held, the group of 13 began working on the PC design, although the project had not been formally approved.

The PC project was officially approved on September 6, 1980 as the result of a meeting between Bill Lowe, key members of development team, Frank Cary, and John Opel at the IBM headquarters in New York. At this meeting a "prototype PC" was demonstrated. The prototype was actually a Datamaster/System 23 motherboard with an 8085 microprocessor, a new graphics display adapter, and a new 5.25-inch floppy disk controller. It was packaged in a wedge-shaped keyboard style enclosure made of wood and painted a glossy black. The demo prototype ran a public domain Tiny Basic from Lawrence Livermore Labs on top of a modified monitor program originally designed for the Motorola 6800 microprocessor. This was the same software that was developed and demonstrated in the small lab in Atlanta nearly two years earlier! At the meeting, a game called "Lunar Lander" was demonstrated, along with several high-resolution graphic images. It actually bore no resemblance to the PC defined by the task force!

As a result of this key meeting, the PC project was approved as a totally independent business unit that reported directly to the chairman and president, bypassing all IBM middle management. The old Datamaster engineers finally got their wish—a new system totally free from IBM's design methodology and technology constraints. They had their second chance to produce the IBM PC they had planned more than two years earlier. Looking back, it is ironic that IBM's decision to enter the PC market was based on the premise of protecting its present mainframe business rather than on creating a whole new industry—an industry that now threatens this very mainframe business!

Why the 8088?

The 16-bit 8086 processor was introduced in June of 1978, more than three years before the introduction of the IBM PC. The IBM PC development group selected the less powerful 8088 microprocessor in an attempt to keep the PC's costs down. The 8088 was similar to the 8086 because it supported an internal 16-bit bus, but its external bus was only 8 bits wide. This made it easier to attach the standard 8-bit peripheral chips and enabled a smaller entry memory size in the PC design. This feature of the 8088 enabled the IBM PC to compete with popular, less costly 8-bit systems, yet have the performance advantage of a large address space and 16-bit internal processor. The 8088 selection also guaranteed compatible performance in the migration path to the 8086 and the 286 processors. The PC development team was aware of the 286 in development at Intel; in fact, it was announced by Intel only six months after the announcement of the PC, and yet was not used by IBM for three years!

The most important reason for selecting the Intel processor family had nothing to do with its performance or cost compared to other alternatives. The Intel processor family had a set of native development tools. This meant that a software developer could actually write software and develop applications on the PC. The other 16-bit processors from IBM or others still required a cross-system environment or the use of a mini-computer or mainframe system to develop software. Most competitive microprocessors did not have development tools that ran on their own microprocessors. This was considered a major obstacle to wide acceptance of the PC and the development of new PC applications. Intel also provided a conversion tool that would semiautomatically convert existing 8080 code to 8086/8088 code. Many of the original applications were 8080 applications converted using this code translator.

The 8088's major distinguishing features over the existing family of 8-bit processors were its internal 16-bit data paths and 1MB address space. The increase in address space was accomplished using a scheme called segmentation. Program instructions could not address any memory location in the 1MB address space directly. A two-step process was used. First, a segment register was loaded that pointed to a 64KB block of data or instructions; this could be on any 16-byte boundary in the 1MB address space. Next, the normal X86 instructions could access any data or instructions in the 64KB. To access data outside the 64KB block, the segment registers needed to be reloaded with new pointers.

Four 16-bit segment registers were provided: one each for instruction accesses, data accesses, and stack accesses, and a special extra segment register. Programmers hated this scheme because it meant that the programmer had to be constantly aware of values of the segment registers and adjust them when spanning a segment boundary. It was not until the introduction of the 80386 processor that new addressing modes permitted full linear addressing in the X86 architecture. The 8088 was implemented with 29,000 transistors and was housed in a 40-pin package. The latest Pentium processors are implemented with 3.1 million transistors and require a 296-pin package.

The PC's Datamaster S/23 Heritage

Many features of the earlier Intel 8085 microprocessor-based Datamaster design were quickly adopted for use in the PC. The adapter-card-on-motherboard packaging approach was adopted from the Datamaster. The PC's card size and right-angle connector bracket mounting was adopted. Even the expansion bus connector and the bus signals were adapted. The 8085 microprocessor's bus was very similar to the newer Intel 8088 microprocessor's interface and only minor changes were made in the Datamaster's expansion bus architecture for use in the PC. It is a little-known fact that the adapter boards designed for the PC would actually fit into and work in an older IBM Datamaster system!

The adoption of the earlier Datamaster's key architectural and packaging features and its prior history of rigorous testing greatly enhanced the PC's development schedule and chances of success. Even after the official formation of the PC development group, many of the Datamaster engineers who were not transferred quietly continued to work on the PC project.

The PC Development Project

As part of the assumptions for meeting cost and schedule targets, Frank Cary and John Opel agreed that the PC development group would have total freedom from IBM's rigid development process. Bill Lowe had seen how the Datamaster project had started with the same assumption and was slowly forced back into the rigid IBM mold. This was attributed to the massive middle management reporting structure in IBM. As each decision moved up the chain, the conclusion was eventually reached to take the safe course and do things the IBM way. To avoid a repeat of this process, the PC project reported directly to IBM's top management, bypassing the middle management bureaucracy entirely.

The PC development group started the project with some very basic assumptions that were totally counter to IBM's product development procedures:

- The group would not use any IBM computer-aided design systems; all schematic, timing verification, and circuit board layout would be done manually according to industry standards.

- Qualification of vendors' components would be dramatically reduced or eliminated. Standard IBM qualification procedures could typically take several months, requiring the vendor to build special higher cost versions for IBM.

- The product testing procedures would be dramatically reduced to a two-stage process testing only preproduction and production level units. The standard IBM product test procedure had four or more phases of testing and typically lasted over two years.

- Case packaging and style did not have to meet IBM guidelines. The PC was the first IBM small system to use a metal case. Plastic cases required tooling of complex molds often requiring a year to develop.

- The PC did not have to maintain compatibility with any existing IBM systems. The earlier Datamaster was forced to use IBM's character set and codes, which precluded any possible use of industry standard software.

- The PC group could ignore requests by internal IBM groups to justify selection of non-IBM technology for use in the PC. The Datamaster project had become bogged down in endless meetings that challenged the use of outside technologies.

- All PC system software was to be purchased from third-party sources. The PC group's software activities were to be limited to developing diagnostic and BIOS routines and testing the procured software.

With the project's goals now well defined, the project needed to be staffed and a home selected. Several IBM sites were candidates for the PC project. Rochester, Minnesota was considered because all low-end business systems were developed there; Atlanta, Georgia was given brief consideration because the original PC work was done there; Boulder, Colorado was given highest priority due to the lack of an existing product mission and a pool of available engineers. In the end, the PC project stayed in Boca Raton. Rochester was too cold, Atlanta meant moving everyone, and Boulder turned down the PC project because it was too risky. However, a number of engineers were recruited from the Boulder site and joined the PC project in Boca Raton.

The PC Project Schedule

Due to the covert work performed by the Datamaster engineers before the project start, the PC development got off to a running start. Shortly after the official start of the project in September 1980, the first true PC prototypes were running, and a few weeks later they were delivered to Microsoft. It quickly became obvious that the development group would have a product and that a more complete organization needed to be put in place to market, service, and manufacture the PC. The search was started for a PC systems manager to organize and run the project as a fully independent business unit. Phillip Don Estridge, the former software development manager for the IBM Series 1 minicomputer, was selected to run the PC business unit.

With the basic PC system unit design completed, the PC group turned to procurement and design of the other system components. The monochrome and color CRT monitors were procured from the Far East, the PC printer was procured from Epson in Japan, and the floppy disk drives from U.S. vendors. The PC group also designed several PC expansion boards, including the Color Graphic Display Adapter, Monochrome Display Adapter, Floppy Disk Drive Adapter, Printer Port Adapter, Asynchronous Communication Port Adapter, Bi-snyc Communications Adapter, and Game Port Adapter. By late spring of 1981, most of the PC product family was ready to be released to manufacturing. It would take approximately three additional months to gear up manufacturing and to build a small stockpile of systems ready to be shipped on announcement day.

The PC Operating System

The Datamaster development team had initially wanted to use Digital Research's CP/M operating system and Microsoft's Basic 80 Basic language interpreter in the Datamaster/System 23. They were very familiar with these products, even though the System 23 eventually used an all-IBM software solution. It was only natural for the PC to follow the path abandoned by the Datamaster. At the time, Bill Gates and Paul Allen, partners in Microsoft, had built a reputation in the microcomputer industry by porting their BASIC language to more than 20 different systems.

IBM met with Bill Gates and presented the PC product and project plans. Gates offered his criticisms and suggestions concerning the PC's designs. He recommended adding a small color palette to the CGA display adapter and graphics characters to the PC character set, and recommended a keyboard layout. All of these suggestions were incorporated into the PC design. Of course, like all software people, he wanted a faster, more powerful processor with more memory, but in the end agreed to the PC's design.

While one IBM group was working with Microsoft on the languages to be supported on the PC, a second group attempted a meeting with Digital Research to explore porting CP/M to the PC. The initial meeting between IBM and Digital Research went poorly when Digital Research refused to sign an IBM nondisclosure agreement. It looked like working with Digital Research would be difficult and could possibly delay the PC schedule. When Bill Gates was asked his advice, he recommended the use of an alternative operating system from Seattle Computer Products, a maker of an 8086 S-100 board product that had an operating system similar to CP/M called QDOS. Microsoft obtained rights to QDOS and began porting it to the PC, thus PC DOS was born. It was agreed that while Microsoft would port QDOS to the PC and modify BASIC for PC, IBM would write the BIOS ROM software. The BIOS was the software that served as the interface between the operating system and the PC's hardware.

When the PC was announced in August 1981, PC DOS was its primary operating system. Although it lacked many of the features that users take for granted today, such as subdirectories and hard disk support, PC DOS 1.0 was very successful. Comparing PC DOS 1.0 to Windows 98 and Windows NT 5.0, one would have to say Microsoft has come a long way!

The Father of the PC

When Don Estridge took over the PC project, most of the PC architecture and product definition had been completed. Still, the PC was a long way from being a sure success. Estridge quickly embraced the maverick spirit of the group and became a strong protector and leader of the PC project, fending off attacks from rival groups within IBM and securing IBM top-level management support. What Estridge did was lay out a step-by-step plan that took the PC from a prototype development to a real product that could be manufactured, serviced, and marketed through nontraditional IBM sales channels. He added just enough organization to the project to ensure its success without stifling its creative energy.

Perhaps Estridge's most enduring contribution was his support of the PC as an open system. This was a concept totally foreign to most people at IBM; why invite competition? The idea that third parties would be allowed to design add-in cards, peripheral devices, and even compatible systems was simply unheard of! The development group wanted an open system; they knew that it would be impossible for IBM to provide all the technology, peripherals, and expansion features needed to make the PC a success. They pointed to the Apple II and the large third-party products market that existed.

Taking the Apple II manuals as a model, IBM finally relented and published the IBM technical reference manuals containing full BIOS listings and system schematics. It is interesting to note how IBM and Apple have swapped positions: IBM used the Apple example to justify an open system, and Apple used the IBM example to justify becoming a closed system. IBM actually had taken some steps that provided a measure of protection against manufacturers of clone systems. First, the BIOS was copyrighted and, second, the PC hardware design was protected by several patents. These initial precautions offered little protection against off-shore clone manufacturers, however. IBM now licenses the patents to clone developers and receives a significant stream of royalties.

Looking back, one would have to say that the PC had many fathers: the small group in Atlanta that built the first PC prototypes and paved the way for the PC; the 5100 development group in Rochester, Minnesota and Los Gatos, California that pioneered small system development in IBM; the Datamaster engineers who tried to build the first PC and kept the idea alive by covertly developing PC technology; Bill Lowe, the PC task force chairman who proposed the PC project; Frank Cary and John Opel, IBM's top management who demanded a PC product; and, of course, Phillip Don Estridge, who managed the PC project to success.

The PC Announcement

In August 1981, IBM officially announced the PC and began volume shipments in October. Many in IBM considered the project to be doomed. Marketing computers through Sears, J.C. Penney, and IBM store-front outlets was crazy! Who would buy a computer that was not attached to a mainframe? One executive even predicted that IBM would have to make a massive recall, making the recall announcement during the half-time of the Super Bowl game. This was predicated on the fact that the PC's design was shabby and unreliable because it had bypassed all the IBM quality tests and design procedures. Of course this dire prediction did not come true, and the PC established a totally new market and revenue stream for IBM. Today, nearly 50 million PCs are produced annually worldwide by IBM and a host of other manufacturers.

B

Some Sample Programs

Peter Norton®

This appendix has two purposes. One is to show you some short samples of source code in several high-level computer programming languages. The second purpose is to give you the answers to the questions I posed at the end of Chapter 6, "Enhancing Your Understanding by Messing Around (Exploring and Tinkering)."

You've already seen examples of two other low-level computer programming languages in Chapter 18, "Understanding How Humans Instruct PCs," in the discussion surrounding Figures 18.1 and 18.2. The first of these figures showed you a program as the CPU "sees" it, in what could be considered its native language, often called *machine language*. That is simply a sequence of numerical values (given there in hexadecimal notation). Figure 18.2 showed the same program expressed in the lowest-level "human-readable" computer programming language, normally called *assembly language*.

Here, I'll show you two simple programs written in a dialect of BASIC (Beginner's All-Purpose Symbolic Instruction Code). Then, I'll show you a fragment of a program for a Web page, written in HTML (Hypertext Markup Language).

BASIC Sample Programs

Since its introduction more than 30 years ago, many different versions, or dialects, of the BASIC programming language have been developed. The early versions required a line number on each line of source code. More modern versions make this optional. The following two programs were created and tested using Microsoft's QuickBASIC, version 4.5, but they should work in any recent version of QBASIC, and they might work in other brands and versions of BASIC as well. (If they don't work in your version, try adding a line number followed by a space at the beginning of each line.) The lines that begin with a single quote mark are *remarks*; that is, they are only meant for humans to read. The BASIC interpreter or compiler ignores them.

The first program example reads the time of day information stored in the BIOS data area near the very bottom of main memory. In this example, the time is first acquired from the system via a special BASIC command, TIME$. And, the number of "timer ticks" since the machine was last rebooted is read from the BIOS data area. This gives a starting point in time for the program to work with. After that, each time you press the spacebar, the program reads the now-current number of time ticks elapsed, and from that and the initial data, computes the current time. It also gets the system's version of that number by another call to TIME$ and then prints both values on the screen so you can compare them. Pressing the Esc key ends the program.

```
'   BIOSTIME.BAS - A program to read timer ticks from BIOS data area.

CLS

'   First get the initial time from BASIC function TIME$
T0$ = TIME$
'   Set Segment to BIOS data area and read values held there.
DEF SEG = &H40
A0% = PEEK(&H6F)
```

```
B0% = PEEK(&H6E)
C0% = PEEK(&H6D)
D0% = PEEK(&H6C)

'  Break down the TIME$ return value to get numerical values for time.
H0% = VAL(MID$(T0$, 1, 2))
M0% = VAL(MID$(T0$, 4, 2))
S0% = VAL(MID$(T0$, 7, 2))

'  Now loop, computing time each time through the loop and compare it
'  to the BASIC TIME$ value, waiting each time through for a space
'  character or an escape character to be received from the keyboard.

TT# = TIMER
I$ = INKEY$
WHILE NOT I$ = CHR$(27)
  '  First get time from BASIC TIME$ function.
  T$ = TIME$
  '  Repeat peeks into BIOS data area. (DEF SEG only needed first time.)
  a% = PEEK(&H6F)
  b% = PEEK(&H6E)
  c% = PEEK(&H6D)
  d% = PEEK(&H6C)

  '  Get differences in all four numbers we peeked from BIOS data area.
  aa% = a% - A0%
  '  If AA% is negative, this implies wraparound, so to get the proper
  '    difference we must add 256.
  IF aa% < 0 THEN aa% = aa% + 256
  bb% = b% - B0%
  cc% = c% - C0%
  dd% = d% - D0%
  '  Compute elapsed time in ticks.
  Ticks& = dd% + 256& * (cc% + 256& * (bb% + 256& * aa%))
  '  Compute elapsed time in seconds since start of program.
  TickTime = .055 * Ticks&

  '  And then, using initial time in numeric form, compute present
  '  time. Seconds are a special case, for which we want to preserve
  '  the fractional part.
  S = S0% + (TickTime MOD 60) + (TickTime - INT(TickTime))
  IF S >= 60 THEN
    S = S - 60
    Mcarry = 1
  ELSE
    Mcarry = 0
  END IF
  '  For minutes and hours we can let MOD function truncate to
  '  integers.
  M = M0% + Mcarry + ((TickTime \ 60) MOD 60)
  IF M >= 60 THEN
    M = M - 60
    Hcarry = 1
  ELSE
    Hcarry = 0
  END IF
  H = H0% + Hcarry + (TickTime \ 3600)
  IF H >= 24 THEN H = H - 24
  '  Don't bother carrying past midnight.
```

```
'  Finally, express numeric times as string values.
SELECT CASE S
  CASE IS < 1
    S$ = "00" + MID$(STR$(S), 2, 4)
  CASE 1 TO 9.9995
    S$ = "0" + MID$(STR$(S), 2, 5)
  CASE IS > 10
    S$ = MID$(STR$(S), 2, 6)
END SELECT
M$ = RIGHT$("0" + MID$(STR$(M), 2), 2)
H$ = RIGHT$("0" + MID$(STR$(H), 2), 2)

PRINT "Time from BASIC = "; T$;
PRINT TAB(40); a%; TAB(50); b%; TAB(60); c%; TAB(70); d%
PRINT "Time from CMOS  = "; H$; ":"; M$; ":"; S$;
PRINT TAB(40); aa%; TAB(50); bb%; TAB(60); cc%; TAB(70); dd%

PRINT

I$ = INKEY$
WHILE NOT (I$ = " " OR I$ = CHR$(27))
  I$ = INKEY$
WEND
WEND
```

The second example is very similar, but this time the actual "real-time clock" data is read from the configuration CMOS.

```
'  CMOSTIME.BAS - A program to read and display time from CMOS.

CLS

'  Now loop, computing time each time through the loop and comparing it to
'  the BASIC TIME$ value, waiting each time through for a space character.

TT# = TIMER
I$ = INKEY$
WHILE NOT I$ = CHR$(27)
  '  First get time from BASIC TIME$ function.
  T$ = TIME$
  '  Send addresses to CMOS for data and read values back.
  OUT &H70, 0
  S = INP(&H71)
  OUT &H70, 2
  M = INP(&H71)
  OUT &H70, 4
  H = INP(&H71)
  '  These numbers are two digit figures in packed BCD format. Next we
  '  need to disassemble them into decimal digits, and combine them to
  '  get string numerals for output.
  S0 = S MOD 16
  S1 = S \ 16
  S$ = MID$(STR$(S1), 2) + MID$(STR$(S0), 2)
  M0 = M MOD 16
  M1 = M \ 16
  M$ = MID$(STR$(M1), 2) + MID$(STR$(M0), 2)
  H0 = H MOD 16
  H1 = H \ 16
  H$ = MID$(STR$(H1), 2) + MID$(STR$(H0), 2)
```

```
      PRINT "Time from BASIC = "; T$
      PRINT "Time from CMOS  = "; H$; ":"; M$; ":"; S$
      PRINT

      I$ = INKEY$
      WHILE NOT (I$ = " " OR I$ = CHR$(27))
         I$ = INKEY$
      WEND
WEND
```

Because this isn't a book on programming, I'll not attempt to teach you what every line means, nor how to create BASIC programs of your own. Plenty of other books do that. If you want to learn BASIC programming, probably the best place to start is with the more modern dialect, Visual Basic.

These examples simply enable you to see how people write source code that is meaningful to suitably trained human beings, and that can then be converted by an appropriate interpreter or compiler into native machine language.

Hypertext Markup Language Sample Program

The last example I'm going to give you is a text file that is a portion of a typical page on the World Wide Web. The computer language used is HTML. I have cut out most of the lines in this example, because they don't shown anything not already evident from other lines. Please go to the URL indicated at the end of this appendix to see the entire page for yourself.

Each Web page can consist of several different elements. The HEAD region of the text defines the page, but its content doesn't end up showing on that page. The TITLE section indicates what is to be shown on the title bar of the browser program's window in which this page is displayed. The BODY region contains all the rest of what gets displayed. Inside the BODY are various subregions indicated by other HTML tags. Some of these set a type size, style, or color. Others indicate where an image is to be included. Still others are hypertext links to other Web pages.

Each HTML tag that marks the beginning of an HTML element consists of a pair of angle brackets enclosing the name of that type of element, plus optionally, some parameters defining aspects of that element's style. A tag marking the end of the element is often not needed. When it is included, it is the same as the start of the element tag with a forward slash character added after the opening angle bracket. Thus, <TITLE> starts the TITLE region and </TITLE> marks its end.

```
<HTML>
<HEAD>

   <META NAME="Description" CONTENT="Exploratorium ExploraNet- the online home
   ➥ of the Exploratorium, a hands-on museum of science, art, and human
   ➥ perception in San Francisco. ExploraNet provides interactive online
```

```
➡ exhibits and exhibitions, activities, science news, and publications,
➡ as well as general information about the museum. Online since 1993.">
  <TITLE>Exploratorium: ExploraNet</TITLE>
</HEAD>
<BODY BGCOLOR="#ffffff" BACKGROUND="images/back.gif" LINK="#bcac58" VLINK=
"#b7acb7">

<TABLE WIDTH="517" BORDER="0" CELLSPACING="0" CELLPADDING="0" HEIGHT="585">
<TR>
<TD WIDTH="122" VALIGN="TOP" HEIGHT="584" ALIGN="CENTER">
➡ <P><IMG SRC="images/palace_anim3.gif" WIDTH="102" HEIGHT="120"
➡ ALT="The Palace of Fine Arts"
ALIGN="BOTTOM" NATURALSIZEFLAG="0"></P>

...

<TABLE WIDTH="90%" BORDER="0" CELLSPACING="2" CELLPADDING="0">
<TR>
<TD WIDTH="8%"></TD>
<TD WIDTH="92%">The Exploratorium is a museum of science, art, and human
➡ perception with over 500 interactive &quot;hands on&quot; exhibits.
➡ Each year more than 600,000 visitors come to the Exploratorium, over
➡ 90,000 students and teachers come on field trips, and more than 2000
➡ teachers attend professional development programs which focus on
➡ inquiry-based teaching and learning in the K-12 classroom. </TD>
➡ </TR>
</TABLE>
</P>

<P><CENTER><FONT SIZE=-1>&copy; The Exploratorium 3601 Lyon Street San
➡ Francisco, CA 94123 Tel: 415-563-7337</FONT></CENTER></TD></TR>
</TABLE>
</BODY>
</HTML>
```

This particular Web page is the home page of one of my favorite institutions, the Exploratorium interactive science museum in San Francisco, California. This extract from their copyrighted source code is included with their permission. You can go there and see the entire page (plus jump to the linked pages) by pointing your Web browser to this URL:

http://www.exploratorium.edu/

Index

MACMILLAN COMPUTER PUBLISHING USA

A VIACOM COMPANY

Technical ---- Support

If you need assistance with the information provided by Macmillan Computer Publishing, please access the information available on our web site at **http://www.mcp.com/feedback.** Our most Frequently Asked Questions are answered there. If you do not find the answers to your questions on our web site, you may contact Macmillan User Services at **(317) 581-3833** or email us at **support@mcp.com.**